XSLT Programmer's Reference, 2nd Edition

Michael Kay

XSLT Programmer's Reference, 2nd Edition

Published by
Wiley Publishing, Inc.
10475 Crosspoint Boulevard
Indianapolis, IN 46256
www.wiley.com

Published simultaneously in Canada

Library of Congress Card Number: 2003107068

ISBN: 0-7645-4381-4

Manufactured in the United States of America

10 9 8 7 6 5 4 3 2 1

1B/RW/QW/QT/IN

For general information on our other products and services or to obtain technical support, please contact our Customer Care Department within the U.S. at (800) 762-2974, outside the U.S. at (317) 572-3993 or fax (317) 572-4002.

Wiley also publishes its books in a variety of electronic formats. Some content that appears in print may not be available in electronic books.

Trademark Acknowledgements

Credits

Author
Michael Kay

Technical Reviewers
David Carlisle
Robert Chang
Michael Corning
Jim MacIntosh
Craig McQueen
Gary L. Peskin
Paul Tchistopolskii
Linda van den Brink
Dmitry E Voytenko
Dan Wahlin

Category Manager
Dave Galloway

Technical Architect
Dianne Parker

Technical Editor
Simon Mackie

Author Agent
Marsha Collins

Project Managers
Avril Corbin
Beckie Stones

Production Manager
Simon Hardware

Production Coordinator
Mark Burdett

Figures
Shabnam Hussein

Cover Design
Shelly Frasier

Proofreader
Ian Allen

About the Author

Michael Kay has recently joined the systems architecture team at Software AG, working on the standards and interfaces for their XML product line, centred around the Tamino database. He also represents Software AG on the W3C XSL Working Group. Until then, he had spent most of his career as a software designer and systems architect with ICL, the IT services supplier. His background (and Ph.D., from the University of Cambridge) is in database technology. He has worked on the design of network, relational, and object-oriented database software products as well as a text search engine. In the XML world he is known as the developer of the open source Saxon product, the first fully-conformant implementation of the XSLT standard.

Michael lives in Reading, Berkshire with his wife and daughter. His hobbies, as you might guess from the examples in this book, include genealogy and choral singing.

Acknowledgements

Firstly, I'd like to acknowledge the work of the W3C XSL Working Group, who created the XSLT language. Without their efforts there would have been no language and no book. I wrote the first edition of this book from an outsider's perspective before I joined the group, and I've tried to keep that flavor in the second edition, despite the fact that I now have to take my share of responsibility for the spec being the way it is.

More specifically, I'm grateful to James Clark, the editor of the XSLT and XPath specifications, who responded courteously and promptly to a great many enquiries.

I've learnt a great deal of what I know about XSLT from the people on the XSL-List; not only from the experts who answer so many of the questions, but also from the many beginners who ask them. Many of the new techniques and explanations in the second edition were prompted by ideas first aired on this list.

I owe a debt both to ICL and to Software AG, my employers during the life of this project, who both offered me every encouragement and support.

My editors at Wrox Press, and the technical reviewers, made an invaluable contribution by pointing out the many places where improvements were needed.

And finally, I'm once again grateful for the support of Penny and Pippa, who took the news that I was planning a second edition with little more than a sigh of resignation.

Table of Contents

Introduction

It wouldn't be too extravagant to claim that XML is the biggest thing to hit the web since the whole thing started less than ten years ago. It's also one of the biggest things to hit the world of information management. Yet on its own, XML doesn't actually **do** anything, all it provides is a way of structuring information and sending it from one piece of software to another. Until now, if you wanted to write applications that took advantage of XML, you had to write some rather low-level code using interfaces (such as DOM and SAX) that required a very detailed knowledge of the way the data is organized.

It reminds me of the way people used to access databases before SQL came along (you've seen the gray hairs on the cover photo) – and when I first saw the XSL Transformation language, XSLT, I realized that this was going to be the SQL of the web, the high-level data manipulation language that would turn XML from being merely a storage and transmission format for data into an active information source that could be queried and manipulated in a flexible, declarative way.

Early in 1998, I was looking at ways of incorporating XML into content management tools for web-based publishing, and I started developing a Java library called Saxon to provide higher-level interfaces for manipulating XML. I was very critical of the first XSL proposals, but as the standardization process gathered pace I started to see a useful and powerful language emerging, and decided to change direction with the Saxon software to turn it into an XSLT processor. When the XSLT version 1.0 Recommendation finally came out on 16th November 1999, I was able to announce a fully-conformant open source implementation just 17 days later.

But although I could see the power and potential of the XSLT language, I could also see that it contained some new and difficult concepts which early users were struggling with. That also reminded me of the early days with SQL – it's hard to remember it now, but when SQL first emerged people had great difficulty understanding its radical new concepts such as inner and outer joins and three-valued logic.

So that's why I wrote the book. XSLT is an exciting and powerful language, but not an easy one to get to grips with. Until now, there have been very few resources available to help, apart from the official W3C specification itself, which is about as readable to most programmers as a piece of tax legislation. So I hope this book will fill the gap, and help to unleash the tremendous potential of this new language.

Who is this Book for?

I've written this book for practising software developers who have used a variety of languages in the past and now want to learn how to use XSLT to create new applications. I'm assuming you will have a basic understanding of XML, though I do recognize that if you ever knew what an external general parsed entity is, you've probably forgotten. I'm also assuming a basic understanding of the architecture of the web and of HTML.

I'm not assuming you are familiar with any particular programming language, though I have written on the basis that you have programming experience. If all the programming you've done is to write HTML pages with a little bit of Javascript, you might find some of the material tough going.

Why a Second Edition?

The main reason for publishing a second edition just a year after the first is that the XSLT language is now so much better supported by products, and a book that describes the language without telling you about the products is only telling half the story. A year ago Microsoft's MSXML3 was an early release that only implemented half the standard; today it is fully supported and fully conformant. And it's not as if Microsoft have the field to themselves; in the appendices to the book I've described a dozen other XSLT processors you can choose from.

There's also been movement on the standards front, with a working draft of XSLT 1.1. We decided to give it full coverage in the book because many features of the draft are already finding their way into products.

Finally, the XSLT community has come up with many inventive ways of using the XSLT 1.0 language – of getting around its limitations, one might argue. In the first edition I stated categorically (and foolishly) that there was no way of constructing the intersection of two node-sets; no sooner had the ink dried than I discovered a solution to the problem. And Steve Muench's brilliant application of the `key()` function to the solution of grouping problems definitely needed to find its place in the book.

What does the Book Cover?

The main body of this book (Chapters 1 to 10) is about XSLT (and with it XPath) as a language, independent of any particular product. In the appendices I've described some of the better known (and a few almost unknown) XSLT-related products. Here I've given most space to the products that I think my readers are most likely to be using: Microsoft's MSXML3, Oracle's XDK, Saxon and Xalan, but I've also tried to give coverage to other processors that are less well-known, such as 4XSLT and Unicorn. The XSLT product scene is vibrant, with new processors being announced every month (some never to be heard of again) so I make no claim to have included everything; this part of the book will inevitably become out of date quite quickly, though with luck the major products such as MSXML3 have now reached a certain level of stability.

The book **doesn't** cover the early dialect of XSL that Microsoft delivered when Internet Explorer 5 came out in 1998 (I refer to this dialect as WD-xsl, for want of a better name). XSLT has moved on a long way since that early draft, and I decided it would be just too confusing to describe two very different versions of a language in one book. Although WD-xsl is widely used and widely installed, Microsoft has moved all its emphasis towards promoting the W3C XSLT 1.0 specification, so WD-xsl clearly has a limited life.

How is the Book Structured?

The material in the body of this book falls naturally into three parts.

The first part comprises Chapters 1 to 3. The purpose of these chapters is to explain the concepts of the XSLT language. Chapter 1 is about the role and purpose of the language, about its history and the factors that motivated its design – I could have called it *Why XSLT?* Chapter 2 explains what the concept of **transformation** means, and describes the processing model in which an XSLT stylesheet describes the relationship of an output tree to an input tree. Then Chapter 3 describes the internal structure of a stylesheet, the way in which stylesheet modules relate to each other, and the main things that you expect to find within a stylesheet.

The second part, Chapters 4 to 8, contains reference information. These chapters aim to give a complete description of every language feature, explaining its detailed syntax rules and its effect, giving usage advice and showing how it works using code examples. I've ordered the material in these chapters for ease of reference rather than for sequential reading: XSLT elements in Chapter 4, XPath expressions in Chapter 5, the syntax of Patterns in Chapter 6, and the standard function library in Chapter 7. Finally, Chapter 8 describes the features introduced in the XSLT 1.1 working draft (which are therefore still subject to change) for invoking external functions written in Java or JavaScript from an XSLT stylesheet. Many of these chapters are arranged alphabetically so you can quickly find the information on a particular language feature.

The third part of the book, Chapters 9 and 10, is designed to help you exploit the XSLT language in developing real industrial applications. Chapter 9 explores a number of design patterns while Chapter 10 contains three in-depth worked examples.

Finally, most of the Appendices describe product-specific information. Microsoft's MSXML3, Oracle, Saxon and Xalan each have an Appendix to themselves, giving information about the APIs used to invoke the products, the relationships with other products from the same vendor, and details of vendor-specific extensions and restrictions. Appendix E gives a less-detailed overview of the capabilities of a wide range of other products, including both XSLT processors such as 4XSLT, Infoteria, Sablotron, Transformiix, and Unicorn, and XSLT development tools including Stylus Studio, Whitehill's XSL Composer, and XML Spy. I'm not trying here to give you all the information you need to use each product, but rather to summarize the characteristics of each product so that you can decide which ones to investigate further.

Appendix F doesn't quite fall into this pattern. It describes the TrAX API, which is a Java API for controlling XSLT transformations. This falls into a middle ground between vendor-neutral specifications and product-specific information (it is published by Sun and is currently implemented by Saxon and Xalan-Java).

At the end of the book is a useful glossary of terms and an index.

Other XSLT Resources

If you can't find what you need in this book, there are several good places to find an answer on the web. Rather than give a long list of XSLT-related sites, I'll just list a few sites that maintain good collections of links:

- http://www.w3.org/Style/XSL/
  This is the official site of the World Wide Web Consortium. It contains all the published specifications and working drafts, plus a good number of news items, articles and white papers.

- http://www.xslinfo.com/
  This is a well-organized site run by James Tauber, consisting almost entirely of classified lists of XSL software, articles, tutorials, and other resources.

- http://www.oasis-open.org/cover/xsl.html
  Robin Cover's link pages provide remarkably comprehensive coverage of everything that's happening or has ever happened in the world of SGML and XML. The link given is to his XSL section.

- http://www.xml.com/
  A good site for opinion articles and news round-up, covering the XML world generally.

- http://msdn.microsoft.com/xml/
  This URL gives a good jumping-off point to Microsoft's view of the XML and XSL world. Many useful articles and white papers, not always confined to their own products.

- http://www.mulberrytech.com/xsl/xsl-list
  The home page of the XSL-List, a very busy but extremely helpful discussion list for all XSLT matters, from beginners' questions to advanced theoretical debates. Even if you can't find time to join the list, use the archives, and follow the links from the home page to various FAQ and tutorial sites.

What do I Need to Use this Book?

Reading about a new language won't make you an expert in it; you also need to try it out and learn from your own experience. There are many examples in this book which I'd encourage you to run, but more importantly I hope they'll stimulate you to try out ideas of your own.

You can download all the code for the worked examples from http://www.wrox.com on the page for this book.

In the appendices I've listed some of the XSLT products available, and the good news is that there's plenty of choice. Most of them are free, though you should always read the license conditions.

One way to get started is with Microsoft's MSXML3 product. You can download this from http://msdn.microsoft.com/xml, and Appendix A gives full installation instructions. MSXML3 allows you to run XSLT stylesheets within the Internet Explorer browser. The product performs well and conforms closely to the XSLT 1.0 language specification. However, it has one major disadvantage: if you get anything wrong, it gives you very unhelpful diagnostics.

For that reason, if you're using a Windows platform, I would suggest starting with:

- **Instant Saxon**, available from: http://users.iclway.co.uk/mhkay/saxon/instant.html
- **Programmer's File Editor (PFE)**, available from various archive sites including: http://www.simtel.net/pub/simtelnet/win95/editor/pfe101i.zip

The recommendation for Instant Saxon is entirely biased; I wrote it. Its merits are that it's a complete implementation of the standard, it's free, and it's easy to install and run. The examples in this book are all tested with Saxon. They should also work with MSXML3, with Xalan and with Oracle XSL, all excellent products that claim 100% conformance to the standard, but I haven't done extensive testing with them.

Like most of the other Java-based processors, Saxon requires you to create and edit your XML and stylesheet files in a text editor, and to run them from the operating system command line. If you've grown up entirely with Windows, that probably seems rather primitive. I recommend PFE because it contains an intuitive text editor that allows you to have lots of files open at once, and because it gives you access to the operating system command line in a Windows-friendly way. If you already have a different favorite, use that instead. I won't be mentioning PFE again.

For non-Windows platforms, several of the products described in the appendices are written in Java and should run on almost anything. You'll have to install a Java Virtual Machine for your particular computer, and you'll have to become familiar with the mechanics of installing and running Java applications in that environment.

Conventions

To help you get the most from the text and keep track of what's happening, a number of conventions have been used throughout the book.

Worked examples – those which you can download and try out for yourself – are generally in a box like this:

A specimen example

Source

This section gives the XML source data, the input to the transformation. If the file name is given as `example.xml`, you will find that file in the archive that you can download from the Wrox web site at http://www.wrox.com/, generally in a subdirectory holding all the examples for one chapter.

```
<source data="xml"/>
```

Stylesheet

This section describes the XSLT stylesheet used to achieve the transformation. Again there will usually be a filename such as `style.xsl` so you can find the stylesheet in the Wrox download archive.

```
<xsl:stylesheet...
```

Output

This section shows the output when you apply this stylesheet to this source data, either as an XML or HTML listing, or as a screenshot.

```
<html>...</html>
```

Any freestanding sections of code are generally shown in a shaded box, like this:

```
<data>
Some XML data or XSLT code
</data>
```

As for styles in the text:

- Important terms, when first introduced, are highlighted as follows: **important words**.
- Filenames, and code within the text appear as: `dummy.xml`.
- Text in user interfaces, and URLs, are shown as: File/Save As…
- French quotation marks (chevrons or guillemets) are used in order to separate a code snippet clearly from the surrounding text, like this: «`a=3;`». These have been used in preference to the usual English single or double quotes partly because they stand out better, and partly to avoid any ambiguity with quotes that are part of the code sample; it means we can write examples such as «`select="'Madrid'"`», where the quotation marks («`"`» and «`'`») are part of the code sample, and the chevrons aren't.
- XML element names, function names and attribute names are written as: `<xsl:value-of>`, `concat()`, `href`.

In addition:

These boxes hold important, not-to-be forgotten information, which is directly relevant to the surrounding text.

While the background style is used for asides to the current discussion.

Syntax rules (which appear mainly in Chapters 5 and 6) stick largely to the conventions used in the W3C standards, except that, again, chevrons have been used to surround literal text. The main notations used in these syntax rules are:

Expression	Meaning
`clause | paragraph`	A `clause` or a `paragraph`. The meaning of `clause` and `paragraph` will be defined in separate rules: these are **non-terminal symbols**. The vertical bar «|» is used to separate alternatives.
`«!» | «?»`	An exclamation mark or a question mark. Words or symbols enclosed by chevrons must be used as written: they are **terminal symbols**.
`adjective noun «.»`	An `adjective` followed by a `noun` followed by a full-stop (period).
`adjective? noun`	Either a `noun` on its own, or an `adjective` followed by a `noun`. The «?» indicates that the preceding symbol is optional.
`adjective* noun`	Zero or more `adjectives` followed by a `noun`.
`adjective+ noun`	One or more `adjectives` followed by a `noun`.
`sentence («?» | «!»)`	A `sentence` followed by either a question mark or an exclamation mark. The parentheses indicate grouping.

Customer Support

Wrox has three ways to support books. You can:

- Check for book errata at www.wrox.com
- Enroll at the peer-to-peer forums at p2p.wrox.com
- E-mail technical support a query or feedback on our books in general

Errata

You can check for errata for the book at our web site www.wrox.com, simply navigate to the page for this book where you will find a link to the list of errata.

P2P Lists

You can enroll in our peer-to-peer discussion forums at p2p.wrox.com where we provide you with a forum where you can put your questions to the author, reviewers and fellow industry professionals. The XSLT list is available in the 'XML' section. You can choose to join the mailing lists or you can receive them as a weekly digest. If you don't have the time or facility to receive the mailing list, then you can search our online archives. You'll find the ability to search on specific subject areas or keywords. As these lists are moderated, you can be confident of finding good, accurate information quickly. Mails can be edited or moved by the moderator into the correct place, making this a most efficient resource. Junk and spam mail are deleted, and your own e-mail address is protected by the unique Lyris system from web-bots that can automatically collect newsgroup mailing list addresses.

E-mail Support

If you wish to point out errata to put up on the web site or directly query a problem in the book with an expert who knows the book in detail, then e-mail support@wrox.com. A typical e-mail should include the following things:

- The name of the book, the last four digits of the book's ISBN, and the page number of the problem in the Subject field
- Your name, contact info and description of the problem in the body of the message

Tell Us What You Think

The author and the Wrox team have worked hard to make this book a pleasure to read as well as being useful and educational, so we'd like to know what you think. Wrox are always keen to hear what you liked best and what improvements you think are possible. We appreciate feedback on our efforts and take both criticism and praise on board in our future editorial efforts. When necessary, we'll forward comments and queries to the author. If you've anything to say, let us know by sending an e-mail to:

feedback@wrox.com

1

XSLT in Context

This chapter is designed to put XSLT in context. It's about the purpose of XSLT and the task it was designed to perform. It's about what kind of language it is, and how it came to be that way; and it's about how XSLT fits in with all the other technologies that you are likely to use in a typical web-based application. I won't be saying much in this chapter about what an XSLT stylesheet actually looks like or how it works: that will come later, in Chapters 2 and 3.

I shall begin by describing the task that XSLT is designed to perform – **transformation** – and why there is the need to transform XML documents. I'll then present a trivial example of a transformation in order to explain what this means in practice.

The chapter then moves on to discuss the relationship of XSLT to other standards in the growing XML family, to put its function into context and explain how it complements the other standards.

I'll describe what kind of language XSLT is, and delve a little into the history of how it came to be like that. If you're impatient you may want to skip the history and get on with using the language, but sooner or later you will ask "why on earth did they design it like that?" and at that stage I hope you will go back and read about the process by which XSLT came into being.

Finally, I'll have a few things to say about the different ways of using XSLT within the overall architecture of an application, in which there will inevitably be many other technologies and components each playing their own part.

What is XSLT?

XSLT, which stands for **eXtensible Stylesheet Language: Transformations**, is a language which, according to the very first sentence in the specification (found at http://www.w3.org/TR/xslt), is primarily designed for transforming one XML document into another. However, XSLT is more than capable of transforming XML to HTML and many other text-based formats, so a more general definition might be as follows:

> **XSLT is a language for transforming the structure of an XML document.**

Why should you want to do that? In order to answer this question properly, we first need to remind ourselves why XML has proved such a success and generated so much excitement.

Why Transform XML?

XML is a simple, standard way to interchange structured textual data between computer programs. Part of its success comes because it is also readable and writable by humans,, using nothing more complicated than a text editor, but this doesn't alter the fact that it is primarily intended for communication between software systems. As such, XML satisfies two compelling requirements:

- **Separating data from presentation**. The need to separate information (such as a weather forecast) from details of the way it is to be presented on a particular device. This need is becoming ever more urgent as the range of internet-capable devices grows. Organizations that have invested in creating valuable information sources need to be able to deliver them not only to the traditional PC-based web browser (which itself now comes in many flavors), but also to TV sets and WAP phones, not to mention the continuing need to produce print-on-paper.

- **Transmitting data between applications**. The need to transmit information (such as orders and invoices) from one organization to another without investing in bespoke software integration projects. As electronic commerce gathers pace, the amount of data exchanged between enterprises increases daily and this need becomes ever more urgent.

Of course, these two ways of using XML are not mutually exclusive. An invoice can be presented on the screen as well as being input to a financial application package, and weather forecasts can be summarized, indexed, and aggregated by the recipient instead of being displayed directly. Another of the key benefits of XML is that it unifies the worlds of documents and data, providing a single way of representing structure regardless of whether the information is intended for human or machine consumption. The main point is that, whether the XML data is ultimately used by people or by a software application, it will very rarely be used directly in the form it arrives: it first has to be transformed into something else.

In order to communicate with a human reader, this something else might be a document that can be displayed or printed: for example an HTML file, a PDF file, or even audible sound. Converting XML to HTML for display is probably the most common application of XSLT today, and it is the one I will use in most of the examples in this book. Once you have the data in HTML format, it can be displayed on any browser.

In order to transfer data between different applications we need to be able to transform data from the data model used by one application to the model used in another. To load the data into an application, the required format might be a comma-separated-values file, a SQL script, an HTTP message, or a sequence of calls on a particular programming interface. Alternatively, it might be another XML file using a different vocabulary from the original. As XML-based electronic commerce becomes widespread, so the role of XSLT in data conversion between applications also becomes ever more important. Just because everyone is using XML does not mean the need for data conversion will disappear. There will always be multiple standards in use. For example, the newspaper industry is likely to use different formats for exchanging news articles from the format used in the broadcasting industry. Equally, there will always be a need to do things like extracting an address from a purchase order and adding it to an invoice. So linking up enterprises to do e-commerce will increasingly become a case of defining how to extract and combine data from one set of XML documents to generate another set of XML documents: and XSLT is the ideal tool for the job.

At the end of this chapter we will come back to specific examples of when XSLT should be used to transform XML. For now, I just wanted to establish a feel for the importance and usefulness of transforming XML. Before we move on to discuss XSLT in more detail and have a first look at how it works, let's take a look at an example that clearly demonstrates the variety of formats to which we can transform XML, using XSLT.

An Example: Transforming Music

There is an excellent registry of XML vocabularies and schemas at http://www.xml.org/xmlorg_registry/index.shtml.

If you look there, you will find half a dozen different XML schemas for describing music. These were all invented with different purposes in mind: a markup language used by a publisher for printing sheet music has different requirements from one designed to let you listen to the music from a browser. MusicML, for example, is oriented to displaying music notation graphically; ChordML is designed for encoding the harmonic accompaniment to vocal lyrics; MusicXML is designed to represent musical scores, specifically western musical notation from the 17th century onwards, while the rather more academic Music Markup Language (MML) from the University of Pretoria is designed for serious musicological analysis, embracing Eastern and African as well as Western musical idioms.

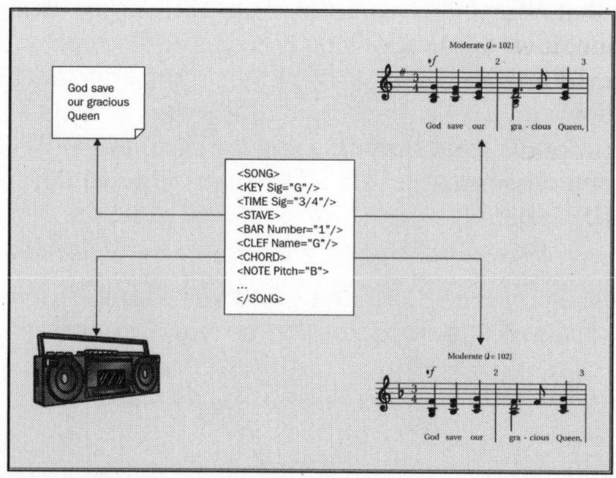

So you could use XSLT to process marked-up music in many different ways:

- You could use XSLT to convert music from one of these representations to another, for example from MusicXML to MML.
- You could use XSLT to convert music from any of these representations into visual music notation, by generating the XML-based vector graphics format SVG.
- You could use XSLT to play the music on a synthesizer, by generating a MIDI (Musical Instrument Digital Interface) file.
- You could use XSLT to perform a musical transformation, such as transposing the music into a different key.
- You could use XSLT to extract the lyrics, into HTML or into a text-only XML document.

As you can see, XSLT is not just for converting XML documents to HTML!

How does XSLT transform XML?

By now you are probably wondering exactly how XSLT goes about processing an XML document in order to convert it into the required output. There are usually two aspects to this process:

- The first stage is a structural transformation, in which the data is converted from the structure of the incoming XML document to a structure that reflects the desired output.
- The second stage is formatting, in which the new structure is output in the required format such as HTML or PDF.

The second stage covers the ground we discussed in the previous section; the data structure that results from the first stage can be output as HTML, a text file or as XML. HTML output allows the information to be viewed directly in a browser by a human user or be input into any modern word processor. Plain text output allows data to be formatted in the way an existing application can accept, for example comma-separated values or one of the many text-based data interchange formats that were developed before XML arrived on the scene. Finally, XML output allows the data to be supplied to one of the new breed of applications that accepts XML directly. Typically this will use a different vocabulary of XML tags from the original document: for example an XSLT transformation might take the monthly sales figures as its XML input and produce a histogram as its XML output, using the XML-based SVG standard for vector graphics. Or you could use an XSLT transformation to generate VoxML output, for aural rendition of your data.

> *Links to information about Motorola's VoxML Voice Markup Language can be found at* http://www.oasis-open.org/cover/voxML.html

Let's now delve into the first stage, transformation – the stage with which XSLT is primarily concerned and which makes it possible to provide output in all of these formats. This stage might involve selecting data, aggregating and grouping it, sorting it, or performing arithmetic conversions such as changing centimeters to inches.

So how does this come about? Before the advent of XSLT, you could only process incoming XML documents by writing a custom application. The application wouldn't actually need to parse the raw XML, but it would need to invoke an XML parser, via a defined Application Programming Interface (API), to get information from the document and do something with it. There are two principal APIs for achieving this: the Simple API for XML (SAX) and the Document Object Model (DOM).

The SAX API is an event-based interface in which the parser notifies the application of each piece of information in the document as it is read. If you use the DOM API, then the parser interrogates the document and builds a tree-like object structure in memory. You would then write a custom application (in a procedural language such as C++, Visual Basic, or Java, for example), which could interrogate this tree structure. It would do so by defining a specific **sequence of steps** to be followed in order to produce the required output. Thus, whatever parser you use, this process has the same principal drawback: every time you want to handle a new kind of XML document, you have to write a new custom program, describing a different sequence of steps, to process the XML.

Both the DOM and the SAX APIs are fully described in the Wrox Press book Professional XML, ISBN 1-861003-11-0.

So how is using XSLT to perform transformations on XML better than writing "custom applications"? Well, the design of XSLT is based on a recognition that these programs are all very similar, and it should therefore be possible to describe what they do using a high-level **declarative** language rather than writing each program from scratch in C++, Visual Basic, or Java. The required transformation can be expressed as a set of rules. These rules are based on defining what output should be generated when particular patterns occur in the input. The language is declarative, in the sense that you describe the transformation you require, rather than providing a sequence of procedural instructions to achieve it. XSLT describes the required transformation and then relies on the XSLT processor to decide the most efficient way to go about it.

XSLT still relies on an XML parser – be it a DOM parser or a SAX-compliant one – to convert the XML document into a tree structure. It is the structure of this tree representation of the document that XSLT manipulates, not the document itself. If you are familiar with the DOM, then you will be happy with the idea of treating every item in an XML document (elements, attributes, processing instructions etc.) as a node in a tree. With XSLT we have a high-level language that can navigate around a node tree, select specific nodes and perform complex manipulations on these nodes.

The XSLT tree model is similar in concept to the DOM but it is not the same. The full XSLT processing model is discussed in Chapter 2.

The description of XSLT given thus far (a declarative language that can navigate to and select specific data and then manipulate that data) may strike you as being similar to that of the standard database query language, SQL. Let's take a closer look at this comparison.

XSLT and SQL: an Analogy

I like to think of an analogy with relational databases. In a relational database, the data consists of a set of tables. By themselves, the tables are not much use, the data might as well be stored in flat files in comma-separated values format. The power of a relational database doesn't come from its data structure; it comes from the language that processes the data, SQL. In the same way, XML on its own just defines a data structure. It's a bit richer than the tables of the relational model, but by itself it doesn't actually do anything very useful. It's when we get a high-level language expressly designed to manipulate the data structure that we start to find we've got something interesting on our hands, and for XML data that language is XSLT.

Superficially, SQL and XSLT are very different languages. But if you look below the surface, they actually have a lot in common. For starters, in order to process specific data, be it in a relational database or an XML document, the processing language must incorporate a declarative query syntax for selecting the data that needs to be processed. In SQL, that's the `SELECT` statement. In XSLT, the equivalent is the **XPath expression**.

The XPath expression language forms an essential part of XSLT, though it is actually defined in a separate W3C Recommendation (http://www.w3.org/TR/xpath) because it can also be used independently of XSLT (the relationship between XPath and XSLT is discussed further on page 26).

The XPath query syntax is designed to retrieve nodes from an XML document, based on a path through the XML document or the context in which the node appears. It allows access to specific nodes, while preserving the hierarchy and structure of the document. XSLT is then used to manipulate the results of these queries (rearranging selected nodes, constructing new nodes etc).

There are further similarities between XSLT and SQL:

- Both languages augment the basic query facilities with useful additions for performing basic arithmetic, string manipulation, and comparison operations.
- Both languages supplement the declarative query syntax with semi-procedural facilities for describing the sequence of processing to be carried out, and they also provide hooks to escape into conventional programming languages where the algorithms start to get too complex.

- Both languages have an important property called **closure**, which means that the output has the same data structure as the input. For SQL, this structure is tables, for XSLT it is trees – the tree representation of XML documents. The closure property is extremely valuable because it means operations performed using the language can be combined end-to-end to define bigger more complex operations: you just take the output of one operation and make it the input of the next operation. In SQL you can do this by defining views or subqueries; in XSLT you can do it by passing your data through a series of stylesheets, or (with the new XSLT 1.1 specification, currently a working draft) by capturing the output of one transformation phase as a temporary tree, and using that temporary tree as the input of another transformation phase.

In the real world, of course, XSLT and SQL have to coexist. There are many possible relationships, but typically data will be stored in relational databases and transmitted between systems in XML. The two languages don't fit together as comfortably as one would like, because the data models are so different. But XSLT transformations can play an important role in bridging the divide. A number of database vendors have delivered products that integrate XML and SQL, though there are no standards in this area as yet. Check the vendor's web sites for the latest releases of Microsoft SQL Server 2000, and Oracle 9i.

Before we move on to look at a simple working example of an XSLT transformation, we need to briefly discuss a few of the XSLT processors that are available to effect these transformations.

XSLT Processors

The principal role of an XSLT processor is to apply an XSLT stylesheet to an XML source document and produce a result document. It is important to note that each of these is an application of XML and so the underlying structure of each is a tree. So, in fact, the XSLT processor handles three trees.

There are several XSLT processors to choose from. Here I'll mention three: Saxon, Xalan, and Microsoft MSXML3. All of these can be downloaded free of charge (but do read the licensing conditions).

These three processors and several others are described in detail in the Appendices to this book.

Saxon is an open source XSLT processor developed by the author of this book. It is a Java application, and can be run directly from the command prompt; no web server or browser is required. The Saxon program will transform the XML document to, say, an HTML document, which can then be placed on a web server. In this example, both the browser and web server only deal with the transformed document.

If you are running Windows (95/98/NT/2000) the simplest way to use it is to download Instant Saxon, which is packaged as a Windows executable. You will need to have Java installed, but that will be there already if you have any recent version of Internet Explorer. On non-Windows platforms you will need to install the full Saxon product and follow the instructions that come with it. You can download Instant Saxon for free from http://users.iclway.co.uk/mhkay/saxon/index.html. Saxon will run with any XML parser that implements the SAX2 interface (in its Java form), but it comes with a copy of the Ælfred parser, so you don't need to install one separately.

Xalan is another open source XSLT processor, available from the Apache organization at http://xml.apache.org/. Xalan was originally derived from an IBM product called LotusXSL , but it has since developed an open-source life of its own. Xalan is available in both Java and C++ versions. Like Saxon, Xalan-Java is a Java application that can be run from the command prompt. Xalan too can operate with any SAX2-compliant parser; it comes with a copy of its stable-mate parser, Xerces.

Saxon and Xalan-Java both implement the same Java interface, known as TrAX, which I will describe in Appendix F: this means you can write applications that work with either processor. Both are highly conformant to the XSLT 1.0 specification, so your stylesheets will be fully portable; but they have different capabilities in terms of what they can do beyond the requirements of the standard. Both products are more fully described in Appendices to this book.

Alternatively, you can run XSLT stylesheets actually within Internet Explorer. The production versions of IE5 and IE5.5 are shipped with a processor that handles a Microsoft dialect of XSLT loosely based on an early 1998 working draft of the W3C specification: this language (which I'll call *working-draft XSL* or *WD-xsl*) is quite different from the final version, and I strongly recommend you to avoid it. Microsoft now provide a fully-conformant implementation of the final XSLT 1.0 specification, which is known as MSXML3. In due course this will probably be shipped as standard with Internet Explorer 6, but in the meantime you can download it separately from http://msdn.microsoft.com and install it for use with IE5 or IE5.5.

Download and install both the SDK and the run-time package. You should also download and install a program called `xmlinst.exe`. Run this program to establish MSXML3 as the default XML processor to be used by Internet Explorer (if you don't do this, IE5 will try to use the old WD-xsl processor). The big advantage of Microsoft's technology is that the XSLT processing can take place on the browser.

I've avoided talking about specific products in most of the book, because the information is likely to change quite rapidly. The products that I've described in the Appendices are reasonably stable by now, but new products are constantly appearing. It's best to get the latest status from the web. Some good places to start are:

- http://www.w3.org/Style/XSL
- http://www.xslinfo.com/
- http://www.xml.com/
- http://www.oasis-open.org/cover

An Example Stylesheet

Now we're ready to take a look at an example of using XSLT to transform a very simple XML document.

Example: A "Hello, world!" XSLT Stylesheet

Kernighan and Ritchie in their classic *The C Programming Language* originated the idea of presenting a trivial but complete program right at the beginning of the book, and ever since then the "Hello world" program has been an honored tradition. Of course, a complete description of how this example works is not possible until all the concepts have been defined, so if you feel I'm not explaining it fully, don't worry – the explanations will come later.

Input

What kind of transformation would we like to do? Let's try transforming the following XML document:

```
<?xml version="1.0" encoding="iso-8859-1"?>
<?xml-stylesheet type="text/xsl" href="hello.xsl"?>
<greeting>Hello, world!</greeting>
```

A simple node-tree-representation of this document would look as follows:

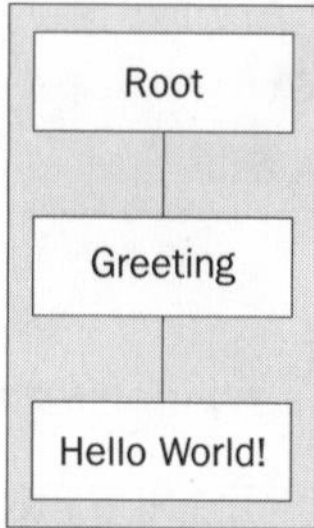

There is one root node per document. The root node in the XSLT model performs the same function as the document node in the DOM model. The XML declaration is not visible to the parser and, therefore, is not included in the tree.

I've deliberately made it easy by including an `<?xml-stylesheet?>` processing instruction in the source XML file. Many XSLT processors will use this to identify the stylesheet if you don't specify a different stylesheet to use. The `href` attribute gives the relative URI of the default stylesheet for this document.

Output

Our required output is the following HTML, which will simply change the browser title to "Today's Greeting" and display whatever greeting is in the source XML file:

```
<html>
<head>
   <title>Today's greeting</title>
</head>
<body>
   <p>Hello, world!</p>
</body>
</html>
```

XSLT Stylesheet

Without any more ado, here's the XSLT stylesheet `hello.xsl` to effect the transformation:

```
<?xml version="1.0" encoding="iso-8859-1"?>
<xsl:stylesheet
   version="1.0"
   xmlns:xsl="http://www.w3.org/1999/XSL/Transform">

<xsl:template match="/">
   <html>
   <head>
      <title>Today's greeting</title>
   </head>
   <body>
      <p><xsl:value-of select="greeting"/></p>
   </body>
   </html>
</xsl:template>

</xsl:stylesheet>
```

Running the Stylesheet

You can run this stylesheet using any of the three processors described in the previous section.

Saxon

With Saxon, the steps (for a Windows platform) are:

- Download the Instant Saxon processor
- Install the executable `saxon.exe` in a suitable directory, and make this the current directory
- Using Notepad, type the two files above into `hello.xml` and `hello.xsl` respectively, within this directory (or get them from the Wrox web site at http://www.wrox.com)
- Bring up an MSDOS-style console window (using Start | Programs | MSDOS Prompt on Windows 98 or NT, or look in the Accessories menu under Windows 2000)

- Type the following at the command prompt:
  `saxon hello.xml hello.xsl`
- Admire the HTML displayed on the standard output

If you want to view the output using your browser, simply save the command line output as an HTML file, in the following manner:

```
saxon hello.xml hello.xsl >hello.html
```

Because you're using the default stylesheet for this source XML document, you could also write:

```
saxon -a hello.xml >hello.html
```

Xalan-Java

The procedure is very similar if you use Xalan-Java. However, Xalan doesn't have a special version packaged for the Windows platform in the way Saxon does, so you'll have to run the application explicitly under Java (you can also do this with Saxon if you use the full version).

You will need to install a Java Virtual Machine. Xalan doesn't support the Microsoft Virtual Machine that comes with Internet Explorer (because it requires features from later versions of Java), so you'll need to do this separately. I usually use Sun's JDK 1.3, which you can get from http://java.sun.com/j2se/1.3/. Installing this is very straightforward, though it's a large download.

Having downloaded Xalan-Java 2 as a `.zip` file, you need to unpack it into a suitable directory. There are two important files that must be accessible to the Java Virtual Machine. These are `xalan.jar` (containing the code of the XSLT processor) and `xerces.jar` (holding the XML parser), both found in the `bin` directory. To tell the Java VM where to find this file, they must be present in the `CLASSPATH` environment variable. You can set this variable in your `autoexec.bat` file, or whatever other script your operating system executes when you log in; on Windows NT and Windows 2000 you set environment variables using the `System` icon on the control panel. An alternative is to enter the classpath as part of the command that invokes the application.

I usually move all the `.jar` files I need to a directory such as `c:\jars` and then set the classpath as follows:

```
SET CLASSPATH=.;c:\jars\xalan.jar;c:\jars\xerces.jar
```

Note that it is the `.jar` files themselves that must be on the classpath, not the directory containing them.

The command to run the "hello world" transformation under Xalan is then:

```
java org.apache.xalan.xslt.Process -in hello.xml -xsl hello.xsl
```

It should give the same result as Saxon. Because you're using the default stylesheet, you could simplify this to:

```
java org.apache.xalan.xslt.Process -in hello.xml
```

If you want to direct the output to a specific file, use the `-out` option.

MSXML3

Finally, you can run the stylesheet actually within Internet Explorer.

Once you have installed MSXML3 as your default XSLT processor, you should simply be able to double-click on the `hello.xml` file, which will bring up IE5 and load `hello.xml` into the browser. IE5 reads the XML file, discovers what stylesheet is needed, loads the stylesheet, executes it to perform the transformation, and displays the resulting HTML. If you don't see the text "Hello, world!" on the screen, but just the XML file, this is because you're using the original WD-xsl interpreter that Microsoft issued with IE5, not the MSXML3 version. If you see the stylesheet displayed, this also indicates that you haven't completed the installation process correctly. Remember to run the `xmlinst.exe` program.

How it Works

If you've succeeded in running this example, or even if you just want to get on with reading the book, you'll want to know how it works. Let's dissect it:

```
<?xml version="1.0" encoding="iso-8859-1"?>
```

This is just the standard XML heading. The interesting point is that an XSLT stylesheet is itself an XML document. I'll have more to say about this later in the chapter. I've used `iso-8859-1` character encoding (which is the official name for the character set that Microsoft sometimes calls "ANSI") because in Western Europe and North America it's the character set that most text editors support. If you've got a text editor that supports `UTF-8` or some other character encoding, feel free to use that instead.

```
<xsl:stylesheet
   version="1.0"
   xmlns:xsl="http://www.w3.org/1999/XSL/Transform">
```

This is the standard XSLT heading. In XML terms it's an element start tag, and it identifies the document as a stylesheet. The **`xmlns:xsl`** attribute is an XML Namespace declaration, which indicates that the prefix **`xsl`** is going to be used for elements defined in the W3C XSLT specification. XSLT makes extensive use of XML namespaces, and all the element names defined in the standard are prefixed with this namespace to avoid any clash with names used in your source document. The **`version`** attribute indicates that the stylesheet is only using features from version 1.0 of the XSLT standard.

Let's move on:

```
<xsl:template match="/">
```

An **`<xsl:template>`** element defines a template rule to be triggered when a particular part of the source document is being processed. The attribute **`match="/"`** indicates that this particular rule is triggered right at the start of processing the source document. Here «/» is an XPath expression which identifies the **root node** of the document: an XML document has a hierarchic structure, and in the same way as UNIX uses the special filename «/» to indicate the root of a hierarchic filestore, XPath uses «/» to represent the root of the XML content hierarchy. The DOM model calls this the Document object, but in XPath it is called the root.

```
<html>
<head>
   <title>Today's greeting</title>
</head>
<body>
   <p><xsl:value-of select="greeting"/></p>
</body>
</html>
```

Once this rule is triggered, the body of the template says what output to generate. Most of the template body here is a sequence of HTML elements and text to be copied into the output file. There's one exception: an **<xsl:value-of>** element, which we recognize as an XSLT instruction because it uses the namespace prefix **xsl**. This particular instruction copies the value of a node in the source document to the output document. The **select** attribute of the element specifies the node for which the value should be evaluated. The XPath expression «**greeting**» means: "find the set of all **<greeting>** elements that are children of the node that this template rule is currently processing". In this case, this means the **<greeting>** element that's the outermost element of the source document. The **<xsl:value-of>** instruction then extracts the text node of this element, and copies it to the output at the relevant place, in other words within the generated **<p>** element.

All that remains is to finish what we started:

```
</xsl:template>

</xsl:stylesheet>
```

In fact, for a simple stylesheet like the one shown above, you can cut out some of the red tape. Since there is only one template rule, the **<xsl:template>** element can actually be omitted. The following is a complete, valid stylesheet equivalent to the preceding one:

```
<html xsl:version="1.0"
      xmlns:xsl="http://www.w3.org/1999/XSL/Transform">
<head>
   <title>Today's greeting</title>
</head>
<body>
   <p><xsl:value-of select="greeting"/></p>
</body>
</html>
```

This simplified syntax is designed to make XSLT look familiar to people who have learned to use proprietary template languages which allow you to write a skeleton HTML page with special tags (analogous to **<xsl:value-of>**) to insert variable data at the appropriate place. But as we'll see, XSLT is much more powerful than that.

Why would you want to place today's greeting in a separate XML file and display it using a stylesheet? One reason is that you might want to show the greeting in different ways depending on the context; for example, it might be shown differently on a different device. In this case you could write a different stylesheet to transform the same source document in a different way. This raises the question of how a stylesheet gets selected at run-time. There is no single answer to this question. As we saw above, Saxon and Xalan have interfaces that allow you to nominate both the stylesheet and the source document to use. The same thing can also be achieved with the Microsoft XSLT product, though it requires you to write an HTML page containing some script code to control the transformation: the **<?xml-stylesheet?>** processing instruction which I used in the example above only works if you want to use the same stylesheet every time.

It's time now to take a closer look at the relationship between XSLT and XPath and other XML-related technologies.

The Place of XSLT in the XML Family

XSLT is published by the World Wide Web Consortium (W3C) and fits into the XML family of standards, most of which are also developed by W3C. In this section I will try to explain the sometimes-confusing relationship of XSLT to other related standards and specifications.

XSLT and XSL

XSLT started life as part of a bigger language called **XSL (Extensible Stylesheet Language)**. As the name implies, XSL was (and is) intended to define the formatting and presentation of XML documents for display on screen, on paper, or in the spoken word. As the development of XSL proceeded, it became clear that this was usually a two-stage process; first a structural transformation, in which elements are selected, grouped and reordered, and then a formatting process in which the resulting elements are rendered as ink on paper, or pixels on the screen. It was recognized that these two stages were quite independent, so XSL was split into two parts, XSLT for defining transformations, and "the rest" – which is still officially called XSL, though some people prefer to call it **XSL-FO (XSL Formatting Objects)** – for the formatting stage.

XSL Formatting is nothing more than another XML vocabulary, in which the objects described are areas of the printed page and their properties. Since this is just another XML vocabulary, XSLT needs no special capabilities to generate this as its output. XSL Formatting is outside the scope of this book. It's a big subject (the draft specification currently available is far longer than XSLT), the standard is not completely finalized, and the products that implement it are still incomplete. What's more, you're far less likely to need it than to need XSLT. XSL Formatting provides wonderful facilities to achieve high-quality typographical output of your documents. However, for most people translating documents into HTML for presentation by a standard browser is quite good enough, and that can be achieved using XSLT alone, or if necessary, by using XSLT in conjunction with Cascading Style Sheets (CSS or CSS2), which I shall return to shortly.

> *The XSL Formatting specifications, which at the time of writing are at Candidate Recommendation status, can be found at* http://www.w3.org/TR/xsl. *A Candidate Recommendation is a specification that W3C has published for final comments, which will normally become a formal Recommendation when those comments have been dealt with. The conditions for XSL Formatting Objects to become a full Recommendation also require evidence that all its constructs have been successfully implemented, and that different implementations are interoperable.*

XSLT and XPath

Halfway through the development of XSLT, it was recognized that there was a significant overlap between the expression syntax in XSLT for selecting parts of a document, and the XPointer language being developed for linking from one document to another. To avoid having two separate but overlapping expression languages, the two committees decided to join forces and define a single language, **XPath**, which would serve both purposes. XPath version 1.0 was published on the same day as XSLT, 16 November 1999.

XPath acts as a sublanguage within an XSLT stylesheet. An XPath expression may be used for numerical calculations or string manipulations, or for testing Boolean conditions, but its most characteristic use (and the one that gives it its name) is to identify parts of the input document to be processed. For example, the following instruction outputs the average price of all the books in the input document:

```
<xsl:value-of select="sum(//book/@price) div count(//book)"/>
```

Here the **`<xsl:value-of>`** element is an instruction defined in the XSLT standard, which causes a value to be written to the output document. The **`select`** attribute contains an XPath expression, which calculates the value to be written: specifically, the total of the **`price`** attributes on all the **`<book>`** elements, divided by the number of **`<book>`** elements.

The XPath specification is increasingly taking on a life of its own, separate from XSLT. For example, several DOM implementations (including Microsoft's) allow you to select nodes within a DOM tree structure using a method such as `selectNodes(XPath)`, and such a feature is being considered for the next version of the standard, DOM3. XPath is also used within other W3C specifications including XPointer and XQuery.

The separation of XPath from XSLT works reasonably well, but there are places where the split seems awkward, and there are many cases where it's difficult to know which document to read to find the answer to a particular question. For example, an XPath expression can contain a reference to a variable, but creating the variable and giving it an initial value is the job of XSLT. Another example: XPath expressions can call functions, and there is a range of standard functions defined. Those whose effect is completely freestanding, such as **`string-length()`**, are defined in the XPath specification, whereas additional functions whose behavior relies on XSLT definitions, such as **`key()`**, are defined in the XSLT specification.

Because the split is awkward, I've written this book as if XSLT+XPath were a single language. For example, all the standard functions are described together in Chapter 7. In the reference sections, I've tried to indicate where each function or other construct is defined in the original standards, but the working assumption is that you are using both languages together and you don't need to know where one stops and the other one takes over. The only downside of this approach is that if you want to use XPath on its own, for example when using the DOM `selectNodes()` method, then you need to check the description of the function in Chapter 7 to see whether it is part of the XPath core or whether it is an XSLT addition.

XSLT and Internet Explorer 5

Very soon after the first draft proposals for XSL were published, back in 1998, Microsoft shipped a partial implementation as a technology preview for use with IE4. This was subsequently replaced with a rather different implementation when IE5 came out. This second implementation, known as MSXSL, remained in the field essentially unchanged until very recently, and is still being shipped with every copy of IE5 and IE5.5, and also with Windows 2000. Unfortunately, though, Microsoft jumped the gun, and the XSLT standard changed and grew, so that when the XSLT Recommendation version 1.0 was finally published on 16 November 1999, it bore very little resemblance to the initial Microsoft product.

> **A Recommendation is the most definitive of documents produced by the W3C. It's not technically a standard, because standards can only be published by government-approved standards organizations. But I will often refer to it loosely as "the standard" in this book.**

Many of the differences, such as changes of keywords, are very superficial but some run much deeper; for example, changes in the way the equals operator is defined.

So the Microsoft IE5 dialect of XSL, which I refer to as WD-xsl, is also outside the scope of this book. Please don't assume that anything in this book is relevant to the original Microsoft XSL as even where the syntax appears similar to XSLT, the meaning of the construct may be completely different.

> *You can find information about WD-xsl in the Wrox book XML IE5 Programmer's Reference, ISBN 1-861001-57-6.*

As we've already seen, Microsoft's MSXML3 is a full implementation of the XSLT 1.0 specification, but at the time of writing you have to download and install this separately. MSXML3 actually supports both the old WD-xsl dialect and the newer XSLT 1.0 language; it decides which is in use based on the namespace URI of the `<xsl:stylesheet>` element.

Microsoft has also released a converter to upgrade stylesheets from WD-xsl to XSLT 1.0. However, this isn't the end of the story, because, of course, there are millions of copies of IE5 installed that only support the old version. If you want to develop a web site that delivers XML to the browser and relies on the browser interpreting its XSLT stylesheet, you've currently got your work cut out to make sure all your users can handle it. Microsoft do provide a CAB file installer to help with the roll-out of MSXML3 — check the MSDN web site for details.

If you are using Microsoft technology on the server, there is an ISAPI extension called XSLISAPI that allows you to do the transformation in the browser where it's supported, and on the server otherwise. Unless you're in control of the browser configuration, however, **server-side** transformation of XML to HTML, driven from ASP pages or from Java servlets, is really the only practical option today for a serious project.

There's more information about Microsoft's XML products in Appendix A – but do be aware that it will become out of date very rapidly.

XSLT and XML

XSLT is essentially a tool for transforming XML documents. At the start of this chapter we discussed the reasons why this is important, but now we need to look a little more precisely at the relationship between the two. There are two particular aspects of XML that XSLT interacts with very closely: one is XML Namespaces; the other is the XML Information Set. These are discussed in the following sections.

XML Namespaces

XSLT is designed on the basis that **XML namespaces** are an essential part of the XML standard. So when the XSLT standard refers to an XML document, it really means an XML document that also conforms to the XML Namespaces specification, which can be found at http://www.w3.org/TR/REC-xml-names.

> *For a full explanation of XML Namespaces, see Chapter 7 of the Wrox Press book* Professional XML, ISBN 1-861003-11-0.

Namespaces play an important role in XSLT. Their purpose is to allow you to mix tags from two different vocabularies in the same XML document. For example, in one vocabulary **`<table>`** might mean a two-dimensional array of data values, while in another vocabulary **`<table>`** refers to a piece of furniture. Here's a quick reminder of how they work:

- Namespaces are identified by a Uniform Resource Identifier (URI). This can take a number of forms. One form is the familiar URL, for example `http://www.wrox.com/namespace`. Another form, not fully standardized but being used in some XML vocabularies (see, for example, http://www.biztalk.org) is a URN, for example `urn:java:com.icl.saxon`. The detailed form of the URI doesn't matter, but it is a good idea to choose one that will be unique. One good way of achieving this is to use the URL of your own web site. But don't let this confuse you into thinking that there must be something on the web site for the URL to point to. The namespace URI is simply a string that you have chosen to be different from other people's namespace URIs; it doesn't need to point to anything.

- Since namespace URIs are often rather long and use special characters such as «/», they are not used in full as part of the element and attribute names. Instead, each namespace used in a document can be given a short nickname, and this nickname is used as a prefix of the element and attribute names. It doesn't matter what prefix you choose, because the real name of the element or attribute is determined only by its namespace URI and its local name (the part of the name after the prefix). For example, all my examples use the prefix **`xsl`** to refer to the namespace URI `http://www.w3.org/1999/XSL/Transform`, but you could equally well use the prefix **`xslt`**, so long as you use it consistently.

- For element names, you can also declare a default namespace URI, which is to be associated with unprefixed element names. The default namespace URI, however, does not apply to unprefixed attribute names.

A namespace prefix is declared using a special pseudo-attribute within any element tag, with the form:

```
xmlns:prefix = "namespace-URI"
```

This declares a namespace prefix, which can be used for the name of that element, for its attributes, and for any element or attribute name contained in that element. The default namespace, which is used for elements having no prefix (but not for attributes), is similarly declared using a pseudo-attribute:

```
xmlns = "namespace-URI"
```

XSLT can't be used to process an XML document unless it conforms to the XML Namespaces Recommendation. In practice this isn't a problem, because most people are treating XML Namespaces as an intrinsic part of the XML standard, rather than a bolt-on optional extra. It does have certain implications, though. In particular, serious use of Namespaces is virtually incompatible with serious use of Document Type Definitions, because DTDs don't recognize the special significance of prefixes in element names; so a consequence of backing Namespaces is that XSLT provides very little support for DTDs, choosing instead to wait for the replacement facility, XML Schemas.

The XML Information Set

XSLT is designed to work on the information carried by an XML document, not on the raw document itself. This means that, as an XSLT programmer, you are given a tree view of the source document in which some aspects are visible and others are not. For example, you can see the attribute names and values, but you can't see whether the attribute was written in single or double quotes, you can't see what order the attributes were in, and you can't tell whether or not they were written on the same line.

One messy detail is that there have been many attempts to define exactly what constitutes the **essential** information content of a well-formed XML document, as distinct from its accidental punctuation. All attempts so far have come up with slightly different answers. The most recent, and the most definitive, attempt to provide a common vocabulary for the content of XML documents is the **XML Information Set** definition (usually called "the infoset"), which may be found at http://www.w3.org/TR/xml-infoset.

Unfortunately this came too late to make all the standards consistent. For example, some treat comments as significant, others not; some treat the choice of namespace prefixes as significant, others take them as irrelevant. I shall describe in Chapter 2 exactly how XSLT (or more accurately, XPath) defines the tree model of XML, and how it differs in finer points of detail from some of the other definitions such as the Document Object Model or DOM.

One piece of jargon you will start hearing more often is the concept of the **post-schema-validation infoset** or PSVI. This contains the significant information from the source document, augmented with information taken from its XML schema. It therefore allows you to find out not only that the value of an attribute was «`17.3`», but also that the attribute was described in the schema as a non-negative decimal number. XSLT isn't yet able to use this information, but it features strongly in the published requirements list for the next version, XSLT 2.0.

XSL and CSS

Why are there two stylesheet languages, XSL (that is, XSLT plus XSL Formatting Objects) as well as Cascading Style Sheets (CSS and CSS2)?

It's only fair to say that in an ideal world there would be a single language in this role, and that the reason there are two is that no-one has been able to invent something that achieved the simplicity and economy of CSS for doing simple things, combined with the power of XSL for doing more complex things.

CSS (by which I include CSS2, which greatly extends the degree to which you can control the final appearance of the page) is mainly used for rendering HTML, but it can also be used for rendering XML directly, by defining the display characteristics of each XML element. However, it has serious limitations. It cannot reorder the elements in the source document, it cannot add text or images, it cannot decide which elements should be displayed and which omitted, it cannot calculate totals or averages or sequence numbers. In other words, it can only be used when the structure of the source document is already very close to the final display form.

Having said this, CSS is simple to write, and it is very economical in machine resources. It doesn't reorder the document, so it doesn't need to build a tree representation of the document in memory, and it can start displaying the document as soon as the first text is received over the network. Perhaps most important of all, CSS is very simple for HTML authors to write, without any programming skills. In comparison, XSLT is far more powerful, but it also consumes a lot more memory and processor power, as well as training budget.

It's often appropriate to use both tools together. Use XSLT to create a representation of the document that is close to its final form, in that it contains the right text in the right order, and then use CSS to add the finishing touches, by selecting font sizes, colors, and so on. Typically (today) you would do the XSLT processing on the server, and the CSS processing on the client (in the browser), so another advantage of this approach is that you reduce the amount of data sent down the line, which should improve response time for your users as well as postponing the next expensive bandwidth increase.

The History of XSL

Like most of the XML family of standards, XSLT was developed by the World Wide Web Consortium (W3C), a coalition of companies orchestrated by Tim Berners-Lee, the inventor of the web. There is an interesting page on the history of XSL, and styling proposals generally, at http://www.w3.org/Style/History/.

Pre-history

HTML was originally conceived by Berners-Lee as a set of tags to mark the logical structure of a document; headings, paragraphs, links, quotes, code sections, and the like. Soon people wanted more control over how the document looked, they wanted to achieve the same control over the appearance of the delivered publication as they had with printing and paper. So HTML acquired more and more tags and attributes to control presentation; fonts, margins, tables, colors, and all the rest that followed. As it evolved, the documents being published became more and more browser-dependent, and it was seen that the original goals of simplicity and universality were starting to slip away.

The remedy was widely seen as separation of content from presentation. This was not a new concept; it had been well developed through the 1980s in the development of **Standard Generalized Markup Language** (**SGML**), whose architecture in turn was influenced by the elaborate (and never implemented) work done in the ISO Open Document Architecture (ODA) standards.

Just as XML was derived as a greatly simplified subset of SGML, so XSLT has its origins in an SGML-based standard called **DSSSL** (**Document Style Semantics and Specification Language**). DSSSL (I pronounce it *Dissel*) was developed primarily to fill the need for a standard device-independent language to define the output rendition of SGML documents, particularly for high-quality typographical presentation. SGML was around for a long time before DSSSL appeared in the early 1990s, but until then the output side had been handled using proprietary and often extremely expensive tools, geared towards driving equally expensive phototypesetters, so that the technology was only really taken up by the big publishing houses.

C. M. Sperberg-McQueen and Robert F. Goldstein presented an influential paper at the WWW '94 conference in Chicago under the title *A Manifesto for Adding SGML Intelligence to the World-Wide Web*. You can find it at: http://www.ncsa.uiuc.edu/SDG/IT94/Proceedings/Autools/sperberg-mcqueen/sperberg.html.

The authors presented a set of requirements for a stylesheet language, which is as good a statement as any of the aims that the XSL designers were trying to meet. As with other proposals from around that time, the concept of a separate transformation language had not yet appeared, and a great deal of the paper is devoted to the rendition capabilities of the language. There are many formative ideas, however, including the concept of fallback processing to cope with situations where particular features are not available in the current environment.

It is worth quoting some extracts from the paper here:

> *Ideally, the style sheet language should be declarative, not procedural, and should allow style sheets to exploit the structure of SGML documents to the fullest. Styles must be able to vary with the structural location of the element: paragraphs within notes may be formatted differently from paragraphs in the main text. Styles must be able to vary with the attribute values of the element in question: a quotation of type "display" may need to be formatted differently from a quotation of type "inline". They may even need to vary with the attribute values of other elements: items in numbered lists will look different from items in bulleted lists.*
>
> *At the same time, the language has to be reasonably easy to interpret in a procedural way: implementing the style sheet language should not become the major challenge in implementing a Web client.*
>
> *The semantics should be additive: It should be possible for users to create new style sheets by adding new specifications to some existing (possibly standard) style sheet. This should not require copying the entire base style sheet; instead, the user should be able to store locally just the user's own changes to the standard style sheet, and they should be added in at browse time. This is particularly important to support local modifications of standard DTDs.*
>
> *Syntactically, the style sheet language must be very simple, preferably trivial to parse. One obvious possibility: formulate the style sheet language as an SGML DTD, so that each style sheet will be an SGML document. Since the browser already knows how to parse SGML, no extra effort will be needed.*
>
> *We recommend strongly that a subset of DSSSL be used to formulate style sheets for use on the World Wide Web; with the completion of the standards work on DSSSL, there is no reason for any community to invent their own style-sheet language from scratch. The full DSSSL standard may well be too demanding to implement in its entirety, but even if that proves true, it provides only an argument for defining a subset of DSSSL that must be supported, not an argument for rolling our own. Unlike home-brew specifications, a subset of a standard comes with an automatically predefined growth path. We expect to work on the formulation of a usable, implementable subset of DSSSL for use in WWW style sheets, and invite all interested parties to join in the effort.*

In late 1995, a W3C-sponsored workshop on stylesheet languages was held in Paris. In view of the subsequent role of James Clark as editor of the XSLT Recommendation, it is interesting to read the notes of his contribution on the goals of DSSSL, which can be found at http://www.w3.org/Style/951106_Workshop/report1.html#clark.

What follows is a few selected paragraphs from these notes:

> *DSSSL contains both a transformation language and a formatting language. Originally the transformation was needed to make certain kinds of styles possible (such as tables of contents). The query language now takes care of that, but the transformation language survives because it is useful in its own right.*

Both simple and complex designs should be possible, and the styles should be suitable for batch formatting as well as interactive applications. Existing systems should be able to support DSSSL with only minimal changes (a DSSSL parser is obviously needed).

The language is strictly declarative, which is achieved by adopting a functional subset of Scheme. Interactive style sheet editors must be possible.

A DSSSL style sheet very precisely describes a function from SGML to a flow object tree. It allows partial style sheets to be combined ('cascaded' as in CSS): some rule may override some other rule, based on implicit and explicit priorities, but there is no blending between conflicting styles.

James Clark closed his talk with the remark:

Creating a good, extensible style language is hard!

One suspects that the effort of editing the XSLT Recommendation didn't cause him to change his mind.

The First XSL Proposal

Following these early discussions, the W3C set up a formal activity to create a stylesheet language proposal. The remit for this group specified that it should be based on DSSSL.

As an output of this activity came the first formal proposal for XSL, dated 21 August 1997. It can be found at http://www.w3.org/TR/NOTE-XSL.html.

There are eleven authors listed. They include five from Microsoft, three from Inso Corporation, plus Paul Grosso of ArborText, James Clark (who works for himself), and Henry Thompson of the University of Edinburgh.

The section describing the purpose of the language is worth reading:

XSL is a stylesheet language designed for the Web community. It provides functionality beyond CSS (e.g. element reordering). We expect that CSS will be used to display simply-structured XML documents and XSL will be used where more powerful formatting capabilities are required or for formatting highly structured information such as XML structured data or XML documents that contain structured data.

Web authors create content at three different levels of sophistication:

- *markup: relies solely on a declarative syntax*
- *script: additionally uses code "snippets" for more complex behaviors*
- *program: uses a full programming language*

> *XSL is intended to be accessible to the "markup" level user by providing a declarative solution to most data description and rendering requirements. Less common tasks are accommodated through a graceful escape to a familiar scripting environment. This approach is familiar to the Web publishing community as it is modeled after the HTML/JavaScript environment.*
>
> *The powerful capabilities provided by XSL allow:*
>
> - *formatting of source elements based on ancestry/descendency, position, and uniqueness*
> - *the creation of formatting constructs including generated text and graphics*
> - *the definition of reusable formatting macros*
> - *writing-direction independent stylesheets*
> - *extensible set of formatting objects*

The authors then explained carefully why they had felt it necessary to diverge from DSSSL, and described why a separate language from CSS (Cascading Style Sheets) was thought necessary.

They then stated some design principles:

- *XSL should be straightforwardly usable over the Internet.*
- *XSL should be expressed in XML syntax.*
- *XSL should provide a declarative language to do all common formatting tasks.*
- *XSL should provide an "escape" into a scripting language to accommodate more sophisticated formatting tasks and to allow for extensibility and completeness.*
- *XSL will be a subset of DSSSL with the proposed amendment.* As XSL was no longer a subset of DSSSL, they cannily proposed amending DSSSL so it would become a superset of XSL.
- *A mechanical mapping of a CSS stylesheet into an XSL stylesheet should be possible.*
- *XSL should be informed by user experience with the FOSI stylesheet language.*
- *The number of optional features in XSL should be kept to a minimum.*
- *XSL stylesheets should be human-legible and reasonably clear.*
- *The XSL design should be prepared quickly.*
- *XSL stylesheets shall be easy to create.*
- *Terseness in XSL markup is of minimal importance.*

As a requirements statement, this doesn't rank among the best. It doesn't read like the kind of list you get when you talk to users and find out what they need. It's much more the kind of list designers write when they know what they want to produce, including a few political concessions to the people who might raise objections. But if you want to understand why XSLT became the language it did, this list is certainly evidence of the thinking.

The language described in this first proposal contains many of the key concepts of XSLT as it finally emerged, but the syntax is virtually unrecognizable. It was already clear that the language should be based on templates that handled nodes in the source document matching a defined pattern, and that the language should be free of side-effects, to allow "progressive rendering and handling of large documents". I'll explore the significance of this requirement in more detail on page 37, and discuss its implications on the way stylesheets are designed in Chapter 9. The basic idea is that if a stylesheet is expressed as a collection of completely independent operations, each of which has no external effect other than generating part of the output from its input (for example, it cannot update global variables), then it becomes possible to generate any part of the output independently if that particular part of the input changes. Whether the XSLT language actually achieves this objective is still an open question.

Microsoft shipped their first technology preview five months after this proposal appeared, in January 1998.

To enable W3C to make an assessment of the proposal, Norman Walsh produced a requirements summary, which was published in May 1998. It is available at http://www.w3.org/TR/WD-XSLReq.

The bulk of his paper is given over to a long list of the typographical features that the language should support, following the tradition both before and since that the formatting side of the language gets a lot more column inches than the transformation side. But as XSLT fans that need not worry us because the success of standards has always been inversely proportional to their length.

What Walsh has to say on the transformation aspects of the language is particularly terse, and although he clearly had reasons for thinking these features were necessary, it's a shame that he doesn't tell us why he put these in and left others, such as sorting, grouping, and totaling, out:

- Ancestors, children, siblings, attributes, content, disjunctions, negation, enumerations, computed select based upon arbitrary query expressions.
- Arithmetic Expressions; arithmetic, simple boolean comparisons, boolean logic, substrings, string concatenation.
- Data Types: Scalar types, units of measure, Flow Objects, XML Objects.
- Side effects: No global side effects.
- Standard Procedures: The expression language should have a set of procedures that are built in to the XSL language. These are still to be identified.
- User Defined Functions: For reuse. Parameterized, but not recursive.

Following this activity, the first Working Draft of XSL (not to be confused with the Proposal) was published on 18 August 1998, and the language started to take shape, gradually converging on the final form it took in the 16 November 1999 Recommendation through a series of Working Drafts, each of which made radical changes, but kept the original design principles intact.

The XSLT 1.0 Recommendation is still the current version at the time of writing, and the one to which most current products conform, although a working draft of XSLT 1.1 was published on December 12th, 2000. I've included the new features of XSLT 1.1 in this book, because they are already starting to appear in some products; but I've flagged them as XSLT 1.1 features to warn you that you won't find them in every product. In most cases, however, these features are based on extensions that many vendors provided in their XSLT 1.0 products, so you are likely to find something similar.

So let's look now at the essential characteristics of XSLT as a language.

XSLT as a Language

What are the most significant characteristics of XSLT as a language, which distinguish it from other languages? In this section I shall pick three of the most striking features: the fact that it is written in XML syntax, the fact that it is a language free of side-effects, and the fact that processing is described as a set of independent pattern-matching rules.

Use of XML Syntax

As we've seen, the use of SGML syntax for stylesheets was proposed as long ago as 1994, and it seems that this idea gradually became the accepted wisdom. It's difficult to trace exactly what the overriding arguments were, and when you find yourself writing something like:

```
<xsl:variable name="y">
   <xsl:call-template name="f">
      <xsl:with-param name="x"/>
   </xsl:call-template>
</xsl:variable>
```

to express what in other languages would be written as « `y = f(x);` », then you may find yourself wondering how such a decision came to be made.

In fact, it could have been worse: in the very early drafts, the syntax for writing what are now XPath expressions was also expressed in XML, so instead of writing `<<select="book/author/first-name">>` you had to write something along the lines of:

```
<select>
   <path>
      <element type="book">
      <element type="author">
      <element type="first-name">
   </path>
</select>
```

The most obvious arguments for expressing XSLT stylesheets in XML are perhaps:

- There is already an XML parser in the browser, so it keeps the footprint small if this can be re-used.
- Everyone had got fed up with the syntactic inconsistencies between HTML/XML and CSS, and didn't want the same thing to happen again.
- The Lisp-like syntax of DSSSL was widely seen as a barrier to its adoption; better to have a syntax that was already familiar in the target community.
- Many existing popular template languages (including simple ASP and JSP pages) are expressed as an outline of the output document with embedded instructions, so this is a familiar concept.
- All the lexical apparatus is reusable, for example Unicode support, character and entity references, whitespace handling, namespaces.
- It's occasionally useful to have a stylesheet as the input or output of a transformation (witness the Microsoft XSL converter as an example), so it's a benefit if a stylesheet can read and write other stylesheets.
- Providing visual development tools easily solves the inconvenience of having to type lots of angle brackets. (Such tools are starting to become available, and I've described some of them in Appendix E.)

Like it or not, the XML-based syntax is now an intrinsic feature of the language that has both benefits and drawbacks. It does require a lot of typing, but in the end, the number of keystrokes has very little bearing on the ease or difficulty of solving particular transformation problems.

No Side-effects

The idea that XSL should be a declarative language free of side-effects appears repeatedly in the early statements about the goals and design principles of the language, but no-one ever seems to explain *why*: what would be the user benefit?

A function or procedure in a programming language is said to have side-effects if it makes changes to its environment; for example, if it can update a global variable that another function or procedure can read, or if it can write messages to a log file, or prompt the user. If functions have side-effects, it becomes important to call them the right number of times and in the correct order. Functions that have no side-effects (sometimes called pure functions) can be called any number of times and in any order. It doesn't matter how many times you evaluate the area of a triangle, you will always get the same answer; but if the function to calculate the area has a side-effect such as changing the size of the triangle, or if you don't know whether it has side-effects or not, then it becomes important to call it once only.

I expand further on this concept in the section on Computational Stylesheets in Chapter 9, page 608.

It is possible to find hints at the reason why this was considered desirable in the statements that the language should be equally suitable for batch or interactive use, and that it should be capable of **progressive rendering**. There is a concern that when you download a large XML document, you won't be able to see anything on your screen until the last byte has been received from the server. Equally, if a small change were made to the XML document, it would be nice to be able to determine the change needed to the screen display, without recalculating the whole thing from scratch. If a language has side effects then the order of execution of the statements in the language has to be defined, or the final result becomes unpredictable. Without side-effects, the statements can be executed in any order, which means it is possible, in principle, to process the parts of a stylesheet selectively and independently.

Whether XSLT has actually achieved these goals is somewhat debatable. Certainly, determining which parts of the output document are affected by a small change to one part of the input document is not easy, given the flexibility of the expressions and patterns that are now permitted in the language. Equally, all existing XSLT processors require the whole document to be loaded into memory. However, it would be a mistake to expect too much too soon. When E. F. Codd published the relational calculus in 1970, he made the claim that a declarative language was desirable because it was possible to optimize it, which was not possible with the navigational data access languages in use at the time. In fact it took another fifteen years before relational optimization techniques (and, to be fair, the price of hardware) reached the point where large relational databases were commercially viable. But in the end he was proved right, and the hope is that the same principle will also eventually deliver similar benefits in the area of transformation and styling languages.

Of course there will always be some transformations where the whole document needs to be available before you can produce any output; examples are where the stylesheet sorts the data, or where it starts with a table of contents. But there are many other transformations where the order of the output directly reflects the order of the input, and progressive rendering should be possible in such cases. At the time of writing, we are starting to see the first signs that implementors are exploiting this capability: Xalan-Java 2, for example, runs a transformation thread in parallel with the parsing thread, so the transformer can produce output before the parser has finished, and MSXML3 (from the evidence of its API) seems to be designed on a similar principle. The Stylus Studio debugging tool, which is described in Appendix E, tracks the dependencies between parts of the output document and the template rules that were used to generate them, so one can start to see the potential to regenerate the output selectively when small changes are made.

What being side-effect free means in practice is that you cannot update the value of a variable. This restriction is something you may find very frustrating at first, and a big price to pay for these rather remote benefits. But as you get the feel of the language and learn to think about using it the way it was designed to be used, rather than the way you are familiar with from other languages, you will find you stop thinking about this as a restriction. In fact, one of the benefits is that it eliminates a whole class of bugs from your code! I shall come back to this subject in Chapter 9, where I outline some of the common design patterns for XSLT stylesheets, and in particular, describe how to use recursive code to handle situations where in the past you would probably have used updateable variables to keep track of the current state.

Rule-based

The dominant feature of a typical XSLT stylesheet is that it consists of a sequence of template rules, each of which describes how a particular element type or other construct should be processed. The rules are not arranged in any particular order; they don't have to match the order of the input or the order of the output, and in fact there are very few clues as to what ordering or nesting of elements the stylesheet author expects to encounter in the source document. It is this that makes XSLT a declarative language, because you specify what output should be produced when particular patterns occur in the input, as distinct from a procedural program where you have to say what tasks to perform in what order.

This rule-based structure is very like CSS, but with the major difference that both the patterns (the description of which nodes a rule applies to) and the actions (the description of what happens when the rule is matched) are much richer in functionality.

Example: Displaying a Poem

Let's see how we can use the rule-based approach to format a poem. Again, we haven't introduced all the concepts yet, so I won't try to explain every detail of how this works, but it's useful to see what the template rules actually look like in practice.

Input

Let's take this poem as our XML source. The source file is called `poem.xml`, and the stylesheet is `poem.xsl`.

```
<poem>
   <author>Rupert Brooke</author>
   <date>1912</date>
   <title>Song</title>
  <stanza>
      <line>And suddenly the wind comes soft,</line>
      <line>And Spring is here again;</line>
      <line>And the hawthorn quickens with buds of green</line>
      <line>And my heart with buds of pain.</line>
   </stanza>
   <stanza>
      <line>My heart all Winter lay so numb,</line>
      <line>The earth so dead and frore,</line>
      <line>That I never thought the Spring would come
again</line>
      <line>Or my heart wake any more.</line>
   </stanza>
   <stanza>
      <line>But Winter's broken and earth has woken,</line>
      <line>And the small birds cry again;</line>
      <line>And the hawthorn hedge puts forth its buds,</line>
      <line>And my heart puts forth its pain.</line>
   </stanza>
</poem>
```

Output

We'll write a stylesheet such that this document appears in the browser as shown below:

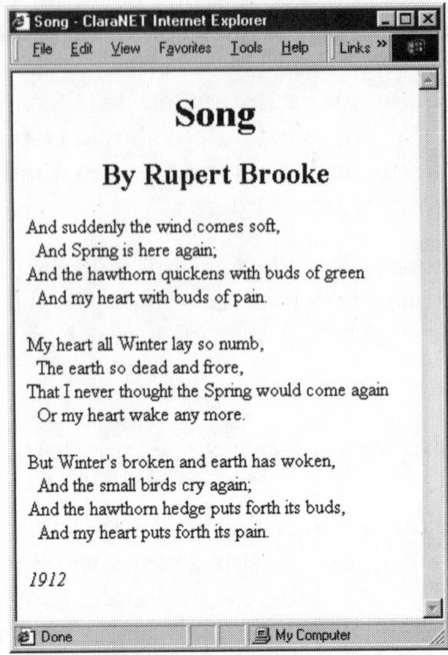

Stylesheet

It starts with the standard header:

```
<xsl:stylesheet
   xmlns:xsl="http://www.w3.org/1999/XSL/Transform"
   version="1.0">
```

Now we'll write one template rule for each element type in the source document. The rule for the **<poem>** element creates the skeleton of the HTML output, defining the ordering of the elements in the output (which doesn't have to be the same as the input order). The **<xsl:value-of>** instruction inserts the value of the selected element at this point in the output. The **<xsl:apply-templates>** instructions cause the selected child elements to be processed, each using its own template rule.

```
<xsl:template match="poem">
   <html>
   <head>
      <title><xsl:value-of select="title"/></title>
   </head>
   <body>
      <xsl:apply-templates select="title"/>
      <xsl:apply-templates select="author"/>
      <xsl:apply-templates select="stanza"/>
      <xsl:apply-templates select="date"/>
   </body>
   </html>
</xsl:template>
```

The template rules for the **<title>**, **<author>**, and **<date>** elements are very simple: they take the content of the element (denoted by «`select="."`»), and surround it within appropriate HTML tags to define its display style:

```
<xsl:template match="title">
   <div align="center"><h1><xsl:value-of select="."/></h1></div>
</xsl:template>

<xsl:template match="author">
   <div align="center"><h2>By <xsl:value-of
select="."/></h2></div>
</xsl:template>

<xsl:template match="date">
   <p><i><xsl:value-of select="."/></i></p>
</xsl:template>
```

The template rule for the **<stanza>** element puts each stanza into an HTML paragraph, and then invokes processing of the lines within the stanza, as defined by the template rule for lines:

```
<xsl:template match="stanza">
  <p><xsl:apply-templates select="line"/></p>
</xsl:template>
```

The rule for **<line>** elements is a little more complex: if the position of the line within the stanza is an even number, it precedes the line with two non-breaking-space characters (` `). The **<xsl:if>** instruction tests a boolean condition, which in this case calls the **position()** function to determine the relative position of the current line. It then outputs the contents of the line, followed by an empty HTML **
** element to end the line.

```
<xsl:template match="line">
   <xsl:if test="position() mod 2 = 0">  </xsl:if>
   <xsl:value-of select="."/><br/>
</xsl:template>
```

And to finish off, we close the **<xsl:stylesheet>** element:

```
</xsl:stylesheet>
```

Although template rules are a characteristic feature of the XSLT language, we'll see that this is not the only way of writing a stylesheet. In Chapter 9, I will describe four different design patterns for XSLT stylesheets, only one of which makes extensive use of template rules. In fact, the *Hello World* stylesheet I presented earlier in this chapter doesn't make any real use of template rules: it fits into the design pattern I call *fill-in-the-blanks,* because the stylesheet essentially contains the fixed part of the output with embedded instructions saying where to get the data to put in the variable parts.

Beyond XSLT 1.0

I've talked about where XSLT 1.0 came from, but where is it going next?

After XSLT 1.0 was published, the XSL Working Group responsible for the language decided to split the requirements for enhancements into two categories; XSLT 1.1 would standardize a small number of urgent features that vendors had already found it necessary to add to their products as extensions, while XSLT 2.0 would handle the more strategic requirements that needed further research.

XSLT 1.1

A working draft of XSLT 1.1 was published on December 12th 2000. It describes four enhancements to the XSLT 1.0 specification:

- Multiple output documents: an **<xsl:document>** instruction, modeled on extensions provided initially in Saxon and subsequently in other products including xt, Xalan and Oracle, allowing a source document to be split into multiple output documents. (All these products are described in the appendices to this book.)
- Temporary trees: the ability to treat a tree created by one phase of processing as input to a subsequent phase of processing. This enhancement was modeled on the **node-set()** extension function introduced first in xt and subsequently copied in other products.
- Standard bindings to extension functions written in Java and ECMAScript. XSLT 1.0 allowed a stylesheet to call external functions, but did not say how such functions should be written, with the result that extension functions written for Xalan would not work with xt or Saxon, or vice versa. XSLT 1.1 defined a general framework for binding extension functions written in any language, with specific mappings for Java and ECMAScript (the official name for JavaScript).
- Support for the **xml:base** construct, a late addition to the XML core standards, which allows an XML document to specify the Base URI that should be used to resolve any relative URIs contained within the document.

At the time of writing, XSLT 1.1 is still a working draft, and there is no official statement about when it is likely to be finalized. There have been suggestions that it would be a good idea to explore in more depth the implications of the XSLT 2.0 requirements before freezing the XSLT 1.1 spec, to avoid constraining the way the XSLT 2.0 requirements are met. One can also speculate that some vendors feel the market is still only really beginning to take XSLT 1.0 on board, and that in reality users want stability more than they want enhancements.

Despite this, we've decided to go ahead and include definitions of XSLT 1.1 facilities in this book. In doing this, we're taking a calculated gamble that the spec will be ratified in very similar form to its published draft, and that it will be implemented in products during the course of the year (2001) – there are signs that is already starting to happen. Meanwhile, we've taken care to flag XSLT 1.1 enhancements for what they are, so that you can check the specifications in this book against the latest W3C recommendations and the facilities offered by your chosen product before using them.

As we went to press, the W3C had decided that XSLT 1.1 would not be progressed further than working draft stage, but would instead be used as a baseline for developing XSLT 2 (see overleaf)

Throughout this book, references to "the XSLT 1.1 working draft" mean the draft dated December 12th 2000.

XSLT 2.0 and XPath 2.0

The W3C XSL Working Group, working closely with other working groups, published the requirements for XSLT 2.0 and XPath 2.0 on 14 February 2001; you can find the documents at the following URLs:

http://www.w3.org/TR/xslt20req
http://www.w3.org/TR/xpath20req

The reason W3C working groups publish requirements documents is to try and get user input into the standardization process, so it would be a mistake to regard these lists of proposed enhancements as definitive. Nevertheless, they give a good indication of the thinking. Broadly, the requirements fall into three categories:

- Features that are obviously missing from the current standards and that would make users' lives much easier; for example, facilities for grouping related nodes, extra string-handling and numeric functions, and the ability to read text files as well as XML documents.
- Addition of features developed by the XML Query working group. XQuery is a specification for an SQL-like language to query a collection of XML documents and return the results, also as an XML document. The first public working draft was released on 15 February 2001 (see http://www.w3.org/TR/2001/WD-xquery-20010215/), but it is based on ideas from a number of previous proposals, notably a language called Quilt, the work of Don Chamberlin, Jonathan Robie, and Daniela Florescu. Although XQuery is designed for use in a different context, there are many overlaps in functionality with XSLT and XPath. W3C likes to keep its different standards as coherent as possible, and there are many features in the proposed XQuery specification which could usefully be added to the XPath specification to keep them in step with each other. There's a heavy dose of compromise involved here, on both sides, because some of the improvements the XML Query group has identified look great in theory, but are difficult to retrofit into a language that is already in widespread use.
- Features designed to exploit and integrate with XML Schema. The W3C XML Schema specification is now at an advanced stage (it became a Candidate Recommendation on 20 October 2000), and implementations are starting to appear in products. The schema acts as a replacement for the DTD, giving a much richer way of specifying the data types of the elements and attributes that may appear in a document. The thinking is that if the schema specifies that a particular element contains a number or a date (for example), then it ought to be possible to use this knowledge when comparing or sorting dates within a stylesheet. Achieving this without turning the current XPath language upside down (at present it is a very loosely typed language) is going to be a major challenge, and for this reason alone I would expect that development of XPath 2.0 may well take a significant length of time.

Where to use XSLT

In the final section of this chapter I shall try and identify what tasks XSLT is good at, and by implication, tasks for which a different tool would be more suitable. I shall also look at alternative ways of using XSLT within the overall architecture of your application.

Broadly speaking, as I discussed at the beginning of the chapter, there are two main scenarios for using XSLT transformations: data conversion, and publishing; and we'll consider each of them separately.

Data Conversion Applications

Data conversion is not something that will go away just because XML has been invented. Even though an increasing number of data transfers between organizations or between applications within an organization are likely to be encoded in XML, there will still be different data models, different ways of representing the same thing, and different subsets of information that are of interest to different people (recall the example at the beginning of the chapter, where we were converting music between different XML representations and different presentation formats). So however enthusiastic we are about XML, the reality is that there are going to be a lot of comma-separated-values files, EDI messages, and any number of other formats in use for a long time to come.

When you have the task of converting one XML data set into another XML data set, then XSLT is an obvious choice.

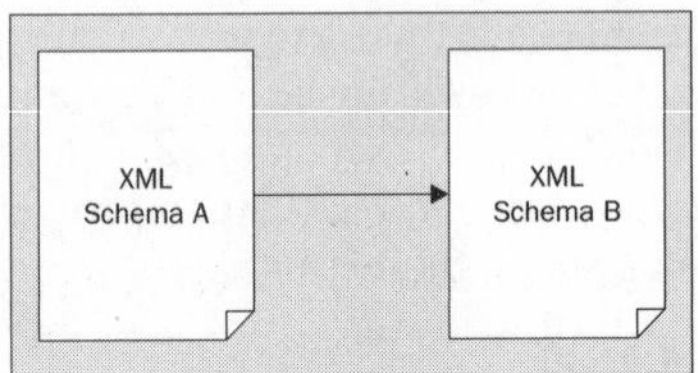

It can be used for extracting the data selectively, reordering it, turning attributes into elements or vice versa, or any number of similar tasks. It can also be used simply for validating the data. As a language, XSLT is best at manipulating the structure of the information as distinct from its content: it's a good language for turning rows into columns, but for string handling (for example removing any text that appears between square brackets) it's rather laborious compared with a language like JavaScript or Perl that supports regular expressions. However, you can always tackle these problems by invoking procedures written in other languages, such as Java or Javascript, from within the stylesheet.

XSLT is also useful for converting XML data into any text-based format, such as comma-separated values, or various EDI message formats. Text output is really just like XML output without the tags, so this creates no particular problems for the language.

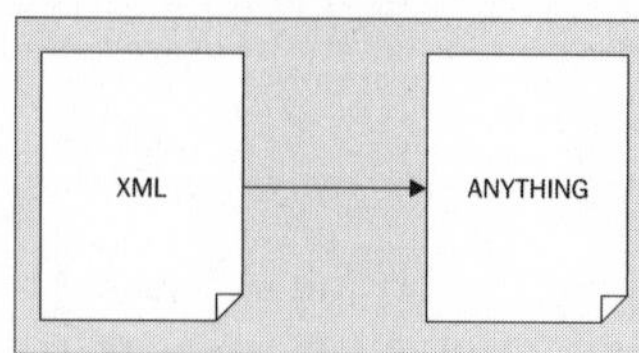

Perhaps more surprising is that XSLT can often be useful to convert from non-XML formats into XML or something else:

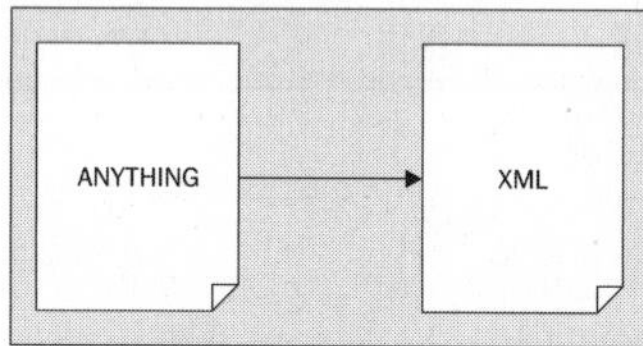

In this case you'll need to write some kind of parser that understands the input format; but you would have had to do that anyway. The benefit is that once you've written the parser, the rest of the data conversion can be expressed in a high-level language. This separation also increases the chances that you'll be able to reuse your parser next time you need to handle that particular input format. I'll show you an example in Chapter 10, page 656, where the input is a rather old-fashioned and distinctly non-XML format widely used for exchanging data between genealogy software packages. It turns out that it isn't even necessary to write the data out as XML before using the XSLT stylesheet to process it: all you need to do is to make your parser look like an XML parser, by making it implement one of the standard parser interfaces: SAX or DOM. Most XSLT processors will accept input from a program that implements the SAX or DOM interfaces, even if the data never saw the light of day as XML.

One caveat about data conversion applications: today's XSLT processors all rely on holding all the data in memory while the transformation is taking place. The tree structure in memory can be as much as ten times the original data size, so in practice, the limit on data size for an XSLT conversion is a few megabytes. Even at this size, a complex conversion can be quite time-consuming, it depends very much on the processing that you actually want to do.

One way around this is to split the data into chunks and convert each chunk separately – assuming, of course, that there is some kind of correspondence between chunks of input and chunks of output. But when this starts to get complicated, there comes a point where XSLT is no longer the best tool for the job. You might be better off, for example, loading the data into a relational or object database, and using the database query language to extract it again in a different sequence.

If you need to process large amounts of data serially, for example extracting selected records from a log of retail transactions, then an application written using the SAX interface might take a little longer to write than the equivalent XSLT stylesheet, but it is likely to run many times faster. Very often the combination of a SAX filter application to do simple data extraction, followed by an XSLT stylesheet to do more complex manipulation, can be the best solution in such cases.

Publishing

The difference between data conversion and publishing is that in the former case, the data is destined for input to another piece of software, while in the latter case it is destined to be read (you hope) by human beings. Publishing in this context doesn't just mean lavish text and multimedia, it also means data; everything from the traditional activity of producing and distributing reports so that managers know what's going on in the business, to producing online phone bills and bank statements for customers, and rail timetables for the general public. XML is ideal for such data publishing applications, as well as the more traditional text publishing, which was the original home territory of SGML.

XML was designed to enable information to be held independently of the way it is presented, which sometimes leads people into the fallacy of thinking that using XML for presentation details is somehow bad. Far from it: if you were designing a new format for downloading fonts to a printer today, you would probably make it XML-based. Presentation details have just as much right to be encoded in XML as any other kind of information. So we can see the role of XSLT in the publishing process as being converting data-without-presentation to data-with-presentation, where both are, at least in principle, XML formats.

The two important vehicles for publishing information today are print-on-paper, and the web. The print-on-paper scene is the more difficult one, because of the high expectations of users for visual quality. XSL Formatting Objects attempts to define an XML-based model of a print file for high quality display on paper or on screen. Because of the sheer number of parameters needed to achieve this, the standard has taken a while to complete, and will probably take even longer to implement in its entirety. But the web is a less demanding environment, where all we need to do is convert the data to HTML and leave the browser to do the best it can on the display available. HTML, of course, is not XML, but it is close enough so that a simple mapping is possible. Converting XML to HTML is the most common application for XSLT today. It's actually a two-stage process: first convert to an XML-based model that is structurally equivalent to the target HTML, and then serialize this in HTML notation rather than strict XML.

The emergence of XHTML 1.0 of course tidies up this process even further, because it is a pure XML format, but how quick the take-up of XHTML will be remains to be seen.

When to do the Conversion?

The process of publishing information to a user is illustrated in the diagram below:

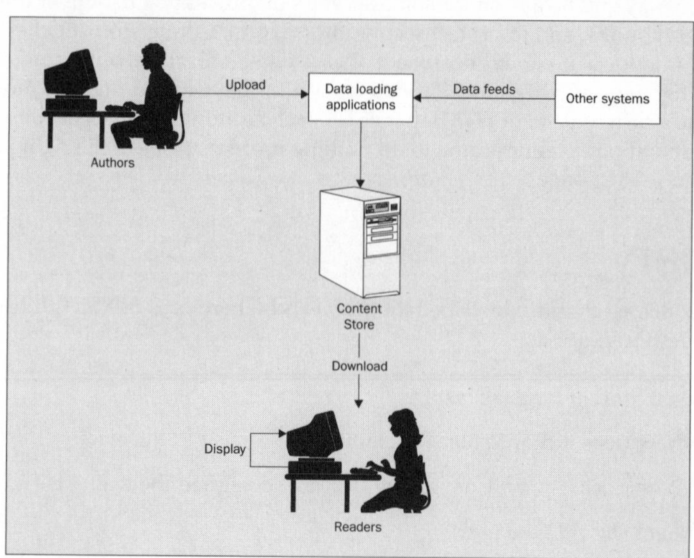

There are several points in such a system where XSLT transformations might be appropriate:

- Information entered by authors using their preferred tools, or customized form-filling interfaces, can be converted to XML and stored in that form in the content store.
- XML information arriving from other systems might be transformed into a different flavor of XML for storage in the content store. For example, it might be broken up into page-size chunks.
- XML can be translated into HTML on the server, when the users request a page. This can be controlled using technology such as Java servlets or Java Server Pages. On a Microsoft server you can use the XSL ISAPI extension available from http://msdn.microsoft.com/xml, or if you want more application control, you can invoke the transformation from script on ASP pages.
- XML can be sent down to the client system, and translated into HTML within the browser. This can give a highly interactive presentation of the information, and remove a lot of the processing load from the server, but it relies on all the users having a browser that can do the job.
- XML data can also be converted into its final display form at publishing time, and stored as HTML within the content store. This minimizes the work that needs to be done at display time, and is ideal when the same displayed page is presented to very many users.

There isn't one right answer, and often a combination of techniques may be appropriate. Conversion in the browser is an attractive option once XSLT becomes widely available within browsers, but that is still some way off. Even when this is done, there may still be a need for some server-side processing to deliver the XML in manageable chunks, and to protect secure information. Conversion at delivery time on the server is a popular choice, because it allows personalization, but it can be a heavy overhead for sites with high traffic. Some busy sites have found that it is more effective to generate a different set of HTML pages for each section of the target audience in advance, and at page request time to do nothing more than select the right pre-constructed HTML page.

Summary

This introductory chapter described the whys and wherefores of XSLT. It tried to answer questions such as:

- What kind of language is it?
- Where does it fit into the XML family?
- Where does it come from and why was it designed the way it is?
- Where should it be used?

You now know that XSLT is a declarative high-level language designed for transforming the structure of XML documents; that it has two major applications: data conversion and presentation; and that it can be used at a number of different points in the overall application architecture, including at data capture time, at delivery time on the server, and at display time on the browser. You also have some idea why XSLT has developed in the way it has.

Now it's time to start taking an in-depth look inside the language to see how it does this job. In the next chapter, we'll look at the way transformation is carried out by treating the input and output as tree structures, and using patterns to match particular nodes in the input tree and define what nodes should be added to the result tree when the pattern is matched.

2

The XSLT Processing Model

In this chapter, we'll take a bird's eye view of what an XSLT processor does. We'll start by looking at a system overview: what are the inputs and outputs of the processor.

Then we'll look in some detail at the data model, in particular the structure of the tree representation of XML documents. An important message here is that XSLT transformations do not operate on XML documents as text, they operate on the abstract tree-like information structure represented by the text.

Having established the data model, I'll describe the processing sequence that occurs when a source document and a stylesheet are brought together. XSLT is not a conventional procedural language: it consists of a collection of template rules defining output that is produced when particular patterns are matched in the input. As seen in Chapter 1, this rule-based processing structure is one of the distinguishing features of the XSLT language.

Finally, we'll look at the way in which variables and expressions can be used in an XSLT stylesheet, and also look at the various data types available.

XSLT: A System Overview

This section looks at the structure of the process performed by XSLT.

A Simplified Overview

The core task of an XSLT processor is to apply a stylesheet to a source document and produce a result document. This is shown in the simplified diagram below:

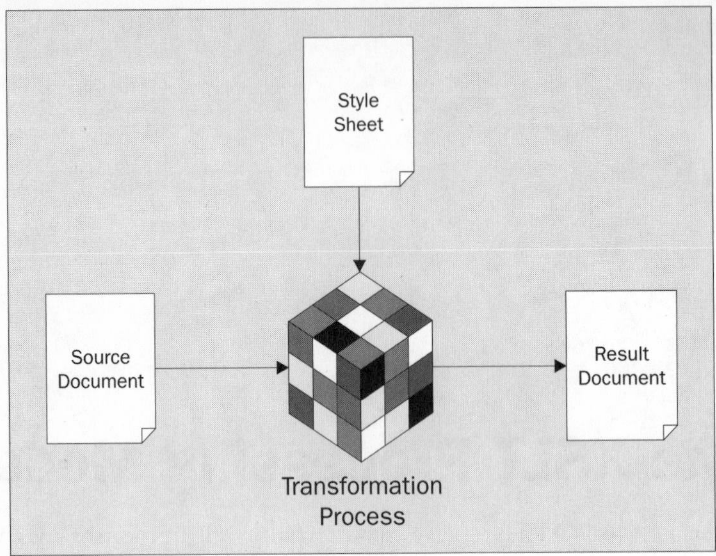

As a first approximation we can think of the source document, the stylesheet, and the result document as each being an XML document. XSLT performs a **transformation** process because the **output** (the result document) is the same kind of object as the **input** (the source document). This has immediate benefits: for example, it is possible to do a complex transformation as a series of simple transformations, and it is possible to do transformations in either direction using the same technology.

The choice of Rubik's cube to illustrate the transformation process is not entirely whimsical. The mathematics of Rubik's cube relies on group theory, which is where the notion of closure comes from: every operation transforms one instance of a type into another instance of the same type. We're transforming XML documents rather than cubes, but the principle is the same.

The name **stylesheet** has stuck for the document that defines the transformation, even though purists prefer to call it a **transformation sheet**. The name reflects the reality that a very common kind of transformation performed using XSLT is to define a display style for the information in the source document, so that the result document contains information from the source document augmented with information controlling the way it is displayed on some output device.

Trees, not Documents

In practice though, we don't always want the input or output to be XML in its textual form. If we want to produce HTML output (a very common requirement) we want to produce it directly, rather than having an XML document as an intermediate form. Similarly, we might want to take input from a database or (say) an LDAP directory, or an EDI message, or a data file using comma-separated values syntax. We don't want to spend a lot of time converting these into XML documents if we can avoid it, nor do we want another raft of converters to install.

So instead, XSLT defines its operations in terms of a representation of an XML document called the **tree**. The tree is an abstract data type. There is no defined API and no defined data representation, only a conceptual model that defines the objects in the tree, their properties and their relationships. The tree is similar in concept to the W3C DOM, except that the DOM does have a defined API. Some implementors do indeed use the DOM as their internal tree structure. Others use a data structure that corresponds more closely to the XPath tree model, while some are experimenting with internal data structures that are only distantly related to this model. It's a conceptual model we are describing, not something that necessarily exists in an implementation.

Taking the inputs and output of the XSLT processors as trees produces a new diagram, as shown below:

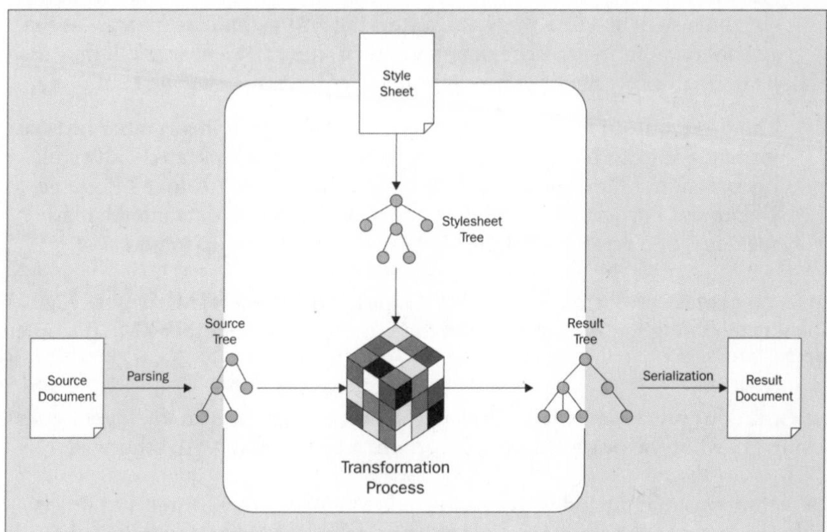

The formal conformance rules say that an XSLT processor must be able to read a stylesheet and use it to transform a source tree into a result tree. This is the part of the system shown in the oval box. There's no official requirement to handle the parts of the process shown outside the box, namely the creation of a source tree from a source XML document (known as parsing), or the creation of a result XML document from the result tree (often called serialization). In practice, though, most real products are likely to handle these parts as well.

Later in this chapter we will examine the data model for the trees in more detail, and see how it relates to the structure of the XML documents.

Different Output Formats

Although the final process of converting the result tree to an output document is outside the conformance rules of the XSLT standard, this doesn't mean that XSLT has nothing to say on the subject. In fact, there is a substantial section of the specification devoted to the subject, and although everything it says is non-binding, most implementations have followed it very closely. The main control over this process is the `<xsl:output>` element, which is described in detail in Chapter 4, page 270.

The **<xsl:output>** element defines three output formats or methods, namely `xml`, `html`, and `text`. In each case the result tree is written to a single output file.

- With the `xml` output method, the output file is an XML document. We'll see later that it need not be a complete XML document; it can also be an XML fragment. The **<xsl:output>** element allows the stylesheet writer some control over the way in which the XML is written, for example the character encoding used, and the use of `CDATA` sections.
- With the `html` output method, the output file is an HTML document, typically HTML 4.0, though products may support other versions if they wish. With HTML output, the XSLT processor will recognize many of the conventions of HTML and structure the output accordingly. For example it will recognize elements such as **<hr>** that have a start tag and no end tag, as well as the special rules for escape characters within a **<script>** element. It may also (if it chooses) generate references to built-in entities such as «`é`».
- The `text` output method is designed to allow output in **any other text-based format**. For example, the output might be a comma-separated-values file, a document in Microsoft's Rich Text Format (RTF) or in Adobe's Portable Document Format (PDF) , or it might be an electronic data interchange message, or a script in SQL or JavaScript. It's entirely up to you.

There is no explicit provision for XHTML output, but since XHTML is pure XML, it can be written using the XML method in the same way as any other XML document type.

If the **<xsl:output>** element is omitted, the processor makes an intelligent guess, choosing HTML if the output starts with an **<html>** tag, and XML otherwise.

Implementations may include output methods other than these three, but this is outside the scope of the standard. One mechanism provided by several products is to feed the result tree to a user-supplied document handler. This will generally be written to conform to the `ContentHandler` interface defined as part of the SAX2 API specification available at http://www.megginson.com/, or the `DocumentHandler` interfaces defined in the earlier SAX1, as described in the Wrox publication *Professional XML*, ISBN 1-861003-11-0.

So, while the bulk of the XSLT Recommendation describes the transformation process from a source tree to a result tree, there is one section (specifically, section 16, *Output*) that describes another process, the output process. This is often called **serialization**, because it turns a tree structure into a stream of characters (but it mustn't be confused with serialization in distributed object systems such as COM and Java, which produces a serial file representation of a COM or Java object). XSLT processors can implement this at their discretion, and it fits into our diagram as shown below:

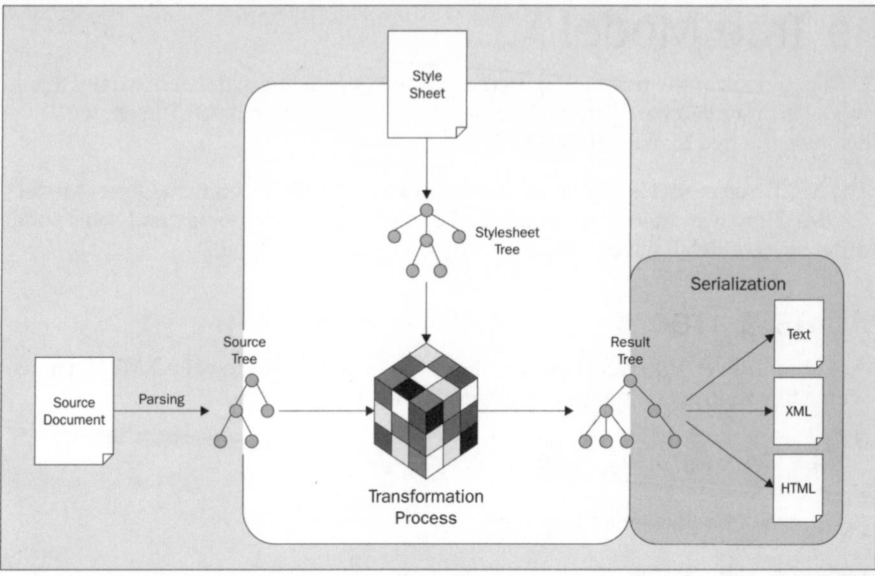

Multiple Inputs and Outputs

In real life the processing model is further complicated because there can be multiple inputs and outputs.

Specifically:

- There can be multiple input documents. The stylesheet can use the **`document()`** function (described in Chapter 7, page 466) to load secondary input documents, based on URI references held in the source document or the stylesheet. Each input document is processed as a tree in its own right, in exactly the same way as the principal input document. It is also possible to supply additional input documents as parameters to the stylesheet.
- The stylesheet too can consist of multiple documents. There are two directives that can be used in the stylesheet, **`<xsl:include>`** and **`<xsl:import>`**, to load additional stylesheet modules and use them as extensions of the principal module. Splitting a stylesheet in this way allows modularity: in a complex environment different aspects of processing can be described in component stylesheets that can be incorporated into several different parent stylesheets. There is a detailed discussion of how to split a stylesheet into modules in Chapter 3.

A single run of the XSLT processor can also produce multiple output documents. This allows a single source document to be split into several output files: for example, the input might contain the text of an entire book, while the output contains one HTML file for each chapter, all connected using suitable hyperlinks. This capability, which is provided by the **`<xsl:document>`** element described in Chapter 4, is standardized in the draft XSLT 1.1 specification, though equivalent facilities are provided in different ways by several XSLT 1.0 products.

The Tree Model

Let's now look at the tree model used in XSLT in a little more detail. Actually this model is described partly in the XPath standard, and partly in XSLT itself: we'll combine the two to make things simpler.

The XSLT tree model is similar in many ways to the XML Document Object Model (DOM). However, there are a number of differences of terminology and some subtle differences of detail. I'll point some of these out as we go along.

XML as a Tree

At a simple level, the equivalence of the textual representation of an XML document with a tree representation is very straightforward.

Example: An XML Tree

Consider a document like this:

```
<definition>
   <word>export</word>
   <part-of-speech>vt</part-of-speech>
   <meaning>Send out (goods) to another country.</meaning>
   <etymology>
      <language>Latin</language>
      <parts>
         <part>
            <prefix>ex</prefix>
            <meaning>out(of)</meaning>
         </part>
         <part>
            <word>portare</word>
            <meaning>to carry</meaning>
         </part>
      </parts>
   </etymology>
</definition>
```

We can consider each piece of text as a leaf node, and each element as a containing node, and build an equivalent tree structure, which looks like the diagram below. I've shown the tree after the stripping of all whitespace nodes: for discussion of this process, see Chapter 3, page 139. In this diagram each node is shown with potentially three pieces of information: in the top cell, the **type** of node, in the middle cell, the **name** of the node, and in the bottom one, its **string-value**. For the root node and for elements, I have shown the string-value simply as an asterisk: in fact, the string-value of these nodes is defined to be the concatenation of the string-values of all the element and text nodes at the next level of the tree.

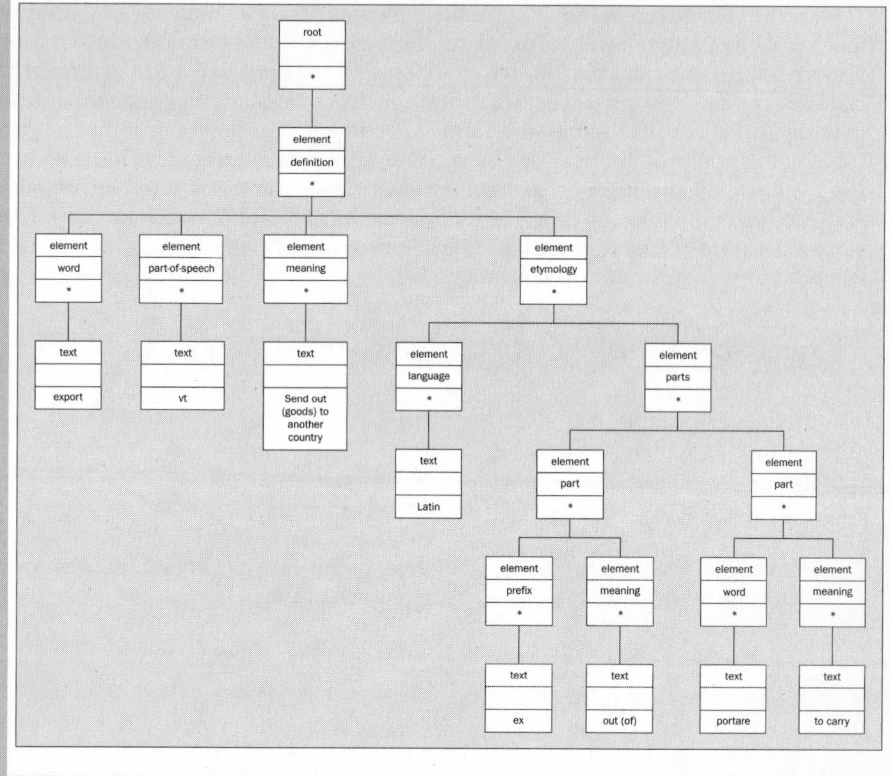

It is easy to see how other aspects of the XML document, for example attributes and processing instructions, can be similarly represented in this tree view by means of additional kinds of node.

At the top of every tree there is a **root** node. This performs the same function as the Document node in the DOM model, in that it doesn't correspond to any particular part of the source document, but you can regard it as representing the document as a whole. The children of the root node are the top level elements, comments, processing instructions and so on.

The root node is not an element. In some other specifications the outermost element is described as the root of the document, but not in XPath or XSLT. In the XPath model the root is the parent of the outermost element, it represents the document as a whole.

The XSLT tree model can represent every well-formed XML document, but it can also represent structures that are not well-formed according to the XML definition. Specifically, in well-formed XML, there must be a single outermost element containing all the other elements and text nodes; this element (the XML specification calls it the document element, though XSLT does not use this term) can be preceded and followed by comments and processing instructions, but cannot be preceded by other elements or text nodes.

The XSLT tree model does not enforce this constraint; the root can have any children that an element might have, including multiple elements and text nodes in any order. The root might also have no children at all. This corresponds to the XML rules for the content of an **external general parsed entity**, which is a freestanding fragment of XML that can be incorporated into a well-formed document by means of an entity reference. I shall sometimes use the term **well balanced** to refer to such an entity. This term is not used in the XSLT specification, rather I have borrowed it from the rarely-mentioned XML fragment interchange proposal (http://www.w3.org/TR/WD-xml-fragment). The essential feature of a well-balanced XML fragment is that every element start tag is balanced by a corresponding element end tag.

Example: Well-balanced XML Fragment

Here is an example of an XML fragment that is well-balanced but not well-formed, as there is no enclosing element:

```
The <noun>cat</noun> <verb>sat</verb> on the <noun>mat</noun>.
```

And here is the corresponding XPath tree. In this case it is important to retain whitespace, so spaces are shown using the symbol ♦:

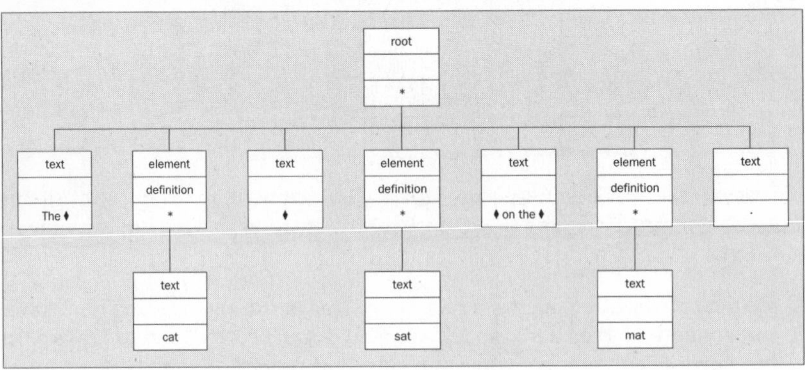

The string-value of the root node in this example is simply «`The cat sat on the mat.`».

In practice the input and output of the transformation will usually be well-formed documents, but it is very common for temporary trees constructed in the course of processing to have more than one element as a child of the root.

Nodes in the Tree Model

An XPath tree is made up of nodes. There are seven types of node. The different types of node correspond fairly directly to the components of the source XML document:

Node Type	Description
Root node	The root node is a singular node; there is one for each document. The root node in the XPath model performs the same function as the document node in the DOM model. Do not confuse the root with the document element, which in a well-formed document is the outermost element that contains all others.
Element node	An element is a part of a document bounded by start and end tags, or represented by a single empty-element tag such as **`<TAG/>`**.
Text node	A text node is a sequence of consecutive characters in a `PCDATA` part of an element. Text nodes are always made as big as possible: there will never be two adjacent text nodes in the tree, because they will have been merged together. In DOM terminology, the text nodes are **normalized**.
Attribute node	An attribute node includes the name and value of an attribute written within an element start tag (or empty element tag). An attribute that was not present in the tag, but which has a default value defined in the DTD, is also represented as an attribute node on each separate element instance. A namespace declaration (an attribute whose name is `xmlns` or whose name begins with `xmlns:`) is, however, **not** represented by an attribute node in the tree.
Comment node	A comment node represents a comment written in the XML source document between the delimiters «`<!--`» and «`-->`».
Processing instruction node	A processing instruction node represents a processing instruction written in the XML source document between the delimiters «`<?`» and «`?>`». The *PITarget* from the XML source is taken as the node's name and the rest of the content as its value. Note that the XML declaration `<?xml version="1.0"?>` is not a processing instruction, even though it looks like one, and it is not represented by a node in the tree.
Namespace node	A namespace node represents a namespace declaration, except that it is copied to each element that it applies to. So each element node has one namespace node for every namespace declaration that is in scope for the element. The namespace nodes belonging to one element are distinct from those belonging to another element, even when they are derived from the same namespace declaration in the source document.

There are several possible ways of classifying these nodes. We could distinguish those that can have children (elements and the root), those that have a parent (everything except the root), those that have a name (elements, attributes, namespaces, and processing instructions) or those that have their own textual content (attributes, text, comments, processing instructions, and namespace nodes). Since each of these criteria gives a different possible class hierarchy, the XSLT tree model instead leaves the hierarchy completely flat, and defines all these characteristics for all nodes, using null or empty values for nodes where the characteristic isn't applicable. So if we show the class hierarchy in UML notation, we get the simple diagram below.

UML (the Unified Modeling Language) is a set of diagrammatic conventions for object-oriented analysis and design. For information about UML, see http://www.omg.org/technology/uml/index.htm*, or the Wrox book Instant UML, by Pierre-Alain Muller, ISBN 1-861000-87-1*

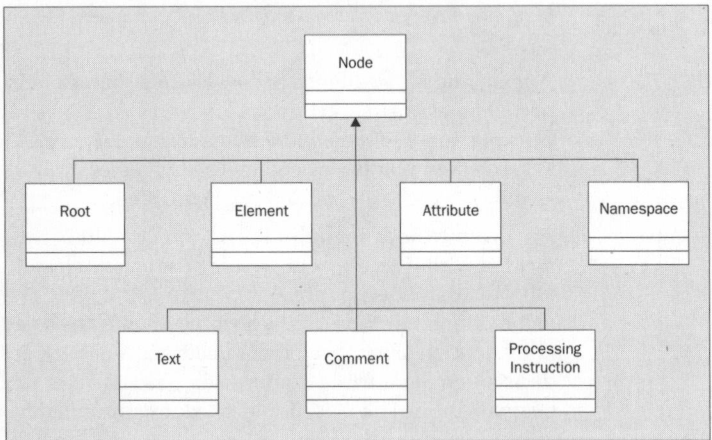

This diagram looks superficially similar to the tree we saw earlier, but this time I'm not showing a specific tree, I'm showing a class hierarchy: the boxes represent classes or types, and the arrow represents an "is-a-kind-of" relationship: for example a comment is-a-kind-of node. The earlier diagram was just one example of a particular tree, whereas now we are considering the structure of all possible trees.

I've already hinted at some of the properties and relationships of these nodes. Let's look at the properties and relationships in more detail, and then add them to the diagram.

The Name of a Node

A node has a name.

For the root node, comments, and text nodes this is the empty string. (Note that this differs from the DOM, where names such as «`#comment`» are used.)

For elements and attributes it is the name that appears in the source XML, expanded using the applicable namespace declarations. For a processing instruction it is the *PITarget* from the source XML: this is not subject to namespace rules.

The name of a namespace node is, by convention, the namespace prefix from the original namespace declaration (without the «`xmlns:`» part). For example, the namespace declaration «`xmlns:acme="http://acme.com/xml"`» generates a namespace node with name «`acme`», while the default namespace declaration «`xmlns="http://acme.com/xml"`» generates a namespace node whose name is the empty string.

A name is written in the source document, and also, of course, in an XML result document, as a `QName`, which is short for **qualified name**. A `QName` has two parts: the prefix, which is the part of the `QName` before the «`:`» as written in the source XML, and the local part, which is the part of the `QName` after the «`:`». If there is no colon, the prefix is the empty string. For example, «`xsl:stylesheet`» is a `QName`, with prefix «`xsl`» and local-name «`stylesheet`».

In the tree model, however, a name is represented by an expanded name. The expanded name also has two parts, though there is no explicit syntax for displaying it. The two parts are the namespace URI, and the local part. The namespace URI is derived from the prefix used in the source document, by finding the namespace declarations that are in scope where it is used, while the local name is again the part of the `QName` after the «`:`». So the expanded name corresponding to the `QName` «`xsl:stylesheet`» has namespace URI «`http://www.w3.org/1999/XSL/Transform`» (assuming the standard namespace declarations are used), and local part «`stylesheet`».

The prefix itself is not officially part of the node name as represented in the tree model. When you look for a node with a particular name, it is only the namespace URI and the local name that the system is interested in, not the prefix.

There are occasions when the system has to generate a `QName` from the expanded name, specifically when you use the **`name()`** function described in Chapter 7, and when you serialize a tree to produce an XML document. On these occasions the system will allocate a prefix by looking at the namespace nodes on the tree. Usually it will keep the same prefix as the one you used in the source document, but there are occasions when it may choose a different one. For example, if you use two different prefixes for the same namespace. However, the processor will always output a prefix that refers to the correct namespace URI.

The String-Value of a Node

A node has a string-value, which is a sequence of Unicode characters.

For a text node this is the text as it appears in the source XML document, except that the XML parser will have replaced every end-of-line sequence by a single new line (`#xA`) character.

For a comment, it is the text of the comment, minus the delimiters.

For a processing instruction, it is the data part of the source processing instruction, not including the white space that separates it from the *PITarget*.

For an attribute, it is the attribute value.

For a root or element node, it is defined as the concatenation of the string-values of all the element and text children of this node. Or to look at it another way: the concatenation of all the PCDATA contained in the element (or for the root node, the document) after stripping out all markup. (This again differs from the DOM, where the **nodeValue** property in these cases is null.)

For a namespace node the string-value is, by convention, the URI of the namespace being declared.

The Base URI of a Node

A node has a base URI. This should not be confused with its namespace URI. The base URI of a node depends on the URI of the source XML document it was loaded from, or more accurately, the URI of the external entity it was loaded from, since different parts of the same document might come from different XML entities. The base URI is used when evaluating a relative URI that occurs as part of the value of this node, for example an **href** attribute: this is always interpreted relative to the base URI of the node it came from.

It is possible in XSLT 1.1 to override this by specifying an explicit base URI using the **xml:base** attribute. For example, if an element has the attribute «xml:base="../index.xml"», then the base URI for this element, and for all its descendants provided they are in the same XML external entity, is the index.xml file in the parent directory of the file that would otherwise have provided the base URI.

The base URI is only maintained explicitly for element nodes and processing instruction nodes. For attributes, text nodes, and comments, the base URI is the same as the URI of its parent node. For the root node, it is the URI of the document entity.

For a namespace node the base URI is implementation dependant. This is rather a curiosity. The only time you might be interested in the base URI of a namespace node is if you are using the namespace URI as the URI of a real resource, for example a schema. But even then, the base URI will only be needed if this is a relative URI. W3C, after fierce debate, had decided that a relative namespace URI was deprecated and implementation defined, so it seemed prudent for the XSL Working Group to steer clear of defining an interpretation.

The fact that text nodes don't have their own base URI is a little ad hoc, since a text node need not come from the same external entity as its parent element, but it reflects the decision that text nodes should be joined up irrespective of entity boundaries.

The base URI of a node in the source document is used for one purpose only: to resolve relative URI references when loading additional input documents using the **document()** function, described in Chapter 7.

The Children of a Node

A node has a list (an ordered set) of child nodes. This one-to-many relationship is defined for all nodes, but the list will be empty for all nodes except the root node and element nodes. So you can ask for the children of an attribute, and you will get an empty node-set returned.

The children of an element are the elements, text nodes, processing instructions, and comments contained textually between its start and end tags, provided that they are not also children of some lower-level element.

The children of the root node are all the elements, text nodes, comments, and processing instructions that aren't contained in another element. For a well-formed document the children of the root node will be the document element plus any comments or processing instructions that come before or after the document element.

The attributes of an element are not regarded as child nodes of the element; neither are its namespace nodes.

The Parent of a Node

Every node, except the root, has a parent. The parent relationship is **not** the exact inverse of the child relationship: specifically, attribute nodes and namespace nodes have an element node as their parent, **but they are not considered to be children of that element**. In other cases, however, the relationship is symmetric: elements, text nodes, processing instructions, and comments are always children of their parent node, which will always be either an element or the root.

The Attributes of a Node

This relationship only exists in a real sense between element nodes and attribute nodes, and this is how it is shown on the diagram below. It is a one-to-many relationship: one element has zero or more attributes. In fact, the relationship `has-attribute` is defined for all nodes, but if you ask for the attributes of any node other than an element, the result will be an empty node-set.

The Namespaces of a Node

This relationship only really exists between element nodes and namespace nodes, and this is how it is shown on the diagram. It is a one-to-many relationship: one element has zero or more namespace nodes. Like the `attributes` relationship, the relationship `namespaces` is defined for all nodes, so if you ask for the namespaces of any node other than an element, the result will be an empty node-set.

Note that each namespace node is owned uniquely by one element. If a namespace declaration in the source document has a scope that includes many elements, then a corresponding namespace node will be generated for each one of these elements. These nodes will all have the same name and string-value, but they will be distinct nodes for the purposes of counting and using the union operator.

Completing the UML Class Diagram

It's now possible to draw a more complete picture of the UML class diagram as follows. In this version:

- I have brought out `Container` as a separate class, to distinguish those nodes that have children (the root, and elements) from those that do not. This is for illustration only: the concept of a container node is not explicit in the formal model.
- I have identified the `parent` relationship between any node and its parent.
- I have identified the separate relationships between an element and its attributes, and between an element and its namespace nodes.

- I have identified the additional class `UnparsedEntity`. This is not itself a node on the tree. It corresponds to an unparsed entity declaration within the document's DTD, and the information is accessible only using the **`unparsed-entity-uri()`** function.
- I have identified two additional properties on the Element node: `BaseURI`, which is the URI of the entity that the element start and end tags were found in, and ID, which is the ID attribute value for this element if it has one.

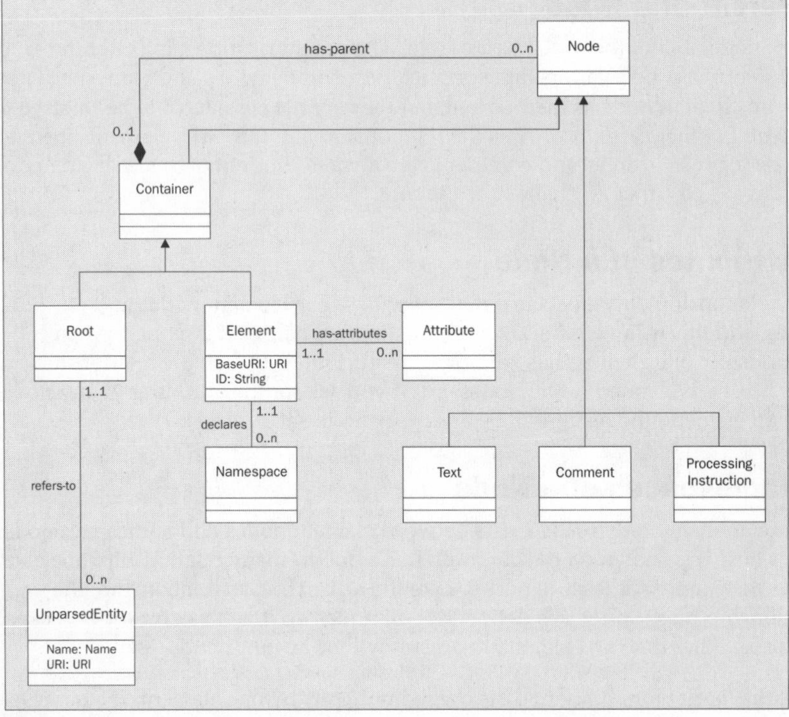

It's worth mentioning that the XSLT tree model never uses null values in the sense that SQL or Java use null values. If a node has no string-value, then the value returned is the empty string; a string of length zero. If a node has no children, then the value returned is the empty node-set; a set containing no members. There's no distinction made between an empty string and an absent string, or between an empty set and an absent set. In the specification, the words null and empty are used interchangeably.

Let's look briefly at some of the features of this model.

Names and Namespaces

XSLT and XPath are designed very much with the use of XML Namespaces in mind, and although many source documents may make little or no use of namespaces, an understanding of the XML Namespaces Recommendation (found in http://www.w3.org/TR/REC-xml-names) is essential.

Expanding on the description in Chapter 1 (page 28), here's a summary of how namespaces work:

- A namespace declaration defines a namespace prefix and a namespace URI. The namespace prefix only needs to be unique within a local scope, but the namespace URI is supposed to be unique globally. Globally here really does mean globally: not just unique in the document, but unique across all documents around the planet. To achieve that, the advice is to use a URI based on a domain name that you control, for example «`http://www.my-domain.com/namespace/billing`». XSLT doesn't impose any particular rules on the URI syntax, though it's a good idea to stick to a standard URI scheme in case this ever changes: in most of our examples we'll use URIs beginning with «`http://`». To avoid any ambiguity, it's also best to avoid relative URIs such as «`billing.dtd`». After a fierce debate on the issue, W3C have issued a belated edict deprecating the use of relative namespace URIs in XML documents, and stating that the effect of using them is implementation-defined. What this actually means is that they couldn't get everyone to agree. However, as far as most XSLT processors are concerned, the namespace URI does not have to conform to any particular syntax. For example, «`abc`», «`42`», and «`?!*`» are all likely to be acceptable as namespace URIs. It is just a character string, and two namespace URIs are considered equal if they contain the same sequence of Unicode characters.

- The namespace URI does not have to identify any particular resource, and although it is recommended to use a URL based on a domain name that you own, there is no implication that there is anything of interest to be found at that address. The two strings «`c:\this.dtd`» and «`C:\THIS.DTD`» are both acceptable as namespace URIs, whether or not there is actually a file of this name; and they represent different namespaces even though when read as filenames they might identify the same file.

> **The fact that every stylesheet uses the namespace URI `http://www.w3.org/1999/XSL/Transform` doesn't mean that you can only run a transformation if your machine has an internet connection. The name is just an elaborate constant: it's not the address of something that the processor has to go and fetch.**

- A namespace declaration for a non-null prefix is written as follows. This associates the namespace prefix `my-prefix` with the namespace URI `http://my.com/namespace`:

```
<a xmlns:my-prefix="http://my.com/namespace">
```

- A namespace declaration may also be present for the null prefix. This is known as the default namespace. The following declaration makes `http://your.com/namespace` the default namespace URI:

```
<a xmlns="http://your.com/namespace">
```

- The scope of a namespace declaration is the element on which it appears and all its children and descendants, excluding any subtree where the same prefix is associated with a different URI. This scope defines where the prefix is available for use. Within this scope, any name with the given prefix is automatically associated with the given namespace URI.

- A name has three properties: the prefix, the local part, and the namespace-URI. If the prefix is not null, the name is written in the source document in the form `prefix:local-part`, for example in the name `xsl:template`, the prefix is `xsl` and the local part is `template`. The namespace-URI of the name is found from the innermost element that carries a namespace declaration of the relevant prefix. (In theory this allows you to use the same prefix with different meanings in different parts of the document, but the only time you'll ever need to do this is if you assemble a document from pieces that were separately authored.)
- The XML Namespaces Recommendation defines two kinds of name that may be qualified by means of a prefix: element names, and attribute names. The XSLT Recommendation extends this to many other kinds of name which appear in the values of XML attributes, for example variable names, template names, names of keys, and so on. All these names can be qualified by a namespace prefix.
- If a name has no prefix, then its namespace URI is considered to be the default namespace URI in the case of an element name, or a null URI in the case of an attribute name or any other kind of name (such as XSLT variable names and template names). However, within an XPath expression, the default namespace URI is never used for unprefixed names, even if the name is an element name.
- Two names are considered equal if they have the same local part and the same namespace URI. The combination of the local part and the namespace URI is called the **expanded name**. The expanded name is never actually written down, and there is no defined syntax for it; it is a conceptual value made up of these two components.

  > *The TrAX Application Programming Interface, described in Appendix F, allows expanded names to be written in the form* «`{namespace.uri}local-name`».

- The prefix of a name is arbitrary in that it does not affect comparison of names; however it is available to applications so it can be used as the default choice of prefix in the result tree, or in diagnostic output messages.

In the XPath tree model, there are two ways namespace declarations are made visible:

- For any node such as an element or attribute, the three components of the name (the prefix, the local part, and the namespace URI) are each available, via the functions **`name()`**, **`local-name()`**, and **`namespace-uri()`**. The application doesn't need to know, and cannot find out, where the relevant namespace was declared. Technically, the prefix is not actually stored as part of the element or attribute name in the tree, but is reconstructed when the **`name()`** function is called. In some situations (for example, if your document uses more than one prefix to refer to the same namespace URI) the system might not use the original prefix, but another prefix that identifies the same namespace URI. In a few cases, typically where the source document uses the same prefix to refer to more than one namespace, it may be necessary for the processor to invent an arbitrary prefix.

- For any element, it is possible to determine all the namespace declarations that were in force for that element, by retrieving the associated namespace nodes. These are all made available as if the namespace declarations were repeated on that specific element. Again the application cannot determine where the namespace declaration actually occurred in the source document. The name of a namespace node is the namespace prefix that was originally written in the source document: unlike the prefix returned by the **`name()`** function, the system is not free to change this.

Although the namespace declarations are originally written in the source document in the form of XML attributes, they are not retained as attribute nodes on the tree, and cannot be processed by looking for all the attribute nodes. Similarly, it is not possible to generate namespace nodes on the result tree by writing attributes with the names «`xmlns:*`» reserved for namespace declarations.

IDs

An `ID` is a string value that identifies an element node uniquely within a document. If an element has an `ID`, it becomes easy and (one hopes) efficient to access that element if the `ID` value is known. The `ID` always appears as the value of an attribute declared in the DTD as being of type `ID`. Each element has zero or one `ID` values and each `ID` value (if it is present at all) identifies one element.

For example, in an XML dataset containing details of employees, each **`<employee>`** element might have a unique **`ssn`** attribute giving the employee's social security number. For example:

```
<personnel>
<employee ssn="SSN-123-45-6789">
   <name>John Doe</name>
   ...
</employee>
<employee ssn="SSN-123-45-6890">
   <name>Jane Stag</name>
   ...
</employee>
</personnel>
```

As the **`ssn`** attribute is unique, it can be declared in the DTD as an `ID` attribute using the following declaration:

```
<!ATTLIST employee ssn ID #REQUIRED>
```

Attributes of type `ID` are often given the name **`ID`** as a reminder of their role; unfortunately this sometimes leads people to believe that the attribute name **`ID`** is somehow special. It isn't; an `ID` attribute is any attribute defined in the DTD as having type `ID`, regardless of the attribute name.

An `ID` value is constrained to take the form of an XML **Name**. This means, for example, that it must start with a letter, and that it may not contain characters such as «`/`» or space.

In XML, attributes can also be defined as being of type `IDREF` or `IDREFS` if they contain `ID` values used to point to other elements in the document (an `IDREF` attribute contains one `ID` value, an `IDREFS` attribute contains a whitespace-separated list of `ID` values). However, XPath does not make any use of this information. XPath provides a function, **`id()`** (see page 496), which can be used to locate an element given its `ID` value. This function is designed so that an `IDREF` or `IDREFS` attribute can be used as input to the function, but equally, so can any other string that happens to contain an `ID`. Therefore, `IDREF` and `IDREFS` attributes do not appear explicitly in the tree model.

There is a slight complication with the use of `ID` values, in that XPath is not constrained to process only valid XML documents. If an XML document is well-formed (or merely well-balanced) but not valid, then values which are supposed to be `ID`s may be duplicated, and they might not obey the syntactic rules for an XML Name. The XPath specification says that if an `ID` value appears more than once, all occurrences except the first are ignored. It doesn't say what happens if the `ID` value contains invalid characters such as spaces, but it's quite likely in this case that the **`id()`** function will fail to find the element but will otherwise appear to work correctly. If you use `ID` values, it's probably a good idea to use a validating XML parser to prevent this situation occurring.

Apart from this special use of `ID` attributes, the attribute type defined in the DTD does not form part of the XPath tree model. You cannot find out, for example, what the declared type of an attribute is. Also, ID attributes can appear only in a tree derived by parsing a source document. They cannot appear in a temporary tree or a result tree, because temporary trees and result trees have no DTD.

XSLT also provides a more flexible approach to finding elements (or other nodes) by content, namely keys. With keys you can do anything that `ID`s achieve, other than enforcing uniqueness. Keys are declared in the stylesheet using the **`<xsl:key>`** element (see Chapter 4, page 241), and they can be used to find a node by means of the **`key()`** function (see Chapter 7, page 499).

Characters

In the **XML Information Set** definition (http://www.w3.org/TR/xml-infoset) each individual character is distinguished as an object (or **information item**). This is a useful model conceptually, because it allows one to talk about the properties of a character and the position of a character relative to other characters, but it would be very expensive to represent each character as a separate object in a real tree implementation.

The XPath model has chosen not to represent characters as nodes. It would be nice if it did, because the XPath syntax could then be extended naturally to do character manipulation within strings, but the designers chose instead to provide a separate set of string-manipulation functions. These functions are described in Chapter 7.

The string-value of any node is a sequence of zero or more characters. Each character is a `Char` as defined in the XML standard. Loosely, this is a Unicode character. More precisely, it is one of the following:

- One of the four whitespace characters tab `#x9`, linefeed `#xA`, carriage return `#xD`, or space `#x20`.

- An ordinary 16-bit Unicode character in the range `#x21` to `#xD7FF` or `#xE000` to `#xFFFD`.
- An extended Unicode character in the range `#x10000` to `#x10FFFF`. Internally such a character is usually represented as a **surrogate pair**, using two 16-bit codes in the range `#xD800` to `#xDFFF`, but as far as XPath is concerned, it is one character rather than two. This affects functions that count characters in a string or that make use of the position of a character in a string, specifically the functions **`string-length()`**, **`substring()`**, and **`translate()`**. Here XPath differs from Java, which counts a surrogate pair as two characters. (Unicode surrogate pairs are not at present widely used, but they are starting to be defined and are likely to be encountered more frequently in the future.)

Note that line endings are normalized to a single newline `#xA` character, regardless of how they appear in the original XML source file.

It is not possible in a stylesheet to determine how a character was written in the source file. For example, the following strings are all identical as far as the XPath data model is concerned:

- `>`
- `>`
- `>`
- `>`
- `>`
- `<![CDATA[>]]>`

The XML parser handles these different character representations. In most implementations, the XSLT processor will use a standard XML parser underneath, and the XSLT processor couldn't treat these representations differently even if it wanted to, because they all look the same once the XML parser has dealt with them.

The only exception to this rule is in the area of whitespace handling. The way in which whitespace in the source XML document is handled, and the interaction of the XML parser and the XSLT processor in this respect, are surprisingly complex topics, and I shall discuss them in some detail in Chapter 3.

On a temporary tree (described later in this chapter on page 93), there is an additional property associated with each character of a text node; a `disable-output-escaping` flag. When you write output using the **`<xsl:text>`** or **`<xsl:value-of>`** instructions, you have the option of specifying **«`disable-output-escaping="yes"`»**; this will cause a special character such as the ampersand («`&`») to be output as «`&`», not as «`&`» as would normally be the case. When the output is directed to a temporary tree, this flag is attached to each character written, so that later, if a text node from the temporary tree is copied to another tree using the **`<xsl:copy>`** or **`<xsl:copy-of>`** instruction, the flag will be copied along with the character. (Of course, most implementations aren't likely to actually store a flag with each character, there are more efficient ways of doing it. But even so, this feature complicates the implementation, and as `disable-output-escaping` is an optional feature of the standard, it's likely that some products won't implement it fully.)

What Does the Tree Leave Out?

The debate in defining a tree model is about what to leave out. What information from the source XML document is significant, and what is an insignificant detail? For example, is it significant whether the CDATA notation was used for text? Are entity boundaries significant? What about comments?

Many newcomers to XSLT ask questions like "How can I get the processor to use single quotes around attribute values rather than double quotes?" or "How can I get it to output « » instead of « »?" – and the answer is that you can't, because these distinctions are considered to be things that the recipient of the document shouldn't care about, and they were therefore left out of the XPath tree model.

Generally the features of an XML document fall into one of three categories: definitely significant, definitely insignificant, and debatable. For example, the order of elements is definitely significant; the order of attributes within a start element tag is definitely insignificant; but the significance of comments is debatable.

The XML standard itself doesn't define these distinctions particularly clearly. It defines certain things that must be reported to the application, and these are certainly significant. There are other things that are obviously significant (such as the order of elements) about which it says nothing. Equally, there are some things that it clearly states are insignificant, such as the choice of CR-LF or LF for line endings, but many others about which it stays silent, such as choice of «"» versus «'» to delimit attribute values.

One result of this is that different standards in the XML family have each made their own decisions on these matters, and XSLT and XPath are no exception.

The debate arises partly because there are two kinds of application. Applications that only want to extract the information content of the document are usually interested only in the core information content. Applications such as XML editing tools tend also to be interested in details of how the XML was written, because when the user makes no change to a section of the document, they want the corresponding output document to be as close to the original as possible.

To resolve these questions and get some commonality across the different standards, the W3C set up an activity to define a common model of the information in an XML document: the so-called XML Information Set (or **InfoSet**, as it is often referred to). Their current conclusions are published at http://www.w3.org/TR/xml-infoset. The latest version as I write is dated 2 February 2001; the spec has been through a long series of changes and it could change again before it's finished.

The XML information set as now defined includes seventeen different information items, listed below. In earlier versions of the Infoset specification, some of these were classified as core information items, and others, by implication, as non-core. However, this classification obviously proved too controversial, because it has disappeared in the latest version of the specification.

The seventeen kinds of information item are as follows:

- Previously classified as core: Document, Element, Attribute, Processing Instruction, Unexpanded Entity, Character, Notation, Namespace Declaration.
- Previously classified as non-core: Comment, Document Type Declaration, Internal Entity, External Entity, Unparsed Entity, Entity Start Marker, Entity End Marker, CDATA Start Marker, CDATA End Marker.

The Information Set started as an attempt to place the content of an XML document into three categories:

- Core information items, which carry information that most applications will be interested in;
- Non-core information items, which some applications may be interested in;
- Lexical details which are not intended to carry information (for example, the whitespace between attribute values in a start tag).

But it seems that it was too difficult to get agreement on this, so the current specification only has two categories: information that is included in the Infoset, and information that is excluded. Even then, it is not written in a prescriptive style. The only conformance rules it imposes are that other specifications must explain which information items are made available to the application and which aren't.

Another attempt to define the core information content of an XML document appears in the specification of Canonical XML (http://www.w3.org/TR/2001/PR-xml-c14n-20010119). This specification approaches the question from a different angle: it tries to define rules for deciding when two lexically-different XML documents have the same information content. To do this, it defines a transformation that can be applied to any XML document to turn it into canonical form; and if two documents have the same canonical form, they are considered equivalent.

The process of turning a document into canonical form is summarized as follows:

- The document is encoded in UTF-8
- Line breaks are normalized to `#xA`
- Attribute values are normalized, depending on the attribute type
- Character references and parsed entity references are expanded
- CDATA sections are replaced with their character content
- The XML declaration and document type declaration (DTD) are removed
- Empty element tags (**`<a/>`**) are converted to tag pairs (**`<a></a>`**)
- Whitespace outside the document element and within tags is normalized
- Attribute value delimiters are set to double quotes
- Special characters in attribute values and character content are replaced by character references
- Redundant namespace declarations are removed
- Default attribute values defined in the DTD are added to each element
- Attributes and namespace declarations are sorted into alphabetical order

This specification has a grey area too: canonical form may or may not retain comments from the original document.

So in place of the Infoset definition, we have an alternative definition of core XML information: namely, information that is retained when a document is turned into canonical form.

The diagram below illustrates the resulting classification: the central core is information that is retained in canonical form; the "peripheral" ring is information that is present in the Infoset but not in canonical XML; while the outer ring represents features of an XML document which are excluded from the information set entirely.

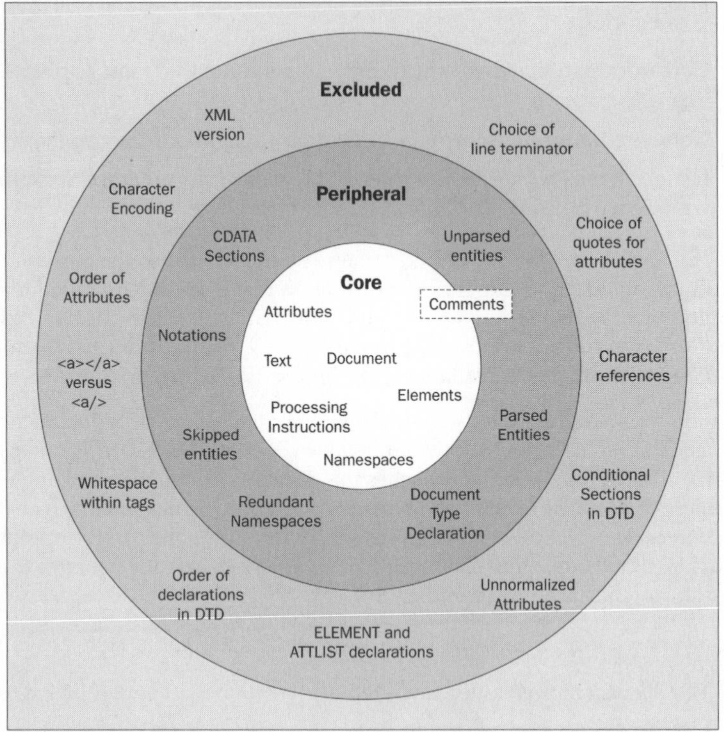

The choice of information items that are present in the XSLT/XPath tree model, and which therefore are accessible to an XSLT stylesheet follows the "core" as shown in the above diagram fairly closely, but there are some very small differences of detail:

- The XSLT model includes comments, which are optional information items in Canonical XML. This can lead to problems when the XSLT processor is built on top of other software, such as a SAX1-compatible XML parser, which treats comments as irrelevant and doesn't pass them on. Fortunately this is fixed in SAX2.
- Canonical XML retains namespace prefixes as originally defined in the source document. In practice most XSLT processors will also retain namespace prefixes, but in theory, according to the specification, the **`name()`** function in XPath can return any namespace prefix so long as it maps to the correct namespace URI.
- The XSLT model retains the base URI as a property of a node: this property is not retained in Canonical XML.

The way in which the textual content of an item is modeled differs between XPath and the Infoset: the Infoset describes each character as an individual information item, whereas the XPath model concatenates adjacent characters into a property called the string-value of a node. In the case of character content within elements this also requires the inclusion of text nodes in the model. However, this is purely a difference in the way the data is described: the information content of both models is the same. The reason the Infoset makes each character a separate information item is that it allows CDATA section boundaries and entity reference boundaries to be placed between the characters. These information items are not retained in Canonical XML, nor are they visible in the XPath model.

Controlling Serialization

The transformation processor, which generates the result tree, generally gives the user control only over the core information items and properties (plus comments) in the output. The output processor or serializer gives a little bit of extra control over how the result tree is converted into a serial XML document. Specifically, it allows control over:

- Use of `CDATA` sections
- XML version
- Character encoding
- The `standalone` property in the XML declaration
- `DOCTYPE` declaration

Some of these things are considered peripheral in our classification above, and some are in the excluded category. The features that can be controlled during serialization do not include all the peripheral information items (for example, it is not possible to generate entity references), and they certainly do not include all the excluded features. For example, there is no way of controlling the order in which attributes are written, or the choice of `<a/>` versus `<a></a>` to represent empty elements, the disposition of whitespace within a start tag, or the presence of a newline character at the end of the document.

In short, the set of things that you can control in the serialization stage of processing bears some resemblance to the classification of features in the Information Set and in Canonical XML, but not as much resemblance as one might expect. Perhaps if the Information Set had been defined earlier, there would be greater consistency between the different W3C specifications.

To underline all this, let's list some of the things you can't see in the input tree, and some of the things you can't control in an XML output file.

Invisible Distinctions

In the table below, the constructs in the two columns are considered equivalent, and in each case you can't tell as a stylesheet writer which one was used in the source document. If one of them doesn't seem to have the required effect, don't bother trying the other because it won't make any difference:

Construct	Equivalent
`<item/>`	`<item></item>`
`>`	`>`
`<e>"</e>`	`<e>"</e>`
`<![CDATA[ a < b ]]>`	`a < b`

`<a xmlns="one.uri">`
`<b/>`
`</a>`
	`<a xmlns="one.uri">`
	`<b xmlns="one.uri"/>`
	`</a>`

`<rectangle x="2" y="4"/>`	`<rectangle y='4'`
	`x='2'`
	`/>`

In all these cases, except CDATA, it's equally true that you have no control over the format of the output. Because the alternatives are equivalent, you aren't supposed to care which is used.

Why make a distinction for CDATA on output? Perhaps because where a passage of text contains a large number of special characters, for example in a book where you want to show examples of XML, the use of character references can become very unreadable. It is after all one of the strengths of XML, and one of the reasons for its success, that XML documents are easy to read and edit by hand. Also, perhaps, because there is actually some controversy about the meaning of CDATA: there have been disputes, for example, about whether «<![CDATA[   ]]>» is allowed in circumstances where XML only permits whitespace.

DTD Information

The XPath designers decided not to include all the DTD information in the tree. Perhaps they were anticipating the introduction of XML Schemas, which are widely expected to replace DTDs, and which represent schema information in XML form, which would allow the same tree model to be used.

The XSLT processor (but not the application) needs to know which attributes are of type ID, so that the relevant elements can be retrieved when the **id()** function is used. It is part of the tree model that a particular element has a particular ID value, but apart from this, there is no information about attribute types explicitly present in the tree model.

The Transformation Process

I've described how the essential process performed by XSLT is to transform a source tree to a result tree under the control of a stylesheet, and we've looked at the structure of these trees. Now it's time to look at how the transformation process actually works, which means taking a look inside the stylesheet.

Template Rules

As we saw in Chapter 1, most stylesheets will contain a number of template rules. Each template rule is expressed in the stylesheet as an **<xsl:template>** element with a **match** attribute. The value of the **match** attribute is a pattern. The pattern determines which nodes in the source tree the template rule matches.

For example, the pattern «/» matches the root node; the pattern «title» matches a **<title>** element, and the pattern «chapter/title» matches a **<title>** element whose parent is a **<chapter>** element.

When you invoke an XSLT processor to apply a particular stylesheet to a particular source document, the first thing it does is to read and parse these documents and create internal tree representations of them in memory. Once this preparation is complete, the transformation process can start.

The first step in the transformation process is to find a template rule that matches the root node of the source tree. If there are several possible candidates, there is a conflict resolution policy to choose the best fit (see page 82 for details). If there is no template rule that matches the root node, a built-in template is used. The XSLT processor then instantiates the contents of this template rule.

The content of the **<xsl:template>** element in the stylesheet is a sequence of elements and text nodes. Comments and processing instructions in the stylesheet are ignored, as are whitespace text nodes, unless they belong to an **<xsl:text>** element or to one with an appropriate **xml:space** attribute. I refer to this sequence as a **template body**. The XSLT specification itself refers to it simply as a template, but this terminology is often confusing, so I have avoided it.

Elements in the template body are classified as either instructions or data, depending on their namespace. Text nodes are always classified as data. When the template is instantiated, the instructions in the template body are executed, and the data nodes are copied to the result tree. Elements that are classified as data are officially termed **literal result elements**.

Contents of a Template Body

Consider the following template rule:

```
<xsl:template match="/">
   <xsl:message>Started!</xsl:message>
   <xsl:comment>Generated from XSLT</xsl:comment>
   <html>
      . . .
   </html>
   The end
</xsl:template>
```

The body of this template rule consists of two instructions (**<xsl:message>** and **<xsl:comment>**), a literal result element (the **<html>** element) and some text («The end»). When this template is instantiated, the instructions are executed according to the rules for each individual instruction, and literal result elements and text nodes are copied (as element nodes and text nodes respectively) to the result tree.

It's simplest to think of this as a sequential process, where instantiating a template body causes instantiation of each of its components in the order they appear. Actually, because XSLT is largely side-effect-free, they could be executed in a different order, or in parallel. The important thing is that after instantiating this template body, the result tree will contain, below its root node, a comment node (produced by the **<xsl:comment>** instruction), an **<html>** element node (produced by the **<html>** literal result element), and the text node «The end».

> *Actually* **<xsl:message>** *is an exception to the rule that XSLT is side-effect-free. If there are several* **<xsl:message>** *instructions in a template body, then the sequence in which the messages appear is not guaranteed.*

If I hadn't included the «...» within the **<html>** element, this would be the end of the matter. But when a literal result element such as **<html>** is instantiated, its content is treated as a template body in its own right, and this is instantiated in the same way. It can again contain a mixture of instructions, literal result elements, and text.

Nested Template Bodies

Now suppose the template rule actually looks like this:

```
<xsl:template match="/">
   <xsl:message>Started!</xsl:message>
   <xsl:comment>Generated from XSLT</xsl:comment>
   <html>
      <head>
         <title>My first generated HTML page</title>
      </head>
      <body>
         <xsl:apply-templates/>
      </body>
   </html>
   The end
</xsl:template>
```

Here the **<html>** element contains two child elements, **<head>** and **<body>**. These are both literal result elements, so they are instantiated by copying them from the stylesheet to the result tree. The **<head>** element contains a **<title>** literal result element, which contains some text, so the whole structure is copied to the result tree.

When the **<body>** element is instantiated, however, it contains an XSLT instruction, namely **<xsl:apply-templates/>**. This particular instruction has critical importance: when written as here, without any attributes, it means "select all the children of the current node in the source tree, and for each one, find the matching template rule in the stylesheet, and instantiate it".

What actually happens at this point depends both on what is found in the source document, and on what other template rules are present in the stylesheet. Typically, because we are currently processing the root node of the source document tree, it will have just one child node, namely the document element (the outermost element of the source XML document). Suppose this is a **<doc>** element. Then the XSLT processor will search the stylesheet looking for a template rule that matches the **<doc>** element.

The simplest situation is where it finds just one rule that matches this element, for example one declared as:

```
<xsl:template match="doc">
```

If it finds more than one matching template rule, it again has to use its conflict resolution policy to choose the best fit. The other possibility is that there is no matching template rule: in this case it invokes the built-in template rule for element nodes, which simply executes **<xsl:apply-templates/>**: in other words, it selects the children of this element, and tries to find template rules that match these children. There's also a built-in template rule for text nodes, which copies the text node to the output. If the element has no children, **<xsl:apply-templates/>** does nothing.

Push Processing

The simplest way to process a source tree is thus to write a template rule for each kind of node that can be encountered, and for that template rule to produce any output required, as well as calling **<xsl:apply-templates>** to process the children of that node.

Example: Push Processing

Here's an example stylesheet that does just that.

Input

The source document, `books.xml`, is a simple book catalog:

```
<?xml version="1.0"?>
<books>
  <book category="reference">
      <author>Nigel Rees</author>
      <title>Sayings of the Century</title>
      <price>8.95</price>
   </book>
   <book category="fiction">
      <author>Evelyn Waugh</author>
      <title>Sword of Honour</title>
      <price>12.99</price>
   </book>
   <book category="fiction">
      <author>Herman Melville</author>
      <title>Moby Dick</title>
      <price>8.99</price>
   </book>
   <book category="fiction">
      <author>J. R. R. Tolkien</author>
      <title>The Lord of the Rings</title>
      <price>22.99</price>
   </book>
</books>
```

Stylesheet

Say you want display this data in the form of a sequentially numbered booklist. The following stylesheet, books.xsl, will do the trick:

```
<xsl:stylesheet
        xmlns:xsl="http://www.w3.org/1999/XSL/Transform"
        version="1.0"
>
<xsl:template match="books">
   <html><body>
   <h1>A list of books</h1>
   <table width="640">
   <xsl:apply-templates/>
   </table>
   </body></html>
</xsl:template>

<xsl:template match="book">
<tr>
   <td><xsl:number/></td>
   <xsl:apply-templates/>
   </tr>
</xsl:template>

<xsl:template match="author | title | price">
   <td><xsl:value-of select="."/></td>
</xsl:template>

</xsl:stylesheet>
```

What's happening here? There's no template for the root node, so the built-in template gets invoked. This processes all the children of the root node.

There's only one child of the root node, the **<books>** element. So the template for the **<books>** element is instantiated. This outputs some standard HTML elements to the result tree, and eventually calls **<xsl:apply-templates/>** to cause its own children to be processed. These children are all **<book>** elements, so they are all processed by the template rule whose match pattern is «match="book"». This template rule outputs an HTML **<tr>** element, and within it a **<td>** element, which it fills by executing the **<xsl:number/>** instruction whose effect is to get the sequence number of the current node (the book element) within its parent element. It then calls **<xsl:apply-templates/>** once again to process the children of the **<book>** element in the source tree.

The children of the **<book>** element in the source document are all **<author>**, **<title>**, or **<price>** elements, so as it happens they all match the template rule whose match pattern is «match="author | title | price"» (you can read «|» as "or"). This template rule outputs an HTML **<td>** element which it fills by executing an instruction: <xsl:value-of select="."/>. This instruction evaluates an XPath expression, and writes its result (a string) as text to the result tree. The expression is «.» which returns the string-value of the current node, that is the textual content of the current **<author>**, **<price>**, or **<title>** element.

This template makes no further call on **<xsl:apply-templates>**, so its own children are not processed, and control returns all the way up.

Output

```
<html>
   <body>
      <h1>A list of books</h1>
      <table width="640">
         <tr>
            <td>1</td>
            <td>Nigel Rees</td>
            <td>Sayings of the Century</td>
            <td>8.95</td>
         </tr>
         <tr>
            <td>2</td>
            <td>Evelyn Waugh</td>
            <td>Sword of Honour</td>
            <td>12.99</td>
         </tr>
   etc..
      </table>
   </body>
</html>
```

This style of processing is called **push** processing. It is as if the processor is pushing the nodes out of the door, saying "is anyone interested in dealing with this one?"

Controlling Which Nodes to Process

Simple push processing works very well when the data in the output is to have the same structure and sequence as the data in the input, and all we want to do is add or remove a few tags or perform other simple editing of values as we go along.

In the above example, it wouldn't work so well if the properties of each book were less predictable, for example if some of the books had no price, or if the title and author could appear in either order. In this case the HTML table that we generated wouldn't be nicely arranged in columns any more, because generating a new cell for each property we encounter is not necessarily the right thing to do.

In such circumstances, we've got two choices:

- We can be more precise about which nodes to process, rather than just saying *process all children of the current node*.
- We can be more precise about how to process them, rather than just saying *choose the best-fit template rule*.

Let's try the first option.

Example: Controlling the Sequence of Processing

We can gain greater control over **which** nodes are to be processed by changing the **<book>** template in books.xsl, as follows:

```
<xsl:template match="book">
    <tr>
    <td><xsl:number/></td>
    <xsl:apply-templates select="author"/>
    <xsl:apply-templates select="title"/>
    <xsl:apply-templates select="price"/>
    </tr>
</xsl:template>
```

Instead of selecting all child elements and finding the appropriate template rule for each one, this now explicitly selects first the **<author>** child element, then the **<title>** child element, and then the **<price>** child element.

This will still work, and it's more robust than our previous attempt, but it will still produce a ragged table if there are any **<book>** elements without an **<author>** (say), or with more than one.

As we want a regular structure in the output and because we know a lot about the structure of the source document, we'd probably be better off in this situation defining all the processing in the **<book>** template rather than relying on templates to match each of its child elements.

Example: Selecting Nodes Explicitly

We can gain greater control over **how** nodes are to be processed by writing the **<book>** template in the following manner:

```
<xsl:template match="book">
    <tr>
    <td><xsl:number/></td>
    <td><xsl:value-of select="author"/></td>
    <td><xsl:value-of select="title"/></td>
    <td><xsl:value-of select="price"/></td>
    </tr>
</xsl:template>
```

Some people call this **pull** processing, because instead of the template pushing nodes out of the door to be picked up by another template, it is pulling the nodes in and handling them itself.

The pattern-matching, or push, style of processing is the most characteristic feature of XSLT, and it works very well in applications where it makes sense to describe the handling of each type of node in the source document independently. However, there are many other techniques available, all of which are equally valuable. From within a template rule that is processing one particular node, the main alternatives if you want access to information in other nodes are:

- Call **<xsl:apply-templates>** to process those nodes using their appropriate template rules.
- Call **<xsl:apply-templates>** in a particular **mode** (see below) to process those nodes using the template rules for the relevant mode.
- Call **<xsl:value-of>** to extract the required information from the nodes directly.
- Call **<xsl:for-each>** to perform explicit processing of each of the nodes in turn.
- Call **<xsl:call-template>** to invoke a specific template by name, rather than relying on pattern matching to decide which template to invoke.

Further discussion of the different approaches to writing a stylesheet is included in Chapter 9, *Design Patterns*.

Modes

Sometimes you want to process the same node in the source tree more than once, in different ways. The classic example is to produce a table of contents. When generating the table of contents, you want to handle all the section headings in one way, and when producing the body of the document, you want to handle them in a different way.

One way around this problem is to use push processing on one of these passes through the data, and pull processing on all the other occasions. However, this could be very constraining. Instead, you can define different modes of processing, one for each pass through the data. You can name the mode of processing when you call **<xsl:apply-templates>**, and the only template rules that will be considered are those that specify the same mode. For example, if you specify:

```
<xsl:apply-templates select="heading-1" mode="table-of-contents"/>
```

Then the selected template rule might be one defined as:

```
<xsl:template match="heading-1" mode="table-of-contents">
. . .
</xsl:template>
```

Further details of how to use modes are in Chapter 4, page 320 and an example of how to use them to generate a table of contents is in Chapter 10, page 639.

Built-in Template Rules

What happens when **<xsl:apply-templates>** is invoked to process a node, and there is no template rule in the stylesheet that matches that node?

The answer is that a **built-in template rule** is invoked.

There is a built-in template rule for each type of node. The built-in rules work as follows:

Node type	Built-in template rule
root	Call **<xsl:apply-templates>** to process the children of the root node, in the same mode as the calling mode
element	Call **<xsl:apply-templates>** to process the children of this node, in the same mode as the calling mode
attribute	Copy the attribute value to the result tree, as text – not as an attribute node
text	Copy the text to the result tree
comment	Do nothing
processing-instruction	Do nothing
namespace	Do nothing

The built-in template rules will only be invoked if there is no rule that matches the node anywhere in the stylesheet.

There is no way to override the built-in template for namespace nodes, because there is no pattern that will match a namespace node. If you call **<xsl:apply-templates>** to process namespace nodes, nothing happens. If you want to process all the namespace nodes for an element, use:

```
<xsl:for-each select="namespace::*">
```

Conflict Resolution Policy

Conversely, what happens when there is more than one template rule whose pattern matches a particular node? As I mentioned earlier, the conflict resolution policy comes into play.

This works as follows:

- First the **import precedence** of each rule is considered. As we will see in Chapter 3, one stylesheet may import another using the **<xsl:import>** element, and this part of the policy basically says that when stylesheet A imports stylesheet B, the rules in A take precedence over the rules in B.
- Then the **priority** of each rule is examined. The priority is a numeric value, and the higher the number, the higher the priority. You can either specify the priority explicitly in the **priority** attribute of the **<xsl:template>** element, or you can leave the system to allocate a default priority. In this case, the system allocates a priority that is designed to reflect whether the pattern is very general or very specific, for example the pattern «subsection/title» (which matches any **<title>** element whose parent is a **<subsection>** element) gets higher priority than the pattern «*», which matches any element. System-allocated priorities are always in the range –0.5 to +0.5: user-allocated priorities will normally be 1 or more, but there are no restrictions. For more details see the description of the **<xsl:template>** element in Chapter 4, page 315.
- Finally, if there is more than one rule with the same import precedence and priority, the XSLT processor has a choice: it can either report an error, or it can choose whichever rule appears last in the stylesheet. Different processors will behave differently in this situation, which gives you a slight portability problem to watch out for: it is best to ensure this ambiguity never happens.

Variables, Expressions, and Data Types

The system of data types lies at the core of any language, and the way expressions are used to compute values and assign these to variables is closely tied up with the type system. So let's look in more detail at these aspects of the language.

Variables

XSLT allows global variables to be defined, which are available throughout the whole stylesheet, as well as local variables, which are available only within a particular template body. The name and value of a variable are defined in an **<xsl:variable>** element. For example:

```
<xsl:variable name="width" select="50"/>
```

This defines a variable whose name is `width` and whose value is the number `50`. The variable can subsequently be referenced in an XPath expression as `$width`. If the **<xsl:variable>** element appears at the top level of the stylesheet (as a child of the **<xsl:stylesheet>** element) then it is a global variable; if it appears within the body of an **<xsl:template>** element then it is a local variable.

Similarly, XSLT also allows global and local parameters to be defined, using an **<xsl:param>** element. Global parameters are set from outside the stylesheet (for example, from the command line or from an API – the actual mechanism is implementor-defined). Local parameters to a template are set using an **<xsl:with-param>** element when the template is called.

Variables and parameters are not statically typed: they take whatever type of value is assigned to them. The five data types defined in XSLT and XPath are:

- **String** (any sequence of Unicode characters permitted in XML).
- **Number** (a double-precision floating point number as defined in IEEE 754).
- **Boolean** (the value true or false).
- **Node-set** (a set of nodes in a source tree).
- **External object** (an object, for example a Java object, returned by an extension function written in a language other than XSLT/XPath). By allowing XSLT variables to identify an external object, external functions are able to pass arbitrary values to each other.

In XSLT 1.0 there is an additional data type, the **Result Tree Fragment**. This is essentially a tree conforming to the model described earlier in this chapter. In the draft XSLT 1.1 specification, the result tree fragment is no longer a separate data type, but is merged into the node-set data type. A tree is manipulated in the form of a node-set containing one node, the root of the tree.

These data types are described in more detail later in the chapter, starting on page 87. The use of variables is superficially very similar to their use in conventional programming and scripting languages. They even have similar scoping rules. However, there is one key difference: once a value has been given to a variable, it cannot be changed. This difference has a profound impact on the way programs are written, so it is discussed in detail in the section *Programming Without Assignment Statements* in Chapter 9, page 609.

Expressions

The syntax of expressions is defined in the XPath Recommendation, and is described in detail in Chapter 5.

XPath expressions are used in a number of contexts in an XSLT stylesheet. They are used as attribute values for many XSLT elements, for example:

```
<xsl:value-of select="($x + $y) * 2"/>
```

In this example `$x` and `$y` are references to variables, and the operators «+» and «*» have their usual meanings of addition and multiplication.

Many XPath expressions, like this one, follow a syntax that is similar to other programming languages. The one that stands out, however, and the one that gave XPath its name, is the **Path Expression**.

A Path Expression defines a navigation path through the document tree. Starting at a defined origin, usually either the current node or the root, it follows a sequence of steps in defined directions. At each stage the path can branch, so for example you can find all the attributes of all the children of the origin node. The result is always a set of nodes. It might be empty or contain only one node, but it is still treated as a set.

The directions of navigation through the tree are called **axes**. The various axes are defined in detail in Chapter 5. They include:

- The child axis, which finds all the children of a node.
- The attribute axis, which finds all the attributes of a node.
- The ancestor axis, which finds all the ancestors of a node.
- The following-siblings axis, which finds the nodes that come after this one and share the same parent.
- The preceding-siblings axis, which finds the nodes that come before this one and share the same parent.

As well as specifying the direction of navigation through the tree, each step in a path expression can also qualify which nodes are to be selected. This can be done in several different ways:

- By defining the name of the nodes (completely or partially).
- By defining the type of nodes (e.g. elements or processing instructions).
- By defining a predicate that the nodes must satisfy – an arbitrary Boolean expression.
- By defining the relative position of the node along the axis: for example, it is possible to select only the immediately preceding sibling.

The syntax of a path expression uses «`/`» as an operator to separate the successive steps. A «`/`» at the start of a path expression indicates that the origin is the root node; otherwise it is generally the current node. Within each step, the axis is written first, separated from the other conditions by the separator «`::`». However, the child axis is the default, so it may be omitted; and the attribute axis may be abbreviated to «`@`».

For example:

```
child::item/attribute::category
```

is a path expression of two steps, the first selects all the child **`<item>`** elements of the current node, and the second step selects their **`category`** attributes. This can be abbreviated to:

```
item/@category
```

Predicates that the nodes must satisfy are written in square brackets, for example:

```
item[@code='T']/@category
```

This selects the **`category`** attributes of those child **`<item>`** elements that have a **`code`** attribute whose value is '`T`'.

There are many ways of abbreviating path expressions to make them easier to write, but the basic structure remains the same. The full detail appears in Chapter 5.

Context

The way in which expressions are evaluated is to some extent context-dependent. For example, the value of the expression `$x` depends on the current value of the variable `x`, and the value of the expression «`.`» depends on which node is currently being processed in the source document.

There are two aspects to the context: the static context, which depends only on where the expression appears in the stylesheet, and the dynamic context, which depends on the state of processing at the time the expression is evaluated.

The static context includes:

- The set of namespace declarations in force at the point where the expression is written. This determines the validity and meaning of any namespace prefixes used in the expression.
- The set of variable declarations (that is, `<xsl:variable>` and `<xsl:param>` elements) in scope at the point where the expression is written. This determines the validity of any variable references used in the expression.
- The set of functions that are available to be called. External function libraries can be set up using vendor-defined mechanisms, or in XSLT 1.1, by using the `<xsl:script>` element (described in Chapter 4 on page 293).
- The Base URI of the stylesheet element containing the XPath expression. This only affects the result if the expression uses the `document()` function, using a relative URI that is interpreted relative to the stylesheet. The `document()` function is described in Chapter 7, page 466.

The dynamic context consists of:

- The current values of all the variables that are in scope for the expression. These may be different each time the expression is evaluated.
- The current location in the source tree. The current location comprises:
  - The **current node**. This is the node in the source tree that is currently being processed. A node becomes the current node when it is processed using the `<xsl:apply-templates>` or `<xsl:for-each>` instructions. The current node can be referenced using the `current()` function.
  - The **context node.** This is normally the same as the current node, except in a predicate used to qualify a step within a path expression, when it is the node currently being tested by the predicate. The context node can be referenced using the expression «`.`», or the longer form «`self::node()`». For example, «`a[.='Madrid']`» selects all the `<a>` elements whose string-value is '`Madrid`'.
  - The **context position**. This is an integer (>=1) that indicates the position of the context node in the current node list. The context position can be referenced using the `position()` function. When `<xsl:apply-templates>` or `<xsl:for-each>` are used to process a list of nodes, that list becomes the current node list, and the context position therefore takes the values 1..n as each of the nodes in the list is processed. When a predicate is used within a path expression, the context position is the position of the node being tested within the set of nodes being tested. So, for example, «`child::a[position() != 1]`» selects all the child elements named `<a>`, except the first.

- The **context size.** This is an integer (>=1) that indicates the number of nodes in the current node list. The context size can be referenced using the **`last()`** function. So, for example, «`child::a[position() != last()]`» selects all the child elements named **`<a>`**, except the last.

The XSLT and XPath specifications use different terminology to describe the context. XSLT uses the concepts of current node and current node list, while XPath uses the concepts of context node, context position, and context size. When the **`<xsl:apply-templates>`** or **`<xsl:for-each>`** instructions are executed, the current node list is set to the list of nodes being processed, and the current node is set to each of these nodes in turn. When an XPath expression is evaluated, the context node is set to the current node; the context position is set to the position of the current node within the current node list; and the context size is set to the size of the current node list.

Some system functions that can be used in expressions have other dependencies on the context, for example the effect of the **`key()`** function depends on the set of **`<xsl:key>`** declarations in force; but the list above covers all the context information that is directly accessible to user-written expressions.

Data Types

XSLT is a dynamically-typed language, in that types are associated with values rather than with variables. In this respect it is similar to VBScript and JavaScript.

Ignoring result tree fragments for the time being, there are five data types available, and conversion between them is generally carried out implicitly when the context requires it. However, the functions **`boolean()`**, **`number()`**, and **`string()`** are also available to carry out explicit conversions. The table below summarizes the conversions between the five data types:

To / From	Boolean	number	string	node-set	external object
Boolean	**not applicable**	false ⇒ 0 true ⇒ 1	false ⇒ 'false' true ⇒ 'true'	not allowed	not allowed
number	0 ⇒ false other ⇒ true	**not applicable**	convert to decimal format	not allowed	not allowed
string	null ⇒ false other ⇒ true	parse as a decimal number	**not applicable**	not allowed	not allowed
node-set	empty⇒false other ⇒ true	convert via string	string-value of first node in document order	**not applicable**	not allowed
external object	not allowed	not allowed	not allowed	not allowed	**not applicable**

More detailed information is given in the descriptions of the functions **`boolean()`**, **`number()`**, and **`string()`** in Chapter 7.

In XSLT 1.1, a temporary tree created using a non-empty **<xsl:variable>** element has a data type of node-set (the node-set contains a single node, the root of the tree), and its conversions to and from other data types are as defined in the table above. With XSLT 1.0, however, temporary trees are represented by an additional data type, the result tree fragment, which behaves in most ways like a node-set, but can't be used in all contexts where node-sets are allowed. Many XSLT 1.0 products provide an extension function to convert a result tree fragment to a node-set when required; in MSXML3, for example, the function is **msxml:node-set()**

See the relevant Appendix for details of extension functions in particular vendors' products.

Conversion of a result tree fragment to a string, number, or boolean happens implicitly, and has the same result as if a node-set containing just the root node of the tree were converted to the required type, using the rules in the table above. The effect of these rules is as follows:

To / From	Boolean	number	string
Result Tree Fragment	always true	convert to a string; then convert the string to a number	the concatenation of all the text nodes in the tree

The following sections describe the core data types, namely Boolean, number, string, and node-set. External objects, which are provided for use by extension functions written in a different programming language, are described in Chapter 8.

Boolean Values

The Boolean data type in XPath contains the values true and false.

There are no constants to represent true and false, instead the values can be written using the function calls **true()** and **false()**.

Boolean values may be obtained by comparing values of other data types using operators such as «=» and «!=», and they may be combined using the two operators «and» and «or» and the function **not()**.

XPath differs from SQL in that it does not use three-valued logic. A Boolean value is always either true or false; it can never be undefined or null. The nearest equivalent to an SQL null value in XPath is an empty node-set, and when you compare an empty node-set to a string or number the result is always false, regardless of which comparison operator you use. For example, if the current element has no **name** attribute, then the expressions «@name='Boston'» and, «@name!='Boston'» both return false. However, the expression «not(@name='Boston')» returns true.

For more information on the sometimes-strange behavior of the equality and inequality operators when applied to node-sets, see the sections EqualityExpr (page 370) and RelationalExpr (page 416) in Chapter 5.

Number Values

A number in XPath is always a double-precision (64-bit) floating-point number, and its behavior is defined to follow the IEEE 754 standard. This standard (*IEEE Standard for Binary Floating-Point Arithmetic. ANSI/IEEE Std. 754-1985*) has been widely implemented by many microprocessors for some years, but it is only through its adoption in the Java language that it has become familiar to high-level language programmers. If you understand how floating point behaves in Java, the contents of this section will be quite familiar; if not, they may be rather strange.

Unlike most other programming languages, XPath does not use scientific notation for floating-point numbers, either on input or on output. If you want to enter the number one trillion, you must write `1000000000000`, not `1.0E12`.

IEEE 754 defines the following range of values for a double-precision number:

Value	Description
Finite nonzero values	These are values of the form $s \times m \times 2^x$, where *s* (the sign) is +1 or –1, *m* (the mantissa) is a positive integer less than 2^{53}, and *x* (the exponent) is an integer between –1075 and 970, inclusive.
Positive zero	This is the result of subtracting a number from itself. It can also result from dividing any positive number by infinity, or from dividing a very small number by a very large number of the same sign.
Negative zero	This is the result of dividing any negative number by infinity. It can also result from dividing a positive number by minus infinity, or from dividing a very small negative number by a very large positive number, or vice versa.
Positive infinity	This is the result of dividing any positive number by zero. It can also result from multiplying two very large numbers with the same sign. Note that division by zero is not an error: it has a well-defined result.
Negative infinity	This is the result of dividing any negative number by zero. It can also result from multiplying two very large numbers with different signs.
NaN	Not a Number. This is the result of attempting to convert a non-numeric string value to a number. It can also be used to mean "unknown" or "not applicable", like the SQL null value.

These values cannot all be written directly as XPath constants. However, they can be expressed as the result of expressions, for example:

Value	XPath expression
Negative zero	–0
Positive Infinity	1 div 0
Negative Infinity	–1 div 0
NaN	number("NaN")

Technically, negative numbers cannot be written directly as constants: «-10» is an expression rather than a number, but in practice it can be used anywhere that a numeric constant can be used. The only thing you need to be careful of is that a space may be needed before the unary minus operator if you write an expression such as «$x div -1».

Except for NaN, number values are **ordered**. Arranged from smallest to largest, they are:

- negative infinity
- negative finite non-zero values
- negative zero
- positive zero
- positive finite non-zero values
- positive infinity

This ordering determines the result of less-than and greater-than comparisons, and also the result of sorting using **<xsl:apply-templates>** or **<xsl:for-each>** with a sort key specified using <xsl:sort data-type="number">.

NaN is **unordered**, so the operators «<», «<=», «>», and «>=» return false if either or both operands are NaN. However, when **<xsl:sort>** is used to sort a sequence of numeric values that includes one or more NaN values, NaN values are collated at the start of the sequence (or at the end if you choose descending order).

The position of NaN in the sort sequence was undefined in the original XSLT 1.0 specification, and this omission was corrected later in an erratum. So you may encounter XSLT processors that don't handle it in this way.

Positive zero and negative zero compare equal. This means that the operators «=», «<=», and «>=» return true, while «!=», «<», and «>» return false. However, other operations can distinguish positive and negative zero; for example, «1.0 div $x» has the value positive infinity if $x is positive zero, and negative infinity if $x is negative zero.

The equals operator «=» returns false if either or both operands are NaN, and the not-equals operator «!=» returns true if either or both operands are NaN. Watch out for the apparent contradictions this leads to; for example «$x=$x» can be false, and «$x<$y» doesn't necessarily give the same answer as «$y>$x».

The simplest way to test whether a value $x is NaN is:

```
<xsl:if test="$x!=$x">
```

If this seems too obscure for your taste, then provided you know that $x is numeric you can write:

```
<xsl:if test="string($x)='NaN'">
```

If you are familiar with null values in SQL, some of this logic might seem familiar, but there are some subtle differences. For example, in SQL the condition «null=null» has the value null, so that «not(null=null)» is also null; while in XPath «NaN=NaN» is false, so that «not(NaN=NaN)» is true.

XPath provides a number of operators and functions that act on numeric values:

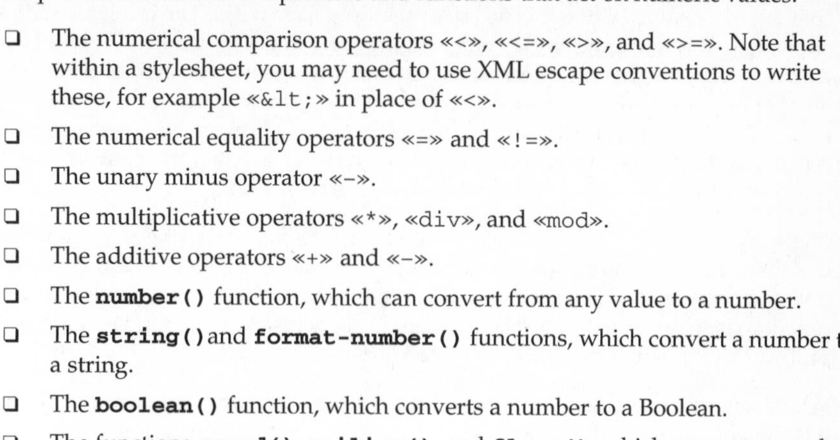

- The numerical comparison operators «<», «<=», «>», and «>=». Note that within a stylesheet, you may need to use XML escape conventions to write these, for example «<» in place of «<».
- The numerical equality operators «=» and «!=».
- The unary minus operator «-».
- The multiplicative operators «*», «div», and «mod».
- The additive operators «+» and «-».
- The **number()** function, which can convert from any value to a number.
- The **string()** and **format-number()** functions, which convert a number to a string.
- The **boolean()** function, which converts a number to a Boolean.
- The functions **round()**, **ceiling()**, and **floor()**, which convert a number to an integer.
- The function **sum()**, which totals the numeric values of a set of nodes.

Operators on numbers behave exactly as specified by IEEE 754. XPath is not as strict as Java in defining exactly what rounding algorithms should be used for inexact results, and in what sequence operations should be performed. Many implementations, however, will follow the Java rules.

XPath numeric operators and functions never produce an error. An operation that overflows produces positive or negative infinity, an operation that underflows produces positive or negative zero, and an operation that has no other sensible result produces NaN. All numeric operations and functions with NaN as an operand produce NaN as a result. For example, if you apply the **sum()** function to a node-set, then if the string value of any of the nodes cannot be converted to a number, the result of the **sum()** function will be NaN.

String Values

A string value in XPath is any sequence of zero or more characters, where the alphabet of possible characters is the same as in XML: essentially the characters defined in Unicode.

String values can be written in XPath expressions in the form of a literal, using either single quotes or double quotes, for example 'John' or "Mary". In theory, the string can contain the opposite quote character as part of the value, for example "John's". In practice, however, XPath expressions are written within XML attributes, so the opposite quote character will generally already be in use for the attribute delimiters. For more details, see the section *Literal* in Chapter 5, page 389.

There is no special null value, as there is in SQL. Where no other value is appropriate, a zero-length string is used. In fact the terms null string and empty string are used interchangeably to refer to a zero-length string.

The only ASCII control characters permitted (codes below #x20) are the whitespace characters #x9, #xA, and #xD (tab, carriage return, and newline).

Strings may be compared using the «=» and «!=» operators. They are compared character by character (there is no space-padding as in SQL). The implementation is allowed to normalize the strings before comparing them, to handle different Unicode representations of the same accented character, but it is not required to do so. There is no operator or function provided to compare two strings ignoring case: the best you can achieve (if you know the strings are restricted to a limited alphabet such as ASCII) is to convert from lowercase to uppercase, or vice versa, using the **`translate()`** function. Otherwise, use an external user-defined function.

There are no operators or functions to compare whether one string is greater than or less than another in alphabetic sequence: the «<» and «>» operators always force a numeric comparison. The only way around this (other than writing an external function) is to do a sort; write both strings as elements on a temporary tree, then process the elements on the tree in sorted order.

When counting characters in a string, for example in the **`string-length()`** function, it is the number of XML characters that is relevant, not the number of 16-bit Unicode codes. This means that Unicode surrogate pairs are counted as a single character. Unicode surrogate pairs, which are used to extend Unicode beyond 65,535 characters, are very rarely encountered in practice, though their use may increase in the future.

Node-set Values

A node-set is a set of nodes in the source document tree. If there are multiple source document trees, a node-set may contain nodes from more than one tree. The nodes may also come from temporary trees, or from trees passed into the stylesheet from external functions or as parameters. The nodes in a node-set may be any type of node, and different types of node can be mixed in the same node-set. It is a pure mathematical set; each node can appear at most once, and there is no intrinsic order.

There is no data type to represent a single node; instead a node-set with a single member is used. For example, when you use the expression «`@name`» to find the value of the **`name`** attribute of the current element, the result is a node-set containing a single attribute node if the element has a **`name`** attribute, or an empty set if it does not.

When a node-set value is converted to a Boolean, an empty node-set is treated as false and a node-set containing one or more nodes as true. So you can use the test:

```
<xsl:if test="@name">
```

to find out whether the current element has a **`name`** attribute.

The nodes in a node-set may have children, but the children are not regarded as members of the node-set. For example, the expression «`/`» returns a node-set containing a single node, the root. The other nodes subordinate to the root can be reached from this node, but they are not themselves members of the node-set, and the value of «`count(/)`» is therefore always 1.

A node-set is not intrinsically ordered, though in many contexts the nodes are processed in **document order**. Where two nodes come from the same document, their relative position in document order is based on their position in the document tree: for example an element precedes its children in document order, and sibling nodes are listed in the same order as they appear in the original source document. Where two nodes come from different documents, their relative order is undefined. The ordering of attribute and namespace nodes is defined only partially: an element node is followed by its namespace nodes, then its attributes, and then its children, but the ordering of the namespace nodes among themselves, and of the attribute nodes among themselves, is undefined.

Temporary Trees

XSLT allows you to construct a new tree, and to refer to this tree using a variable. In XSLT 1.0, such trees are considered to be a data type in their own right, known as a result tree fragment. A result tree fragment behaves exactly like a node-set containing a single node, the root of the tree, but it cannot be used in every context where node-sets are allowed. Specifically, there are only two things you can do with a result tree fragment: you can copy it to another tree using the **<xsl:copy-of>** instruction, or you can extract its string value (the concatenation of all text nodes in the tree). Many vendors, however, provide an extension function to convert a result tree fragment to the equivalent node-set.

With XSLT 1.1, a temporary tree behaves exactly like a node-set, and can be used anywhere that a node-set can be used. The conversion to a node-set is implicit, whenever you use a tree-valued variable in a context that expects a node-set. So the additional data type has disappeared, and with it the rather awkward term "result tree fragment".

> *In fact, XSLT 1.1 no longer has a name for this concept at all. I've found I need a name to explain the concept in this book, so I've invented the terms "temporary tree" and "tree-valued variable". These terms aren't found in the XSLT Recommendation.*

A temporary tree always contains a root node, and the root node may have children. A tree does not necessarily correspond to a well-formed XML document, for example the root node can own text nodes directly, and it can have more than one element node among its children. However, it must conform to the same rules as an XML external parsed entity: for example, all the attributes belonging to an element node must have distinct names.

Example: Temporary Trees

A temporary tree is constructed by instantiating the body of an **<xsl:variable>** declaration, for example:

```
<xsl:variable name="tree"
   >AAA<xsl:element name="x">
   <xsl:attribute name="att">att-value</xsl:attribute
      >BBB</xsl:element>
   <xsl:element name="y"
   />CCC</xsl:variable>
```

(The strange layout is to ensure there is no white space adjacent to the text values, because that would be difficult to show on the tree diagram. The effects of whitespace are discussed in Chapter 3.)

This creates the tree illustrated in the diagram below. Each box shows a node; the three layers are respectively the node type, the node name, and the string-value of the node. Once again, an asterisk indicates that the string-value is the concatenation of the string-values of the child nodes.

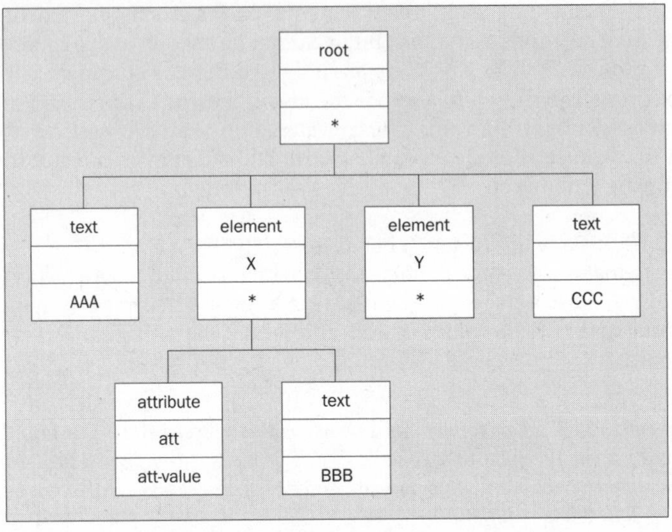

In XSLT 1.0, as we have seen, there are only two things you can do with this tree once it has been constructed: you can copy it to the current destination tree (which might be the final result tree or another temporary tree) using the **<xsl:copy-of>** instruction, or you could convert its value to a string. Converting it to a string gives the concatenation of all the text nodes in the tree: in the above example this is «AAABBBCCC».

In XSLT 1.1 you can manipulate the tree in many other ways. For example:

- You can apply templates to process its nodes, using **<xsl:apply-templates>**. It's a good idea to use a different mode, so that you know which template rules are supposed to apply to which tree.
- You can access its nodes explicitly using a path expression, for example `<xsl:value-of select="$tree/x/@att"/>` will output the text «att-value».
- You can use the **sum()** and **count()** functions, for example «count($tree//*)» will return 2 (the number of element nodes on the tree).

This means, for example, that you can use a temporary tree as a lookup table. The following stylesheet fragment uses data held in a temporary tree to get the name of the month, given its number held in a variable $mm:

```
<xsl:variable name="months">
  <January/><February/><March/><April/><May/><June/>
  <July/><August/><September/><October/><November/><December/>
</xsl:variable>
. . .
  <xsl:value-of select="name($months/*[position()=$mm"/>
```

With XSLT 1.0 you can usually achieve the same effect by writing something like:

```
<xsl:value-of select="name(xx:node-set($months)/*[position()=$mm)/>
```

but the details depend on which processor you are using.

Summary

In this chapter we explored the important concepts needed to understand what an XSLT processor does.

- We examined the overall system architecture, in which a stylesheet controls the transformation of a source tree into a result tree.
- We saw in some detail the tree model used in XSLT, and the way it relates to the XML standards: also some of the ways it differs from the DOM model.
- We learned how template rules are used to define the action to be taken by the XSLT processor when it encounters particular kinds of node in the tree.
- We looked at the way in which expressions, data types, and variables are used in the XSLT language to calculate values.

In the next chapter we will look at the structure of an XSLT stylesheet in more detail.

3

Stylesheet Structure

This chapter describes the overall structure of a stylesheet. The aim of the chapter is to explain some of the concepts used in writing stylesheets, before we get into the main reference section of the book in Chapters 4 through 8. Some of these concepts are tricky; they are areas that often cause confusion, which is why I have tried to explain them in some detail. However, it's not necessary to master everything in this chapter before you can write your first stylesheet – so use it as a reference, coming back to topics as and when you need to understand them more deeply.

The topics covered in this chapter are:

- **Stylesheet modules**: we will discuss how a stylesheet program can be made up of one or more stylesheet modules, linked together with `<xsl:import>` and `<xsl:include>` elements.
- The `<xsl:stylesheet>` (or `<xsl:transform>` element), which is the outermost element of most stylesheet modules.
- The `<?xml-stylesheet?>` processing instruction which can be used to link a source document to its associated stylesheet, and which also allows stylesheets to be embedded directly in the source document whose style they define.
- A brief description of the **top-level elements** found in the stylesheet, that is, the immediate children of the `<xsl:stylesheet>` or `<xsl:transform>` element: the full specifications are in Chapter 4.
- Simplified stylesheets, in which the `<xsl:stylesheet>` and `<xsl:template match="/">` elements are omitted, to make an XSLT stylesheet look more like the simple template languages that some users may be familiar with.
- The idea of a **template body**, a sequence of text nodes and literal result elements to be copied to the result tree, and instructions and extension elements to be executed.
- **Attribute value templates**, which are used to define variable attributes not only of literal result elements, but of certain XSLT elements as well.
- Facilities allowing the specification to be extended, both by vendors and by W3C itself, without adversely affecting the portability of stylesheets.
- Handling of **whitespace** in the source document, in the stylesheet itself, and in the result tree.

The Modular Structure of a Stylesheet

In the previous chapter we described the XSLT processing model, in which a stylesheet defines the rules by which a source tree is transformed into a result tree.

Stylesheets, like programs in other languages, can become quite long and complex, and so there is a need to allow them to be divided into separate modules. This allows modules to be reused, and combined in different ways for different purposes: for example, we might want to use two different stylesheets to display press releases on screen and on paper, but there might be components that both of these stylesheets share in common. These shared components can go in a separate module that is used in both cases.

We can regard the complete collection of modules as a **stylesheet program**, and refer to its components as **stylesheet modules**.

> *The XSLT standard does not use this terminology. In fact it uses the term stylesheet sometimes for the stylesheet program and sometimes for the stylesheet module as defined here.*

One of the stylesheet modules is the **principal stylesheet module**. This is in effect the main program, the module which is identified to the stylesheet processor by the use of an **`<?xml-stylesheet?>`** processing instruction in the source document, or whatever command line parameters or API the vendor chooses to provide. The principal stylesheet module may fetch other stylesheet modules using **`<xsl:include>`** and **`<xsl:import>`** elements. These may in turn fetch others, and so on.

Example: Using <xsl:include>

Source

The input document, `sample.xml`, looks like this:

```
<?xml version="1.0" encoding="iso-8859-1"?>
<document>
    <author>Michael Kay</author>
    <title>XSLT Programmer's Reference</title>
    <copyright/>
    <date/>
    <abstract>A comprehensive guide to the XSLT 1.1 and XPath 1.0
      recommendations published by the World Wide Web Consortium
       </abstract>
</document>
```

Stylesheets

The stylesheet uses **<xsl:include>**. The effect of this stylesheet is to copy the source document unchanged to the result, except that any **<date>** elements are set to the current date, and any **<copyright>** elements are set to a string identifying the copyright owner.

The three modules of this stylesheet program are as follows: `principal.xsl`, `date.xsl`, and `copyright.xsl`. The `date.xsl` module uses an extension function, it is written to work with any XSLT 1.1 processor that supports extension functions written in Java.

You only need to name the principal stylesheet module as your stylesheet, the other modules will be fetched automatically. The way this stylesheet is written, all the modules must be in the same directory.

principal.xsl

The first module, `principal.xsl`, contains the main logic of the stylesheet:

```
<?xml version="1.0" encoding="iso-8859-1"?>
<xsl:stylesheet
     xmlns:xsl="http://www.w3.org/1999/XSL/Transform"
     version="1.0"
>
<xsl:include href="date.xsl"/>
<xsl:include href="copyright.xsl"/>

<xsl:output method="xml" encoding="iso-8859-1" indent="yes"/>
<xsl:strip-space elements="*"/>

<xsl:template match="date">
    <date><xsl:value-of select="$date"/></date>
</xsl:template>

<xsl:template match="copyright">
    <copyright><xsl:call-template
name="copyright"/></copyright>
</xsl:template>

<xsl:template match="*">
    <xsl:copy>
        <xsl:copy-of select="@*"/>
        <xsl:apply-templates/>
    </xsl:copy>
</xsl:template>

</xsl:stylesheet>
```

It starts with two **<xsl:include>** elements to bring in the other modules. The **<xsl:output>** element indicates that the output should be in XML format, using the ISO 8859/1 character set (which makes it easy to view with a text editor), and with indentation to show the XML structure. The **<xsl:strip-space>** element indicates that whitespace nodes in the source document are to be ignored: I'll have a lot more to say about whitespace handling later in this chapter. Then there are three template rules, one for **<date>** elements, one for **<copyright>** elements, and one for everything else.

The template rule for **<date>** elements outputs the value of the variable named `$date`. This variable isn't defined in this stylesheet module, but it is present in the module `date.xsl`, so it can be accessed from here.

The template rule for **<copyright>** elements similarly calls the template named `copyright`. Again, there is no template of this name in this module, but there is one in the module `copyright.xsl`, so it can be called from here.

Finally, the template rule that matches all other elements («`match="*"`») has the effect of copying the element unchanged from the source document to the output. The **<xsl:copy>** (page 192) and **<xsl:copy-of>** (page 195) instructions are explained in Chapter 4.

date.xsl

The next module, `date.xsl`, declares a global variable containing today's date. This calls the Java «`java.util.Date`» class to get the date, referencing it as an external function. External functions are introduced later in this chapter. This stylesheet module uses the **<xsl:script>** element introduced with XSLT version 1.1.

```
<xsl:stylesheet
      xmlns:xsl="http://www.w3.org/1999/XSL/Transform"
      version="1.1"
      xmlns:Date="java:java.util.Date"
>
<xsl:script implements-prefix="Date"
      language="java" src="java:java.util.Date"/>
<xsl:variable name="date"
      select="Date:to-string(Date:new())"/>

</xsl:stylesheet>
```

At present, there are not many XSLT processors that support **<xsl:script>**, because it was only introduced in the XSLT 1.1 specification, which at the time of writing is still only a draft. But there are equivalent vendor-specific facilities in all the Java-based processors: see the relevant Appendix for details.

copyright.xsl

Finally, the module `copyright.xsl` contains a named template that outputs a copyright statement. This template is called by the **<xsl:call-template>** instruction in the principal stylesheet. The template uses a variable `$owner` to construct the copyright statement: we'll see later how this is useful.

The rather strange way of writing the **<xsl:template>** start tag is to avoid outputting a newline before the copyright text. Later in the chapter I'll describe other ways of achieving this.

```
<?xml version="1.0" encoding="iso-8859-1"?>
<xsl:stylesheet
      xmlns:xsl="http://www.w3.org/1999/XSL/Transform"
      version="1.0"
>
<xsl:variable name="owner">Wrox Press</xsl:variable>

<xsl:template name="copyright"
>Copyright © <xsl:value-of select="$owner"/>
2001</xsl:template>

</xsl:stylesheet>
```

The reason for separating this stylesheet program into three modules is that the `date.xsl` and `copyright.xsl` modules are reusable in other stylesheets. Functionally, the stylesheet would have exactly the same effect if the variable `$date` and the template named `copyright` were defined directly in the principal stylesheet.

Output

```
<?xml version="1.0" encoding="iso-8859-1" ?>
<document>
   <author>Michael Kay</author>
   <title>XSLT Programmer's Reference</title>
   <copyright>Copyright © Wrox Press 2001</copyright>
   <date>Thu Jan 18 10:27:44 GMT+00:00 2001</date>
   <abstract>A comprehensive guide to the XSLT 1.1 and XPath
1.0          recommendations
   published by the World Wide Web Consortium </abstract>
</document>
```

There is no syntactic difference between a principal stylesheet module and any other module; in fact any module can be used as a principal module.

This means that **<xsl:include>** and **<xsl:import>** can be used in any module, not only the principal module. So the stylesheet program is actually a tree of stylesheet modules, with the principal module at its root.

A stylesheet module is generally a complete XML document (the exception, an **embedded stylesheet**, will be described later on page 108). The document element (the outermost element of the XML document) is then either an **<xsl:stylesheet>** element or an **<xsl:transform>** element: the two names are synonymous. The elements immediately subordinate to the **<xsl:stylesheet>** or **<xsl:transform>** element are called **top-level** elements (it might have been clearer to call them second-level elements, but top-level is the term the standard uses). The XSLT-defined top-level elements are listed on page 111.

The **<xsl:include>** and **<xsl:import>** elements are always top-level elements. Usually, top-level elements can appear in any order, but **<xsl:import>** is an exception: it must appear before any other top-level element. Both elements take an **href** attribute whose value is a URI. Most commonly, it will be a relative URL, defining the location of the included or imported stylesheet module relative to the parent module. For example, **<xsl:include href="mod1.xsl"/>** causes the module named mod1.xsl, located in the same directory as the parent module, to be fetched.

The difference between **<xsl:include>** and **<xsl:import>** is that conflicting definitions are resolved differently:

- **<xsl:include>** effectively does a textual inclusion of the referenced stylesheet module, minus its containing **<xsl:stylesheet>** element, at the point where the **<xsl:include>** element is written. The included module is treated exactly as if its top-level elements, with their contents, appeared in the parent module in place of the **<xsl:include>** element itself.
- **<xsl:import>** also incorporates the top-level elements from the referenced stylesheet module, but in this case the definitions in the imported module have lower **import precedence** than the definitions in the parent module. If there are conflicting definitions, the one with higher import precedence will generally win. The detailed rules actually depend on the type of definition, and are given in the specification of **<xsl:import>** on page 226, in Chapter 4. Importing a module is thus rather like defining a subclass, in that the parent module can use some definitions unchanged from the imported module, and override others with definitions of its own.

The most obvious kind of definition is the definition of a template rule, using an **<xsl:template>** element with a **match** attribute. As we saw in the previous chapter, if there are several template rules that match a particular node in the source tree, the first step in deciding which to use is to look at their import precedence, and discard all those with import precedence less than the highest. So a template rule defined in a particular stylesheet module will automatically take precedence over another matching rule in a module that it imports.

Where one module A imports two others, B and C, as shown in the diagram below, then A takes precedence over both B and C, and C also takes precedence over B, assuming that the **<xsl:import>** element that loads B precedes the **<xsl:import>** element that loads C.

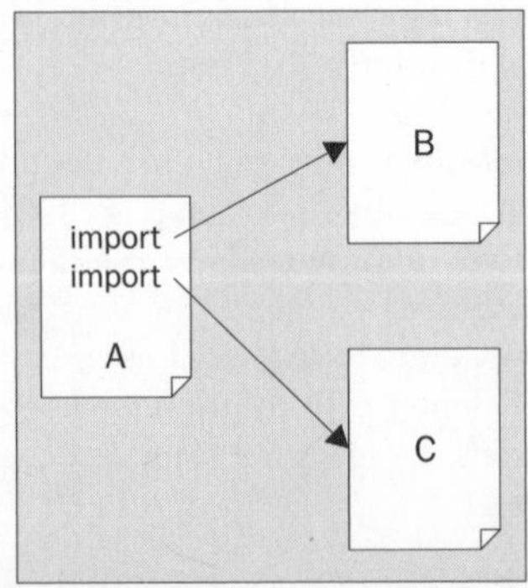

When a stylesheet incorporates another using **<xsl:include>**, the definitions in the included stylesheet have the same import precedence as those in the parent stylesheet.

Where two definitions have the same import precedence (because they were in the same stylesheet module, or because one was in a module incorporated in the other using **<xsl:include>**), the rules for resolving conflicts depend on the kind of definition. In some cases, for example definitions of named templates or variables, duplicate definitions with the same name are always reported as an error. In other cases, for example definitions of template rules, the implementor has the choice of reporting an error or choosing the definition that occurs later in the stylesheet. Some implementors may pass this choice on to the user. The detailed rules are given in Chapter 4 for each kind of top-level element, and they are summarized in the section for **<xsl:import>**, page 226.

Example: Using <xsl:import>

This extends the previous **<xsl:include>** example, showing how to use **<xsl:import>** to incorporate the definitions in another stylesheet module while overriding some of them.

Source

The input document for this example is `sample.xml`.

Stylesheet

Recall that the `copyright.xsl` module used a variable, `$owner`, to hold the name of the copyright owner. Suppose that we want to use the `copyright` template, but with a different copyright owner. We can achieve this by writing a revised principal stylesheet as follows (this is called `principal2.xsl` in the downloadable sample files).

This stylesheet uses **<xsl:import>** instead of **<xsl:include>** to incorporate the `copyright.xsl` module, and it then contains a new declaration of the `$owner` variable, which will override the declaration in the imported module. Note that the **<xsl:import>** element must come first.

```
<?xml version="1.0" encoding="iso-8859-1"?>
<xsl:stylesheet
      xmlns:xsl="http://www.w3.org/1999/XSL/Transform"
      version="1.0"
>
<xsl:import href="copyright.xsl"/>
<xsl:variable name="owner">Wrox Press Ltd</xsl:variable>
<xsl:include href="date.xsl"/>

<xsl:output method="xml" encoding="iso-8859-1" indent="yes"/>
<xsl:strip-space elements="*"/>

<xsl:template match="date">
   <date><xsl:value-of select="$date"/></date>
</xsl:template>
```

```
<xsl:template match="copyright">
   <copyright><xsl:call-template name="copyright"/></copyright>
</xsl:template>

<xsl:template match="*">
   <xsl:copy>
      <xsl:copy-of select="@*"/>
      <xsl:apply-templates/>
   </xsl:copy>
</xsl:template>

</xsl:stylesheet>
```

Output

```
<?xml version="1.0" encoding="iso-8859-1" ?>
<document>
   <author>Michael Kay</author>
   <title>XSLT Programmer's Reference</title>
   <copyright>Copyright © Wrox Press Ltd 2001</copyright>
   <date> Thu Jan 18 10:27:44 GMT+00:00 2001</date>
   <abstract>A comprehensive guide to the XSLT 1.1 and XPath 1.0
   recommendations published by the World Wide Web Consortium
</abstract>
</document>
```

This example wouldn't work if you used **<xsl:include>** rather than **<xsl:import>**. It would complain that the variable `$owner` was declared twice. This is because with **<xsl:include>**, the two declarations have the same import precedence, so neither can override the other.

It is an error for a stylesheet module to import or include itself, directly or indirectly, because doing so would define an infinite loop.

It isn't an error, however, for a stylesheet module to be included or imported at more than one place in the stylesheet program. The following isn't an error:

```
<xsl:stylesheet xmlns:xsl="http://www.w3.org/1999/XSL/Transform"
version="1.0">
   <xsl:import href="date.xsl"/>
   <xsl:import href="date.xsl"/>
</xsl:stylesheet>
```

This may seem rather pointless, but in a highly modular structure it can sometimes happen by accident and be harmless. For example, several of your stylesheet modules might independently reference a commonly used module such as `date.xsl`. The effect is simply to load two copies of all the definitions in `date.xsl`, exactly as if two identical files with different names had been imported.

If the same module is fetched twice using **<xsl:include>**, the included definitions will have the same import precedence, which is likely to cause an error. If, for example, the included module defines a global variable or a named template, duplicate definitions will be reported. In other cases, for example where the file uses the **<xsl:attribute-set>** element to define named attribute sets, the duplicate definitions are harmless (the **<xsl:attribute-set>** element is described on page 173, in Chapter 4). However, if there is a risk of loading the same module twice, it makes sense to use **<xsl:import>** rather than **<xsl:include>**.

Note that with both **<xsl:include>** and **<xsl:import>**, the **href** attribute is fixed: it is possible for a stylesheet compiler to assemble all the modules in a stylesheet well before a source document is supplied to actually run the transformation. People often ask for some kind of facility to load stylesheet modules dynamically, based on a decision made while the transformation is running. The simple answer is that you can't do this.

Sometimes, this requirement arises when people try to use **<xsl:import>** "the wrong way round". It's fairly natural to think in terms of writing a general-purpose stylesheet G that imports A in some circumstances (say if the user is French) and imports B in other circumstances (if the user is Spanish). But that's the wrong way to do it: you should select A or B as the principal stylesheet module, and have both of these import the general-purpose module G. The special-purpose stylesheet module should always import the general-purpose module, not the other way around.

The <xsl:stylesheet> Element

The **<xsl:stylesheet>** element (or **<xsl:transform>**, which is a synonym) is the outermost element of every stylesheet module.

The name **<xsl:stylesheet>** is a conventional name. The first part, `xsl`, is a prefix that identifies the namespace to which the element name belongs. Any prefix can be used so long as it is mapped, using a namespace declaration, to the URI `http://www.w3.org/1999/XSL/Transform`. There is also a mandatory **version** attribute. So the start tag of the **<xsl:stylesheet>** element will usually look like this:

```
<xsl:stylesheet
   xmlns:xsl="http://www.w3.org/1999/XSL/Transform"
   version="1.0"
>
```

If you come across a stylesheet that uses the namespace URI `http://www.w3.org/TR/WD-xsl`, *then the stylesheet is written in a Microsoft dialect based on an early working draft of the XSLT standard. This version was released with Internet Explorer 5. There are many differences between the IE5 dialect (which I refer to as* **WD-xsl**, *but which Microsoft usually refer to simply as "XSL") and the final XSLT specification described in this book. For details of WD-xsl, see the Wrox Press book* XML IE5 Programmer's Reference, *ISBN 1-861001-57-6. Microsoft has since released an updated version of their MSXML processor, which supports the full XSLT 1.0 specification, details of which can be found in Appendix A.*

The other attributes that may appear on this element are described under **<xsl:stylesheet>** in Chapter 4, page 302. Specifically, they are:

- **id**, to identify the stylesheet if it appears as an embedded stylesheet within another document. Embedded stylesheets are described in the next section.
- **extension-element-prefixes**, a list of namespace prefixes that denote elements used for vendor-defined or user-defined extensions to the XSLT language.

- **`exclude-result-prefixes`**, a list of namespaces used in the stylesheet that should not be copied to the result tree unless they are actually needed. I'll explain how this works in the section *Literal Result Elements* on page 118.

These attributes affect only the stylesheet module in which this **`<xsl:stylesheet>`** element appears; they do not affect what happens in included or imported stylesheet modules.

The **`<xsl:stylesheet>`** element will often contain further namespace declarations. Indeed, if the **`extension-element-prefixes`** or **`exclude-result-prefixes`** attributes are used, then any namespace prefixes they mention must be declared by means of a namespace declaration on the **`<xsl:stylesheet>`** element. For example, if you want to declare «`saxon`» as an extension element prefix, the start tag of the **`<xsl:stylesheet>`** element would look like this:

```
<xsl:stylesheet
   xmlns:xsl="http://www.w3.org/1999/XSL/Transform"
   xmlns:saxon="http://icl.com/saxon"
   version="1.0"
   extension-element-prefixes="saxon"
>
```

Namespace declarations on the **`<xsl:stylesheet>`** element, and indeed anywhere else in the stylesheet, apply only to the stylesheet module in which they appear. They are not inherited by included or imported modules.

The <?xml-stylesheet?> Processing Instruction

This processing instruction is not part of the XSLT or XPath standard, rather it has a short W3C Recommendation all to itself, which you can find at http://www.w3.org/TR/xml-stylesheet. XSLT mentions it, but only in an example, so there is no implication that an XSLT processor is required to support it, but an increasing number of processors do.

The **`<?xml-stylesheet?>`** processing instruction is used within a source XML document to identify the stylesheet that should be used to process it. There can be several **`<?xml-stylesheet?>`** processing instructions present, defining different stylesheets to be used under different circumstances.

The processing instruction has an **`href`** attribute whose value is the URI of the stylesheet (that is, the principal stylesheet module), and a **`type`** attribute that indicates the language in which the stylesheet is written. This doesn't have to be an XSLT stylesheet, it could be CSS. The W3C Recommendation says that for XSLT the media type should be either `text/xml` or `application/xml`; however, with Microsoft's implementation in Internet Explorer 5 it must be `text/xsl`.

Technically, XML processing instructions do not contain attributes, they contain a name (here `xml-stylesheet`*) followed by character data. However, many people like to structure the character data as a sequence of* `name="value"` *pairs, like the attributes in an element start tag, and the xml-stylesheet recommendation follows this practice. It refers to the* `name="value"` *pairs as* pseudo-attributes.

The full list of pseudo-attributes in the **`<?xml-stylesheet?>`** processing instruction is as follows:

Attribute name	Value	Meaning
`href` mandatory	URI	The URI of the stylesheet. This may be an absolute or relative URL of the XML document containing the stylesheet, or it may contain a fragment identifier (for example `#styleB`) used to locate the stylesheet within a larger file. See *Embedded Stylesheets* on page 108.
`type` mandatory	Mime type	Identifies the language in which the stylesheet is written; typically `text/xml` or `text/xsl` (see discussion above).
`title` optional	String	If there are several **`<?xml-stylesheet?>`** processing instructions, each should be given a title to distinguish them. The user can then be allowed to choose which stylesheet is wanted. For example, there may be special stylesheets that produce large print or aural rendition.
`media` optional	String	Description of the output medium, for example "`print`", "`projection`", or "`aural`". The list of possible values is defined in the HTML 4.0 specification. This value can be used to select from the available stylesheets.
`charset` optional	Character encoding name, for example `iso-8859-1`	This attribute is not useful with XSLT stylesheets, since as XML documents they define their character encoding themselves.
`alternate` optional	"`yes`" or "`no`"	If "`no`" is specified, this is the preferred stylesheet. If "`yes`" is specified, it is an alternative stylesheet.

An **`<?xml-stylesheet?>`** processing instruction must appear, if it appears at all, as part of the document prolog, that is, before the start tag of the document element. The **`href`** attribute identifies the location of the stylesheet by an absolute or relative URL. For example:

```
<?xml-stylesheet type="text/xsl" href="../style.xsl"?>
```

As with CSS, it is possible to have several `<?xml-stylesheet?>` processing instructions that match the required criteria. If you do this, though, you start to discover variations between different products. With some, this has exactly the same effect as if there were a single stylesheet that imported the selected stylesheet modules, in order, using `<xsl:import>` elements. The typical way of using this is to have one stylesheet containing common template rules, followed by more specific stylesheet modules distinguished using the title or media pseudo-attributes. But other products, notably Microsoft's MSXML3, simply use the first stylesheet and ignore the others.

It isn't mandatory to use the `<?xml-stylesheet?>` processing instruction, and most products will offer some other way of saying which stylesheet you want to apply to a particular document. It's mainly useful when you want to apply a stylesheet to an XML document within the browser; specifying this processing instruction means that the browser can apply a default stylesheet to the document without any extra scripting being needed.

Clearly, one of the reasons for separating the stylesheet from the source XML document is so that the same information can be transformed or presented in different ways depending on the user, their equipment, or the particular mode of access. The various attributes of the `<?xml-stylesheet?>` processing instruction are designed to define the rules controlling the selection of an appropriate stylesheet. The mechanism is geared towards stylesheets that are used to display information to users: it has less relevance to the more general use of XSLT for performing data transformations.

Embedded Stylesheets

There is one exception to the rule that the stylesheet module must be an XML document. The principal stylesheet module can be **embedded** within another XML document, typically the document whose style it is defining.

The ability to embed stylesheets within the source document is best regarded as a carryover from CSS. It can be useful if you have a freestanding document that you want to distribute as a self-contained unit, but in most situations it is better to use an external stylesheet that can be used for many different source documents. Some people like to embed stylesheets to reduce download time, but this can be counter-productive, because it means the browser cannot spot that the stylesheet is already present in its cache.

> **Not all XSLT processors support embedded stylesheets. Check the documentation for your particular product before using them.**

The outermost element of the stylesheet is still an `<xsl:stylesheet>` or `<xsl:transform>` element, but it will no longer be the outermost element of the XML document (that is, the document element). The `<xsl:stylesheet>` element will generally have an `id` attribute to identify it, and will be referenced within its containing document using the `<?xml-stylesheet?>` processing instruction, for example:

Example: Embedded Stylesheets

This example shows a stylesheet embedded within an XML source document containing a list of books.

Source

The data file, embedded.xsl, containing both source document and stylesheet, is as follows:

```
<?xml version="1.0"?>
<?xml-stylesheet type="text/xml" href="#style1"?>
<books>
   <book category="reference">
      <author>Nigel Rees</author>
      <title>Sayings of the Century</title>
      <price>8.95</price>
   </book>
   <book category="fiction">
      <author>Evelyn Waugh</author>
      <title>Sword of Honour</title>
      <price>12.99</price>
   </book>
   <book category="fiction">
      <author>Herman Melville</author>
      <title>Moby Dick</title>
      <price>8.99</price>
   </book>
   <book category="fiction">
      <author>J. R. R. Tolkien</author>
      <title>The Lord of the Rings</title>
      <price>22.99</price>
   </book>

   <xsl:stylesheet id="style1" version="1.0"
      xmlns:xsl="http://www.w3.org/1999/XSL/Transform">

   <xsl:template match="xsl:stylesheet"/>

   <xsl:template match="books">
      <html><body>
         <h1>A list of books</h1>
         <table>
            <xsl:apply-templates/>
         </table>
      </body></html>
   </xsl:template>

   <xsl:template match="book">
      <tr><xsl:apply-templates/></tr>
   </xsl:template>

   <xsl:template match="author | title | price">
      <td><xsl:value-of select="."/></td>
   </xsl:template>

   </xsl:stylesheet>
</books>
```

You can run this stylesheet using Saxon with a command of the form (at the time of writing, this doesn't work in Saxon 6):

```
saxon -a embedded.xsl
```

The -a option tells Saxon to look for an **<?xml-stylesheet?>** processing instruction in the supplied source document, and to process the source document using that stylesheet. Saxon doesn't allow you (when using the command line interface) to specify the criteria for selecting a specific stylesheet, so if there are several, it uses a composite stylesheet that imports all of them.

Output

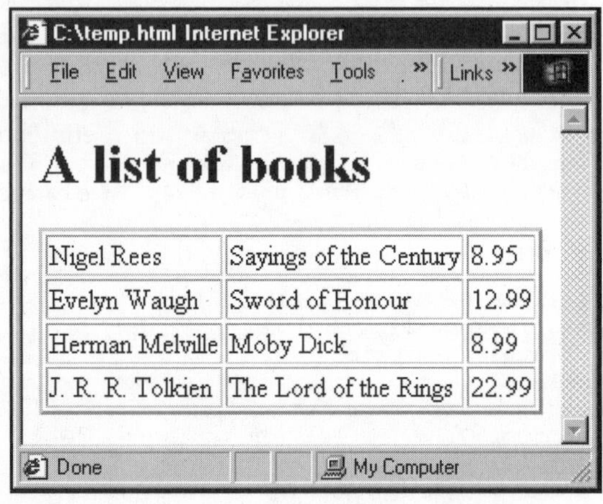

Note the empty template rule that matches the **<xsl:stylesheet>** element. This is needed because without it, the stylesheet will try to process itself along with the rest of the document. The empty template rule ensures that when the **<xsl:stylesheet>** element is matched, no output is generated, and its child elements are not processed. You may need to take care to avoid matching other elements in the stylesheet as well. For example, if the stylesheet looks for book titles using an expression such as «//title», this could accidentally match a **<title>** literal result element within the embedded stylesheet.

An embedded stylesheet module will generally be used as the principal stylesheet module. The standard doesn't explicitly say whether or not an embedded stylesheet can be included or imported into another. In practice, the details of what is supported are likely to vary from one product to another; few of the current products have much to say about embedded stylesheets in their documentation.

If namespace declarations occur outside the embedded stylesheet, they will still be in scope within the embedded stylesheet, which may result in extra namespace nodes being copied into the result tree. You can suppress such namespaces using the exclude-result-prefixes attribute on the **<xsl:stylesheet>** element.

Top-Level Elements

The term **top-level element** means an element that is an immediate child of the **<xsl:stylesheet>** or **<xsl:transform>** element. The term second-level element might have been more accurate, but **top-level element** is the one used in the standard.

It is not permitted to have text nodes as immediate children of the **<xsl:stylesheet>** or **<xsl:transform>** element, unless they consist entirely of whitespace characters. Processing instructions and comments may appear, and the XSLT processor will ignore them.

Top-level elements can appear in any order in the stylesheet, except that if there are any **<xsl:import>** elements, they must come first. In most cases the order in which the elements appear is of no significance; however, if there are conflicting definitions, the XSLT processor sometimes has the option of either reporting an error or taking whichever definition comes last. If you want your stylesheet to be portable, you cannot rely on this behavior, and should ensure that conflicting definitions don't arise.

The elements that may appear at the top level fall into three categories:

- XSLT-defined top-level elements
- Implementor-defined top-level elements
- User-defined top-level elements

Let's now examine these three categories further.

XSLT-Defined Top-Level Elements

An XSLT-defined top-level element must be one of the elements listed below:

```
<xsl:attribute-set>
<xsl:decimal-format>
<xsl:import>
<xsl:include>
<xsl:key>
<xsl:namespace-alias>
<xsl:output>
<xsl:param>
<xsl:preserve-space>
<xsl:script>
<xsl:strip-space>
<xsl:template>
<xsl:variable>
```

The meaning of these elements is explained in Chapter 4. No other XSLT element (that is, no other element with the namespace URI http://www.w3.org/1999/XSL/Transform) may be used at the top level.

Implementor-Defined Top-Level Elements

An implementor-defined top-level element must belong to a namespace with a non-null URI, different from the XSLT namespace. This will generally be a namespace defined by the vendor: for example with the Saxon product, the relevant namespace URI is `http://icl.com/saxon`. The meaning of elements in this category is entirely at the discretion of the vendor, though the specification states a rule that such elements must not be used to change the meaning of any standard XSLT constructs. Note that these top-level elements are not technically extension elements, and their namespace does not have to be declared in the **extension-element-prefixes** attribute for them to be effective.

Several vendors supply top-level elements that allow you to define external functions that can be invoked from XPath expressions in the stylesheet (but now that XSLT 1.1 supports the **<xsl:script>** element, such extensions should start to disappear). Others might use such elements to define debugging or tracing options. Such extensions are described in the relevant Appendix for the particular product.

User-Defined Top-Level Elements

A **user-defined top-level element** must also belong to a namespace with a non-null URI, different from the XSLT namespace, and preferably different from the namespace URI used by any vendor. These elements are ignored by the XSLT processor.

With XSLT 1.0, user-defined top-level elements are useful as a place to put lookup data, error messages, and the like. It is possible to reference these elements from within the stylesheet by treating the stylesheet as an additional source document, and loading it using the **document()** function, which is described in Chapter 7, page 466. If the first argument to this function is an empty string, it is interpreted as a reference to the stylesheet module in which the **document()** function appears.

So for example, if the stylesheet contains a user-defined top-level element as follows:

```
<user:data xmlns:user="http://acme.com/">
   <message nr="1">Source document is empty</message>
   <message nr="2">Invalid date</message>
   <message nr="3">Sales value is not numeric</message>
</user:data>
```

then the same stylesheet can contain a named template to display a numbered message as follows:

```
<xsl:template name="display-message">
   <xsl:param name="message-nr"/>
   <xsl:message xmlns:user="http://acme.com/">
      <xsl:value-of
       select="document('')/*/user:data/message[@nr=$message-nr]"/>
   </xsl:message>
</xsl:template>
```

The **<xsl:value-of>** element evaluates the XPath expression in its **select** attribute as a string, and writes the value to the result tree. In this case the XPath expression is a path expression starting with «`document('')`», which selects the root node of the stylesheet module, followed by «`*`», which selects its first child (the **<xsl:stylesheet>** element), followed by «`user:data`», which selects the **<user:data>** element, followed by «`message[@nr=$message-nr]`», which selects the **<message>** element whose **nr** attribute is equal to the value of the `$message-nr` parameter in the stylesheet.

This named template might be invoked from elsewhere in the stylesheet using a sequence such as:

```
<xsl:if test="string(number(@sales))='NaN'">
   <xsl:call-template name="display-message">
      <xsl:with-param name="message-nr" select="3"/>
   </xsl:call-template>
</xsl:if>
```

The **<xsl:if>** element tests whether the **sales** attribute of the current source element is numeric: if not, the result of converting it to a number and then to a string will be the value NaN, meaning Not-A-Number. In this case, the code will call the template we defined earlier to display the message "Sales value is not numeric". (The destination of messages output using **<xsl:message>** is not defined in the standard. It might produce an alert box, or simply a message in the web server log file.)

The advantage of this technique is that it gathers all the messages together in one place, for ease of maintenance. The technique can also be readily extended to use different sets of messages depending on the user's preferred language.

With XSLT 1.1, this technique will no longer be necessary, since it becomes more convenient to define fixed data as part of a global variable definition. Instead of writing:

```
<user:data xmlns:user="http://acme.com/">
   <message nr="1">Source document is empty</message>
   <message nr="2">Invalid date</message>
   <message nr="3">Sales value is not numeric</message>
</user:data>
```

you can write:

```
<xsl:variable name="data">
   <message nr="1">Source document is empty</message>
   <message nr="2">Invalid date</message>
   <message nr="3">Sales value is not numeric</message>
</xsl:variable>
```

and instead of :

```
<xsl:value-of
select="document('')/*/user:data/message[@nr=$message-nr]"/>
```

you can write:

```
<xsl:value-of select="$data/message[@nr=$message-nr]"/>
```

Simplified Stylesheets

A simplified stylesheet uses an abbreviated syntax in which the **<xsl:stylesheet>** element and all the top-level elements are omitted.

The XSLT specification calls this facility **Literal Result Element As Stylesheet.** Its purpose is to allow people with HTML authoring skills but no programming experience to write simple stylesheets with a minimum of training. A simplified stylesheet has a skeleton that looks like the target document (which is usually HTML, though it doesn't have to be), and uses XSLT instructions to fill in the variable parts.

A stylesheet module is interpreted as a simplified stylesheet if the outermost element is not **<xsl:stylesheet>** or **<xsl:transform>**. The outermost element can have any name, provided it is not in the XSLT namespace. It must still contain a declaration of the XSLT namespace, and it must have an **xsl:version** attribute. For XSLT 1.1 the value should be «1.0» or «1.1» (use «1.1» if your stylesheet depends on features defined in XSLT 1.1, or «1.0» if you also want it to work with XSLT 1.0 processors). When the **xsl:version** attribute is not equal to «1.0» or «1.1», forwards compatible processing mode is enabled. This is discussed later on page 137.

Example: A Simplified Stylesheet

This example shows a stylesheet that takes the form of an HTML skeleton page, with XSL instructions embedded within it to pull data from the source document. The stylesheet is i the download file obtainable from http://www.wrox.com. It has the filename `simplified.xsl`, and can be used together with the data file `books.xml`.

The complete stylesheet is as follows:

```
<html xmlns:xsl="http://www.w3.org/1999/XSL/Transform"
      xsl:version="1.0">
<head><title>A list of books</title></head>
<body>
<h1>A list of books</h1>
   <table border="2">
   <xsl:for-each select="//book">
      <xsl:sort select="author"/>
      <tr>
        <td><xsl:value-of select="author"/></td>
        <td><xsl:value-of select="title"/></td>
        <td><xsl:value-of select="@category"/></td>
        <td><xsl:value-of select="price"/></td>
      </tr>
   </xsl:for-each>
   </table>
</body>
</html>
```

When you run this against the file `books.xml` (which is listed on page 77 in Chapter 2), the output is a sorted table showing the books, as follows:

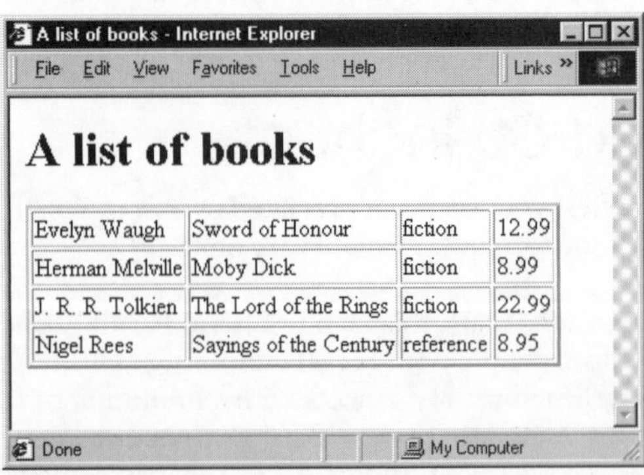

A simplified stylesheet is equivalent to a stylesheet in which the outermost element (typically the **<html>** element) is wrapped first in an **<xsl:template>** element with «match="/"», and then in an **<xsl:stylesheet>** element. The **xsl:version** attribute of the outermost element becomes the **version** attribute of the **<xsl:stylesheet>**. So the expanded form of the above example would be:

```
<xsl:stylesheet xmlns:xsl="http://www.w3.org/1999/XSL/Transform"
version="1.0">
<xsl:template match="/">
<html>
<head><title>A list of books</title></head>
<body>
<h1>A list of books</h1>
   <table border="2">
   <xsl:for-each select="//book">
      <xsl:sort select="author"/>
      <tr>
         <td><xsl:value-of select="author"/></td>
         <td><xsl:value-of select="title"/></td>
         <td><xsl:value-of select="@category"/></td>
         <td><xsl:value-of select="price"/></td>
      </tr>
   </xsl:for-each>
   </table>
</body>
</html>
</xsl:template>
</xsl:stylesheet>
```

The significance of «match="/"» is that this identifies the template rule as the first one to be processed when the stylesheet is activated. As we saw in Chapter 2, processing always starts at the root node of the source document tree, and whichever template rule matches the root node is the first one to be invoked. The match pattern «/» matches the root node. In a simplified stylesheet, this will be the only template rule invoked.

There are many things a simplified stylesheet cannot do, because it cannot have any top-level XSLT elements. For example, a simplified stylesheet can't include or import another stylesheet, it can't have global variables or parameters, and it can't define keys. But when you need these extra capabilities, you can always "unsimplify" the stylesheet by adding the surrounding **<xsl:stylesheet>** and **<xsl:template>** elements.

It is possible in theory for a stylesheet to include or import a simplified stylesheet, which would be expanded exactly as described above – but it would be a rather unusual thing to do.

Template Bodies

The content of an **<xsl:template>** element, after any parameter definitions contained in **<xsl:param>** elements, is a **template body**. The XSLT specification calls this simply a **template**, but since this term is often used casually to mean an **<xsl:template>** element, I have avoided this usage.

Many other XSLT elements are also defined to have a template body as their content. This simply refers to the rules for what contents may appear within the element, it does not mean that there must actually be an **<xsl:template>** element present. For example, the contents of an **<xsl:variable>** or **<xsl:if>** element follow exactly the same rules as the content of an **<xsl:template>** (ignoring **<xsl:param>** elements), and these too are template bodies. It follows that one template body may be contained within another. For example, consider the following template rule:

```
<xsl:template match="para">
   <xsl:if test="position()=1">
      <hr/>- o - 0 - o -<hr/>
   </xsl:if>
   <xsl:apply-templates/>
   <xsl:if test="position()=last()">
      <hr/>- o - 0 - o -<hr/>
   </xsl:if>
</xsl:template>
```

Viewed as a tree, using the notation introduced in Chapter 2, this has the structure shown in the diagram below. There are three template bodies, indicated by the dotted lines. Within the template bodies on this tree, there are three kinds of nodes: text nodes, XSLT instructions (such as **<xsl:if>**), and literal result elements (such as **<hr>**) which are elements to be written to the result tree.

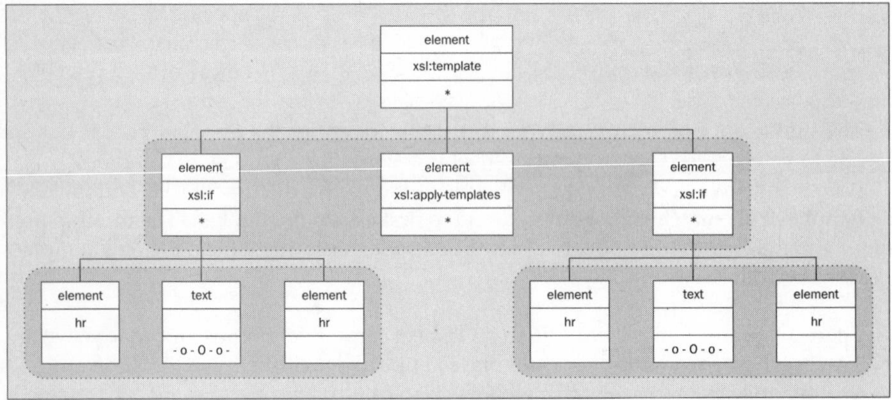

A template body is the nearest equivalent in XSLT to a block or compound statement in a block-structured programming language such as C or Java; and like blocks in C or Java, it defines the scope of any local variables declared within the block.

A template body is a sequence of sibling nodes in the stylesheet. Comment and processing instruction nodes are allowed, but the XSLT processor ignores them. The nodes of interest are text nodes and element nodes.

Text nodes appearing within a template body are copied to the result tree when the template body is instantiated. However, text nodes in a template body that consist entirely of whitespace will be ignored, unless the **xml:space** attribute is used on an enclosing element to define them as significant.

Text nodes containing whitespace only are also significant if they appear as the content of an **<xsl:text>** *element, but in that case they are not part of a template body.*

Element nodes within a template body are one of three kinds: XSLT instructions, extension elements, and literal result elements. I'll describe these in the next three sections.

XSLT Instructions

An XSLT instruction is one of the following elements:

```
<xsl:apply-imports>
<xsl:apply-templates>
<xsl:attribute>
<xsl:call-template>
<xsl:choose>
<xsl:comment>
<xsl:copy>
<xsl:copy-of>
<xsl:document>*
<xsl:element>
<xsl:fallback>
<xsl:for-each>
<xsl:if>
<xsl:message>
<xsl:number>
<xsl:processing-instruction>
<xsl:text>
<xsl:value-of>
<xsl:variable>
```

* **<xsl:document>** is new in XSLT 1.1; the others are all available in XSLT 1.0.

No other element in the XSLT namespace may appear directly in a template body. Other XSLT elements, for example **<xsl:with-param>**, **<xsl:sort>**, and **<xsl:otherwise>**, are not regarded as instructions, because they cannot appear directly in a template body – they may only appear in very specific contexts. The **<xsl:param>** element is a bit anomalous as it can appear as a child of an **<xsl:template>** element, but it is constrained to appear before other elements, and is therefore not considered to be part of the template body. So, it is not classified as an instruction.

I shall explain the meaning of all these XSLT instructions in Chapter 4.

If an unknown element in the XSLT namespace is encountered in a template body, the action taken depends on whether **forwards-compatible mode** is enabled. This is discussed later on page 137.

Extension Elements

An **extension element** is an instruction defined by the vendor or the user, as distinct from one defined in the XSLT standard. In both cases, they are recognized as extension elements because they belong to a namespace that is listed in the **extension-element-prefixes** attribute of the containing **<xsl:stylesheet>** element, or in the **xsl:extension-element-prefixes** attribute of the element itself, or of a containing literal result element or extension element.

In practice, extension elements are more likely to be defined by vendors than by users. With XSLT 1.0, several vendors have provided extension elements to direct the stylesheet output to multiple output files (with XSLT 1.1, this is superseded by a standard facility, the **<xsl:document>** instruction). Another example: the Saxon product provides the **<saxon:group>** extension element to perform grouping (like the SQL `GROUP BY` construct), a capability which is awkward and inefficient to achieve using standard XSLT facilities.

Not all products allow users to implement their own extension elements, and with those that do, it may well involve some rather complex system-level programming. In practice, it is usually simpler to escape to user-written code by using extension functions, which are much easier to write. At XSLT 1.1, it even becomes possible to write extension functions that are portable between XSLT processors; at any rate, between those that support Java or JavaScript.

The following example shows an <**acme:instruction**> element which would be treated as a literal result element were it not for the **xsl:extension-element-prefixes** attribute, which turns it into an extension element:

```
<acme:instruction
   xmlns:acme="http://acme.co.jp/xslt"
   xsl:extension-element-prefixes="acme"/>
```

The way in which new extension elements are implemented is not defined in the XSLT specification, and is likely to vary for each vendor. In fact, XSLT processors are not required to provide a mechanism for defining new extension elements. The only requirement is that they should recognize an extension element when they see one, and distinguish it from a literal result element.

What happens if a stylesheet that uses an extension element defined in the Xalan product (say) is processed using a different product (say Microsoft's)? If the processor encounters an extension element that it cannot instantiate (typically because it was invented by a different vendor), the action it must take is clearly defined in the XSLT standard: if the stylesheet author has defined an **<xsl:fallback>** action, it must execute that, otherwise it must report an error. The one thing it must not do is to treat the extension element as a literal result element and copy it to the result tree.

> *The* **<xsl:fallback>** *instruction allows you to define how an XSLT processor should deal with extension elements it does not recognize. It is described in more detail on page 137, and full specifications are on page 214, in Chapter 4.*

Any element found in a template body that is not an XSLT instruction or an extension element is interpreted as a **literal result element** (for example, the **<hr/>** elements in the previous template bodies example above). When the template body is instantiated, the literal result element will be copied to the result tree.

So in effect there are two kinds of nodes in a template body: instructions and data. Instructions are obeyed according to the rules of the particular instruction, and data nodes (text nodes and literal result elements) are copied to the result tree.

Literal result elements play an important role in the structure of a stylesheet, so the next section examines them in more detail.

Literal Result Elements

A literal result element is an element within a template body in the stylesheet that cannot be interpreted as an instruction, and which is therefore treated as data to be copied to the current output destination.

I'll describe literal result elements using the same structure as I'll be using to describe XSLT elements in Chapter 4.

Format

Position

A literal result element always appears directly within a template body.

Attributes

Name	Value	Meaning
xsl:exclude-result-prefixes optional	Whitespace-separated list of namespace prefixes (see note below)	Each prefix in the list must identify a namespace that is in scope at this point in the stylesheet module. The namespace identified is not to be copied to the result tree.
xsl: extension-element-prefixes optional	Whitespace-separated list of namespace prefixes (see note below)	Each prefix in the list must identify a namespace that is in scope at this point in the stylesheet module. Elements that are a descendant of this literal result element, and whose names are in one of these identified namespaces, are treated as extension elements rather than literal result elements.
xsl:version optional	Number	For an XSLT 1.0 processor, if the value is «1.0», then any XSLT element that is a descendant of the literal result element must be an XSLT element defined in version 1.0 of the Recommendation. If the value is any other value, forwards-compatible mode is enabled, see below. For an XSLT 1.1 processor, the values «1.0» and «1.1» are synonymous; both allow any XSLT element defined in the XSLT 1.1 specification.
xsl:use-attribute-sets optional	Whitespace-separated list of QNames identifying named **<xsl:attribute-set>** elements (see note below)	The attributes defined in the named attribute sets are instantiated and copied as attributes of this literal result element in the output destination.

Name	Value	Meaning
other attributes optional	Attribute value template	Any XPath expressions occurring between curly braces in the value are evaluated, and the resulting string forms the value of an attribute copied to the current output destination. Attribute Value Templates are described on page 127.

Note

Several of the attributes take the form of whitespace-separated lists. This is simply a list of names (or prefixes) in which the various names are separated by any of the XML-defined whitespace characters; tab, carriage return, newline, or space. For example, you could write:

```
<TD xsl:use-attribute-sets="blue italic centered"/>
```

Here the names `blue`, `italic`, and `centered` must match the names of **`<xsl:attribute-set>`** elements elsewhere in the stylesheet.

Content

The content of a literal result element is a template body. It may thus contain XSLT instructions, extension elements, literal result elements, and/or text nodes.

Usage

The literal result element is copied to the result tree, and its content is instantiated.

Consider a template body containing a single literal result element:

```
<TD>Product code</TD>
```

In this case a **`<TD>`** element will be written to the result tree with a child text node whose content is «`Product code`». When the result tree is output to an XML or HTML file, it will regenerate the text as it appeared in the stylesheet – or something equivalent. There is no guarantee that it will be character-for-character identical, for example the processor may add or remove whitespace within the tags, or it may represent characters using character or entity references.

If the literal result element has content, then the content must be another template body, and this template body is itself instantiated; any nodes generated in the result tree in the course of this process will become children of the element created from the literal result element.

For example, if the template body is:

```
<TD><xsl:value-of select="."/></TD>
```

then when the **<TD>** element is instantiated, its content will also be instantiated. The content in this case is a template body consisting of a single XSLT instruction, and the effect is that this instruction is instantiated to create a text node which will be a child of the **<TD>** element in the result tree. The instruction `<xsl:value-of select=".">` outputs the string-value of the current node in the source tree. So if this value is «`$83.99`», the result would be:

```
<TD>$83.99</TD>
```

It is tempting to think of this as a sequence of three steps:

- The **<TD>** start tag causes a **<TD>** start tag to be written to the output
- The **`<xsl:value-of>`** element is evaluated and the result («`$83.99`») is written to the output
- The **</TD>** end tag causes a **</TD>** end tag to be written to the output

However, this is not a true picture of what is going on, and it is best not to think about it this way, because otherwise you will start wondering, for example, how to delay writing the end tag until some condition is encountered in the input.

> **The transformation process writes nodes to the result tree, it does not write tags to a sequential file. The `<TD>` element in the stylesheet causes a `<TD>` element to be written to the result tree. You cannot write half a node to the tree – the start and end tags are not written as separate operations. The `<TD>` and `</TD>` tags are generated only when the result tree is serialized as XML or HTML.**

The following diagram might help to illustrate this:

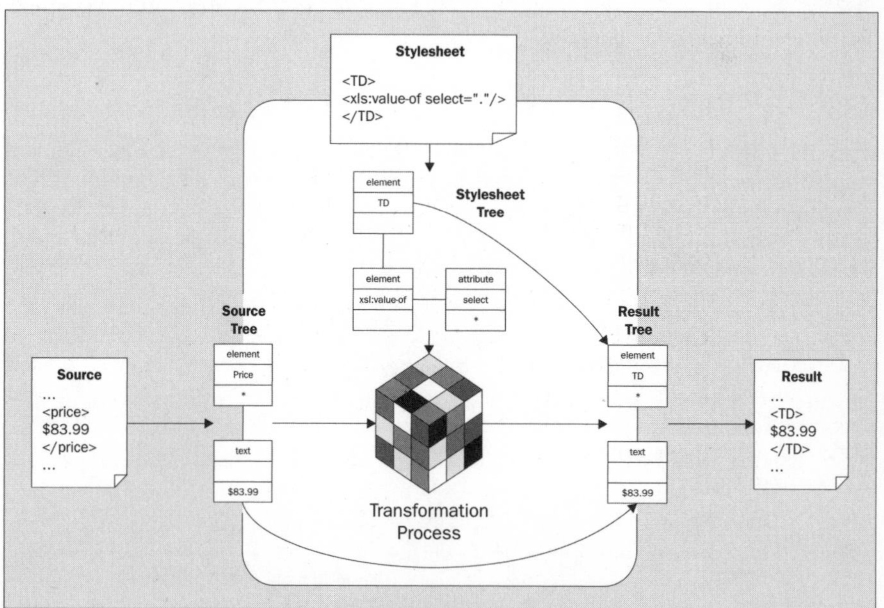

If you do find yourself thinking about where you want tags to appear in the output, it is a good idea to draw a sketch showing the required shape of the result tree, and then think about how to write the stylesheet to produce the required nodes on the tree. Since the element in the result tree will always be produced by instantiating one template body in the stylesheet, this amounts to asking "what condition in the input tree should cause this result element to be generated?".

For example, suppose you want to generate an HTML table with five columns, arranging the **<item>** elements from the source XML five to a row. Then the condition in the source XML that causes an output row to be generated is an **<item>** element whose position is 1, 6, 11, etc. The logic can be written:

```
<xsl:template match="item[position() mod 5 = 1]">
<tr>
  <xsl:for-each select=". | following-sibling::item[position() &lt;
5]">
    <td><xsl:value-of select="."/></td>
  </xsl:for-each>
</tr>
</xsl:template>

<xsl:template match="item"/>
```

The first template rule matches **<item> elements** that should appear at the start of a new row; it outputs the **<tr>** element, and five **<td>** elements corresponding to this **<item>** and its four following siblings. The second rule matches **<item> elements** that should **not** appear at the start of a new row, and does nothing, because these will already have been processed by the first template rule.

Attributes of a Literal Result Element

If the literal result element has attributes, other than the special `xsl`-prefixed ones in the list above, then these attributes too will be copied to the current output destination. So if the template body contains:

```
<TD><IMG src="picture1.gif"/></TD>
```

then the output will contain a copy of this whole structure. The outer **<TD>** element is copied to the result tree as before, and this time its content consists of another literal result element, the **<IMG>** element, which is copied to the result tree as a child of the **<TD>** element, along with its **src** attribute. This time both the stylesheet tree and the result tree take the form shown below:

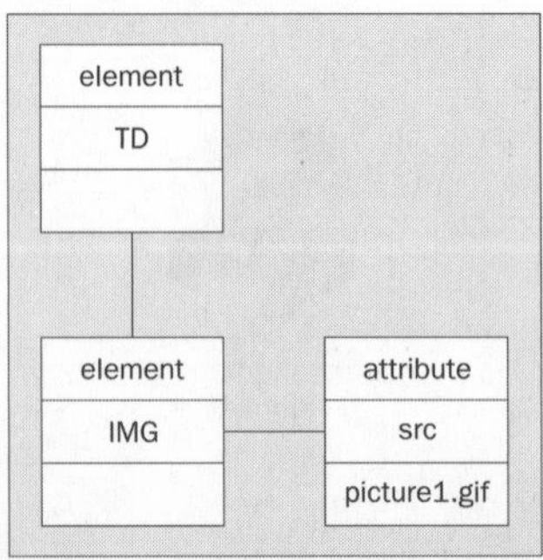

If the value of an attribute of a literal result element contains curly braces («{» and «}»), then it is treated as an **attribute value template** (discussed further in the next section). The text between the curly braces is treated as an XPath expression, and is evaluated as a string; the attribute written to the result tree contains this string in place of the expression. For example, suppose we apply the following template to the `books.xml` file used earlier:

```
<xsl:template match="/">
<xsl:for-each select="//book">
<div id="div{position()}">
    <xsl:value-of select="title"/>
</div>
</xsl:for-each>
</xsl:template>
```

Because the **`position()`** function takes the values 1, 2, 3, and 4, as we move through the set of books, the output will take the form:

```
<div id="div1">Sayings of the Century</div>
<div id="div2">Sword of Honour</div>
<div id="div3">Moby Dick</div>
<div id="div4">The Lord of the Rings</div>
```

It is also possible to generate attributes for a literal result element by two other mechanisms:

- The attribute can be generated by an **`<xsl:attribute>`** instruction. This instruction does not need to be textually within the content of the literal result element in the stylesheet, but it must be instantiated before any child nodes (elements or children) have been generated.

  The reason for this rule is to allow the XSLT processor to avoid building the result tree in memory. Many processors will serialize XML syntax directly to an output file as the nodes are generated, and the rule that attributes must be generated before child elements or text nodes ensures that this is possible. The rule is phrased as if execution of the stylesheet has to be sequential, but of course any implementation strategy that produces the same effect is acceptable.

- A collection of attributes can be generated by use of a named attribute set. The literal result element must contain an **`xsl:use-attribute-sets`** attribute that names the attribute sets to be incorporated: these names must correspond to **`<xsl:attribute-set>`** elements at the top level of the stylesheet. The named attribute sets each contain a sequence of **`<xsl:attribute>`** instructions, and these cause attributes to be added to the generated element as if they were present directly in the content of the literal result element. Named attribute sets are useful to maintain a collection of related attributes such as font name, color, and size, which together define a style that will be used repeatedly in the output document; they are a direct parallel to the styles found in simpler languages such as CSS.

Attributes are added to the generated element node in a defined order: first attributes incorporated using **xsl:use-attribute-sets**, then attributes present on the literal result element itself, and finally attributes added using **<xsl:attribute>** instructions. The significance of this sequence is that if two or more attributes with the same name are added, it is the last one that counts. It doesn't mean that they will necessarily appear in this order when the result tree is serialized.

Namespaces for a Literal Result Element

The namespace nodes of a literal result element are also copied to the current output destination. This is often the source of some confusion. The literal result element in the stylesheet will have a namespace node for every namespace declaration that is in scope: that is, every **xmlns** attribute or **xmlns:*** attribute on the literal result element itself, or on any of its ancestor elements in the stylesheet. The only exception is that the attribute «`xmlns=""`» does not act as a namespace declaration, rather it cancels any earlier declaration for the default namespace.

In the result tree, the element created from the literal result element is guaranteed to have a namespace node for every namespace node that was present on the literal result element in the stylesheet, except the following:

- a namespace node for the XSLT namespace URI `http://www.w3.org/1999/XSL/Transform` will not be copied.
- a namespace node for a namespace declared as an extension element namespace will not be copied. A namespace is declared as an extension element namespace by including its prefix in the value of the **extension-element-prefixes** attribute of the **<xsl:stylesheet>** element, or in the value of the **xsl:extension-element-prefixes** attribute of this literal result element or of any ancestor literal result element or extension element.
- a namespace node for an excluded namespace will not be copied. A namespace is declared as an excluded namespace by including its prefix in the value of the **exclude-result-prefixes** attribute of the **<xsl:stylesheet>** element, or in the value of the **xsl:exclude-result-prefixes** attribute of this literal result element or of any ancestor literal result element.

For example, consider the following stylesheet:

```
<xsl:stylesheet
   xmlns:xsl="http://www.w3.org/1999/XSL/Transform"
   version="1.1"
   xmlns:Date="java:java.util.Date"
>

<xsl:script implements-prefix="Date" language="java"
    src="java:java.util.Date"/>

<xsl:template match="/"
      xmlns = "urn:acme-com:gregorian">
    <date><xsl:value-of select="$today"/></date>
</xsl:template>

<xsl:param name="today" select="Date:toString(Date:new())"/>

</xsl:stylesheet>
```

There are three namespaces in scope for the **<date>** element, namely the XSLT namespace, the namespace «java:java.util.Date, and the default namespace «urn:acme-com:gregorian». The XSLT namespace is not copied to the result tree, but the other two are. So the **<date>** element added to the result tree is guaranteed to have these two namespaces «java:java.util.Date», and «urn:acme-com:gregorian» in scope.

> *The stylesheet above uses two extension functions* «Date:new()» *and* «Date:toString()»*. It has been written to use the* **<xsl:script>** *element specified in the XSLT 1.1 working draft. To run it with an XSLT 1.0 processor, you will need to make minor changes: see the relevant product appendix for details.*

If the $today parameter is supplied as the value «2000-13-18», the output would be as follows (regardless of the source document):

```
<date xmlns="urn:acme-com:gregorian"
      xmlns:Date="java:java.util.Date">2000-13-18</date>
```

The first namespace declaration is necessary, because it defines the namespace for the element name **<date>**. However, you probably don't really want the **xmlns:Date** declaration here. It's not doing any harm, but it's not doing any good either. It's there because the XSLT processor can't tell that it's unwanted. If you want this declaration to be omitted, use the **xsl:exclude-result-prefixes** attribute as follows:

```
<xsl:stylesheet
   xmlns:xsl="http://www.w3.org/1999/XSL/Transform"
   version="1.1"
   xmlns:Date="java:java.util.Date"
>

<xsl:script implements-prefix="Date" language="java"
    src="java:java.util.Date"/>

<xsl:template match="/"
      xmlns = "urn:acme-com:gregorian">
      <date xsl:exclude-result-prefixes="Date">
         <xsl:value-of select="$today"/>
      </date>
</xsl:template>

<xsl:param name="today" select="Date:toString(Date:new())"/>

</xsl:stylesheet>
```

The fact that an element in the result tree has a namespace node does not necessarily mean that when the result tree is written out as an XML document, the corresponding element will have a namespace declaration for that namespace. The XSLT processor is likely to omit the namespace declaration if it is redundant, in other words, if it duplicates a namespace declaration on a containing element. It can't be omitted, however, simply on the basis that it is not used. This is because namespace declarations might affect the meaning of the data in the output document in a way that the XSLT processor is unaware of. Applications are perfectly entitled to use namespace declarations to scope identifiers and names appearing in attribute values or text.

An element in the result tree generated from a literal result element may also have additional namespace nodes beyond those described above. For example, it may well inherit namespace nodes that were generated on a containing element. In addition, because the XSLT processor is required to generate output that conforms to the XML Namespaces Recommendation, the generated element will also have namespace nodes corresponding to any namespace prefixes used in the element name or in any attribute name, even if these have been declared as excluded namespaces.

> *The* **`xsl:exclude-result-prefixes`** *attribute is used to remove namespace declarations that are unused and unwanted. It can't be used to remove the declaration of namespace prefixes that are actually used in the result tree. And it isn't used to remove duplicate namespace declarations, as most processors will do that automatically.*

Namespace Prefixes

When a literal result element is copied to the result tree, the element name and attribute names of the new nodes in the result tree will have the same expanded name (that is, local name and namespace URI) as the corresponding nodes in the stylesheet. Usually, the names that are eventually output will also use the same namespace prefix.

There are unusual circumstances when the XSLT processor may need to change the prefix for a namespace. For example, it is possible to create two attributes that use the same namespace prefix to refer to different namespace URIs, as in the following example:

```
<output>
   <xsl:attribute name="out:file"
      xmlns:out="http://domain-a.com/">a</xsl:attribute>
   <xsl:attribute name="out:dir"
      xmlns:out="http://domain-b.com/">b</xsl:attribute>
</output>
```

The generated output in this case will look something like this:

```
<output
   out:file="a"
   ns1:dir="b"
   xmlns:out="http://domain-a.com/"
   xmlns:ns1="http://domain-b.com/"/>
```

The XSLT processor has no choice but to invent a prefix for one of the namespaces, because the supplied prefix is already in use with a different meaning. But because namespace prefixes are essentially arbitrary (it's only the URI that has any real significance) the meaning of the output file is not affected.

> *When namespace nodes are copied from the source or stylesheet tree to the result tree, the namespace prefix and namespace URI are both copied unchanged. When element or attribute nodes are copied, the expanded name of the element or attribute (that is, its local name and namespace URI) is always preserved, but the namespace prefix may occasionally need to be changed. If this happens, however, an extra namespace node will be added to the result tree to associate the new namespace prefix with the correct namespace URI.*

Namespace Aliasing

In some circumstances, instead of changing the namespace prefix when a literal result element is copied to the result tree, it is necessary to change the namespace URI.

The most obvious situation where this arises is when the output document is itself a stylesheet. This isn't as esoteric a requirement as it may appear; generating a stylesheet can be a very useful technique. For example, if your company changes its house-style to use different fonts and colors, you could write an XSLT transformation to convert all your existing stylesheets to the new standard.

When you generate a stylesheet, you will want to generate XSLT elements such as **`<xsl:template>`** in the result tree; but you can't include such elements as literal result elements in the stylesheet, because they would be mistaken for instructions. So the answer is to include them in the stylesheet with a different namespace, and to declare in an **`<xsl:namespace-alias>`** element that the URI should be changed when the literal result element is copied to the result tree.

For more details, see **`<xsl:namespace-alias>`** in Chapter 4, on page 252.

Attribute Value Templates

As we've seen, an attribute value template is a special form of parameterized attribute value. There are two ways they can be used:

- On a literal result element, an attribute value template provides a way of generating an attribute whose value is computed at run-time rather than always taking the same value, for example `<TD WIDTH="{$width}">`. You could achieve the same effect with the **`<xsl:attribute>`** instruction, but attribute value templates are easier to write and easier to understand.
- On some XSLT elements, certain attributes can be computed at run-time. For example, when sorting, instead of writing «`order="ascending"`» or «`order="descending"`», you could write «`order="{$order}"`» so that the order varies depending on a run-time parameter. Note that there are very few attributes where this facility is available. They are listed later in this section.

The term **template** here has nothing to do with XSLT template rules, template bodies, or **`<xsl:template>`** elements. Attribute value templates are simply a notation for embedding variable components into an otherwise fixed attribute value.

An attribute value template is a string in which XPath expressions may be embedded within curly braces («`{`» and «`}`»). The XPath expression is evaluated, the result is converted to a string using the conversion rules described on page 87 in Chapter 2, and this string is then substituted into the attribute value in place of the expression.

For example, suppose you have a set of images representing an alphabet such as the following, and you want to use these to represent the first character of a paragraph of text.

You could write a template rule to achieve this as follows (ignoring practical details such as how to deal with paragraphs that don't start with a capital letter). It uses the **`substring()`** function, which is described in Chapter 7, on page 545.

```
<xsl:template match="para">
   <p><img src="fancy{substring(.,1,1)}.gif"/>
   <xsl:value-of select="substring(.,2)" /></p>
</xsl:template>
```

A paragraph that starts with the letter A (like this one) will cause the **`src`** attribute of the **`<img>`** element to be evaluated as «`img src="fancyA.gif"`», so it will be displayed in the browser like this:

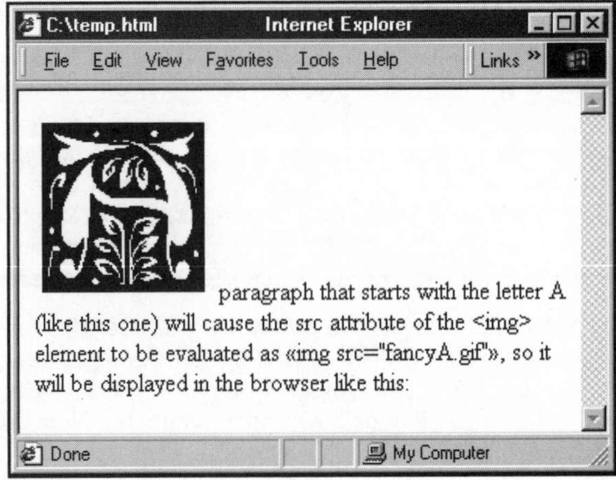

If you want to include the characters «`{`» or «`}`» in an attribute value with their ordinary meaning (this is sometimes useful when generating dynamic HTML), they should be doubled as «`{{`» or «`}}`». However, you should only do this in an attribute that is being interpreted as an attribute value template. In other attributes, curly braces have no special meaning.

Curly brackets can never be nested. You can only use them to include an XPath expression in the text of a stylesheet attribute; they cannot be used within an XPath expression itself. You can always achieve the required effect some other way; for example, instead of:

```
<a href="#{id( 'A{@nr}' )}">  /* WRONG */
```

write:

```
<a href="#{id( concat('A', @nr) )}">
```

The **concat()** function, described on page 456, in Chapter 7, performs concatenation of strings.

Attribute value templates cannot be used anywhere you like in the stylesheet. They can only be used for those attributes that are specifically identified as attribute value templates in the XSLT Recommendation. The following table gives a complete list of all the places you can use Attribute Value Templates:

Element	Attributes interpreted as attribute value templates
Literal result elements	All attributes except those in the XSLT namespace
Extension elements	As defined by the specification of each extension element
<xsl:attribute>	**name**, **namespace**
<xsl:document>	All attributes (note, this element is new in XSLT 1.1)
<xsl:element>	**name**, **namespace**
<xsl:number>	**format**, **lang**, **letter-value**, **grouping-separator**, **grouping-size**
<xsl:output>	All attributes (at XSLT 1.1: with XSLT 1.0, none of the attributes are interpreted as attribute value templates)
<xsl:processing-instruction>	**name**
<xsl:sort>	**lang**, **data-type**, **order**, **case-order**

In all other contexts, don't even think of trying to use them because the curly braces will either be ignored, or will cause an error to be reported. It can be very tempting, if you want to use **<xsl:call-template>**, for example, and the name of the template you want to call is in a variable, to want to write:

```
<!-WRONG-->
<xsl:param name="tname"/>
<xsl:call-template name="{$tname}"/>
<!-WRONG-->
```

However, you can't, because the **name** attribute (or any other attribute of <**xsl:call-template**> for that matter) of **<xsl:call-template>** is not in the above list of places where attribute value templates can be used.

Why are attribute value templates rationed so severely? A few of the restrictions do appear to be purely arbitrary, but most are there deliberately to make life easier for the XSLT processor:

- Attribute value templates are generally not allowed for attributes of top-level elements. This ensures that the values are known before the source document is read, and are constant for each run of the stylesheet. However, in the XSLT 1.1 working draft this constraint has been relaxed in the case of **<xsl:output>**, which will allow all its attributes to be specified as attribute value templates.

- Attribute value templates are never allowed for attributes whose value is an XPath expression or a pattern. This ensures that expressions and patterns can be compiled when the stylesheet is read, and do not need to be re-parsed each time they are evaluated.
- Attribute value templates are generally not allowed for attributes whose value is the name of another object in the stylesheet, for example a named template or a named attribute set. This ensures that references from one stylesheet object to another can be resolved once and for all when the stylesheet is first read. They are allowed, however, for names of objects being written to the result tree.
- Attribute value templates are not allowed for attributes interpreted by the XML parser, specifically **`xml:space`**, **`xml:lang`**, and namespace declarations (**`xmlns`** and **`xmlns:prefix`**). This is because the XML parser reads the value before the XSLT processor gets a chance to expand it. The **`xml:base`** attribute, when used on a literal result element, is anomalous: the value of the attribute as seen by the XML parser will be the value before any attribute-value-template expansion, while the value copied to the result tree will be the value after attribute-value-template expansion. It's therefore best to avoid using curly braces within the value of the **`xml:base`** attribute. (The **`xml:base`** attribute, whose meaning is defined in a separate W3C Recommendation called XML Base, is explicitly supported only in XSLT 1.1.)

The remaining restrictions must be seen as arbitrary. For example it is hard to see any good reason why the **`terminate`** attribute of **`<xsl:message>`** can't be an attribute value template, but the fact is that the spec doesn't allow it.

When an XPath expression within an attribute value template is evaluated, the context is the same as for any other expression in the stylesheet. The idea of an expression having a context was introduced in Chapter 2, on page 85: it determines the meaning of constructs such as «`.`», which refers to the context node, and «`position()`», which refers to the context position. Variables and namespace prefixes may only be used within the expression if they are in scope at that point in the stylesheet. The context node, context position, and context size are determined from the current node and current node list being processed in the most recent call of **`<xsl:apply-templates>`** or **`<xsl:for-each>`**; if there is no such call (which can happen while a global variable is being evaluated, or while the attributes of the **`<xsl:output>`** element are being evaluated), the current node and current node list contain just the root node.

Extensibility

Bitten by years of experience with proprietary vendor extensions to HTML, the W3C committee responsible for XSLT took great care to allow vendor extensions in a tightly controlled way.

The extensibility mechanisms in XSLT are governed by several unstated design principles:

- Namespaces are used to ensure that vendor extensions cannot clash with facilities in the standard (including facilities introduced in future versions), or with extensions defined by a different vendor.
- It is possible for an XSLT processor to recognize where extensions have been used, including extensions defined by a different vendor, and to fail cleanly if it cannot implement those extensions.
- It is possible for the writer of a stylesheet to test whether particular extensions are available, and to define fallback behavior if they are not. For example, the stylesheet might be able to achieve the same effect in a different way, or it might make do without some special effect in the output.

The principal extension mechanisms, which I will describe below, are extension functions and extension elements. However, it is also possible for vendors to define other kinds of extensions, or to provide mechanisms for users or third parties to do so. These include the following:

- XSLT-defined elements can have additional vendor-defined attributes, provided they use a non-null namespace URI, and that they do not change the behavior of standard elements and attributes. For example, a vendor could add an attribute such as **`acme:debug`** to the **`<xsl:template>`** element, whose effect is to pause execution when the template is instantiated. But adding an attribute **`acme:repeat="2"`** whose effect is to execute the template twice would be against the conformance rules. (Whether vendors will pay any attention to the conformance rules, of course, is another matter.)
- Vendors can define additional top-level elements; again provided that they use a non-null namespace URI, and that they do not change the behavior of standard elements and attributes. An example of such an element is Microsoft's **`<msxsl:script>`** element, for defining external functions in VBScript or JScript (this is a precursor to the standard **`<xsl:script>`** element in XSLT 1.1). Any processor that doesn't recognize the namespace URI will ignore such top-level elements.
- Certain XSLT-defined attributes have an open-ended set of values, where vendors have discretion on the range of values to be supported. Examples are the **`lang`** attribute of **`<xsl:number>`** and **`<xsl:sort>`**, which provides language-dependent numbering and sorting, the **`method`** attribute of **`<xsl:output>`**, which defines how the result tree is output to a file, and the **`format`** attribute of **`<xsl:number>`**, which allows the vendor to provide additional numbering sequences beyond those defined in the standard. The list of system properties supplied in the first argument of the **`system-property()`** function is similarly open-ended, as is the set of language names allowed in the **`language`** attribute of the XSLT 1.1 **`<xsl:script>`** element.

Extension Functions

Extension functions provide a mechanism for extending the capabilities of XSLT by escaping into another language such as Java or JavaScript. The most usual reasons for doing this are:

- To improve performance (for example when doing complex string manipulations)
- To exploit system capabilities and services
- To reuse code that already exists in another language
- For convenience, as complex algorithms and computations can be very verbose when written in XSLT

The term **extension function** is used both for functions supplied by the vendor beyond the core functions defined in the XSLT and XPath standards (those described in Chapter 7), and for functions written by users and third parties.

The XSLT 1.0 Recommendation allows extension functions to be called, but does not define how they were written, or how they should be bound to the stylesheet, or which languages should be supported. This means that with XSLT 1.0, it is quite difficult to write extension functions that work with more than one vendor's XSLT processor, even though there are some conventions that several vendors have adopted.

With the XSLT 1.1 working draft this situation is much improved. The XSLT 1.1 working draft defines a standard interface for calling extension functions written in Java or JavaScript (technically, ECMAScript). It doesn't require that processors support these two languages, and it allows them to support additional languages if they wish, but Java extension functions should now be portable between all XSLT processors that support a Java interface, and JavaScript extension functions should be portable between those that support JavaScript. There are a few minor limitations to this portability in terms of the way the XPath data model is mapped to the DOM. The language bindings, and these limitations, are described in Chapter 8.

A function name in the XPath expression syntax (see Chapter 5) is a `QName`, that is, a name with an optional namespace prefix. If there is no prefix, the name must be one of the core functions defined in the standard: for example the core function **`not()`** can be invoked as:

```
<xsl:if test="not( @name = 'Mozart' )">
```

If there is a prefix, the function is assumed to be an extension function. The namespace URI associated with the prefix is used to locate an **`<xsl:script>`** element in the stylesheet, which in turn identifies where the implementation of the function can be found. For example, the following stylesheet declares a global variable and initializes its value to a random number between zero and one, by using the relevant method in the `java.lang.Math` class in the Java run-time library:

```
<xsl:stylesheet version="1.1"
   xmlns:xsl="http://www.w3.org/1999/XSL/Transform"
   xmlns:Math="java:java.lang.Math">
<xsl:script implements-prefix="Math" language="java"
src="java:java.lang.Math"/>
<xsl:variable name="random-number" select="Math:random()"/>
```

When a function is called, the relevant Java class is loaded and inspected (using Java's introspection mechanisms) to find a method whose name and parameters match the name and arguments used in the XSLT call, and the relevant method is then called.

Prior to the introduction of the **<xsl:script>** element in XSLT 1.1, several XSLT 1.0 processors have provided a mechanism in which the namespace URI ends with the fully qualified name of a Java class. This mechanism means all the information needed to identify and call the function is contained within the namespace URI itself. The above example can be written using the xt processor as follows:

```
<xsl:stylesheet version="1.0"
   xmlns:xsl="http://www.w3.org/1999/XSL/Transform">
<xsl:variable name="random-number" select="Math:random()"
    xmlns:Math="http://www.jclark.com/xt/java/java.util.Date"/>
```

Similar mechanisms are available in other processors including Saxon and Xalan, but in each case the rules for forming the namespace URI are slightly different, so it's best to use the **<xsl:script>** element when it's supported.

You can pass the result of one external function to another, even when it's an object that can't be represented directly as one of the XPath data types. This is known as an **external object**.

As the following example shows, this allows you to output the current date and time by using the standard Java class «java.util.Date». The default constructor for this class creates a Date object whose value is the current date, and the «toString()» method on this object creates a default string representation of the date. So you can write in your stylesheet:

```
<xsl:stylesheet version="1.1"
   xmlns:xsl="http://www.w3.org/1999/XSL/Transform"
   xmlns:Date="java:java.util.Date">

<xsl:script implements-prefix="Date" language="java"
src="java:java.util.Date"/>

<xsl:variable name="today" select="Date:new()"/>

<xsl:template name="show-todays-date">
    <xsl:value-of select="Date:toString($today)"/>
</xsl:template>
. . .
```

In the expression «Date:new()», Date is a namespace prefix referring to a namespace URI that refers to the class «java.util.Date», so the processor knows that it is being asked to create an instance of this Java class. As a result, the variable «$today» will hold a external object which is a Java object of type «java.util.Date». To output the date using **<xsl:value-of>**, we need to convert it to a string, so we pass it to the «toString()» method on the same class (because it too has the namespace prefix «Date»). By convention, the object that is the target of the method is written as its first argument; so writing «Date:toString($today)» in an XPath expression is the equivalent of writing «today.toString()» in Java. The effect is that the named template writes the current date to the result tree.

The XSLT 1.1 working draft also provides a standard interface for JavaScript functions: instead of being loaded from a separate file holding the compiled code, the JavaScript can be written inline within the **<xsl:script>** element itself. Microsoft's MSXML3 product is (at the time of writing) an XSLT 1.0 implementation, but it provides its own very similar mechanism using the **<msxsl:script>** element in place of **<xsl:script>**.

Here is an example of a simple extension function implemented using this mechanism with Microsoft's XSLT processor, and an expression that calls it:

```
<xsl:stylesheet version="1.0"
   xmlns:xsl="http://www.w3.org/1999/XSL/Transform"
   xmlns:ms="javascript:my-extensions">

<msxsl:script
   xmlns:msxsl="urn:schemas-microsoft-com:xslt"
   language="VBScript"
   implements-prefix="ms"
>
Function ToMillimetres(inches)
   ToMillimetres = inches * 25.4
End Function
</msxsl:script>
```

```
<xsl:template match="/" >
   <xsl:variable name="test" select="12"/>
   <size><xsl:value-of select="ms:ToMillimetres($test)"/></size>
</xsl:template>
</xsl:stylesheet>
```

You can test whether a particular extension function is available by using the **function-available()** function. For example:

```
<xsl:choose xmlns:acme="http://acme.co.jp/xslt">
   <xsl:when test="function-available('acme:moonshine')">
      <xsl:value-of select="acme:moonshine($x)"/>
   </xsl:when>
   <xsl:otherwise>
      <xsl:text>*** Sorry, moonshine is off today ***</xsl:text>
   </xsl:otherwise>
</xsl:choose>
```

The specification says that an XSLT processor that doesn't recognize the extension function **acme:moonshine()** shouldn't fail simply because the stylesheet references it, it should only fail if it is actually called. In this situation no failure should occur, because **function-available()** is used first to check the availability of the function, and will return false if the function is not present.

Extension functions, because they are written in general-purpose programming languages, can have side effects. For example, they can write to databases, they can ask the user for input, or they can maintain counters. One product, Xalan, includes a sample application that implements a counter using extension functions, effectively circumventing the restriction that XSLT variables cannot be modified in situ. However, extension functions with side effects should be used with great care, because the XSLT specification doesn't say what order things are supposed to happen in. For example, it doesn't say whether a variable is evaluated when its declaration is first encountered, or when its value is first used. One product in particular, xt, adopts a lazy evaluation strategy in which variables are never evaluated until they are used. If extension functions with side effects are used to evaluate such variables, the results can be very surprising, because the order in which the extension functions are called becomes quite unpredictable. For example, if one function writes to a log file and another closes this file, you could find that the log file is closed before it is written to.

I'll have a lot more to say about writing extension functions in Chapter 8.

Extension Elements

An extension element is an element occurring within a template body, that belongs to a namespace designated as an extension namespace. A namespace is designated as an extension namespace by including its namespace prefix in the **extension-element-prefixes** attribute of the **<xsl:stylesheet>** element, or in the **xsl:extension-element-prefixes** attribute of the element itself, or of a containing extension element or literal result element.

For example, Saxon provides an extension element **<saxon:while>** to perform looping while a condition remains true. There is no standard XSLT construct for this because without side effects, a condition once true can never become false. But when used in conjunction with extension functions, **<saxon:while>** can be a useful addition.

The following named template takes a string as a parameter and splits it up into words, outputting each word as a separate element. It uses the standard Java class `java.util.StringTokenizer` to provide extension functions:

```
<xsl:stylesheet version="1.1"
   xmlns:xsl="http://www.w3.org/1999/XSL/Transform"
   xmlns:Tokenizer="java:java.util.StringTokenizer">

<xsl:script implements-prefix="Tokenizer"
   language="java" src="java:java.util.StringTokenizer"/>

<xsl:template name="tokenize">
   <xsl:param name="sentence"/>
   <xsl:variable name="tok" select="Tokenizer:new($sentence)"/>
   <saxon:while test="Tokenizer:hasMoreTokens($tok)"
          xsl:extension-element-prefixes="saxon"
          xsl:exclude-result-prefixes="Tokenizer"
          xmlns:saxon="http://icl.com/saxon">
      <word>
        <xsl:value-of select="Tokenizer:nextToken($tok)"/>
      </word>
   </saxon:while>
</xsl:template>
</xsl:stylesheet>
```

Note that for this to work, «saxon» must be declared as an extension element prefix, otherwise **<saxon:while>** would be interpreted as a literal result element and would be copied to the output. The **xsl:exclude-result-prefixes** attribute is not strictly necessary, but it prevents the output being cluttered with unnecessary namespace declarations.

If this template is called with the parameter value "The cat sat on the mat", as follows:

```
<xsl:template match="/">
  <xsl:call-template name="tokenize">
    <xsl:with-param name="sentence">The cat sat on the
mat</xsl:with-param>
  </xsl:call-template>
</xsl:template>
```

it will produce the output:

```
<word>The</word><word>cat</word><word>sat</word><word>on</word>
<word>the</word><word>mat</word>
```

> *If you have extra namespaces declared on the* **<xsl:stylesheet>** *element, they will be copied into the* **<word>** *elements. To get rid of them, add the unwanted namespace prefix to the* **xsl:exclude-result-prefixes** *attribute.*

As with extension functions, the term **extension element** covers both non-standard elements provided by the vendor, and non-standard elements implemented by a user or third party. There is no requirement that an XSLT implementation must allow users to define new extension elements, only that it should behave in a particular way when it encounters extension elements that it cannot process.

Where a product does allow users to implement extension elements (two products that do so are Saxon and Xalan), the mechanisms and APIs involved are likely to be rather more complex than those for extension functions, and the task is not one to be undertaken lightly. However, extension elements can offer capabilities that would be very hard to provide with extension functions alone.

If there is an extension element in a stylesheet, then all XSLT processors will recognize it as such, but in general some will be able to handle it and others won't (because it is defined by a different vendor). As with extension functions, the rule is that a processor mustn't fail merely because an extension element is present, it should fail only if an attempt is made to instantiate it.

There are two mechanisms to allow stylesheet authors to test whether a particular extension element is available; the **element-available()** function, and the **<xsl:fallback>** instruction.

The **element-available()** function works in a very similar way to **function-available()**. For example:

```
<xsl:choose xmlns:acme="http://acme.co.jp/xslt">
   <xsl:when test="element-available('acme:moonshine')">
      <acme:moonshine select="$x" xsl:extension-element-
prefixes="acme"/>
   </xsl:when>
   <xsl:otherwise>
      <xsl:text>*** Sorry, moonshine is off today ***</xsl:text>
   </xsl:otherwise>
</xsl:choose>
```

Note that at the time **element-available()** is called, the prefix for the extension element (here «acme») must have been declared in a namespace declaration, but it does not need to have been designated as an extension element.

The **<xsl:fallback>** instruction (which is fully described on page 214,in Chapter 4) provides an alternative way of specifying what should happen when an extension element is not available. The following example is equivalent to the previous one:

```
<acme:moonshine select="$x"
   xmlns:acme="http://acme.co.jp/xslt" xsl:extension-element-
prefixes="acme">
   <xsl:fallback>
      <xsl:text>*** Sorry, moonshine is off today ***</xsl:text>
   </xsl:fallback>
</acme:moonshine>
```

When an extension element is instantiated, and the XSLT processor does not know what to do with it, it should instantiate any child **<xsl:fallback>** element. If there are several **<xsl:fallback>** children, it should instantiate each of them. Only if there is no **<xsl:fallback>** element should it report an error. Conversely, if the XSLT processor can instantiate the element, it should ignore any child **<xsl:fallback>** element.

> *The specification doesn't actually say that an extension element must allow an* **<xsl:fallback>** *child to be present. There are plenty of XSLT instructions that do not allow* **<xsl:fallback>** *as a child, for example* **<xsl:copy-of>** *and* **<xsl:value-of>**. *However, an extension element that didn't allow* **<xsl:fallback>** *would certainly be against the spirit of the standard.*

Vendor-defined or user-defined elements at the top level of the stylesheet are not technically extension elements, because they don't appear within a template body; therefore the namespace they appear in does not need to be designated as an extension namespace.

Forwards Compatibility

Whereas extensibility, as discussed in the previous section, is about how to write stylesheets that are resilient to vendor and user extensions to the XSLT language, forwards compatibility is about how to achieve resilience to differences between versions of the XSLT standard. The two questions are, of course, closely related.

There are currently two versions of the XSLT Recommendation, version 1.0, and a working draft of version 1.1 (the six working drafts that preceded version 1.0 don't count). So compatibility between versions will soon become an issue. However, the language designers had the foresight to anticipate that it would become an issue, and made provision even in version 1.0 to allow stylesheets to be written in a portable way.

The stylesheet is required to carry a version number (typically «`version=1.0`» or «`version=1.1`») as an attribute of the **`<xsl:stylesheet>`** element. Specifying «`version=1.0`» declares that the stylesheet will only be using facilities defined in XSLT version 1.0, while specifying «`version=1.1`» indicates that it may require facilities defined in version 1.1.

If you only use facilities defined in XSLT version 1.0, then you should specify «`version=1.0`», and every conformant XSLT processor will then handle the stylesheet correctly. This is the policy we have followed in all the examples in this book.

If you use facilities that were first defined in XSLT version 1.1, then you should specify «`version=1.1`». A conformant XSLT 1.1 processor will then handle the stylesheet correctly as defined in the XSLT 1.1 specification, but an XSLT 1.0 processor will process the stylesheet in **forwards-compatible mode**. Equally, an XSLT 1.1 processor will switch into forwards-compatible mode if the stylesheet specifies «`version=2.0`», or any other version that it does not recognize.

In forwards-compatible mode, the XSLT processor must assume that the stylesheet is using XSLT facilities defined in a version of the standard that has been published since the software was released. The processor, of course, won't know what to do with these facilities, but it must assume that the stylesheet author is using them deliberately. It treats them in much the same way as vendor extensions that it doesn't understand:

- It must report an error for XSLT elements it doesn't understand only if they are instantiated, and if there is no child **`<xsl:fallback>`** instruction.
- It must ignore attributes it doesn't recognize, and unrecognized values for recognized attributes.
- It must report an error for functions it doesn't recognize, or that have the wrong number or arguments, only if the function is actually called. You can avoid this error condition by using **`function-available()`** to test whether the function exists before calling it.
- It must report syntax errors in XPath expressions that use syntax that isn't allowed in XPath version 1.0 only if the expression is actually evaluated. (XSLT 1.0 and XSLT 1.1 both reference XPath 1.0; the XPath syntax is unchanged between the two versions.)

This behavior only occurs when forwards-compatible mode is enabled, which happens only if the **`<xsl:stylesheet>`** element specifies a version other than «`1.0`» or (for XSLT 1.1 only) «`1.1`». Forwards-compatible mode can also be specified for a portion of a stylesheet by specifying the **`xsl:version`** attribute on any literal result element, again with a value other than «`1.0`» or «`1.1`». If forwards-compatible mode is not enabled, that is, if the version is specified as «`1.0`» or «`1.1`», then any use of an XSLT element, attribute, or function that isn't in the XSLT version 1.1 standard, or of XPath syntax that isn't in the XPath 1.0 standard, is an error and must be reported, whether it is actually executed or not.

If you specify «version=1.0» and then use XSLT 1.1 facilities such as **<xsl:document>**, then an XSLT 1.0 processor will reject this as an error. An XSLT 1.1 processor, however, will process your stylesheet successfully. XSLT processors are not expected to remember which facilities were introduced at each version of the standard.

Forwards-compatible processing was specified to allow you to write a stylesheet that exploits facilities in version 1.1 while still behaving sensibly when run with an XSLT processor that only supports version 1.0, or, at some point in the future, to use facilities in version 2.0 and still behave sensibly with an XSLT 1.1 processor. To achieve this, you can use the same mechanisms as you use for handling vendor extensions: the **function-available()** and **element-available()** functions, and the **<xsl:fallback>** element.

There is also one other mechanism you can use: you can use the **system-property()** function (described on page 557, in Chapter 7) to discover which version of XSLT the processor implements, or which processor is being used. For example, you could write code such as:

```
<xsl:if test="system-property('xsl:version')=2.0 or
      starts-with(system-property('xsl:vendor'), 'xalan')">
   <xsl:new-facility/>
</xsl:if>
```

Relying on the version number this returns is a rather crude mechanism: there are plenty of processors still in the field that return «1.0» as the value of «system-property('xsl:version')» but which do not implement the XSLT standard in full, and no doubt this will remain true. But testing which vendor's processor is in use is handy for portability, especially when vendors have not kept strictly to the conformance rules.

Technically, a processor that implements some of the new XSLT 1.1 features but not all doesn't conform either with XSLT 1.0 or with XSLT 1.1. But since many XSLT processors are developed incrementally with new releases every few weeks, you might well find products that occupy this no-man's-land. A product will presumably return «1.1» as the value of «system-property('xsl-version')» when the vendor is confident that the product is "almost" conformant: past experience suggests that different vendors will interpret this in different ways!

Whitespace

Whitespace handling can be a considerable source of confusion. When the output is HTML, you can get away without worrying too much about it, because except in some very specific contexts HTML generally treats any sequence of spaces and newlines in the same way as a single space. But with other output formats, getting spaces and newlines where you want them, and avoiding them where you don't, can be crucial.

There are two issues:

- ❑ Controlling which whitespace in the source document is significant, and therefore visible to the stylesheet.
- ❑ Controlling which whitespace in the stylesheet is significant, because significant whitespace in the stylesheet is likely to get copied to the output.

Whitespace is defined as any sequence of the following four characters:

Character	Unicode Symbol
tab	#x9
newline	#xA
carriage return	#xD
space	#x20

The definition in XSLT is exactly the same as in XML itself. Other characters such as non-breaking-space (#xA0), which is familiar to HTML authors as the entity reference « », may use just as little black ink as these four, but they are not included in the definition.

There are some additional complications about the definition. Writing a character reference « » is in many ways exactly the same as hitting the space bar on the keyboard, but in some circumstances it behaves differently. The character reference « » will be treated as whitespace by the XSLT processor, but not by the XML parser, so you need to understand which rules are applied at which stage of processing.

The XML standard makes some attempt to distinguish between significant and insignificant whitespace. Whitespace in elements with element-only content is considered insignificant, whereas whitespace in elements that allow #PCDATA content is significant. However, the distinction depends on whether a validating parser is used or not, and in any case, the standard requires both kinds of whitespace to be notified to the application. The writers of the XSLT specification decided that the handling of whitespace should not depend on anything in the DTD, and should not depend on whether a validating or non-validating parser was used. Instead the handling of whitespace is controlled entirely from the source document (using the **xml:space** attribute) or from the stylesheet (using the **<xsl:strip-space>** and **<xsl:preserve-space>** directives), which are fully described in Chapter 4.

The first stages in whitespace handling are the job of the XML parser, and are done long before the XSLT processor gets to see the data:

- End-of-line appearing in the textual content of an element is always normalized to a single newline «#xA» character. This eliminates the differences between line endings on Unix, Windows, and Macintosh systems.
- The XML parser will normalize attribute values. A tab or newline will always be replaced by a single space, unless it is written as a character reference such as «	» or «&#A;»; for some types of attribute (anything except type CDATA), the XML parser will also remove leading and trailing whitespace, and normalize other sequences of whitespace to a single space character.

This attribute normalization can be significant when the attribute in question is an XPath expression in the stylesheet. For example, suppose you want to test whether a string value contains a newline character. You can write this as:

```
<xsl:if test="contains(address, '&#xA')">
```

It's important to use the character reference «`
`» here, rather than a real newline, because a newline character would be converted to a space by the XML parser, and the expression would then actually test whether the supplied string contains a space.

What this means in practice is that if you want to be specific about whitespace characters, write them as character references; if you just want to use them as separators and padding, use the whitespace characters directly.

> **The XSLT specification assumes that the XML parser will hand over all whitespace text nodes to the XSLT processor. However, the input to the XSLT processor is technically a tree, and the XSLT specification claims no control over how this tree is built. If you use Microsoft's MSXML3, the tree is supplied in the form of a DOM, and the default option when building a DOM in MSXML3 is to remove whitespace text nodes. If you want the parser to behave the way that the XSLT specification expects, you must set the `preserveWhitespace` property on the `Document` object to `true` before you load the document.**

Once the XML parser has done its work, the XSLT processor then applies some processing of its own. By this time entity and character references have been expanded, so there is no difference between a space written as a space and one written as «` `»:

- Adjacent text nodes are merged into a single text node (**normalized** in the terminology of the DOM).
- Then, if a text node consists entirely of whitespace, it is removed (or **stripped**) from the tree if the containing element is listed in an **`<xsl:strip-space>`** definition in the stylesheet. The detailed rules are more complex than this, and also take into account the presence of the **`xml:space`** attribute in the source document, see the **`<xsl:text>`** element on page 323, in Chapter 4, for details.

This process never removes whitespace characters that are adjacent to non-whitespace characters. For example, consider:

```
<article>
   <title>Abelard and Heloise</title>
   <subtitle>Some notes towards a family tree</subtitle>
   <author>Brenda M Cook</author>
   <abstract>
      The story of Abelard and Heloise is best recalled
nowadays from the stage drama of 1970 and it is perhaps inevitable
that Diana Rigg stripping off for Keith Mitchell should be the most
enduring image of this historic couple in some people's minds.
   </abstract>
</article>
```

There are five whitespace-only text nodes in this fragment, one before each of the child elements **<title>**, **<subtitle>**, **<author>**, and **<abstract>**, and another between the end of the **<abstract>** and the end of the **<article>**. The whitespace in these nodes is passed by the XML parser to the XSLT processor, and it is up to the stylesheet whether to take any notice of it or not. Typically in this situation this whitespace is of no interest and it can be stripped from the tree by specifying `<xsl:strip-space elements="article"/>`.

The whitespace within the **<abstract>** cannot be removed by the same process. The newline characters at the start and end of the abstract, and at the end of each line, are part of the text passed by the parser to the application, and it is not possible in the stylesheet to declare them as being irrelevant. They will always be present in the tree model of the source document. What you can do is to call the **normalize-space()** function when processing these nodes on the source tree, which will remove leading and trailing whitespace and replace all other sequences of one or more whitespace characters by a single space. The **normalize-space()** function is described on page 524 in Chapter 7.

To emphasize this, XSLT makes a very firm distinction between text nodes that comprise whitespace only, and those that hold something other than whitespace. A whitespace text node can only exist where there is nothing between two pieces of markup other than whitespace characters.

To take another example, consider the following document.

```
<person>
   <name>Prudence Flowers</name>
   <employer>Lloyds Bank</employer>
   <place-of-work>
      71 Lombard Street
      London, UK
      <zip>EC3P 3BS</zip>
   </place-of-work>
</person>
```

Where are the whitespace nodes? Let's look at it again, this time making the whitespace characters visible:

```
<person>↵
→<name>Prudence Flowers</name>↵
→<employer>Lloyds Bank</employer>↵
→<place-of-work>↵
→♦♦♦71 Lombard Street↵
→♦♦♦London, UK↵
→♦♦♦<zip>EC3P 3BS</zip>↵
→</place-of-work>↵
</person>↵
```

The newline and tab between `<person>` and `<name>` are not adjacent to any non-whitespace characters, so they constitute a whitespace node. So do the characters between **</name>** and <**employer**>, and between **</employer>** and **<place-of-work>**. However, most of the whitespace characters within the <**place-of-work**> element are in the same text node as non-whitespace characters, so they do not constitute a whitespace node. To make it even clearer, let's show the characters in whitespace nodes in white on a black background:

```
<person>↵
→<name>Prudence Flowers</name>↵
→<employer>Lloyds Bank</employer>↵
→<place-of-work>↵
→◆◆◆71 Lombard Street↵
→◆◆◆London, UK↵
→◆◆◆<zip>EC3P 3BS</zip>◆↵
→</place-of-work>↵
</person>
```

Why is all this relevant? As we've seen, the **<xsl:strip-space>** element allows you to control what happens to whitespace nodes (those shown in white on black above), but it doesn't let you do anything special with whitespace characters that appear in ordinary text nodes (those shown in black on white).

All the whitespace nodes in this example are immediate children of the **<person>** element, so they could be stripped by writing:

```
<xsl:strip-space elements="person"/>
```

Whitespace nodes are retained on the source tree unless you ask for them to be stripped.

Whitespace Nodes in the Stylesheet

For the stylesheet itself, whitespace nodes are all stripped, with one exception, namely whitespace within an **<xsl:text>** element. So if you explicitly want to copy a whitespace text node from the stylesheet to the result tree, write it within an **<xsl:text>** element, like this:

```
<xsl:value-of select="address-line[1]"/>
<xsl:text>&#xA;</xsl:text>
<xsl:value-of select="address-line[2]"/>
```

The only reason for using «`
`» here rather than an actual newline is that it's more clearly visible to the reader; it's also less likely to be accidentally turned into a newline followed by tabs or spaces. Writing the whitespace as a character reference doesn't stop it being treated as whitespace by XSLT, because the character references will have been expanded by the XML parser before the XSLT processor gets to see them.

The Effect of Stripping Whitespace Nodes

There are two main effects of stripping whitespace nodes, say on the **<person>** element in the example above:

- When you use **<xsl:apply-templates/>** to process all the children of the <**person**> element, the whitespace nodes aren't there, so they don't get selected. If they had been left on the source tree, then by default they would be copied to the result tree.
- When you use **<xsl:number>** or the **position()** or **count()** functions to count nodes, the whitespace nodes aren't there, so they aren't counted. If you had left the whitespace nodes on the tree, then the **<name>**, **<employer>** and **<place-of-work>** elements would be nodes 2, 4, and 6 instead of 1, 2, and 3.

There are cases where it's important to keep the whitespace nodes. Consider the following:

```
<para>
Edited by <name>James Clark</name>♦<email>jjc@jclark.com</email>
</para>
```

The diamond represents a space character that needs to be preserved, but because it is not adjacent to any other text, it would be eligible for stripping. In fact, whitespace is nearly always significant in elements that have mixed content (that is, elements that have both element and text nodes as children).

If you want to strip all the whitespace nodes from the source tree, you can write:

```
<xsl:strip-space elements="*"/>
```

If you want to strip all the whitespace nodes except those within certain named elements, you can write:

```
<xsl:strip-space elements="*"/>
<xsl:preserve-space elements="para h1 h2 h3 h4"/>
```

If any elements in the document (either the source document or the stylesheet) use the XML-defined attribute «`xml:space="preserve"`», this takes precedence over these rules: whitespace nodes in that element, and in all its descendants, will be kept on the tree unless the attribute is cancelled on a descendant element by specifying «`xml:space="default"`». This allows you to control on a per-instance basis whether whitespace is kept, whereas **`<xsl:strip-space>`** controls it at the element-type level.

Solving Whitespace Problems

There are two typical problems with whitespace in the output, which are too much of it, or too little.

If you are generating HTML, a bit of extra whitespace usually doesn't matter, though there are some places where it can slightly distort the layout of your page. With some text formats, however (a classic example is comma-separated values) you need to be very careful to output whitespace in exactly the right places.

Too Much Whitespace

If you are getting too much whitespace, there are three possible places it can be coming from:

- The source document
- The stylesheet
- Output indentation

First ensure that you set «indent="no"» on the **<xsl:output>** element, to eliminate the last of these possibilities.

If the output whitespace is adjacent to text, then it probably comes from the same place as that text.

- If this text comes from the stylesheet, use **<xsl:text>** to control more precisely what is output. For example, the following code outputs a comma between the items in a list, but it also outputs a newline after the comma, because the newline is part of the same text node as the comma:

```
<xsl:for-each select="item">
   <xsl:value-of select="."/>,
</xsl:for-each>
```

  If you want the comma but not the newline, change this so that the newline is in a text node of its own, and is therefore stripped:

```
<xsl:for-each select="item">
   <xsl:value-of select="."/>,<xsl:text/>
</xsl:for-each>
```

- If the text comes from the source document, use **normalize-space()** to trim leading and trailing spaces from the text before outputting it.

If the offending whitespace is between tags in the output, then it probably comes from whitespace nodes in the source tree that have not been stripped, and the remedy is to add an **<xsl:strip-space>** element to the stylesheet.

Too Little Whitespace

If you want whitespace in the output and aren't getting it, use **<xsl:text>** to generate it at the appropriate point. For example, the following code will output the lines of a poem in HTML, with each line of the poem being shown on a new line:

```
<xsl:for-each select="line">
     <xsl:value-of select="."/><br/>
</xsl:for-each>
```

This will display perfectly correctly in the browser, but if you want to view the HTML in a text editor, it will be difficult because everything goes on a single line. It would be useful to start a newline after each **
** element – you can do this as follows:

```
<xsl:for-each select="line">
   <xsl:value-of select="."/><br/><xsl:text>&#xa;</xsl:text>
</xsl:for-each>
```

Another trick I have used to achieve this is to exploit the fact that the non-breaking-space character (#xa0), although invisible, is not classified as whitespace. So you can achieve the required effect by writing:

```
<xsl:for-each select="line">
   <xsl:value-of select="."/><br/> 
</xsl:for-each>
```

This works because the newline after the « » is now part of a non-whitespace node.

Summary

The purpose of this chapter was to study the overall structure of a stylesheet, before going into the detailed specification of each element in the next chapter.

- First I explained how a stylesheet program can be made up of one or more stylesheet modules, linked together with **<xsl:import>** and **<xsl:include>** elements. I described how the concept of import precedence allows one stylesheet to override definitions in those it imports.
- I introduced the **<xsl:stylesheet>** (or **<xsl:transform>**) element, which is the outermost element of most stylesheet modules.
- I described the **<?xml-stylesheet?>** processing instruction which can be used to link from a source document to its associated stylesheets, and explained how this can be used to allow a stylesheet to be embedded directly in the source document whose style it defines.
- I then covered the top-level elements found in the stylesheet, that is, the immediate children of the **<xsl:stylesheet>** or **<xsl:transform>** element, including the ability to have user-defined or vendor-defined elements here.
- Very simple stylesheets can be written as a single template, so you saw how the **<xsl:stylesheet>** and **<xsl:template match="/">** elements can be omitted, to make an XSLT stylesheet look more like the simple template languages that some users may be familiar with.
- A structure that occurs throughout a stylesheet is the idea of a template body, a sequence of text nodes and literal result elements to be copied to the result tree, and instructions and extension elements to be executed. This led naturally to a discussion of literal result elements, and of attribute value templates, which are used to define variable attributes not only of literal result elements, but of certain XSLT elements as well.
- I then explained how the W3C standards committee has tried to ensure that the specification can be extended, both by vendors and by W3C itself, without adversely affecting the portability of stylesheets. You saw how to make a stylesheet work even if it uses proprietary extension functions and extension elements that may not be available in all implementations.
- Finally I discussed, in some detail, how XSLT stylesheets handle whitespace in the source document, in the stylesheet itself, and in the result tree.

You have now reached the end of the preamble. The next four chapters contain detailed specifications of the XSLT elements you can use in a stylesheet, the XPath expressions you can use in the attributes of some of these elements, the node-matching patterns you can use to establish template rules, and the standard functions that are available for use within XPath expressions.

4

XSLT Elements

This chapter provides an alphabetical list of reference entries, one for each of the XSLT elements. Each entry gives:

- a short description of the purpose of the element
- an indication of where in the XSLT specification the element is described
- a pro forma summary of the format, defining where the element may appear in the stylesheet, what its permitted attributes are, and what its content (child elements) may be
- a definition of the formal rules defining how this element behaves
- a section giving usage advice on how to exploit this XSLT element
- finally, coding examples of the element, showing the context in which it might be used

The *Format* section for each element includes a syntax skeleton designed to provide a quick reminder of the names and types of the attributes and any constraints on the context. The format of this is designed to be intuitive: it only gives a summary of the rules, because you will find these in full in the *Position*, *Attributes*, and *Content* sections which follow.

There are a number of specialized terms used in this chapter, and it is worth becoming familiar with them before you get in too deeply. There are fuller explanations in Chapters 2 and 3, and the following descriptions are really intended just as a quick memory-jogger.

For a more comprehensive definition of terms, refer to the glossary.

Term	Description
attribute value template	An attribute whose value may contain expressions nested with curly braces, for example «`url="../{$href}"`». The term *template* here has nothing to do with any other kind of template in XSLT. Embedded expressions may only be used in an attribute value (or are only recognized as such) if the attribute is one that is explicitly designated as an attribute value template. Attribute value templates are described in more detail in Chapter 3, page 127.
document order	An ordering of the nodes in the source tree which corresponds to the order in which the corresponding items appeared in the source XML document: an element precedes its children, and the children are ordered as they appeared in the source.
`Expression`	Many XSLT elements have attributes whose value is an `Expression`. This always means an XPath expression: a full definition of XPath `Expressions` is given in Chapter 5. An expression returns a value, which may be a string, a number, a Boolean, a node-set, or an external object. These data types are described fully in Chapter 2, page 87.
instantiate	Instructions and template bodies can be instantiated. This may seem a rather grandiose way of saying that the instruction is obeyed or executed, but there is some logic to it: we can regard a template body in the stylesheet as being a pro forma for lots of pieces of the output document, each of which is formed by creating a new instance of the pro forma.
instruction	Any element used in a template body that is not a literal result element: specifically, an XSLT instruction or an extension element. The **`<xsl:if>`** element is an instruction, but **`<xsl:strip-space>`** isn't, because **`<xsl:if>`** appears in a template body and **`<xsl:strip-space>`** doesn't. Extension elements are described in Chapter 3, page 117.
literal result element	An element in the stylesheet, used in a *template body*, which is copied to the output document: for example (if you are generating HTML) **`<p>`** or **`<td>`**. Literal result elements are described in Chapter 3, page 118.
`Pattern`	Some XSLT elements have attributes whose value must be a `Pattern`. the syntax of `Patterns` is defined in Chapter 6. A `Pattern` is a test that can be applied to nodes to see if they match. For example, the `Pattern` «`title`» matches all **`<title>`** elements, and the `Pattern` «`text()`» matches all text nodes.
`QName`	An XML name, optionally qualified by a namespace prefix. Examples of `QNames` with no prefix are «`color`» and «`date-due`». Examples of prefixed names are «`xsl:choose`» and «`html:table`». Where the name has a prefix, this must always match a namespace declaration that is in scope at the place in the stylesheet where the `QName` is used. For more information on namespaces see Chapter 2, page 64.

stylesheet	In general, references to the **stylesheet** mean the principal stylesheet module plus all the stylesheet modules incorporated into it using **`<xsl:include>`** and **`<xsl:import>`** elements. When I want to refer to one of these components individually, I call it a **stylesheet module**.
template body	A sequence of instructions and literal result elements contained within (that is, that are children of) another XSLT element. The containing element need not be an **`<xsl:template>`** element; many other XSLT elements, such as **`<xsl:if>`** and **`<xsl:variable>`**, also have a template body as their content. The XSLT specification calls this simply a **template**, but I have avoided this because it is easily confused with a **template rule** (an **`<xsl:template>`** element with a **`match`** attribute) and a **named template** (an **`<xsl:template>`** element with a **`name`** attribute).
template rule	An **`<xsl:template>`** element that has a **`match`** attribute.
temporary tree	The value of a variable established using an **`<xsl:variable>`** element that contains a template body, for example `<xsl:variable>A <b>very</b> nice language</xsl:variable>` This construct is referred to in the XSLT 1.0 specification as a **result tree fragment**, and it has a different data type from any other value. In XSLT 1.1, however, the term result tree fragment is no longer used, and the data type of this value is simply a node-set (it actually consists of a single node, the root of the tree).
XSLT element	Any of the standard elements in the XSLT namespace listed in this chapter, for example **`<xsl:template>`** or **`<xsl:if>`**.

I decided to list the different XSLT elements in alphabetical order for ease of reference, because I know how difficult it is to find them in the XSLT Recommendation, where they are organised on functional lines. This is fine when you know what you are looking for, but if you are using this book as your introduction to XSLT, it does create the problem that related things won't be found together. And if you try to read sequentially, you'll start with **`<xsl:apply-imports>`**, which on a training course is something I would probably cover rather quickly on the Friday afternoon.

So here's an attempt at some kind of ordering and grouping, to suggest which entries you might look at first if you're new to the subject:

Grouping	**Elements**
Elements used to define template rules and control the way they are invoked	**`<xsl:template>`** **`<xsl:apply-templates>`** **`<xsl:call-template>`**
Elements defining the structure of the stylesheet	**`<xsl:stylesheet>`** **`<xsl:include>`** **`<xsl:import>`**
Elements used to generate output	**`<xsl:value-of>`** **`<xsl:element>`** **`<xsl:attribute>`** **`<xsl:comment>`** **`<xsl:processing-instruction>`** **`<xsl:text>`**

Grouping	Elements
Elements used to define variables and parameters	**<xsl:variable>** **<xsl:param>** **<xsl:with-param>**
Elements used to copy information from the source document to the result	**<xsl:copy>** **<xsl:copy-of>**
Elements used for conditional processing and iteration	**<xsl:if>** **<xsl:choose>** **<xsl:when>** **<xsl:otherwise>** **<xsl:for-each>**
Elements to control sorting and numbering	**<xsl:sort>** **<xsl:number>**
Elements used to control the final output format	**<xsl:output>** **<xsl:document>**

This covers all the most commonly-used elements; the rest can only really be classified as 'miscellaneous'.

xsl:apply-imports

The **<xsl:apply-imports>** instruction is used in conjunction with imported stylesheets. A template rule in one stylesheet module can override a template rule in an imported stylesheet module. Sometimes, you want to supplement the functionality of the rule in the imported module, not to replace it entirely. **<xsl:apply-imports>** is provided so that the overriding template rule can invoke the overridden template rule in the imported module.

There is a clear analogy here with object-oriented programming. Writing a stylesheet module that imports another is like writing a subclass, whose methods override the methods of the superclass. **<xsl:apply-imports>** behaves analogously to the **super()** function in object-oriented programming languages, allowing the functionality of the superclass to be incorporated in the functionality of the subclass.

Defined in

XSLT section 5.6

Format

XSLT 1.0 Format:

```
<xsl:apply-imports/>
```

XSLT 1.1 Format:

```
<xsl:apply-imports>
   <xsl:with-param> *
</xsl:apply-imports>
```

Position

<xsl:apply-imports> is an instruction, and is always used within a template body.

Attributes

None.

Content

The element must either be empty or (with XSLT 1.1 only) it may contain one or more **<xsl:with-param>** elements.

Effect

<xsl:apply-imports> relies on the concept of a *current template rule*. A template rule becomes the current template rule when it is invoked using **<xsl:apply-templates>**. Using **<xsl:call-template>** does not change the current template rule. However, using **<xsl:for-each>** makes the current template rule null, until such time as the **<xsl:for-each>** terminates, at which time the previous value is reinstated. The current template rule is also null while global variables are being evaluated.

<xsl:apply-imports> searches for a template rule that matches the current node, using the same search rules as **<xsl:apply-templates>**, but considering only those template rules that (a) have the same mode as the current template rule and (b) are defined in a stylesheet that was imported into the stylesheet containing the current template rule. For details of import precedence, see **<xsl:import>** on page 226.

> *The specification doesn't say exactly what* **imported into** *means. A reasonable interpretation is a stylesheet module that is a descendant of this one in the import tree. A stylesheet module S becomes a child of another stylesheet module T in the import tree by being referenced in an* **<xsl:import>** *statement within T, or within a module that is included in T directly or indirectly by means of* **<xsl:include>** *statements. If module S is imported into module T, then templates defined in S will always have lower import precedence than templates defined in T.*

With the draft XSLT 1.1 specification it becomes possible to specify parameters to be supplied to the called template, using **<xsl:with-param>** elements contained within the **<xsl:apply-imports>** element. These work in the same way as parameters for **<xsl:call-template>** and **<xsl:apply-templates>**; if the name of the supplied parameter matches the name of an **<xsl:param>** element within the called template, the parameter will take that value, otherwise it will take the default value supplied in the **<xsl:param>** element. It is not an error to supply parameters that don't match any **<xsl:param>** element in the called template rule, they will simply be ignored.

Usage and Examples

The intended usage pattern behind **<xsl:apply-imports>** is illustrated by the following example.

One stylesheet, `a.xsl`, contains general-purpose rules for rendering elements. For example, it might contain a general-purpose template rule for displaying dates, as follows:

```
<xsl:template match="date">
   <xsl:value-of select="day"/>
   <xsl:text>/</xsl:text>
   <xsl:value-of select="month"/>
   <xsl:text>/</xsl:text>
   <xsl:value-of select="year"/>
</xsl:template>
```

A second stylesheet, `b.xsl`, contains special-purpose rules for rendering elements. For example, you might want it to display dates that occur in a particular context in the same way, but in bold face. It could write:

```
<xsl:template match="timeline/date">
   <b>
   <xsl:value-of select="day"/>
   <xsl:text>/</xsl:text>
   <xsl:value-of select="month"/>
   <xsl:text>/</xsl:text>
   <xsl:value-of select="year"/>
   </b>
</xsl:template>
```

However, this involves duplicating most of the template body, which is a bad idea from a maintenance point of view. So, in `b.xsl` we could import `a.xsl`, and write instead:

```
<xsl:import href="a.xsl"/>
<xsl:template match="timeline/date">
   <b>
   <xsl:apply-imports/>
   </b>
</xsl:template>
```

Note that the facility only allows a template rule to invoke one of lower **import precedence**, not one of lower **priority**. The import precedence depends on how the stylesheet module was loaded, as explained under **`<xsl:import>`** on page 226. The priority can be specified individually for each template rule, as explained under **`<xsl:template>`** on page 312. The code above will work only if the «`timeline/date`» template rule is in a stylesheet that directly or indirectly imports the «`date`» template rule. It will not work, for example, if they are in the same stylesheet but defined with different priority.

In many situations the same effect can be achieved equally well by giving the general-purpose template rule a name, and invoking it from the special-purpose template rule by using **`<xsl:call-template>`** (see page 179). This technique also works when overriding a template rule of lower priority (and equal import precedence). The one time this alternative technique is not possible is when the general-purpose template rule was written by someone else and cannot be changed. For example this situation might arise if users of web pages were allowed to create XSLT stylesheets that modified the behavior of an author-supplied stylesheet.

But that approach doesn't work if you want one rule that overrides or supplements many others. One example I encountered was a developer who had a working stylesheet, but wanted to add the rule "output an HTML **`<a>`** tag for any source element that has an `anchor` attribute". Rather than modifying every rule in the existing stylesheet, this can be achieved by defining a new stylesheet module that imports the original one, and contains the single rule:

```
<xsl:template match="*[@anchor]">
  <a name="{@anchor}"/>
  <xsl:apply-imports/>
</xsl:template>
```

There is a more complete example of the use of **<xsl:apply-imports>** in the section for **<xsl:import>**.

See also

<xsl:import> on page 226
<xsl:param> on page 283
<xsl:with-param> on page 345

xsl:apply-templates

The **<xsl:apply-templates>** instruction defines a set of nodes to be processed, and causes the system to process them by selecting an appropriate template rule for each one.

Defined in

XSLT section 5.4

Format

```
<xsl:apply-templates select=Expression mode=QName >
   ( <xsl:with-param> | <xsl:sort> ) *
</xsl:apply-templates>
```

Position

<xsl:apply-templates> is an instruction, and is always used within a template body.

Attributes

Name	Value	Meaning
select optional	Expression	The node-set to be processed. If omitted, all children of the current node are processed.
mode optional	QName	The processing mode. Template rules used to process the selected nodes must have a matching mode.

The constructs `Expression` and `QName` are defined at the beginning of this chapter and more formally in Chapter 5.

Content

Zero or more **<xsl:sort>** elements.
Zero or more **<xsl:with-param>** elements.

Effect

The **<xsl:apply-templates>** element selects a set of nodes in the input tree, and processes each of them individually by finding a matching template rule for that node. The set of nodes is determined by the **select** attribute; the order in which they are processed is determined by the **<xsl:sort>** elements (if present), and the parameters passed to the template rules are determined by the **<xsl:with-param>** elements (if present). The behavior is explained in detail in the following sections.

The select Attribute

If the **select** attribute is present, the `Expression` defines the nodes that will be processed. This must be an XPath `Expression` that returns a node-set. (The concept of a node-set is explained along with other XSLT data types in Chapter 2, page 59). For example `<xsl:apply-templates select="*"/>` selects the set of all element nodes that are children of the current node. Writing `<xsl:apply-templates select="@width+3"/>` would be an error, because the value of the expression is a number, not a node-set.

The expression may select nodes relative to the current node (the node currently being processed), as in the example above. Alternatively it may make an absolute selection from the root node (for example `<xsl:apply-templates select="//item"/>`), or it may simply select the nodes by reference to a variable initialized earlier (for example `<xsl:apply-templates select="$sales-figures"/>`). For further details of XPath expressions, see Chapter 5.

If the **select** attribute is omitted, the nodes processed will be the children of the current node: that is, the elements, text nodes, comments, and processing instructions that occur directly within the current node. Text nodes that consist only of whitespace will be processed along with the others, unless they have been stripped from the tree; for details, see **<xsl:strip-space>** on page 301. In the XPath tree model, described in Chapter 2, attribute nodes and namespace nodes are **not** regarded as children of the containing element, so they are not processed: if you want to process attribute nodes, you must include an explicit **select** attribute, for example `<xsl:apply-templates select="@*"/>`. However, it is more usual to get the attribute values directly using the **<xsl:value-of>** instruction, described on page 329.

Omitting the **select** attribute has exactly the same effect as specifying a node-set expression of «`child::node()`». This selects all the nodes (elements, text nodes, comments, and processing instructions) that are children of the current node. If the current node is anything other than a root node or an element node, then it has no children, so **<xsl:apply-templates/>** does nothing, because there are no nodes to process.

For each node in the selected node-set, in turn, one template rule is selected and its template body is instantiated. In general this may be a different template rule for each selected node. Within this template body, this node becomes the new current node, so it can be referred to using the XPath expression «`.`».

The called template can also determine the relative position of this node within the list of nodes selected for processing: specifically, it can use the **position()** function to give the position of that node in the list of nodes being processed (the first node processed has `position()=1`, and so on), and the **last()** function to give the number of nodes in the list being processed. These two functions are described (with examples) in Chapter 7, pages 533 and 510 respectively. They enable the called template to output sequence numbers for the nodes as they are processed, or to take different action for the first and the last nodes, or perhaps to use different background colors for odd-numbered and even-numbered nodes.

Sorting

If there are no child **<xsl:sort>** instructions, the selected nodes are processed in *document order*. In the normal case where the nodes all come from the same input document this means they will be processed in the order they are encountered in the original source document: for example, an element node is processed before its children. Attribute nodes belonging to the same element, however, may be processed in any order, because the order of attributes in XML is not considered significant. If there are nodes from several different documents in the node-set, which can happen when you use the **document()** function (described in Chapter 7, page 466), the relative order of nodes from different documents is not defined, though it is consistent if the same node-set is processed more than once.

If there are one or more **<xsl:sort>** instructions as children of the **<xsl:apply-templates>** instruction, the nodes are sorted before processing. Each **<xsl:sort>** instruction defines one sort key. For details of how sorting is controlled, see **<xsl:sort>** on page 300. If there are several sort keys defined, they apply in major-to-minor order. For example if the first **<xsl:sort>** defines sorting by Country and the second by State, then the nodes will be processed in order of State within Country. If two nodes have equal sort keys, they will be processed in document order.

Note that the direction of the axis used to select the nodes is irrelevant. (The direction of different axes is described in Chapter 5.) For example, «`select="preceding-sibling::*"`» will process the preceding siblings of the current node in document order (starting with the first sibling) even though the preceding-sibling axis is in reverse document order. The axis direction affects only the meaning of any positional qualifiers used within the select expression. For example, «`select="preceding-sibling::*[1]"`» will select the first preceding sibling element in the direction of the axis, which is the element immediately before the current node, if there is one.

Choosing a Template Rule

For each node to be processed, a template rule is selected. The choice of a template rule is made independently for each selected node; they may all be processed by the same template rule, or a different template rule may be chosen for each one.

The template rule selected for processing a node will always be either an **<xsl:template>** element with a **match** attribute, or a built-in template rule provided by the XSLT processor.

An **<xsl:template>** element will be used to process a node only if it has a matching *mode*: that is, the **mode** attribute of the **<xsl:apply-templates>** element must match the **mode** attribute of the **<xsl:template>** element. This means they must both be absent, or they must both be present. If they are both present, they must be matching names: if the mode name contains a namespace prefix, it is the namespace URI that must match, not necessarily the prefix itself.

Note that if the **mode** attribute is omitted, it makes no difference what mode was originally used to select the template rule containing the **<xsl:apply-templates>** instruction. The mode is not sticky; it reverts to the default mode as soon as **<xsl:apply-templates>** is used with no **mode** attribute.

An **<xsl:template>** element will be used to process a node only if the node matches the pattern defined in the **match** attribute of the **<xsl:template>** element.

If there is more than one **<xsl:template>** element that matches a selected node, one of them is selected based on its **import precedence** and **priority**, as detailed under **<xsl:template>** on page 312.

If there is no **<xsl:template>** element that matches a selected node, a built-in template rule is used. The action of the built-in template rule depends on the type of node, as follows:

Node Type	Action of Built-In Template Rule
root	Call apply-templates to process each child of the root node, using the mode specified on the call to **<xsl:apply-templates>**. This is as if the contents of the template were: `<xsl:apply-templates mode="mode"/>`
element	Call apply-templates to process each child node of the element, using the mode specified on the call to **<xsl:apply-templates>**. This is as if the contents of the template were: `<xsl:apply-templates mode="mode"/>`
text	Copy the text value of the node to the output. This is as if the contents of the template were: `<xsl:value-of select=".">`
attribute	Copy the value of the attribute to the output, as text. This is as if the contents of the template were: `<xsl:value-of select=".">`
processing instruction	No action
comment	No action
namespace	No action

For the root node and for element nodes, the built-in template rule processes the children of the selected node in document order, matching each one against the available template rules as if the template body contained an explicit **<xsl:apply-templates>** element with no **select** attribute. Unlike the situation with explicit template rules, the mode *is* sticky; it is carried through automatically to the template rules that are called. So if you execute `<xsl:apply-templates mode="m"/>` for an element that has no matching template rule, the built-in template rule will execute `<xsl:apply-templates mode="m"/>` for each of its children. This process can of course recurse to process the grandchildren, and so on.

Although the built-in template rules pass on the mode they were called with, the same is not true for parameters. They are not passed on by built-in template rules; see the section below.

Parameters

If there are any **<xsl:with-param>** elements present as children of the **<xsl:apply-templates>** element, they define parameters which are made available to the called template rules. The same parameters are made available to each template rule that is instantiated, even though different template rules may be invoked to process different nodes in the list.

Each **<xsl:with-param>** element is evaluated in the same way as an **<xsl:variable>** element. Specifically:

- if it has a **select** attribute, this is evaluated as an XPath expression.
- if there is no **select** attribute and the **<xsl:with-param>** element is empty, the value is an empty string.
- otherwise, the value of the parameter is a temporary tree. The tree is built by instantiating the template body making up the content of the **<xsl:with-param>** element, and the value is a node-set containing one node, the root of this tree. Tree-valued variables are described in Chapter 2, and again more formally under **<xsl:variable>** on page 333.

It is not defined whether the parameter is evaluated once only, or whether it is evaluated repeatedly, once for each node in the node-set. If the value isn't needed (for example, because the node-set is empty, or because none of the nodes match a template that uses this parameter) then it isn't defined whether the parameter is evaluated at all. Usually this doesn't matter, because evaluating the parameter repeatedly will have exactly the same effect each time. But it's something to watch out for if the parameter is obtained by calling an external function that has a side effect, such as reading the next record from a database.

If the name of a child **<xsl:with-param>** element matches the name of an **<xsl:param>** element in the selected template rule, then the value of the **<xsl:with-param>** element is assigned to the relevant **<xsl:param>** variable name.

If there is a child **<xsl:with-param>** element that does not match the name of any **<xsl:param>** element in the selected template rule, then it is ignored. This is not treated as an error.

If there is an **<xsl:param>** element in the selected template rule with no matching **<xsl:with-param>** element in the **<xsl:apply-templates>** element, then the parameter is given a default value: see **<xsl:param>** on page 283 for details. Again, this is not an error.

If the selected template rule is a built-in rule, then any parameters that are supplied are ignored. They are not passed on to any template rules called by the built-in rule, in the way that the mode is passed on. This can cause perplexing problems, when you have two rules like this:

```
<xsl:template match="section">
<ol>
  <xsl:apply-templates>
    <xsl:with-param name="in-section" select="true()"/>
  </xsl:apply-templates>
</ol>
</xsl:template>

<xsl:template match="clause">
  <xsl:param name="in-section" select="false()"/>
  . . .
</xsl:template>
```

When a **<clause>** is contained directly within a **<section>**, the parameter `$in-section` will take the value «`true`» as expected. But if there is an intervening element, with no explicit template rule, so that the **<clause>** is the grandchild of the **<section>** element, the **<clause>** template rule will still be invoked, but the parameter `$in-section` will have the value «`false`». The reason is that the built-in template rule for the intermediate element calls **<xsl:apply-templates>** to process its **<clause>** children, but without supplying any parameters.

Output Destination

A called template rule does not return a result in the conventional way that functions in many programming languages (and indeed in XPath) return a result. The only thing a template rule can do to leave a record of its existence is to write nodes to the current output destination.

When execution of the stylesheet starts, the current output destination is the principal result tree produced by executing the stylesheet, so any output produced by a template goes to the principal output document.

Within the body of an **<xsl:variable>**, **<xsl:param>**, or **<xsl:with-param>** element, the current output destination is changed to be a new temporary tree. When construction of this tree is complete, the variable or parameter will have a value that is a node-set containing a single node, this being the root node of the temporary tree.

XSLT 1.1 also allows multiple result trees. When an **<xsl:document>** instruction (described on page 204) is encountered within a template body, a new tree is started, which becomes the current output destination. On completion this tree will be serialized in the same way as the principal result tree.

Some other XSLT instructions also change the output destination. Examples are **<xsl:attribute>**, **<xsl:comment>**, and **<xsl:processing-instruction>**. In these cases the new output destination is the text value of the node being created, and it is an error if nodes other than text nodes are written to the destination. Another example is **<xsl:message>**, where the new output destination is the text of the message to be written. In this case it is permitted to write nodes other than text nodes, but it's up to the implementation to decide what to do with them.

Calling **<xsl:apply-templates>** does not change the current output destination. So if **<xsl:apply-templates>** is called within the body of an **<xsl:variable>** element, the output from the called template rules, and from any template rules which they in turn call, is added to the temporary tree that becomes the value of this variable.

Note that it's quite legitimate to use **<xsl:apply-templates>** within the body of a global variable definition, for example:

```
<xsl:variable name="table-of-contents">
   <xsl:apply-templates mode="toc"/>
</xsl:variable>
```

In this situation the current node is taken as the root of the principal source document, so the **<xsl:apply-templates>** processes the children of the root node. It's not defined what happens if a template instantiated in this way attempts to reference the value of the global variable, but it's likely to cause an error of some kind.

Usage

The following sections give some hints and tips about using **<xsl:apply-templates>**. First I'll discuss when to use **<xsl:apply-templates>** and when to use **<xsl:for-each>**. Then I'll explain how to use modes.

<xsl:apply-templates> Versus <xsl:for-each>

<xsl:apply-templates> is most useful when processing an element that may contain children of a variety of different types in an unpredictable sequence. This is a *rule-based* design pattern: the body of each individual template rule declares which nodes it is interested in, rather than the template rule for the parent node defining in detail how each of its children should be processed. The rule-based approach works particularly well when the document design is likely to evolve over time. As new child elements are added, template rules to process them can also be added, without changing the logic for the parent elements in which they might appear.

This style of processing is sometimes called **push** processing. It will be familiar if you have used text processing languages such as awk or Perl, but it may be unfamiliar if you are more used to procedural programming in C++ or Visual Basic.

Where the structure is more regular and predictable, it may be simpler to navigate around the document using **<xsl:for-each>**, or by accessing the required data directly using **<xsl:value-of>**. This is sometimes called **pull** processing. The **<xsl-value-of>** instruction allows you to fetch data from the XML document using an arbitrarily complex XPath expression. In this sense it is similar to a `SELECT` statement in SQL.

A unique strength of XSLT is the ability to mix these two styles of programming. I'll discuss both approaches, and their relative merits, in more detail in Chapter 9.

Modes

Modes are useful where the same data is to be processed more than once.

A classic example is when building a table of contents. The main body of the output can be produced by processing the nodes in default mode, while the table of contents is produced by processing the same nodes with «`mode="TOC"`».

The following example does something very similar to this: it displays a scene from a play, adding at the start of the page a list of the characters who appear in this scene:

Example: Using Modes

Source

The source file, `scene.xml`, contains a scene from a play (specifically, Act I Scene 1 of Shakespeare's *Othello* – marked up in XML by Jon Bosak).

It starts like this:

```
<?xml version="1.0"?>
<SCENE><TITLE>SCENE I.  Venice. A street.</TITLE>
<STAGEDIR>Enter RODERIGO and IAGO</STAGEDIR>

<SPEECH>
<SPEAKER>RODERIGO</SPEAKER>
<LINE>Tush! never tell me; I take it much unkindly</LINE>
<LINE>That thou, Iago, who hast had my purse</LINE>
<LINE>As if the strings were thine, shouldst know of this.</LINE>
</SPEECH>

<SPEECH>
<SPEAKER>IAGO</SPEAKER>
<LINE>'Sblood, but you will not hear me:</LINE>
<LINE>If ever I did dream of such a matter, Abhor me.</LINE>
</SPEECH>
etc.
</SCENE>
```

Stylesheet

The stylesheet `scene.xsl` is designed to display this scene in HTML. This is how it starts:

```
<xsl:transform
 xmlns:xsl="http://www.w3.org/1999/XSL/Transform"
 version="1.0"
>
<xsl:template match="SCENE">
<html><body>
   <xsl:apply-templates select="TITLE"/>
   <xsl:variable name="speakers"
         select="//SPEAKER[not(.=preceding::SPEAKER)]"/>
   <h2>Cast: <xsl:apply-templates
         select="$speakers" mode="cast-list"/></h2>
   <xsl:apply-templates select="*[not(self::TITLE)]"/>
</body></html>
</xsl:template>
```

The template rule shown above matches the **<SCENE>** element. It first displays the **<TITLE>** element (if there is one) using the appropriate template rule. Then it sets up a variable called «speakers» to be a node-set containing all the distinct **<SPEAKER>** elements that appear in the document. The rather complex **select** attribute uses the expression «//SPEAKER» to select all **<SPEAKER>** elements that are descendants of the root (in other words, all of them), and then qualifies this with a predicate in square brackets that eliminates those speakers that are the same as a previous speaker. The result is a list of the speakers in which each one appears once only.

The template rule then calls **<xsl:apply-templates>** to process this set of speakers in mode «cast-list» (a nice side effect is that they will be listed in order of appearance). Finally it calls **<xsl:apply-templates>** again, this time in the default mode, to process all elements («*») that are not **<TITLE>** elements (because the title has already been processed).

The stylesheet carries on as follows:

```
<xsl:template match="SPEAKER" mode="cast-list">
    <xsl:value-of select="."/>
    <xsl:if test="not(position()=last())">, </xsl:if>
</xsl:template>
```

This template rule defines how the **<SPEAKER>** element should be processed when it is being processed in «cast-list» mode. The template body has the effect of outputting the speaker's name, followed by a comma if it is not the last speaker in the list.

Finally the remaining template rules define how each element should be output, when processed in default mode:

```
<xsl:template match="TITLE">
<h1><xsl:apply-templates/></h1>
</xsl:template>

<xsl:template match="STAGEDIR">
<i><xsl:apply-templates/></i>
</xsl:template>

<xsl:template match="SPEECH">
<p><xsl:apply-templates/></p>
</xsl:template>

<xsl:template match="SPEAKER">
<b><xsl:apply-templates/></b><br/>
</xsl:template>
```

```
<xsl:template match="LINE">
<xsl:apply-templates/><br/>
</xsl:template>
</xsl:transform>
```

Output

The precise layout of the HTML will depend on which XSLT processor you are using, but apart from layout details it should start like this:

```
<html>
   <body>
      <h1>SCENE I.  Venice. A street.</h1>
      <h2>Cast: RODERIGO, IAGO, BRABANTIO</h2>
      <i>Enter RODERIGO and IAGO</i>
      <p>
         <b>RODERIGO</b><br>
         Tush! never tell me; I take it much unkindly<br>
         That thou, Iago, who hast had my purse<br>
         As if the strings were thine, shouldst know of this.<br>
      </p>
      <p>
         <b>IAGO</b><br>
         'Sblood, but you will not hear me:<br>
         If ever I did dream of such a matter, Abhor me.<br>
      </p>
   </body>
</html>
```

It is sometimes useful to use named modes, even where they are not strictly necessary, to document more clearly the relationship between calling templates and called templates, and to constrain the selection of template rules rather more visibly than can be achieved by relying on template rule priorities. This might even improve performance by reducing the number of rules to be considered, though the effect is likely to be marginal.

For example, suppose that a **<poem>** consists of a number of **<stanza>** elements, and that the first **<stanza>** is to be output using a different style from the rest. The orthodox way to achieve this would be as follows:

```
<xsl:template match="poem">
. . .
   <xsl:apply-templates select="stanza"/>
. . .
</xsl:template>
<xsl:template match="stanza[1]">
. . .
</xsl:template>
```

```
<xsl:template match="stanza">
. . .
</xsl:template>
```

This relies on the default priority rules to ensure that the correct template rule is applied to each stanza – as explained under **<xsl:template>** on page 312, the default priority for the pattern «stanza[1]» is higher than the default priority for «stanza».

Another way of doing it, perhaps less orthodox but equally effective, is as follows:

```
<xsl:template match="poem">
. . .
   <xsl:apply-templates select="stanza[1]" mode="first"/>
   <xsl:apply-templates select="stanza[position() &gt; 1]"
mode="rest"/>
. . .
</xsl:template>

<xsl:template match="stanza" mode="first">
. . .
</xsl:template>

<xsl:template match="stanza" mode="rest">
. . .
</xsl:template>
```

Another solution, giving even finer control, would be to use **<xsl:for-each>** and **<xsl:call-template>** to control precisely which template rules are applied to which nodes, avoiding the pattern-matching mechanisms of **<xsl:apply-templates>** altogether.

Which you choose is largely a matter of personal style, and it is very hard to argue that one is better than the other in all cases. However, if you find that the match patterns used in defining a template rule are becoming extremely complex and context-dependent, then you probably have both a performance and a maintenance problem on your hands, and controlling the selection of template rules in the calling code, by using modes or by calling templates by name, may well be the answer.

Examples

`<xsl:apply-templates/>`	Processes all the children of the current node.
`<xsl:apply-templates select="para"/>`	Process all the **<para>** elements that are children of the current node.
`<xsl:apply-templates select="//*" mode="toc"/>`	Processes every element in the document in mode «toc».

`<xsl:apply-templates select="para"> <xsl:with-param name="indent" select="$n+4"/> </xsl:apply-templates>`	Process all the **<para>** elements that are children of the current node, setting the value of the `indent` parameter in each called template to the value of the variable `$n` plus 4.
`<xsl:apply-templates select="//book "> <xsl:sort select="@isbn"/> </xsl:apply-templates>`	Process all the **<book>** elements in the document, sorting them in ascending order of their **isbn** attribute.

See also

<xsl:for-each> on page 219
<xsl:template> on page 312
<xsl:with-param> on page 345

xsl:attribute

The **<xsl:attribute>** element outputs an attribute name and value to the current output destination. It is successful only if an element node has been added to this output tree and if no nodes other than attributes have been added since the element was added.

Defined in

XSLT section 7.1.3

Format

```
<xsl:attribute name={QName} namespace={uri}>
    template body
</xsl:attribute>
```

Position

<xsl:attribute> may be used either as an instruction within a *template body*, or within an **<xsl:attribute-set>** element.

Attributes

Name	Value	Meaning
name mandatory	Attribute value template returning a `QName`	The name of the attribute to be generated
namespace optional	Attribute value template returning a URI	The namespace URI of the generated attribute

Content

A template body.

Effect

An **<xsl:attribute>** instruction may appear within a template body, or within an **<xsl:attribute-set>** element.

Both the **name** and the **namespace** attributes may be written as attribute value templates: that is, they may contain expressions nested within curly braces, for example `<xsl:attribute name="{$chosenName}"/>`. Attribute value templates are explained in detail in Chapter 3, page 127.

The **<xsl:attribute>** instruction must only be instantiated in the course of instantiating an instruction to add an element node to the result tree. This might be an **<xsl:element>** or **<xsl:copy>** instruction, or a literal result element. Moreover, the attribute must be output before any child nodes (text nodes, elements, comments, or processing instructions) are added to the element node. Very often the **<xsl:attribute>** instruction will be contained directly in the instruction that writes the element, for example:

```
<table>
<xsl:attribute name="border">2</xsl attribute>
</table>
```

but this is not essential, for example you could also do:

```
<table>
   <xsl:call-template name="set-border"/>
</table>
```

and then create the attribute from within the «`set-border`» template.

The rule that the attributes of an element must be written to the result tree before any children are added is there for the convenience of implementors. It means that the XSLT processor doesn't actually need to build the result tree in memory, instead each node can be written out to an XML file as soon as it is generated. If it weren't for this rule, the software wouldn't be able to write the first start tag until right at the end, because there would always be a chance of an attribute being added to it.

If, at the time **<xsl:attribute>** is instantiated, there is already an attribute on the current element node with the same name as this one (that is, another attribute whose name has the same local part and namespace URI), then the new attribute overwrites the earlier one. This is not an error: in fact, when named attribute sets are used to add attributes to an output element, it is an important mechanism. Named attribute sets are described under **<xsl:attribute-set>** on page 173.

Attribute Name

The name of the new attribute is obtained by expanding the **name** attribute. The result of expanding the attribute value template must be a `QName`, which is a valid XML name with optional namespace prefix. In the most common case, this will be a simple name with no colon, and the output attribute name is then the same as this `QName`.

The local part of the name of the output attribute will always be the same as the local part of the `QName` supplied as the value of the **name** attribute. The prefix may be different, as discussed below.

Attribute Namespace

I introduced XML namespaces in Chapter 2 (page 64). The **namespace** attribute of the **<xsl:attribute>** instruction lets you define the namespace URI of the attribute being generated.

The XSLT specification explicitly states that you cannot use **<xsl:attribute>** to generate namespace declarations by giving an attribute name of «`xmlns`» or «`xmlns:*`». Namespace declarations will be added to the output automatically whenever you generate elements or attributes that require them.

If the **<xsl:attribute>** element has a **namespace** attribute, then its value (after expanding the attribute value template) should be a URI identifying a namespace. However, the system does not check that it conforms to any particular URI syntax, so in effect any string can be used.

The prefix of the name of the output attribute will normally be the same as the prefix of the supplied `QName`, but this is not guaranteed, and there are some circumstances where the system may need to allocate a different prefix. One such situation is when two attributes are added to the same element using the same prefix but with different namespace URIs; another is when the prefix takes the reserved value «`xmlns`». If this happens, the system can allocate any namespace prefix it likes. Whatever prefix the system chooses, it must also ensure that the relevant element on the result tree has a namespace node that maps this prefix to the correct namespace URI. This ensures that the final output will contain a namespace declaration for this prefix. It is also relevant when you are writing attributes to a temporary tree that you later read: it means that the **name()** function will always return a `QName` whose prefix correctly identifies the namespace URI of the attribute node.

If there is no **namespace** attribute:

- If the supplied `QName` includes a prefix, the prefix must be a namespace prefix that is in scope at this point in the stylesheet. The namespace URI in the output will be that of the namespace associated with this prefix in the stylesheet.
- Otherwise, the supplied `QName` is used directly as the output attribute name. The default namespace (as declared using «`xmlns="uri"`») is **not** used.

If there is a **namespace** attribute and its value is an empty string, then the output attribute will have a null namespace URI. It will therefore be output without a prefix. Any prefix in the value of the **name** attribute will be ignored.

If there is a **namespace** attribute and its value is not an empty string, the name of the output attribute will have the namespace URI obtained by evaluating the **namespace** attribute. The namespace URI associated with any prefix in the `QName` obtained from the **name** attribute will then be ignored (though it must still be valid). The XSLT processor may need to generate a prefix for the output attribute name if none was supplied. For example, if you write:

```
<table>
<xsl:attribute name="width" namespace="http://acme.org/">
   <xsl:text>200</xsl:text>
</xsl:attribute>
</table>
```

then the output might be:

```
<table ns0001:width="100" xmlns:ns0001="http://acme.org"/>
```

Attribute Value

The value of the new attribute is the string value obtained by instantiating the template body.

It is an error if instantiating the template body generates any nodes other than text nodes (for example, elements or comments). The system may report this as a fatal error, or it may recover by simply ignoring these nodes and anything they contain.

Usage

Developers familiar with Microsoft's WD-xsl dialect often use the **<xsl:attribute>** instruction whenever they need to output an attribute value. However, in XSLT there are many different ways to generate an attribute in the result tree. This section compares the different approaches.

Where an output element is generated using a literal result element, the simplest way to specify attributes is normally to include them as attributes on the literal result element itself. You can do this even when the value is derived from information in the source document, because the value can be generated using an attribute value template, for example:

```
<body bgcolor="#{@red}{@green}{@blue}">
```

This concatenates three attributes of the current node in the source tree to create a single attribute in the result tree. Attribute value templates are described in Chapter 3, page 127.

Using **<xsl:attribute>** gives you more control than writing the attribute directly using attribute value templates. It is useful where one of the following conditions applies:

- The parent element is output using **<xsl:element>** or **<xsl:copy>** (rather than a literal result element)
- There is conditional logic to decide whether to output the attribute or not
- The name of the attribute is computed at run-time

- There is complex logic to calculate the value of the attribute
- The attribute is one of a set that can conveniently be grouped together using an **<xsl:attribute-set>**
- The output attribute belongs to a namespace that is not present in the source document or the stylesheet

A third way to output attributes is to copy them from the source tree to the result tree by using **<xsl:copy>** or **<xsl:copy-of>**. This works only if the attribute you want to generate has the same name and same value as an attribute in the source. **<xsl:copy>** can be used when the current node in the source document is an attribute node. It's not necessary that the owning element was output using **<xsl:copy>**, for example the following code ensures that the **width**, **height**, and **depth** attributes of the source **<parcel>** element are copied to the output **<package>** element, but its **value** and **owner** attributes are discarded:

```
<xsl:template match="parcel">
<package>
   <xsl:apply-templates select="@*"/>
</package>
</xsl:template>

<xsl:template match="parcel/@width | parcel/@height | parcel/@depth">
   <xsl:copy/>
</xsl:template>

<xsl:template match="parcel/@value | parcel/@owner"/>
```

This example uses **<xsl:apply-templates>** to process all the attributes of the **<parcel>** element. Some of these match one template rule, which copies the attribute to the output element, while others match an empty template rule that does nothing.

The same effect could be achieved more easily with **<xsl:copy-of>**, as follows:

```
<xsl:template match="parcel">
<package>
   <xsl:copy-of select="@width | @height | @depth"/>
</package>
</xsl:template>
```

The **select** expression here selects a node-set that contains all the **width**, **height**, and **depth** attributes of the current node, and the **<xsl:copy-of>** instruction copies this node-set. The «|» operator, described in Chapter 5, creates the union of two node-sets.

If you want to copy all attributes of the current node to the result tree, the simplest way to achieve it is `<xsl:copy-of select="@*"/>`. If you want to copy all the attributes except certain particular ones, you can either use the rule-based approach described above, or write something like:

```
<xsl:copy-of select=@* [not(name() = 'value' or name()='owner')]"/>
```

It's best to avoid this, however, if the attributes are in a namespace, because the result of the **name()** function could then vary depending on the choice of prefix. You can't use «`not(self::value)`» here, as you would with an element, because «`self::value`» will only match an element called **value**, never an attribute. A safer solution is to test both the **local-name()** and **namespace-uri()**.

Examples

The following example outputs an HTML **<OPTION>** element, with a **SELECTED** attribute included only if the Boolean variable `$selected` is true. (The XML output would be `<OPTION SELECTED="SELECTED">`, but the HTML output method will convert this to `<OPTION SELECTED>`.)

Example: Generating an Attribute Conditionally

Source

The source file is `countries.xml`.

```
<?xml version="1.0"?>
<countries>
<country name="France"/>
<country name="Germany"/>
<country name="Israel"/>
<country name="Japan"/>
<country name="Poland"/>
<country name="United States" selected="yes"/>
<country name="Venezuela"/>
</countries>
```

Stylesheet

The stylesheet file is `options.xsl`.

This is a complete stylesheet using the simplified stylesheet syntax described in Chapter 3, page 113. It outputs an HTML selection box in which the `selected` attribute is set for the option marked as «`selected="yes"`» in the XML source document.

```
<html version="1.0"
      xmlns:xsl="http://www.w3.org/1999/XSL/Transform">
<body>
<h1>Please select a country:</h1>
<select id="country">
<xsl:for-each select="//country">
    <option value="{@name}">
   <xsl:if test="@selected='yes'">
       <xsl:attribute name="selected">selected</xsl:attribute>
   </xsl:if>
    <xsl:value-of select="@name"/>
    </option>
</xsl:for-each>
</select>
<hr/>
</body>
</html>
```

Output

The output (shown with the selection box opened) is as follows:

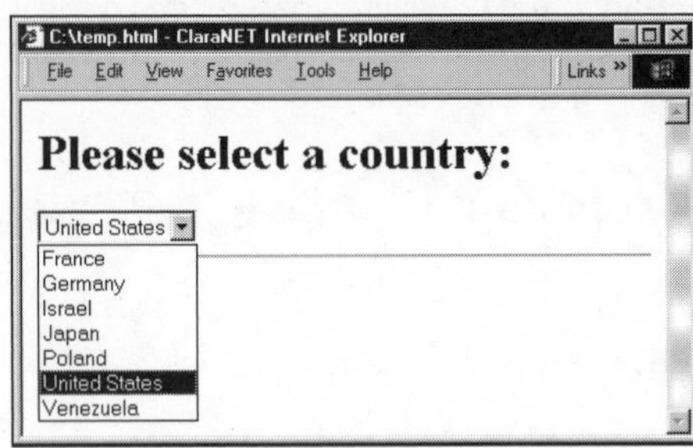

The following example outputs a **<promotion>** element with either a **code** or **reason-code** attribute depending on the variable `$schema-version`. This kind of logic can be useful in an application that has to handle different versions of the output document schema.

Example: Deciding the Attribute Name at Run-Time

Source

This example works with any source file.

Stylesheet

The stylesheet can be found in file `conditional.xsl`.

The stylesheet declares a global parameter «`schema-version`» which controls the name of the attribute used in the output file.

```
<xsl:stylesheet version="1.0"
      xmlns:xsl="http://www.w3.org/1999/XSL/Transform">

<xsl:param name="schema-version" select="4.0"/>

<xsl:template match="/">
<promotion>
   <xsl:variable name="attname">
       <xsl:choose>
       <xsl:when test="$schema-version &lt; 3.0">code</xsl:when>
       <xsl:otherwise>reason-code</xsl:otherwise>
       </xsl:choose>
   </xsl:variable>
   <xsl:attribute name="{$attname}">17</xsl:attribute>
</promotion>

</xsl:template>
</xsl:stylesheet>
```

Output

With the default value of the parameter «schema-version», the output is:

```
<promotion reason-code="17"/>
```

When run with the parameter «schema-version» set to 2.0, the output is:

```
<promotion code="17"/>
```


In the above example it would be equally valid, of course, to use **<xsl:attribute>** with a fixed attribute name in both arms of the **<xsl:choose>** element; the advantage of doing it the way we have shown would start to become apparent if the template body of the **<xsl:attribute>** instruction were more complicated than the simple constant «17».

This leads naturally to the next example, where **<xsl:attribute>** is used because the value requires a calculation. In this example, the value of the output attribute is a whitespace-separated list of the **id** attributes of the child **<item>** elements of the current node:

```
<basket>
   <xsl:attribute name="value">
      <xsl:for-each select="item">
         <xsl:value-of select="@id"/>
         <xsl:if test="not(position()=last())">
            <xsl:text> </xsl:text>
         </xsl:if>
      </xsl:for-each>
   </xsl:attribute>
</basket>
```

See also

<xsl:element> on page 209
<xsl:copy> on page 192
<xsl:copy-of> on page 195

xsl:attribute-set

The **<xsl:attribute-set>** element is a top-level XSLT element used to define a named set of attribute names and values. The resulting attribute set can be applied as a whole to any output element, providing a way of defining commonly-used sets of attributes in a single place.

Named attribute sets provide a capability similar to named styles in CSS .

Defined in

XSLT section 7.1.4

Format

```
<xsl:attribute-set   name=QName
   use-attribute-sets=list-of-QNames >
      <xsl:attribute> *
</xsl:attribute-set>
```

Position

<xsl:attribute-set> is a top-level element, so it must always occur as a child of the **<xsl:stylesheet>** element.

Attributes

Name	Value	Meaning
name mandatory	QName	The name of the attribute set
use-attribute-sets optional	Whitespace-separated list of QName	The names of other attribute sets to be incorporated into this attribute set

Content

Zero or more **<xsl:attribute>** elements.

Effect

The **name** attribute is mandatory, and defines the name of the attribute set. It must be a QName; a name with or without a namespace prefix. If the name uses a prefix, it must refer to a namespace declaration that is in scope at this point in the stylesheet, and as usual it is the namespace URI rather than the prefix that is used when matching names. The name does not need to be unique; if there are several attribute sets with the same name, they are effectively merged.

The **use-attribute-sets** attribute is optional. It is used to build up one attribute set from a number of others. If present, its value must be a whitespace-separated list of tokens each of which is a valid QName that refers to another named attribute set in the stylesheet. For example:

```
<xsl:attribute-set name="table-cell"
   use-attribute-sets="small-font gray-background centered"/>
<xsl:attribute-set name="small-font">
   <xsl:attribute name="font-name">Verdana</xsl:attribute>
   <xsl:attribute name="font-size">6pt</xsl:attribute>
</xsl:attribute-set>
<xsl:attribute-set name="gray-background">
   <xsl:attribute name="bgcolor">#xBBBBBB</xsl:attribute>
</xsl:attribute-set>
<xsl:attribute-set name="centered">
   <xsl:attribute name="align">center</xsl:attribute>
</xsl:attribute-set>
```

The references must not be circular: if A refers to B, then B must not refer directly or indirectly to A. The order is significant: specifying a list of named attribute sets is equivalent to copying the **`<xsl:attribute>`** elements that they contain, in order, to the **beginning** of the list of **`<xsl:attribute>`** elements contained in this **`<xsl:attribute-set>`** element.

If several attribute sets have the same name, they are merged. If this merging finds two attributes with the same name, then the one in the attribute set with higher import precedence will take precedence. Import precedence is discussed under **`<xsl:import>`** on page 226. If they both have the same precedence, the XSLT processor has the option of using the one that came later in the stylesheet, or reporting an error. (Note that it isn't generally possible to detect this error at compile time, because the attribute names can be calculated at run-time using an attribute value template.)

The order in which this merging process takes place can affect the outcome. When `use-attribute-sets` appears on an **`<xsl:attribute-set>`** or **`<xsl:copy>`** element, or `xsl:use-attribute-sets` on a literal result element, it is expanded to create an equivalent sequence of **`<xsl:attribute>`** instructions. The precise rules are tortuous, even in the corrected version that appears in the XSLT 1.0 errata. They are best explained by example.

Suppose you have the following attribute-set definition:

```
<xsl:attribute-set name="B" use-attribute-sets="A1 A2">
  <xsl:attribute name="p">percy</xsl:attribute>
  <xsl:attribute name="q">queenie</xsl:attribute>
  <xsl:attribute name="r">rory</xsl:attribute>
</xsl:attribute-set>
```

If there is more than one attribute-set named `A1` these must be merged first (taking import precedence into account), and then the merged contents must be substituted into `B`.

Then the same process is applied to `A2`. The referenced attribute sets are expanded in order. The attributes that result from expanding `A1` are output before those that result from expanding `A2`. This means that attributes from `A2` take priority over those from `A1` if there is a clash.

In turn, this attribute-set `B` must be fully expanded before it is merged with any other attribute-set called `B`. That is, the processor must replace the references to attribute-sets `A1` and `A2` with an equivalent list of **`<xsl:attribute>`** instructions before it merges this `B` with other attribute sets of the same name.

When `B` is expanded, the attributes derived from `A1` and `A2` will be output before the attributes `p`, `q`, and `r`, so if expanding `A1` and `A2` generates any attributes called `p`, `q`, and `r`, these will be overwritten by the values specified within `B` (`percy`, `queenie`, and `rory`).

In general, duplicate attribute names or attribute set names do not cause an error; if several attributes have the same name, the one that comes last (in the order produced by the merging rules given above) will take precedence. There is one situation only that is defined as an error, namely if two different attribute-sets with the same name and the same import precedence both produce attributes with the same name. Another way of saying this is: it is an error if the final result depends on the relative positions of the attribute-set definitions in the stylesheet. However, the processor is allowed to recover from this error by taking the definitions in stylesheet order, and in this particular case it's so much easier to take the recovery action than to detect the error that I suspect this is what most processors are likely to do.

Usage

The most common use of attribute sets is to define packages of attributes that constitute a display style, for example a collection of attributes for a font or for a table.

A named attribute set is used by referring to it in the **`use-attribute-sets`** attribute of the **`<xsl:element>`** or **`<xsl:copy>`** elements, or in the **`xsl:use-attribute-sets`** attribute of a literal result element, or, of course, in the **`use-attribute-sets`** attribute of another **`<xsl:attribute-set>`**. The first three cases all write an element node to the current output destination, and have the effect of adding the attributes in the named attribute set to that element node. Any attributes added implicitly from a named attribute set can be overridden by attribute nodes added explicitly by the invoking code.

An attribute set is not simply a textual macro. The attributes contained in the attribute set each have a template body to define the value, and although this will often be a simple text node, it may also, for example, declare variables or invoke other XSLT instructions such as **`<xsl:call-template>`** and **`<xsl:apply-templates>`**.

The rules for the scope of variables, described under **`<xsl:variable>`** on page 333, are the same as anywhere else, and are defined by the position of the definitions in the source stylesheet document. This means that the only way to parameterize the values of attributes in a named attribute set is by reference to global variables and parameters: there is no other way of passing parameters to an attribute set. However, the value of the generated attributes may depend on the context in the source document. The context is not changed when the attribute-set is used, so the current node («.») and current node list are exactly the same as in the calling template.

This is shown in the following example:

Example: Using an Attribute Set for Numbering

Let's suppose we want to copy an XML file containing a poem, but with the **<line>** elements in the poem output in the form `<line number="3" of="18">` within the stanza.

Source

The source file `poem.xml` has the following structure (I'm only showing the first stanza):

```
<?xml version="1.0"?>
<poem>
<author>Rupert Brooke</author>
<date>1912</date>
<title>Song</title>
<stanza>
<line>And suddenly the wind comes soft,</line>
<line>And Spring is here again;</line>
<line>And the hawthorn quickens with buds of green</line>
<line>And my heart with buds of pain.</line>
</stanza>
</poem>
```

Stylesheet

The stylesheet `number-lines.xsl` copies everything unchanged except the **<line>** elements, which are copied with a named attribute set:

```
<xsl:transform
 xmlns:xsl="http://www.w3.org/1999/XSL/Transform"
 version="1.0"
>
<xsl:strip-space elements="*"/>
<xsl:output method="xml" indent="yes"/>

<xsl:template match="*">
   <xsl:copy>
   <xsl:apply-templates/>
   </xsl:copy>
</xsl:template>

<xsl:template match="line">
   <xsl:copy use-attribute-sets="sequence">
   <xsl:apply-templates/>
   </xsl:copy>
</xsl:template>
```

4

XSLT Elements

```
<xsl:attribute-set name="sequence">
   <xsl:attribute name="number"><xsl:value-of
                select="position()"/></xsl:attribute>
   <xsl:attribute name="of"><xsl:value-of
                select="last()"/></xsl:attribute>
</xsl:attribute-set>
</xsl:transform>
```

Output

The output (again showing only the first stanza) looks like this:

```
<poem>
   <author>Rupert Brooke</author>
   <date>1912</date>
   <title>Song</title>
   <stanza>
      <line number="1" of="4">And suddenly the wind comes
soft,</line>
      <line number="2" of="4">And Spring is here again;</line>
      <line number="3" of="4">And the hawthorn quickens with
                    buds of green</line>
      <line number="4" of="4">And my heart with buds of
pain.</line>
   </stanza>
</poem>
```

Examples

The following example defines an attribute set designed for generated HTML **<table>** elements:

```
<xsl:attribute-set name="full-width-table">
   <xsl:attribute name="border">1</xsl:attribute>
   <xsl:attribute name="cellpadding">3</xsl:attribute>
   <xsl:attribute name="cellspacing">0</xsl:attribute>
   <xsl:attribute name="width">100%</xsl:attribute>
</xsl:attribute-set>
```

This attribute set can be used when generating an output element, as follows:

```
<table xsl:use-attribute-sets="full-width-table">
<tr></tr>
</table>
```

This produces the following output:

```
<table border="1" cellpadding="3" cellspacing="0" width="100%">
<tr></tr>
</table>
```

Alternatively it is possible to use the attribute set while overriding some of its definitions and adding others, for example:

```
<table border="2" rules="cols" xsl:use-attribute-sets="full-width-
table">
<tr></tr>
</table>
```

The output now becomes:

```
<table border="2" rules="cols" cellpadding="3"
                               cellspacing="0" width="100%">
<tr></tr>
</table>
```


If this combination of attributes is also used repeatedly, it could be defined as an attribute set in its own right, as:

```
<xsl:attribute-set name="ruled-table" use-attribute-set="full-width-
table">
    <xsl:attribute name="border">2</xsl:attribute>
    <xsl:attribute name="rules">cols</xsl:attribute>
</xsl:attribute-set>
```

Then this new attribute set could also be invoked by name from a literal result element, an **<xsl:element>** instruction, or an **<xsl:copy>** instruction.

See also

<xsl:element> on page 209
<xsl:copy> on page 192
Literal Result Elements in Chapter 3, page 118

xsl:call-template

The **<xsl:call-template>** instruction is used to invoke a named template. Its effect is analogous to a procedure call or subroutine call in other programming languages.

Defined in

XSLT section 6

Format

```
<xsl:call-template name=QName>
   <xsl:with-param> *
</xsl:call-template>
```

Position

<xsl:call-template> is an instruction; it is always used within a template body.

Attributes

Name	Value	Meaning
name mandatory	QName	The name of the template to be called

Content

Zero or more **<xsl:with-param>** elements.

Effect

The sections below describe the rules for the template name, the rules for supplying parameters to the called template, and the way the context is affected.

The Template Name

The mandatory **name** attribute must be a QName, and it must match the **name** attribute of an **<xsl:template>** element in the stylesheet. If the name has a namespace prefix, the names are compared using the corresponding namespace URI in the usual way. If there is no prefix, the namespace URI is null (the default namespace is not used). It is an error if there is no **<xsl:template>** element with a matching name.

If there is more than one **<xsl:template>** in the stylesheet with a matching name, they must have different **import precedence**, and the one with highest import precedence is used. For information about import precedence, see **<xsl:import>** on page 226.

The name of the template to be called must be written explicitly in the **name** attribute. There is no way of writing this name as a variable or expression to be evaluated at run-time. If you want to make a run-time decision which of several named templates to call, the only way to achieve this is to write an **<xsl:choose>** instruction.

Parameters

If the name of a child **<xsl:with-param>** element matches the name of an **<xsl:param>** element in the called **<xsl:template>**, then the **<xsl:with-param>** element is evaluated (in the same way as an **<xsl:variable>** element) and the value is assigned to the relevant **<xsl:param>** variable name within that named template.

If there is a child **<xsl:with-param>** element that does not match the name of any **<xsl:param>** element in the selected **<xsl:template>**, then it is ignored. This is not treated as an error.

If there is an **<xsl:param>** element in the selected **<xsl:template>** with no matching **<xsl:with-param>** element in the **<xsl:call-template>** element, then the **<xsl:param>** variable is given a default value. See **<xsl:param>** on page 283 for details. Again, this is not an error.

Context

The selected `<xsl:template>` is executed with no change to the context; it uses the same current node and current node list, and the same output destination, as the calling template. There is also no change to the *current template rule* (a concept that is used only by `<xsl:apply-imports>`, described on page 152).

Usage and Examples

The `<xsl:call-template>` element is similar to a subroutine call in conventional programming languages, and the parameters behave in the same way as conventional call-by-value parameters. It is useful wherever there is common logic to be called from different places in the stylesheet.

Output Destination

There is no direct way of returning a result from `<xsl:call-template>`. However, if `<xsl:call-template>` is called from within an `<xsl:variable>` element, that variable becomes the current output destination, so any data written by the called template (for example, using `<xsl:value-of>`) will be accessible as part of the value of this variable. The value of the variable will always be a node-set containing a temporary tree, but in practice it will often be used simply as a string.

For example, the following template outputs the supplied string enclosed in parentheses:

```
<xsl:template name="parenthesize">
   <xsl:param name="string"/>
   <xsl:value-of select="concat('(',$string,')')"/>
</xsl:template>
```

This may be called as follows:

```
<xsl:variable name="credit-in-paren">
   <xsl:call-template name="parenthesize">
      <xsl:with-param name="string" select="@credit"/>
   </xsl:call-template>
</xsl:variable>
```

If the value of the **credit** attribute is «`120.00`», the resulting value of the variable «`$credit-in-paren`» will be «`(120.00)`». More strictly, it will be a temporary tree consisting of a root node which owns a single text node, and the contents of that text node will be «`(120.00)`»; but for all practical purposes the value can be used as if it were a string.

Changing the Current Node

If you want to use `<xsl:call-template>` to process a node that is not the current node, the easiest way to achieve this is to nest the `<xsl:call-template>` inside an `<xsl:for-each>` element. An alternative, however, is to give the target template a distinctive mode name, and call it using `<xsl:apply-templates>` with the specified mode.

For example, suppose you have written a template that outputs the depth of the current node (the number of ancestors it has). The template has been given a unique name and an identical mode name:

```
   <xsl:template name="depth-of-node" mode="depth-of-node"
match="node()">
      <xsl:value-of select="count(ancestor::node())"/>
   </xsl:template>
```

Now, suppose you want to obtain the depth of a node other than the current node – let's say the depth of the next node in document order, which need not be on the same level as the current node. You can call this template in either of two ways.

Using **<xsl:call-template>**:

```
   <xsl:variable name="next-depth">
      <xsl:for-each select="following::node()[1]">
         <xsl:call-template name="depth-of-node"/>
      </xsl:for-each>
   </xsl:variable>
```

or using **<xsl:apply-templates>** with a special mode:

```
   <xsl:variable name="next-depth">
      <xsl:apply-templates select="following::node()[1]" mode="depth-of-
node"/>
   </xsl:variable>
```

In both cases the variable `$next-depth` will, on return, hold a value which is the depth in the tree of the node following the current node. Technically the value will be a temporary tree, but because such a tree can be freely converted to a string or a number where the context requires it, it can be used without formality in contexts such as arithmetic expressions. For example, you could write a test such as `<xsl:if test="$next-depth > 4">`.

Recursion: Processing a List of Values

Named templates are sometimes used to process a list of values. As XSLT has no updateable variables like a conventional programming language, it also has no conventional *for* or *while* loop, because these constructs can only terminate if there is a control variable whose value is changing. Instead, to process a list of items in XSLT you need to use recursion.

The typical logic used is illustrated by the following pseudo-code:

```
   function process-list(list L) {
      if (not-empty(L)) {
         process(first(L));
         process-list(remainder(L));
      }
   }
```

That is, the function does nothing if the list is empty; otherwise it processes the first item in the list, and then calls itself to process the list containing all items except the first. The net effect is that each item in the list will be processed and the function will then exit.

There are two main kinds of list that this logic is applied to: node-sets, and strings containing separator characters. I will show one example of each kind; there are further, more complex, examples in Chapters 9 and 10.

Example: Using Recursion to Process a Node-Set

Here's an example for processing a node-set. XPath 1.0 provides built-in functions for counting nodes and for totaling their values, but it doesn't provide a **max()** or **min()** function, so to do this we have to walk through the set of nodes comparing the value with the previous highest or lowest. Of course we can't use a variable to record the highest or lowest so far, so we need to turn to recursion for the solution.

Conceptually it's trivial: the maximum value of a set of numbers is either the first number or the maximum of the set of the numbers after the first, whichever is larger. We use XPath predicates for manipulating the node-sets: in particular, «[1]» to find the first node in the set, and «[position()!=1]» to find the remainder.

Let's use this approach to find the longest speech in a scene of a play.

Source

The source file scene.xml is the scene of a play. It starts like this:

```
<?xml version="1.0"?>
<SCENE><TITLE>SCENE I.  Venice. A street.</TITLE>
<STAGEDIR>Enter RODERIGO and IAGO</STAGEDIR>

<SPEECH>
<SPEAKER>RODERIGO</SPEAKER>
<LINE>Tush! never tell me; I take it much unkindly</LINE>
<LINE>That thou, Iago, who hast had my purse</LINE>
<LINE>As if the strings were thine, shouldst know of this.</LINE>
</SPEECH>

<SPEECH>
<SPEAKER>IAGO</SPEAKER>
<LINE>'Sblood, but you will not hear me:</LINE>
<LINE>If ever I did dream of such a matter, Abhor me.</LINE>
</SPEECH>
etc.
</SCENE>
```

Stylesheet

The stylesheet `longest-speech.xsl` is shown below. It starts by defining a named template «`max`». This template takes a node-set called «`list`» as its parameter.

The first thing it does is to test whether this node-set is non-empty (`<xsl:when test="$list">`). If it isn't, it gets the number of **`<LINE>`** element children of the first node in the list into a variable «`$first`». Then the template calls itself recursively, passing all nodes except the first as the parameter, to determine the maximum value for the rest of the list. It then returns either the first value, or the maximum for the rest of the list, whichever is greater. Finally, if the supplied list was empty, it returns zero.

The template rule for the root node of the source document simply calls the «`max`» template, passing the list of all **`<SPEECH>`** elements as a parameter.

```
<xsl:transform
 xmlns:xsl="http://www.w3.org/1999/XSL/Transform"
 version="1.0"
>
<xsl:template name="max">
<xsl:param name="list"/>
<xsl:choose>
<xsl:when test="$list">
   <xsl:variable name="first" select="count($list[1]/LINE)"/>
   <xsl:variable name="max-of-rest">
      <xsl:call-template name="max">
         <xsl:with-param name="list"
select="$list[position()!=1]"/>
      </xsl:call-template>
   </xsl:variable>
   <xsl:choose>
   <xsl:when test="$first &gt; $max-of-rest">
      <xsl:value-of select="$first"/>
   </xsl:when>
   <xsl:otherwise>
      <xsl:value-of select="$max-of-rest"/>
   </xsl:otherwise>
   </xsl:choose>
</xsl:when>
<xsl:otherwise>0</xsl:otherwise>
</xsl:choose>
</xsl:template>

<xsl:template match="/">
Longest speech is <xsl:text/>
   <xsl:call-template name="max">
        <xsl:with-param name="list" select="//SPEECH"/>
   </xsl:call-template>
<xsl:text/> lines.
</xsl:template>
</xsl:transform>
```

Output

The output is simply a message giving the length of the longest speech in this scene:

```
<?xml version="1.0" encoding="utf-8" ?>
Longest speech is 26 lines.
```

I should mention that there is another solution to this problem which may be more appropriate depending on the circumstances. This involves sorting the node-set, and taking the first or last element. It goes like this:

```
<xsl:variable name="longest-speech">
   <xsl:for-each select="SPEECH">
     <xsl:sort select="count(LINE)"data-type="number"/>
     <xsl:if test="position()=last()">
       <xsl:value-of select="count(LINE)"/>
     </xsl:if>
   </xsl:for-each>
</xsl:variable>
```

In principle, the recursive solution should be faster, because it only looks at each node once, whereas sorting all the values requires far more work than is strictly necessary to find the largest. In practice, though, it rather depends on how efficiently recursion is implemented in the particular processor.

Another case where recursion is useful is to process a list presented in the form of a string containing a list of tokens. The easiest form to process is a whitespace-separated list, because the **normalize-space()** function is available to ensure that each item in the list is separated by exactly one space character.

Example: Using Recursion to Process a Separated String

In this example we will print out all lines in `scene.xml` where the line contains the name of a person appearing in that scene. An example of such a line is:

```
<LINE>That thou, Iago, who hast had my purse</LINE>
```

To do this we will first need to normalize the line to convert punctuation into spaces and to convert lower-case into upper-case. Then we will need to process the line word by word. The only way to do this is by recursion: test whether the first word in the line is the name of a speaker, then apply the same logic to the rest of the line after the first word.

Source

The source file `scene.xml` is the same as in the previous example.

Stylesheet

The stylesheet `naming-lines.xsl` starts by declaring a global variable whose value is the set of **<SPEAKER>** elements anywhere in the document:

```
<xsl:transform
 xmlns:xsl="http://www.w3.org/1999/XSL/Transform"
 version="1.0"
>

<xsl:variable name="speakers" select="//SPEAKER"/>
```

Now comes the recursive named template. It takes a parameter called «`line`». The first thing it does is to massage this line, first by converting lower case to upper case and punctuation to spaces using the **translate()** function, and then by replacing multiple spaces by a single space, and adding another single space at the end, using the **normalize-space()** and **concat()** functions. (These functions are all described in Chapter 7.)

Then the template extracts the first word in the line by using **substring-before()**. If this word is present in the global node-set «$speakers» it returns the value «true». Otherwise it applies the same test to the rest of the line (obtained using **substring-after()**) by calling itself recursively.

If the end of the line is reached, the template returns the value «false».

```
<xsl:template name="contains-name">
    <xsl:param name="line"/>
    <xsl:variable name="line1"
         select="translate($line,
                          'abcdefghijklmnopqrstuvwxyz.,:?!;',
                          'ABCDEFGHIJKLMNOPQRSTUVWXYZ       ')"/>
    <xsl:variable name="line2"
         select="concat(normalize-space($line1), ' ')"/>
    <xsl:variable name="first" select="substring-before($line2,'
')"/>
    <xsl:choose>
    <xsl:when test="$first">
        <xsl:choose>
        <xsl:when test="$speakers[.=$first]">true</xsl:when>
        <xsl:otherwise>
            <xsl:variable name="rest" select="substring-
after($line2,' ')"/>
            <xsl:call-template name="contains-name">
                <xsl:with-param name="line" select="$rest"/>
            </xsl:call-template>
        </xsl:otherwise>
        </xsl:choose>
    </xsl:when>
    <xsl:otherwise>false</xsl:otherwise>
    </xsl:choose>
</xsl:template>
```

Then comes the "main program", the template rule that matches the root node. This simply calls the named template for each **<LINE>** element in the document, copying the element to the output if the named template returns the value «true»:

```
<xsl:template match="/">

<xsl:for-each select="//LINE">
    <xsl:variable name="contains-name">
        <xsl:call-template name="contains-name">
            <xsl:with-param name="line" select="."/>
        </xsl:call-template>
    </xsl:variable>
    <xsl:if test="$contains-name='true'">
        <xsl:copy-of select="."/>;
    </xsl:if>
</xsl:for-each>
</xsl:template>
</xsl:transform>
```

Output

The output lists all the **<LINE>** elements containing the name of a **<SPEAKER>** in the scene:

```
<?xml version="1.0" encoding="utf-8" ?>
      <LINE>That thou, Iago, who hast had my purse</LINE>;
      <LINE>It is as sure as you are Roderigo,</LINE>;
      <LINE>Were I the Moor, I would not be Iago:</LINE>;
      <LINE>What, ho, Brabantio! Signior Brabantio, ho!</LINE>;
      <LINE>Awake! what, ho, Brabantio! thieves! thieves!
thieves!</LINE>;
      <LINE>My name is Roderigo.</LINE>;
      <LINE>Most grave Brabantio,</LINE>;
      <LINE>This thou shalt answer; I know thee, Roderigo.</LINE>;
      <LINE>Is nought but bitterness. Now, Roderigo,</LINE>;
      <LINE>May be abused? Have you not read, Roderigo,</LINE>;
      <LINE>On, good Roderigo: I'll deserve your pains.</LINE>;
```

When processing strings in this way, the only thing you need to be especially careful about is ensuring that there is a single space between each pair of words and another one at the end (because otherwise the **substring-before()** call would fail when there is one word left in the list). This is achieved using the **normalize-space()** and **concat()** functions. The way these are used here is rather inefficient, because the line only needs to be normalized once, not on each recursive call, but I have left that inefficiency in to keep the example code simpler.

One other case where recursion is needed is the simple matter of doing something a fixed number of times. For example, suppose you need to create four empty cells in a table. The following code achieves this, by producing one cell, and then calling itself to produce the rest, stopping only when the number requested reaches zero.

```
<xsl:template name="produce-empty-cells">
    <xsl:param name="count"/>
    <xsl:if test="$count != 0">
        <td> </td>
        <xsl:call-template name="produce-empty-cells">
            <xsl:with-param name="count" select="$count - 1"/>
        </xsl:call-template>
    </xsl:if>
</xsl:template>
```

To produce four empty cells, call this with the «count» parameter set to four, thus:

```
<xsl:call-template name="produce-empty-cells">
    <xsl:with-param name="count" select="4"/>
</xsl:call-template>
```

See also

<xsl:apply-templates> on page 155
<xsl:param> on page 283
<xsl:with-param> on page 345

xsl:choose

The **<xsl:choose>** instruction defines a choice between a number of alternatives.

If there are two alternatives it performs the equivalent of `if-then-else` in other languages; if there are more than two, it performs the equivalent of a `switch` or `select` statement.

Defined in

XSLT section 9.2

Format

```
<xsl:choose>
   <xsl:when> +
   <xsl:otherwise> ?
</xsl:choose>
```

Position

<xsl:choose> is an instruction; it is always used within a template body.

Attributes

None.

Content

One or more **<xsl:when>** elements.
Optionally, an **<xsl:otherwise>** element, which must come last if it is present at all.

Effect

The **<xsl:choose>** element is instantiated as follows:

- The first **<xsl:when>** element whose **test** *expression* is true is selected. Subsequent **<xsl:when>** elements are ignored whether or not their **test** *expression* is true.
- If none of the **<xsl:when>** elements has a **test** *expression* that is true, the **<xsl:otherwise>** element is selected. If there is no **<xsl:otherwise>** element, no element is selected, and the **<xsl:choose>** element therefore has no effect.
- The selected child element (if any) is executed by instantiating its template body in the current context. So the effect is as if the relevant template body appeared in place of the **<xsl:choose>** instruction.

It is not defined whether the **test** *expression* in a **<xsl:when>** element after the selected one is evaluated or not, so if it calls extension functions that have side-effects, or if it contains errors, the result is undefined.

Usage

The **<xsl:choose>** instruction is useful where there is a choice of two or more alternative courses of action. It thus performs the functions of both the `if-then-else` and `switch` or `Select Case` constructs found in other programming languages.

Using **<xsl:choose>** with a single **<xsl:when>** instruction and no **<xsl:otherwise>** is permitted, and means exactly the same as **<xsl:if>**. Some people suggest writing every **<xsl:if>** instruction this way, to save rewriting it later when you discover that you want an `else` branch after all.

When **<xsl:choose>** is used within the body of an **<xsl:variable>** (or **<xsl:param>** or **<xsl:with-param>**) element, the effect is a conditional assignment: the relevant variable is assigned a different value depending on the conditions. Note however that the value of the variable in such cases will always be a temporary tree.

Examples

The following example outputs the name of a State in the USA based on a two-letter abbreviation for the State. If the abbreviation is not that of a recognized State, it outputs the abbreviation itself.

```
<xsl:choose>
   <xsl:when test="state='AZ'">Arizona</xsl:when>
   <xsl:when test="state='CA'">California</xsl:when>
   <xsl:when test="state='DC'">Washington DC</xsl:when>
   ......
   <xsl:otherwise><xsl:value-of select="state"/></xsl:otherwise>
</xsl:choose>
```

The following example declares a variable called `width` and initializes its value to the **width** attribute of the current node, if there is one, or to 100 otherwise.

```
<xsl:variable name="width">
   <xsl:choose>
      <xsl:when test="@width">
         <xsl:value-of select="@width"/>
      </xsl:when>
      <xsl:otherwise>100</xsl:otherwise>
   </xsl:choose>
</xsl:variable>
```

Note: you might be tempted to write this as follows:

```
<!--WRONG-->
<xsl:choose>
   <xsl:when test="@width">
      <xsl:variable name="width">
         <xsl:value-of select="@width"/>
      </xsl:variable>
   </xsl:when>
   <xsl:otherwise>
```

```
        <xsl:variable name="width" select="100"/>
    </xsl:otherwise>
</xsl:choose>
<!--WRONG-->
```

This is legal XSLT, but it does not achieve the required effect. This is because both the variables called «width» have a scope which is bounded by the containing element, so they are inaccessible outside the **<xsl:choose>** instruction.

See also

<xsl:when> on page 343
<xsl:otherwise> on page 269
<xsl:if> on page 223

xsl:comment

The **<xsl:comment>** instruction is used to write a comment to the current output destination.

Defined in

XSLT section 7.4

Format

```
<xsl:comment>
   template body
</xsl:comment>
```

Position

<xsl:comment> is an instruction; it is always used within a template body.

Attributes

None.

Content

A template body.

Effect

The template body contained in the **<xsl:comment>** instruction may only generate text nodes, it is an error if it generates other nodes such as elements, attributes, or nested comments. The XSLT processor may treat this as a fatal error, or it may recover silently by ignoring the offending nodes and their content.

The comment should not include the sequence «--», and it should not end in «-», because these sequences are not allowed in XML comments. Again, the XSLT processor may recover from these errors by adding extra spaces to the comment or it may report an error. If you want your stylesheet to be portable, you must therefore avoid generating these sequences.

In XML or HTML output, the comment will appear as:

```
<!-- comment text -->
```

Usage

In theory, a comment has no meaning to the software that processes the output document, it is intended only for human readers. Comments are therefore useful to record when and how the document was generated, or perhaps to explain the meaning of the tags.

Comments can be particularly useful for debugging the stylesheet. If each **<xsl:template>** in the stylesheet starts with an **<xsl:comment>** instruction, you will find it much easier to trace back from the output to your stylesheet.

Comments in HTML output are used for some special markup conventions, for example surrounding Dynamic HTML scripts. The purpose of the comment here is to ensure that browsers that don't understand the script will skip over it rather than display it as text. An example is shown below.

Examples

The following example uses an extension function, if it is available, to output a comment containing the date at which the stylesheet was generated. Extension functions are described in Chapter 8. Because of the extension function, this example will not work with all processors.

```
<xsl:if test="function-available(Date:toString)"
                                   xmlns:Date="java:java.util.Date">
   <xsl:comment>Generated at:
      <xsl:value-of select="Date:toString()"/>
   </xsl:comment>
</xsl:if>
```

Typical output might be:

```
<!--Generated at Tue Dec 07 23:38:08 GMT 1999-->
```

The following example outputs a piece of client-side JavaScript to an HTML output file:

```
<script language="JavaScript">
   <xsl:comment>
      function bk(n) {
         parent.frames['content'].location="chap" + n + ".1.html";
      }
   //</xsl:comment>
</script>
```

The output will look like this:

```
<script language="JavaScript">
   <!--
      function bk(n) {
         parent.frames['content'].location="chap" + n + ".1.html";
      }
   //-->
</script>
```

The comment cannot be written as a comment in the stylesheet, of course, because then the XSLT processor would ignore it entirely. Comments in the stylesheet are not copied to the output destination.

See also

`function-available()` in Chapter 7, page 487.

xsl:copy

The **`<xsl:copy>`** instruction copies the current node in the source document to the current output destination. This is a shallow copy; it does not copy the children, descendants, or attributes of the current node, only the current node and (if it is an element) its namespaces. For a deep copy, you need to use **`<xsl:copy-of>`**, see page 195.

Defined in

XSLT section 7.5

Format

```
<xsl:copy use-attribute-sets=list-of-QNames >
   template body
</xsl:copy>
```

Position

`<xsl:copy>` is an instruction. It is always used within a template body.

Attributes

Name	Value	Meaning
`use-attribute-sets` optional	Whitespace-separated list of `QNames`	The names of attribute sets to be applied to the generated node, if it is an element

Content

An optional template body, which is used only if the current node is a root node or an element.

Effect

The action depends on the node type of the current node, as follows:

Type of current node in source document	Action
root	Nothing is written to the output destination (it is never necessary to write a root node to the output destination, because it is created implicitly). The **`use-attribute-sets`** attribute is ignored. The only effect of calling **`<xsl:copy>`** is that the template body is instantiated.
element	An element node is added to the current output destination, as if by a call on **`<xsl:element>`**. This will have the same name as the current element node in the source document. The namespace nodes associated with the current element node are also copied. The **`use-attribute-sets`** attribute is expanded: it must be a whitespace-separated list of `QNames` that identify named attribute-sets in the stylesheet. The attributes within these named attribute sets are evaluated in the order they appear, and added to the new element node. The template body is then instantiated.
text	A new text node is written to the output destination, with the same value as the current text node in the source document. The **`use-attribute-sets`** attribute and the template body are ignored.
attribute	An attribute node is added to the current output destination, as if by a call on **`<xsl:attribute>`**. This will have the same name and value as the current attribute node in the source document. If the output destination does not currently have an open element node to hold this attribute, an error is reported. If the open element node already holds an attribute with the same name, the new attribute overwrites the old. The **`use-attribute-sets`** attribute and the template body are ignored. Although the local name, namespace URI, and value of the output attribute are guaranteed to be the same as the original, the prefix may change (for example, if two attributes added to the same element use the same prefix to refer to different namespace URIs). The rules governing the consistency of namespace nodes on a tree ensure that the owning element on the result tree will have a namespace node that maps some namespace prefix to the namespace URI of the attribute, but there is no guarantee what this prefix will be.
processing instruction	A processing instruction node is added to the current output destination, with the same name and value (target and data in XML terminology) as the current processing instruction node in the source document. The **`use-attribute-sets`** attribute and the template body are ignored.

Type of current node in source document	Action
comment	A comment node is added to the current output destination, with the same content as the current comment node in the source document. The **use-attribute-sets** attribute and the template body are ignored.
namespace	The namespace node is copied to the output destination. The new namespace node will have the same name and value (that is, the same namespace prefix and URI) as the original. If the output destination does not currently have an open element node to hold this namespace node, an error is reported: for this purpose an element remains open until its first child node or attribute is added, or until the instruction that is instantiating the element node completes. This means that it is an error to add a namespace node to an element after attributes or children have been added to it. It is also an error if the element node already has a namespace node for the same namespace prefix but with a different namespace URI, or if the element name uses the default namespace and the new namespace node changes the URI for the default namespace. If there is an existing namespace node with the same prefix and the same URI, the duplicate namespace node is ignored.

Usage

The main use of **<xsl:copy>** is when doing an XML-to-XML transformation in which parts of the document are to remain unchanged. It is also useful when the source XML document contains XHTML fragments within it, for example if the simple HTML formatting elements such as **<i>** and **<b>** are used within textual data in the source, and are to be copied unchanged to an HTML output document.

Although **<xsl:copy>** does a shallow copy, it is easy to construct a deep copy by applying it recursively. The typical manner of use is to write a template rule that effectively calls itself:

```
<xsl:template match="@*|node()" mode="copy">
   <xsl:copy>
      <xsl:apply-templates select="@*" mode="copy"/>
      <xsl:apply-templates mode="copy"/>
   </xsl:copy>
</xsl:template>
```

This template rule matches any node except a namespace or root node. This is because «@*» matches any attribute node, and «node()», which is short for «child::node()», matches any node that is the child of something. Once this template rule is applied to a node, it copies that node, and if it is an element node, it applies the same template rule first to its attributes and then to its child nodes – I am assuming there is no other template rule with mode="copy" that has a higher priority.

An easier way of doing a deep copy is to use **<xsl:copy-of>**. However, the recursive use of **<xsl:copy>** allows control over exactly which nodes are to be included in the output.

Examples

The following template rule is useful if the source document contains HTML-like tables that are to be copied directly to the output, without change to the structure.

```
<xsl:template match=" table | tbody | tr | th | td ">
   <xsl:copy>
      <xsl:for-each select="@*">
         <xsl:copy/>
      </xsl:for-each>
      <xsl:apply-templates/>
   </xsl:copy>
</xsl:template>
```

The effect is that all of these elements are copied to the output destination, along with their attributes, but their child elements are processed using whatever template rule is appropriate, which might be this one in the case of a child element that is part of the table model, or it might be a different template for some other element. This template rule could be simplified by copying the attributes using **<xsl:copy-of>**, thus:

```
<xsl:template match=" table | tbody | tr | th | td ">
   <xsl:copy>
      <xsl:copy-of select="@*"/>
      <xsl:apply-templates/>
   </xsl:copy>
</xsl:template>
```

The following template rule matches any elements in the source document that are in the SVG namespace, and copies them unchanged to the output, along with their attributes. The SVG namespace node itself will also be included automatically in the output tree. (SVG stands for Scalable Vector Graphics, it is an XML-based standard, currently a Candidate Recommendation, that is designed to fill the long-standing need for including vector graphics in web pages.)

```
<xsl:template match="svg:*"
              xmlns:svg="http://www.w3.org/2000/svg">
   <xsl:copy>
      <xsl:copy-of select="@*">

      <xsl:apply-templates/>
   </xsl:copy>
</xsl:template>
```

See also

<xsl:copy-of> below.

xsl:copy-of

The main purpose of the **<xsl:copy-of>** instruction is to copy a node-set to the current output destination. This is a deep copy – when a node is copied, its descendants are also copied.

Defined in

XSLT section 11.3

Format

```
<xsl:copy-of select=Expression />
```

Position

<xsl:copy-of> is an instruction. It is always used within a template body.

Attributes

Name	Value	Meaning
select mandatory	Expression	The node-set or other value to be copied to the output destination

Content

None; the element is always empty.

Effect

If the result of evaluating the **select** expression is a node-set, each of the nodes in the node-set is copied, in document order, to the current output destination. This is a deep copy: copying a node copies its namespaces, its attributes, and its children, recursively.

When the value of the select expression is a reference to a variable whose value is a temporary tree, the effect of this rule is that the entire tree is copied to the output destination. The root node of the tree is not copied (because a tree can only have one root) but all the nodes that are children of this root are copied, in the order they appear, together with their namespaces, their attributes, and their children, recursively.

If the tree being copied includes text that was written with the `disable-output-escaping="yes"` (on an **<xsl:text>** or **<xsl:value-of>** instruction) directive, then this directive is copied to the new tree along with the text it applies to, and will take effect if and when that tree is finally serialized.

If the result is any other type (string, number, or boolean), **<xsl:copy-of>** has the same effect as **<xsl:value-of>**. The value is converted to a string using the rules of the **string()** function, and the string is written to the current output destination as a text node.

Usage and Examples

There are two principal uses for **<xsl:copy-of>**: it can be used when the same data is needed in more than one place in the output document, and it can be used for copying a subtree unchanged from the input document to the output.

Repeated Output Fragments

The use of **<xsl:copy-of>** in conjunction with temporary trees arises primarily when you want to write the same collection of nodes to the output in more than one place. This might arise, for example, with page headers and footers. The construct allows you to assemble the required output fragment as the value of a variable, and then copy it to the final output destination as often as required.

Example: Using <xsl:copy-of> for Repeated Output

Source

The source file `soccer.xml` holds details of a number of soccer matches played during the World Cup finals in 1998.

```
<?xml version="1.0"?>
<results group="A">
<match>
<date>10-Jun-98</date>
<team score="2">Brazil</team>
<team score="1">Scotland</team>
</match>
<match>
<date>10-Jun-98</date>
<team score="2">Morocco</team>
<team score="2">Norway</team>
</match>
<match>
<date>16-Jun-98</date>
<team score="1">Scotland</team>
<team score="1">Norway</team>
</match>
<match>
<date>16-Jun-98</date>
<team score="3">Brazil</team>
<team score="0">Morocco</team>
</match>
<match>
<date>23-Jun-98</date>
<team score="1">Brazil</team>
<team score="2">Norway</team>
</match>
<match>
<date>23-Jun-98</date>
<team score="0">Scotland</team>
<team score="3">Morocco</team>
</match>
</results>
```

Stylesheet

The stylesheet is in file `soccer.xsl`.

It constructs an HTML table heading as a global tree-valued variable, and then uses **<xsl:copy-of>** every time it wants to output this heading. In this particular case the heading is fixed, but it could contain data from the source document, so long as the heading is the same each time it is output. If it contained calculated values, there would be a possible performance benefit by coding it this way rather than regenerating the heading each time.

```
<xsl:stylesheet version="1.0"
     xmlns:xsl="http://www.w3.org/1999/XSL/Transform">

<xsl:variable name="table-heading">
    <tr>
        <td><b>Date</b></td>
        <td><b>Home Team</b></td>
        <td><b>Away Team</b></td>
        <td><b>Result</b></td>
    </tr>
</xsl:variable>

<xsl:template match="/">
<html><body>
    <h1>Matches in Group <xsl:value-of select="/*/@group"/></h1>
    <xsl:for-each select="//match">
    <h2><xsl:value-of select="concat(team[1], ' versus ',
team[2])"/></h2>
    <table bgcolor="#cccccc" border="1" cellpadding="5">
        <xsl:copy-of select="$table-heading"/>
        <tr>
        <td><xsl:value-of select="date"/> </td>
        <td><xsl:value-of select="team[1]"/> </td>
        <td><xsl:value-of select="team[2]"/> </td>
        <td><xsl:value-of
          select="concat(team[1]/@score, '-',
team[2]/@score)"/> </td>
        </tr>
    </table>
    </xsl:for-each>
</body></html>
</xsl:template>

</xsl:stylesheet>
```

Output

(Apologies to soccer fans who know full well that all these matches were played in France, on neither team's home territory. It's only an example!)

In XSLT 1.0, temporary trees (known as result tree fragments; the term has been dropped in XSLT 1.1) are very limited in functionality. There are only two things you can do with them: you can copy them to another tree using **<xsl:copy-of>**, and you can convert them to a string. Several XSLT 1.0 implementations have provided an extension function to convert a result tree fragment to a node-set, which greatly increases the usefulness of result tree fragments because it allowed them to be used as working data structures. In XSLT 1.1, this capability has become part of the standard, so a temporary tree can be used anywhere a node-set can be used. In fact, in XSLT 1.1 a temporary tree **is** a node-set, so there is no need for a special conversion function.

Deep Copy

The other use for **<xsl:copy-of>**, which is easily overlooked because of the way the XSLT specification describes its use, is that it provides a simple way of copying an entire sub-tree of the input document directly to the output. As **<xsl:copy-of>** does a deep copy, this is simpler than using **<xsl:copy>**, although it can only be used when the whole subtree is to be copied without change. For example, an XML document defining a product description might have an element called **<overview>** whose content is pure XHTML. You could copy this to the output HTML document with a template rule such as:

```
<xsl:template match="overview">
   <div>
      <xsl:copy-of select="node()"/>
   </div>
</xsl:template>
```

Unlike the examples using **<xsl:copy>**, there is no recursive application of template rules here: each child node of the **<overview>** element is copied to the output destination in a single operation, along with all its children.

The most common example of this technique is using **<xsl:copy-of select="@*"/>** to copy all the attributes of the current element. You can also use this selectively. To copy specific attributes:

```
<xsl:copy-of select="@name | @height | @width"/>
```

to copy all the attributes with named exceptions is a little more difficult. Perhaps the best approach is to use the **generate-id()** function, described in Chapter 7 on page 491:

```
<xsl:variable name="note-id" select="generate-id(@note)"/>
<xsl:copy-of select="@*[generate-id() != $node-id]"/>
```

See also

<xsl:copy> on page 192
<xsl:variable> on page 334

xsl:decimal-format

The **<xsl:decimal-format>** element is used to define the characters and symbols used when converting numbers into strings using the **format-number()** function.

Note that **<xsl:decimal-format>** only applies to the **format-number()** function. It has no effect on the way **<xsl:number>** formats numbers for display, nor on the default number-to-string conversion used by the **string()** function, nor on the format used when **<xsl:value-of>** is used to output a number as a string.

Defined in

XSLT section 12.3

Format

```
<xsl:decimal-format
    name=QName
    decimal-separator=character
    grouping-separator=character
    infinity=string
    minus-sign=character
    NaN=string
    percent=character
    per-mille=character
    zero-digit=character
    digit=character
    pattern-separator=character  />
```

Position

<xsl:decimal-format> is a top-level element. It may appear any number of times in a stylesheet, but only as an immediate child of the **<xsl:stylesheet>** element.

Attributes

Name	Value	Meaning
name optional	QName	The name of this decimal format. If omitted, the attributes apply to the default decimal format.
decimal-separator optional	character	Character to be used to separate the integer and the fraction part of a number. Default is «.».
grouping-separator optional	character	Character used to separate groups of digits. Default is «,».
infinity optional	string	String used to represent the numeric value infinity. Default value is «Infinity».
minus-sign optional	character	Character used as the default minus sign. Default is «-».
NaN optional	string	String used to represent the numeric value NaN (not a number). Default value is «NaN».
percent optional	character	Character used to represent a percentage sign. Default value is «%».
per-mille optional	character	Character used to represent a per-mille (per-thousand) sign. Default value is «‰».
zero-digit optional	character	Character used in a format pattern to indicate a place where a leading or trailing zero digit is required, even if it is not significant. Default value is «0».
digit optional	character	Character used in a format pattern to indicate a place where a digit will appear, provided it is a significant digit. Default value is «#».
pattern-separator optional	character	Character used in a format pattern to separate the subpattern for positive numbers from the subpattern for negative numbers. Default value is «;».

Content

None; the element is always empty.

Effect

If a **name** attribute is supplied, the **<xsl:decimal-format>** element defines a named decimal format; otherwise it defines attributes of the default decimal format. A named decimal format is used by the **format-number()** function when it is called with three arguments (the third argument is the name of a decimal format); the default decimal format is used when the **format-number()** function is called without a third argument.

It is an error to have more than one **<xsl:decimal-format>** element for the default decimal format, or more than one for a decimal format with a given name, unless all non-default attribute values are identical. This is true even if the different **<xsl:decimal-format>** elements have different import precedence.

The **<xsl:decimal-format>** element does not directly define the display format of a number. Rather it defines the characters and strings used to represent different logical symbols. Some of these logical symbols occur in the *format pattern* used as an argument to the **format-number()** function, some of them occur in the final output number itself, and some are used in both. The actual display format of a number depends both on the format pattern and on the choice of decimal format symbols.

For example, if there is a **<xsl:decimal-format>** element as follows:

```
<xsl:decimal-format name="european"
                    decimal-separator=","
                    grouping-separator="." >
```

then the function call:

```
format-number(1234.5, '#.##0,00', 'european')
```

will produce the output:

```
1.234,50
```

The use of the «.» and «,» characters in both the format pattern and the output display is determined by the named **<xsl:decimal-format>** element, but the number of digits displayed, and the use of leading and trailing zeros is determined solely by the format pattern.

The structure of a format pattern is defined in the description of the **format-number()** function in Chapter 7, page 484. The syntax of the format pattern uses a number of special symbols: the actual characters used for these symbols are defined in the relevant **<xsl:decimal-format>** element. These symbols are:

```
decimal-separator
grouping-separator
percent
per-mille
zero-digit
digit
pattern-separator
```

The **<xsl:decimal-format>** element also defines characters and strings which are used, when required, in the actual output value. Some of these are the same as characters used in the format pattern, others are different. These characters and strings are:

```
decimal-separator
grouping-separator
infinity
minus-sign
NaN
percent
per-mille
zero-digit
```

For example, if the **<xsl:decimal-format>** element defines the infinity string as «`***`», then the output of «`format-number(1 div 0, $format)`» will be «`***`», regardless of the format pattern.

Usage

The **<xsl:decimal-format>** element is used in conjunction with the **format-number()** function to output numeric information. It is designed primarily to provide localization of the format for display to human readers, but it can also be useful when you need to produce an output data file using, for example, a fixed number of leading zeroes. It is typically used for numbers in the source data or computed from the source data, whereas the **<xsl:number>** element, which has its own formatting capabilities, is generally used for sequence numbers.

Each **<xsl:decimal-format>** element defines a style of localized numbering, catering for the variations that occur in different countries and languages, and for other local preferences such as the convention in the accountancy profession whereby parentheses are used to indicate negative numbers.

Examples

The following tables illustrate some of the effects achievable using the **<xsl:decimal-format>** element in conjunction with different format patterns.

Example 1

This decimal format is used in many Western European countries; it uses a comma as a decimal point and a period (full stop) as a thousands separator, the reverse of the custom in Britain and North America.

The left hand column shows the number as it would be written in XSLT. The middle column shows the format pattern supplied as the second argument to the **format-number()** function. The right-hand column shows the string value returned by the **format-number()** function.

The patterns used in this example use the following symbols:

- «.» which I have defined as my thousands separator
- «,» which I have defined as my decimal point
- «#» which is a position where a digit can occur, but where the digit is omitted if it is an insignificant zero
- «0» which is a position where a digit will always occur, even if it is an insignificant zero
- «%» which indicates that the number should be expressed as a percentage
- «;» which separates the pattern used for positive numbers from the pattern used for negative numbers

```
<xsl:decimal-format decimal-separator="," grouping-separator="."/>
```

Number	Format Pattern	Result
1234.5	#.##0,00	1.234,50
123.456	#.##0,00	123,46
1000000	#.##0,00	1.000.000,00
-59	#.##0,00	-59,00
1 div 0	#.##0,00	Infinity
1234	###0,0###	1234,0
1234.5	###0,0###	1234,5
.00035	###0,0###	0,0004
0.25	#00%	25%
0.736	#00%	74%
1	#00%	100%
-42	#00%	-4200%
-3.12	#,00;(#,00)	(3,12)
-3.12	#,00;#,00CR	3,12CR

Example 2

This example shows how digits other than the Western digits 0–9 can be used. Since such digits will be unfamiliar to most readers, I'll illustrate the effect using letters instead. This works perfectly well, though it isn't very useful:

```
<xsl:decimal-format zero-digit="a" minus-sign="~"/>
```

Number	Format Pattern	Result
10	aa	ba
12.34	##.##	bc.de
-9999999	#,###,###	~j,jjj,jjj

Example 3

This example shows how the exceptional numeric values NaN and Infinity can be shown, for example in a statistical table.

```
<xsl:decimal-format NaN="Not Applicable" infinity="Out of Range"/>
```

Number	Format Pattern	Result
'a'	any	Not Applicable
1 div 0	any	Out of Range
-1 div 0	any	-Out of Range

See also

format-number() function in Chapter 7, page 484
<xsl:number> on page 256.

xsl:document

The **<xsl:document>** instruction is used to create a new output file. This is a new instruction introduced in the draft XSLT 1.1 specification, but similar facilities have been provided in a proprietary way by several popular XSLT 1.0 processors. The facility allows a transformation to produce multiple output files, so you can write a stylesheet that splits a large XML file into smaller XML files, or into multiple HTML files, perhaps connected to each other by hyperlinks.

Defined in

XSLT 1.1, section 16.5

Format

```
<xsl:document
   href= { uri }
   method= { "xml" | "html" | "text" | QName }
   version= { NMtoken }
   encoding= { string }

   omit-xml-declaration= { "yes" | "no" }
   standalone= { "yes" | "no" }
   doctype-public= { string }
   doctype-system= { string }
   cdata-section-elements= { list-of-QNames }
   indent= { "yes" | "no" }
   media-type= { string } >
         template body
</xsl:document>
```

Position

<xsl:document> is an instruction, which means it may occur anywhere in a template body.

Attributes

With the exception of the href attribute, the attributes of <xsl:document> are the same as those of the <xsl:output> element, described on page 270. These attributes control the formatting of the secondary output document created using this instruction.

All the attributes of <xsl:document> can be written as attribute value templates, that is, as XPath expressions within curly braces. This allows the values to be supplied as parameters to the stylesheet, or to be determined by examining the source document.

Name	Value after expanding attribute value template	Meaning
href mandatory	Relative or absolute URI	Defines the location where the output document will be written after serialization
method optional	«xml» | «html» | «text» | QName	Defines the required output format
version optional	NMtoken	Defines the version of the output format
encoding optional	string	Defines the character encoding
omit-xml-declaration optional	«yes» | «no»	Indicates whether an XML declaration is to be included in the output
standalone optional	«yes» | «no»	Indicates that a **standalone** declaration is to be included in the output, and gives its value
doctype-public optional	string	Indicates the public identifier to be used in the DOCTYPE declaration in the output file
doctype-system optional	string	Indicates the system identifier to be used in the DOCTYPE declaration in the output file
cdata-section-elements optional	Whitespace- separated list of QNames	Names those elements whose text content is to be output in the form of CDATA sections
indent optional	«yes» | «no»	Indicates whether the output should be indented to indicate its hierarchic structure
media-type optional	string	Indicates the media-type (often called MIME type) to be associated with the output file

Content

The content of the **<xsl:document>** element is a template body.

The **<xsl:document>** element may contain an **<xsl:fallback>** element. If it does, the **<xsl:fallback>** element defines the action that an XSLT 1.0 processor will take when it encounters the **<xsl:document>** instruction. Note that the fallback processing only applies if the stylesheet is executing in forwards-compatible mode, which will be the case if you set «`version="1.1"`» on the **<xsl:stylesheet>** element, or «`xsl:version="1.1"`» on any enclosing literal result element.

Effect

When the **<xsl:document>** instruction is instantiated, a new result tree is created, and the new result tree becomes the current output destination for all the nodes output until the **<xsl:document>** element completes.

Normally, this will result in a new output file being created. This output file is the result of serializing the result tree, and it is controlled by the various attributes of the **<xsl:document>** element in the same way as the **<xsl:output>** element controls the serialization of the principal output document.

The location of the new output file is determined by the value of the **href** attribute.

- If this is an absolute URI, the file will be written so that it is accessible using this absolute URI. (This will only work in practice if the XSLT processor has access to this location via the protocol scheme used by the specified URI. The only absolute URIs that you can be confident will work are those beginning «`file:/`», and even then it will only work if the permissions are set up correctly. In some environments, though, you may be able to write to URIs starting with, say, «`ftp:`» or «`webdav:`» – useful when you are running the transformation as part of a document publishing process.)
- If you specify a relative URI, the file will be written so that it is accessible using this URI, relative to the URI of the parent output document.

The concept of the parent output document is more complicated than it might seem. The most common situation is where your stylesheet generates a principal output document, perhaps to serve as a front page or index, and a collection of secondary output documents, each of which is created using an **<xsl:document>** instruction at a point where the current output destination was the principal output document. In this case the parent output document is always the principal output. The URI of the principal output is not controlled from the stylesheet itself, it is typically set from the command line or the API used to invoke the transformation. If the principal document is written to `file:/c:/results/index.html`, then a secondary document created using `<xsl:document href="chapter1.html">` will be written to `file:/c:/results/chapter1.html`.

It is possible to instantiate an **<xsl:document>** instruction while the current output destination is another secondary document created using another **<xsl:document>** element. You might do this to create a complex structure of HTML pages containing pages within sections within chapters. In this case the relative URI in the **href** attribute is interpreted relative to the file created by the currently-active **<xsl:document>** instruction.

The real complications arise when you use **<xsl:document>** at a point where the current output destination is neither the principal output document, nor a secondary output document created using **<xsl:document>**, but rather a temporary tree. For example, when you write:

```
<xsl:variable name="tree">
  <xsl:document href="chap{$nr}.html" method="html">
    <xsl:apply-templates select="content"/>
  </xsl:document>
</xsl:variable>
```

What happens in this situation is that the secondary output document is not written out immediately; it is stored as a tree in memory, linked to the temporary tree. It isn't actually part of the temporary tree, so there is no way of accessing it from the stylesheet, but when you use **<xsl:copy-of>** to copy the temporary tree to another output destination, the secondary documents are transferred along with it. If that output destination is serialized, then the secondary documents are serialized too, to a destination determined by interpreting their **href** attributes relative to the parent document they are now linked to.

This means you can create two copies of the secondary output document, in different places in filestore, by using **<xsl:copy-of>** more than once. Conversely, if the tree-valued variable is never copied to a serialized output tree, then the secondary output documents will never be serialized at all. You need to take care if you are doing this that each time a tree is serialized it is written to a different place, because writing two trees to the same URI in the course of a single transformation is an error.

Usage

Generating multiple output files is something I have often found useful when doing transformations. A typical scenario is that a weighty publication, such as a dictionary, is managed as a single XML file, which would be far too big to download to a user who only wants to see a few entries. So the first stage in preparing it for human consumption is to split it up into bite-sized chunks, perhaps one document per letter of the alphabet or even one per dictionary headword. You can make these chunks individual HTML pages, but I usually find it's better to do the transformation in two stages: first split the big XML document into lots of small XML documents, then convert each of these into HTML independently.

The usual model is to generate one principal output file and a whole family of secondary output files. The principal output file can then serve as an index. Often you'll need to keep links between the files so that you can easily assemble them again (using the **document()** function described on page 466 in Chapter 7), or so that you can generate hyperlinks for the user to follow.

Examples

This feature is often used to break up large documents into manageable chunks, but we don't really want to use a big document as an example, so we'll illustrate the principle with a small one.

Example: Creating Multiple Output Files

This example takes a poem as input, and outputs each stanza to a separate file. A more realistic example would be to split a book into its chapters, but I wanted to keep the files small.

Source

The source file is `poem.xml`. It starts:

```
<poem>
<author>Rupert Brooke</author>
<date>1912</date>
<title>Song</title>
<stanza>
<line>And suddenly the wind comes soft,</line>
<line>And Spring is here again;</line>
<line>And the hawthorn quickens with buds of green</line>
<line>And my heart with buds of pain.</line>
</stanza>
<stanza>
<line>My heart all Winter lay so numb,</line>
<line>The earth so dead and frore,</line>
. . .
```

Stylesheet

The stylesheet is `split.xsl`.

We want to start a new output document for each stanza, so we use the **`<xsl:document>`** instruction in the template rule for the `<stanza>` element. Its effect is to switch all output produced by its template body to a different output file. In fact, it's very similar to the effect of an **`<xsl:variable>`** element that creates a tree, except that the tree, instead of being a temporary tree, is serialized directly to an output file of its own.

```
<?xml version="1.0"?>
<xsl:stylesheet xmlns:xsl="http://www.w3.org/1999/XSL/Transform"
                version="1.1">

<xsl:template match="poem">
   <poem>
      <xsl:copy-of select="title"/>
      <xsl:copy-of select="author"/>
      <xsl:copy-of select="date"/>
      <xsl:apply-templates select="stanza"/>
   </poem>
</xsl:template>

<xsl:template match="stanza">
   <xsl:variable name="file" select="concat('verse', position(),
'.xml')"/>
   <verse number="{position()}" href="{$file}"/>
   <xsl:document href="{$file}">
        <xsl:copy-of select="."/>
   </xsl:document>
</xsl:template>
</xsl:stylesheet>
```

Output

The principal output file contains the skeletal poem below (new lines added for legibility):

```
<?xml version="1.0" encoding="utf-8" ?>
<poem>
<title>Song</title>
<author>Rupert Brooke</author>
<date>1912</date>
<verse number="1" href="verse1.xml"/>
<verse number="2" href="verse2.xml"/>
<verse number="3" href="verse3.xml"/>
</poem>
```

Three further output files `verse1.xml`, `verse2.xml`, and `verse3.xml` are created in the same directory as the principal output file. Here is `verse1.xml`:

```
<?xml version="1.0" encoding="utf-8" ?>
<stanza>
<line>And suddenly the wind comes soft,</line>
<line>And Spring is here again;</line>
<line>And the hawthorn quickens with buds of green</line>
<line>And my heart with buds of pain.</line>
</stanza>
```

For another version of this example, which uses the **`element-available()`** function to test whether the **`<xsl:document>`** instruction is implemented and takes fallback action if not, see the entry for **`element-available()`** on page 476 in Chapter 7.

See Also

`<xsl:output>` on page 270

xsl:element

The **`<xsl:element>`** instruction is used to output an element node to the current output destination.

It provides an alternative to using a literal result element, and is useful especially when the element name or namespace are to be calculated at run-time.

Defined in

XSLT section 7.1.2

Format

```
<xsl:element name={QName} namespace={uri}
   use-attribute-sets=list-of-QNames  >
      template body
</xsl:element>
```

Position

`<xsl:element>` is used as an instruction within a template body.

Attributes

Name	Value	Meaning
name mandatory	Attribute value template returning a QName	The name of the element to be generated
namespace optional	Attribute value template returning a URI	The namespace URI of the generated element
use-attribute-sets optional	Whitespace-separated list of QNames	List of named attribute sets containing attributes to be added to this output element

Content

A template body.

Effect

The name of the generated element node is determined using the **name** and **namespace** attributes.

Attributes may be added to the element node either by using the **use-attribute-sets** attribute, or by writing attribute nodes to the output destination using **<xsl:attribute>** or **<xsl:copy>** or **<xsl:copy-of>**: this must be done before anything else is written to the output destination. Any attributes written using **<xsl:attribute>** or **<xsl:copy>** or **<xsl:copy-of>** will overwrite attributes of the same name written using the **use-attribute-sets** attribute.

The child nodes of the element are produced by instantiating the contained template body.

The XSLT specification is written in terms of writing nodes to a result tree. Sometimes it is convenient to think in terms of the start tag of the **<xsl:element>** element producing a start tag in the output XML file and the end tag of the **<xsl:element>** element producing the corresponding end tag, with the intervening template body producing the contents of the output element. However, it is dangerous to extend this analogy too far, because writing the start tag and end tag are not separate operations that can be individually controlled, they are simply two things that happen together as a consequence of the **<xsl:element>** instruction being instantiated. This is explained in more detail in the section on *Literal Result Elements* in Chapter 3, page 118.

Both the **name** and the **namespace** attributes may be given as attribute value templates; that is, they may contain expressions nested within curly braces.

Element Name

The name of the new element is obtained by expanding the **name** attribute. The result of expanding the attribute value template must be a `QName`; that is, a valid XML name with an optional namespace prefix. For example, «`table`» or «`fo:block`». If there is a prefix, it must correspond to a namespace declaration that is in scope at this point in the stylesheet, unless there is also a **namespace** attribute, in which case it is taken as referring to that namespace.

If the name is not a valid `QName`, the XSLT processor is required either to report the error, or to leave this element node out of the generated tree, while still including its children. Different processors may thus handle this error differently.

The local part of the name of the output element will always be the same as the local part of the `QName` supplied as the value of the **name** attribute.

Element Namespace

As explained in Chapter 2, the result tree will always conform to the XML Namespaces specification. Sometimes, of course, you can generate all the output elements in the default namespace, but as namespaces become more widely used you may need to define the namespace URI of the generated element name.

If the **<xsl:element>** instruction has a **namespace** attribute, it is evaluated (expanding the attribute value template if necessary):

- If the value is an empty string, the element will have a null namespace URI.
- Otherwise, the value should be a URI identifying a namespace. This namespace does **not** need to be in scope at this point in the stylesheet, in fact it usually won't be. The system does not check that the value conforms to any particular URI syntax, so in effect any string can be used. The XSLT processor will output any necessary namespace nodes to ensure that the element name is associated with this namespace URI in the result tree.
- The prefix of the name of the output element will normally be the same as the prefix of the supplied `QName`, but the XSLT processor is allowed to allocate a different prefix if it chooses, so long as it is associated with the correct URI. This might happen, for example, if there are several different prefixes associated with the same namespace URI.

If there is no **namespace** attribute:

- If the supplied `QName` includes a prefix, the prefix must be a namespace prefix that is in scope at this point in the stylesheet: in other words, there must be an **xmlns:prefix** attribute either on the **<xsl:element>** instruction itself or on some containing element. The namespace URI in the output will be that of the namespace associated with this prefix in the stylesheet.
- Otherwise, the default namespace is used. This is the namespace declared, in some containing element in the stylesheet, with an «`xmlns="uri"`» declaration. Note that this is one of the few places in XSLT where the default namespace is used to expand a `QName` having no prefix; in nearly all other cases, a null namespace URI is used. The reason is to ensure that the behavior is consistent with that of an element name used in the start tag of a literal result element.

The generated element node will automatically contain all the namespace nodes it needs to define the prefixes used on its own name and on the names of all its attributes, as well as copies of namespace nodes written to the element's ancestors in the result tree. These nodes will only be visible directly if the current output destination is a temporary tree that you then explore using XPath expressions such as `<xsl:for-each select="namespace::*">`. When the output destination is serialized to a file, the importance of the namespace nodes is that they determine the namespace declarations that will appear in the XML output.

Generating Attributes

If the **`use-attribute-sets`** attribute is present it must be a whitespace-separated list of `QNames` that identify named **`<xsl:attribute-set>`** elements in the stylesheet. The attributes within these named attribute sets are instantiated in the order they appear, and are added to the new element node. If two attributes with the same name are added during this process, the last one added overwrites any earlier ones.

Subsequently, further attribute nodes may be added to the element using **`<xsl:attribute>`**. The **`<xsl:attribute>`** instruction will often be a child of the **`<xsl:element>`** instruction, but it does not need to be; it could be invoked, for example, by using **`<xsl:call-template>`**. Once a node other than an attribute node is added to the element (typically a text node or a child element node), no further attributes can be added.

> *The reason for this rule is to allow the implementation the flexibility to generate the output as an XML file, without having to build the result tree in memory first. If attributes could be added at any time, the whole result tree would need to be kept in memory.*

Again, if any attribute is added with the same name as an attribute already present on the element node, the new value takes precedence.

Element Content

The contents of the new element, that is, its child and descendant nodes, are the nodes produced by instantiating the template body contained in the **`<xsl:element>`** instruction.

Usage

In most cases, output elements can be generated either using literal result elements in the stylesheet, or by copying a node from the source document using **`<xsl:copy>`**.

The only situations where **`<xsl:element>`** is absolutely needed are therefore where the element type in the output file is not fixed, and is not the same as the element type in the source document.

Using **`<xsl:element>`** rather than a literal result element can also be useful where different namespaces are in use. It allows the namespace URI of the generated element to be specified explicitly, rather than being referenced via a prefix. This means the namespace does not have to be present in the stylesheet itself, thus giving greater control over exactly which elements the namespace declarations are attached to.

Example: Converting Attributes to Child Elements

Source

The source document `book.xml` contains a single **<book>** element with several attributes:

```
<?xml version="1.0"?>
<book title="Object-oriented Languages"
   author="Michel Beaudouin-Lafon"
   translator="Jack Howlett"
   publisher="Chapman &amp; Hall"
   isbn="0 412 55800 9"
   date="1994"/>
```

Stylesheet

The stylesheet `atts-to-elements.xsl` handles the book element by processing each of the attributes in turn (the expression «`@*`» selects all the attribute nodes). For each one, it outputs an element whose name is the same as the attribute name and whose content is the same as the attribute value.

The stylesheet is as follows:

```
<xsl:transform
 xmlns:xsl="http://www.w3.org/1999/XSL/Transform"
 version="1.0"
>
<xsl:output indent="yes"/>
<xsl:template match="book">
  <book>
     <xsl:for-each select="@*">
       <xsl:element name="{name()}">
       <xsl:value-of select="."/>
       </xsl:element>
     </xsl:for-each>
  </book>
</xsl:template>
</xsl:transform>
```

This selects all the attributes of the **<book>** element (using the expression «`@*`»), and for each one, it generates an element whose name is the same as the name of that attribute, and whose content is the value of that attribute.

Output

The XML output (from Saxon) is shown below. Actually, this stylesheet isn't guaranteed to produce exactly this output. This is because the order of attributes is undefined. This means that the **<xsl:for-each>** loop might process the attributes in any order, so the order of child elements in the output is also unpredictable.

4

XSLT Elements

```
<book>
   <author>Michel Beaudouin-Lafon</author>
   <date>1994</date>
   <isbn>0 412 55800 9</isbn>
   <publisher>Chapman &amp; Hall</publisher>
   <title>Object-oriented Languages</title>
   <translator>Jack Howlett</translator>
</book>
```

See also

<xsl:attribute> on page 166
<xsl:copy> on page 192
Literal Result Elements in Chapter 3, page 118

xsl:fallback

The **<xsl:fallback>** instruction is used to define processing that should occur if no implementation of its parent instruction is available.

Defined in

XSLT section 15

Format

```
<xsl:fallback>
   template body
</xsl:fallback>
```

Position

<xsl:fallback> is an instruction. It is always used within a template body.

Attributes

None.

Content

A template body.

Effect

There are two circumstances where **<xsl:fallback>** can be useful:

- In a stylesheet that uses XSLT features defined in a version later than 1.0, to indicate what should happen if the stylesheet is used with an XSLT processor that implements an earlier version of the standard (for example, version 1.0). For example, the draft XSLT 1.1 specification introduces one new instruction, **`<xsl:document>`**. If you want to use the **`<xsl:document>`** instruction in a stylesheet, and also want to specify what an XSLT 1.0 processor that doesn't understand this instruction should do, you can define the required behavior using **`<xsl:fallback>`**.
- In a stylesheet that uses extension elements provided by a vendor, by the user, or by a third party, to indicate what should happen if the stylesheet is used with an XSLT processor that does not support these extensions.

If the **`<xsl:fallback>`** instruction is encountered in a template body that the processor can instantiate normally, it is ignored, along with its contents.

An XSLT processor recognizes an element as an instruction if it occurs in a template body **and** it is:

- either in the XSLT namespace
- or in a namespace designated as an extension namespace by its inclusion in:
  - the **`extension-element-prefixes`** attribute of the **`<xsl:stylesheet>`** element
  - or the **`xsl:extension-element-prefixes`** attribute of the element itself, or of a containing literal result element or extension element

If an element recognized as an instruction is known to the XSLT processor, it is instantiated. The standard doesn't define exactly what "known to the XSLT processor" means. Typically it means that either the instruction is a vendor-specific extension implemented by that vendor, or it is a user-defined extension that has been installed or configured according to the instructions given by the vendor.

If an element is recognized as an instruction but is **not** known to the XSLT processor, the action taken by an XSLT 1.0 processor is as follows:

- For an element in the XSLT namespace, if the effective version is «`1.0`», an error is reported. If the effective version is anything other than «`1.0`», fallback processing is invoked.
- For an extension element, fallback processing is invoked.

For an XSLT 1.1 processor, unknown elements in the XSLT namespace are treated this way if the effective version is anything other than «`1.0`» or «`1.1`».

The effective version is the value of the **`xsl:version`** attribute on the nearest enclosing literal result element that has such an attribute, or the **`version`** attribute on the **`<xsl:stylesheet>`** element otherwise. The comparison is a string comparison not a numeric one, so you should write the version number strictly as «`1.0`» or «`1.1`», and not for example «`1`» or «`1.10`». The idea is that a stylesheet, or a portion of a stylesheet, that uses facilities defined in some future XSLT version, 2.1 (say), should be given an effective version of «`2.1`».

Fallback processing means that if the unknown instruction has an **<xsl:fallback>** child element, the **<xsl:fallback>** instruction is instantiated; otherwise, an error is reported. If there is more than one **<xsl:fallback>** instruction, they are all instantiated.

<xsl:fallback> is concerned only with fallback behavior for instructions within templates. Top-level elements that the implementation doesn't recognize are simply ignored. An unrecognized element in another context (for example, an unrecognized child of an **<xsl:choose>** or **<xsl:call-template>** instruction) is an error.

Note that both the **version** (or **xsl:version**) attribute and the **extension-element-prefixes** (or **xsl:extension-element-prefixes**) attribute apply only within the stylesheet module in which they occur: they do not apply to stylesheet modules incorporated using **<xsl:include>** or **<xsl:import>**.

Usage

The **<xsl:fallback>** mechanism allows a stylesheet to be written that behaves sensibly with XSLT processors that handle different versions of XSLT. This is motivated very much by the experience of web developers with HTML, and especially by the difficulty of writing web pages that work correctly on different browsers. Once XSLT support becomes widespread within browsers, you will need to think about how to ensure that your stylesheet runs correctly in any browser.

Similarly, it is very likely that each vendor of an XSLT processor (or each browser vendor) will add some bells and whistles of their own – indeed, this is already happening. For server-side stylesheet processing you might be prepared to use such proprietary extensions and thus lock yourself into the products of one vendor; but more likely, you want to keep your stylesheets portable. The **<xsl:fallback>** mechanism allows you to do this by defining within any proprietary extension element what the XSLT processor should do if it doesn't understand it. This might be, for example:

- do nothing, if the behavior is inessential, such as keeping statistics
- invoke an alternative implementation that achieves the same effect
- output fallback text to the user explaining that a particular facility cannot be offered and suggesting how they should upgrade

An alternative way of defining fallback behavior when facilities are not available is to use the **element-available()** function, and to avoid executing the relevant parts of a stylesheet. This function is described in Chapter 7, page 476. The two mechanisms are overlapping, so use whichever you find most convenient.

Examples

Example 1: XSLT Forwards Compatibility

The following example shows a stylesheet written to exploit a hypothetical new XSLT feature in version 6.1 of the standard that inserts a document identified by URI straight into the result tree (this is one of the features that appears in the list of possible enhancements published as an appendix to the XSLT 1.0 Recommendation). The stylesheet is written so that if this feature is not available, the same effect is achieved using existing facilities.

```
<xsl:template match="boilerplate">
   <div id="boilerplate" xsl:version="6.1">
      <xsl:copy-to-output href="boilerplate.xhtml">
         <xsl:fallback>
            <xsl:copy-of select="document('boilerplate.xhtml')"/>
         </xsl:fallback>
      </xsl:copy-to-output>
   </div>
</xsl:template>
```


Example 2: Vendor Portability

Writing a stylesheet that uses vendor extensions but is still portable is not particularly easy, but the mechanisms are there to achieve it, especially in the case where several vendors provide similar extensions but in slightly different ways.

For example, several XSLT 1.0 processors (certainly xt, Saxon, and Xalan) provide a feature to generate multiple output files from a single stylesheet. With XSLT 1.1 this popular facility has made it into the XSLT standard, but before that happened, each product had to invent its own syntax. If you want to write a stylesheet that uses the XSLT 1.1 facility when it is available, but with fallback implementations for these three products, you could do it like this:

```
<xsl:template match="preface">
<a href="preface.html" xsl:version="1.1"
      xmlns:saxon="http://icl.com/saxon"
      xmlns:xt="http://www.jclark.com/xt"
      xmlns:xalan="com.lotus.xsl.extensions.Redirect"
      xsl:extension-element-prefixes="saxon xt xalan">
  <xsl:document href="preface.html">
   <xsl:call-template name="write-preface"/>
   <xsl:fallback>
     <saxon:output file="preface.html">
        <xsl:call-template name="write-preface"/>
        <xsl:fallback/>
     </saxon:output>
     <xt:document href="preface.html">
        <xsl:call-template name="write-preface"/>
        <xsl:fallback/>
     </xt:document>
     <xalan:write file="preface.html">
        <xsl:call-template name="write-preface"/>
        <xsl:fallback/>
     </xalan:write>
   </xsl:fallback>
 </xsl:document>
Preface</a>
</xsl:template>
```

Hopefully this little nightmare will disappear once XSLT 1.1 is finalized and becomes widely implemented. However, by then the vendors, no doubt, will have thought of other good ideas to include as non-standard extensions.

Example 3: Temporary Trees

This example doesn't actually use **<xsl:fallback>**; it's an example of where the same effect needs to be achieved by different means.

One of the most important new features introduced in XSLT 1.1 is the ability to process a tree-valued variable as a node-set in its own right, using facilities such as XPath path expressions and `<xsl:for-each>`. The following code, which is perfectly legal in XSLT 1.1, will be flagged as an error by an XSLT 1.0 processor:

```
<xsl:variable name="us-states">
  <state abbr="AZ" name="Arizona"/>
  <state abbr="CA" name="California"/>
  <state abbr="NY" name="New York"/>
</xsl:variable>
. . .
<xsl:value-of select="$us-states/state[@abbr='CA']/@name"/>
```

The change to make this legal in XSLT 1.1 involves no new instructions, so it isn't possible to write an **<xsl:fallback>** template that defines what an XSLT 1.0 processor should do with this code: there's no suitable instruction to contain it. The only way of defining fallback behavior in this case is to test the XSLT version using the **system-property()** function. The following stylesheet will work with both XSLT 1.0 and XSLT 1.1. This accesses a lookup table defined as a global variable in the stylesheet. With a 1.1 processor, it accesses the variable containing the lookup table directly. With a 1.0 processor, it does it by using the **document('')** construct to read the stylesheet as a secondary input document.

```
<xsl:stylesheet version="1.1"
     xmlns:xsl="http://www.w3.org/1999/XSL/Transform">

<xsl:variable name="us-states">
  <state abbr="AZ" name="Arizona"/>
  <state abbr="CA" name="California"/>
  <state abbr="NY" name="New York"/>
</xsl:variable>

<xsl:param name="state" select="'AZ'"/>

<xsl:variable name="is-1.0" select="system-
property('xsl:version')=1.0"/>

<xsl:variable name="lookup-table-1.0"
  select="document('')/*/xsl:variable[@name='us-states']"/>

<xsl:template match="/">
  <xsl:choose>
    <xsl:when test="$is-1.0">
      <xsl:value-of select="$lookup-table-
1.0/state[@abbr=$state]/@name"/>
    </xsl:when>
    <xsl:otherwise>
      <xsl:value-of select="$us-states/state[@abbr=$state]/@name"/>
    </xsl:otherwise>
  </xsl:choose>
</xsl:template>

</xsl:stylesheet>
```

I used «version="1.1"» on the <xsl:stylesheet> element here, but in fact «version="1.0"» works just as well, because there is nothing in the forwards compatibility rules that relates to this situation, where the syntax is legal at both versions but the run-time behavior is an error with version 1.0. In theory, an XSLT 1.0 processor could legitimately reject the above stylesheet at compile time, regardless whether it specifies «version="1.0"» or «version="1.1"», but fortunately the XSLT 1.0 processors that I've tried it on accept it without quibble.

In this example I used the standard **document()** function to provide fallback processing that works with all XSLT 1.0 processors. In more complex examples, the fallback processing might need to use vendor extensions such as Microsoft's **msxml:node-set()** extension function. In this situation different fallback mechanisms would be needed for different processors.

See also

Extensibility in Chapter 3, page 130
Literal Result Elements in Chapter 3, page 111814
element-available() function in Chapter 7, page 476
system-property() function in Chapter 7, page 557

xsl:for-each

The **<xsl:for-each>** instruction selects a set of nodes using an XPath expression, and performs the same processing for each node in the set.

Defined in

XSLT section 8

Format

```
<xsl:for-each select=Expression>
   <xsl:sort> *
   template body
</xsl:for-each>
```

Position

<xsl:for-each> is an instruction, it is always used within a template body.

Attributes

Name	Value	Meaning
select mandatory	Expression returning a node-set	The set of nodes to be processed

Content

Zero or more **<xsl:sort>** elements, followed by a template body.

Effect

The effect of the **<xsl:for-each>** instruction is to instantiate the template body that it contains once for each node in the selected node-set. The following sections describe how this is done.

The select Attribute

The **select** attribute is mandatory. The `Expression` defines the nodes that will be processed. This may be any XPath expression, as defined in Chapter 5, so long as it returns a node-set. The expression may select nodes relative to the current node (the node currently being processed) or it may make an absolute selection from the root node, or it may simply select the nodes by reference to a variable initialized earlier. By referencing a tree-valued variable, or by using the **document()** function (described in Chapter 7, page 466) it may also select the root node of another XML document.

The template body contained within the **<xsl:for-each>** element is instantiated once for each node selected. Within this template body, the current node is the node being processed (one of the selected nodes); the **position()** function gives the position of that node in order of processing (the first node processed has `position()=1`, and so on), and the **last()** function gives the number of nodes being processed.

A common mistake is to forget that **<xsl:for-each>** changes the current node. For example, the following code will probably produce no output:

```
<xsl:for-each select="para">
  <p><xsl:value-of select="para"/></p>
</xsl:for-each>
```

Why? Because within the **<xsl:for-each>** element, the current node is a `<para>` element, so the **<xsl:value-of>** instruction is trying to display another `<para>` element that is a child of the first one. What the author probably intended was:

```
<xsl:for-each select="para">
  <p><xsl:value-of select="."/></p>
</xsl:for-each>
```

Sorting

If there are no child **<xsl:sort>** elements, the selected nodes are processed in *document order*. In the normal case where the nodes all come from the same input document this means they will be processed in the order they are encountered in the original source document: for example, an element node is processed before its children. Attribute nodes belonging to the same element, however, may be processed in any order. If there are nodes from several different documents in the list, the relative order of nodes from different documents is not defined (and may therefore differ from one product to another).

If there are one or more **<xsl:sort>** elements as children of the **<xsl:for-each>** instruction, the nodes are sorted before processing. Each **<xsl:sort>** element defines one sort key. For details of how sorting is controlled, see **<xsl:sort>** on page 296. If there are several sort keys defined, they apply in major-to-minor order. For example if the first **<xsl:sort>** defines sorting by Country and the second by State, then the nodes will be processed in order of State within Country. If two selected nodes have equal sort keys, they will be processed in document order.

Note that the direction of the axis used to select the nodes is irrelevant (the various axes, and the way they are ordered, are described in Chapter 5). For example, «`select="preceding-sibling::*"`» will process the preceding siblings of the current node in document order (starting with the first sibling) even though the preceding-sibling axis is in reverse document order. The axis direction affects only the meaning of any positional qualifiers used within the select expression. So «`preceding-sibling::*[1]`» will select the first preceding sibling element in axis order – that is, the element immediately before the current node, if there is one.

If you want to process the nodes in reverse document order, specify:

```
<xsl:sort select="position()" order="descending" data-type="number">
```

Usage and Examples

The main purpose of **<xsl:for-each>** is to iterate over a set of nodes. It can also be used, however, simply to change the current node. These two styles of use are illustrated in the following sections.

Iterating over a Set of Nodes

The principal use of **<xsl:for-each>** is to iterate over a set of nodes. As such it provides an alternative to **<xsl:apply-templates>**. Which you use is largely a matter of personal style, arguably **<xsl:apply-templates>** (*push* processing) ties the stylesheet less strongly to the detailed structure of the source document and makes it easier to write a stylesheet that can accommodate some flexibility in the structures that will be encountered, while **<xsl:for-each>** (*pull* processing) makes the logic clearer to the reader. It may even improve performance because it bypasses the need to identify template rules by pattern matching, though the effect is likely to be very small.

The following example processes all the attributes of the current element node, writing them out as elements to the result tree. This example is presented in greater detail under **<xsl:element>** on page 209.

```
<xsl:template match="book">
   <book>
      <xsl:for-each select="@*">
         <xsl:element name="{name()}">
            <xsl:value-of select="."/>
         </xsl:element>
      </xsl:for-each>
   </book>
</xsl:template>
```

The next example is a general one that can be applied to any XML document.

Example: Showing the Ancestors of a Node

The following example stylesheet can be applied to any XML document. For each element it processes all its ancestor elements, in reverse document order (that is, starting with the parent node and ending with the document element), and outputs their names to a comment that shows the position of the current node.

Source

This stylesheet can be applied to any source document.

Stylesheet

This stylesheet is in file `nesting.xsl`.

```
<xsl:transform
 xmlns:xsl="http://www.w3.org/1999/XSL/Transform"
 version="1.0"
>
<xsl:template match="*">
   <xsl:comment>
      <xsl:value-of select="name()"/>
      <xsl:for-each select="ancestor::*">
         <xsl:sort select="position()" order="descending"
                   data-type="number"/>
         <xsl:text> within </xsl:text>
         <xsl:value-of select="name()"/>
      </xsl:for-each>
   </xsl:comment>
   <xsl:apply-templates/>
</xsl:template>

</xsl:transform>
```

Output

An example of the output this might produce is:

```
<!--BOOKS within BOOKLIST-->
   <!--ITEM within BOOKS within BOOKLIST-->
   <!--TITLE within ITEM within BOOKS within BOOKLIST-->Number, the
                                                Language of Science
   <!--AUTHOR within ITEM within BOOKS within BOOKLIST-->Danzig
   <!--PRICE within ITEM within BOOKS within BOOKLIST-->5.95
   <!--QUANTITY within ITEM within BOOKS within BOOKLIST-->3
```

Changing the Current Node

Another use of **`<xsl:for-each>`** is simply to change the current node. For example, if you want to use the **`key()`** function (described in Chapter 7, page 499) to locate nodes in some ancillary document, you must first establish some node in that document (typically the root) as the current node, because the **`key()`** function will only find nodes in the same document as the current node.

For example, you might write:

```
<xsl:variable name="county">
   <xsl:for-each select="document('county-code.xml')">
      <xsl:value-of select="key('county-code', $code)/@name"/>
   </xsl:for-each>
</xsl:variable>
```

The effect is to assign to the variable the value of the **name** attribute of the first element whose county-code key matches the value of the `$code` variable.

The **<xsl:for-each>** statement here selects a single node, because the **document()** function when used like this will return at most one node. We don't even use the node that it returns; the only effect is to make this the current node, which affects the result of the **key()** function.

In a stylesheet that handles multiple input documents, it is always a good idea to declare a global variable:

```
<xsl:variable name="root" select="/"/>
```

Then you can always return to the original source document by writing:

```
<xsl:for-each select="$root">
   . . .
</xsl:for-each>
```

See also

<xsl:apply-templates> on page 155
<xsl:sort> on page 296
document() function in Chapter 7, page 466
key() function in Chapter 7, page 499

xsl:if

The **<xsl:if>** instruction encloses a template body that will be instantiated only if a specified condition is true.

<xsl:if> is analogous to the *if* statement found in many programming languages.

Defined in

XSLT section 9.1

Format

```
<xsl:if test=Expression >
   template body
</xsl:if>
```

Position

<xsl:if> is an instruction. It is always used within a template body.

Attributes

Name	Value	Meaning
test mandatory	Expression	The Boolean condition to be tested

Content

A template body.

Effect

The **test** expression is evaluated and the result is converted if necessary to a Boolean using the rules defined for the **boolean()** function. If the result is true, the contained template body is instantiated; otherwise, no action is taken.

Any XPath value may be converted to a Boolean. In brief, the rules are:

- if the expression is a node-set, it is treated as true if the node-set contains at least one node. (This means that a reference to a temporary tree is always treated as true.)
- if the expression is a string, it is treated as true if the string is not empty.
- if the expression is a number, it is treated as true if the number is non-zero.

Usage

The **<xsl:if>** instruction is useful where an action is to be performed conditionally. It performs the functions of the `if-then` construct found in other programming languages. If there are two or more alternative actions (the equivalent of an `if-then-else` or `switch` or `Select Case` in other languages), use **<xsl:choose>** instead.

One common use of **<xsl:if>** is to test for error conditions. In this case it is often used with **<xsl:message>**.

Try to avoid using **<xsl:if>** immediately within **<xsl:for-each>**. It's better to use a predicate instead, because that gives the processor more scope for optimization. For example:

```
<xsl:for-each select="para">
  <xsl:if test="@display='yes'">
   <p><xsl:apply-templates/></p>
  </xsl:if>
</xsl:for-each>
```

can be rewritten as:

```
<xsl:for-each select="para[@display='yes']">
   <p><xsl:apply-templates/></p>
</xsl:for-each>
```

Examples

The following example outputs an **<hr>** element after processing the last of a sequence of **<para>** elements:

```
<xsl:template match="para">
   <p><xsl:apply-templates/></p>
   <xsl:if test="position()=last()">
      <hr/>
   </xsl:if>
</xsl:template>
```

The following example reports an error if the **percent** attribute of the current element is not a number between 0 and 100. The expression returns true if:

- the **percent** attribute does not exist, or
- the value cannot be interpreted as a number (so that «number(@percent)» is NaN), or
- the numeric value is less than zero, or
- the numeric value is greater than 100

```
<xsl:if test="not(@percent) or
                        (string(number(@percent))='NaN') or
                        (number(@percent) &lt; 0) or
                        (number(@percent) &gt; 100)">
   <xsl:message>
      percent attribute must be a number between 0 and 100
   </xsl:message>
</xsl:if>
```

The following example formats a list of names, using **<xsl:if>** to produce punctuation that depends on the position of each name in the list.

Example: Formatting a List of Names

Source

The source file authors.xml contains a single **<book>** element with a list of authors.

```
<?xml version="1.0"?>
<book>
     <title>Design Patterns</title>
     <author>Erich Gamma</author>
     <author>Richard Helm</author>
     <author>Ralph Johnson</author>
     <author>John Vlissides</author>
</book>
```

Stylesheet

The stylesheet `authors.xsl` processes the list of authors, adding punctuation depending on the position of each author in the list.

```
<xsl:transform
 xmlns:xsl="http://www.w3.org/1999/XSL/Transform"
 version="1.0"
>

<xsl:template match="book">
   <xsl:value-of select="title"/>
   by <xsl:for-each select="author">
      <xsl:value-of select="."/>
      <xsl:if test="position()!=last()">, </xsl:if>
      <xsl:if test="position()=last()-1">and </xsl:if>
</xsl:for-each>
</xsl:template>

</xsl:transform>
```

Output

```
Design Patterns
by Erich Gamma, Richard Helm, Ralph Johnson, and John Vlissides
```

See also

<xsl:choose> on page 188

xsl:import

<xsl:import> is a top-level element used to import the contents of one stylesheet module into another. The definitions in the importing stylesheet module have a higher *import precedence* than those in the imported module, which usually means that they will be used in preference, but the detailed rules vary for each top-level element type.

Defined in

XSLT section 2.6.2

Format

```
<xsl:import href=uri />
```

Position

<xsl:import> is a top-level element, which means that it must appear as a child of the **<xsl:stylesheet>** element. Within an **<xsl:stylesheet>** element, the **<xsl:import>** child elements must come before any other children.

Attributes

Name	Value	Meaning
href mandatory	URI	The URI of the stylesheet to be imported

Content

None; the element is always empty.

Effect

The URI contained in the **href** attribute may be an absolute URI or a relative URI. If relative, it is interpreted relative to the base URI of the XML document or external entity containing the **<xsl:import>** element. For example, if a file `main.xsl` contains the element `<xsl:import href="date.xsl"/>` then the system will by default look for `date.xsl` in the same directory as `main.xsl`. With XSLT 1.1 you can change this behavior by using the **xml:base** attribute, as described in Chapter 2 on page 62. This allows you to specify a different base URI for resolving the relative URI.

The URI must identify an XML document that is a valid XSLT stylesheet module. The top-level elements of this stylesheet are logically inserted into the importing stylesheet at the point where the **<xsl:import>** element appears. However:

- Imported top-level elements have lower import precedence than the top-level elements defined directly in the importing stylesheet, or incorporated into it using **<xsl:include>**. This is explained in more detail below.
- Imported elements retain their base URI, so anything that involves referencing a relative URI is done relative to the original URI of the imported stylesheet. This includes, for example, expansion of further **<xsl:import>** elements, or use of URIs as arguments to the **document()** function.
- When a namespace prefix is used (typically within a `QName`, but it also applies to freestanding prefixes such as those in the **xsl:exclude-result-prefixes** attribute of a literal result element) it is interpreted using only the namespace declarations in the original stylesheet module in which the `QName` occurred. An imported stylesheet module does not inherit namespace declarations from the module that imports it. This includes `QNames` constructed at execution time as the result of evaluating an expression, for example an expression used within an attribute value template for the **name** or **namespace** attribute of **<xsl:element>**.
- The values of the **version**, **extension-element-prefixes**, and **exclude-result-prefixes** attributes that apply to an element in the imported stylesheet, as well as **xml:lang** and **xml:space**, are those that were defined in the **<xsl:stylesheet>** element of their own stylesheet module, not those on the **<xsl:stylesheet>** element of the importing module.

The imported stylesheet module may use the simplified stylesheet (*literal-result-element-as-stylesheet)* syntax described in Chapter 3. This allows an entire module to be defined as the content of an element such as **<HTML>**. It is then treated as if it were a stylesheet module containing a single template, whose match pattern is «/» and whose content is the literal result element.

The imported stylesheet module may contain `<xsl:include>` statements to include further stylesheet modules, or `<xsl:import>` statements to import them. A stylesheet module must not directly or indirectly import itself.

It is not an error to import the same stylesheet module more than once, either directly or indirectly, but it is not usually a useful thing to do. The effect is that the same definitions or templates will be present with several different import precedences. The situation is exactly the same as if two stylesheet modules with different names but identical contents had been imported.

Import Precedence

Each stylesheet module that is imported has an import precedence. The rules are:

- The precedence of a module that is imported is always lower than the precedence of the module importing it
- If one module imports several others, then the one it imports first has lower precedence than the next, and so on

This means that in the structure shown here, the highest precedence module is A; after that C, then F, then B, then E and finally D.

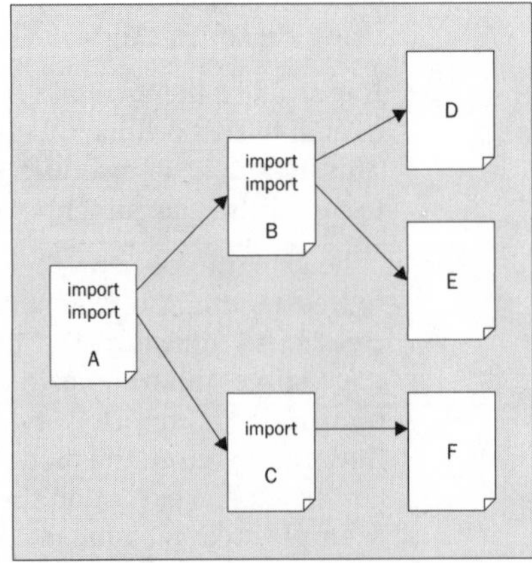

If one stylesheet module incorporates another using `<xsl:include>` rather than `<xsl:import>`, then it has the same import precedence as the module that includes it. This is shown in this diagram.

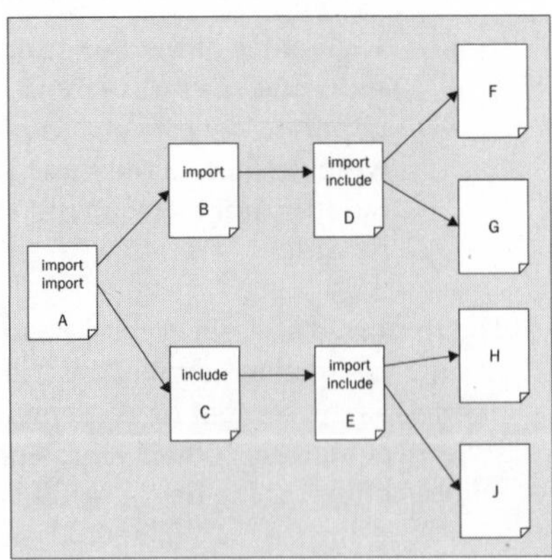

Here J is included in E, so it has the same import precedence as E, and similarly E has the same import precedence as C. If we attach numeric values to the import precedence to indicate the ordering (the absolute values don't matter, the only significance is that a higher number indicates higher precedence) we could do so as follows:

A	B	C	D	E	F	G	H	J
6	3	5	2	5	1	2	4	5

The import precedence of a stylesheet module applies to all the top-level elements in that module, so for example the **<xsl:template>** elements in module E have a higher import precedence than those in G.

As **<xsl:import>** statements must occur before any other top-level elements in a stylesheet module, the effect of these rules is that if each **<xsl:import>** statement were to be replaced by the content of the module it imports, the top-level elements in the resulting combined stylesheet would be in increasing order of import precedence. This makes life rather easier for implementors. However, it does not mean that **<xsl:import>** is a straightforward textual substitution process, because there is still a need to distinguish cases where two objects (for example template rules) have the same import precedence because they came originally from the same stylesheet or from stylesheets that were included rather than imported.

Effect of Import Precedence

The import precedence of a top-level element affects its standing relative to other top-level elements of the same type, and may be used to resolve conflicts. The effect is as shown in the table below for each kind of top-level element.

Element type	Rules
`<xsl:attribute-set>`	If there are two attribute sets with the same expanded name, they are merged. If there is an attribute that is present in both, then the one from the attribute set with higher import precedence wins. It is an error if there is no clear winner from this process (that is, if there are two or more values for an attribute that have the same precedence, and this is the highest precedence). The XSLT processor has the choice of reporting the error or choosing the one that was specified last.

Element type	Rules
<xsl:decimal-format>	The import precedence of an **<xsl:decimal-format>** element is of no significance. It is an error to include more than one **<xsl:decimal-format>** element with the same name (or with no name) unless the definitions are equivalent. On this occasion the XSLT processor is required to report the error.
<xsl:import> and <xsl:include>	No conflicts arise; the import precedence of these elements is immaterial, except in determining the import precedence of the referenced stylesheet module.
<xsl:key>	All the key definitions are used, regardless of their import precedence. See **<xsl:key>** on page 241 for details.
<xsl:namespace-alias>	If several aliases for the same stylesheet prefix are defined, the one with the highest import precedence is used. It is an error if there is no clear winner. The XSLT processor has the choice of reporting the error or choosing the one that was specified last.
<xsl:output>	All the **<xsl:output>** elements in the stylesheet are effectively merged. In the case of the **cdata-section-elements** attribute, an element is output in CDATA format if it is declared as such on any of the **<xsl:output>** elements. For all the other attributes, if the value is explicitly present on more than one **<xsl:output>** element then the one with highest import precedence wins. It is an error if there is no clear winner. The XSLT processor has the choice of reporting the error or choosing the one that was specified last.
<xsl:strip-space> and <xsl:preserve-space>	If there is more than one **<xsl:strip-space>** or **<xsl:preserve-space>** element that matches a particular element name in the source document, then the one with highest import precedence is used. If this still leaves several that match, each one is assigned a priority, using the same rules as for the **match** pattern in **<xsl:template>**. Specifically, an explicit `QName` has higher priority than the form «`prefix:*`», which in turn has higher priority than «`*`». The one with highest priority is then used.

Element type	Rules
`<xsl:strip-space>` and `<xsl:preserve-space>` (continued)	It is an error if this leaves more than one match (even if they all give the same answer). The XSLT processor has the choice of reporting the error or choosing the one that was specified last. If there are no matches for an element, whitespace nodes are preserved.
`<xsl:template>`	When selecting a template rule for use with `<xsl:apply-templates>`, firstly all the template rules with a matching **mode** are taken. Of these, all those with a **match** pattern that matches the selected node are considered. If this leaves more than one, only those with the highest import precedence are considered. If this still leaves more than one, the one with highest priority is chosen: the rules for deciding the priority are given under `<xsl:template>` on page 312. It is an error if this still doesn't identify a clear winner. The XSLT processor has the choice of reporting the error or choosing the template rule that was specified last. (In practice, several processors output a warning message.) When selecting a template for use with `<xsl:call-template>`, all the named templates with a matching name are considered. If there are several, the one with highest import precedence is used. It is an error to have several named templates with the same name and the same import precedence; the XSLT processor is required to report this error, even if the templates are never referenced.
`<xsl:variable>` and `<xsl:param>`	In resolving a `VariableReference` in an expression or pattern, the XSLT processor first tries to find a matching local variable or parameter definition, that is, one defined in a template. If it can't find one that is in scope, it looks for a global variable or parameter – that is, a top-level `<xsl:variable>` or `<xsl:param>` element with the same expanded name as the `VariableReference`. This may occur anywhere in the stylesheet, either in the same module or in a different module, and there is no restriction on forward references. If there is more than one global variable or parameter that matches, the one with highest import precedence is used.

Element type	Rules
`<xsl:variable>` and `<xsl:param>` **(continued)**	It is an error to have more than one global variable or parameter in the stylesheet with the same expanded name and the same import precedence. This is true even if the variable is never referenced, or if it is masked by another variable of the same name with higher import precedence. The XSLT processor must report this error.

Usage

The rules for **<xsl:import>** are so pervasive that one would imagine the facility is central to the use of XSLT, rather in the way inheritance is central to writing in Java. In practice, many stylesheets never need to use **<xsl:import>**, but you will almost certainly need it once you start to develop a family of stylesheets to handle a wide range of source document types.

Like inheritance in object-oriented languages, **<xsl:import>** is designed to allow the creation of a library or reusable components, only in this case, the components are modules of stylesheets. And the mechanism works in a very similar way to inheritance. For example, you might have a stylesheet that simply defines your corporate color scheme, as a set of global variables defining color names. Another stylesheet might be defined to produce the basic framesets for your site, referring to these color names to supply the background detail. Now if you want to use this general structure but to vary some detail, for example to modify one of the colors because it clashes with an image you are displaying on a particular page, you can define a stylesheet for this particular page that does nothing apart from redefining that one color. This is illustrated in the diagram below.

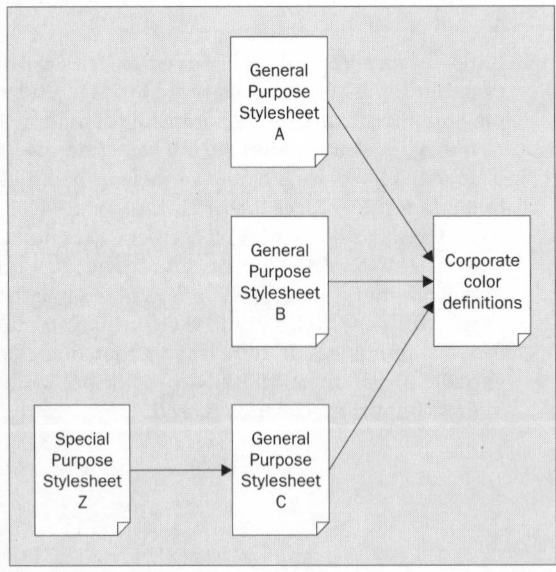

Suppose the stylesheet module for corporate color definitions looks like this:

```
<xsl:stylesheet xmlns:xsl="http://www.w3.org/1999/XSL/Transform"
    xmlns:color="http://acme.co.nz/colors"
       version="1.0">
<xsl:variable name="color:blue" select="'#0088ff'"/>
<xsl:variable name="color:pink" select="'#ff0088'"/>
<xsl:variable name="color:lilac" select="'#ff00ff'"/>
</xsl:stylesheet>
```


Now all the general-purpose stylesheets could **<xsl:include>** these definitions (no need to **<xsl:import>** them unless they are being modified). This makes it easier to maintain the corporate brand image, because things are defined in one place only.

However, there are cases where we want to depart from the general rule, and we can do so quite easily. If a particular document wants to use stylesheet C, but needs to vary the colors used, we can define stylesheet Z for it, as follows:

```
<xsl:stylesheet xmlns:xsl="http://www.w3.org/1999/XSL/Transform"
    xmlns:color="http://acme.co.nz/colors"
       version="1.0">
<xsl:import href="general-stylesheet-C.xsl"/>
<xsl:variable name="color:lilac" select="'#cc00cc'"/>
</xsl:stylesheet>
```

In fact, this might be the entire stylesheet (apart from the **<xsl:stylesheet>** element, of course). In common English, style Z is the same as style C but with a different shade of lilac. Note that all the references to variable «`color:lilac`» are interpreted as references to the definition in Z, even if the references occur in the same stylesheet module as a different definition of «`color:lilac`».

As a general principle, to incorporate standard content into a stylesheet without change, use **<xsl:include>**. If there are definitions you want to override, use **<xsl:import>.**

Examples

The first example is designed to show the effect of **<xsl:import>** on variables.

Example 1: Precedence of Variables

This example demonstrates the precedence of global variables when the principal stylesheet module and an imported module declare variables with the same name.

Source

This example can be run with any source XML file.

Stylesheet

The principal stylesheet module is `variables.xsl`.

```
<?xml version="1.0" encoding="iso-8859-1"?>
<xsl:stylesheet version="1.0"
    xmlns:xsl="http://www.w3.org/1999/XSL/Transform"
    xmlns:acme="http://acme.com/xslt"
    exclude-result-prefixes="acme">

<xsl:import href="boilerplate.xsl"/>
<xsl:output encoding="iso-8859-1" indent="yes"/>

<xsl:variable name="acme:company-name" select="'Acme Widgets
Limited'"/>

<xsl:template match="/">
<c><xsl:value-of select="$acme:copyright"/></c>
</xsl:template>

</xsl:stylesheet>
```

The imported stylesheet module is `boilerplate.xsl`.

```
<?xml version="1.0" encoding="iso-8859-1"?>
<xsl:stylesheet version="1.0"

xmlns:xsl="http://www.w3.org/1999/XSL/Transform"
                              xmlns:co="http://acme.com/xslt">

<xsl:variable name="co:company-name" select="'Acme Widgets
Incorporated'"/>

<xsl:variable name="co:copyright"
                              select="concat('Copyright © ', $co:company-
name)"/>

</xsl:stylesheet>
```

Output

The output of this stylesheet will be:

```
<?xml version="1.0" encoding="iso-8859-1" ?>
<c>Copyright © Acme Widgets Limited</c>
```

This is because in the variable declaration of «`$co:copyright`», the reference to variable «`$co:company-name`» matches the declaration of this variable in the principal stylesheet, because that has higher import precedence than the declaration in `boilerplate.xsl`.

The fact that different namespace prefixes are used in the two stylesheets is, of course, irrelevant: the prefix «`acme`» in the principal stylesheet maps to the same namespace URI as the prefix «`co`» in `boilerplate.xsl`, so the names are considered equivalent.

This example explicitly specifies `encoding="iso-8859-1"` for both the stylesheet modules and the output. Most of my examples only use ASCII characters, and since the default character encoding UTF-8 is a superset of ASCII, that works fine. This time, though, I've used the copyright symbol «©», which is not an ASCII character, so it's important to specify the character encoding that my text editor uses, which is iso-8859-1 (actually it's the Microsoft variant of it known as Windows ANSI, but that's close enough not to make a difference).

The second example shows the effect of **<xsl:import>** on template rules.

Example 2: Precedence of Template Rules

In this example I shall define a complete stylesheet `standard-style.xsl` to display poems in HTML, and then override one of its rules in an importing stylesheet. The files required are all in the subdirectory `import` in the download file for this chapter.

Source

This example works with the poem that we used in Chapter 1. In the download file it's available as `poem.xml`. It starts like this:

```
<?xml version="1.0"?>
<poem>
<author>Rupert Brooke</author>
<date>1912</date>
<title>Song</title>
<stanza>
<line>And suddenly the wind comes soft,</line>
<line>And Spring is here again;</line>
<line>And the hawthorn quickens with buds of green</line>
<line>And my heart with buds of pain.</line>
</stanza>
etc.
</poem>
```

Stylesheet A

Here is `standard-style.xsl`:

```
<xsl:stylesheet version="1.0"

xmlns:xsl="http://www.w3.org/1999/XSL/Transform">

<xsl:template match="/">
   <html>
   <head>
   <title><xsl:value-of select="//title"/></title>
   </head>
   <body>
```

```
         <xsl:apply-templates/>
      </body>
      </html>
   </xsl:template>

   <xsl:template match="title">
      <h1><xsl:apply-templates/></h1>
   </xsl:template>

   <xsl:template match="author">
      <div align="right"><i>by </i>
         <xsl:apply-templates/>
      </div>
   </xsl:template>

   <xsl:template match="stanza">
      <p><xsl:apply-templates/></p>
   </xsl:template>

   <xsl:template match="line">
      <xsl:apply-templates/><br/>
   </xsl:template>

   <xsl:template match="date"/>
   </xsl:stylesheet>
```

Output A

When you run this stylesheet, the output starts like this (the actual layout may vary, of course, depending on which XSLT processor you use):

```
<html>
   <head>
   <title>Song</title>
   </head>
   <body>
      <div align="right"><i>by </i>Rupert Brooke</div>
      <h1>Song</h1>
      <p>
         And suddenly the wind comes soft,<br>
         And Spring is here again;<br>
         And the hawthorn quickens with buds of green<br>
         And my heart with buds of pain.<br>
      </p>
```

Stylesheet B

Now we want to create a variant of this in which the lines of the poem are numbered. This will act as the principal style sheet when we want this form of output. Here it is in `numbered-style.xsl`:

```
<xsl:stylesheet version="1.0"

xmlns:xsl="http://www.w3.org/1999/XSL/Transform">

<xsl:import href="standard-style.xsl"/>

<xsl:template match="line">
   <xsl:number level="any" format="001"/>  
   <xsl:apply-imports/>
</xsl:template>

</xsl:stylesheet>
```

Note the use of the character reference «` `» to output a non-breaking space. In HTML this is normally done by writing «` `». You can use this entity reference in the stylesheet if you like (it's simply a symbolic name for the Unicode character `#xa0`), but only if you declare it as an entity in the DTD. It's usually simpler just to use the numeric character reference.

Output B

This time the output starts like this. Again, the precise format depends on the processor (for example, some processors may output «` `»; or «` `» instead of «` `») but it should look the same when displayed in the browser.

```
<html>
   <head>
   <title>Song</title>
   </head>
   <body>
      <div align="right"><i>by </i>Rupert Brooke</div>
      <h1>Song</h1>
      <p>
         001  
         And suddenly the wind comes soft,<br>
         002  
         And Spring is here again;<br>
         003  
         And the hawthorn quickens with buds of green<br>
         004  
         And my heart with buds of pain.<br>
      </p>
```

All the template rules defined in `standard-style.xsl` are used as normal, except where the current node matches the pattern «`line`». In this situation there are two possible templates that match the node, so the one with higher import precedence is chosen. This is the one in the importing stylesheet module, namely `numbered-style.xsl`. As a result, the lines of the poem are output with a preceding line number, calculated using the **`<xsl:number>`** instruction, which is described on page 257. The use of **`<xsl:apply-imports>`** means that once the line number has been output, the line is then displayed in the normal way, using the template rule from the `standard-style.xsl` stylesheet.

See also

<xsl:include> in the section below
<xsl:apply-imports> on page 152

xsl:include

<xsl:include> is a top-level element used to include the contents of one stylesheet module within another. The definitions in the included stylesheet module have the same *import precedence* as those in the including module, so the effect is exactly as if these definitions were textually included at the point in the including module where the **<xsl:include>** element appears.

Defined in

XSLT section 2.6.1

Format

```
<xsl:include href=uri />
```

Position

<xsl:include> is a top-level element, which means that it must appear as a child of the **<xsl:stylesheet>** element. There are no constraints on its ordering relative to other top-level elements in the stylesheet.

Attributes

Name	Value	Meaning
href mandatory	URI	The URI of the stylesheet to be included

Content

None; the element is always empty.

Effect

The URI contained in the **href** attribute may be an absolute URI or a relative URI. If relative, it is interpreted relative to the the base URI of the XML document or external entity containing the **<xsl:include>** element. For example, if a file `main.xsl` contains the element `<xsl:include href="date.xsl"/>` then by default the system will look for `date.xsl` in the same directory as `main.xsl`. With XSLT 1.1 you can change this behavior by using the **xml:base** attribute to specify a base URI explicitly, as described in Chapter 2 on page 62.

The URI must identify an XML document that is a valid XSLT stylesheet. The top level elements of this stylesheet are logically inserted into the including stylesheet module at the point where the **<xsl:include>** element appears. However:

- These elements retain their base URI, so anything that involves referencing a relative URI is done relative to the original URI of the included stylesheet. This rule applies, for example, when expanding further **<xsl:include>** and **<xsl:import>** elements, or when using relative URIs as arguments to the **document()** function.
- When a namespace prefix is used (typically within a QName, but it also applies to freestanding prefixes such as those in the **xsl:exclude-result-prefixes** attribute of a literal result element) it is interpreted using only the namespace declarations in the original stylesheet module in which the QName occurred. An included stylesheet module does not inherit namespace declarations from the module that includes it. This even applies to QNames constructed at execution time as the result of evaluating an expression, for example an expression used within an attribute value template for the **name** or **namespace** attribute of **<xsl:element>**.
- The values of the **version**, **extension-element-prefixes**, and **exclude-result-prefixes** attributes that apply to an element in the included stylesheet module, as well as **xml:lang** and **xml:space**, are those that were defined on its own **<xsl:stylesheet>** element, not those on the **<xsl:stylesheet>** element of the including stylesheet module.
- An exception is made for **<xsl:import>** elements in the included stylesheet module. **<xsl:import>** elements must come before any other top-level elements, so instead of placing them in their natural sequence in the including module, they are promoted so they appear after any **<xsl:import>** elements, but before any other top-level elements, in the including stylesheet module. This is relevant to situations where there are duplicate definitions and the XSLT processor is allowed to choose the one that comes last.

The included stylesheet module may use the simplified (*literal-result-element-as-stylesheet*) stylesheet syntax, described in Chapter 3. This allows an entire stylesheet module to be defined as the content of an element such as **<HTML>**. It is then treated as if it were a module containing a single template, whose match pattern is «/» and whose content is the literal result element.

The included stylesheet module may contain **<xsl:include>** statements to include further stylesheets, or **<xsl:import>** statements to import them. A stylesheet must not directly or indirectly include itself.

It is not an error to include the same stylesheet module more than once, either directly or indirectly, but it is not a useful thing to do. It may well cause errors due to the presence of duplicate declarations, in fact if the stylesheet contains definitions of global variables or named templates, and is included more than once at the same import precedence, such errors are inevitable. In some other situations it is implementation-defined whether an XSLT processor will report duplicate declarations as an error, so the behavior may vary from one product to another.

Usage

<xsl:include> provides a simple textual inclusion facility analagous to the #include directive in C, it is purely a way of writing a stylesheet in a modular way so that commonly used definitions can be held in a library and used wherever they are needed.

If you are handling a wide range of different document types, the chances are they will have some elements in common, which are to be processed in the same way regardless of where they occur. For example, these might include standard definitions of toolbars, backgrounds, and navigation buttons to go on your web pages, as well as standard styles applied to data elements such as product names, e-mail contact addresses, or dates.

To incorporate such standard content into a stylesheet without change, use **<xsl:include>**. If there are definitions you want to override, use **<xsl:import>**.

<xsl:include> is a compile-time facility; it is used to assemble the complete stylesheet before you start executing it. People sometimes ask how to include other stylesheets conditionally at run-time, based on conditions found in the source document. The answer is simple: you can't. It would be like writing a program in Visual Basic that modifies itself as it executes. If you do want different sets of rules to be active at different times, consider using modes, or consider inverting the logic, so that instead of having an all-purpose stylesheet that tries to include different sets of rules on different occasions, you make your principal stylesheet module the one that is most closely tailored to the circumstances, and use **<xsl:import>** to import the all-purpose rules into it, at a lower import precedence than the specialized rules.

It can make a difference where in your stylesheet the **<xsl:include>** statement is placed. There are some kinds of objects – notably, template rules – where if there is no other way of deciding which one to use, the XSLT processor has the option of giving priority to the one that occurs last in the stylesheet. This isn't something you can easily take advantage of, because in all these cases the processor also has the option of reporting an error. As a general principle, it's probably best to place **<xsl:include>** statements near the beginning of the file, because then if there are any accidental overlaps in the definitions, the ones in your principal stylesheet will either override those included from elsewhere, or be reported as errors.

Examples

Example: Using <xsl:include> with Named Attribute Sets

Source

This example can be used with any source document.

Stylesheet

Consider a principal stylesheet `picture.xsl` that includes a stylesheet `attributes.xsl`, as follows:

Module `picture.xsl`:

```
<xsl:stylesheet version="1.0"

xmlns:xsl="http://www.w3.org/1999/XSL/Transform">

<xsl:include href="attributes.xsl"/>

<xsl:template match="/">
   <picture xsl:use-attribute-sets="picture-attributes">
      <xsl:attribute name="color">red</xsl:attribute>
   </picture>
```

```
</xsl:template>
</xsl:stylesheet>
```

Module attributes.xsl:

```
<xsl:stylesheet version="1.0"

xmlns:xsl="http://www.w3.org/1999/XSL/Transform">

<xsl:attribute-set name="picture-attributes">
   <xsl:attribute name="color">blue</xsl:attribute>
   <xsl:attribute name="transparency">100</xsl:attribute>
</xsl:attribute-set>

</xsl:stylesheet>
```

The named attribute set in the included stylesheet is used exactly as if it were defined in the principal stylesheet, at the point where the **<xsl:include>** statement appears.

Output

The resulting output is:

```
<picture transparency="100" color="red"/>
```

This is because attributes generated using **<xsl:attribute>** override those generated by using a named attribute set; it has nothing to do with the fact that the attribute set came from an included stylesheet.

See also

<xsl:import> on page 226

xsl:key

The **<xsl:key>** element is a top-level element used to declare a named key, for use with the **key()** function in expressions and patterns.

Defined in

XSLT section 12.2

Format

```
<xsl:key  name=QName  match=Pattern  use=Expression />
```

Position

<xsl:key> is a top-level element, which means that it must be a child of the **<xsl:stylesheet>** element. It may appear any number of times in a stylesheet.

Attributes

Name	Value	Meaning
name mandatory	`QName`	The name of the key
match mandatory	`Pattern`	Defines the nodes to which this key is applicable
use mandatory	`Expression`	The expression used to determine the value of the key for each of these nodes

The constructs `QName` and `Expression` are defined in Chapter 5, and `Pattern` is defined in Chapter 6.

Neither the `Pattern` in the **`match`** attribute, nor the `Expression` in the **`use`** attribute, may contain a `VariableReference`. This is to prevent circular definitions. Key definitions are effectively processed before global variable definitions, which means you can use keys when defining the value of a global variable, but you cannot use global variables when defining a key.

A further restriction to prevent circular definitions is that neither the **`match`** pattern nor the **`use`** expression can use the **`key()`** function.

Content

None, the element is always empty.

Effect

The **`name`** attribute specifies the name of the key. It must be a valid `QName`; if it contains a namespace prefix, the prefix must identify a namespace declaration that is in scope on the **`<xsl:key>`** element. The effective name of the key is the expanded name, consisting of the namespace URI and the local part of the name. Namespaces are described in Chapter 2, page 64.

The **`match`** attribute specifies the nodes to which the key applies. The value is a `Pattern`, as described in Chapter 6. If a node doesn't match the pattern, then it will have no values for the named key. If a node does match the pattern, then the node will have zero or more values for the named key, as determined by the **`use`** attribute.

The simplest case is where the key values are unique. For example, consider the following source document:

```
<vehicles>
<vehicle reg="P427AGH" owner="Joe Karloff"/>
<vehicle reg="T788PHT" owner="Prunella Higgs"/>
<vehicle reg="V932TXQ" owner="William D. Abikombo"/>
</vehicles>
```

In the stylesheet you can define a key for the registration number of these vehicles, as follows:

```
<xsl:key name="vehicle-registration" match="vehicle" use="@reg"/>
```


The **`use`** attribute specifies an expression used to determine the value or values of the key. This expression doesn't have to be an attribute, like «`@reg`» in the example above. For example, it could be a child element. If this is a repeating child element, you can create an index entry for each instance. The formal rules are as follows. For each node that matches the pattern, the expression is evaluated with that node as the current node, and with the current node list containing that node only, and then:

- If the result is a node-set, each node in the result contributes one value for the key. The value of the key is the string-value of that node.
- Otherwise, the result is converted to a string, and this string acts as the value of the key.

There is no rule that stops two nodes having the same key value. For example, declaring a key for vehicle registration numbers in the example above does not mean that each registration number must be different. So a node can have more than one key value, and a key value can refer to more than one node.

More formally, each named key can be considered as a set of node-value pairs. A node can be associated with multiple values and a value can be associated with multiple nodes. The value is always a string. A node-value pair (N, V) is added to the set if node N matches the pattern specified in the **`match`** attribute, and if the expression in the **`use`** attribute, when applied to node N, produces either a node-set containing a node whose string-value is V, or a value that is not a node-set and which, on conversion to a string, is equal to V. To complicate things a bit further, there can be more than one key definition in the stylesheet with the same name. The set of node-value pairs for the key is then the union of the sets produced by each key definition independently. The import precedence of the key definitions makes no difference.

A key can be used to select nodes in any document, not just the principal source document. The **`key()`** function always returns nodes that are in the same document as the context node at the time it is called. It is therefore best to think of there being one set of node-value pairs for each named key for each document.

The effect of calling `key(K, V)`, where `K` is a key name and `V` is a string value, is to locate the set of node-value pairs for the key named `K` and the context document, and to return a node-set containing the node from each pair where the value is `V`.

If you like to think in SQL terms, imagine a table `KEY-VALUES` with four columns, `KEY-NAME`, `DOCUMENT`, `NODE`, and `VALUE`. Then calling `key('K', 'V')` is equivalent to the SQL statement:

```
SELECT DISTINCT NODE FROM KEY-VALUES WHERE
   KEY-NAME='K' AND
   VALUE='V' AND
   DOCUMENT=current-document;
```

Usage and Examples

Declaring a key has two effects; it simplifies the code you need to write to find the nodes with given values, and it is likely to make access faster.

The performance effect, of course, depends entirely on the implementation. It would be quite legitimate for an implementation to conduct a full search of the document each time the **key()** function was called. In practice, however, most implementations are likely to build an index or hash table, so there will be a one-time cost in building the index (for each document), but after that, access to nodes whose key value is known should be very fast.

The **<xsl:key>** element is usually used to index elements, but in principle it can be used to index any kind of node except namespace nodes.

Using a Simple Key

The detailed rules for keys seem complicated, but most practical applications of keys are very simple. Consider the following key definition:

```
<xsl:key name="product-code" match="product" use="@code"/>
```

This defines a key whose name is «product-code», and which can be used to find **<product>** elements given the value of their **code** attribute. If a product has no **code** attribute, it won't be possible to find it using this key.

To find the product with code value «ABC-456», you can write, for example:

```
<xsl:apply-templates select="key('product-code', 'ABC-456')"/>
```

Note that you could just as well choose to index the attribute nodes:

```
<xsl:key name="product-code" match="product/@code" use="."/>
```

To find the relevant product you would then write:

```
<xsl:apply-templates select="key('product-code', 'ABC-456')/.."/>
```

I've used **<xsl:apply-templates>** here as an example. This will select all the **<product>** elements in the current document that have code «ABC-456» (I never said it had to be a unique identifier) and apply the matching template to each one in turn, processing them in document order, as usual. I could equally have used any other instruction that uses an XPath expression; for example, I could have assigned the node-set to a variable, or used it in an **<xsl:value-of>** element.

The second argument to the key function is normally a string. It won't usually be a literal, as in my example, but is more likely to be a string obtained from somewhere else in the source document, or perhaps supplied as a parameter to the stylesheet. It may well have been passed as one of the parameters in the URL used to select this stylesheet in the first place; for example, a web page might display a list of available products such as:

Select from the following list of products:
Baked Beans
Tomato Ketchup
Fish Fingers
Cornflakes

Behind each of these hyperlinks shown to the user might be a URL such as:

```
http://www.cheap-food.com/servlet/product?code=ABC-456
```

You then write a servlet (or an ASP page if you prefer) on your web server that extracts the query parameter code, and fires off your favorite XSLT processor specifying products.xml as the source document, show-product.xsl as the stylesheet, and «ABC-456» as the value to be supplied for the global stylesheet parameter called prod-code. Your stylesheet then would look like this:

```
<xsl:param name="prod-code"/>
<xsl:key name="product-code" match="product" use="@code"/>
<xsl:template match="/">
   <html>
   <body>
   <xsl:variable name="product"
                        select="key('product-code', $prod-code)"/>
   <xsl:if test="not($product)">
      <p>There is no product with this code</p>
   </xsl:if>
   <xsl:apply-templates select="$product"/>
   </body>
   </html>
</xsl:template>
```


Multi-valued Keys

A key can be multi-valued, in that a single node can have several values each of which can be used to find the node independently. For example, a book may have several authors, and each author's name can be used as a key value. This could be defined as follows:

```
<xsl:key name="book-author" match="book" use="author/name"/>
```

The **use** expression, «author/name», is a node-set expression, so the string value of each of its nodes (that is, the name of each author of the book) is used as one of the values in the set of node-value pairs that makes up the key.

In this particular example, as well as one book having several authors, each author may have written several books, so when we use an XPath expression such as:

```
<xsl:for-each select="key('book-author', 'Agatha Christie')">
```

we will be selecting all the books in which Agatha Christie was one of the authors. What if you want to find all the books in which Alex Homer and David Sussman are joint authors? There's no direct way of combining the results of two different keys, but there is an indirect way.

At least two products, Saxon and xt, support an extension function **intersection()**, allowing you to write the XPath expression:

```
prefix:intersection(
       key('book-author', 'Alex Homer'),
       key('book-author', 'David Sussman'))
```

However, this isn't in the standard. Instead, if you need to find the intersection of two keys, you can write the rather convoluted expression:

```
    <xsl:variable name="set1" select="key('book-author', 'Alex Homer')"/>
    <xsl:variable name="set2" select="key('book-author', 'David Sussman')"/>
    <xsl:variable name="result" select="$set1[ count(.|$set2) =
count($set2)]"/>
```

This works because «count(X|Y)» will only be the same as «count(Y)» if X is a subset of Y (recall that «|» is the set union operator); so the predicate filters the contents of $set1, selecting only those elements that are also in $set2.

You can supply a node-set as the second argument to the **key()** function. For example, you might write:

```
    <xsl:variable name="ac" select="key('book-author', 'Agatha Christie')">
    <xsl:for-each select="key('book-author', $ac/author/name)">
```

The result of the **select** expression in the **<xsl:for-each>** instruction is the set of all books in which one of the authors is either Agatha Christie or a co-author of Agatha Christie. This is because $ac is the set of all books of which Agatha Christie is an author, so «$ac/author/name» is the set of all authors of these books, and using this set of named authors as the value of the key produces the set of books in which **any** of them is an author. As we have already mentioned, there is no direct way of finding books in which they are **all** named as authors.

Example: Multi-valued Non-unique Keys

This example shows how a node can have several values for one key, and a given key value can identify more than one node. It uses author name as a key to locate **<book>** elements.

Source

The source file is booklist.xml:

```
<booklist>
<book>
    <title>Design Patterns</title>
    <author>Erich Gamma</author>
    <author>Richard Helm</author>
    <author>Ralph Johnson</author>
    <author>John Vlissides</author>
</book>
<book>
    <title>Pattern Hatching</title>
    <author>John Vlissides</author>
</book>
<book>
    <title>Building Applications Frameworks</title>
    <author>Mohamed Fayad</author>
    <author>Douglas C. Schmidt</author>
    <author>Ralph Johnson</author>
</book>
<book>
    <title>Implementing Applications Frameworks</title>
    <author>Mohamed Fayad</author>
    <author>Douglas C. Schmidt</author>
    <author>Ralph Johnson</author>
</book>
</booklist>
```

Stylesheet

The stylesheet is `author-key.xsl`.

It declares the key and then simply copies the **<book>** elements that match the author name supplied as a parameter. So you can call this stylesheet with a call such as:

```
saxon booklist.xml author-key.xsl author="Ralph Johnson"
```

Note that parameters containing spaces have to be written in quotes on the command line. The detailed syntax for each processor is different, see the relevant Appendices for details. For convenience in trying out this stylesheet, a default value has been supplied for the parameter.

```
<xsl:transform
 xmlns:xsl="http://www.w3.org/1999/XSL/Transform"
 version="1.0"
>

<xsl:key name="author-name" match="book" use="author"/>

<xsl:param name="author" select="'John Vlissides'"/>

<xsl:template match="/">
<xsl:copy-of select="key('author-name', $author)"/>
</xsl:template>

</xsl:transform>
```

Output

With the parameter set to its default value «`John Vlissides`», the output is as follows:

```
<?xml version="1.0" encoding="utf-8" ?>
<book>
    <title>Design Patterns</title>
    <author>Erich Gamma</author>
    <author>Richard Helm</author>
    <author>Ralph Johnson</author>
    <author>John Vlissides</author>
</book>
<book>
    <title>Pattern Hatching</title>
    <author>John Vlissides</author>
</book>
```

Multiple Named Keys

There is nothing to stop you defining several keys for the same nodes. For example:

```
<xsl:key name="book-isbn" match="book" use="isbn"/>
<xsl:key name="book-author" match="book" use="author/surname"/>
```

This allows you to find a book if either the author or the ISBN is known.

It's worth thinking twice before doing this, however. Assuming the XSLT processor implements the key by building an index or hash table, rather than by searching the whole document each time, you have to weigh the cost of building the index against the cost of finding the information by a search. If your transformation only needs to find a single book using its ISBN number, it might be simpler and faster to write:

```
<xsl:for-each select="//book[isbn='0-13-082676-6']"/>
```

and not use a key at all.

Multiple Definitions for the Same Key

It's also possible to have several key definitions with the same name. For example:

```
<xsl:key name="artist-key" match="book" use="author/name"/>
<xsl:key name="artist-key" match="CD" use="composer"/>
<xsl:key name="artist-key" match="CD" use="performer"/>
```

Now you can use the **key()** function in an expression such as:

```
<xsl:apply-templates select="key('artist-key', 'Ringo Starr')"/>
```

The set of nodes this returns will be either **<book>** elements or **<CD>** elements or a mixture of the two; the only thing we know for certain is that each one will either be a book with Ringo Starr as one of the authors, or a CD with Ringo Starr listed either as the composer or as a performer.

If the **use** expression were the same in each case, we could simplify this. For example to find books and CDs with a particular publisher, you could write:

```
<xsl:key name="publisher-key" match="book | CD" use="publisher"/>
```

This example uses the `Pattern` «`book | CD`» which matches all **<book>** elements and all **<CD>** elements. The `Pattern` is described on page 434 in Chapter 6.

The different definitions do not all need to be in the same stylesheet module; all the key definitions in included and imported stylesheets are merged together regardless of their import precedence.

See also

key() function in Chapter 7, page 499

xsl:message

The **<xsl:message>** instruction outputs a message, and optionally terminates execution of the stylesheet.

Defined in

XSLT section 13

Format

```
<xsl:message  terminate="yes" | "no" >
   template body
</xsl:message>
```

Position

<xsl:message> is an instruction. It is always used as part of a template body.

Attributes

Name	Value	Meaning
terminate optional	«yes» | «no»	The value «yes» indicates that processing is terminated after the message is output. The default is «no».

Content

A template body. There is no requirement that this should only generate text nodes; it can produce any XML fragment. What happens to any markup, however, is not defined in the standard.

Effect

If the **terminate** attribute is omitted, the value «no» is assumed.

The value obtained by expanding the template is output where the user can be expected to see it. The XSLT specification does not actually say where it goes; this is implementation-dependent, and it might be determined by configuration options. The specification suggests an alert box on the screen and a log file as two possible destinations.

If the **terminate** attribute has the value «yes», execution of the stylesheet is abandoned immediately, and any output generated so far is discarded.

Usage

The **<xsl:message>** instruction is generally used to report error conditions detected by the stylesheet logic. An example might be where an element such as **<sales>** is expected to have a numeric value, but is found to have a non-numeric value.

- With «terminate="no"» (the default), the stylesheet can report the error and continue processing.
- With «terminate="yes"», the stylesheet can report the error and quit.

Before using **<xsl:message>** in a production environment, check what happens to the messages and whether they can be redirected. You need to be particularly clear about whether your messages are intended to be read by the source document author, the stylesheet author, or the end user: this will affect the way in which you write the text of the message.

The output produced by **<xsl:message>** can be unpredictable, because the sequence of execution of a stylesheet is not defined in the standard. For example, some products (notably xt) defer evaluation of a variable until the variable is first used, which means that the order in which different variables are evaluated is difficult to predict. If evaluation of a variable triggers execution of **<xsl:message>**, the order of the messages may be surprising. Certainly, it can vary from one XSLT processor to another.

A common use of **<xsl:message>** is to generate diagnostic output so you can work out why your stylesheet isn't behaving as expected. This works well with products like Saxon and Xalan that have a fairly predictable sequence of execution, but it can be rather bewildering with xt, which often does things in a different order from the one you would expect. Placing diagnostics as comments into the result tree (using **<xsl:comment>**) is probably a more flexible solution. Some products, of course, have vendor-defined debugging aids built-in.

> **Microsoft's MSXML3 parser currently ignores <xsl:message terminate="no"> so the message is not reported anywhere. If «terminate="yes"», it generates an error, which can be handled through the script on the HTML page that invoked the transformation.**

Examples

The following example issues a message and quits if the value of the **<sales>** element is non-numeric:

```
<xsl:if test="string(number(sales))='NaN'">
   <xsl:message terminate="yes">
      <xsl:text>Sales value is not numeric</xsl:text>
   </xsl:message>
</xsl:if>
```

Unfortunately there is no mechanism defined in the XSLT standard that allows the location of the error in the source document to be included in the message.

The following example extends this by allowing several such errors to be reported in a single run, terminating the run only after all errors have been reported. It works by assigning a global variable to the set of nodes in error.

```
   <xsl:variable name="bad-sales"

select="//sales[string(number(current()))='NaN']"/>
   <xsl:template match="/">
      <xsl:for-each select="$bad-sales">
         <xsl:message>Sales value <xsl:value-of select="."/>
            is not numeric
         </xsl:message>
      </xsl:for-each>
   ...
      <xsl:if test="$bad-sales">
         <xsl:message terminate="yes">
            <xsl:text>Processing abandoned</xsl:text>
         </xsl:message>
      </xsl:if>
   </xsl:template>
```


Localized Messages

XSLT is designed very much with internationalization in mind, and no doubt the requirement to localize message text was discussed by the working group. They clearly decided that no special facilities were needed, and instead included a detailed example in the XSLT specification showing how the message text can be localized (output in the user's native language). The example is worth repeating because it shows a general technique.

Messages for a particular language are stored in a file whose name identifies the language, for example German messages might be in `messages/de.xml`. The message file might have the structure:

```
<messages>
   <message name="started">Angefangen</message>
   <message name="please-wait"/>Bitte warten!</message>
   <message name="finished"/>Fertig</message>
</messages>
```

A stylesheet that wishes to produce messages in the appropriate local language will need a parameter to identify that language (it might also be obtainable via the **`system-property()`** function described in Chapter 7, on page 557, but not in a portable way). It can then get access to the messages file for the appropriate language, and read the messages from there:

```
<xsl:param name="language" select="'en'"/>
<xsl:template name="output-message">
   <xsl:param name="name"/>
   <xsl:variable name="message-file"
                 select="concat('messages/', $language, '.xml')"/>
   <xsl:variable name="message-text"
                 select="document($message-file)/messages"/>
   <xsl:message>
      <xsl:value-of select="$message-text/message[@name=$name]"/>
   </xsl:message>
</xsl:template>
```

The same technique can of course be used for producing localized text to include in the output file from the stylesheet.

xsl:namespace-alias

The **<xsl:namespace-alias>** element allows a namespace used in the stylesheet to be mapped to a different namespace used in the output. It is most commonly used when writing transformations that produce an XSLT stylesheet as their output.

Defined in

XSLT section 7.1.1

Format

```
<xsl:namespace-alias
      stylesheet-prefix=NCName
      result-prefix=NCName />
```

Position

<xsl:namespace-alias> is a top-level element, which means it must be a child of the **<xsl:stylesheet>** element. It may be repeated any number of times in a stylesheet.

Attributes

Name	Value	Meaning
stylesheet-prefix mandatory	NCName | «#default»	A namespace prefix used in the stylesheet
result-prefix mandatory	NCName | «#default»	The prefix of the corresponding namespace to be used in the output

Content

None. The **<xsl:namespace-alias>** element is always empty.

Effect

The **<xsl:namespace-alias>** element affects the treatment of namespaces on literal result elements.

Normally, when an element node is output by processing a literal result element, the output element name will have the same local part, the same prefix, and the same namespace URI as the literal result element itself. It isn't guaranteed that it should have the same prefix, but it usually will. The same applies to the attributes of the literal result element. The namespace nodes on the literal result element must be copied unchanged to the result tree, using the same prefix and namespace URI. (The XSLT specification states that when processing a literal result element, all the namespaces that are in scope for the element in the stylesheet, with certain defined exceptions, will also be present in the output, even if they aren't used. Redundant namespace nodes can be suppressed by using the **xsl:exclude-result-prefixes** attribute. For more details on this, see the section *Literal Result Elements*, on page 118, in Chapter 3.)

Suppose you want the output document to be an XSLT stylesheet. Then you need to create elements such as **<xsl:template>** that are in the XSLT namespace. However, you can't use **<xsl:template>** as a literal result element, because by definition, if an element uses the XSLT namespace, it is treated as an XSLT element.

The answer is to use a different namespace on the literal result element in the stylesheet, and include an **<xsl:namespace-alias>** declaration to cause this to be mapped to the XSLT namespace when the literal result element is output. So your literal result element might be **<out:template>**, and you could use an **<xsl:namespace-alias>** element to indicate that the stylesheet prefix «out» should be mapped to the result prefix «xsl».

The **<xsl:namespace-alias>** element declares that one namespace URI, the stylesheet URI, should be replaced by a different URI, the result URI, when literal result elements are output. The namespace URIs are not given directly, but are referred to by using prefixes that are bound to these namespace URIs as a result of namespace declarations that are currently in force. Either one of the namespace URIs may be the default namespace URI, which is referred to using the pseudo-prefix «#default».

So although the **<xsl:namespace-alias>** element describes the mapping in terms of prefixes, it is not the prefix that is changed, but the URI.

The substitution of one namespace URI for another affects the names of literal result elements themselves, and the names of all attributes of literal result elements. It also affects the URIs of namespace nodes copied into the result tree from a literal result element. It does not affect elements created using **<xsl:element>**, attributes created using **<xsl:attribute>**, or nodes copied using **<xsl:copy>**. The prefix of namespace nodes is unchanged (it will be the **stylesheet-prefix**, not the **result-prefix**) and it is therefore likely that the prefixes of elements and attributes will be unchanged also, but as always, the processor has discretion to choose a different prefix on these names so long as it maps to the right namespace URI.

If there are several **<xsl:namespace-alias>** elements that specify the same **stylesheet-prefix**, the one with highest import precedence is used; if there is more than one with this import precedence, the implementation can either report an error or choose the one that comes last in the stylesheet.

The aliasing of namespace URIs applies when a literal result element in the stylesheet is instantiated to create an element in the result tree. It applies whether the result tree is the final output destination or a temporary tree. This means that if you examine a temporary tree into which literal result elements have been copied, the corresponding elements and attributes will use the namespace URI associated with the result prefix, not the stylesheet prefix.

Usage and Examples

The main justification for this facility is to enable stylesheets to be written that generate stylesheets as output. This is not as improbable a scenario as it sounds; there are many possible reasons for using this technique, including the following:

- There are many proprietary template languages currently in use. Translating these templates into XSLT stylesheets creates an attractive migration route, and there is no reason why these translators should not be written in XSLT.
- There may be a continuing need for a template language that is less complex and powerful than XSLT, for use by non-programmers. Again, these simple templates can easily be translated into XSLT stylesheets.
- There are some parts of an XSLT stylesheet that cannot easily be parameterized. For example, it is not possible to construct an XPath expression programmatically and then execute it (XSLT is not a reflexive language). The requirement to do this arises when visual tools are developed to define queries and reports interactively. One way of implementing such tools is to construct a customized stylesheet from a generic stylesheet, and again this is a transformation that can be assisted by using XSLT.
- You might have developed a large number of stylesheets that all have some common characteristic, for example they might all generate HTML that uses the **`<CENTER>`** tag. As the **`<CENTER>`** tag is deprecated, you now want to modify these stylesheets to use `<DIV ALIGN="CENTER">`. Why not write an XSLT transformation to convert them?
- There are already tools appearing that make it possible to generate XSLT stylesheets from a schema (see for example Schematron at http://www.ascc.net/xml/resource/schematron/schematron.html). Since both the schema and the stylesheet are XML documents, this is an XML to XML transformation, so it should be possible to write it in XSLT.

In fact, having gone to all the trouble of defining XSLT stylesheets as well-formed XML documents, it would be very surprising if it then proved impossible to manipulate them using XSLT itself.

There may be other situations where **`<xsl:namespace-alias>`** is useful. The XSLT specification mentions one, the need to avoid using namespace URIs that have recognized security implications in the area of digital signatures. Another might arise if stylesheets and other documents are held in a configuration management system; there might be a need to ensure that namespaces recognized by the configuration management system, for example to describe the authorship and change history of a document, are not used directly in the stylesheet.

Example of <xsl:namespace-alias>

The following example generates an XSLT stylesheet consisting only of a single global variable declaration, whose name and default value are supplied as parameters. Although this is a trivial stylesheet, it could be useful when incorporated into another more useful stylesheet using **<xsl:include>** or **<xsl:import>**.

This example is available in the code download as `alias.xsl`.

Source

This stylesheet can be used with any source XML document. The source document is not used (though it must exist).

Stylesheet

```
<xsl:stylesheet version="1.0"

xmlns:xsl="http://www.w3.org/1999/XSL/Transform"
                         xmlns:xslt="output.xsl">

   <xsl:param name="variable-name">v</xsl:param>
   <xsl:param name="default-value"/>
   <xsl:output indent="yes"/>

   <xsl:namespace-alias
               stylesheet-prefix="xslt"
               result-prefix="xsl"/>

   <xsl:template match="/">
      <xslt:stylesheet version="1.0">
      <xslt:variable name="{$variable-name}">
         <xsl:value-of select="$default-value"/>
      </xslt:variable>
      </xslt:stylesheet>
   </xsl:template>

</xsl:stylesheet>
```

Output

If you default the values of the parameters «`variable-name`» and «`default-value`», the output might be as follows. This is the output Saxon generates; other processors may vary it slightly.

```
<?xml version="1.0" encoding="utf-8"?>
<xslt:stylesheet
      xmlns:xslt="http://www.w3.org/1999/XSL/Transform"
      xmlns:xsl="http://www.w3.org/1999/XSL/Transform"
      version="1.0">
   <xslt:variable name="v"/>
</xslt:stylesheet>
```

> Why the two namespace declarations, in particular the one for prefix «xsl»? This is probably a Saxon oddity: although the rules are expressed differently in XSLT 1.0 and in XSLT 1.1, both are clear that this namespace declaration is allowed but not required. Saxon outputs it because its algorithm for eliminating unnecessary namespace declarations only considers namespace URIs, not namespace prefixes.
>
> The fact that a processor is allowed to output the namespace declaration for the «xsl» prefix also means that it can use this prefix, if it wishes, on the element names **<xslt:variable>** and **<xslt:stylesheet>**. However, it must output the namespace declaration for the «xslt» prefix, even if it is not used, because this corresponds directly to a namespace node on the result tree.

See also

Literal result elements in Chapter 3, on page 118.

xsl:number

The **<xsl:number>** element performs two functions. It can be used to allocate a sequential number to the current node, and it can be used to format a number for output. These functions are often performed together, but they can also be done separately.

Note that the facilities for number formatting in the **<xsl:number>** element are quite separate from those offered by the **format-number()** function and the **<xsl:decimal-format>** element.

Defined in

XSLT section 7.7

Format

```
<xsl:number
   level="single" | "multiple" | "any"
   count=Pattern
   from=Pattern
   value=Expression
   format={format-string}
   lang={language-code)
   letter-value={ "alphabetic" | "traditional" }
   grouping-separator={character}
   grouping-size={number} />
```

Position

<xsl:number> is an instruction. It is always used within a template body.

Attributes

Name	Value	Meaning
`level` optional	`«single» | «multiple» | «any»`	Controls the way in which a sequence number is allocated based on the position of the node in the tree
`count` optional	`Pattern`	Determines which nodes are counted to determine a sequence number
`from` optional	`Pattern`	Determines a cut-off point, a point in the document from which sequence numbering starts afresh
`value` optional	`Expression`	A user-supplied number to be formatted (instead of using a node sequence number)
`format` optional	Attribute value template, returning a format string, as defined below	Determines the output format of the number
`lang` optional	Attribute value template, returning a language code, as defined in XML for the **`xml:lang`** attribute	Indicates a language whose conventions for number formatting should be used
`letter-value` optional	Attribute value template, returning `«alphabetic» | «traditional»`	Distinguishes between different numbering schemes used with the same language
`grouping-separator` optional	Attribute value template, returning a single character	A character to be used to separate groups of digits (for example, a comma as a thousands separator)
`grouping-size` optional	Attribute value template, returning a number	The number of digits in each group, indicating where the grouping-separator should be inserted

For the syntax of an `Expression`, see Chapter 5.
For the syntax of a `Pattern`, see Chapter 6.

Content

None, the element is always empty.

Effect

The `<xsl:number>` instruction performs four tasks:

- Determine a sequence number
- Analyze the format string into a sequence of format tokens
- Format each part of the sequence number using the appropriate format token
- Write the resulting string to the current output destination as a text node

These steps are considered individually in the following sections.

Determining a Sequence Number

If the **value** attribute is specified, the sequence number is obtained by evaluating the expression in the **value** attribute, converting the result if necessary to a number using the rules for the **number()** function (page 531), and then rounding it to an integer using the rules for the **round()** function (page 537) . In this case, the **level**, **count**, and **from** attributes are ignored.

It is an error if the number is infinite, NaN, zero, or negative (or indeed, less than 0.5) because **<xsl:number>** is designed to handle positive integers. The XSLT processor may treat this error as fatal, or it may produce a fallback representation of the number, using the same conversion rules as apply to the **string()** function. The **<xsl:number>** element is designed for handling the natural numbers that arise from counting nodes, so if you want to handle other cases, it's better to use the **format-number()** function described in Chapter 7, on page 484.

If no **value** attribute is specified, **<xsl:number>** determines a sequence number based on the position of the current node in the source document.

The rules for determining a sequence number depend on the value of the **level**, **count**, and **from** attributes. If any of these attributes is omitted, the default is as follows:

Attribute	Default value
level	«single».
count	A pattern that matches nodes of the same node type as the current node; and if the current node has a name, that matches nodes with the same name. As always, names with namespace prefixes are matched using the relevant namespace URI rather than the prefix.
from	A pattern that matches no nodes, for example «*[false()]».

The sequence number is in general a list of positive integers. If the **level** attribute is «single» or «any» the sequence number will normally contain a single integer, if it is «multiple» then it may contain several (for example «3.6.1»). It is also possible for the list to be empty.

The sequence number is determined as follows:

level	Rules
`single`	This is designed for numbering of peer nodes at the same level in the structure, for example the items in a list. If the current node matches the **`count`** pattern, the target node is the current node. Otherwise, the processor searches for an ancestor of the current node that matches the **`count`** pattern, and makes that the target node. It stops the search when an ancestor is found that matches the **`from`** pattern, if there is one. If a target node is found, the sequence number is determined by counting how many preceding siblings of the target node match the **`count`** pattern, and adding one for the target node itself. For example, if the target node has six preceding siblings that match the **`count`** pattern then the sequence number is 7. If no target node is found, the sequence number will be an empty list.
`any`	This is designed for numbering nodes that can appear at any level of the structure, for example the footnotes or equations in a chapter of a book. Starting at the current node, the processor walks backwards through the document in reverse document order, counting the number of nodes that match the **`count`** pattern, and stopping when a node is found that matches the **`from`** pattern, if there is one. The nodes considered are those on the preceding, ancestor, and self axes. The sequence number is the number of nodes counted. If none of these nodes matches the **`count`** pattern, the sequence number will be an empty list. Attribute and namespace nodes are never counted.
multiple	This is designed to produce a composite sequence number that reflects the hierarchic position of a node, for example «`2.17.1`». The processor makes a list of all the ancestors of the current node, plus the current node itself, but stopping when an ancestor is reached that matches the **`from`** pattern, if there is one. The node that matches the **`from`** pattern is not included in the list. It puts this list into document order, that is, with the outermost ancestor first. For each node in this list that matches the **`count`** pattern, the processor counts how many preceding siblings it has that also match the **`count`** pattern, and adds one for the node itself. The resulting list of numbers makes up the composite sequence number. Once again, it is possible for the list to be empty.

These rules appear complex but in practice most common cases are quite straightforward, as the following examples demonstrate.

Analysing the Format String

Once the sequence number has been determined, the next stage is to format it into a string.

The sequence number, as we have seen, is a list of zero or more positive integers. The formatting is controlled primarily using the format string supplied in the **`format`** attribute. If this is omitted, the default value is «`1`».

The format string consists of a sequence of alternating formatting tokens and punctuation tokens. Any sequence of consecutive alphanumeric characters is taken as a formatting token, any other sequence is taken as a punctuation token. For example, if the format attribute is «`1((a))`», this is broken up into a formatting token «`1`», a punctuation token «`((`», a formatting token «`a`», and a punctuation token «`))`». The term alphanumeric is based on Unicode character categories, and is defined to include letters and digits from any language.

In the most common case the sequence number is a single number. In this situation, the output string consists of the initial punctuation token if there is one, followed by the result of formatting the number using the first format token, followed by the final punctuation token if there is one. So if the sequence number is «`42`» and the format attribute is «`[1]`», then the final output is «`[42]`».

Where the sequence number is a list of numbers, the rules are a little more complex but still have intuitive results, for example if the list of numbers is «`3, 1, 6`» and the format attribute is «`1.1(a)`» then the final output is «`3.1(f)`» (because «`f`» is the sixth letter in the alphabet). The detailed rules are as follows:

- The *n*th formatting token is used to format the *n*th number in the list where possible, using the rules in the following section.
- If there are more numbers in the list than formatting tokens, then the excess numbers are formatted using the last formatting token. For example, if the list is «`3,1,2,5`» and the format attribute is «`A.1`», then the output will be «`C.1.2.5`».
- If there are no formatting tokens, then a formatting token of «`1`» is used.
- If there are more formatting tokens than numbers in the list, the excess formatting tokens are ignored.

- Each number is preceded in the output by the punctuation token that precedes the formatting token used to format that number, if there is one. If there is no preceding punctuation token, and the number is not the first in the list, it is preceded by «.».
- If the formatting string ends with a punctuation token, this is added to the end of the output string.

Note that if the sequence number is an empty list, the result will consist of the initial and final punctuation tokens. For example if the format string is « [1] », an empty list will be formatted as « [] ». The most likely reason for an empty list is that no nodes matched the **`count`** pattern.

Formatting the Parts of the Sequence Number

This section describes how a single number is formatted using a single formatting token to construct a string that will form part of the final output string.

The XSLT specification defines this process only partially. There are some definitive rules, some guidance for the implementor, and many other cases that are left unspecified.

The definitive cases are listed in the table below:

Formatting token	Output sequence
1	1, 2, 3, 4…
01	01, 02, 03, … 10, 11, 12... More generally, if the format token is a «1» preceded by *n* zeros, the output numbers will be in decimal notation with a minimum of *n+1* digits.
other Unicode digits	The above two rules also apply to any other Unicode digits equivalent to zero and one, for example Thai or Tamil digits. The number is output using the same family of digits as are used in the formatting token.
a	a, b, c, d, … x, y, z, aa, ab, ac …
A	A, B, C, D, … X, Y, Z, AA, AB, AC …
i	i, ii, iii, iv, … x, xi, xii, xiii, xiv, …
I	I, II, III, IV, … X, XI, XII, XIII, XIV, …

The specification doesn't define these sequences in detail, for example it doesn't say how you represent numbers above 1000 in roman numerals (the Romans themselves had various conventions, such as putting horizontal lines above the letters or boxes around them; effects that would be difficult to achieve in XML output).

The attributes **`grouping-separator`** and **`grouping-size`** can be used to control the separation of groups of digits. For example, setting «`grouping-separator=" "`» (a single space) and «`grouping-size="2"`» would cause the number 12345 to be output as «`1 23 45`». The groups will always be formed by counting digits from the right-hand side.

For other formatting tokens, the XSLT specification is not prescriptive. It indicates that any formatting token may be used to indicate a sequence starting with that token, provided the implementation supports such a sequence; if the implementation does not support such a sequence, it may format the number using the format token «1». So, for example, if an implementation supports the numbering sequence «eins, zwei, drei, vier», then you can invoke this sequence using a format token of «eins»; if it supports the numbering sequence «α, β, γ, δ», then you can invoke this sequence with a format token of «α».

In case the format token does not identify a numbering sequence unambiguously, two attributes are provided to give greater control.

- The **lang** attribute is intended to indicate the target language: for example the sequence starting «a» might be different for English («lang="en"») and for Swedish («lang="se"»). The language code is intended to take the same form as the **xml:lang** attribute defined in the XML specification.
- The **letter-value** attribute is intended for languages such as Hebrew that have several possible sequences starting with the same token. The two permitted values are «alphabetic» and «traditional».

The detailed effect of these attributes is left entirely to the implementor, so you can't expect different products necessarily to behave in the same way.

All the attributes controlling formatting are attribute value templates, so they can be parameterized using expressions enclosed in curly braces. This is mainly useful if you want to select the values from a localization file based on the preferred language of the current user. To achieve this, you can use the same techniques as are described for localizing messages: see **<xsl:message>** on page 249.

Outputting the Number

The final action of **<xsl:number>** is to write the generated string to the current output destination, as a text node.

If you want to do something else with the number (perhaps to write it as an attribute or to copy it to every page heading), you can save it as the value of a variable, as follows:

```
<xsl:variable name="section-number"><xsl:number/></xsl:variable>
```

Writing the value to a variable also allows you to perform further manipulation. For example, if you want to use the traditional numbering sequence for footnotes (*, †, ‡, §, ¶) you cannot do this directly in **<xsl:number>** because these characters are punctuation symbols rather than alphanumerics. What you can do, however, is to use conventional decimal numbering and then convert, for example:

```
<xsl:template match="footnote"/>
<xsl:variable name="footnote-number">
   <xsl:number level="any" from="section"/>
</xsl:variable>
<xsl:value-of select="translate($footnote-number, '12345', '*†‡§¶')"/>
```

In practice it might be safer to use character references for these special characters to avoid them being mangled by a text editor that doesn't understand Unicode. The **translate()** function replaces characters in its second argument by the corresponding character in the third argument: it is described on page 560, in Chapter 7.

I have dodged a tricky question here, which is that if you want footnote numbers to start at 1 on each page, you can't allocate them until you have paginated the document. Some kinds of numbering are really the domain of XSL Formatting rather than XSL Transformations.

Usage and Examples

Although the rules for **<xsl:number>** are very general and sometimes complex, most common cases are quite straightforward.

The general rules allow for numbering any kind of node, but in practice the **<xsl:number>** instruction is almost invariably used for numbering elements. So in this section, I'll assume that the current node is an element.

level="single"

This option (the default) is used to number sibling elements.

The simplest way of using **<xsl:number>** is without any attributes:

```
<xsl:number/>
```

If the current element is the eighth **<item>** element owned by its parent element, say, then this will write the text value «8» to the current output destination. Technically, the processor is counting all the elements that match the pattern in the **count** attribute, and the default for the **count** attribute in this case is a pattern that matches **<item>** elements.

For this simple kind of numbering, it is often better to use the **position()** function, particularly if there are many nodes to be numbered. This is because with a typical implementation, each node that is numbered using **<xsl:number>** will result in the preceding siblings being counted, which will take an increasingly long time as the number of siblings increases. With the **position()** function, it is much more likely that the system already knows the position and doesn't have to do any special walking around the tree and pattern matching. Of course this is only possible where «`position()`» and `<xsl:number/>` produce the same answer, which will happen when the current node list being processed consists of all the sibling elements of a particular element type.

Another option for numbering is to use the **count()** function, for example «`count(preceding-sibling::item)+1`». This is often simpler if you want to use the number for further processing, rather than formatting it for output.

The **count** attribute of **<xsl:number>** can be used in two ways.

Firstly, it is useful if there are several different kinds of sibling elements that you want to count. For example, you might have an element containing a mixture of **<item>** and **<special-item>** children, as follows:

```
<shopping-list>
   <item>bananas</item>
   <item>apples</item>
   <special-item>flowers for Grandma</special-item>
   <item>grapes</item>
   <special-item>chocolate for Aunt Maud</special-item>
   <item>cherries</item>
</shopping-list>
```

If you want to number these in a single sequence, you can write:

```
<xsl:template match="item | special-item">
   <xsl:number count="item | special-item"/>
   <xsl:text> </xsl:text>
   <xsl:value-of select="."/><br/>
</xsl:template>
```

which, when you process the `<shopping-list>` element, will result in the output:

```
1 bananas<br/>
2 apples<br/>
3 flowers for Grandma<br/>
4 grapes<br/>
5 chocolate for Aunt Maud<br/>
6 cherries<br/>
```

In this case you could also use «`count="*"`» to achieve this effect. If you omitted the **`count`** attribute, the output would be:

```
1 bananas<br/>
2 apples<br/>
1 flowers for Grandma<br/>
3 grapes<br/>
2 chocolate for Aunt Maud<br/>
4 cherries<br/>
```

because each element is numbered taking into account only other elements with the same name.

Another use for the **`count`** attribute is to specify that it is not the current node that should be counted, but an ancestor node. For example, in the template rule for a **`<title>`** element you can use **`<xsl:number>`** to determine the number of the section that the title belongs to, by writing:

```
<xsl:template match="title">
   <xsl:number count="section"/>
. . .
</xsl:template>
```

This usage is less common: it would be just as easy in most cases to output the section number from the template rule that handles the **`<section>`** element itself.

The **`from`** attribute is rarely needed with «`level="single"`». In fact, it's difficult to construct an example that isn't completely artificial.

If you want numbering to start at a value other than one, or perhaps to proceed in increments other than one, you can capture the result of **<xsl:number>** in a variable and manipulate it using XPath expressions. For example, the following template rule numbers the items in a list starting at an offset passed in as a parameter:

```
<xsl:template match="item">
   <xsl:param name="first-number" select="1"/>
   <xsl:variable name="number"><xsl:number/></xsl:variable>
   <xsl:value-of select="$first-number + $number - 1"/>
. . .
</xsl:template>
```


level="any"

This option is useful when numbering objects within a document that have a numbering sequence of their own, independent of their position within the hierarchic structure. Examples are figures and illustrations, tables, equations, footnotes, and actions from a meeting.

The **count** attribute can usually be defaulted. For example, to number quotations within a document, you can write a template rule such as:

```
<xsl:template match="quotation">
<table><tr>
<td width="90%" valign="top">
   <i><xsl:value-of select="."/></i></td>
<td><xsl:number level="any"/></td>
</tr></table>
</xsl:template>
```

Again, the **count** attribute is useful when several different element types are included in the same numbering sequence, for example there might be a single sequence that includes both diagrams and photographs.

Note that each evaluation of **<xsl:number>** is quite independent of any previous evaluations. The result depends only on the relative position of the current element in the source document, and not on how many times the **<xsl:number>** element has been evaluated. So there is no guarantee that the numbers in the output document will be consecutive. In fact, if the output order is different from the input order then the numbers definitely won't be consecutive. If you want to number things based on their position in the output document, you can often achieve this by using the **position()** function. If this isn't adequate, the alternative is to perform a second pass, to add the sequence numbers.

With the facilities in the XSLT 1.1 draft, you can do this by writing the result of the first pass to a temporary tree. The following example extracts all the **<glossary-item>** elements from a document, sorts them alphabetically, and numbers them in their output sequence. The variable `glossary` is used to hold the temporary tree. To achieve the same effect with an XSLT 1.0 processor, you'll need to use the vendor-specific **node-set()** extension function.

Imagine a source document that contains glossary definitions scattered throughout the document, in the form:

```
<glossary-item>
     <term>XML</term>
     <definition>Extensible Markup Language</definition>
</glossary-item>
```

The relevant template looks like this:

```
<xsl:template name="make-glossary">
  <xsl:variable name="glossary">
    <xsl:for-each select="//glossary-item">
    <xsl:sort select="term"/>
      <xsl:copy-of select="."/>
    </xsl:for-each>
  </xsl:variable>
  <table>
    <xsl:for-each select="$glossary/glossary-item">
     <tr>
       <td><xsl:number format="[1]"/></td>
       <td><xsl:value-of select="term"/></td>
       <td><xsl:value-of select="definition"/></td>
     </tr>
    </xsl:for-each>
  </table>
</xsl:template>
```

In this example, however, the numbers could equally well have been generated on the first pass using the **position()** function.

The **from** attribute is useful to indicate where numbering should restart:

```
<xsl:template match="footnote">
   <xsl:number level="any" from="chapter"/>
   <xsl:text> </xsl:text>
   <xsl:value-of select="."/>
</xsl:template>
```

The above code would number footnotes consecutively within a chapter, starting again at 1 for each chapter.

Example: Numbering the Lines of a Poem

The following example numbers the lines of a poem, showing the number to the right of every third line. We assume the input structure contains a **<poem>** element, a **<stanza>** element, and a **<line>** element: the lines are to be numbered within the poem as a whole, not within each stanza.

Source

This stylesheet can be used with the source file `poem.xml` used in Chapter 1.

Stylesheet

This stylesheet is `poem.xsl`. It uses **<xsl:number>** to get the number of every line, but displays it only every third line, using the «mod» operator to get the remainder when the line number is divided by three.

```
<xsl:stylesheet version="1.0"
     xmlns:xsl="http://www.w3.org/1999/XSL/Transform">

<xsl:template match="/">
<html><body>
<p><xsl:apply-templates select="/poem/stanza"/></p>
</body></html>
</xsl:template>

<xsl:template match="stanza">
<p><table><xsl:apply-templates/></table></p>
</xsl:template>

<xsl:template match="line">
<tr>
<td width="350"><xsl:value-of select="."/></td>
<td width="50">
   <xsl:variable name="line-nr">
      <xsl:number level="any" from="poem"/>
   </xsl:variable>
   <xsl:if test="$line-nr mod 3 = 0">
      <xsl:value-of select="$line-nr"/>
   </xsl:if>
</td>
</tr>
</xsl:template>
</xsl:stylesheet>
```

Output

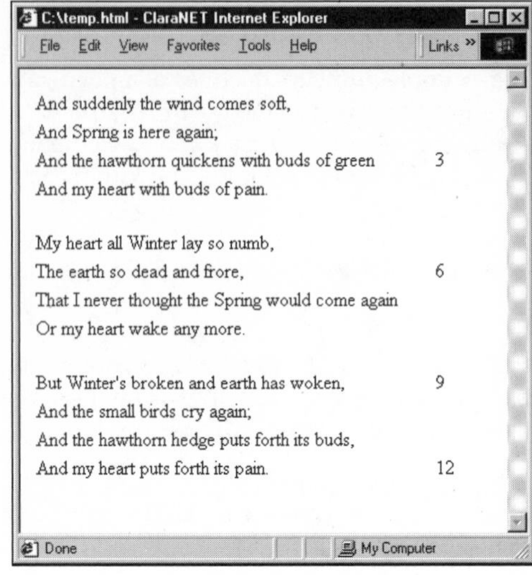

level="multiple"

This option is typically used to produce the hierarchic sequence numbers often found in technical or legal documents, for example 1.12.3, or A2(iii).

Note that an alternative way to produce such numbers is to use several calls on **`<xsl:number>`** with «`level="single"`» and different **`count`** attributes, for example:

```
<xsl:number count="chapter"/>.<xsl:number count="section"/>
   (<xsl:number count="clause"/>)
```

Another technique, which might be marginally faster, is to evaluate the chapter number once and pass it as a parameter to the template handling the section, and then pass both the chapter number and section number (or their concatenation) as parameters to the template handling each clause.

However, using «`level="multiple"`» is convenient, and in some cases (particularly with recursive structures, where **`<section>`** elements are contained within **`<section>`** elements) may be the only way of achieving the required effect.

The **`count`** attribute defines which ancestor elements should be included. Usually this is expressed as a union pattern, as in the example below:

```
<xsl:template match="clause">
   <xsl:number
      format="1.1.1. "
      level="multiple"
      count="chapter | section | clause"/>
   <xsl:apply-templates/>
</xsl:template>
```

The effect of the rules is that a composite sequence number will be formed containing one component number for each ancestor (or the element itself) that is a **<chapter>**, **<section>**, or **<clause>**. If the structure is regular, so that chapters, sections and clauses are neatly nested, then each clause will be output preceded by a number such as 1.13.5, where 1 is the chapter number, 13 is the number of the section within the chapter, and 5 is the number of the clause within the section.

If the structure isn't regular, for example if there are sections that don't belong to a chapter, or if there are clauses that have sections as siblings at the same level, or if there are sections nested within other sections, then the effects can be surprising, but a careful reading of the rules should explain what's going on.

A problem that sometimes occurs is that the numbering is context-sensitive. For example, within a regular chapter, clauses are numbered 1.2.3, but in an appendix, they are numbered A.2.3. It's possible to achieve this effect by exploiting the fact that the format pattern is an attribute value template; for example, you could write:

```
<xsl:template match="clause">
   <xsl:variable name="format">
      <xsl:choose>
         <xsl:when test="ancestor::chapter">1.1.1. </xsl:when>
         <xsl:otherwise>A.1.1 </xsl:otherwise>
      </xsl:choose>
   </xsl:variable>
   <xsl:number
      format="{$format}"
      level="multiple"
      count="appendix | chapter | section | clause"/>
   <xsl:apply-templates/>
</xsl:template>
```

See also

count() function in Chapter 7, on page 460
position() function in Chapter 7, on page 532
format-number() function, in Chapter 7 on page 484
<xsl:decimal-format> on page 199

xsl:otherwise

The **<xsl:otherwise>** element is used within an **<xsl:choose>** instruction to indicate the action that should be taken when none of the **<xsl:when>** conditions is satisfied.

Defined in

XSLT section 9.2

Format

```
<xsl:otherwise>
   template body
</xsl:otherwise>
```

Position

`<xsl:otherwise>` can only appear as a child of an `<xsl:choose>` element. If it is present at all, it must be the last child of the `<xsl:choose>` element, and it may not appear more than once.

Attributes

None.

Content

A template body.

Effect

The template body of the `<xsl:otherwise>` element is instantiated if (and only if) none of the `<xsl:when>` elements in the containing `<xsl:choose>` element evaluates to true.

Usage and Examples

See `<xsl:choose>` on page 188.

See also

`<xsl:choose>` on page 188
`<xsl:when>` on page 343

xsl:output

The `<xsl:output>` element is a top-level element used to control the format of the stylesheet output. An XSLT stylesheet is processed conceptually in two stages: the first stage is to build a result tree, and the second is to write out the result tree to a serial output file. The `<xsl:output>` element controls this second stage, which is often referred to as *serialization*.

This second stage of processing, to serialize the tree as an output document, is not a mandatory requirement for an XSLT processor; the standard allows the processor to make the tree available in some other way, for example via the DOM API. A processor that does not write the tree to an output file is allowed to ignore this element. Some processors that do provide serialization also allow the definitions in this element to be overridden by parameters set in the API when the processor is invoked. See the Appendix F for details of the TrAX API.

Defined in

XSLT section 16

Format

```
<xsl:output
   method= { "xml" | "html" | "text" | QName }
   version= { NMtoken }
   encoding= { string }
```

```
    omit-xml-declaration= { "yes" | "no" }
    standalone= { "yes" | "no" }
    doctype-public= { string }
    doctype-system= { string }
    cdata-section-elements= { list-of-QNames }
    indent= { "yes" | "no" }
    media-type= { string } />
```


Position

<xsl:output> is a top-level element, which means it must be a child of the **<xsl:stylesheet>** element. It may appear any number of times in a stylesheet.

Attributes

With XSLT 1.0, all the attributes of the **<xsl:output>** element must be written literally: it is not possible to use attribute value templates to parameterize them.

This changes in the draft XSLT 1.1 specification, which permits all the attributes of **<xsl:output>** to be written as attribute value templates, that is, as XPath expressions within curly braces. This allows the values to be supplied as parameters to the stylesheet, or to be determined by examining the source document. The rules given in the table below then apply to the attribute value after expanding any attribute value template.

Name	Value	Meaning
method optional	«xml» | «html» | «text» | QName	Defines the required output format
version optional	NMtoken	Defines the version of the output format
encoding optional	string	Defines the character encoding
omit-xml-declaration optional	«yes» | «no»	Indicates whether an XML declaration is to be included in the output
standalone optional	«yes» | «no»	Indicates that a **standalone** declaration is to be included in the output, and gives its value
doctype-public optional	string	Indicates the public identifier to be used in the DOCTYPE declaration in the output file
doctype-system optional	string	Indicates the system identifier to be used in the DOCTYPE declaration in the output file
cdata-section-elements optional	Whitespace - separated list of QNames	Names those elements whose text content is to be output in the form of CDATA sections
indent optional	«yes» | «no»	Indicates whether the output should be indented to indicate its hierarchic structure
media-type optional	string	Indicates the media-type (often called MIME type) to be associated with the output file

Content

None, the element is always empty.

Effect

There may be more than one **<xsl:output>** element in the stylesheet. If there are several, the attributes they define are in effect combined into a single conceptual **<xsl:output>** element as follows:

- For the **cdata-section-elements** attribute, the lists of `QNames` supplied on the separate **<xsl:output>** elements are merged – if an element name is present in any of the lists, it will be treated as a `CDATA` section element.
- For all other attributes, an **<xsl:output>** element that specifies a value for the attribute takes precedence over one that leaves it defaulted. If several **<xsl:output>** elements specify a value for the attribute, the one with highest import precedence is used. If this leaves more than one value (and even if they are identical), the XSLT processor may either report an error, or use the one that occurs last in the stylesheet.

The **method** attribute controls the format of the output, and this in turn affects the detailed meaning and the default values of the other attributes.

Three output formats are defined in the specification: «`xml`», «`html`», and «`text`». Alternatively, the output format may be given as a `QName`, which must include a non-null prefix that identifies a namespace that is currently in scope. This option is provided for vendor extensions, and the meaning is not defined in the standard. A vendor-defined format can attach its own interpretations to the meanings of the other attributes on the **<xsl:output>** element, and it can also define additional attributes on the **<xsl:output>** element, provided they are not in the default namespace.

If the **method** attribute is omitted, the output will be in XML format, unless the result tree is recognizably HTML. The result tree is recognized as HTML if:

- The root node has at least one element child, and
- The first element child of the root node is named **<html>**, in any combination of upper and lower case, and has a null namespace URI, and
- There are no text nodes before the **<html>** element, other than, optionally, a text node containing whitespace only

Rules for XML output

When the output method is «`xml`», the output file will usually be a well-formed XML document, but the actual requirement is only that it should be a well-formed XML external general parsed entity; in other words, something that could be incorporated into an XML document by using an entity reference such as «`&doc;`». The following example shows a well-formed external general parsed entity that is not a well-formed document:

```
A <b>bold</b> and <emph>emphatic</emph> statement
```

The specification is a little bit ambiguous in this area. Although it states that the output will always be a well-formed external general parsed entity, the context makes it clear that it can also include things such as a standalone document declaration and a document type declaration which, according to XML syntax, can only appear in a document entity, and not in an external general parsed entity.

An example of a well-formed document that is not a well-formed external general parsed entity is:

```
<?xml version="1.0" encoding="utf-8" standalone="yes"?>
<p>A <b>bold</b> and <emph>emphatic</emph> statement</p>
```

The rules for document entities and external general parsed entities overlap, as shown in the following diagram:

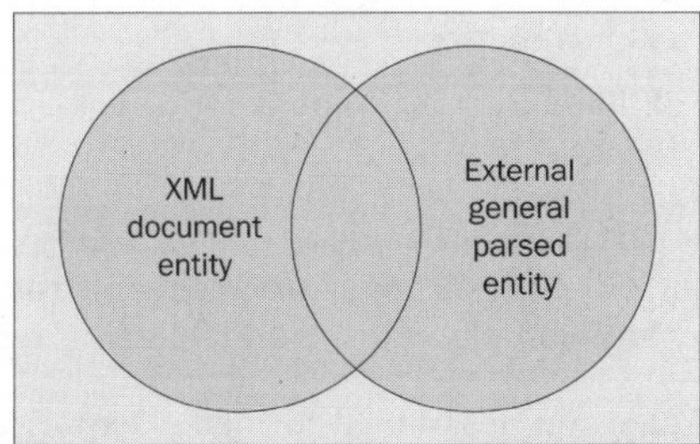

Essentially, an XSLT stylesheet can output anything that fits in the darker shaded area; anything that is a well-formed XML document entity, a well-formed external general parsed entity, or both.

Well, almost anything:

- It must also conform to the namespaces Recommendation
- There is no explicit provision for generating an internal DTD subset, although it can be achieved, with difficulty, by generating text and disabling output escaping
- Similarly, there is no explicit provision for generating entity references, though this can also be achieved by generating text and disabling output escaping

In the XML standard, the rules for an external general parsed entity are given as:

```
extParsedEnt    TextDecl ? content
```

while the rule for the document entity is effectively:

```
document    XMLDecl ?  Misc *  doctypedecl ?  Misc *  element  Misc *
```

where `Misc` permits whitespace, comments, and processing instructions.

So the principal differences between the two cases are:

- A `TextDecl` (text declaration) is not quite the same thing as an `XMLDecl` (XML declaration), as discussed below.

- A document may contain a `doctypedecl` (document type declaration), but an external general parsed entity must not. A document type declaration is the `<!DOCTYPE ... >` header identifying the DTD and possibly including an internal DTD subset.
- The body of a document is an `element`, while the body of an external parsed entity is `content`. Here `content` is effectively the contents of an element but without the start and end tags.

The `TextDecl` (text declaration) looks at first sight very like an XML declaration; for example `<?xml version="1.0" encoding="utf-8"?>` could be used either as an XML declaration or as a text declaration. There are differences, however:

- In an XML declaration, the **`version`** attribute is mandatory, but in a text declaration it is optional
- In an XML declaration, the **`encoding`** attribute is optional, but in a text declaration it is mandatory
- An XML declaration may include a **`standalone`** attribute, but a text declaration may not

The `content` part is a sequence of components including child elements, character data, entity references, CDATA sections, processing instructions, and comments, each of which may appear any number of times and in any order.

So the following are all examples of well-formed external general parsed entities:

```
<quote>Hello!</quote>
```

```
<quote>Hello!</quote><quote>Goodbye!</quote>
```

```
Hello!
```

```
<?xml version="1.0" encoding="utf-8"?>Hello!
```

The following is a well-formed XML document, but it is *not* a well-formed external general parsed entity, both because of the **`standalone`** attribute, and because of the document type declaration. This is also legitimate output:

```
<?xml version="1.0" encoding="utf-8" standalone="no"?>
<!DOCTYPE quote SYSTEM "hello.dtd">
<quote>Hello!</quote>
```

The following is neither a well-formed XML document nor a well-formed external general parsed entity.

```
<?xml version="1.0" encoding="utf-8" standalone="no"?>
<!DOCTYPE quote SYSTEM "hello.dtd">
<quote>Hello!</quote>
<quote>Goodbye!</quote>
```

It cannot be an XML document because it has more than one top-level element, and it cannot be an external general parsed entity because it has a `<!DOCTYPE>` declaration. An erratum to XSLT 1.0 makes it clear that a stylesheet attempting to produce this output is in error.

The XSLT specification also places two other constraints on the form of the output, although these are rules for the implementor to follow rather than rules that directly affect the stylesheet author. These rules are:

- The output must conform to the rules of the XML Namespaces Recommendation. If it is an XML document, the meaning of this is clear enough, but if it is merely an external entity, some further explanation is needed. The standard provides this by saying that when the entity is pulled into a document by adding an element tag around its content, the resulting document must conform with the XML Namespaces rules.
- The output file must faithfully reflect the result tree. This requirement is easy to state informally, but the specification includes a more formal statement of the requirement, which is surprisingly complex.

Between XSLT 1.0 and XSLT 1.1 there is a change in the way the rules concerning namespace declarations are described. At XSLT 1.0, it is up to the serializer to generate namespace declarations, not only for namespace nodes that are explicitly present on the result tree, but also for any namespaces that are used in the result document, but that are not represented by namespace nodes. This can happen because there is nothing in the rules for **`<xsl:element>`** and **`<xsl:attribute>`**, for example, that require namespace nodes to be created on the tree for the namespace URI used in the names of these nodes. At XSLT 1.1, however, the specification describes a process called namespace fixup, which ensures that an element in the result tree always has a namespace node for every namespace that is used either in the element name or in the name of any of its attributes. This means that it is no longer the responsibility of the serializer to create these namespace declarations. The reason for this change is that with XSLT 1.1, the content of temporary trees (including their namespace nodes) becomes visible to the stylesheet, so the rules had to be tightened up.

Although the output is required to be well-formed XML, there is no rule that says it has to be valid XML (recall that a valid XML document is, roughly speaking, an XML document that conforms to the rules in its own DTD). If you generate a document type declaration that refers to a specific DTD, don't expect the XSLT processor to check that the output document actually conforms to that DTD; that's entirely your responsibility as the stylesheet author.

With the «`xml`» output method, the other attributes of **`<xsl:output>`** are interpreted as follows:

Attribute	Interpretation
`version`	The version of XML used in the output document. Currently the only version of XML that exists is version 1.0, but this anticipates the possibility that there will be other versions in the future. The default value, and the only value you should consider using at present, is «`1.0`».

Attribute	Interpretation
`encoding`	This specifies the preferred character encoding for the output document. All XSLT processors are required to support the values «`UTF-8`» and «`UTF-16`» (which are also the only values that XML parsers are required to support). This encoding name will be used in the encoding attribute of the XML or Text declaration at the start of the output file, and all characters in the file will be encoded using these conventions. The standard encoding names are not case-sensitive. If the encoding is one that does not allow all XML characters to be represented directly, for example «`iso-8859-1`», then characters outside this subset will be represented where possible using XML character references (such as «`₤`»). It is an error if such characters appear in contexts where character references are not recognized (for example within a processing instruction or comment, or in an element or attribute name).
`indent`	If this attribute has the value «`yes`», the idea is that the XML output should be indented to show its hierarchic structure. The XSLT processor is not obliged to respect this request, and if it does so, the precise form of the output is not defined. There are some constraints on how indentation should be achieved. In effect, it can only be done by adding whitespace-only text nodes to the tree, and these cannot be added adjacent to an existing text node. Whitespace that is already in the result tree cannot be removed, so if the output already contains multi-line text nodes, the scope to produce aesthetically-pleasing output is limited. Note that even with these restrictions, adding whitespace nodes to the output may affect the way the recipient interprets it. This is particularly true with mixed content models where an element can have both elements and text nodes as its children.
`cdata-section-elements`	This is a list of element names, each expressed as a `QName`, separated by whitespace. Any prefix in a `QName` is treated as a reference to the corresponding namespace URI in the normal way, using the namespace declarations in effect on the actual **`<xsl:output>`** element where the **`cdata-section-elements`** attribute appears; because these are element names, the default namespace is assumed where the name has no prefix. When a text node is output, if the parent element of the text node is identified by a name in this list, then the text node is output as a `CDATA` section. For example, the text value «`James`» is output as «`<![CDATA[James]]>`», and the text value «`AT&T`» is output as «`<![CDATA[AT&T]]>`».

Attribute	Interpretation
cdata-section-elements (continued)	Otherwise, this value would probably be output as «AT&T». The XSLT processor is free to choose other equivalent representations if it wishes, for example a character reference, but the standard says that it should not use CDATA unless it is explicitly requested. (However, note the word *should*; this means the rule is advisory, not a conformance requirement.) The CDATA section will be split into parts if necessary, perhaps because the terminator sequence «]]>» appears in the data, or because there is a character that can only be output using a character reference because it is not supported directly in the chosen encoding.
omit-xml-declaration	If this attribute has the value «yes», the XSLT processor should not output an XML declaration (or, by implication, a text declaration; recall that XML declarations are used at the start of the document entity, text declarations at the start of an external general parsed entity). If the attribute is omitted, or has the value «no», then a declaration should be output. The declaration should include both the **version** and **encoding** attributes (to ensure that it is valid both as an XML declaration and as a text declaration). It should include a **standalone** attribute only if a **standalone** attribute is specified in the **<xsl:output>** element.
standalone	If this attribute is set to «yes», then the XML declaration will specify «standalone="yes"». If this attribute is set to «no», then the XML declaration will specify «standalone="no"». If the attribute is omitted, then the XML declaration will not include a **standalone** attribute. This will make it a valid text declaration, enabling its use in an external general parsed entity. This attribute should not be used unless the output is a well-formed XML document.
doctype-system	If this attribute is specified, the output file should include a document type declaration (that is, **<!DOCTYPE>**) after the XML declaration and before the first element start tag. The name of the document type will be the same as the name of the first element. The value of this attribute will be used as the system identifier in the document type declaration. This attribute should not be used unless the output is a well-formed XML document.
doctype-public	This attribute is ignored unless the **doctype-system** attribute is also specified. It defines the value of the public identifier to go in the document type declaration. If no public identifier is specified, none is included in the document type declaration.

Attribute	Interpretation
`media-type`	This attribute defines the media type of the output file (often referred to as its MIME type). The default value is «text/xml». The specification doesn't say what use is made of this information: it doesn't affect the contents of the output file, but it may affect the way it is named, stored, or transmitted, depending on the environment. For example, the information might find its way into an HTTP protocol header.

Do remember that the specifications in the **<xsl:output>** element will only be effective if you actually use the XSLT processor to serialize the XML. If you write the output of the transformation to a DOM, and then use a serializer that comes with your DOM implementation (for example by using the **save** method or the **xml** property in the case of the Microsoft DOM implementation), then the **<xsl:output>** specifications will have no effect.

Rules for HTML output

When the method attribute is set to «html», or when it is defaulted and the result tree is recognized as representing HTML, the output will be an HTML file. By default, it will conform to HTML 4.0.

The XSLT specification doesn't mention the possibility of producing XHTML output, which is not really surprising as it was published before the XHTML specification. XHTML is pure XML, so if you want to generate XHTML, use the «xml» output method. Some vendors have customized the XML output for XHTML, to make it acceptable to legacy HTML browsers, for example by generating empty tags such as `<hr />` with a space after the element name. However, this is outside the scope of the XSLT standard.

HTML is output in the same way as XML, except where specific differences are noted. These differences are:

- Certain elements are recognized as empty elements. They are recognized in any combination of upper and lower case. These elements are output with a start tag and no end tag. For HTML 4.0 these elements are:

  ```
  <area>        <frame>      <isindex>
  <base>        <hr>         <link>
  <basefont>    <img>        <meta>
  <br>          <input>      <param>
  <col>
  ```

- The **<script>** and **<style>** elements (again in any combination of upper and lower case) do not require escaping of special characters. In the text content of these elements, a «<» character will be output as «<», not as «<».

- HTML attributes whose value is a URI (for example, the **href** attribute of the **<a>** element, or the **src** attribute of the **<img>** element) are recognized, and special characters within the URI are escaped as defined in the HTML specification. Specifically, non-ASCII characters in the URI should be represented by converting each byte of the UTF-8 representation of the character to «%HH» where HH represents the byte value in hexadecimal.

- Special characters may be output using entity references such as «`é`» where these are defined in the relevant version of HTML. This is at the discretion of the XSLT processor, it doesn't have to use these entity names.
- Processing instructions are terminated with «`>`» rather than «`?>`». Processing instructions are not often used in HTML, but the HTML 4.0 standard recommends that any vendor extensions should be implemented this way, rather than by adding element tags to the language. So it is possible they will be seen more frequently in the future.
- Attributes that are conventionally written with a keyword only, and no value, will be recognized and output in this form. Common examples are `<TEXTAREA READONLY>` and `<OPTION SELECTED>`. This is shorthand, permitted in SGML but not in XML, for an attribute that has only one permitted value, which is the same as the attribute name. In XML, these tags must be written as `<TABLE BORDER="BORDER">` and `<OPTION SELECTED="SELECTED">`. The HTML output method will normally use the abbreviated form, as this is the only form that older HTML browsers will recognize.
- The special use of the ampersand character in dynamic HTML attributes is recognized. For example, the tag `<TD WIDTH="&{width};">` is correct HTML, though it would not be correct in XML, because of the ampersand character. To produce this output from a literal result element, the tag in the stylesheet would need to be written as `<TD WIDTH="&{{width}};">`: note the double curly braces, to prevent them being interpreted with their special meaning in attribute value templates.

A common source of anxiety with HTML output is the use of ampersands in URLs. For example, suppose you want to generate the output:

```
<a href="http://www.acme.com/search.asp?product=widgets&country=spain>
Spanish Widgets
</a>
```

It's not actually possible to produce this using standard XSLT; the ampersand will always come out as «`&`». The reason for this is simple: «`&`», although commonly used and widely accepted, is not actually correct HTML, and according to the standard it must be escaped as «`&`». All respectable browsers accept the correct escaped form, so the answer is: don't worry about it.

The attributes on the **`<xsl:output>`** element are interpreted as follows when HTML output is selected:

Attribute	Interpretation
`version`	The version of HTML used in the output document. It is up to the implementation which versions of HTML should be supported, though all implementations can be expected to support the default version, namely version 4.0.
`encoding`	This specifies the preferred character encoding for the output document. This will be used to generate a **`charset`** attribute of a **`<META>`** element inserted immediately after the start tag of the **`<HEAD>`** element, if there is one. If the encoding is one that does not allow all XML characters to be represented directly, for example «`iso-8859-1`», then characters outside this subset will be represented where possible using either entity references or numeric character references. The processor is allowed to use such references even for characters that are within the encoding: for example, the non-breaking space character may be output as itself (it looks just like an ordinary space) or as «` `», «`&#a0;`», or «` `». It is an error if characters that can't be represented directly appear in contexts where character references are not recognized (for example within a script element, within a comment, or in an element or attribute name).
`indent`	If this attribute has the value «`yes`», the idea is that the HTML output should be indented to show its hierarchic structure. The XSLT processor is not obliged to respect this request, and if it does so, the precise form of the output is not defined. When producing indented output, the processor has much more freedom to add or remove whitespace than in the XML case, because of the way whitespace is handled in HTML. The processor can add or remove whitespace anywhere it likes so long as it doesn't change the way a browser would display the HTML.
`cdata-section-elements`	This attribute is not applicable to HTML output.
`omit-xml-declaration`	This attribute is not applicable to HTML output.
`standalone`	This attribute is not applicable to HTML output.
`doctype-system`	If this attribute is specified, the output file will include a document type declaration immediately before the first element start tag. The name of the document type will be «`HTML`» or «`html`». The value of the attribute will be used as the system identifier in the document type declaration.
`doctype-public`	If this attribute is specified, the output file will include a document type declaration immediately before the first element start tag. The name of the document type will be «`HTML`» or «`html`». The value of the attribute will be used as the public identifier in the document type declaration.

Attribute	Interpretation
`media-type`	This attribute defines the media type of the output file (often referred to as its MIME type). The default value is «`text/html`». The specification doesn't say what use is made of this information; it doesn't affect the contents of the output file, but it may affect the way it is named, stored, or transmitted, depending on the environment. For example, the information might find its way into an HTTP protocol header.

Rules for Text Output

When «`method="text"`», the result tree is output as a plain text file. The values of the text nodes of the tree are copied to the output, and all other nodes are ignored. Within text nodes, all character values are output using the relevant encoding as determined by the **`encoding`** attribute; there are no special characters such as «`&`» to be escaped.

The way in which line endings are output (for example LF or CRLF) is not defined; the implementation might choose to use the default line-ending conventions of the platform on which it is running.

The attributes that are relevant to text output are listed below. All other attributes are ignored.

Attribute	Interpretation
`encoding`	This specifies the preferred character encoding for the output document. The default value is implementation-defined, and may depend on the platform on which it is running. If the encoding is one that does not allow all XML characters to be represented directly, for example «`iso-8859-1`», then any character outside this subset will be reported as an error.
`media-type`	This attribute defines the media type of the output file (often referred to as its MIME type). The default value is «`text/plain`». The specification doesn't say what use is made of this information: it doesn't affect the contents of the output file, but it may affect the way it is named, stored, or transmitted, depending on the environment. For example, the information might find its way into an HTTP protocol header.

Usage

The defaulting mechanisms ensure that it is usually not necessary to include an **`<xsl:output>`** element in the stylesheet. By default, the XML output method is used unless the first thing output is an **`<HTML>`** element, in which case the HTML output method is assumed.

The `<xsl:output>` element is concerned with how your result tree is turned into an output file. If the XSLT processor allows you to do something else with the result tree, for example passing it to the application as a DOM Document or as a stream of SAX events, then the `<xsl:output>` element is irrelevant.

The **encoding** attribute can be very useful to ensure that the output file can be easily viewed and edited. Unfortunately, though, the set of possible values varies from one XSLT implementation to another, and may also depend on the environment. For example, many XSLT processors are written in Java and use the Java facilities for encoding the output stream, but the set of encodings supported by each Java VM is different. However, support for iso-8859-1 encoding is fairly universal, so if you have trouble viewing the output file because it contains UTF-8 Unicode characters, setting the encoding to iso-8859-1 is often a good remedy.

> **If your stylesheet generates accented letters or other special characters, and it looks as if they have come out incorrectly in the output, the chances are they are correctly represented in UTF-8, but you are looking at them with a text editor that doesn't understand UTF-8.**

The **encoding** attribute determines how the XSLT processor serializes the output as a stream of bytes, but it says nothing about what happens to the bytes afterwards. If the processor writes to a file, the file will probably be written in the chosen encoding. But if the output is accessed as a character string through an API, or is written to a character field in a database, the encoding of the characters may be changed before you get to see them. A classic example of this effect is the Microsoft **transformNode()** interface (see Appendix A), which returns the result of the transformation as a `BSTR` string. Because this is a `BSTR`, it will always be encoded in UTF-16, regardless of the encoding you request. The same thing will happen with the TrAX interface (see Appendix F); if you supply a `StreamResult` based on a `Writer` the encoding then depends on how the particular `Writer` encodes Unicode characters, and the XSLT processor has no control over the matter.

Examples

The following example requests XML output using iso- 8859-1 encoding. The output will be indented for readability, and the contents of the `<script>` element, because it is expected to contain many special characters, will be output as a CDATA section. The output file will reference the DTD `booklist.dtd`: note that it is entirely the user's responsibility to ensure that the output of the stylesheet actually conforms to this DTD, and, indeed, that it is a well-formed XML document.

```
<xsl:output
   method="xml"
   indent="yes"
   encoding="iso-8859-1"
   cdata-section-elements="script"
   doctype-system="booklist.dtd" />
```

The following example might be used if the output of the stylesheet is a comma-separated-values file using US ASCII characters only:

```
<xsl:output
   method="text"
   encoding="us-ascii" />
```

xsl:param

The **<xsl:param>** element is used either at the top level, to describe a global parameter, or immediately within an **<xsl:template>** element, to describe a local parameter to a template. It specifies a name for the parameter and a default value, which is used if the caller supplies no value for the parameter.

Defined in

XSLT section 11

Format

```
<xsl:param name=QName select=Expression >
   template body
</xsl:param>
```

Position

<xsl:param> may appear as a top-level element (a child of the **<xsl:stylesheet>** element), or as an immediate child element of **<xsl:template>**. In the latter case, **<xsl:param>** elements must come before any other child elements.

Attributes

Name	Value	Meaning
name mandatory	QName	The name of the parameter
select optional	Expression	The default value of the parameter if no explicit value is supplied by the caller

The constructs `QName` (on page 414) and `Expression` (on page 377) are defined in Chapter 5.

Content

An optional template body. If a **select** attribute is present, the element should be empty.

Effect

An **<xsl:param>** element at the top level of the stylesheet declares a global parameter; an **<xsl:param>** element appearing as a child of an **<xsl:template>** element declares a local parameter for that template.

The **<xsl:param>** element defines the name of the parameter, and a default value. The default value is used only if no other value is explicitly supplied by the caller.

An explicit value can be supplied for a local parameter by using the **<xsl:with-param>** element when the template is invoked using **<xsl:apply-templates>**, **<xsl:call-template>**, or (with XSLT 1.1 only) **<xsl:apply-imports>**.

The way in which explicit values are supplied for global parameters is implementor defined (for example, they may be defined on the command line or through environment variables, or they may be supplied via a vendor-defined API). Details are given for particular products in the relevant appendix, and in Appendix F for the TrAX API.

The Value of the Parameter

The default value of the parameter may be given either by the `Expression` in the **`select`** attribute, or by the contents of the contained template body. If there is a **`select`** attribute, the **<xsl:param>** element should be empty. If there is no **`select`** attribute and the template body is empty, the default value of the parameter is an empty string.

If the value is given by an `Expression`, the data type of the value will be Boolean, number, string, or node-set, depending on the expression. If the value is given by a non-empty template body, a temporary tree will be constructed. With XSLT 1.0, the value will have the data type result tree fragment; with XSLT 1.1 it will be a node-set, containing the root of this tree as its only member. This is all exactly the same as with the **<xsl:variable>** element, described on page 333.

The Name of the Parameter

The name of the parameter is defined by the `QName`. Normally this will be a simple name (such as «`num`» or «`list-of-names`»), but it may be a name qualified with a prefix, for example «`my:value`». If it has a prefix, the prefix must correspond to a namespace that is in scope at that point in the stylesheet. The true name of the parameter, for the purpose of testing whether two names are the same, is determined not by the prefix but by the namespace URI corresponding to the prefix, so two variables «`my:value`» and «`your:value`» have the same name if the prefixes «`my`» and «`your`» refer to the same namespace URI. If the name has no prefix, it is treated like an attribute name; that is, it has a null namespace URI – it does not use the default namespace URI.

Parameter names are referenced in exactly the same way as variables, by prefixing the name with a dollar sign (for example «`$num`») and all the rules for uniqueness and scope of names are exactly as if the **<xsl:param>** element was replaced by an **<xsl:variable>** element. The only difference between parameters and variables is the way they acquire an initial value.

Usage

Global parameters are particularly useful to select which part of the source document to process. A common scenario is that the XSLT processor will be running within a web server. The user request will be accepted by a Java Server Page or by a Java servlet, or indeed by an ASP page, the request parameters will be accepted, and the stylesheet processing will be kicked off using an API defined by each vendor. Generally this API will provide some way of passing the parameters that came from the HTTP request into the stylesheet as the initial values of global **<xsl:param>** elements.

If the API supports it, a global parameter may take any value: a string, number, Boolean, node-set, or external object. Because it can be a node-set, this provides another way of supplying secondary source documents for use by the stylesheet, as an alternative to the **document()** function. Many products allow such a parameter to be supplied as a DOM `Document` object.

Local parameters are used more often with **<xsl:call-template>** than with **<xsl:apply-templates>**, though they are available to both, and in XSLT 1.1 they can also be used with **<xsl:apply-imports>**. The actual value of the parameter is set by the caller using an **<xsl:with-param>** element. Parameters are often needed by the recursive algorithms used in XSLT to handle lists of items: there are examples of such algorithms under **<xsl:call-template>** on page 179.

Examples

Example: Using <xsl:param> with a Default Value

Source

This stylesheet works with any XML source file.

Stylesheet

The stylesheet is `call.xsl`.

It contains a named template that outputs the depth of a node (defined as the number of ancestors). The node may be supplied as a parameter; if it is not supplied, the parameter defaults to the current node.

The stylesheet includes a template rule for the root node that invokes this named template, defaulting the parameter, to display the name and depth of every element in the source document.

```
<xsl:transform
 xmlns:xsl="http://www.w3.org/1999/XSL/Transform"
 version="1.0"
>
<xsl:output method="text"/>

<xsl:template match="/">
<xsl:for-each select="//*">
    <xsl:value-of select="concat(name(), ' -- ')"/>
    <xsl:call-template name="depth"/>;
</xsl:for-each>
</xsl:template>

<xsl:template name="depth">
    <xsl:param name="node" select="."/>
    <xsl:value-of select="count($node/ancestor::node())"/>
</xsl:template>
</xsl:transform>
```

Output

If the stylesheet is run against the file `poem.xml` used in Chapter 1, the output is as follows:

```
poem -- 1;
author -- 2;
date -- 2;
title -- 2;
stanza -- 2;
line -- 3;
line -- 3;
line -- 3;
line -- 3;
stanza -- 2;
line -- 3;
line -- 3;
line -- 3;
line -- 3;
stanza -- 2;
line -- 3;
line -- 3;
line -- 3;
line -- 3;
```

See also

<xsl:apply-templates> on page 155
<xsl:call-template> on page 179
<xsl:variable> on page 333
<xsl:with-param> on page 345

xsl:preserve-space

The **<xsl:preserve-space>** element, along with **<xsl:strip-space>**, is used to control the way in which whitespace nodes in the source document are handled.

Defined in

XSLT section 3.4

Format

```
<xsl:preserve-space elements=list-of-NameTests />
```

Position

<xsl:preserve-space> is a top-level element, meaning that it must be a child of the **<xsl:stylesheet>** element. There are no constraints on its ordering relative to other top-level elements.

Attributes

Name	Value	Meaning
elements mandatory	Whitespace-separated list of NameTests	Defines the elements in the source document whose whitespace-only text nodes are to be preserved

The NameTest construct is defined on page 394, in Chapter 5. It may be an actual element name, the symbol «*» meaning all elements, or the construct «prefix:*» meaning all elements in a particular namespace.

Content

None, the element is always empty.

Effect

This element, together with **<xsl:strip-space>** defines the way that whitespace-only text nodes in the source document are handled. Unless contradicted by an **<xsl:strip-space>** element, **<xsl:preserve-space>** indicates that whitespace-only text nodes occurring as children of a specified element are to be retained in the source tree.

Preserving whitespace-only text nodes is the default action, so this element only needs to be used where it is necessary to contradict an **<xsl:strip-space>** element. The interaction of the two is explained below.

The concept of whitespace-only text nodes is explained at some length, starting on page 139, in Chapter 3.

This element also affects the handling of whitespace-only text nodes in any document loaded using the **document()** function. It does not affect the handling of whitespace-only text nodes in the stylesheet when used in its role as a stylesheet, but it does affect the stylesheet in the same way as any other document if a copy of the stylesheet is loaded using the **document()** function.

The element does not affect whitespace nodes in documents returned as the result of extension functions or passed to the stylesheet as the value of a global parameter. Also, the element does not affect anything that happens to the source document before the XSLT processor gets to see it, so if you create the source tree using an XML parser that strips whitespace nodes (as Microsoft's MSXML3 does, by default), then specifying **<xsl:preserve-space>** in the stylesheet isn't going to get these nodes back – they are already gone.

A whitespace-only text node is a text node whose text consists **entirely** of a sequence of whitespace characters, these being space, tab, carriage return, and linefeed (#x20, #x9, #xD, and #xA). The **<xsl:preserve-space>** element has no effect on whitespace contained in text nodes that also contain non-whitespace characters; such whitespace is always preserved and is part of the value of the text node.

Before a node is classified as a whitespace-only text node, the tree is normalized by concatenating all adjacent text nodes. This includes the merging of text that originated in different XML entities.

A whitespace-only text node may either be stripped or preserved. If it is stripped, it is removed from the tree. This means it will never be matched, it will never be copied to the output, and it will never be counted when nodes are numbered. If it is preserved, it is retained on the tree in its original form, subject only to the end-of-line normalization performed by the XML parser.

If a whitespace-only text node has an ancestor with an **xml:space** attribute and the nearest ancestor with such an attribute has the value «xml:space="preserve"», then the text node is preserved regardless of the **<xsl:preserve-space>** and **<xsl:strip-space>** elements in the stylesheet.

The **elements** attribute of **<xsl:preserve-space>** must contain a whitespace-separated list of NameTests. The form of a NameTest is defined in the XPath expression language; see Chapter 5, page 394. Each form of NameTest has an associated priority. The different forms of NameTest and their meanings are:

Syntax	Examples	Meaning	Priority
QName	title svg:width	Matches the full element name, including its namespace URI	0
NCName «:*»	svg:*	Matches all elements in the namespace whose URI corresponds to the given prefix	–0.25
«*»	*	Matches all elements	–0.5

The priority is used when conflicts arise. For example, if the stylesheet specifies:

```
<xsl:strip-space elements="*"/>
<xsl:preserve-space elements="para clause"/>
```

then whitespace-only text nodes appearing within a **<para>** or **<clause>** will be preserved. Even though these elements match both the **<xsl:strip-space>** and the **<xsl:preserve-space>**, the NameTest in the latter has higher priority (0 as compared to –0.5).

An **<xsl:strip-space>** or **<xsl:preserve-space>** element containing several NameTests is equivalent to writing a separate **<xsl:strip-space>** or **<xsl:preserve-space>** element for each NameTest individually.

A whitespace-only text node is preserved if there is no **<xsl:strip-space>** element in the stylesheet that matches its parent element.

A whitespace-only text node is removed from the tree if there is an **<xsl:strip-space>** element that matches the parent element, and no **<xsl:preserve-space>** element that matches.

If there is both an **<xsl:strip-space>** element that matches the parent element, and an **<xsl:preserve-space>** element that matches, then the decision depends on the import precedence and priority of the respective rules. Taking into consideration all the **<xsl:strip-space>** and **<xsl:preserve-space>** elements that match the parent element of the whitespace-only text node, the XSLT processor takes the one with highest import precedence (as defined in the rules for **<xsl:import>** on page 226). If there is more than one with this import precedence, it takes the one with highest priority, as defined in the table above. If there is still more than one, it may either report an error, or choose the one that occurs last in the stylesheet. If the chosen element is **<xsl:preserve-space>**, the whitespace-only text node is preserved on the tree: if it is **<xsl:strip-space>**, it is removed from the tree.

In deciding whether to strip or preserve a whitespace-only text node, only its immediate parent element is considered in the above rules. The rules for its other ancestors make no difference. The element itself, of course, is never removed from the tree: the stripping process will only ever remove text nodes.

If an individual element has the XML-defined attribute «`xml:space="preserve"`» or «`xml:space="default"`» this overrides anything defined in the stylesheet. These values, unlike **<xsl:preserve-space>** and **<xsl:strip-space>**, do affect descendant elements as well as the element on which the attribute appears. If an **<xsl:strip-space>** doesn't seem to be having any effect, one possible reason is that the element type in question is declared in the DTD to have an **`xml:space`** attribute with a default value of «`preserve`». There is no way of overriding this in the stylesheet.

Usage

For many categories of source document, especially those used to represent data structures, whitespace-only text nodes are never significant, so it is useful to specify:

```
<xsl:strip-space elements="*"/>
```

which will remove them all from the tree. There are two main advantages in stripping these unwanted nodes:

- When **<xsl:apply-templates>** is used with a default **`select`** attribute, all child nodes will be processed. If whitespace-only text nodes are not stripped, they too will be processed, probably leading to the whitespace being copied to the output destination.
- When the **`position()`** function is used to determine the position of an element relative to its siblings, the whitespace-only text nodes are included in the count. This often leads to the significant nodes being numbered 2, 4, 6, 8 …

Generally speaking, it is a good idea to strip whitespace-only text nodes belonging to elements that have element content, that is, elements declared in the DTD as containing child elements but no `#PCDATA`.

It also usually does no harm to strip whitespace-only text nodes from elements declared as having `#PCDATA` content; that is, elements whose only children are text nodes. In most cases, an element containing whitespace text is equivalent to an empty element, so stylesheet logic can be simplified if elements containing whitespace only are normalized to be empty by removing the text node.

By contrast, stripping whitespace-only text nodes from elements with mixed content, elements declared in the DTD to contain both child elements and `#PCDATA`, is often a bad idea. For example, consider the element below:

```
<quote>He went to <edu>Balliol College</edu> <city>Oxford</city> to read
<subject>Greats</subject></quote>
```

The space between the **<edu>** element and the **<city>** element is a whitespace-only text node, and it should be preserved, because otherwise when the tags are removed by an application that's only interested in the text, the words «`College`» and «`Oxford`» will run together.

Examples

To strip whitespace nodes from all elements of the source tree:

```
<xsl:strip-space elements="*"/>
```

To strip whitespace nodes from selected elements:

```
<xsl:strip-space elements="book author title price"/>
```

To strip whitespace nodes from all elements except the **<description>** element:

```
<xsl:strip-space elements="*"/>
<xsl:preserve-space elements="description"/>
```

To strip whitespace nodes from all elements except those in the namespace with URI `http://mednet.org/text`:

```
<xsl:strip-space elements="*"/>
<xsl:preserve-space elements="mednet:*"
                              xmlns:mednet="http://mednet.org/text" />
```

See also

<xsl:strip-space> on page 301

xsl:processing-instruction

The **<xsl:processing-instruction>** instruction is used to write a processing instruction node to the current output destination.

Defined in

XSLT section 7.3

Format

```
<xsl:processing-instruction name=NCName >
   template body
</xsl:processing-instruction>
```

Position

<xsl:processing-instruction> is an instruction. It is always used as part of a template body.

Attributes

Name	Value	Meaning
name mandatory	Attribute value template returning an NCName	The name (target) of the generated processing instruction.

Content

A template body.

Effect

The name of the generated processing instruction (in XML terms, the PITarget), is determined by the **name** attribute. This may be expressed as an attribute value template. The name must be valid as a PITarget as defined in the XML specification, and XSLT imposes the additional rule that it must be a valid NCName, as defined in the XML Namespaces Recommendation. This means it must be an XML Name that doesn't contain a colon (to make it an NCName) and that isn't the name «xml» in any mixture of upper and lower case (to make it a PITarget).

The specification is quite explicit that **<xsl:processing-instruction>** cannot be used to generate an XML declaration at the start of the output file. The XML declaration looks like a processing instruction, but technically it isn't one; and the ban on using the name «xml» makes this quite explicit. The XML declaration in the output file is generated automatically by the XSLT processor, and can be controlled to a limited extent using the **<xsl:output>** element.

The data part of the processing instruction is generated from the contained template body. The space that separates the PITarget from the data is output automatically. The output generated by the template body must contain text nodes only, and it must not contain the string «?>» which terminates a processing instruction. Implementations are allowed to trap the «?>» and replace it by «? >» (with an embedded space); unfortunately they are also allowed to report this as an error, so if you want your stylesheet to be portable, you need to make sure this condition can't happen.

The data part of a processing instruction cannot contain character references such as «₤», so it is an error to output any characters that can't be represented directly in the chosen character encoding of the output file. Some processing instructions may accept data that looks like a character reference, but that's an application-level convention, not something defined in the XML standard, so the XSLT processor will never generate such a reference automatically.

Usage

Use this instruction when you want to output a processing instruction.

Processing instructions are not widely used in most XML applications, so you will probably not need to use this instruction very often. They are used even less in HTML, though HTML 4.0 does recommend that any vendor-specific extensions should be implemented this way. In HTML the terminator for a processing instruction is «>» rather than «?>», and this difference is handled automatically by the HTML output method; see **<xsl:output>** on page 270.

Note that you cannot generate a processing instruction in the output by writing a processing instruction in the stylesheet. Processing instructions in the stylesheet are ignored completely. You can, however, use **<xsl:copy>** or **<xsl:copy-of>** to copy processing instructions from the source tree to the result tree.

Examples

The following example outputs an **<?xml-stylesheet?>** processing instruction at the start of the output file.

```
<xsl:processing-instruction name="xml-stylesheet">
<xsl:text>href="housestyle.css" type="text/css"</xsl:text>
</xsl:processing-instruction>
```

The generated output is:

```
<?xml-stylesheet href="housestyle.css" type="text/css"?>
```

Writing an XSLT stylesheet that produces an XML document which itself refers to a CSS stylesheet isn't such a crazy thing to do as it might seem. It often makes sense to do the first stage of processing of an XML file on the server, and the second stage on the client (in other words, in the browser). The first stage will extract the data that the user wants to see – and, most importantly, remove any information they are not allowed to see. The second stage applies the detailed rules for output formatting. The second stage can often be done just as easily with CSS as with XSLT, because anything CSS can't cope with, such as adding or reordering textual content, can be done in the first stage with XSLT.

One point to watch out for in generating an <?xml-stylesheet?> processing instruction, and which might well apply to other processing instructions, is the use of pseudo-attributes and pseudo-character and entity references. The text «href="housestyle.css"» in the above example is designed to look like an XML attribute, but it is not actually an XML attribute, it is purely part of the processing instruction data. It is parsed by the application, not by the XML parser. As it is not a true XML attribute, you cannot generate it as an attribute node using the **<xsl:attribute>** instruction; rather, it is generated as text.

The rules for the <?xml-stylesheet?> processing instruction are defined in a short W3C Recommendation called *Associating Style Sheets with XML Documents*, available at http://www.w3.org/TR/xml-stylesheet. As well as defining the data part of this processing instruction in the form of pseudo-attributes, the rules also allow the use of numeric character references such as «₤» and predefined entity references such as «>» and «&». Again, these are not true character references and entity references that the XML parser will recognize, and as a result they will not be generated by the XSLT processor either. If you want to include «₤» as part of the data of the processing instruction, you can write, for example,

```
<xsl:processing-instruction name="xml-stylesheet">
<xsl:text>href="housestyle.css" type="text/css" </xsl:text>
<xsl:text>title="A title containing &amp;#x20A4;" </xsl:text>
</xsl:processing-instruction>
```

xsl:script

The **<xsl:script>** element is a top-level element used to define extension functions that can be invoked from XPath expressions. The **<xsl:script>** element is new in the draft XSLT 1.1 specification. Several XSLT 1.0 processors provide equivalent vendor-defined mechanisms, for example Microsoft's MSXML3 has an **<msxml:script>** element whose specification is quite similar.

The XSLT 1.1 working draft provides standard ways of writing extension functions in Java or in JavaScript, though XSLT processors are not required to support either of these languages, and can if they wish support other languages whose language binding is not defined in the standard.

Defined in

XSLT 1.1 section 14.4

Format

```
<xsl:script
   implements-prefix = NCName
   language = "ecmascript" | "javascript" | "java" | QName
   src = URI
   archive = list of URIs >
         text
</xsl:script>
```

Position

<xsl:script> is a top-level element, so it must be contained immediately within the **<xsl:stylesheet>** or **<xsl:transform>** element.

There can be more than one **<xsl:script>** element in a stylesheet; the only constraint is that you cannot have two **<xsl:script>** elements with the same `language` and the same `implements-prefix` (or, more accurately, prefixes that map to the same namespace URI) unless they have different import precedence. The order of **<xsl:script>** elements makes no difference.

Attributes

Name	Value	Meaning
implements-prefix mandatory	Namespace prefix	Matches the prefix used in the extension function call. (Prefixes match if they relate to the same namespace URI.)
language mandatory	«ecmascript» | «javascript» | «java» | *QName*	Defines the language in which the extension function is implemented. A *QName* (which must have a non-null prefix) is used for vendor-defined languages.
src optional	URI	Identifies the code (source code or compiled code) that implements the function. If omitted, the source code can be found in the text content of the **<xsl:script>** element.
archive optional	Whitespace-separated list of URIs	Defines locations to be searched for code needed to support the extension function.

Content

If the **src** attribute is present, the element must be empty.

If the **src** attribute is omitted, the element must contain the code of one or more extension functions, in the language specified. The content is text-only, it may not contain any elements. Since code often makes use of XML special characters such as «<» or «&», it is a good idea to write it as a `CDATA` section between the delimiters «<![CDATA[» and «]]>», but this is not mandatory.

Effect

The **<xsl:script>** element tells the processor where to find implementations of extension functions referenced within the stylesheet.

An extension function is called from within an XPath expression using a prefixed function name, for example «`my:function()`». The prefix «`my`» must correspond to a namespace URI that is in scope at the point where the XPath expression is written; the processor searches for an implementation of the function by looking for an **`<xsl:script>`** element that implements a prefix corresponding to this same namespace URI.

If the search finds implementations for the namespace URI in more than one language, the processor can choose whichever of these it prefers. The idea here is that the stylesheet can provide alternative implementations of the same function in different languages, so different XSLT processors can each find a version they can handle. It's up to the stylesheet author to make sure that the alternative implementations are equivalent.

If the search finds more than one implementation in the same language, then they must have different import precedences. In an ideal world, the processor would look for the implementation of the required function that has the highest import precedence; however, the specification recognizes that this is not practical for all languages, so it allows the behavior to vary from one language to another.

It is possible for a collection of functions with the same namespace URI to be defined in a single **`<xsl:script>`** element. In an object-oriented language such as Java where method names are unique within a class, a separate namespace URI, and therefore a separate **`<xsl:script>`** element, will be needed for each class containing extension functions, but all the methods within this class will be accessible via a single **`<xsl:script>`** element. In languages such as JavaScript that allow functions to exist within a global namespace, it is possible to use a single **`<xsl:script>`** element for all extension functions.

The actual code can either be written in the stylesheet itself, or loaded from a separate file.

- For an interpreted language such as JavaScript, both options are feasible; you can write the code within the **`<xsl:script>`** element, or in a file referenced using the **`src`** attribute, for example «`src="date-routines.js"`».
- With a compiled language such as Java, the only feasible option is to tell the XSLT processor where to load the compiled Java code for the relevant classes, and this is done by giving a URI that identifies the class (for example «`src="java:com.acme.toolslib.Widget"`», possibly supplemented by the **`archive`** attribute which specifies a list of directories or JAR files to be searched, in the form of a classpath.

The **`<xsl:script>`** element has been designed to be extensible for different languages. Initially only JavaScript and Java are defined (the name must be written in lowercase, and «`ecmascript`» is allowed as a synonym of «`javascript`», for those who like to use the official name of the language). Other languages such as VB or Perl may be offered by vendors but the details are outside the scope of the standard.

Usage and Examples

Examples of the use of this element are provided in Chapter 8.

See also

Further information on writing extension functions in Java and JavaScript is provided in Chapter 8 of this book.

xsl:sort

The **<xsl:sort>** element is used to define a sort key, to specify the order in which nodes selected by **<xsl:apply-templates>** or **<xsl:for-each>** are processed.

Defined in

XSLT section 10

Format

```
<xsl:sort
    select=Expression
    order={"ascending" | "descending"}
    case-order={"upper-first" | "lower-first"}
    lang={language-code}
    data-type={"text" | "number" | QName }/>
```

Position

<xsl:sort> is always a child of **<xsl:apply-templates>** or **<xsl:for-each>**. Any number of sort keys may be specified, in major-to-minor order. When used in **<xsl:for-each>**, any **<xsl:sort>** elements must appear before the template body of the **<xsl:for-each>** statement. When used in **<xsl:apply-templates>**, the **<xsl:sort>** elements can come before or after any **<xsl:with-param>** elements.

Attributes

Name	Value	Meaning
select optional	`Expression`	Defines the sort key. The default is the string value of the node (the expression «`string(.)`»).
order optional	Attribute value template returning: «`ascending`» | «`descending`»	Defines whether the nodes are processed in ascending or descending order of this key. The default is «`ascending`».
case-order optional	Attribute value template returning: «`upper-first`» | «`lower-first`»	Defines whether upper-case letters are to be collated before or after lower-case letters. The default is language-dependent.

Name	Value	Meaning
lang optional	Attribute value template returning a language code	Defines the language whose collating conventions are to be used. The default depends on the processing environment.
data-type optional	Attribute value template returning: «text» | «number» | QName	Defines whether the values are to be collated alphabetically or numerically, or using a user-defined data type. The default is «text».

Content

None, the element is always empty.

Effect

The list of **<xsl:sort>** elements within an **<xsl:apply-templates>** or **<xsl:for-each>** element determines the order in which the selected nodes are processed. The nodes are sorted first by the first sort key; any group of nodes that have duplicate values for the first sort key are then sorted by the second sort key, and so on. If a group of nodes have duplicate values for all the sort keys, this group is sorted in document order. Similarly, when no sort keys are specified at all, the nodes are processed in document order.

The value of the sort key for each node in the node-set is established by evaluating the expression given in the **select** attribute. This is evaluated with that node as the current node, and with the current node list being the complete node-set, in document order.

This means that if you want to process the nodes in reverse document order, you can specify a sort key as:

```
<xsl:sort select="position()"
          data-type="number"
          order="descending" />
```

The result of the expression is always converted to a string, and if the **data-type** is «number» this string will then be converted to a number.

The way in which sort keys are compared is determined by the other attributes of the **<xsl:sort>** element. Some of these rules are defined precisely in the XSLT specification, some are given merely as guidance for the implementor, and some are left entirely implementation-defined. The specification explicitly warns that different implementations may produce different results.

Note that the **select** attribute must be an expression which is evaluated for each node, with that node as the context node, to give the value that determines that node's position in the sequence. There's no direct way of specifying that you want to use different sort keys on different occasions. I've seen people try to write things like:

```
<xsl:param name="sort-key" >
. . .
     <xsl:for-each select="BOOK">
        <xsl:sort select="$sort-key"/>
```

hoping that if `$sort-key` is set to «`TITLE`», the elements will be sorted by title, and that if `$sort-key` is set to «`AUTHOR`», they will be sorted by author. This doesn't work: the variable `$sort-key` will have the same value for every `<BOOK>` element, so the books will always be output in unsorted order. In this case, where the sort key is always a child element of the elements being sorted, you can achieve the required effect by writing:

```
<xsl:sort select="*[local-name()=$sort-key]">
```

Another way of making the sort conditional is to use a conditional expression as the sort key. This gets more complicated, but if there is a fixed range of possibilities, you could write something like:

```
<xsl:sort select="title[$sort-key='title'] |
                  author[$sort-key='author'] |
                  @isbn[$sort-key='isbn']">
```

Here the union expression (constructed using the union operator, « | ») is being used to combine several node-sets, all but one of which will be empty, because the predicates are mutually exclusive.

The **`data-type`** may be either «`text`» or «`number`». With «`text`» order, you would expect to see «`10`» appear before «`5`», while with «`number`» order, you would expect «`5`» to come before «`10`».

- Ordering of numbers is well defined. The specification says that they are sorted according to the numeric value. Any values that are NaN (not a number) are placed at the start of the sequence. (The rule for sorting of NaN values was left undefined in the original XSLT 1.0 specification, so you may find that not all processors handle it this way.)
- By contrast, ordering of text strings is rather loosely defined. The concept of alphabetic order is language-dependent, so the intention is that it should be controlled by the **`lang`** attribute. For example, in modern German «ä» is collated immediately after «a» (in older works, it is collated as if it were the pair of letters «`ae`»), while in Swedish, «ä» is a separate letter that appears at the end of the alphabet after «`z`». The XSLT specification refers implementors for guidance to a Unicode white paper on international sorting, Unicode Technical Report #10, *Unicode Collation Algorithm*. (See http://www.unicode.org/unicode/reports/tr10/index.html). However, it doesn't make any of the rules mandatory.

Knowing the language doesn't help you decide whether upper-case or lower-case letters should come first (every dictionary in the world has its own rules on this), so XSLT makes this a separate attribute, **`case-order`**. Generally case-order will be used only to decide the ordering of two words that compare equal if case is ignored. For example, in German, where an initial upper-case letter can change the meaning of a word, some dictionaries list the adjective *drall* (meaning plump or buxom) before the unrelated noun *Drall* (a swerve, twist, or bias), while others reverse the order. Specifying «`case-order="lower-first"`» would place *drall* immediately before *Drall*, while «`case-order="upper-first"`» would have *Drall* immediately followed by *drall*.

The **order** attribute specifies whether the order is ascending or descending. Descending order will produce the opposite result of ascending order. This means, for example, that NaN values will appear last rather than first, and it also means that the effect of the `case-order` attribute is reversed: if you specify «`case-order="upper-first"`» with «`order="descending"`», then *drall* will come **before** *Drall*. (Again, this is something that was clarified after the initial publication of XSLT 1.0, so you may come across a processor that interprets the rules differently.)

The option to set «`data-type="QName"`» was a last-minute addition to the language before version 1.0 was frozen, and its behavior is not precisely defined. It's really a hook to allow vendor extensions, or perhaps to allow extensions in a subsequent addendum to the standard. There is a recognized requirement to enable sorting of data types such as dates and times that are defined in the XML Schema Recommendation, and support for XML Schema data types is high on the shopping list for XSLT 2.0.

The final sorted order of the nodes determines the sequence in which they are processed by the containing **<xsl:apply-templates>** or **<xsl:for-each>** statement, and also the value of the **position()** function when each node comes to be processed. The value of **position()** will reflect its position in the sorted list.

Usage

XSLT is designed to be capable of handling serious professional publishing applications, and clearly this requires some fairly powerful sorting capabilities. In practice, however, the most demanding applications almost invariably have domain-specific collating rules; for instance, the rules for sorting personal names in a telephone directory are unlikely to work well for geographical names in a gazetteer. For these applications, vendors are already providing hooks to allow user-defined collating algorithms.

Examples

I'll start with a couple of simple examples, and then show a full working example which you can download and try yourself.

Example 1: To process all the **<book>** children of the current node, sorting them by the value of the **isbn** attribute:

```
<xsl:apply-templates select="book">
   <xsl:sort select="@isbn"/>
</xsl:apply-templates>
```

Example 2: To output the contents of all the **<city>** elements in the document, in alphabetical order, including each distinct city once only:

```
<ul>
<xsl:for-each select="//city[not(.=preceding::city)]">
   <xsl:sort select="."/>
   <li><xsl:value-of select="."/></li>
</xsl:for-each>
</ul>
```

If «select="."» was omitted from the **<xsl:sort>** element, the effect would be the same, because this is the default; however, I prefer to include it for clarity.

Example: Sorting on the Result of a Calculation

This example outputs a list of products, sorted by the total sales of each product, in descending order.

Source

This is the file products.xml:

```
<products>
<product name="strawberry jam">
   <region name="south" sales="20.00"/>
   <region name="north" sales="50.00"/>
</product>
<product name="raspberry jam">
   <region name="south" sales="205.16"/>
   <region name="north" sales="10.50"/>
</product>
<product name="plum jam">
   <region name="east" sales="320.20"/>
   <region name="north" sales="39.50"/>
</product>
</products>
```

Stylesheet

products.xsl is a complete stylesheet written using the simplified stylesheet syntax, in which the entire stylesheet module is written as a single literal result element. Simplified stylesheets are described in Chapter 3, on page 113.

The **<xsl:sort>** element sorts the selected node-set (containing all the **<product>** elements) in descending order of the numerical total of the **sales** attribute over all their **<region>** child elements. The total is calculated using the **sum()** function (discussed on Chapter 7, page 553), and displayed using the **format-number()** function (shown Chapter 7, on page 484).

```
<products xsl:version="1.0"
       xmlns:xsl="http://www.w3.org/1999/XSL/Transform">
<xsl:for-each select="products/product">
   <xsl:sort select="sum(region/@sales)"
                                    data-type="number"
                                    order="descending"/>
   <product name="{@name}"
            sales="{format-number(sum(region/@sales), '$####0.00')}"/>
</xsl:for-each>
</products>
```

Output

I have added line breaks for readability:

```
<products>
<product name="plum jam" sales="$359.70"/>
<product name="raspberry jam" sales="$215.66"/>
<product name="strawberry jam" sales="$70.00"/>
</products>
```


See also

<xsl:apply-templates> on page 155
<xsl:for-each> on page 219

xsl:strip-space

The **<xsl:strip-space>** element, along with **<xsl:preserve-space>**, is used to control the way in which whitespace nodes in the source document are handled. The **<xsl:strip-space>** element identifies elements in which whitespace-only text nodes are considered insignificant, so they can be removed from the source tree.

Defined in

XSLT section 3.4

Format

```
<xsl:strip-space elements=list-of-NameTests />
```

Position

<xsl:strip-space> is a top-level element, which means it is always a child of the **<xsl:stylesheet>** element. There are no constraints on where it appears relative to other top-level elements.

Attributes

Name	Value	Meaning
elements mandatory	Whitespace-separated list of `NameTests`	Defines elements in the source document whose whitespace-only text nodes are to be removed

The construct `NameTest` is defined in Chapter 5, on page 394.

Content

None, the element is always empty.

Effect, Usage, and Examples

See **<xsl:preserve-space>** on page 286. The two elements **<xsl:strip-space>** and **<xsl:preserve-space>** are closely related, so I have presented the rules and usage guidance in one place.

See also

<xsl:preserve-space> on page 286
<xsl:text> on page 323

xsl:stylesheet

The **<xsl:stylesheet>** element is the outermost element of a stylesheet. The synonym **<xsl:transform>** can be used as an alternative.

Defined in

XSLT section 2.2

Format

```
<xsl:stylesheet
   id=identifier
   version="1.1"
   xmlns:xsl="http://www.w3.org/1999/XSL/Transform"
   extension-element-prefixes=list-of-prefixes
   exclude-result-prefixes=list-of-prefixes >
      top-level-element *
</xsl:stylesheet>
```

Position

<xsl:stylesheet> appears as the outermost element of every stylesheet module, except one that uses the *literal-result-element-as-stylesheet* syntax described on page 113, in Chapter 3. It is used both on a principal stylesheet and on one that is imported or included into another stylesheet.

As well as being the outermost element of the stylesheet module, the **<xsl:stylesheet>** element is usually the document element of an XML document – but not always; as described in Chapter 3, a stylesheet can also be embedded in another XML document.

Namespace Declarations

There will always be at least one namespace declaration on the **<xsl:stylesheet>** element, typically:

```
xmlns:xsl="http://www.w3.org/1999/XSL/Transform"
```

This is necessary to identify the document as an XSLT stylesheet. The URI part must be written exactly as shown. The prefix «xsl» is conventional, and is used in all XSLT documentation including this book and the standard itself, but you could choose a different prefix if you wanted, for example «XSLT». You would then have to name the element **<XSLT:stylesheet>** instead of **<xsl:stylesheet>**.

You can also make this the default namespace by using the following declaration:

```
xmlns="http://www.w3.org/1999/XSL/Transform"
```

In this case the element name will simply be **<stylesheet>**, and other XSLT elements will similarly be unprefixed, for example **<template>** rather than **<xsl:template>**. Although this works, it is not generally recommended, because the default namespace is then not available for literal result elements. The technique that works best is to reserve the default namespace for literal result elements that you want to go in the default namespace of the output document.

> **If you come across a stylesheet that uses the namespace declaration:**
>
> **xmlns:xsl="http://www.w3.org/TR/WD-xsl"**
>
> **then it is not an XSLT stylesheet at all, but one written in WD-xsl, the working-draft dialect of XSL that Microsoft shipped in 1998 with Internet Explorer 5. This is a very different language, and is not described in this book. See Appendix A for details of current Microsoft XSL products.**

Attributes

Name	Value	Meaning
id optional	XML Name	An identifier used to identify the **<xsl:stylesheet>** element when it is embedded in another XML document.
version mandatory	Number	Defines the version of XSLT required by this stylesheet. Use «1.1» for a stylesheet that requires XSLT 1.1 features, or «1.0» if you want the stylesheet to be portable between XSLT 1.0 and XSLT 1.1 processors.
extension-element-prefixes optional	Whitespace-separated list of NCNames	Defines any namespaces used in this stylesheet to identify extension elements.
exclude-result-prefixes optional	Whitespace-separated list of NCNames	Defines any namespaces used in this stylesheet that should not be copied to the output destination, unless they are actually used in the result document.

Content

The **<xsl:stylesheet>** element may contain XSLT elements referred to as **top-level elements**. These elements are:

<xsl:attribute-set>	**<xsl:key>**	**<xsl:preserve-space>**
<xsl:decimal-format>	**<xsl:namespace-alias>**	**<xsl:script> ***
<xsl:import>	**<xsl:output>**	**<xsl:strip-space>**
<xsl:include>	**<xsl:param>**	**<xsl:template>**
		<xsl:variable>

* Note: **<xsl:script>** is new in XSLT 1.1.

If there are any **<xsl:import>** elements, they must come before other top-level elements.

The **<xsl:stylesheet>** element may also contain other elements provided they use a non-null namespace URI which is different from the XSLT namespace URI. If the namespace URI is recognized by the XSLT processor, it may interpret such elements in any way the vendor chooses, provided that the correct functioning of the stylesheet is not affected. If it does not recognize these elements, it should ignore them.

Effect

The rules are described below for each of the attributes.

The id Attribute

This attribute is there to allow an **<xsl:stylesheet>** element to be referenced when it is contained within another XML document.

The precise usage is not defined in the standard, but the expectation is that this **id** attribute will allow an embedded stylesheet to be referenced in an `<?xml-stylesheet?>` processing instruction. An example is given in Chapter 3.

The version Attribute

The **version** attribute defines the version of the XSLT specification that the stylesheet is relying on. At present there are two published versions of the XSLT standard, namely versions 1.0 and 1.1, so this attribute should take either of these values.

Implementations of XSLT, even if they only implement version 1.0 of the standard, are required to behave in a particular way if the version specified is anything other than 1.0.

- If the **version** attribute is «`1.0`», an XSLT 1.0 processor must report as errors any elements in the XSLT namespace that it doesn't recognize. For example, if it encounters the element **<xsl:apply_template>** it will flag this as an error (because the correct spelling is **<xsl:apply-templates>**). Similarly, an XSLT 1.1 processor must reject unrecognized XSLT elements if the version attribute is set to «`1.0`» or «`1.1`».

- If the **version** attribute is any other value (including, oddly, a lower value than 1.0), the implementation must assume that the stylesheet is trying to use features defined in some version of XSLT that the software is unaware of. So if the version attribute is «2.1», and the element **<xsl:apply_template>** appears, the software has to assume that this is a new element defined in version 2.1 of the standard, rather than a misspelling of **<xsl:apply-templates>**. The XSLT specification calls this *forwards-compatible processing mode*. In this mode, the **<xsl:apply_template>** element will be rejected only if (a) an attempt is made to instantiate it, and (b) it has no **<xsl:fallback>** child element. If it does have an **<xsl:fallback>** child element, this will be instantiated in place of the unrecognized parent element. This is described in greater detail under **<xsl:fallback>** on page 214.

Forwards compatible mode also affects the handling of other apparent errors. For example if the **version** attribute is «1.0» (or in the case of an XSLT 1.1 processor, «1.1»), then any unrecognized attributes or values of attributes on an XSLT element are reported as errors, but in forwards compatible mode, such attributes are ignored. Similarly, in forwards compatible mode a misplaced XSLT element such as **<xsl:sort>**, if found within a template body, will not be reported as an error until you try to instantiate it.

The **version** attribute applies to the entire stylesheet, except any parts contained within a literal result element that has an **xsl:version** attribute. Its scope is the stylesheet module, not the full stylesheet tree constructed by applying **<xsl:include>** and **<xsl:import>** elements.

The extension-element-prefixes Attribute

This attribute identifies a set of namespaces used for extension elements. Extension elements may be defined by an implementor, by a user, or by a third party. They can be used anywhere an instruction can be used, that is, within a template body. If an element is found in a template body that is not in the XSLT namespace, then it must either be an extension element or a literal result element. If its namespace is the same as a namespace identified in the **extension-element-prefixes** attribute of the containing **<xsl:stylesheet>** element, then it will be treated as an extension element, otherwise it will be treated as a literal result element.

The value of the attribute is a whitespace-separated list of prefixes; each of these prefixes must identify a namespace declaration present on the **<xsl:stylesheet>** element. The default namespace (the namespace declared using the **xmlns** attribute) may be designated as an extension element namespace by including the pseudo-prefix «#default».

The list of namespaces used for extension elements may be augmented for a section of the stylesheet by using the **xsl:extension-element-prefixes** attribute of a literal result element or an extension element. This does not override the declarations at the stylesheet level, it supplements them.

The scope of the **extension-element-prefixes** attribute is the stylesheet module, not the full stylesheet tree constructed by applying **<xsl:include>** and **<xsl:import>** elements.

If a namespace is designated as an extension element namespace, then every XSLT processor will recognize that these elements are extension elements. However, some XSLT processors may be unable to instantiate them. For example, if the namespace `http://www.jclark.com/xt/extensions` is designated as an extension namespace, then both xt and Xalan will recognize that these elements are extensions, but the likelihood is that xt will know how to handle them and Xalan won't. If the processor knows how to instantiate the element, it does so; otherwise, it looks to see if the element contains an **<xsl:fallback>** instruction. If it does, the **<xsl:fallback>** instruction is instantiated, otherwise, an error is reported.

It is only necessary to designate a namespace as an extension element namespace to distinguish extension elements from literal result elements. At the top level of the stylesheet, there is no risk of confusion. Any implementation can define its own top-level elements, using its own namespace, and other implementations will simply ignore these elements, treating them as data. So the **extension-element-prefixes** attribute is not needed to identify top-level elements used as vendor or user extensions. For example, you can use **<msxml:script>** as a top-level element, and processors other than Microsoft MSXML3 will probably ignore it (though there is nothing that says they have to).

The exclude-result-prefixes Attribute

This attribute defines a set of namespaces which are **not** to be copied into the result tree.

The XSLT processor is required to produce a correct tree that conforms with the data model (as described on page 52, in Chapter 2) and with the XML Namespaces rules, so you will never find yourself with an output file using namespace prefixes that have not been declared. However, you can easily find yourself with a file containing unnecessary and unwanted namespace declarations, for example, declarations of namespaces that occur on nodes in your source document but which are not used in the output document, or namespaces for extension functions that are used only in the stylesheet. These extra namespace declarations usually don't matter, because they don't affect the meaning of the output file, but they can clutter it up. They can also affect validation if you are trying to create a result document that conforms to a particular DTD. So this attribute is provided to help you get rid of them.

More specifically, the XSLT specification requires that when a literal result element in the stylesheet is instantiated, the element is copied into the result tree along with all its namespace nodes, except for the XSLT namespace and any namespace that defines extension elements. An element has a namespace node for every namespace that is in scope, including namespaces defined on ancestor elements as well as on the element itself, so the namespaces copied over include not only the namespaces defined on the literal result element, and those that are actually used on the literal result element, but even those that are merely *available* for use.

Very often, of course, one literal result element will be a child or descendant of another, and the namespace nodes on the child element will include copies of all the namespace nodes on the parent element. For example, consider the stylesheet below:

```
<xsl:stylesheet version="1.0"
                xmlns:xsl="http://www.w3.org/1999/XSL/Transform"/>

<xsl:template match="/">
   <acme:document xmlns:acme="http://acme.com/xslt">
      <acme:chapter>
         Once upon a time ...
      </acme:chapter>
   </acme:document>
</xsl:template>

</xsl:stylesheet>
```


This can be represented by the tree shown in the diagram below, using the same notation as previously seen in Chapters 2 and 3. Although there are only two namespace declarations, these are propagated to all the descendant elements, so for example the **<acme:chapter>** element has two namespace nodes even though there are no namespace declarations on the element. (It also has a namespace node for the «xml» namespace, not shown on the diagram.)

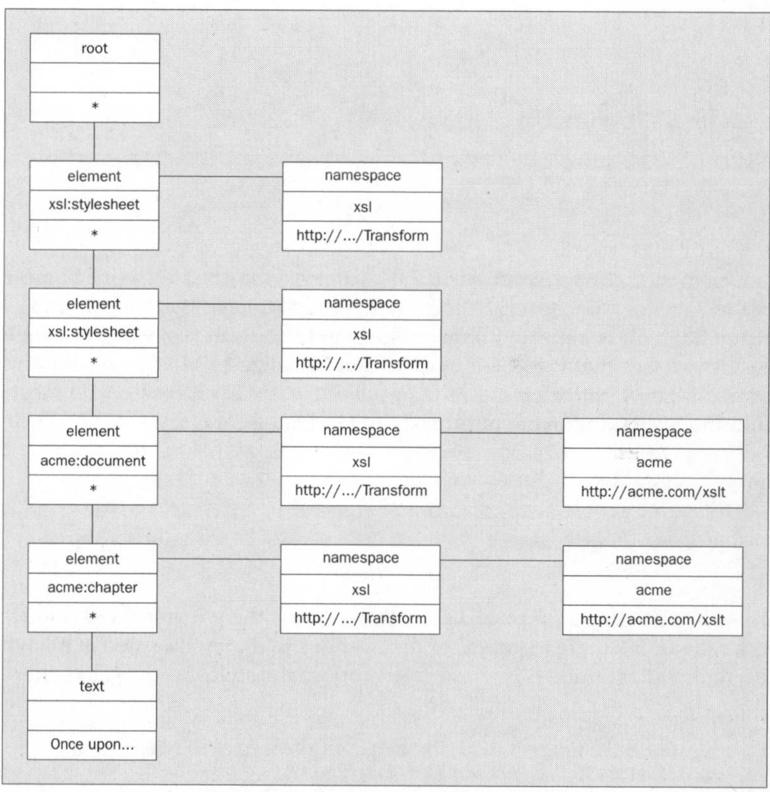

The specification says that each literal result element is copied with all its namespace nodes (but excluding the XSLT namespace), so the result tree will look like this (again, the «xml» namespace nodes are omitted):

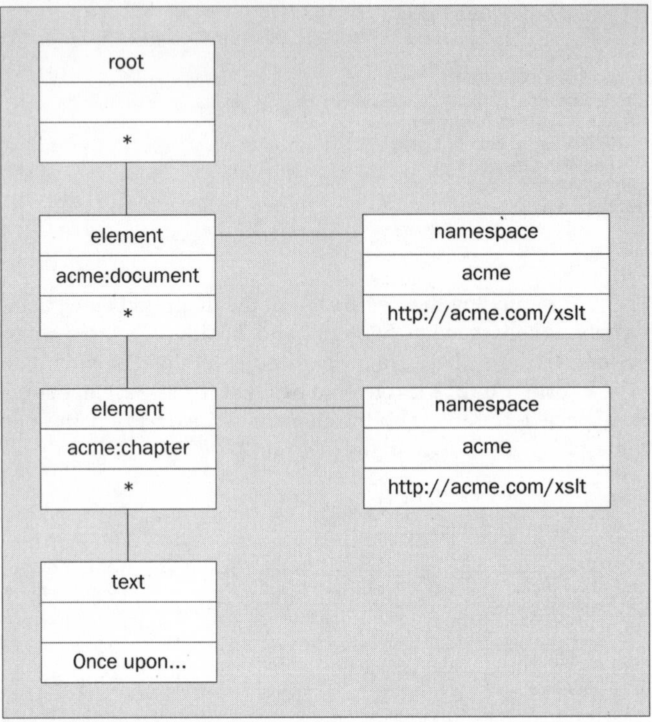

Both elements, **<acme:document>** and **<acme:chapter>**, have a namespace node for the «acme» namespace. However, this doesn't mean that the namespace declaration will be repeated unnecessarily in the output file: we're talking here about the abstract tree that is created, not the final serialized XML file. Avoiding duplicate namespace declarations is entirely the job of the XSLT processor, and most processors will produce the following output, shown indented for clarity:

```
<acme:document xmlns:acme="http://acme.com/xslt">
   <acme:chapter>
      Once upon a time ...
   </acme:chapter>
</acme:document>
```

The **exclude-result-prefixes** attribute isn't there to get rid of duplicate declarations, it's there to get rid of declarations that aren't wanted at all, which is a different matter entirely. For example suppose the stylesheet was like this:

```
<xsl:stylesheet version="1.0"
   xmlns:xsl="http://www.w3.org/1999/XSL/Transform"
   xmlns:var="http://another.org/xslt"
/>

<xsl:variable name="var:x" select="17"/>
```

```
<xsl:template match="/">
   <acme:document xmlns:acme="http://acme.com/xslt">
      <acme:chapter>
         Once upon a time ...
      </acme:chapter>
   </acme:document>
</xsl:template>

</xsl:stylesheet>
```


Then although the template body has not changed, the **<acme:document>** and **<acme:chapter>** elements each now have an extra namespace node, and this will be copied to the output file even though it is unused, resulting in the output:

```
<acme:document xmlns:acme="http://acme.com/xslt"
               xmlns:var="http://another.org/xslt">
   <acme:chapter>
      Once upon a time ...
   </acme:chapter>
</acme:document>
```

Why can't the XSLT processor simply include all the namespaces that are actually used in element and attribute names, and omit the rest? The thinking is that many XML applications, like XSLT itself, will use the namespace mechanism to create unique values within their own data. For example, namespace prefixes might be used in attribute values as well as attribute names. The XSLT processor can't distinguish these from ordinary values, so it has to play safe.

So if there are namespaces you don't want in the output tree, you can specify them in the **exclude-result-prefixes** attribute of the **<xsl:stylesheet>** element. The attribute is a list of namespace prefixes, separated by whitespace, and with the option to include the default namespace under the pseudo-prefix «#default».

The prefix, as always, is simply a way of referring to the associated namespace URI: it is the namespace URI that is really being excluded, not the prefix itself. So if the same namespace URI is declared again with a different prefix, it is still an excluded namespace.

The **exclude-result-prefixes** attribute on the **<xsl:stylesheet>** element provides a way of controlling namespace exclusion for the entire stylesheet. Additional prefixes to be excluded may be specified in the **xsl:exclude-result-prefixes** attribute of the literal result element itself: these only affect that element and its descendants.

The **xsl:exclude-result-prefixes** and **exclude-result-prefixes** attributes apply only to namespace nodes copied from the stylesheet using literal result elements. They do not affect namespace nodes copied from the source document using **<xsl:copy>** or **<xsl:copy-of>**; there is no way of suppressing these.

Like the other attributes on the **<xsl:stylesheet>** element, the **exclude-result-prefixes** attribute applies only to elements within the stylesheet module, not to those brought in using **<xsl:include>** or **<xsl:import>**.

What happens if you try to exclude a namespace that is actually needed because it is used in the result tree? The XSLT processor is obliged to generate output that conforms to the Namespaces Recommendation, so it will ignore the request to exclude this namespace. (The XSLT 1.0 specification technically gives the serializer free rein to generate any extra namespace declarations it feels like. At XSLT 1.1 the rules are more restrictive: namespace nodes must be generated in the result tree only where they are actually needed to declare a prefix for a namespace URI used in the expanded name of an element or attribute node.)

Usage and Examples

The **<xsl:stylesheet>** element is always the outermost element of the stylesheet (though the stylesheet may be embedded in another document). It will always include:

```
<xsl:stylesheet
         xmlns:xsl="http://www.w3.org/1999/XSL/Transform"
         version="1.0"
>
```

The various possible attributes are considered in the sections that follow.

The id Attribute

If the XSLT processor you are using supports embedding of stylesheets within the source document that they are to transform, then the typical layout will be like this:

```
<?xml version="1.0"?>
<?xml-stylesheet href="#style" type="text/xsl"?>
<data>
...
...
   <xsl:stylesheet id="style" version="1.0"
      xmlns:xsl="http://www.w3.org/1999/XSL/Transform"
   >
   <xsl:include href="module1.xsl"/>
   <xsl:include href="module2.xsl"/>
   <xsl:template match="xsl:*"/>
   </xsl:stylesheet>
</data>
```

Note that when this structure is used, the stylesheet will be presented with the entire source document, including a copy of itself. The stylesheet therefore needs to be written to handle its own elements in an appropriate way, hence the null template that matches all elements in the XSLT namespace.

The version Attribute

If your stylesheet only uses features from XSLT 1.0, you should specify «`version="1.0"`» on the **<xsl:stylesheet>** element. Then it will work with any XSLT processor that conforms to XSLT 1.0 or a later version of the standard.

If you use features first defined in XSLT 1.1, you must either specify «`version="1.1"`» on the **<xsl:stylesheet>** element, or specify «`xsl:version="1.1"`» on a literal result element that encloses the part of the stylesheet where version 1.1 features are used. This is not an option, of course, if you use **<xsl:script>**, which is a top-level element and is therefore never enclosed by a literal result element: an alternative in this case is to put the **<xsl:script>** element in an included stylesheet module, and specify «`version="1.1"`» on the **<xsl:stylesheet>** element of that module.

The extension-element-prefixes Attribute

This attribute should be set to a list of all the prefixes you are using for extension elements in your stylesheet. The most common cases are either to omit it entirely, or to include a single prefix for the namespace used by the vendor for their own proprietary extensions. There will always be a namespace declaration for that namespace on the **<xsl:stylesheet>** element as well.

For example, if you are using Saxon:

```
<xsl:stylesheet
          version="1.0"
          xmlns:xsl="http://www.w3.org/1999/XSL/Transform"
          xmlns:saxon="http://icl.com/saxon"
          extension-element-prefixes="saxon"
          >
```

Don't include the vendor's prefix unless you are actually using their proprietary extensions in the stylesheet. You don't need to include this attribute to use proprietary top-level elements such as **<msxml:script>**, only if you want to use proprietary features such as instructions within a template body, where they would otherwise be assumed to be literal result elements.

If your usage of vendor extensions is highly localized within the stylesheet, it is better to identify them using the **xsl:extension-element-prefixes** attribute of the extension element itself, or of a literal result element that surrounds the template body where the extensions are actually used. This aids portability and makes it easier to see which parts of the stylesheet are standard and which parts use proprietary extensions.

If you want to use extensions supplied by several different vendors, you can list them all in this attribute. An XSLT processor from one vendor won't object to finding another vendor's namespace in the list, it will only object if it is actually asked to instantiate a proprietary instruction that it doesn't understand, and even then if there is an **<xsl:fallback>** child element that defines the fallback behavior it will carry on calmly executing that in place of the unrecognized instruction.

Although extension elements supplied by XSLT product vendors are likely to be the most common case, it's also possible in principle to install third-party extensions or to write your own (the APIs for doing so will be different for each vendor, however). So everything we've said about the vendor's extensions applies equally to your own extensions or those acquired from a third party.

For more information about the extensions provided by various vendors in their products, see the appendix for the relevant product.

An inventive way of using the **extension-element-prefixes** attribute is to flag elements that you want to reserve for debugging or annotation. For example, if you include the following element within a template body anywhere in the stylesheet, then the normal action will be to output an element to the result tree, showing the current values of the variables `$var1 and $var2`.

```
<debug:write var1="{$var1}" var2="{$var2}"><xsl:fallback/></debug:write>
```

When you no longer need to use this debugging instruction, you can disable it simply by declaring «`debug`» as an extension element prefix. This time the `<xsl:fallback/>` action will be taken, because the processor doesn't recognize the extension element.

The exclude-result-prefixes Attribute

The simplest way to decide which namespace prefixes to list here is by trial and error; run the stylesheet, and if the output document contains namespace declarations that clearly serve no useful purpose, add them to the **exclude-result-prefixes** attribute and run the stylesheet again.

Namespaces that are used only within the stylesheet will normally be excluded automatically. These include the XSLT namespace itself, and namespaces used for extension elements. It may not apply, however, to namespaces used for your own top-level elements in the stylesheet.

The most common cause of unwanted namespace declarations finding their way into the result document is where your stylesheet needs to refer to namespaces used in the source document, for example in a template **match** pattern, but where none of these elements is copied into the destination document.

For example:

```
<xsl:stylesheet
          version="1.0"
          xmlns:xsl="http://www.w3.org/1999/XSL/Transform"
          xmlns:po="http://accounting.org/xslt"
          exclude-result-prefixes="po"
>
<xsl:template match="po:purchase-order">
   <order-details>
   ...
   </order-details>
</xsl:template>
</xsl:stylesheet>
```

Here the «po» namespace would be copied into the result document if it weren't for the **exclude-result-prefixes** attribute, because it is in scope when the literal result element **<order-details>** is instantiated.

As with the other **<xsl:stylesheet>** attributes, you don't have to apply the exclusion to the whole stylesheet if you don't want to, you can also apply it to any part of the stylesheet by using the **xsl:exclude-result-prefixes** attribute on any literal result element. It's probably a good idea in practice to keep the declaration of a namespace and the directive that excludes it from the result document together in one place.

See also

<xsl:transform> on page 328

xsl:template

The **<xsl:template>** element defines a template for producing output. It may be invoked either by matching nodes against a pattern, or explicitly by name.

Defined in

XSLT section 5.3

Format

```
<xsl:template
        name=QName
        match=Pattern
        mode=QName
        priority=Number >
    <xsl:param> *
    template body
</xsl:template>
```

Position

<xsl:template> is a top-level element, which means that it always appears as a child of the **<xsl:stylesheet>** element.

Attributes

Name	Value	Meaning
match optional	Pattern	A pattern that determines which nodes are eligible to be processed by this template. If this attribute is absent, there must be a **name** attribute.
name optional	QName	The name of the template. If this attribute is absent, there must be a **match** attribute.
priority optional	Number	A number (positive or negative, integer or real) that denotes the priority of this template, used when several templates match the same node.
mode optional	QName	The mode. When **<xsl:apply-templates>** is used to process a set of nodes, the only templates considered are those with a matching mode.

The constructs `QName` (page 414) and `Number` (page 401) are defined in Chapter 5. The construct `Pattern` is defined in Chapter 6.

Content

Zero or more **<xsl:param>** elements, followed by a template body.

Effect

There must be either a **match** attribute, or a **name** attribute, or both.

- If there is a **match** attribute, the **<xsl:template>** element defines a template rule that can be invoked using the **<xsl:apply-templates>** instruction.
- If there is a **name** attribute, the **<xsl:template>** element defines a named template that can be invoked using the **<xsl:call-template>** instruction.
- If both attributes are present, the template can be invoked in either of these ways.

The match Attribute

The match attribute is a `Pattern`, as defined in Chapter 6. The pattern is used to define which nodes this template rule applies to.

The pattern must not contain a `VariableReference`, that is, a reference to a variable such as «`$var`». This is to prevent circular definitions; the template body of a global variable is allowed to include an **<xsl:apply-templates>** instruction, so it must be possible to evaluate the pattern before the values of global variables are known.

To see what might happen if variables were allowed in the **match** attribute, consider the following:

```
<xsl:variable name="x">
   <xsl:apply-templates select="//item"/>
</xsl:variable>
<!-- WRONG -->
<xsl:template match="item[$x]">
   <xsl:value-of select="3"/>
</xsl:template>
<!-- WRONG -->
```

Clearly, while the variable x is being evaluated, it is impossible to determine whether this template rule matches a particular `<item>` or not.

When **<xsl:apply-templates>** is used to process a selected set of nodes, each node is processed using the best-fit template rule for that node, as described under **<xsl:apply-templates>** on page 155.

A template is only considered as a candidate if the node matches the pattern supplied in the **match** attribute and if the value of the **mode** attribute is the same name as the **mode** attribute of the **<xsl:apply-templates>** instruction.

If more than one template rule meets these criteria, they are first considered in order of import precedence (as described under **<xsl:import>** on page 226), and only those templates with the highest import precedence are considered further.

If there is still more than one template rule (in other words, if two template rules that both match the node have the same import precedence) they are next considered in order of priority. The priority is given either by the value of the **priority** attribute, described below, or is a default priority that depends on the **match** pattern.

If this leaves one pattern with a numerically higher priority than all the others, that one is chosen. If there are several with the same priority, which is higher than all the others, the XSLT processor has the choice of reporting an error, or choosing from the remaining templates the one that appears last in the stylesheet. Several processors in practice report a warning, which you can ignore if you wish. In my experience, however, this condition often indicates that the stylesheet author has overlooked something.

The name Attribute

The **name** attribute is a `Qname`; that is, a name optionally qualified with a namespace prefix. If there is a prefix, it must correspond to a namespace declaration that is in scope on this element (which means it must be defined either on this element itself, or on the **<xsl:stylesheet>** element). If there is no prefix, the namespace URI is null; the default namespace is not used.

This name is used when the template is invoked using **<xsl:call-template>**. The **name** attribute of the **<xsl:call-template>** element must match the **name** attribute of the **<xsl:template>** element. Two names match if they have the same local part and the same namespace URI, but the prefix can be different.

If there is more than one named template in the stylesheet with the same name, the one with higher import precedence is used; for details, see **<xsl:import>** on page 226. It is an error to have two templates in the stylesheet with the same name and the same import precedence, even if the template is never called.

The priority Attribute

The **priority** attribute is a number, for example `«17»`, `«0.5»`, or `«-3»`: more specifically, a `Number` as defined on page 401 in the XPath expression syntax given in Chapter 5, with an optional leading minus sign.

The **priority** attribute is used to decide which template to invoke when **<xsl:apply-templates>** is called and there are several possible candidates. For each selected node, a template is chosen using the following procedure:

- First select all the templates that have a **match** attribute.
- From these, select all the templates that have the same mode as is used on the call of **<xsl:apply-templates>**. If the **<xsl:apply-templates>** element has no **mode** attribute, the selected templates must have no mode attribute.
- From these, select all those whose pattern matches the selected node.
- If there is more than one, select those that have the highest import precedence.
- If there is still more than one, select those that have the numerically highest priority.

If there are several matching templates left, and they all have the same import precedence and priority, the XSLT processor can either choose the one that occurs last in the stylesheet, or report an error.

If there are no templates that match the selected node, the built-in template for the relevant node type is used. Built-in templates are described under **<xsl:apply-templates>** on page 158.

The default priority depends on the pattern, and is decided according to the following rules. A numerically higher value indicates a higher priority.

Pattern syntax	Default priority
`Pattern1 «|» Pattern2`	Treat it as if there were two completely separate template rules specified, one for `Pattern1` and one for `Pattern2`, and calculate the default priority of `Pattern1` and `Pattern2` independently

`QName`
`«@» QName`
`«child::» QName`
`«attribute::» QName`
`«processing-instruction» «(» Literal «)»`
	0.0

`NCName «:*»`
`«@» NCName «:*»`
`«child::» NCName «:*»`
`«attribute::» NCName «:*»`
	–0.25

`NodeTest`
`«@» NodeTest`
`«child::» NodeTest`
`«attribute::» NodeTest`
	–0.5

otherwise	0.5

These default priorities are carefully chosen. They reflect the selectivity of the pattern:

- The patterns «`node()`» and «`text()`» and «`*`» are not very selective at all, they match any node of the right node type, so they have a low priority of –0.5.
- Patterns of the form «`abc:*`» or «`@xyz.*`» are more selective, they will only match element or attribute nodes belonging to a particular namespace, so they have a higher priority than the previous category.
- Patterns such as «`title`» or «`@isbn`» are the ones most commonly encountered; their default priority of 0.0 reflects the fact that in terms of selectivity, they are typical.
- Patterns that are more specific than this, for example «`book[@isbn]`» or «`chapter/title`» or «`para[1]`» have a higher priority, so they will be chosen in preference to templates whose patterns are respectively «`book`», «`title`», or «`para`». Note however that this category can also include patterns that turn out not to be very selective at all, for example «`//node()`».

All these values are chosen to leave you free to allocate your own priorities as natural numbers, for example «`1`», «`2`», «`3`», and such templates will always be chosen ahead of those with a system-allocated default priority.

You may find that stylesheets are easier to understand and less error-prone if you avoid relying on default priorities, and use explicit priorities whenever you have more than one template rule that can match the same node.

The mode Attribute

If present, the **mode** attribute must be a QName, that is, a name with an optional namespace prefix. When **<xsl:apply-templates>** is used with a specific mode, only template rules with that same mode will be considered, and when **<xsl:apply-templates>** is used with no **mode** attribute, only template rules with no **mode** attribute will be considered.

The modes are compared using the usual rules for Qnames; both names are expanded using the namespace declarations in effect on their respective stylesheet elements (not including any default namespace declaration), and they match if the local name and namespace URI both match.

The mode specified on the **<xsl:template>** template is **not** propagated to any **<xsl:apply-templates>** elements within its body. Although it is common practice to process an entire subtree in a single mode, and therefore for a template to continue using the mode it was called in, this is not the default behavior except in the case of built-in templates.

If you have a **mode** attribute on a template but no **match** attribute, this is not an error, but it is redundant because the mode will never be used.

If you have a **mode** attribute on a template and there is no **<xsl:apply-templates>** element with the same mode anywhere in the stylesheet, this again is not an error, though it means the template will never be selected by any **<xsl:apply-templates>** call. This can be a handy way of commenting out a template rule.

Instantiating a Template

Once an **<xsl:template>** element is selected for processing the following occurs:

- If called using **<xsl:apply-templates>**, the current node and current node list are set up as required.
- A new stack frame is allocated, to hold a new instance of each local variable defined within the template.
- All parameters listed in **<xsl:param>** elements contained within the **<xsl:template>** element are evaluated. These **<xsl:param>** elements must come before any instructions in the template body. For each parameter, if a value was supplied by the caller (using an **<xsl:with-param>** element with matching name), that value is assigned to the parameter, otherwise the **<xsl:param>** element is evaluated directly: see **<xsl:param>** on page 283 for details.
- The template body is instantiated. This means that the child nodes of the **<xsl:template>** element are instantiated in turn. XSLT instructions and extension elements are processed using their individual rules; literal result elements and text nodes are written to the current output destination.

When processing of the template body is complete, the stack frame containing its local variables is deleted, control returns to the calling template, and the current node and current node list revert to their previous values.

The implementation, of course, is free to do things in a different order if it has the same effect. Some products use lazy evaluation, *where the parameters are only evaluated when they are first used. This will only show up if you use extension functions that have side effects, or if you use* **<xsl:message>** *to trace the sequence of execution.*

Usage and Examples

We'll look first at using template rules, then give some advice on the use of modes, and finally discuss named templates.

Using Template Rules

A **template rule** is an **<xsl:template>** element with a **match** attribute, which can therefore be invoked using the **<xsl:apply-templates>** instruction.

This rule-based approach to processing is the characteristic way of writing XSLT stylesheets, though it is by no means the only way. Its biggest advantage is that the output for each element type can be defined independently of the context that the element appears in, which makes it very easy to reuse element types in different contexts, or to add new element types to an existing document definition without rewriting the stylesheet templates for all the possible containing elements. A classic example of this approach to processing arises when converting semantic markup in a document to rendition markup, as the following example demonstrates.

Example: Template Rules

Source

The source file is `soloist.xml`.

In this text featuring the work of a singer, the name of a composer is tagged **<composer>**, the title of a musical work is tagged **<work>**, and the name of a publication is tagged **<publication>**. Sections of text relating to the same performance are marked with a **<performance>** tag. So a fragment of marked up text might read:

```
<cv>
<para>
<performance>
<publication>Early Music Review</publication> said of his debut
<venue>Wigmore</venue> concert with <group>Ensemble
Sonnerie</group> in <date>1998</date>: <quote>One of the
finest concerts I have ever heard ... a singer to watch out for</quote>.
</performance>
<performance>
Other highlights include a televised production of
<composer>Bach</composer>'s <work>St. Matthew Passion</work> conducted by
<artist>Jonathan Miller</artist>, in which he played <role>Judas</role>.
</performance>
</para>
</cv>
```

Stylesheet

The stylesheet file is `soloist.xsl`.

In presenting this text to a human reader, the main task is to select typographical conventions to be used for each piece of semantic markup. The designer might choose, for example, to display the titles of works in italics, titles of publications in a sans serif font, and composers' names in the ordinary paragraph font. This could be achieved by the following stylesheet definitions (assuming the output is HTML):

```
<xsl:stylesheet version="1.0"
    xmlns:xsl="http://www.w3.org/1999/XSL/Transform">

<xsl:template match="/">
<html><body>
<xsl:apply-templates/>
</body></html>
</xsl:template>

<xsl:template match="para">
   <p><xsl:apply-templates/></p>
</xsl:template>

<xsl:template match="publication">
   <font face="arial"><xsl:apply-templates/></font>
</xsl:template>

<xsl:template match="quote">
   <xsl:text/>"<xsl:apply-templates/>"<xsl:text/>
</xsl:template>

<xsl:template match="work">
   <I><xsl:apply-templates/></i>
</xsl:template>

<xsl:template match="role">
   <u><xsl:apply-templates/></u>
</xsl:template>

</xsl:stylesheet>
```

Note that some of the markup is ignored, for example **`<artist>`**. The default template for elements simply discards the tags and outputs the text, which is exactly what we want here.

Output

If the generated HTML is copied into a word processor, it will look like this:

> Early Music Review said of his debut Wigmore concert with Ensemble Sonnerie in 1998: "One of the finest concerts I have ever heard ... a singer to watch out for". Other highlights include a televised production of Bach's *St. Matthew Passion* conducted by Jonathan Miller, in which he played Judas.

(Incidentally, this way of getting printed output from an XSLT stylesheet is often overlooked. It won't give nearly as much control as the advanced features of the XSL Formatting proposals, but while you're waiting for that standard to be finished and for products to appear, using HTML as an intermediate format is not a bad compromise.)

The great advantage of this approach is that the rules are written making no assumptions about the way the markup tags are nested in the source document. It is very easy to add new rules for new tags, and to reuse rules if an existing tag is used in a new context.

With document structures where the nesting of elements is more rigid, for example in some data interchange files, this very flexible rule-based (or **push**) style of processing may have fewer benefits, and a **pull** programming style using conventional flow-of-control constructs such as `<xsl:for-each>`, `<xsl:if>`, and `<xsl:call-template>` may be preferable. For more discussion of the different design approaches, see Chapter 9.

Using Modes

The classic reason for using modes is to enable the same content to be processed more than once in different ways: for example, the first pass through the document might generate the table of contents, the second pass the actual text, and the third pass an index.

Example: Using modes

The source document is a biography of a singer, in the same format as the previous example. This time, however, we want to produce at the end of the biography a list of works mentioned in the text.

Source

The source file is `soloist.xml`. See previous example.

Stylesheet

The stylesheet file is `soloist+index.xsl`.

This stylesheet extends the previous one using **<xsl:import>**. After outputting the text as before, it now creates a table listing the singer's performances, completing what information is known about the composer, the work, the date of the performance, and the venue.

The «` `» characters (better known to HTML authors as a non-breaking space, «` `»), are used to ensure that there is something in each table cell: this gives a cleaner appearance in the browser. It would be quite possible to use the entity reference «` `» in the stylesheet so long as it was properly declared as an XML entity in a **<!DOCTYPE>** declaration at the start of the file.

```
<xsl:stylesheet version="1.0"
     xmlns:xsl="http://www.w3.org/1999/XSL/Transform">

<xsl:import href="soloist.xsl"/>

<xsl:template match="/">
<html><body>
    <xsl:apply-templates/>
    <table bgcolor="#cccccc" border="1" cellpadding="5">
    <tr>
        <td><b>Date</b></td>
        <td><b>Venue</b></td>
        <td><b>Composer</b></td>
        <td><b>Work</b></td>
        <td><b>Role</b></td>
    </tr>
    <xsl:apply-templates mode="index"/>
    </table>
</body></html>
</xsl:template>

<xsl:template match="performance" mode="index">
    <tr>
    <td><xsl:value-of select="date"/> </td>
    <td><xsl:value-of select="venue"/> </td>
    <td><xsl:value-of select="composer"/> </td>
    <td><xsl:value-of select="work"/> </td>
    <td><xsl:value-of select="role"/> </td>
    </tr>
</xsl:template>

</xsl:stylesheet>
```

Output

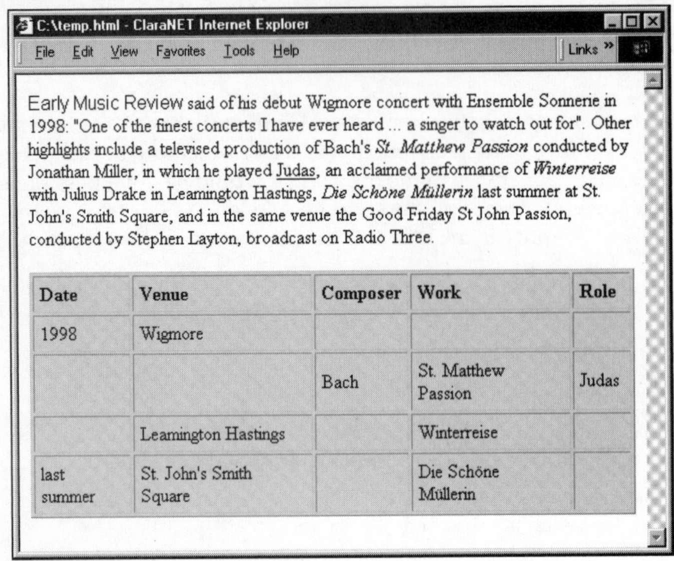

Early Music Review said of his debut Wigmore concert with Ensemble Sonnerie in 1998: "One of the finest concerts I have ever heard ... a singer to watch out for". Other highlights include a televised production of Bach's *St. Matthew Passion* conducted by Jonathan Miller, in which he played Judas, an acclaimed performance of *Winterreise* with Julius Drake in Leamington Hastings, *Die Schöne Müllerin* last summer at St. John's Smith Square, and in the same venue the Good Friday St John Passion, conducted by Stephen Layton, broadcast on Radio Three.

Date	Venue	Composer	Work	Role
1998	Wigmore			
		Bach	St. Matthew Passion	Judas
	Leamington Hastings		Winterreise	
last summer	St. John's Smith Square		Die Schöne Müllerin	

Using Named Templates

Named templates provide the equivalent of a subroutine mechanism in XSLT. If a template has a name attribute, it can be invoked using the **`<xsl:call-template>`** instruction.

For examples of the use of named templates, see **`<xsl:call-template>`** on page 179.

See also

`<xsl:apply-templates>` on page 155
`<xsl:apply-imports>` on page 152
`<xsl:call-template>` on page 179
`generate-id()` function in Chapter 7, on page 491

xsl:text

The **<xsl:text>** instruction is used within a template body to output literal text to the current output destination.

Defined in

XSLT section 7.2

Format

```
<xsl:text disable-output-escaping="yes" | "no">
   text ?
</xsl:text>
```

Position

<xsl:text> is an instruction. It is always used as part of a template body.

Attributes

Name	Value	Meaning
disable-output-escaping optional	«yes» | «no»	The value «yes» indicates that special characters in the output (such as «<») should be output as is, rather than using an XML escape form such as «<». Default is «no».

Content

A text node. The element may also be empty. It may not contain other elements such as **<xsl:value-of>**.

Effect

Text appearing within a template body in the stylesheet is copied to the current output destination whether it is enclosed by **<xsl:text>** or not. The only direct effect of enclosing text in an **<xsl:text>** element is that the handling of whitespace is different. A whitespace node appearing in the stylesheet (that is, a text node which consists only of whitespace) is copied to the result tree only if :

- it appears within an **<xsl:text>** element, or
- an enclosing element has the attribute «`xml:space="preserve"`», and this is not overridden by an inner enclosing element specifying «`xml:space="default"`»

The **`disable-output-escaping`** attribute controls whether special characters such as «<» should be escaped (that is, converted to a character reference or entity reference such as «`<`») if they appear in the text. The default value is «`no`». The value «`yes`» may be ignored in some circumstances, for example if the result of the transformation is written to a DOM rather than being serialized as an XML file.

Usage

There are two main reasons for using **<xsl:text>**, which are to control the output of whitespace, and to disable escaping of special characters. These are discussed in the next two sections.

Whitespace Control

The most obvious case where **<xsl:text>** is useful is to force output of whitespace. An example is given in the XSLT specification. If you write:

```
<xsl:value-of select="first-name"/> <xsl:value-of select="last-name"/>
```

the space between the first name and last name will be lost, because it is part of a node that contains whitespace only (a single space character). To force a space to appear between the first name and last name, write:

```
<xsl:value-of select="first-name"/>
<xsl:text> </xsl:text>
<xsl:value-of select="last-name"/>
```

The arrangement on three lines here is purely for readability, but it does not affect the output, because the newline characters are now in whitespace-only nodes that will not be output.

If you find this long-winded, another way of achieving the same effect is to write:

```
<xsl:value-of select="concat(first-name, ' ', last-name)"/>
```

The **`concat()`** function forms a string by concatenating its arguments; it is described on page 456 in Chapter 7.

The other side of the problem is to prevent the output of unwanted whitespace. Fortunately in HTML output extra whitespace usually doesn't matter, because the browser will ignore it. For XML or text output, however, avoiding unwanted whitespace can be important.

If you are suffering from excess whitespace in your output, the first thing to establish is whether it comes from the source document or from the stylesheet. If the whitespace is adjacent to text copied from the source document, then it probably comes from the source document; if it is adjacent to text that appears in the stylesheet, then that is the most likely source.

If the unwanted whitespace comes from the source document, consider using **<xsl:strip-space>** to remove nodes consisting entirely of whitespace, or the **normalize-space()** function to remove leading and trailing spaces around visible text.

The **<xsl:text>** element can be used to suppress unwanted whitespace that originates in the stylesheet. For example, consider the following template:


```
<xsl:template match="stage-direction">
   [ <xsl:value-of select="."/> ]
</xsl:template>
```

The intention here is to output a stage direction enclosed in square brackets. But the text nodes containing the opening and closing square brackets also contain a newline character and several spaces, which will be written to the output destination along with the brackets themselves. To prevent this behavior, the simplest way is to use empty **<xsl:text>** elements before and after, thus:

```
<xsl:template match="stage-direction">
   <xsl:text/>[ <xsl:value-of select="."/> ]<xsl:text/>
</xsl:template>
```

The effect of this is that the extra newlines and spaces now belong to whitespace-only nodes, which are stripped from the stylesheet and ignored.

Note that it is incorrect to use an **<xsl:text>** element around the **<xsl:value-of>** element, as **<xsl:text>** elements must contain text data only. So the following is wrong:

```
<!-- WRONG -->
      <xsl:text>[ <xsl:value-of select="."/> ]</xsl:text>
<!-- WRONG -->
```

Controlling Output Escaping

Normally, when you try to output a special character such as «<» or «&» in a text node, the special character will be escaped in the output file using the normal XML escaping mechanisms. The XSLT processor is free to choose whichever mechanism it wants, for example it can write «<» as «<» or «<» or «<![CDATA[<]]>», because these are all equivalent according to the XML standard. The one thing it will not write is «<». So, it doesn't matter how you write the «<» in your input: the XSLT processor sees a «<» and escapes it in the output.

There are several valid reasons why you might not want this behavior. For example:

- The output is not XML or HTML at all; it is (say) a data file in comma-separated-values format.
- The output is HTML and you want to exploit one of the many HTML quirks where special characters are needed without escaping, for example a «<» sign in a piece of client-side JavaScript on your HTML page.

- The output is XML and you want to achieve some special effect that the XSLT processor won't let you do, for example to output an entity reference such as «`¤t-date;`» or a document type declaration containing an entity declaration.
- The output is some format that uses angle-bracket syntax but is not pure XML or HTML; for example, ASP pages or Java Server Pages, which both use «`<%`» and «`%>`» as delimiters. (But if you are generating Java Server Pages, note that these have an alternative syntax that is pure XML.)

If the output is not XML or HTML at all, then rather than using **`disable-output-escaping`** it is better to set «`method="text"`» on the **`<xsl:output>`** element.

Now here's an example of a bad reason for disabling output escaping. You want to get markup tags into the output document that you can't see how to achieve with the regular facilities of **`<xsl:element>`** or literal result elements. For example, you might want to do something like:

```
<!-- WRONG -->
<xsl:template match="bullet"/>
   <xsl:if test='not(preceding::*[self::list-item])'>
      <ul>
   </xsl:if>
   <li><xsl:value-of select="."/></li>
   <xsl:if test='not(following::*[self::list-item])'>
      </ul>
   </xsl:if>
</xsl:template>
<!-- WRONG -->
```

The intended effect here is to output a `<ul>` tag if the preceding element is not a list-item, and to output a `</ul>` tag when the following element is not a list-item. Of course it doesn't work, because the `<ul>` and `</ul>` tags are not properly nested: this template will be thrown out by the XML parser before the XSLT processor even gets to look at it.

So your next thought might be to write the tags as text, as follows:

```
<xsl:template match="bullet"/>
   <xsl:if test='not(preceding::*[self::list-item])'>
      <xsl:text disable-output-escaping="yes">&lt;ul&gt;</xsl:text>
   </xsl:if>
   <li><xsl:value-of select="."/></li>
   <xsl:if test='not(following::*[self::list-item])'>
      <xsl:text disable-output-escaping="yes">/&lt;ul&gt;</xsl:text>
   </xsl:if>
</xsl:template>
```

You now have something which is legal XML and indeed legal XSLT, but it's not guaranteed to work in all circumstances. In particular, it may fail if there is something downstream that cares about the structure of the output XML. So it's a trick that may or may not work.

With a bit of thought you can usually find a way to achieve the output you want without resorting to such devices.

The first thing is to think in terms of outputting a result tree containing nodes, not a text file containing tags. Don't try to generate the <ul> start tag and the </ul> end tag as two separate actions; try to generate a **<ul>** element node as a single action, and then generate its children.

The aim is to produce a **<ul>** element for every **<bullet>** in the source that is not preceded by another bullet, so we can start by writing:

```
<xsl:template match="bullet[not(preceding-sibling::*[1][self::bullet])]">
   <ul>
      . . .
   </ul>
</xsl:template>
```

This template rule matches every **<bullet>** element that either has no preceding sibling, or whose immediately preceding sibling is not a **<bullet>** element.

For each such bullet, we want to process the list of following siblings until the next non-bullet is reached. The best way to do this is with a recursive template:

```
<xsl:template
         match="bullet[not(preceding-sibling::bullet)]">
   <ul>
      <xsl:call-template name="bullet-list"/>
   </ul>
</xsl:template>

<xsl:template name="bullet-list">
   <li>
      <xsl:value-of select="."/>
   </li>
   <xsl:variable name="next" select="following-sibling::*[1]"/>
   <xsl:for-each select="$next[self::bullet]">
      <xsl:call-template name="bullet-list"/>
   </xsl:for-each>
</xsl:template>
```

Rather than processing the following bullets in a loop, we process them by recursion: the bullet-list template outputs the current <bullet> element, and if the next element is also a <bullet>, it calls itself to process that one. Note that the <xsl:for-each> element here is not actually looping, it is processing a node-set which will contain one element if the next element is a <bullet>, and zero elements otherwise.

Examples

1) Output first-name and last-name, separated by a space:

```
<xsl:value-of select="first-name"/>
<xsl:text> </xsl:text>
<xsl:value-of select-"last-name"/>
```

Another way to achieve the same effect is to use the **concat()** function:

```
<xsl:value-of select="concat(first-name, ' ', last-name)"/>
```

2) Output a comma-separated list of values:

```
<xsl:output method="text"/>
<xsl:template match="book">
   <xsl:value-of select="title"/>,<xsl:text/>
   <xsl:value-of select="author"/>,<xsl:text/>
   <xsl:value-of select="price"/>,<xsl:text/>
   <xsl:value-of select="isbn"/><xsl:text>
</xsl:text>
</xsl:template>
```

The purpose of the empty **<xsl:text/>** elements is to split the comma and the following newline character into separate text nodes; this ensures that the newline character becomes part of a whitespace-only node, and is therefore not copied to the output. The final **<xsl:text>** element ensures that a newline is written at the end of each record.

3) Output an «` `» entity reference:

```
<xsl:text disable-output-escaping="yes">&amp;nbsp;</xsl:text>
```

Note that outputting a #xa0 (or #160) character will generally have exactly the same effect, to do this you can simply write:

```
<xsl:text> </xsl:text>
```

See also

<xsl:value-of> on page 329

xsl:transform

This is a synonym of **<xsl:stylesheet>**, described on page 302. The two element names may be used interchangeably.

Why is it useful to have two names for the same thing? Probably because it's the easiest way for a standards committee to keep all its members happy. More seriously, the existence of these two names is indicative of the fact that some people see XSLT as being primarily a language for transforming trees, while others see its main role as defining presentation styles. Take your pick.

Format

```
<xsl:transform
   id=identifier
   version="1.0" or "1.1"
   xmlns:xsl="http://www.w3.org/1999/XSL/Transform"
   extension-element-prefixes=list-of-prefixes
   exclude-result-prefixes=list-of-prefixes >
      top-level-element *
</xsl:transform>
```


Defined in

XSLT section 2.2

See also

<xsl:stylesheet> on page 302

xsl:value-of

The **<xsl:value-of>** instruction writes the string value of an expression to the result tree.

Defined in

XSLT section 7.6.1

Format

```
<xsl:value-of select=Expression
disable-output-escaping="yes" | "no"/>
```

Position

<xsl:value-of> is an instruction. It is always used as part of a template body.

Attributes

Name	Value	Meaning
select mandatory	Expression	The value to be output.
disable-output-escaping optional	«yes» | «no»	The value «yes» indicates that special characters in the output (such as «<») should be output as is, rather than using an XML escape form such as «<». Default is «no».

Content

None, the element is always empty.

Effect

The expression is evaluated as a string, and the result is output to the result tree as a text node. If necessary the value is first converted to a string, as follows:

- If the value is a Boolean, the output will be one of the strings «`true`» or «`false`».
- If the value is a number, it is converted to a string representation of the number in decimal notation, for example «`93.7`». (If you want to control the formatting of the number, use the **`<xsl:number>`** element or the **`format-number()`** function instead.)
- If the value is a node-set, **all nodes other than the first (in document order) are ignored**. If the node-set is empty, nothing is output. Otherwise, the string value of the first node is output. The string value of a node depends on the type of node: for a text node, it is the textual content; for an attribute node, it is the attribute value; for a comment, it is the text of the comment; for a processing instruction, it is the data part of the processing instruction (excluding the *target*). For an element node, it is the concatenation of the values of all the descendant text nodes: in other words, the text contained in the element, without any markup or attributes. Similarly for the root, the string-value is all the text in the document, with markup removed.

  Note the very different behavior between a node-set that contains many elements and a node-set that contains a single element which itself has many children. The expression «`//para`» returns a node-set containing all the **`<para>`** elements in the document. The string value of this is the string-value of the first **`<para>`** element, so `<xsl:value-of select="//para">` will only display one paragraph. By contrast, the expression «`/`» represents a node-set containing one node only, namely the root. The string-value of this is all the text in the document, so `<xsl:value-of select="/"/>` will output all this text.
- If the value is a temporary tree, the output is the string-value of the root node of the tree. In effect this means that the result is the concatenation of all the text nodes within the tree. If you want to copy the nodes in the tree to the output destination, rather than just their string value, use **`<xsl:copy-of>`** described on page 195.

The **`disable-output-escaping`** attribute has the same effect as with **`<xsl:text>`**. Special characters such as «`<`» in the string value of the select expression will be escaped just as if they occurred in literal text, and the **`disable-output-escaping`** attribute can be used to suppress this in the same way. For details, see **`<xsl:text>`** on page 323.

Usage

The **<xsl:value-of>** element is the most common way of writing text to the result tree (or to the current output destination, if that is different).

The other ways of writing text nodes to the result tree are to include text literally in the stylesheet (perhaps within an **<xsl:text>** instruction) or to use **<xsl:copy>** or **<xsl:copy-of>**. Surprisingly, you could make do without using **<xsl:value-of>** at all, because `<xsl:value-of select="X"/>` can always be rewritten as `<xsl:copy-of select="string(X)"/>`.

Another alternative is to use **<xsl:apply-templates>** on a text node and rely on the built-in template for text nodes, which is equivalent to `<xsl:value-of select="."/>`

The **<xsl:value-of>** instruction is often an effective alternative to navigating the source tree recursively using **<xsl:apply-templates>**. For example:

```
<xsl:template match="book">
   <book>
      <publisher><xsl:value-of select="../@name"/></publisher>
      <title><xsl:value-of select="@title"/></title>
      <author><xsl:value-of select="@author"/></author>
      <isbn><xsl:value-of select="@isbn"/></isbn>
   </book>
</xsl:template>
```

As **<xsl:value-of>** writes to the current output destination, not necessarily the final result tree, it is used to return a result from a called template. For example you can write a named template that replaces characters in a filename as follows:

```
<xsl:template name="change-filename">
   <xsl:param name="filename"/>
   <xsl:value-of select="translate($filename, '\', '/')"/>
</xsl:template>
```

This template can then be called as follows, to get the result into the variable `$new-filename`:

```
<xsl:variable name="$new-filename">
   <xsl:call-template name="change-filename">
      <xsl:with-param name="$old-filename"/>
   </xsl:call-template>
</xsl:variable>
```

The value of variable `$new-filename` is actually a temporary tree, but for all practical purposes it can be treated as a string.

Using disable-output-escaping

One technique used quite often is to wrap HTML inside an XML document, for example:

```
<message>
  <header>
    <sent-by>Dept 178</sent-by>
    <recipient>App 263</recipient>
  </header>
  <content type="text/html">
    <![CDATA[
       <html>
          <head><title>An HTML page with unmatched tags</title></head>
          <body>HTML authors are often lazy!<p></body>
       </html>
    ]]>
  </content>
</message>
```

One way you can include the HTML within the XML message is to put it through a program such as Dave Raggett's **html tidy** utility (available from http://www.w3.org/), which converts it to well-formed XHTML. But you may not want to risk changing it, so using a CDATA section as shown here is the only alternative. When you do this, however, the «<» and «>» characters are no longer treated as mark up characters, they are now ordinary text. If you try to run an XSLT transformation that outputs the HTML enclosed in this message, these characters will therefore be escaped, typically by writing them as «<» and «>». This isn't what you want; so you can solve the problem by writing:

```
<xsl:template match="content[@type='text/html']">
  <xsl:value-of select="." disable-output-escaping="yes"/>
</xsl:template>
```

But remember that this is only likely if the output is serialized by the XSLT processor; it won't work if you write the result to a DOM.

Examples

`<xsl:value-of select="."/>`	Output the string-value of the current node.
`<xsl:value-of select="title"/>`	Output the string-value of the first child **<title>** element of the current node.
`<xsl:value-of select="sum(@*)"/>`	Output the sum of the values of the attributes of the current node, converted to a string. If there is any non-numeric attribute, the result will be "NaN".
`<xsl:value-of select="$x"/>`	Output the value of variable $x, after converting it to a string.

See also

<xsl:copy-of> on page 195
<xsl:text> on page 323

xsl:variable

The **<xsl:variable>** element is used to declare a local or global variable in a stylesheet, and to give it a value.

Defined in

XSLT section 11

Format

```
<xsl:variable name=QName select=Expression >
   template body
</xsl:variable>
```

Position

The **<xsl:variable>** element may appear either as a top-level element (that is, as a child of the **<xsl:stylesheet>** element), or as an instruction within a template body.

Attributes

Name	Value	Meaning
name mandatory	QName	The name of the variable
select optional	Expression	An expression that is evaluated to give the value of the variable. If omitted, the value is determined from the contents of the **<xsl:variable>** element

The constructs `QName` (page 414) and `Expression` (page 377) are defined in Chapter 5.

Content

An optional template body. If a **select** attribute is present, the **<xsl:variable>** element should be empty.

Effect

An **<xsl:variable>** element may appear either at the top level of the stylesheet (in which case it declares a global variable) or as an instruction within a template body (in which case it declares a local variable).

The Value of the Variable

The value of the variable may be given either by the `Expression` in the **`select`** attribute, or by the contents of the contained template body. If there is a **`select`** attribute, the **`<xsl:variable>`** element should be empty. If there is no **`select`** attribute and the template body is empty, the value of the variable is an empty string.

If the value is given by an `Expression`, the data type of the value will be Boolean, number, string, or node-set, depending on the expression. Or if the expression is a call to an extension function, the value may also be an *external object*. If the value is given by a non-empty template body, the value will be a temporary tree. With XSLT 1.0 this is regarded as a separate data type, the **result tree fragment**. With XSLT 1.1, however, a temporary tree is regarded as a node-set value, one that always contains a single node, the root node of the temporary tree.

Note that if an expression is used to assign a literal string value to a variable, the string literal must be enclosed in quotes, and these quotes are additional to the quotes used around the XML attribute. So to assign the value «`London`» to the variable named «`city`», you can write either of the following:

```
<xsl:variable name="city" select="'London'"/>
<xsl:variable name="city" select='"London"'/>
```

You can also write:

```
<xsl:variable name="city">London</xsl:variable>
```

Technically the value is then a node-set rather than a string, but it can be used exactly as if it were a string, so there is no difference in practice.

> *A common mistake is to write:*
>
> ```
> <xsl:variable name="city" select="London"/> <!-- WRONG -->
> ```
>
> *This sets the value of «`$city`» to a node-set containing all the element children of the current node that have element name* **`<London>`**. *This will probably be an empty set, so if you use the variable as a string, its value will be the empty string. You won't get any error message if you make this mistake, because it's a perfectly valid thing to write, it will just cause your stylesheet to produce the wrong output.*
>
> *You won't be alone if you make this mistake, there's an example of it in the original XSLT 1.0 specification, which had to be fixed in the subsequent errata.*

You don't need the extra quotes if you want the value to be a number:

```
<xsl:variable name="max-size" select="255"/>
```

The Name of the Variable

The name of the variable is defined by a `QName`. Normally this will be a simple name such as «`city`» or «`total-sales`», but it may be a name qualified with a prefix, for example «`my:value`». If it has a prefix, the prefix must correspond to a namespace that is in scope at that point in the stylesheet. The true name of the variable, for the purpose of testing whether two names are the same, is determined not by the prefix but by the namespace URI corresponding to the prefix: so two variables «`my:value`» and «`your:value`» have the same name if the prefixes «`my`» and «`your`» refer to the same namespace URI. If the name has no prefix, it has a null namespace URI – it does not use the default namespace URI.

The scope of a global variable is the entire stylesheet, including any stylesheets that are included or imported. A global variable may even be referenced before it is declared. The only constraint is that circular definitions are not allowed; if variable *x* is defined in terms of *y*, then *y* may not be defined directly or indirectly in terms of *x*.

The scope of a local variable is block-structured; it may be referenced in any following sibling element or in a descendant of a following sibling. This is illustrated in the diagram below.

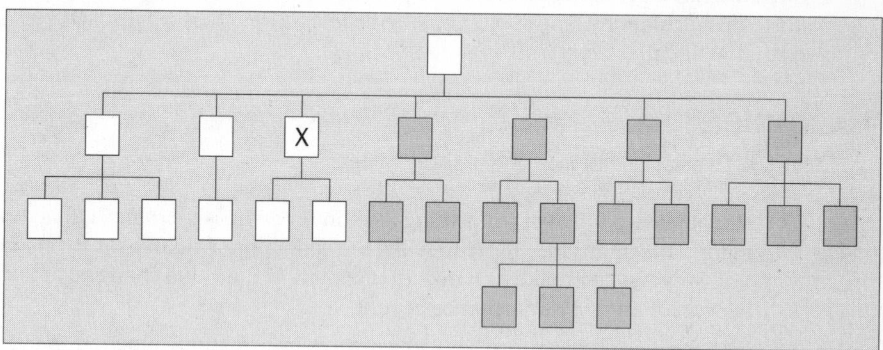

The diagram shows for a variable X, the elements that may contain a reference to X; the shaded elements may refer to X, the unshaded elements may not. Specifically, a local variable may be referenced in any following sibling element, or in a descendant of a following sibling. It cannot be referenced within its own descendants, and it goes out of scope when the end tag for its parent element is encountered. Unlike global variables, a forwards reference to a local variable is not allowed. If you think of XSLT instructions as being like the statements in a block-structured language like C, Java, or JavaScript, and the enclosing element as being like a block enclosed in those languages by curly braces, the scope rules will seem very familiar.

Two global variables may have the same name only if they have different *import precedence*; in other words, if one of them was in an imported stylesheet (for further details, see **`<xsl:import>`** on page 226). In this case, the definition with higher import precedence wins (the original XSLT 1.0 spec forgot to say this, but the omission has been fixed by an erratum). Note that the higher-precedence definition applies everywhere, even within the imported stylesheet that contains the lower-precedence definition. This means it is not a good idea to rely on precedence to resolve accidental name clashes between independently-developed modules, it's better to use namespaces.

Two local variables may have the same name only if neither variable is defined within the scope of the other. However, a local variable may have the same name as a global variable, in which case the global variable is inaccessible within the scope of the local variable.

These rules on uniqueness and scope of names apply equally to parameters declared using **`<xsl:param>`**; the **`<xsl:param>`** instruction is effectively just another way of declaring a variable.

Usage

Variables are useful, as in any programming language, to avoid calculating the same result more than once.

Global variables are useful for defining constants, such as a color value, that will be used in many places throughout the stylesheet.

Unlike variables in many programming languages, **XSLT variables cannot be updated**. Once they are given an initial value, they retain that value until they go out of scope. This feature has a profound effect on the programming style used when a stylesheet needs to do calculations. The subject of *programming without assignment statements* is discussed in detail in Chapter 9.

Examples

Most XSLT variables fall into one of three categories:

- Variables used to avoid repeating a common expression in more than one place. This might be simply to make the code more readable, or to ensure that you only have to make a change in one place if the value changes, or perhaps because it gives a performance benefit.
- Variables used to capture context-sensitive information, allowing the variable to be used after the context has changed.
- Variables holding a temporary tree (a result tree fragment as it used to be known).

In each case the variable might be local or global. I'll show some examples of each kind.

Convenience Variables

Consider this example, which calculates the number of goals scored by, and against, a soccer team.

```
<xsl:variable name="for"
              select="sum($matches/team[.=$this]/@score)"/>
<xsl:variable name="against"
              select="sum($matches[team=$this]/team/@score) - $for"/>
. . .
<td><xsl:value-of select="$for"/></td>
<td><xsl:value-of select="$against"/></td>
```

This uses two rather complex expressions to construct the variables «for» and «against», which calculate the number of goals scored by, and against, the team identified by the variable «$team». If you want to understand the logic in more detail, it is given as a fully worked example under the description of the **sum()** function in Chapter 7, on page 555.

It would be quite possible in this case to avoid using the variable «against». The expression that calculates its value could equally be written at the point where the variable is used, in the second **<xsl:value-of>** instruction. The same is true of the «for» variable, though this time the expression would need to be written twice, in both places where the variable is used, and this might give a performance penalty. However, these variables are really being used only for clarity; it would be quite possible to write the stylesheet without them.

This is true because nothing can change between the variables being defined and being used. The source document can't change, and the values of the variables $team and $matches can't change. The context (for example the current position in the source document) can change, but in this example (a) it doesn't, and (b) the expressions don't depend on the context anyway.

I call these *convenience variables* because you could get by without them if you had to (though there might be a performance hit). They can be used either as global variables or as local variables. Creating global convenience variables that refer to node-sets in the source document is often a useful programming technique, for example:

```
<xsl:variable name="group-A-matches" select="//match[@group='A']"/>
```

These act rather like views in an SQL database.

Variables to capture context-sensitive Values

These variables are most often useful in conjunction with **<xsl:for-each>**, which changes the current node. Consider the following example:

Example: Using a Variable for Context-sensitive Values

Source

The source file is opera.xml. It contains a list of operas and details of their composers.

```
<?xml version="1.0"?>
<programme>
   <opera>
      <title>The Magic Flute</title>
      <composer>Mozart</composer>
      <date>1791</date>
   </opera>
   <opera>
      <title>Don Giovanni</title>
      <composer>Mozart</composer>
      <date>1787</date>
```

```
    </opera>
    <opera>
        <title>Ernani</title>
        <composer>Verdi</composer>
        <date>1843</date>
    </opera>
    <opera>
        <title>Rigoletto</title>
        <composer>Verdi</composer>
        <date>1850</date>
    </opera>
    <opera>
        <title>Tosca</title>
        <composer>Puccini</composer>
        <date>1897</date>
    </opera>
    <composer name="Mozart">
        <fullname>Wolfgang Amadeus Mozart</fullname>
        <born>1756</born>
        <died>1791</died>
    </composer>
    <composer name="Verdi">
        <fullname>Guiseppe Verdi</fullname>
        <born>1813</born>
        <died>1901</died>
    </composer>
    <composer name="Puccini">
        <fullname>Giacomo Puccini</fullname>
        <born>1858</born>
        <died>1924</died>
    </composer>
</programme>
```

Stylesheet

The stylesheet is file `opera.xsl`. This is a complete stylesheet; it uses the simplified stylesheet syntax described on page 113, in Chapter 3.

The stylesheet contains two nested **`<xsl:for-each>`** loops. In the outer loop, it sets a variable «c» to the context node (the current composer). In the expression controlling the inner loop, this variable is used. It would not be correct to use «`.`» in place of «`$c`», because the **`<composer>`** element is no longer the context node. In this example it would be possible to use the **`current()`** function here (this function is described on page 463, in Chapter 7), but there are other cases where a variable is necessary.

```
<html
    xmlns:xsl="http://www.w3.org/1999/XSL/Transform"
    xsl:version="1.0">

<body><center>
    <h1>Programme</h1>
    <xsl:for-each select="/programme/composer">
        <h2><xsl:value-of
            select="concat(fullname, ' (', born, '-', died, ')')"/></h2>
        <xsl:variable name="c" select="."/>
        <xsl:for-each select="/programme/opera[composer=$c/@name]">
            <p><xsl:value-of select="title"/></p>
        </xsl:for-each>
    </xsl:for-each>
</center></body>
</html>
```

Output

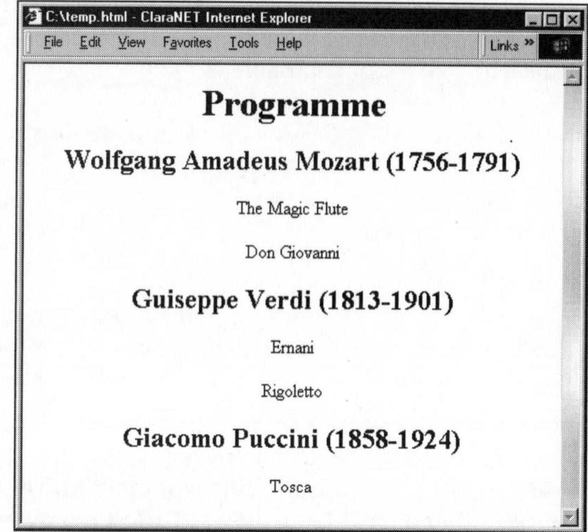

One case where context variables are very useful is when handling multiple source documents.

In any stylesheet that handles multiple source documents, it is useful to include a global variable that refers to the root node of the principal source document, thus:

```
<xsl:variable name="root" select="/"/>
```

This means it is always possible to refer to the source document by using this variable. Without this, when the context node is in a secondary document, there is no way of accessing data from the principal document.

For example, the expression «`//item`» refers to all **`<item>`** elements in the same document as the context node. If you actually want all **`<item>`** elements in the principal source document, then (provided you have included the global variable declaration above) you can use the expression «`$root//item`».

If there is a document referenced from the stylesheet, for example to hold lookup data such as messages or tax rates, it is also useful to define this in a global variable, for example:

```
<xsl:variable name="tax-rates" select="document('tax-rates.xml')"/>
```

Temporary Trees

The value of a variable is a temporary tree (or result tree fragment as it was known in XSLT 1.0) if it is defined using the content of the **<xsl:variable>** element rather than the **select** attribute. In many cases the tree will only contain a single text node, in which case it behaves almost exactly like a string variable.

A local variable can often be useful for expanding the default value of an attribute. For example:

```
<xsl:variable name="width">
   <xsl:choose>
      <xsl:when test="@width">
         <xsl:value-of select="@width"/>
      </xsl:when>
      <xsl:otherwise>0</xsl:otherwise>
   </xsl:choose>
</xsl:variable>
```

Subsequently the variable `$width` can be used in calculations in place of the attribute `@width`, without worrying about the case where the attribute was omitted. The fact that the variable is technically a tree rather than a string does not affect the way it can be used.

Beginners often try to write this as:

```
   <xsl:choose>
   <xsl:when test="@width">
      <xsl:variable name="width"
                    select="@width"/>
   </xsl:when>
   <xsl:otherwise>
      <xsl:variable name="width" select="0"/>
   </xsl:otherwise>
 </xsl:choose>
```

This won't work, because when you get to the end tag of the ***<xsl:choose>*** *element, both variable declarations will have gone out of scope!*

If you prefer terseness to clarity, an alternative way to initialize the variable is:

```
<xsl:variable name="width"
select="concat(@width, substring('0', 1, not(@width)))"/>
```

To see how this works, see the description of the ***substring()*** *function on page 544 in Chapter 7.*

Tree-valued variables are also needed whenever you want to use **<xsl:call-template>** to calculate a value which you then want to manipulate further, as shown in the next example.

Example: Getting the Result of <xsl:call-template> in a Variable

Source

The source file is the list of operas and composers used in the previous example, `operas.xml`.

Stylesheet

The stylesheet is the file `composers.xsl`.

This stylesheet uses a general-purpose named template («`make-list`») to output a list of names in the form «`A; B; C; and D`». It passes this template a node-set containing the names of all the composers in the source document. On return from the «`make-list`» template, it extracts the result of this template into a variable (which will be a temporary tree containing a single text node), and passes this variable into the **`translate()`** function (described in Chapter 7 page 560) to convert the commas to semicolons. The **`translate()`** function converts its first argument to a string, which in this case extracts the value of the text node from the tree.

```
<xsl:stylesheet
   xmlns:xsl="http://www.w3.org/1999/XSL/Transform"
   version="1.0">

<xsl:template match="/">
    <xsl:variable name="list">
        <xsl:call-template name="make-list">
            <xsl:with-param name="names"

select="/programme/composer/fullname"/>
        </xsl:call-template>
    </xsl:variable>
    This week's composers are:
    <xsl:value-of select="translate($list, ',', ';')"/>
</xsl:template>

<xsl:template name="make-list">
    <xsl:param name="names"/>
    <xsl:for-each select="$names">
        <xsl:value-of select="."/>
        <xsl:if test="position()!=last()">, </xsl:if>
        <xsl:if test="position()=last()-1">and </xsl:if>
    </xsl:for-each>
</xsl:template>

</xsl:stylesheet>
```

Output

```
This week's composers are:
Wolfgang Amadeus Mozart; Guiseppe Verdi; and Giacomo Puccini
```

4

XSLT Elements

With XSLT 1.1, it is possible to perform any operation on a temporary tree that you can perform on the principal source document, or on a document loaded using the **document()** function. This greatly increases their usefulness. Some examples of the way you can use this are:

- Perform a transformation in several phases. The output of the first phase is directed to a temporary tree, and the second phase uses this temporary tree as its input. This can help to break up a complex transformation into a number of simple steps; for example, if you need to do sorting and grouping, and then number the sorted groups, a three-phase transformation that does grouping first, then sorting, and finally numbering may be the answer. To do a multi-phase transformation you may want to use a stylesheet structure like this:

```
<xsl:template match="/">
  <xsl:variable name="phase1output">
      <xsl:apply-templates select="." mode="phase1"/>
  </xsl:variable>
  <xsl:variable name="phase2output">
      <xsl:apply-templates select="$phase1output"
                mode="phase2"/>
  </xsl:variable>
  <xsl:apply-templates select="$phase2output"
                mode="phase3"/>
</xsl:template>
```

  As well as using a distinct mode for each phase of the transformation, you may find it useful to keep the template rules for each phase in a separate stylesheet module, linked to the principal stylesheet module using **<xsl:include>**.

- Use a temporary tree to hold fixed lookup tables. An example of this is shown in the entry for the **document()** function, on page 466 in Chapter 7. With XSLT 1.0, you can hold such data in a user-defined top-level element within the stylesheet, accessing it using «**document('')**», which makes the stylesheet accessible as a secondary source document. In XSLT 1.1, instead of using a user-defined top-level element, such data can be held in a global tree-valued variable, and accessed directly.

- Use a temporary tree to hold complex working data structures, which can be passed to a named template as a parameter for processing. For example, in Chapter 10 one of the worked examples calculates a knight's tour of the chessboard, and this requires a named template that takes the current state of the board as an input parameter. In XSLT 1.0 (without using vendor extensions) it is necessary to encode this information as a string. With XSLT 1.1 as currently defined, it can be represented as a tree structure, making it much more amenable to processing. (But note, this doesn't change the basic rule that variables can't be updated; once you have built a temporary tree, it is immutable. The only thing you can do is copy it to a new tree, making changes as you do so.)

- Build a temporary tree to represent a list of items, so that you can use **<xsl:for-each>** to iterate over this list. For example, if you want to produce an output file for each color of the rainbow, you could start by defining a variable thus:

```
<xsl:variable name="rainbow">
  <color>red</color>
  <color>orange</color>
  <color>yellow</color>
  <color>green</color>
  <color>blue</color>
  <color>indigo</color>
  <color>violet</color>
</xsl:variable>
```

  and then iterate over it like this:

```
<xsl:for-each select="$rainbow/color">
   <xsl:document href="{.}.xml">
     . . .
   </xsl:document>
</xsl:for-each>
```

It doesn't have to be a fixed list, of course, it could equally well be a list of all the colors of the products you currently have in stock.

See also

<xsl:param> on page 283

xsl:when

The **<xsl:when>** element always appears as a child of **<xsl:choose>**. It defines a condition to be tested and the action to be performed if the condition is true.

Defined in

XSLT section 9.2

Format

```
<xsl:when test=Expression>
   template body
</xsl:when>
```

Position

<xsl:when> is always a child element of **<xsl:choose>**. There must be at least one **<xsl:when>** element within an **<xsl:choose>** element.

Attributes

Name	Value	Meaning
`test` mandatory	`Expression`	The Boolean condition to be tested

Content

A template body.

Effect

The **`<xsl:choose>`** element is instantiated as follows:

- The first **`<xsl:when>`** element whose **`test`** `Expression` is true is selected; subsequent **`<xsl:when>`** elements are ignored whether or not their `Expression` is true.
- If none of the **`<xsl:when>`** elements has a **`test`** `Expression` that is true, the **`<xsl:otherwise>`** element is selected. If there is no **`<xsl:otherwise>`** instruction, no element is selected.
- The selected child element (if any) is executed by instantiating its template body in the current context: that is, the effect is as if the relevant template body appeared in place of the **`<xsl:choose>`** instruction.

It is not defined whether the **`test`** `Expression` in a **`<xsl:when>`** element after the selected one is evaluated or not, so if it calls functions that have side-effects, or if it contains errors, the result is undefined.

Any XPath value may be converted to a Boolean. In brief, the rules are:

- If the expression is a node-set, it is treated as true if the node-set is not empty
- If the expression is a string or a result tree fragment, it is treated as true if the string value is not empty
- If the expression is a number, it is treated as true if the number is non-zero

Usage and Examples

See **`<xsl:choose>`** on page 188

See also

`<xsl:choose>` on page 188
`<xsl:otherwise>` on page 269
`<xsl:if>` on page 223

xsl:with-param

The **<xsl:with-param>** element is used to set the values of parameters when calling a template, either when using **<xsl:call-template>**, or when using **<xsl:apply-templates>**. With XSLT 1.1 it can also be used with **<xsl:apply-imports>**.

Defined in

XSLT section 11.6

Format

```
<xsl:with-param name=QName select=Expression >
   template body
</xsl:with-param>
```

Position

<xsl:with-param> is always a child of either **<xsl:apply-templates>**, **<xsl:call-template>**, or (with XSLT 1.1 only) **<xsl:apply-imports>**.

Attributes

Name	Value	Meaning
name mandatory	`QName`	The name of the parameter
select optional	`Expression`	The value of the parameter to be supplied to the called template

The constructs `QName` (page 414) and `Expression` (page 377) are defined in Chapter 5.

Content

An optional template body. If a **select** attribute is present, the **<xsl:with-param>** element should be empty.

Effect

An **<xsl:with-param>** element can appear only as the immediate child of an **<xsl:call-template>**, **<xsl:apply-templates>**, or (with XSLT 1.1 only) an **<xsl:apply-imports>** instruction.

The **<xsl:with-param>** element assigns a value to a parameter. The value of the parameter can be used within the called template.

The value of the parameter is established in exactly the same way as for the **<xsl:variable>** element. That is, the value is taken from the **select** expression if present, or by instantiating the template body if not.

If the called template has an **<xsl:param>** element whose name matches that of the **<xsl:with-param>** element, then the value assigned to the **<xsl:with-param>** element is available within the template. If the called template has no such parameter, the value is ignored: this is not an error. In the case of **<xsl:apply-templates>**, the parameter value is available in each of the templates that is called (one per selected node). The parameter is effectively evaluated once only – it will have the same value for each of these templates.

The name of the parameter is defined by a `QName`. Normally this will be a simple name such as «`city`» or «`total-sales`», but it may be a name qualified with a prefix, for example «`my:value`». If it has a prefix, the prefix must correspond to a namespace that is in scope at that point in the stylesheet. The true name of the parameter, for the purpose of matching it with an **<xsl:param>** element in the called template, is determined not by the prefix but by the namespace URI corresponding to the prefix; so the name «`my:value`» will match a parameter declared as «`your:value`» if the prefixes «`my`» and «`your`» refer to the same namespace URI. If the name has no prefix, it has a null namespace URI – it does not use the default namespace URI.

It is an error for two sibling **<xsl:with-param>** elements to have the same name, after namespace prefixes are replaced with namespace URIs. In other words, you can't supply two values for the same parameter.

The **<xsl:with-param>** element does not actually declare a variable, so there is no problem if the name is the same as that of a variable that is currently in scope. In fact it is quite normal to pass a parameter in the form:

```
<xsl:with-param name="current-user" select="$current-user"/>
```

This is used to ensure that the variable «`$current-user`» in the called template has the same value as the variable «`$current-user`» in the calling template.

Usage and Examples

Parameters to templates take on considerable significance in XSLT because variables cannot be updated. This means that many tasks which in conventional programming languages are done by updating variables in a loop are done instead in XSLT using recursive calls and parameters. The consequences of this are explained in Chapter 9, and there are some detailed examples of the technique in Chapter 10.

Examples of recursive calls are also included in this chapter under **<xsl:call-template>** on page 179.

See also:

<xsl:apply-imports> on page 152
<xsl:apply-templates> on page 155
<xsl:call-template> on page 179
<xsl:param> on page 283

Summary

This has been a long chapter, but I hope you'll agree that every page was worth it! We have examined all of the XSLT elements in detail and have provided working examples to bolster your understanding of how they are used. We will now move on to look at *Expressions* in the same way.

5

Expressions

This chapter defines the syntax and meaning of **XPath expressions**. XPath expressions are used in many places within an XSLT stylesheet to select data from the source document and to manipulate it to generate data to go in the result document. XPath is defined by W3C as a free-standing language, so it can also be used in other contexts, for example in defining links from one XML document to another (see the W3C XLink and XPointer specifications); however, all our examples will concentrate on the way it is used in XSLT.

As with other programming languages, the syntax is defined in a set of **production rules**. Each rule defines the structure of a particular construct as a set of choices, sequences, or repetitions. There is one section in this chapter for each production rule.

I have taken the formal production rules directly from the XPath specification document, http://www.w3.org/TR/xpath. I have reordered the rules into alphabetical order for ease of reference, and I have made minor changes to the typography for ease of reading. I have also pulled in those rules from the XML and XML Namespaces standards that the XPath syntax references. I've also included a reference to allow you to find the relevant rule in the original specification if you need to. However, I have tried to include all the information you need from the XPath specification, so this should only be necessary if you need to see the precise wording of the standard.

Most of the information you need to write XPath expressions is in this chapter. The key concepts were explained in Chapter 2, in particular the tree model (page 56) and the idea of the context of an expression (page 85) – both concepts are essential to a full understanding of this chapter. The system of data types was also explained in Chapter 2 (page 87). XPath expressions can include function calls: the standard functions defined within the XPath and XSLT Recommendations are described in Chapter 7 of this book, and the way in which you can add your own functions is described in Chapter 8.

The current version of the XPath specification, at the time of writing, is still version 1.0: although a draft of XSLT 1.1 has been published, this did not require any changes to XPath itself. However, I have incorporated the latest errata to XPath 1.0 (though most of the errors and omissions were things the average user would never come across).

Notation

As in the rest of the book, I have used French quotation marks «`thus`» (also known as chevrons or guillemots) to surround pieces of XPath text that you write: I chose this convention partly because these marks stand out more clearly, but more importantly to distinguish these quotation marks unambiguously from quotation marks that are actually part of the expression. So if we write, for example, that literals can be enclosed either in «`"`» or «`'`» marks, then it's clear that you don't actually write the chevrons. XPath syntax doesn't use chevrons with any special meaning (though like any other Unicode character, you can use them in literals), so you can be sure that any chevron you see is not to be included in the expression.

The production rules in XPath implicitly define the precedence of the different operators. For example the rule for `OrExpr` defines it as a sequence of `AndExpr` operands separated by «`or`» operators. This is a convenient way of defining that the «`and`» operator binds more tightly than «`or`».

One consequence of this style of definition is that the simplest `OrExpr` consists of a single `AndExpr` with no «`or`» operator present at all. This gives us a problem, because when we want to talk about an expression that uses an «`or`» operator, we can't call it an `OrExpr`. So we'll refer to an `OrExpr` with no «`or`» operator as a **trivial** `OrExpr`, and to a real one (with one or more «`or`» operators) as a **non-trivial** `OrExpr`. In the section of text that describes the effect of an `OrExpr`, we'll always concentrate on the non-trivial case. The same situation arises for many other constructs.

Although the production rules in XPath define the operator precedence, they do not impose any type checking. This would be hard to achieve, because variables are untyped, and because in most contexts a value of one type can be implicitly converted to a value of the required type, so for example «`3 or 'bread'`» is a perfectly legal expression (and evaluates to `true`). There are contexts that require a value that is a node-set, and values of other types cannot be converted to node-sets; however, the designers of the language chose not to build this in to any of the production rules. This means that the expression «`3|'bread'`» (where «`|`» is the set union operator) is also syntactically valid according to the production rules, though it is clearly an error because it violates the rule that the operands of «`|`» must be node-sets. Think of an analogy with English – there are sentences that are perfectly correct grammatically, but still nonsense: "An easy apple only trumpets yesterday."

Where to Start

Some people prefer to present the syntax of a language bottom-up, starting with the simplest constructs such as numbers and names, while others prefer to start at the top, with a construct like `Program` or `Expression`. As no single order of presentation suits everyone, and because you're likely to have to follow cross-references from one section to another anyway, we've chosen to list the production rules in alphabetical order. If you're the sort of person who likes the serendipity of browsing at random through an encyclopedia, you might enjoy reading the sections sequentially; or you could just as sensibly start at the end and work backwards. For a top-down approach, start with `Expr` on page 377 as this is the top-level production rule for an XPath expression. For a bottom-up approach, look at the syntax tree shown on the following page and select the terms that are furthest from the root. Or if you want to start in the middle, take a look at `Step` (page 420), which is one of the key concepts that gives XPath its power.

Many languages distinguish the lexical rules, which define the format of basic tokens such as names, numbers, and operators, from the syntactic rules, which define how these tokens are combined to form expressions and other higher-level constructs.

The XPath specification includes both syntactic and lexical production rules, but they are not quite as clearly separated as in some languages. As some constructs appear in both, I've kept them bundled together, showing the lexical rules in the same alphabetical sequence as the syntax rules, but distinguishing them in the text. The main distinction between the two kinds of rule is that whitespace can be freely used between lexical tokens but not within a lexical token. The top-level lexical rule is `ExprToken`.

A Syntax Tree

To help you find your way around the syntax, I have compiled the charts below, which show all the syntax rules (but not the purely lexical rules) arranged in a hierarchy. The children of each syntactic construct are the other constructs it references in its syntax rule.

The first chart contains all the expressions down to `PathExpr`. This part of the hierarchy is very straightforward; apart from `MultiplyOperator`, each construct defines a type of expression constructed using operands and operators, and the hierarchy reflects the precedence of the operators. For example, the chart shows that an `AndExpr` can contain an `EqualityExpr`, which implies that an operator used in an `EqualityExpr` (such as «=») has higher precedence and therefore binds more tightly than the «and» operator used in an `AndExpr`.

```
Expr
   OrExpr
      AndExpr
         EqualityExpr
            RelationalExpr
               AdditiveExpr
                  MultiplicativeExpr
                     MultiplyOperator
                     UnaryExpr
                        UnionExpr
                           PathExpr
```

The next chart expands `PathExpr`. Where a name is followed by an asterisk, its expansion is to be found in the heirarchy

```
PathExpr
   LocationPath
      RelativeLocationPath *
      AbsoluteLocationPath
         RelativeLocationPath *
         AbbreviatedAbsoluteLocationPath
            RelativeLocationPath *
   FilterExpr
      PrimaryExpr
         VariableReference
         Expr *
```

```
                Literal
                Number
                   Digits
                FunctionCall
                   FunctionName
                      QName
                   Argument
                      Expr *
             Predicate
                PredicateExpr
                   Expr *
          RelativeLocationPath
             Step
                AxisSpecifier
                   AxisName
                   AbbreviatedAxisSpecifier
                NodeTest
                   NameTest
                      NCName
                      QName
                   NodeType
                   Literal *
                Predicate *
                AbbreviatedStep
             AbbreviatedRelativeLocationPath
             RelativeLocationPath *
```

Notice how once you hit `PathExpr`, the syntax gets much more complicated. Perhaps this isn't surprising in a language called XPath, because the main purpose of the language is to define paths through an XML document, and this is specifically what a `PathExpr` does. The reason the syntax gets messy below this level is that it's full of shortcuts, which make it much easier to write commonly-used path expressions, but which are difficult to define formally. For more details see the section `PathExpr` on page 405.

The following sections describe the syntactic constructs in alphabetical order.

AbbreviatedAbsoluteLocationPath

An `AbbreviatedAbsoluteLocationPath` is an expression used to select all nodes in the document that satisfy some condition.

Expression	Syntax
`AbbreviatedAbsoluteLocationPath`	`«//» RelativeLocationPath`

Defined in

XPath section 2.5, rule 10

Used in

`AbsoluteLocationPath`

Usage

The initial «//» indicates that the selection path starts at the document root; the relative location path indicates how it then proceeds.

This form of expression can be expensive to evaluate, because the XSLT processor will generally have to search the whole document to find the selected nodes. If you can specify a more restricted search it is generally a good idea to do so – for example, if you know that all the **<book>** elements are children of the document element, then specifying «/*/book» will generally be more efficient than writing «//book». Of course, actual performance characteristics of different products may vary.

Examples

Expression	Description
`//figure`	Selects all **<figure>** elements in the document.
`//book[@category = 'fiction']`	Selects all **<book>** elements in the document that have a **category** attribute with the value «fiction».
`//*/*`	Selects all element nodes that have an element as a parent, in other words all elements except those that are immediate children of the root node. Here «*» is a `NameTest` that matches any element.
`//book/title`	Selects all **<title>** elements that have a **<book>** element as their parent.

Technically «//X» is an abbreviation for «/descendant-or-self::node()/X». So «//figure[1]» means «/descendant-or-self::node()/figure[1]»; that is, any **<figure>** element in the document that is the first **<figure>** child of its parent element. If you want to select the first figure element in the document, write «/descendant::figure[1]», or «(//figure)[1]».

AbbreviatedAxisSpecifier

An `AbbreviatedAxisSpecifier` indicates that the axis for selecting nodes in a path expression is either the child axis, or the attribute axis.

Expression	Syntax
`AbbreviatedAxisSpecifier`	«@» ?

Note the question mark: this means the «@» is optional. In other words, an `AbbreviatedAxisSpecifier` may be a completely empty string.

Defined in

XPath section 2.5, rule 13

Used in

`AxisSpecifier`

Usage

An abbreviated axis specifier may be either «@», to indicate the attribute axis, or nothing, to indicate the child axis. The abbreviated axis specifier «@» is an abbreviation for «attribute::», while the empty abbreviated axis specifier «» is an abbreviation for «child::». Looking at the syntax for AxisSpecifier on page 368, we see that an AxisSpecifier itself can be empty, which means (looking now at Step on page 420) that a Step can consist of a NodeTest on its own, or followed by one or more Predicates.

What this means in practice is that in a path expression «A/@B», B is referring to an attribute of A, while in the path expression «A/B», B is referring to a child element of A.

> **Take care when using the «self::» axis. You can write «self::title» to test whether the context node is a <title> element, but you can't write «self::@title» to test whether it is a title attribute. This is because «@» is short for «attribute::», and «self::attribute::title» doesn't make sense: you can either look on the self axis, or the attribute axis, but not both at once.**

Examples in Context

Expression	Description
@category	This is a RelativeLocationPath consisting of a single Step, which itself consists of an AbbreviatedAxisSpecifier «@» followed by a NodeTest that is a NameTest, or more specifically a QName. The effect of the expression is to select any attribute node of the context node that is named «category». The full form of the expression would be «./attribute::category».
title	This is a RelativeLocationPath consisting of a single Step, which itself consists of an empty AbbreviatedAxisSpecifier followed by a NodeTest that is a NameTest, or more specifically a QName. The effect of the expression is to select any child element of the context node that is named «title». The full form of the expression would be «./child::title».

AbbreviatedRelativeLocationPath

An AbbreviatedRelativeLocationPath is a relative location path that uses the «//» operator, which is a shorthand way of requesting all the descendants of a node rather than just the immediate children.

Expression	Syntax
AbbreviatedRelativeLocationPath	RelativeLocationPath «//» Step

Defined in

XPath section 2.5, rule 11.

Used in

`RelativeLocationPath`

Usage

An abbreviated relative location path is a shorthand notation for selecting the descendants of a given node.

As with «//» used at the beginning of a path, this construct may be expensive, because the XSLT processor has to search all the descendants of the given node. If you can restrict the search it is a good idea to do so, for example if you know that the required nodes are all grandchildren of the starting node it is better to write «$A/*/B» rather than «$A//B». Of course, the actual performance may vary between different products.

Technically an expression such as «$chapters//diagram» is an abbreviation for «$chapters/descendant-or-self::node()/diagram». This means: for each element in the node-set «$chapters», find all the descendant nodes of that element, and for each of these descendant nodes, find any children that are **<diagram>** elements. At first sight this seems to be the same as «$chapters/descendant::diagram», but there is a subtle difference when positional predicates are used, as seen in the example below:

Example: Comparing the // Operator with /descendant::

Consider the two expressions «$chapters//diagram[1]» and «$chapters/descendant::diagram[1]»:

- «$chapters//diagram[1]» means «$chapters/descendant-or-self::node()/diagram[1]», that is, every <**diagram**> element that is the first <**diagram**> child of its parent element and that is a descendant of a node in $chapters.
- «$chapters/descendant::diagram[1]» means the first <**diagram**> element (taking them in document order) that is a descendant of a node in $chapters. Another way of writing this is «($chapters//diagram)[1]».

To see the difference, consider the following source document:

```
<chapter>
   <section>
      <diagram nr="12"/>
      <diagram nr="13"/>
   </section>
      <diagram nr="14"/>
   <section>
      <diagram nr="15"/>
      <diagram nr="16"/>
   </section>
</chapter>
```

> With this document, if the node-set `$chapters` contains only the outer <**chapter**> element, «`$chapters//diagram[1]`» will select diagrams 12, 14, and 15, while both «`$chapters/descendant::diagram[1]`» and «`($chapters//diagram)[1]`» will select diagram 12 only.

Examples

Expression	Description
`chapter//footnote`	Selects all **<footnote>** elements that are descendants of a **<chapter>** element that itself is a child of the context node. The context node is explained in the entry for `Expr` on page 377.
`.//footnote`	Selects all **<footnote>** elements that are descendants of the context node.
`document('lookup.xml')//entry`	Selects all **<entry>** elements within the document identified by the relative URL `lookup.xml`. The **`document()`** function is described in Chapter 7, page 466.
`$winners//*/@name`	Selects the **`name`** attribute of all elements that are descendants of a node that belongs to the node-set identified by the variable `$winners`.
`.//..`	This strange but perfectly legal expression combines «`//`» which finds the descendants of a node, and «`..`» which finds its parent. The effect is to find all nodes that are the parent of a descendant of the context node, plus the parent of the context node itself.

AbbreviatedStep

An `AbbreviatedStep` is a shorthand way to select the context node or the parent of the context node.

Expression	Syntax
`AbbreviatedStep`	«`.`» | «`..`»

Defined in

XPath section 2.5, rule 12.

Used in

`Step`

Usage

The production rule `AbbreviatedStep` defines the two common symbols «`.`» which refers to the context node, and «`..`» which refers to the parent of the context node. (For a discussion of the meaning of `context node`, see `Expr` on page 377.) These symbols are abbreviations for «`self::node()`» and «`parent::node()`» respectively.

Although «`.`» is technically a `Step`, and can thus be used on the right-hand side of the path operator «`/`», it rarely makes sense to do so, since it is in effect a null step, a step that goes nowhere. The two places where «`.`» is commonly used are:

- with the operator «`//`» in a relative path expression such as «`.//A`», which (loosely speaking) selects all the descendant **<A>** elements of the context node. The «`.`» is necessary here because if the expression started with «`//`» it would select all descendants of the root node.
- On its own, to mean a node-set containing the context node only. This usually arises in expressions such as «`.=3`» or «`string-length(.)`» where we want to test the value of the context node, or in the XSLT instruction `<xsl:value-of select="."/>`, which outputs the string-value of the context node to the result tree.

Some people also like to use the «`.`» operator for clarity at the start of a relative path expression such as «`./TITLE`», but in fact this is precisely equivalent to «`TITLE`» on its own.

The «`..`» notation to refer to the parent is also found most commonly at the start of a relative path expression, for example «`../@name`» selects the name attribute of the parent of the context node. It is possible to use «`..`» anywhere in a path expression, though the need rarely arises. For example, «`//@width/..`» selects all elements in the document that have a **`width`** attribute. The same result could be achieved, perhaps more naturally, by writing «`//*[@width]`».

Note that every node except the root node has a parent (so «`/..`» is always an empty node-set; and «`not(..)`» is a simple way of testing whether the context node is the root). As explained in Chapter 2, the element containing an attribute is considered to be the parent of the attribute, even though the attribute is not a child of the element. So you can select all elements containing an attribute named **`ID`** with an expression such as «`//@ID/..`» (though «`//*[@ID]`» achieves the same thing and might be more efficient). Unlike biological relationships, in XPath the "parent" and "child" relationships are not the inverse of each other. The same applies to namespace nodes.

Note that neither «`.`» nor «`..`» can be followed by a predicate: it is an error to write, for example, `<xsl:if test=".[@color='black']">`. You may be used to writing this if you have used the Microsoft WD-xsl dialect of XSL, which did not support Boolean expressions; with XSLT you can write simply `<xsl:if test="@color='black'">`.

5

Expressions

Examples in Context

XSLT Instruction	Description
`<xsl:value-of select="."/>`	Outputs the string-value of the context node
`<xsl:value-of select="../@name"/>`	Outputs the value of the **name** attribute of the parent of the context node

AbsoluteLocationPath

An AbsoluteLocationPath represents a location path starting at the root node.

Expression	Syntax
AbsoluteLocationPath	«/» RelativeLocationPath ? | AbbreviatedAbsoluteLocationPath

Defined in

XPath section 2, rule 2

Used in

LocationPath

Usage

The simplest AbsoluteLocationPath is «/», which selects the root node. More specifically, when there are multiple input documents, it selects the root node of the document that contains the context node. (So the term absolute is something of a misnomer.)

This syntax is familiar to anyone who has used UNIX filenames, though it is not actually very logical. The symbol «/» is used both as an expression to refer to the root node, and as an operator to separate the parts of a path. I find it helpful to think of an AbsoluteLocationPath «/X» as an abbreviation for an imaginary expression «®/X», and «/» as an abbreviation for «®», where «®» represents the document root node.

The AbbreviatedAbsoluteLocationPath, which takes the form «//X», is discussed in its own section on page 352.

If you are writing a stylesheet that loads several source documents using the **document()** function, there is no direct way of selecting the root of the principal source document when the context node is in a different one. To solve this problem it is useful to include in your stylesheet a global variable declaration of the form `<xsl:variable name="root" select="/"/>`. You can then refer to the root of the principal document at any time as «$root».

Examples

Expression	Description
/	Selects the root node of the document containing the context node.
/price-list	Selects the document element, provided its name is **<price-list>**.
/*	Selects the document element, whatever its type.
/child::node()	Selects all nodes that are immediate children of the document root, which is the document element plus any comments or processing instructions that come before or after the document element. (However, note that the <?xml version="1.0"?> at the start of a document is **not** a processing instruction; in fact it is not a node at all, and is not accessible using XPath.)
/*/xsl:*	Selects all element nodes with names in the namespace associated with the «xsl:» namespace prefix that are immediate children of the document element. (If applied to an XSLT stylesheet, this would select all the top-level XSL elements.)
//figure	This AbbreviatedAbsoluteLocationPath selects all the **<figure>** elements in the document.

AdditiveExpr

A non-trivial AdditiveExpr is used to add or subtract numeric values.

Expression	Syntax
AdditiveExpr	MultiplicativeExpr | AdditiveExpr «+» MultiplicativeExpr | AdditiveExpr «-» MultiplicativeExpr

Defined in

XPath section 3.5, rule 25

Used in

RelationalExpr

Usage

A non-trivial AdditiveExpr consists of two or more MultiplicativeExpr operands separated by the plus «+» or minus «-» operators. A trivial AdditiveExpr consists of a single MultiplicativeExpr with no plus or minus operator.

When using the minus operator, take care that it does not get confused with a hyphen within a name. If it immediately follows a name, use a space to separate it. Note that «price-discount» (without spaces) is a single hyphenated name, whereas «price - discount» (with spaces) performs a subtraction.

Numbers in XSLT are always double-length floating point, so the calculation is carried out using floating point arithmetic, according to the rules of IEEE 754. See the description of the number data type in Chapter 2, page 89.

If an operand of the AdditiveExpr is not already a number, it is converted to a number as if the **number()** function was used. If the value cannot be converted to an ordinary number, it is converted to the special value NaN (Not-a-Number), and in this case the result of the addition or subtraction will also be NaN.

Examples in Context

Expression	Description
`$X + 1`	The result of adding 1 to the value of the variable $X.
`last()-1`	One less than the position of the last node in the context list.
`@price - @discount`	The value of the **price** attribute of the context node, converted to a number, minus the value of the **discount** attribute of the context node, converted to a number.
`count($list) mod 5 + 1`	The number of nodes in the node-set $list modulo 5, plus one. The result will be a number in the range 1 to 5. (For more on modulo, see page 393.)
`42`	The number 42 is a trivial AdditiveExpr, so it can be used anywhere that an AdditiveExpr is allowed.

AndExpr

A non-trivial AndExpr is used to test whether two or more Boolean conditions are all true.

Expression	Syntax
AndExpr	EqualityExpr | AndExpr «and» EqualityExpr

Defined in

XPath section 3.4, rule 22

Used in

OrExpr

Usage

A non-trivial AndExpr consists of two or more EqualityExpr operands separated by the «and» operator. A trivial AndExpr consists of a single EqualityExpr with no «and» operator.

An AndExpr is evaluated by evaluating each EqualityExpr in turn, from left to right, and converting it to a Boolean value, until one is found that is false. As soon as one is found that is false, evaluation stops and the expression returns false. If each EqualityExpr is true, the final result is true.

The rules for converting the value to a Boolean are the same as for the **boolean()** function, described in Chapter 7, page 452. For example, a string is false if it is zero-length, and a node-set is false if it is empty.

The XPath specification is quite explicit about the order of evaluation; however, since XPath expressions are free of side effects, it normally makes no difference. One case where it might affect the outcome is if an operand invokes user-defined extension functions that have side-effects. Another is where evaluating one of the operands might cause an error. This means you can safely write:


```
<xsl:if test="function-available('my:trace') and my:trace('Here we are!')"/>
```

This will call the extension function my:trace() if it is available, and won't call it otherwise. It doesn't matter what result my:trace() returns, because the content of the **<xsl:if>** is empty.

Examples

Expression	Description
$x > 3 and $x < 8	True if the value of variable $x is greater than 3 and less than 8.
@name and @address	True if the context node has both a **name** and an **address** attribute. (Both the operands are node-sets, which are converted to the Boolean true if they contain a node, and to false if they are empty.)
string(@name) and string(@address)	True if the context node has both a **name** and an **address** attribute and if neither is a zero length string. (Both the operands are strings, which are converted to the Boolean true if their length is non-zero. If an attribute is absent, the node-set will be empty, and its string value will therefore be the empty string.)
true()	A trivial AndExpr consisting of a single function call.

Argument

An Argument is used to represent the value supplied as input to a FunctionCall.

Expression	Syntax
Argument	Expr

Defined in

XPath section 3.2, rule 17

Used in

`FunctionCall`

Usage

Any expression can be used as an argument to a function. The only reason for defining a separate production rule for `Argument` is to make the rules easier to read.

Note that some expressions when used as arguments might look rather strange if you are thinking in terms of conventional languages. For example, «`string-length(..)`» returns the length of the string-value of the parent of the context node, and «`document(@*,/)`» returns a node-set containing the root nodes of the documents whose URIs are contained in attributes of the context node, using the base URI of the root of the source document as the base for resolving these URIs, if they are relative URIs.

The XPath specification uses the term `Arguments` for the input to an XPath `FunctionCall`. The term **parameters** has a different meaning – it is used in XSLT for the values supplied to a template.

If the function is an external one, written for example in Java or JavaScript, the arguments may need to be converted from XPath values to Java or JavaScript values. The rules for doing this (as defined in the XSLT 1.1 working draft) are given in Chapter 8.

Most functions will automatically convert the supplied argument to the required data type, for example the `concat()` function will automatically convert each of its arguments to a string. This doesn't work where the required argument is a node-set (examples being the `count()` and `sum()` functions), because values of other data types cannot be converted to node-sets. Some functions, such as `id()` and `key()`, are polymorphic: they behave differently depending on the data type of the argument supplied. In this case you may need to do the conversion explicitly (using one of the functions `string()`, `number()`, or `boolean()`) to achieve the required effect. All these functions are described in Chapter 7.

Examples in Context

Any expression can be used as an argument to a function call. Here are some examples of function calls that exploit this flexibility:

Expression	Description
`count(@*)`	Returns the number of attributes on the context node.
`id(string(@idref))`	Returns a node-set containing the element (if there is one) whose ID is equal to the value of the **`idref`** attribute of the context node.
`not(isbn)`	Returns true if the context node has no child element node named **`<isbn>`**. The argument here is a `RelativeLocationPath` and is equivalent to «`./child::isbn`».
`generate-id(/)`	Returns a string that uniquely identifies the root node of the document containing the context node.

AxisName

An `AxisName` is used within a `Step` to identify a path to be followed from a given node to other related nodes.

Expression	Syntax

`AxisName`	`«ancestor» |`
	`«ancestor-or-self» |`
	`«attribute» |`
	`«child» |`
	`«descendant» |`
	`«descendant-or-self» |`
	`«following» |`
	`«following-sibling» |`
	`«namespace» |`
	`«parent» |`
	`«preceding» |`
	`«preceding-sibling» |`
	`«self»`

Defined in

XPath section 2.2, rule 6

Used in

`AxisSpecifier`

Usage

An **axis** is a path through the document tree, starting at a particular node (which I'll call the origin) and following a particular relationship between nodes.

The various axis names have the following meaning:

Axis	Description
`ancestor`	Selects all the nodes that are ancestors of the starting node, in reverse document order. The first node on the axis is the parent of the origin node, the second is its grandparent, and so on; the last node on the axis is the document root.
`ancestor-or-self`	Selects the same nodes as the ancestor axis, but starting with the origin node rather than with its parent.
`attribute`	If the origin node is an element, this axis selects all its attribute nodes, in some arbitrary order. Otherwise, it selects nothing.
`child`	Selects all the children of the origin node, in document order. For any node except a root node or element node, this selects nothing. Note that the children of an element node do not include its attributes or namespace nodes, only the text nodes, element nodes, processing instructions and comments that make up its content.

Axis	Description
`descendant`	Selects all the children of the origin node, and their children, and so on recursively. The resulting nodes are in document order. If the origin is an element, this effectively means that the descendant axis contains all the text nodes, element nodes, comments and processing instructions that appear in the original source document between that element's start and end tags, in their original sequence.
`descendant-or-self`	This is the same as the descendant axis, except that the first node selected is the origin node itself.
`following`	This selects all the nodes that appear after the origin node in document order, excluding the descendants of the origin node. If the origin is an element node, for example, this effectively means that it contains all the text nodes, element nodes, comments and processing instructions in the document that start after the end tag of the origin element. The following axis will never contain attribute or namespace nodes.
`following-sibling`	This selects all the nodes that follow the origin node in document order, and that are children of the same parent node. If the origin is a root node, an attribute node, or a namespace node, then the following-sibling axis will always be empty.
`namespace`	If the origin node is an element, this axis selects all the namespace nodes that are in scope for that element; otherwise it is empty. The order of the namespace nodes is undefined. The namespace nodes correspond to namespace declarations (`xmlns="x"` or `xmlns:y="z"`) on the element itself or on one of its ancestor elements, but excluding any namespace declaration that cannot be used on this element because it is masked by another declaration of the same namespace prefix. For more information about namespace nodes, including the rules for creating namespace nodes on result trees, see Chapter 2.
`parent`	This axis selects a single node, the parent of the origin node. If the origin node is a root node, the parent axis is empty.
`preceding`	This selects all the nodes that appear before the origin node, excluding the ancestors of the origin node, in reverse document order. If the origin is an element node, this effectively means that it contains all the text nodes, element nodes, comments and processing instructions in the document that finish before the start tag of the origin element. The preceding axis will never contain attribute or namespace nodes.
`preceding-sibling`	This selects all the nodes that precede the origin node, and that are children of the same parent node, in reverse document order. If the origin is a root node, an attribute node, or a namespace node, then the preceding-sibling axis will always be empty.

Axis	Description
`self`	This selects a single node, the origin node itself. This axis will never be empty.

The various axes can also be shown diagrammatically. In each case in the table below the diagram shows the origin node in dark shading, while the nodes on the axis are numbered in the sequence they appear on the axis. The diagram does not show attribute and namespace nodes, and the attribute and namespace axes are therefore excluded from the table.

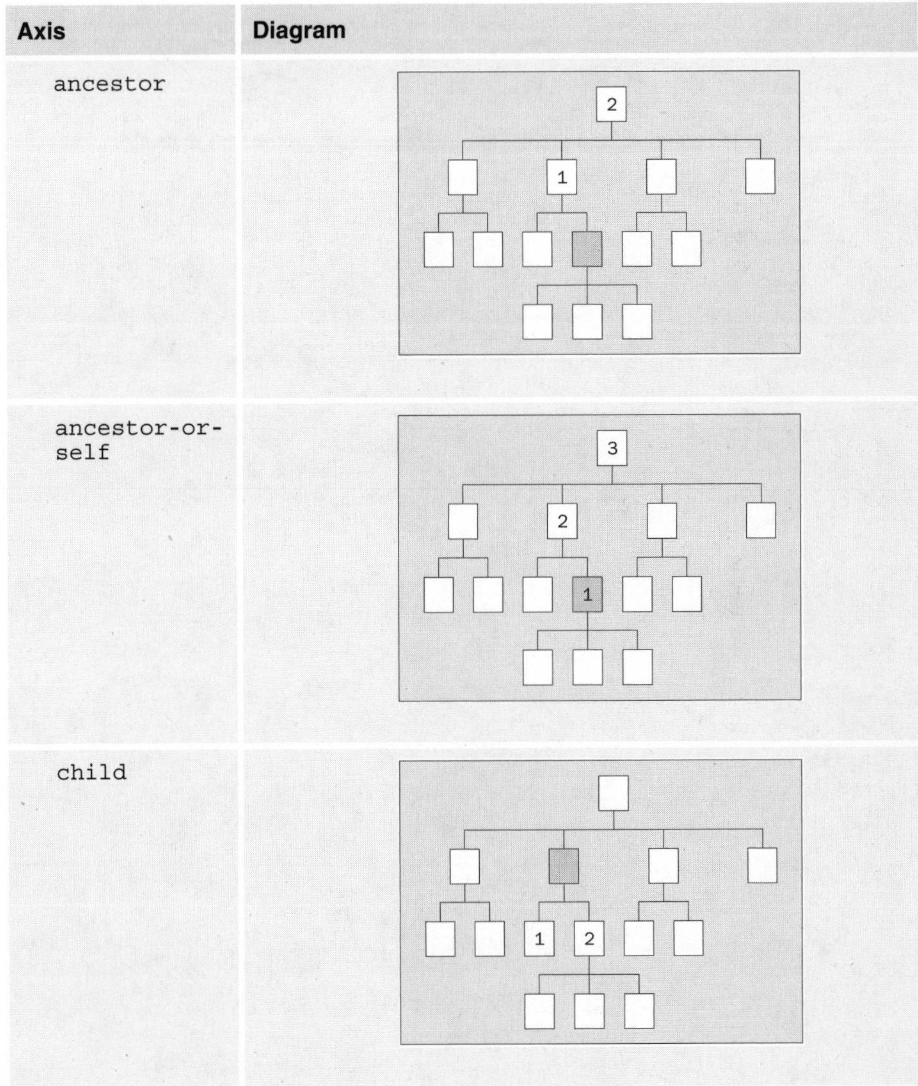

Axis	Diagram
`ancestor`	
`ancestor-or-self`	
`child`	

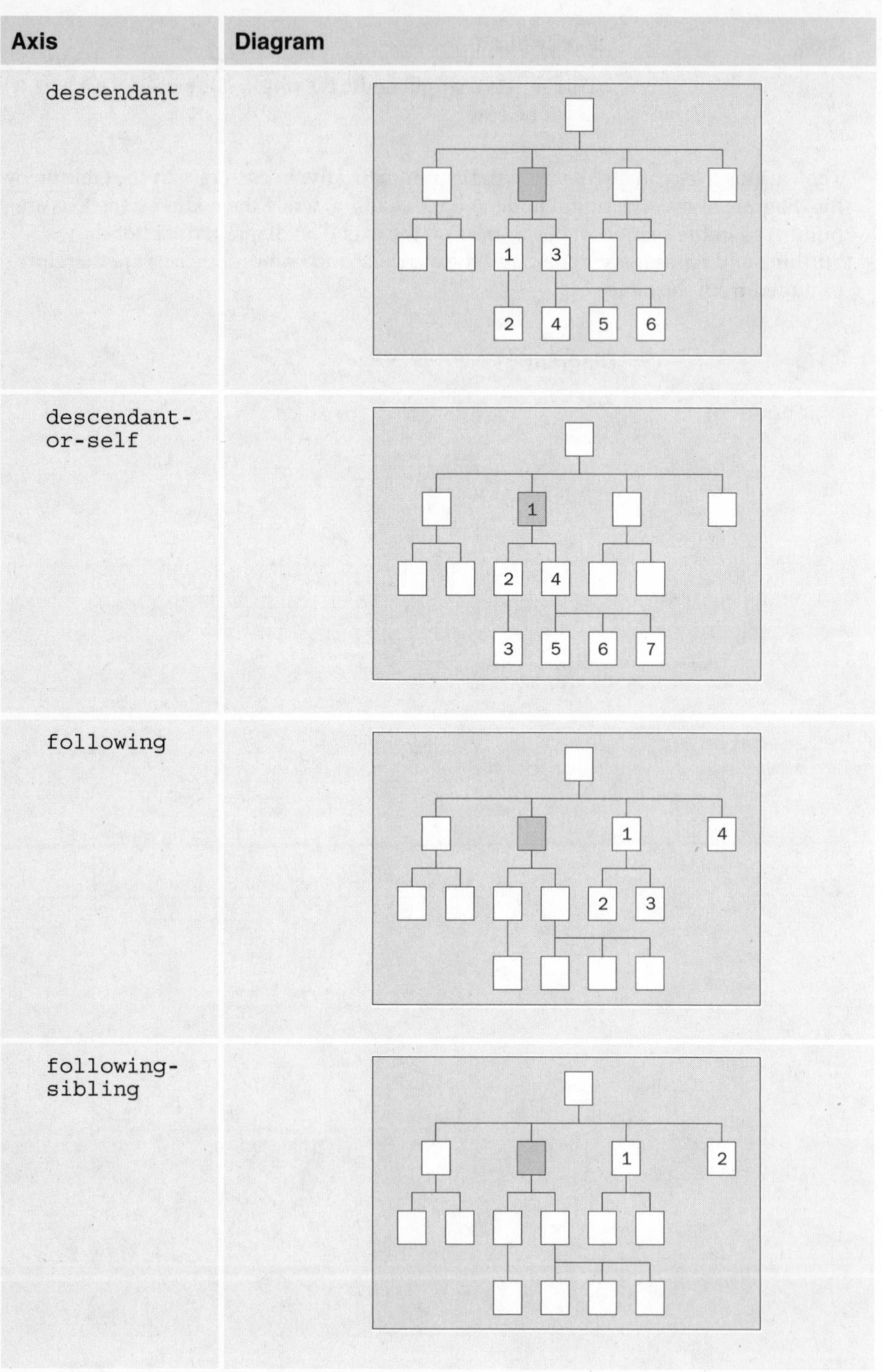

Axis	Diagram
descendant	
descendant-or-self	
following	
following-sibling	

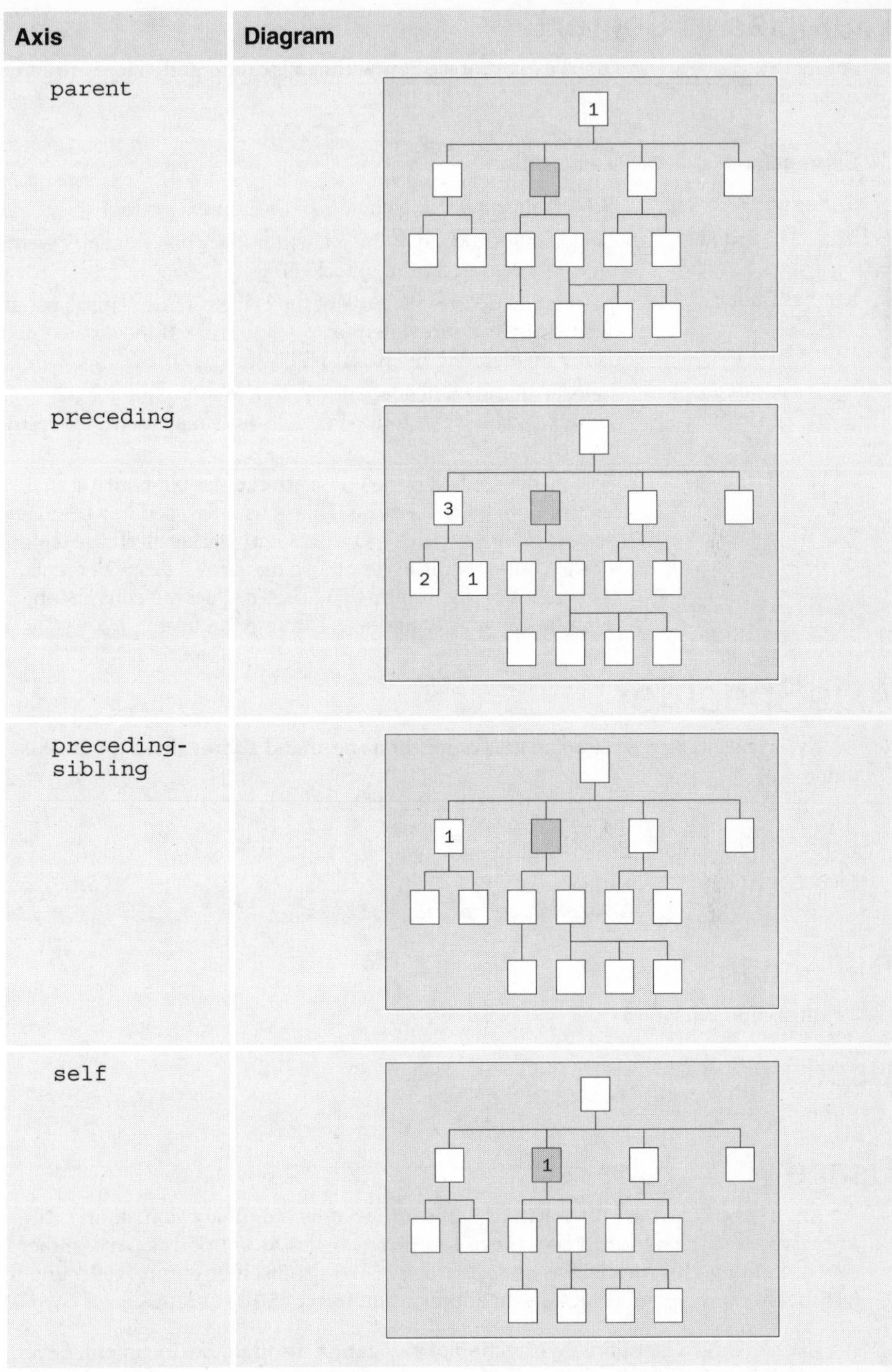

Axis	Diagram
parent	
preceding	
preceding-sibling	
self	

For details of how axes are used in a location path, and examples, see `Step` on page 420.

Examples in Context

An AxisName is always used as part of a Step within a location path. Here are some examples.

Expression	Description
ancestor::*	Selects the ancestor elements of the context node.
child::node()	Selects the children of the context node. This is usually written in its abbreviated form, «node()».
attribute::color	Selects the color attribute of the context node. This is usually written in its abbreviated form, «@color». If the context node is not an element, the result will be empty.
namespace::*	Selects all the namespace nodes that are in scope for the context node. If the context node is not an element, the result will be empty.
self::item	Selects the context node if it is an **<item>** element, or an empty node-set otherwise. This is usually used in a predicate, for example «*[not(self::item)]» selects all the children of the context node except those that are <item> elements. This relies on the implicit node-set-to-Boolean conversion, whereby an empty node-set is treated as false.

AxisSpecifier

An AxisSpecifier is either an axis name, or a shorthand abbreviation for an axis name.

Expression	Syntax
AxisSpecifier	AxisName «::» | AbbreviatedAxisSpecifier

Defined in

XPath section 2.1, rule 5

Used in

Step

Usage

An AxisSpecifier is either an axis name followed by a double colon, or an AbbreviatedAxisSpecifier. Since an AbbreviatedAxisSpecifier is either «@» or nothing, this means that an AxisSpecifier can itself be empty, reflecting the fact that in this context «PARA» is an abbreviation for «child::PARA».

An AxisSpecifier defines a direction of navigation through the document. Given a start node in the document, an AxisSpecifier defines an ordered list of nodes that can be visited in turn. Details of each axis are given in the section AxisName on page 363.

Examples

Expression	Description
`ancestor::`	Specifies the ancestor axis.
`preceding-sibling::`	Specifies the preceding-sibling axis.
`@`	Specifies the attribute axis.
	Specifies the child axis. (Yes, the entry on the left is blank!)

Digits

`Digits` is a sequence of decimal digits in the range 0 through 9. The sequence is used as part of a number: either the whole number, or the part before the decimal point, or the part after the decimal point.

Expression	Syntax
`Digits`	`[0-9]+`

This production rule is written as a **regular expression** and means that `Digits` is a sequence of one or more characters, each in the range zero to nine. The square brackets do not mean that the construct is optional, as in some other syntax notations: rather they indicate a range of characters.

Defined in

XPath section 3.7 (Lexical Structure), rule 31

Used in

`Number`

Usage

An instance of `Digits` is simply a sequence of one or more of the decimal digits 0 through 9.

As `Number` is a lexical token, it cannot contain embedded whitespace; therefore `Digits` cannot contain whitespace either.

Examples in Context

Expression	Description
`89`	This `Number` consists of a single sequence of digits, that is, one instance of `Digits`.
`3.14159`	This `Number` contains two sequences of digits, that is two instances of `Digits`. The first instance of `Digits` is «`3`», the second instance of `Digits` is «`14159`».

EqualityExpr

A non-trivial `EqualityExpr` is used to determine whether two values are equal, or not equal.

Note: for the other comparison operators «<», «<=», «>», and «>=», see `RelationalExpr` on page 416.

Expression	Syntax

`EqualityExpr`	`RelationalExpr |`
	`EqualityExpr «=» RelationalExpr |`
	`EqualityExpr «!=» RelationalExpr`

Defined in

XPath section 3.4, rule 23

Used in

`AndExpr`

Usage

A non-trivial `EqualityExpr` consists of one or more `RelationalExpr` operands separated by «=» (equals) or «!=» (not equals) operators. A trivial `EqualityExpr` consists of a single `RelationalExpr` without any «=» or «!=» operator.

The result of an equals (or not equals) test is always a Boolean value true or false. However, there are many situations where the result of the expression is not obvious, so I'll explain the different cases in some detail.

The harmless looking «=» operator holds many surprises in XPath, so it is well worth studying the rules carefully, even if they seem complicated. Just to warn you of the dangers that lie in wait for the unwary, here are some particular elephant traps:

- You can't assume that «`$X=$X`» is true. It usually will be, but if «`$X`» is an empty node-set, it will be false.
- You can't assume that «`$X!=3`» means the same as «`not($X=3)`». When «`$X`» is a node-set, the first expression is true if any node in the node-set is not equal to 3, while the second is true if no node in the node-set is equal to 3.
- You can't assume that if «`$X=$Y and $Y=$Z`», then «`$X=$Z`». Again, node-sets are the culprit. Two node-sets are considered equal if there is a value that both have in common, so {2, 3} = {3, 4} is true, and {3, 4} = {4, 5} is true, but {2, 3} = {4, 5} is false.

In this strange Orwellian world where some values seem to be more equal than others, the one consolation is that «`$X=$Y`» always means the same as «`$Y=$X`».

The left-hand operand of an `EqualityExpr` may be another `EqualityExpr`. This means that the expression «`$A = $B = $C`» is legal. However, it isn't particularly useful, and probably doesn't have the expected effect. It means the same as «`($A=$B)=$C`», and tests whether the value of `$C`, when converted to a Boolean, is the same as the result of comparing `$A` and `$B`. This means, for example, that «`2=1=0`» is true, because «`2=1`» is false, and `0` when converted to a Boolean is false, and «`2=1`» therefore equals «`boolean(0)`».

Comparing Simple Values

First, consider the case where both operands are simple values: Booleans, numbers, or strings. If the two values are of different type, then:

- if one is a Boolean, the other is converted to a Boolean, and they are compared as Booleans
- otherwise, if one is a number, the other is converted to a number, and they are compared as numbers
- otherwise, they are compared as strings

The effect of these rules is summarized in the following table:

«=»	**Boolean**	**Number**	**String**
Boolean	True if both operands are true or if both are false. False if one operand is true and the other is false.	True if the Boolean is true and the number is not zero and not `NaN`; or if the Boolean is false and the number is zero or `NaN`.	True if the Boolean is true and the string is not empty, or if the Boolean is false and the string is empty.
Number	True if the Boolean is true and the number is not zero and not `NaN`; or if the Boolean is false and the number is zero or `NaN`.	True only if the two operands are numerically equal as defined in IEEE 754.	True only if the string, when converted to a number using the rules for the **`number()`** function, is numerically equal to the number as defined in IEEE 754.

«=»	Boolean	Number	String
String	True if the Boolean is true and the string is not empty, or if the Boolean is false and the string is empty.	True only if the string, when converted to a number using the rules for the **number()** function, is numerically equal to the number as defined in IEEE 754.	True only if the two operands contain the same sequence of Unicode characters.

See Chapter 2, page 89 for details of how IEEE 754 defines numerical equality. For example, positive zero and negative zero are considered equal, but NaN and NaN are considered unequal.

For simple values (including special numeric values such as NaN), the result of applying the «!=» (not equals) operator is always the opposite of applying the «=» operator: if the result of an «=» test is true, the result of «!=» will be false, and vice versa.

Comparisons Involving Node-sets

Now consider the case where at least one operand is a node-set. (And remember that an expression as innocent as «TITLE» or «@HREF» is actually a node-set, even if it only contains a single node.) The result of an «=» or «!=» test is now as shown in the table below. Given that one operand is a node-set (it doesn't matter which), choose the row according to the data type of the other operand.

Data Type of Other Operand	= (equals)	!= (not equals)
Boolean	True if the Boolean is true and the node-set contains at least one node; or if the Boolean is false and the node-set is empty.	True if the Boolean is true and the node-set is empty; or if the Boolean is false and the node-set contains at least one node.
Number	True if the node-set contains a node whose string-value, after converting to a number using the **number()** function, is numerically equal to the number operand as defined in IEEE 754.	True if the node-set contains a node whose string-value, after converting to a number using the **number()** function, is numerically not equal to the number operand as defined in IEEE 754.

Data Type of Other Operand	= (equals)	!= (not equals)
string	True if the node-set contains a node whose string-value is equal to the string operand.	True if the node-set contains a node whose string-value is not equal to the string operand.
Node-set	True if there is a pair of nodes, one from each node-set, that have the same string-value. Note that this means that if either or both node-sets are empty, the result is always false. If there is a node that is present in both node-sets, the result will always be true.	True if there is a pair of nodes, one from each node-set, that have different string-values. Note that this means that if either or both node-sets are empty, the result is always false. It also means that if either node-set contains more than one node, then unless the nodes all have the same string-value the result will always be true.

So where a node-set «`$N`» is compared with a string «`'mary'`», the test «`$N='mary'`» is effectively a shorthand for "if there is a node n in `$N` such that `string-value(n) = 'mary'`". Similarly, the test «`$N!='mary'`» is effectively a shorthand for "if there is a node `n` in `$N` such that `string-value(n) != 'mary'`". If `$N` contains two nodes, whose string-values are "`mary`" and "`john`", then «`$N='mary'`» and «`$N!='mary'`» will both be true, because there is a node that is equal to `'mary'` and another that is not. If `$N` is an empty node-set, then «`$N='mary'`» and «`$N!='mary'`» will both be false, because there is no node that is equal to `'mary'`, but there is also no node that is not equal to `'mary'`.

Note that when we talk about the nodes in a node-set, we are only concerned with the nodes that are members of the node-set in their own right. The children of these nodes are not members of the node-set.

Example: Node-set Comparisons

For example, consider the following piece of XML:

```
<booklist>
   <book><author>Adam</author><title>Penguins</title></book>
   <book><author>Betty</author><title>Giraffes</title></book>
</booklist>
```

Suppose we create a variable whose value is the node-set containing all <**book**> elements, as follows:

```
<xsl:variable name="all-books" select="//book"/>
```

And now suppose we do the following test:

```
<xsl:if test="$all-books = 'Adam'"/>
```

The result is false, because the node-set `$all-books` contains two <**book**> nodes, and neither has a string-value of "`Adam`". The first **<book>** element has the string-value "`AdamPenguins`", and the second has the string-value "`BettyGiraffes`". The fact that one of them has a child whose string-value is "`Adam`" is of no consequence: the child is not a member of the node-set.

The string-value of a node depends on the type of node. For a text node, it is the actual characters in the value. For an element node, it is the concatenation of the text in all text nodes that are descendants of the element. For an attribute node, it is the value of the attribute. See Chapter 2 for the detailed rules.

An interesting consequence of the rules for comparing node-sets is that if `$N` is an empty node-set, the result of the test «`$N=$N`» is false, because there is no node in the first node-set whose string-value is equal to that of a node in the second node-set.

It is very easy to trip up on these rules, by assuming for example that `<xsl:if test="@name!= 'James'">` means the same as `<xsl:if test="not(@name = 'James')">`. It doesn't; if there is no **name** attribute, the first test is false, while the second is true.

Generally speaking, it is best to steer clear of the «`!=`» operator unless you know exactly what you are doing. Use «`not(x=y)`» instead; it is more likely to match the intuitive meaning.

One situation where «`!=`» can be useful with node-sets, however, is to test whether all values in a node-set have the same value. For example, writing `<xsl:if test="not($documents//version!=1.0)">` tests whether there is any node in the node-set «`$documents//version`» whose numeric value is not 1.0.

It is important to remember that an equality test compares the string values of the nodes, not their identity. For example, «`..=/`» might seem to be a natural way of testing whether the parent of the context node is the root. In fact this test will also return true if the parent node is the document element, because in a well-formed tree the string-value of the document element is the same as the string-value of the root. Not only is the test wrong, it could also be very expensive: the string-value of the root contains all the text in the document, so you might be constructing two strings each a million characters long and then comparing them.

A better way to test if the current node's parent node is the root is to write «`parent::*[not(..)]`»: this is true only for a node that has a parent and no grandparent. Another possibility, which can be used to compare any single-member node-sets, is «`generate-id(..)=generate-id(/)`». This relies on the **`generate-id()`** function, described in Chapter 7, page 491, which returns a string that uniquely identifies a node. Finally, tests on node identity can be done using the union operator «|» together with the **`count()`** function: thus «`count(..| / )=1 and ..`» will be true only if the parent node and the root node are the same node. The «`and ..`» is needed because without it the test would also be true for a node that has no parent, namely the root node itself.

Comparisons Involving Trees

When one of the operands of an `EqualityExpr` is the root of a tree, it follows the rules described above for node-sets. However, such a node-set will always contain exactly one node, so in many ways the actual behavior is much more like that described for strings.

Trees can arise in various ways. The root expression «/» refers to a tree; so does the result of the **`document()`** function (though this can also be a node-set containing the roots of several trees). You can also construct a temporary tree using an **`<xsl:variable>`** or **`<xsl:param>`** element with no **`select`** attribute. One difference from the source document tree is that the source tree usually represents a well-formed XML document, whose root node has a single element child and no text node children, whereas a temporary tree only has to be well-balanced: the root may have any number of element nodes and text nodes as its children.

These rules mean that if you compare a tree-valued variable with a string, the result will be true if the string-value of the root of the tree is equal to the string. So a simple tree valued variable declared as

```
<xsl:variable name="city">Osaka</xsl:variable>
```

behaves just like a string declared as

```
<xsl:variable name="city" select="'Osaka'"/>
```

In both cases «`$city='Osaka'`» will be true and «`$city='Tokyo'`» will be false.

A tree-valued variable can also be more complex, for example:

```
<xsl:variable name="tree">A <emph>very</emph> important
person</xsl:variable>
```

The tree in this example is a root node with three child nodes: a text node for "`A♦`" (where ♦ represents a space character), an **`<emph>`** element node, and a text node for "`♦important♦person`". The string value of this variable is the string «`A♦very♦important♦person`». An «=» or «!=» comparison with `$tree` will give the same result as a comparison with this string.

To summarize, where one of the operands of the «`=`» or «`!=`» comparison is a tree, it is treated as if the comparison was done with a node-set containing a single node, the root of the tree. So the result of the comparison will be as follows:

	= (equals)	!= (not equals)
Boolean	True if the Boolean is true, false if it is false; the contents of the tree are immaterial, because it always contains a node.	True if the Boolean is false, false if it is true; the contents of the tree are immaterial, because it always contains a node.
Number	True if the string-value of the tree, after converting to a number using the **`number()`** function, is numerically equal to the number operand as defined in IEEE 754.	True if the string-value of the tree, after converting to a number using the **`number()`** function, is numerically not equal to the number operand as defined in IEEE 754.
String	True if the string-value of the tree is equal to the string operand.	True if the string-value of the tree is not equal to the string operand.
Node-set	True if the node-set contains a node whose string-value is equal to the string-value of the tree.	True if the node-set contains a node whose string-value is not equal to the string-value of the tree.

These rules actually mean that for all practical purposes, a variable defined as:

```
<xsl:variable name="city">Johannesburg</xsl:variable>
```

behaves in exactly the same way as the string variable:

```
<xsl:variable name="city" select="'Johannesburg'"/>
```

In fact there is only one case where the result is different: namely comparison with a Boolean. The result of «`$city=false()`» is true if `$city` is a zero-length string, but it is always false if `$city` is a tree, regardless of its value.

Note that this doesn't change with the XSLT 1.1 draft; although result tree fragments cease to be a separate data type, the semantics of equality comparisons remain the same.

Examples

Expression	Description
`@width = 3`	Tests whether the **`width`** attribute of the context node, after converting to a number, has the numeric value 3. The result will be true if the **`width`** attribute is say «`3`» or «`3.00`». It will be false if there is no **`width`** attribute.

Expression	Description
`@width = @height`	Tests whether the **`width`** attribute and the **`height`** attribute of the context node have the same string value. If **`width`** is «`3`» and **`height`** is «`3.00`», the result will be false. It will also be false if either or both attributes are absent. If you want a numeric comparison, use the **`number()`** function (described in Chapter 7, page 530) to force a conversion.
`@width != $x`	If the variable `$x` holds a numeric value, a numeric comparison is performed; if it holds a string value, a string comparison is performed. The result will be true if the values are different. It will be false if there is no **`width`** attribute. If `$x` holds a node-set, the result will be true if there is any node in the node-set whose string-value is equal to the **`width`** attribute, using string comparison; it will be false if the node-set is empty or if there is no **`width`** attribute.

Expr

`Expr` is the top-level production rule, representing an XPath expression.

Expression	Syntax
`Expr`	`OrExpr`

Defined in

XPath section 3.1, rule 14

Used in

`Expr` is the top-level rule for the syntax of an XPath expression.

A nested `Expr` is also used in the production rules for `Argument`, `PrimaryExpr`, and `PredicateExpr`.

Within an XSLT stylesheet, XPath expressions are used in the following contexts:

Context	Result data type
Attribute value templates. The expression is written between curly braces «{» and «}» in any attribute where attribute value templates are permitted. A list of these attributes is included in Chapter 3, page 129.	string

Context	Result data type
`<xsl:apply-templates select="">`	node-set
`<xsl:copy-of select="">`	node-set
`<xsl:for-each select="">`	node-set
`<xsl:if test="">`	Boolean
`<xsl:key use="">`	node-set or string
`<xsl:number value="">`	number
`<xsl:param select="">`	Any
`<xsl:sort select="">`	string
`<xsl:value-of select="">`	string
`<xsl:variable select="">`	Any
`<xsl:when test="">`	Boolean
`<xsl:with-param select="">`	Any

Usage

`Expr` (short for *Expression*) is the top-level construct in the production rules defined in this chapter. What the syntax rule says is that every `Expr` is an `OrExpr` (and vice versa, every `OrExpr` is an `Expr`). So it merely delegates the rules to `OrExpr`. The construct `OrExpr` is described on page 404.

The designers of XPath chose to specify the syntax of the language in such a way that the precedence of the various operators is inherent in the production rules. So this rule also tells us that «`or`» is the lowest-precedence operator. The production rule for `OrExpr` defines it in terms of `AndExpr`, which tells us that «`and`» is a higher precedence operator than «`or`», and so on. A consequence of this style of definition is that an `OrExpr` does not necessarily contain an «`or`» operator; it is merely an expression that occurs in a context where an «`or`» operator would be recognized.

In XSLT, expressions (that is, sentences conforming to the production rule for `Expr`) occur within stylesheets, and the stylesheet context imposes rules on the `Expr` that are not inherent in the XPath syntax. These include data type rules (for example, certain stylesheet contexts require a node-set, as described in the table above), and also rules about the scope of variables and the assignment of namespace prefixes. For example, «`2+2`» is a perfectly valid XPath expression, but if you try to write `<xsl:for-each select="2+2"/>` the XSLT processor will report an error, telling you that a node-set is required in this context.

The stylesheet context imposes constraints on the syntactic validity of the expression, and also provides a run-time context when the time comes to evaluate the expression. So we can consider the context of the expression in two parts, a static part and a dynamic part.

The static context of the expression, which can be determined merely by examining the stylesheet, includes:

- The list of variable names that are in scope at the point where the expression appears.
- The list of namespace prefixes that are in scope at the point where the expression appears, and the corresponding namespace URI for each one. This affects the validity and indeed the meaning of any `QName` (loosely, a namespace-qualified name) occurring in the expression, as described in the section `QName` on page 414.
- The required data type (for example **`<xsl:if>`** requires a `Boolean`, **`<xsl:for-each>`** requires a node-set, and an expression contained within an attribute value template evaluates to a string).
- The set of extension functions (user- or vendor-defined external functions) that is available in the current stylesheet context.
- The URI of the stylesheet containing the expression: or more precisely, the Base URI of the actual element in which the expression appears. Normally this is the URL of the XML entity containing this part of the stylesheet (the stylesheet may consist of several separate entities, linked either using **`<xsl:include>`** and **`<xsl:import>`**, or using XML external general entity references). XSLT 1.1 also allows the base URI to be modified using the **`xml:base`** attribute, as described in Chapter 2. In fact this Base URI is needed for one purpose only, to resolve a relative URI used in the **`document()`** function, which is described in Chapter 7 page 466.

The dynamic context of the expression, which can only be established while the stylesheet is being used to process a specific source document, includes:

- The current values of all variables that are referenced in the expression.
- The context node, context position, and context size, which together identify the set of nodes in the source document that the stylesheet is currently processing. These important concepts were explained in Chapter 2.

The XSLT processor may also need information about the static context at run-time. For example, certain functions (such as **`system-property()`** and **`key()`**) can generate a `QName` (a name potentially in the form «`prefix:localname`») as a result of an expression, and just like a `QName` written directly in the expression, any namespace prefixes this uses must be in scope.

As explained in Chapter 1, it's a general principle of XPath that expression evaluation is free of side effects; evaluating an expression isn't going to change the values of any variables, write information to log files, or prompt the user for their credit card number. Therefore evaluating the same expression more than once, in the same context, shouldn't make any difference to the answer or to the final output, and equally it shouldn't make any difference in which order expressions are evaluated. As a result, the XSLT and XPath specifications generally say nothing about order of evaluation. The only exceptions are `OrExpr` and `AndExpr`, where left-to-right evaluation is explicitly mandated.

The only way side effects can occur from evaluating an expression is if the expression calls user-written (or vendor-written) extension functions, because the XPath specification doesn't constrain what an extension function can do. Equally, it makes no guarantees about when, and in what order, extension functions are called.

Examples

Examples of expressions occur throughout this chapter. Here is a selection, brought together to indicate the variety of constructs that fall under this heading:

Expression	Description
`$x + ($y * 2)`	Returns the result of multiplying `$y` by two and adding the value of `$x`
`//book | //magazine`	Returns a node-set containing all of the **`<book>`** and **`<magazine>`** elements in the same document as the context node
`substring-before(author, ' ')`	Finds the string-value of the first **`<author>`** child of the context node, and returns that part of the string-value that precedes the first space character.
`chapter and verse`	Returns the Boolean value true if the context node has a child **`<chapter>`** element and also a child **`<verse>`** element
`93.7`	Returns the numeric value `93.7`

ExprToken

An `ExprToken` is a lexical unit of the XPath expression language. `ExprToken` defines the lexical rules for separating tokens using whitespace; it is not itself a syntactic unit used in any other production rule.

Expression	Syntax

`ExprToken`	`«(» | «)» | «[» | «]» |`
	`«.» | «..» | «@» |`
	`«,» | «::» |`
	`NameTest |`
	`NodeType |`
	`Operator |`
	`FunctionName |`
	`AxisName |`
	`Literal |`
	`Number |`
	`VariableReference`

Defined in

XPath section 3.7 (Lexical Structure), rule 28

Used in

The production rule is the top-level lexical rule; it is not referenced from anywhere else.

Usage

The production rule defines those constructs in the language that are regarded as lexical tokens. If a construct is a lexical token, it is indivisible: its components must be contiguous and cannot be separated by whitespace. Higher-level constructs consist of a sequence of lexical tokens and are allowed to contain whitespace to separate the tokens. So for example, the expression «child::xsl:*» contains three tokens, «child», «::», and «xsl:*». Spaces and newlines can be used between these tokens, but not within them. This means the expression can contain optional whitespace at all the points marked here with a diamond: «♦child♦::♦xsl:*♦».

> *The spec doesn't explicitly say so, but by implication, whitespace cannot be freely used in the middle of an* ExprToken; *except, of course, within a* Literal. *This means, for example, that there can be no space between the two colons in* «child::node()», *because* «::» *is a single token.*

This doesn't mean that you always have to include whitespace between tokens. It's only necessary where one token could otherwise be misread as part of the previous token, for example in an expression such as «$x div 2» or «price - discount».

Whitespace itself is defined by the ExprWhitespace rule. It's perfectly OK to spread an XPath expression over several lines; a newline can be used as a separator wherever a space can appear.

Examples

Here are some examples of ExprTokens. No whitespace is permitted within the token, except in the case of a Literal.

Token	Description
[	A punctuation symbol used as part of a Predicate.
item	An NCName.
my-namespace:*	A NameTest. No spaces are permitted before or after the colon.
$weekly-sales-total	A VariableReference. No spaces are permitted after the «$» sign.
93.7	A Number.
"a pinch of salt"	A Literal. Any whitespace occurring within the Literal is significant, it is part of the string value.

ExprWhitespace

The ExprWhitespace rule defines precisely what constitutes whitespace within an XPath expression.

Expression	Syntax
ExprWhitespace	S
S	(#x20 | #x9 | #xD | #xA)+

Defined in

XPath section 3.7, rule 39
The rule for S is from the XML Recommendation

Used in

This production rule is not actually referenced from any other. It is used only in the narrative text of the XPath specification.

Usage

The definition of whitespace is taken directly from the XML standard: whitespace is any sequence of space, tab, carriage return, and linefeed (newline) characters.

XPath allows whitespace to be used before or after any `ExprToken`. See the section `ExprToken` above for a list of constructs that are considered to be lexical tokens and that may therefore not contain any embedded whitespace. It is not intuitively obvious which composite symbols in XPath are tokens and which are not; for example «`self::x`» consists of three tokens (so spaces can appear before or after the double colon, but not between the two colons), while «`xsl:*`» is a single token, with no embedded whitespace allowed anywhere. This is because «`xsl:*`» is a `NameTest`, and `NameTest` is one of the constructs listed in the production rule for `ExprToken`.

The lexical rules for XPath say that any token swallows as many characters as it can. If a character can be treated as part of the previous token, then it is treated as such, even if this causes a syntax error later on. This means it is necessary in some circumstances to insert whitespace to separate tokens; the most common example being the need to use a space before a minus sign to distinguish an arithmetic expression such as «`price - discount`» from the hyphenated name «`price-discount`». Whitespace is also required, of course, to separate names from the operators «`or`», «`and`», «`div`», and «`mod`». In the expression «`5 mod 2`», the space before «`mod`» is optional, because «`5mod`» would not be a valid token; but the space after «`mod`» is necessary, because «`mod2`» would otherwise be read as a `QName`.

Although it is common practice to write XPath expressions on a single line, because this is how XML attributes are normally written, there is nothing to stop whitespace characters such as tab and newline being used as an alternative to spaces.

Examples

Expression	Description
	The box on the left shows what whitespace usually looks like.
`
`	If you really want to see your whitespace characters, you can write them like this.

FilterExpr

A `FilterExpr` is used to apply one or more `Predicates` to a node-set, selecting a subset of those nodes that satisfy some condition.

Expression	Syntax
FilterExpr	PrimaryExpr | FilterExpr Predicate

Defined in

XPath section 3.3, rule 20

Used in

PathExpr

Usage

A non-trivial FilterExpr consists of a PrimaryExpr whose value is a node-set, followed by one or more Predicates that select a subset of the nodes in the node-set. Each predicate consists of an expression enclosed in square brackets, for example «[@name='London']» or «[position()=1]».

The way the syntax is defined, every PrimaryExpr is also a trivial FilterExpr, including simple expressions such as «23», «'Washington'», and «true()».

If there are any Predicates, the value of the PrimaryExpr must be a node-set. Each of the predicates is applied to the node-set in turn; only those nodes in the node-set for which the predicate is true pass through to the next stage. The final result consists of those nodes in the original node-set that satisfy each of the predicates.

A predicate may be either a numeric predicate (for example «[1]» or «[last()-1]»), or a Boolean predicate (for example «[count(*) > 5]» or «[@name and @address]»). If the value of the expression is a number, it is treated as a numeric predicate; otherwise it is converted if necessary to a Boolean (using the **boolean()** function), and is treated as a Boolean predicate. A numeric predicate whose value is N is equivalent to the Boolean predicate «[position()=N]». So, for example, the numeric predicate «[1]» means «[position()=1]», and the numeric predicate «[last()]» means «[position()=last()]».

It's important to remember that this implicit testing of **position()** happens only when the predicate expression actually evaluates to a number. For example, «$paras[1 or last()]» does not mean «$paras[position()=1 or position()=last()]», because the result of evaluating «1 or last()» is a Boolean, not a number (and as it happens, it will always be true). Similarly, «book[../@book-nr]» does not mean «book[position()=../@book-nr]», because the result of «../@book-nr» is a node-set, not a number.

In nearly all practical cases, a numeric predicate selects either a single node from the node-set, or no node at all, but this is not part of the definition: for example, «$x[count(*)]» selects every node whose position is the same as the number of children it has.

As discussed in Chapter 2, every XPath expression is evaluated in some context. For an expression used as a predicate, the context is different from the context of the containing expression. While evaluating each predicate, the context is established as follows:

- The **context node** (the node referenced as «.») is the node being tested
- The **context position** (the value of the **position()** function) is the position of that node within the set of nodes surviving from the previous stage, taken in document order
- The **context size** (the value of the **last()** function) is the number of nodes surviving from the previous stage

To see how this works, consider the FilterExpr «$headings [self::h1] [last()]». This starts with the node-set that is the value of the variable «$headings» (it is an error if this value is not a node-set). The first predicate is «[self::h1]». This is applied to each node in «$headings» in turn. While it is being applied, the context node is that particular node. The expression «self::h1» is a RelativeLocationPath consisting of a single Step: it selects a node-set. If the context node is an **<h1>** element this node-set will contain a single node – the context node. Otherwise, the node-set will be empty. When this node-set is converted to a Boolean, it will be true if it contains a node, and false if it is empty. So the first predicate is actually filtering through those nodes in «$headings» that are **<h1>** elements.

The second predicate is now applied to each node in this set of **<h1>** elements. In each case the predicate «[last()]» returns the same value: a number indicating how many **<h1>** elements there are in the set. As this is a numeric predicate, a node passes the test when «[position()=last()]», that is, when the position of the node in the set (taken in document order) is equal to the number of nodes in the set. So the meaning of «$headings [self::h1] [last()]» is "the last **<h1>** element in the node-set $headings, taking the nodes in document order".

Note that this isn't the same as «$headings [last()] [self::h1]», which means "the node-set containing the last node in $headings, provided it is an **<h1>** element".

The operation of a Predicate in a FilterExpr is very similar to the application of a Predicate to a Step in a LocationPath, and although they are not directly related in the XPath grammar rules, you can often use Predicates without being fully aware that you are using a FilterExpr or a LocationPath. For example, «$para[1]» is a FilterExpr, while «para[1]» is a RelativeLocationPath consisting of a single Step. The main differences to watch out for are firstly, that in a LocationPath the predicates apply only to the most recent Step (for example in «book/author[1]» the «[1]» means the first author within each book), and secondly, that in a FilterExpr the nodes are always considered in document order (whereas in a Step they can be in forwards or reverse document order depending on the direction of the axis).

Examples

Expression	Description
$paragraphs	This FilterExpr comprises a single VariableReference. It is not necessarily a node-set.
$paragraphs[23]	This FilterExpr consists of a VariableReference filtered by a Predicate. It selects the 23rd node in the node-set that is the value of variable $paragraphs, taking them in document order.

Expression	Description
`document('lookup.xml')`	This `FilterExpr` comprises a single `FunctionCall`. It selects the root node of the document identified by the URI `lookup.xml`.
`key('empname', 'John Smith')[@loc='Sydney']`	This `FilterExpr` comprises a `FunctionCall` filtered by a `Predicate`. Assuming that the key «`empname`» has been defined in the obvious way, it selects all employees named `John Smith` who are located in `Sydney`.
`(//section|//subsection) [title='Introduction']`	This `FilterExpr` consists of a parenthesized `UnionExpr` filtered by a `Predicate`. It selects all **<section>** and **<subsection>** elements that have a child **<title>** element with the content «`Introduction`».
`document(//@href) [pricelist][1]`	This `FilterExpr` first selects all documents referenced by URLs contained in **href** attributes anywhere in the source document; from this set of documents it selects those whose outermost element is named **<pricelist>**, and from these it selects the first. The order of nodes that are in different documents is not defined, so if there are several price lists referenced, it is unpredictable which will be selected.

5

Expressions

FunctionCall

A `FunctionCall` invokes either a system-defined function or a vendor- or user-supplied extension function.

Expression	Syntax
`FunctionCall`	`FunctionName` «`(`» (`Argument` («`,`» `Argument`)*)? «`)`»

Defined in

XPath section 3.2, rule 16

Used in

`PrimaryExpr`

Usage

There are two kinds of function call: calls on the standard functions listed in Chapter 7, which will be present in every conforming XSLT product, and calls on extension functions which may be supplied either by the product vendor or by the user, as described in Chapter 8. The two kinds can be readily distinguished, because in a call on a standard function, the function name will always be a simple name with no colon, while the name of an extension function will always be in some non-default namespace and will therefore be recognizable by having a name of the form «`prefix:localname`». The prefix must refer to a namespace declaration that is in scope for the expression containing this function call.

Technically there are two kinds of standard function, core functions which are defined in the XPath specification itself, and additional functions which are defined in the XSLT specification. If you are only using XPath in the context of XSLT stylesheets, however, the difference is of no importance.

A `FunctionCall` with no arguments takes the form `FunctionName` «`(`» «`)`», while in a call with arguments, the arguments are separated by commas in the usual way. The arguments themselves can be any XPath expression, subject to any type-checking rules or other constraints defined for the particular function in question. This includes expressions such as «`/`», «`.`» or «`@*`», which are not found in conventional programming languages.

A `FunctionCall` has very similar syntax to a `NodeTest` such as «`node()`» or «`comment()`», but is distinguished simply by use of a set of reserved names for the different node types.

In the case of standard functions, the supplied values will always be converted to the required types if conversion is necessary. Many of the standard functions take a fixed number of arguments. In some, an argument is optional, which usually defaults to a node-set containing the context node. The **`concat()`** function, which concatenates strings, is exceptional in that the number of arguments is open-ended.

A `FunctionCall` always returns a result. This may be a value of any of the four XPath data types: Boolean, number, string, or node-set. With XSLT 1.0, a function can in principle return a result tree fragment, though none of the standard functions does this. In the case of an extension function, the result may also be an *external object*, as described below. There is nothing to say that the same function will always return the same type of result: for example the **`system-property()`** function sometimes returns a string and sometimes a number.

For use with extension functions, the XSLT 1.1 draft defines an additional data type : the external object. This is just an XPath handle or wrapper for an object created in another language such as Java or JavaScript. External objects can be returned by one external function call and passed on as an argument to another, but there's nothing else the stylesheet can do with them; it's not even possible to convert them to a string for display, unless another external function is available to do this.

None of the standard functions have side effects; they don't change the values of variables, they don't produce any output, and they don't change any settings in the browser or the operating system. There is nothing to stop an extension function from having side-effects; for example, an extension function could print a message or increment a counter, or even do something more radical such as modify the source document or the stylesheet itself. However, extension functions with side effects are likely to be rather unpredictable, since there is nothing to say in which order things happen. For example, you can't assume that global variables are evaluated in any particular order or that they are evaluated only once; and a global variable that is never accessed might never be evaluated at all.

Calling a function that is not available is an error. However, it is not necessarily an error for a stylesheet to contain an expression that references a function that is not available. You can test whether a particular function is available using the system function **`function-available()`**, and use the result to avoid calling functions that are not provided. The **`function-available()`** mechanism works both for extension functions and for system functions: this will be useful as the standard develops, because if new functions are added in a future version of XPath or XSLT, you may want to write stylesheets that still work with products that only implement the current version.

Examples

Expression	Description
`true()`	A call on a standard function that always returns the Boolean value true.
`string-length($x)`	A call on a standard function that converts the argument to a string, and returns the number of characters it contains.
`count(*)`	A call on a standard function that evaluates the node-set «`*`» (the set of all element children of the context node) and returns a number indicating how many nodes there are in this node-set.
`xt:intersection($x, $y)`	A call on an extension function. It is identified as an extension function by the presence of a prefix «`xt:`» which must correspond to a namespace declaration that is in scope. The rules for locating an implementation of this extension function are implementor-defined.
`function-available ('xt:intersection')`	A call on the standard function named `function-available`, which tests whether the extension function named «`xt:intersection`» is available for use. Note that a positive response doesn't mean that a call on this function will necessarily succeed; for example, there is no way of asking how many arguments are expected.

FunctionName

A `FunctionName` can be any valid name other than a name reserved for a node type.

Expression	Syntax
`FunctionName`	`QName - NodeType`

The "-" sign in this production rule means "but not a"; in other words, a `FunctionName` may be any name other than one used for a `NodeType`. In practice the choice is a lot more limited than this, since names in the default namespace (names with no colon) can be used only for standard functions, of which there is a fixed list defined in the XPath and XSLT specifications.

Defined in

XPath section 3.7 (Lexical Structure), rule 35

Used in

`PrimaryExpr`

Usage

Syntactically, a function name can be any name other than one of the four `NodeType` names «`comment`», «`text`», «`processing-instruction`», or «`node`». A function name is recognized in the syntax as a name that is followed by a left parenthesis.

The only function names with no namespace prefix are the system-defined functions listed in Chapter 7. User-defined (or vendor-defined) extension functions will always include a namespace prefix. The prefix is interpreted using the namespace definitions in scope for the stylesheet element containing the expression in which the function name appears.

Examples

Expression	Definition

`concat`
`string-length`
`namespace-uri`
	These are system function names.

`saxon:intersection`
`xt:node-set`
`irs:get-tax-rate`
	These are extension function names.

Literal

A `Literal` represents a constant string.

Expression	Syntax
`Literal`	«"» [^"]* «"» | «'» [^']* «'»

Unless you are familiar with regular expressions you may find this production rule difficult to read, but what it is saying is actually quite simple; a `Literal` is either a sequence of any characters other than double-quotes, enclosed between double-quotes, or a sequence of any characters other than single-quotes, enclosed between single-quotes.

A `Literal` is a lexical token. Whitespace within a `Literal` is allowed, and is significant (whitespace characters are part of the value). Some care is needed when using tab, carriage-return, and newline characters within a literal, because the XML parser is required to replace these by space characters before the XPath expression parser ever gets to see them, as part of the process of *attribute value normalization*. Use character references such as «`	`», «`
`», and «`
`» to prevent this.

Defined in

XPath section 3.7 (Lexical Structure), rule 29.

Used in

`PrimaryExpr`
`NodeTest`

The appearance of `Literal` within the syntax rules for `NodeTest` is for testing the name of a processing instruction: for details of this anomaly, see `NodeTest`, page 398.

Usage

A literal represents a constant string value (note that unlike some other languages, numeric constants are not regarded as literals). It is written enclosed in either single quotes or double quotes; if single quotes are used, there must be no single-quote within the string, while if double-quotes are used, there must be no double-quotes within the string.

It is not possible for a literal to contain both single quotes and double quotes; if such a string is required, use the system function **`concat()`**, described in Chapter 7, page 456. Using character entities or entity references doesn't solve the problem, because these are expanded by the XML parser before the XPath parser gets to see them.

In practice the ability to use single and double quotes is further constrained by the fact that in an XSLT context, XPath expressions are always written within XML attributes in the stylesheet. If the XML attribute is written with single quotes, the XPath literal must be in double quotes, and it cannot contain a single quote because that would terminate the attribute value; equally, if the XML attribute is in double quotes, the XPath literal must be in single quotes, and it cannot contain a double quote for the same reasons.

The best way round this problem is to avoid it by using tree-valued variables in place of the literal. For example, rather than trying to write the expression «`message[text="I won't"]`», declare a variable as follows:

```
<xsl:variable name="msg-text">I won't</xsl:variable>
```

and write the expression as «`message[text=$msg-text]`».

Where a literal is used as the entire value of an XPath expression, two pairs of quotes are needed, for example:

```
<xsl:variable name="html-dialect" select="'netscape'"/>
```

If the extra quotes are omitted, «`netscape`» is assumed to be a node-set expression that finds all **`<netscape>`** element children of the context node. This means you won't get a sensible error message when you make this mistake, instead it will probably just lead to your stylesheet producing incorrect results. It's probably clearer to write:

```
<xsl:variable name="html-dialect">netscape</xsl:variable>
```

Although technically this isn't quite the same thing (because the value is now a temporary tree rather than a string), in practice the tree can be used anywhere the string could be used, with the same meaning. (The only exception is that conversion to a Boolean works differently.)

Examples

The following are examples of literals allowed in XPath:

```
'London'
"Los Angeles"
"O'Connor"
'Never say "never"'
```

Note that the last two examples are fine as far as XPath is concerned, but to write them in an XSLT stylesheet it will be necessary to use XML character or entity references for either the single quotes or the double quotes: whichever kind is used for delimiting the surrounding XML attribute. For example:

```
<xsl:value-of select='"O&apos;Connor"'/>
<xsl:value-of select="'Never say &quot;never&quot;'"/>
```

You cannot use character or entity references to represent the quotation mark that delimits the literal itself, for example:

```
<xsl:value-of select='"Never say &quot;never&quot;"'/> <!--WRONG -->
```

because once the XML parser has expanded the entity references, the XPath expression seen by the XSLT processor will look like this:

```
"Never say "never""
```

which is clearly wrong. Using tree-valued variables and the **concat()** function, as suggested above, is usually simpler.

LocationPath

A LocationPath is a PathExpr that selects nodes by following a path starting either at the root node (an AbsoluteLocationPath) or at the context node (a RelativeLocationPath).

Expression	Syntax
LocationPath	RelativeLocationPath | AbsoluteLocationPath

Defined in

XPath section 2, rule 1

Used in

PathExpr

Usage

A RelativeLocationPath, when used as a LocationPath, is used to select a set of nodes based on their position relative to the context node.

An AbsoluteLocationPath is used to select a set of nodes based on their position in the source document relative to the root node. (If there are several source documents, this will always be the root node of the document that contains the context node, so "absolute" is rather a misnomer.)

Examples

Expression	Description
/contract/clause[3]/subclause[2]	This AbsoluteLocationPath selects the second **<subclause>** of the third **<clause>** of the **<contract>** that is the document element. If the document element is not a **<contract>**, or if any of the other components are missing, it produces an empty node-set.

Expression	Description
//figure	The AbsoluteLocationPath selects all the **<figure>** elements in the document. (See the section AbsoluteLocationPath for advice about the possible poor performance of this construct.)
@title	This RelativeLocationPath selects all the **title** attributes of the context node. The result will either be empty or contain a single attribute node.
book/author/ first-name	This RelativeLocationPath selects the **<first-name>** elements that are children of the **<author>** elements that are children of the **<book>** elements that are children of the context node.
city[not(@name= preceding-sibling ::city/@name)]	This RelativeLocationPath selects all the child **<city>** elements of the context node that do not have a **name** attribute that is the same as the **name** attribute of a preceding **<city>** element with the same parent. It thus selects a set of child **<city>** elements with unique names. This is the nearest equivalent in XPath to the SELECT DISTINCT clause in SQL.

MultiplicativeExpr

A non-trivial MultiplicativeExpr performs a multiplication, division, or remainder operation on two numeric operands.

Defined in

XPath section 3.5, rule 26.

Syntax

Expression	Syntax
MultiplicativeExpr	UnaryExpr | MultiplicativeExpr MultiplyOperator UnaryExpr | MultiplicativeExpr «div» UnaryExpr | MultiplicativeExpr «mod» UnaryExpr

Used in

AdditiveExpr

Usage

A non-trivial MultiplicativeExpr consists of two or more UnaryExpr operands separated by the multiply «*», divide «div», or modulo «mod» operators, whose detailed effect is explained below. A trivial MultiplicativeExpr consists of a single UnaryExpr with no operators.

The reason the MultiplyOperator, alone among all the XPath operators, is singled out to have a syntax rule in its own right, is because the meaning of the asterisk character in XPath is very context-dependant; as well as being used as a multiplication operator, it is also used as a wild-card in a NameTest.

The «/» character is not used for division because it is already used for the path operator and as an expression representing the root node.

Although XPath is not intended primarily for doing computations, simple arithmetic functions can be very useful, for example to enable positioning of objects on the output medium.

If either operand of the MultiplicativeExpr is not numeric, it is converted to a number as if the **number()** function was used. If the value cannot be converted to an ordinary number, it is converted to the special value NaN (not a number), and in this case the result of the calculation will also be NaN.

Numbers in XSLT are always double-length floating point, so the calculation is carried out using floating point arithmetic. The multiplication and division operations are defined to follow the rules of IEEE 754, which are summarized in Chapter 2. The modulo operation returns the remainder from a division. More technically, it is defined to return "the remainder from a truncating division", which is a division that doesn't use decimals: since it is difficult to understand exactly what this means in all cases, the specification helpfully explains it by example as follows:

Expression	Result
5 mod 2	1
5 mod –2	1
–5 mod 2	–1
–5 mod –2	–1

To perform an integer division, use «floor($X div $Y)»

Arithmetic in XPath never produces an error condition. For example division by zero is not an error, it produces the special number infinity (or minus infinity) as a result.

Examples

Expression	Description
`ceil(count(item) div 3)`	One-third of the number of child **<item>** elements of the context node, rounded upwards. (Useful if you are arranging the items in three columns.)
`@margin*2`	Twice the value of the **margin** attribute of the context node.
`item[position() mod 2 = 0]`	Selects the even-numbered child **<item>** elements of the context node.

MultiplyOperator

A `MultiplyOperator` is the symbol used to represent a multiplication sign: an asterisk.

Expression	Syntax
`MultiplyOperator`	«*»

The reason the `MultiplyOperator`, alone among all the XPath operators, is singled out to have a production rule in its own right, is because the meaning of the asterisk character in XPath is context-dependant; as well as being used as a multiplication operator, it is also used as a wild-card in a `NameTest`.

Defined in

XPath section 3.7 (Lexical Structure), rule 34

Used in

`MultiplicativeExpr`

Usage

See `MultiplicativeExpr` on page 392

The lexical rules for XPath state that «*» is recognized as a `MultiplyOperator` if there is a preceding token and the preceding token is not one of «@», «::», «,», «(», «[», or an `Operator`. Otherwise, it is assumed to be part of a `NameTest`.

Examples

Expression	Description
`item[$x * 2]`	Selects the **`<item>`** element whose position is `$x` multiplied by 2.
`***`	Converts the string-value of the first child element of the context node to a number, and multiplies it by itself. (Only the second of the three asterisks is recognized as a multiplication operator, by virtue of the rules above. The other two are abbreviations for «`child::*`».)

NameTest

A `NameTest` is either a name, or a generic name specified using wild-cards.

Defined in

XPath section 3.7 (Lexical Rules), rule 37

Expression	Syntax
NameTest	«*» | NCName «:» «*» | QName

Note that a NameTest is a token, which means it cannot contain embedded whitespace. This means the second option in the production rule might have been more naturally written as NCName «:*».

Used in

NodeTest

A NameTest, as well as being used in XPath *Expressions*, is also used in some other XSLT contexts. For example, the **<xsl:preserve-space>** and **<xsl:strip-space>** elements have an attribute whose value is a whitespace-separated list of NameTests.

Usage

In general a NameTest will match some names and will not match others.

The NameTest «*» matches any name. (But when used as an expression on its own, «*» is short for «child::*», which selects all child elements of the context node. The fact that the result is restricted to element nodes only is because «*», when used in a Step, selects only nodes of the principal node type for the axis: and for all axes except the attribute and namespace axes, the principal node type is element nodes.)

> **A surprising effect of this rule is that you can't write:**
> ```
> <xsl:copy-of select="@*[not(self::title)]"/>
> ```
> **to copy all attributes of an element except the title attribute. Why? Because the principal node type for the self axis is element nodes, so if the context node is an attribute named title, «self::title» won't select it. Instead, write:**
> ```
> <xsl:variable name="title" select="generate-
> id(@title)"/>
> <xsl:copy-of select="@*[generate-id(.)!=$title]"/>
> ```

The NameTest «xyz:*» matches any name whose namespace is the one currently bound to the namespace prefix «xyz». It is not necessary that the name being tested should use the same prefix, only that the prefix should refer to the same namespace URI.

The NameTest «xyz:item» matches any name whose namespace is the one currently bound to the namespace prefix «xyz», and whose local part is «item». It is not necessary that the name being tested should use the same prefix, only that the prefix should refer to the same namespace URI.

The NameTest «item» (with no namespace prefix) matches any name whose local part is «item» and whose namespace URI is null. The default namespace is not used.

> **If your source document uses a default namespace declaration such as «xmlns="some.uri"», then an <item> element in the source document will not be selected by an XPath expression such as «//item», even if the stylesheet contains the same namespace declaration «xmlns="some.uri"». This is because in the XPath expression, the default namespace is ignored. You will need to specify an explicit namespace declaration such as «xmlns:x="some.uri"» and refer to the element as «//x:item».**

Examples

Expression	Description
`*`	Matches any name. If «*» is used on its own, it represents the RelativeLocationPath «child::*», which selects all child elements of the context node, regardless of their name.
`xt:*`	Matches any name in the namespace bound to the prefix «xt». If «xt:*» is used on its own, it represents the RelativeLocationPath «child::xt:*», which selects all child elements of the context node that are in the namespace bound to the prefix «xt».
`title`	Matches a node whose local name is name «title» and whose namespace URI is null.
`wrox:title`	Matches the name that has local part «title» and whose namespace is the namespace currently bound to the prefix «wrox».

NCName and NCNameChar

An NCName is a name, or part of a name, that contains no colon. XPath adopts the definition from the XML Namespaces Recommendation.

There is no official explanation of the abbreviation NCName but "no-colon-name" is a plausible expansion.

An NCNameChar is a character that may appear in an NCName.

Expression	Syntax
NCName	(Letter | «_») (NCNameChar) *
NCNameChar	Letter | Digit | «.» | «-» | «_» | CombiningChar | Extender

The rules for Letter, Digit, CombiningChar, and Extender are given in the XML specification. The definitions are in the form of long lists of Unicode characters, and little would be gained by repeating them here. The basic principle is that if a name is valid in XML, then it is also valid in XPath.

Informally, an NCName starts with a letter or underscore, and continues with zero or more NCNameChars, which may be letters, digits, or the three punctuation characters dot, hyphen, and underscore. The «Letter» and «Digit» categories include a wide variety of characters and ideographs in non-Latin scripts as well as accented Latin letters, while the «CombiningChar» and «Extender» categories cover accents and diacritics in many different languages.

Defined in

XML Namespaces Recommendation

Used in

```
QName
NameTest
```

Usage

An NCName is used in two places in the XPath syntax: as part of a QName, discussed in detail on page 414, and as part of a NameTest, described on page 394.

In both contexts the name is used to match names that appear in the source XML document, which is why the syntax has to match the XML syntax for names.

As well as the XML-defined rules for names, XPath incorporates the additional rules defined in XML Namespaces. The designers of the XPath language made the decision that it would not be possible to use XPath to manipulate an XML document unless the XML document also conformed to the rules defined in XML Namespaces, for example the fact that a name may contain only a single colon.

As in XML, names are case-sensitive, and names are only considered to match when they consist of exactly the same sequence of characters. This is true even when the Unicode standards describe characters as equivalent, for example different ways of writing accented letters.

Examples

The following are examples of valid NCNames:

```
A
a
π
א
_system-id
iso-8859-1
billing.address
Straßenüberführung
ΕΛΛΑΣ
 ... --- ...
```

NodeTest

A NodeTest tests whether a node satisfies specified constraints on the type of node or the name of the node.

Expression	Syntax
NodeTest	NameTest | NodeType «(» «)» | «processing-instruction» «(» Literal «)»

Note that the second option permits «processing-instruction()»; the third option is needed only when it is necessary to give the name of the processing instruction.

The third form is unusual in that it is the only place in XPath where the name of a node in the source document is written in quotes. The reason for this is apparently that the language designers wanted to retain the freedom in future versions of the specification to use constructs like node() and comment() as function calls; if an NCName had been specified here in place of a literal, it would make the semantics inconsistent with the rules for function calls.

Defined in

XPath section 2.3, rule 7

Used in

Step

Usage

A NodeTest is used in a Step to specify the type and/or the name of the nodes to be selected by the Step.

In general you specify either the name of the nodes, or their type. If you specify a NameTest, this implicitly selects nodes of the principal node type for the axis used in the Step. For the attribute axis, this selects attribute nodes; for the namespace axis, it selects namespace nodes, and for all other axes, it selects element nodes.

Specifying «node()» as the NodeType selects all nodes on the axis. You must specify «node()» if you want the Step to select nodes of more than one type.

Specifying «processing-instruction()» or «comment()» or «text()» as the NodeType selects nodes of the specified type. It doesn't make sense to specify any of these on the attribute or namespace axes, because they can't occur there. These nodes are unnamed, except for processing instructions, which is why there is an option in this single case to specify both the node type and the node name required.

There is no node test for the root node. If an axis (for example the ancestor or parent axis) includes the root node, it will be selected if and only if the `NodeTest` is «`node()`». If you're looking specifically for the root node, you don't need an axis to find it, because the special `LocationPath` «`/`» is available.

Examples

Expression	Description
`TITLE`	This `NameTest` selects all **<TITLE>** elements, unless it is used with the attribute axis (in the form «`attribute::TITLE`» or «`@TITLE`»), when it selects the **TITLE** attribute, or with the namespace axis (as «`namespace::TITLE`»), when it selects the namespace node whose prefix is `TITLE`.
`news:article`	This `NameTest` selects all nodes with local name «`article`» within the «`news`» namespace. These may be attribute nodes or element nodes, depending on the axis. There must be an enclosing element in the stylesheet that declares the «`news`» prefix, by having an attribute of the form «`xmlns:news="`*uri*`"`». The node in the source document must have a name that uses this namespace URI, but it does not need to use the same prefix.
`MathML:*`	This `NameTest` selects all nodes whose names are in the MathML namespace. These may be attribute nodes or element nodes, depending on the axis. There must be an enclosing element in the stylesheet that declares this prefix, by having an attribute of the form «`xmlns:MathML="`*uri*`"`».
`*`	This `NameTest` selects all elements, unless it is used with the attribute axis (in the form «`attribute::*`» or «`@*`» when it selects all attributes, or with the namespace axis (as «`namespace::*`»), when it selects all namespaces.
`text()`	This `NodeTest` selects all text nodes on the relevant axis.
`processing-instruction()`	This `NodeTest` selects all processing instructions on the relevant axis. Note that the XML declaration at the start of the document is *not* a processing instruction, even though it looks like one.
`processing-instruction('ckpt')`	This `NodeTest` selects all processing instructions that have the name (or `PITarget` as the XML specification calls it) «`ckpt`»: for example the processing instruction `<?ckpt frequency=daily?>`.
`node()`	This `NodeTest` selects all nodes on the relevant axis.

NodeType

A `NodeType` represents a constraint on the type of a node.

Expression	Syntax
NodeType	«comment» | «text» | «processing-instruction» | «node»

A NodeType is a token, so it can contain whitespace before and after the name, but not within it.

Note that the four NodeType names cannot be used as function names, but apart from this, they are not reserved words. It is quite possible to have elements or attributes called «text» or «node» in your source XML document, and therefore you can use «text» or «node» as ordinary names in XPath. This is why the names are flagged in a NodeTest by the following parentheses, for example «text()».

Defined in

XPath section 3.7 (Lexical Rules), rule 38

Used in

NodeTest

Usage

A NodeType can be used within a NodeTest (which in turn is used within a Step) to restrict a Step to return nodes of a particular type. The keywords «comment», «text», and «processing-instruction» are self-explanatory: they restrict the selection to nodes of that particular type. The keyword «node» selects nodes of any type, and is useful because a Step has to include some kind of NodeTest, so if you want all the nodes on the axis, you can specify «node()». For example, if you want all child nodes, specify «child::node()».

Note that there is no way of referring to the other four node types, namely root, element, attribute, and namespace. In the case of the root node, this is because if you only want the root node, you don't need to find it using an axis, just use the special expression «/». In the case of the attribute and namespace nodes, it is because these types of node are exclusive to the attribute and namespace axes: you can only find these nodes by using the axis of the same name, and all the nodes on that axis will be nodes of the appropriate type. In the case of element nodes, all the axes that can contain elements have element as their principal node type, and you can select the nodes of the principal node type using the special NameTest «*».

Examples in Context

Expression	Description
`parent::node()`	Selects the parent of the context node, whether this is an element node or the root node. This differs from «`parent::*`», which selects the parent node only if it is an element. The expression «`parent::node()`» is usually abbreviated to «`..`».
`//comment()`	Selects all comment nodes in the document.
`child::text()`	Selects all text node children of the context node. This is usually abbreviated to «`text()`».
`@comment()`	A strange but legal way of getting an empty node-set: it looks for all comment nodes on the attribute axis, and of course finds none.

Number

A `Number` represents a constant numeric (floating-point) value.

Expression	Syntax
`Number`	`Digits` («`.`» `Digits`?)? | «`.`» `Digits`

Defined in

XPath section 3.7 (Lexical Rules), rule 30

Used in

`PrimaryExpr`

Usage and Examples

A `Number` is a constant numeric value, and is expressed in decimal notation. The production rule is a rather complicated way of saying that there are four ways of writing a number:

Format	Example
`Digits`	839
`Digits` «`.`»	10.
`Digits` «`.`» `Digits`	3.14159
«`.`» `Digits`	.001

Note that all numeric values in XPath are treated as double-length floating point values. A more precise definition of the range of possible values is given in Chapter 2, page 89. Functions such as **`round()`**, **`ceiling()`**, and **`floor()`** are available to convert these to integers when required: these are described in Chapter 7.

A `Number` as such may not have a leading minus sign. However, in any context where a number may sensibly be used, it is also possible to use a `UnaryExpr`, which can consist of a minus sign followed by a number.

Unlike many programming languages, XPath does **not** allow a number to be expressed in scientific notation; you must write one million as «`1000000`», not as «`1.0e6`».

Operator

An `Operator` is a symbol or name used to denote a processing operation.

Expression	Syntax
`Operator`	`OperatorName` | `MultiplyOperator` | «`/`» | «`//`» | «`|`» | «`+`» | «`-`» | «`=`» | «`!=`» | «`<`» | «`<=`» | «`>`» | «`>=`»

Defined in

XPath section 3.7 (Lexical Rules), rule 32

Used in

Each of the operators appears in a different production rule, for example «`=`» appears in `EqualityExpr`.

Usage

The production rule for `Operator` is part of the lexical rules for XPath; an operator is one example of an `ExprToken`, that is, a lexical token. As operators are tokens, they may always be preceded and followed by whitespace, and must not include any embedded whitespace.

In some cases it is necessary to precede or follow an operator by whitespace to ensure it is recognized. This applies not only to the named operators (such as «`and`» and «`or`»), but also to the minus sign «`-`» which could be mistaken for a hyphen if written with no preceding space.

The numeric comparison operators are written here as XPath sees them; when they appear in an XSLT stylesheet the special characters «`<`» and «`>`» can be written «`<`» and «`>`» respectively.

The «/» and «//» symbols are regarded as operators, though they have an unusual feature: the right-hand operand is not an expression, but a `Step`.

Examples

```
and  or  div
*  /  =  !=  <
```

OperatorName

An `Operator` that is written as a name.

Expression	Syntax
`OperatorName`	«and» | «or» | «mod» | «div»

Defined in

XPath section 3.7 (Lexical Rules), rule 33

Used in

`ExprToken`

Usage

The production rule for `OperatorName` is part of the lexical rules for XPath; an `OperatorName` is one example of an `ExprToken`, that is, a lexical token. As operator names are tokens, they may always be preceded and followed by whitespace. In practice the whitespace may be necessary to separate the `OperatorName` from the adjacent token if that is also made up of letters and digits.

The four operator names are not reserved words. It is perfectly legitimate to have an element in the source XML document named **`<div>`** (indeed XHTML defines such an element), and it is possible to refer to that element in the normal way using a path expression such as «`ancestor::div`» or simply «`div`». The decision as to whether «`div`» (or indeed «`and`», «`or`», or «`mod`») is an `NCName` or an `OperatorName` is therefore based on context: the rule is that it is recognized as an `NCName` if it is the first token in the expression, or if the preceding token is «`@`», «`::`», «`,`», «`(`», «`[`», or an `Operator`.

Examples in Context

Expression	Description
`$x = 5 or $x = 10`	True if the variable `$x`, after converting to a number, has the value 5 or 10

Expression	Description
`position() mod 2`	Zero if the context position is an even number, one if it is odd
`floor( string-length(@name) div 2)`	Half the length of the value of the **`name`** attribute, rounded down
`@name and @id`	True if the context node has both a **`name`** attribute and an **`id`** attribute

OrExpr

A non-trivial `OrExpr` represents a Boolean expression, which is true if either of its operands is true.

Expression	Syntax
`OrExpr`	`AndExpr` | `OrExpr «or» AndExpr`

Defined in

XPath section 3.4, rule 21

Used in

`Expr`

Usage

A non-trivial `OrExpr` consists of two or more `AndExpr` operands separated by the operator «`or`». A trivial `OrExpr` consists of a single `AndExpr` without any «`or`» operator.

The «`or`» operator has its usual meaning in Boolean logic: if either or both of the operands are true, the result is true. The operands are first converted to Booleans if necessary by an implicit call of the **`boolean()`** function.

The language specification explicitly states that the right-hand operand of an «`or`» operator is not evaluated if the left-hand operand evaluates to true. (This is one of very few places where the order of evaluation is specified.)

Note that there are no null values in XPath, as there are for example in SQL, and there is therefore no need for three-valued logic to handle unknown or absent data. Instead, you may need to test explicitly for absent values, as shown in some of the examples below.

Examples

Expression	Description
`$x = 5 or $x = 10`	True if the variable `$x`, after converting to a number, has the value 5 or 10
`@name or @id`	True if the context node has a **`name`** attribute, an **`id`** attribute, or both
`not(@id) or @id=""`	True if the context node has no **`id`** attribute or if it has an **`id`** attribute and the value is an empty string.
`//para[position()=1 or position()=last()]`	Selects the **`<para>`** elements that are either the first or the last (or the only) **`<para>`** children of their parent node

PathExpr

A `PathExpr` is an expression for selecting a set of nodes by following a path (a sequence of one or more steps) from a given starting point. The starting point may be the context node, the root node, or an arbitrary node-set given, say, by the value of a variable or the result of a function call.

Expression	Syntax
`PathExpr`	`LocationPath` | `FilterExpr` | `FilterExpr «/» RelativeLocationPath` | `FilterExpr «//» RelativeLocationPath`

Defined in

XPath section 3.3, rule 19

Used in

`UnionExpr`

Usage

A non-trivial `PathExpr` identifies a node-set. However, because a trivial `FilterExpr` may consist simply of a `Number` or `Literal`, a trivial `PathExpr` may identify a value of any type.

In a non-trivial PathExpr, there are several different ways the node-set can be identified:

- By a LocationPath, representing a set of nodes selected by following a sequence of steps starting either at the document root or at the context node.
- By a FilterExpr, which might be a variable reference that identifies a node-set, a function call that evaluates to a node-set, a bracketed expression such as «($a | $b)», or any of these followed by one or more predicates.
- By a FilterExpr followed by the path operator «/» followed by a RelativeLocationPath; the RelativeLocationPath identifies a sequence of steps in the same way as the LocationPath, but starts with the set of nodes identified by the FilterExpr, instead of starting at the document root or at the context node.
- By a FilterExpr followed by the shorthand path operator «//» followed by a RelativeLocationPath: as in other contexts, «//» is an abbreviation for «/descendant-or-self::node()/».

Examples

Expression	Description
para	This PathExpr is a LocationPath, and selects all the **<para>** element children of the context node.
para[@id]	This PathExpr is a LocationPath, and selects all the **<para>** element children of the context node that have an **id** attribute.
para/@id	This PathExpr is a LocationPath, and selects the **id** attributes of all the **<para>** element children of the context node. This differs from the previous example in that the result is a set of attribute nodes rather than a set of element nodes.
/*/para	This PathExpr is a LocationPath, and selects all the **<para>** element children of the document element (the outermost element of the document).
$paragraphs	This PathExpr consists of a FilterExpr comprising a single VariableReference. It is not necessarily a node-set.
$paragraphs[23]	This PathExpr consists of a FilterExpr comprising a VariableReference filtered by a Predicate. It selects the 23rd node in the node-set that is the value of variable $paragraphs.
document('lookup.xml')	This PathExpr consists of a FilterExpr comprising a single FunctionCall. It selects the root node of the XML document identified by the URI lookup.xml.

Expression	Description
`key('empname', 'John Smith') [@location='Sydney']`	This `PathExpr` consists of a `FilterExpr` comprising a `FunctionCall` filtered by a `Predicate`. Assuming that the key `empname` has been defined in the obvious way, it selects all employees named John Smith who are located in Sydney.
`(//section | //subsection) [title='Introduction']`	This `PathExpr` consists of a `FilterExpr` comprising a parenthesized `UnionExpr` filtered by a `Predicate`. It selects all **<section>** and **<subsection>** elements that have a child **<title>** element with the content «`Introduction`».
`$sections/body`	This `PathExpr` selects all **<body>** element children of nodes in the node-set identified by the variable `$sections`.
`$sections[3]/body`	This `PathExpr` selects all **<body>** element children of the third node in the node-set identified by the variable `$sections`.
`(//section|//subsection) //para`	This `PathExpr` selects all **<para>** descendants of **<section>** and **<subsection>** elements.
`((//section|//subsection) // para)[last()]`	This `PathExpr` selects the last **<para>** element (in document order) that is a descendant of a **<section>** or **<subsection>** element.

As is evident from the chart at the beginning of this chapter, it's the `PathExpr` construct that accounts for most of the syntactic complexity in the XPath language. The actual production rules are quite complicated and hard to follow, but they are there to make path expressions easy to write, especially if you are familiar with UNIX-style path names for directories and files.

If we forget for a moment the «`//`» abbreviation, and if we imagine a function call **`root()`** that finds the root node, then it would become possible to write every path expression in the form `FilterExpr` («`/`» `Step`)* , which would greatly simplify the production rules. The other options are there to allow the root node to be written as «`/`», to allow absolute path expressions to be written starting with a «`/`», and to allow relative path expressions to omit the initial «`./`».

Predicate

A predicate is a qualifying expression used to select a subset of the nodes in a node-set or a `Step`.

5 Expressions

Expression	Syntax
`Predicate`	«`[`» `PredicateExpr` «`]`»

Defined in

XPath section 2.4, rule 8

Used in

`Step`
`FilterExpr`

Usage

There are two places in the syntax where a predicate can appear: as part of a `Step` in a `PathExpr`, or as part of a `FilterExpr`. The meaning of the two cases is very similar, and it's easy to use them without always being aware of the difference.

For example:

Expression	Description
`para[3]`	Here the predicate «`[3]`» is being applied to the `Step` «`para`», which is short for «`./child::para`». It selects the third child **`<para>`** element of the context node.
`$para[3]`	Here the predicate «`[3]`» is being applied to the variable-reference «`$para`». Assuming this variable refers to a node-set, the expression selects the third node in the node-set, in document order.

In both cases the effect of a predicate is to select a subset of the nodes in a node-set. The difference comes when a predicate is used with a path expression of more than one step. For example:

Expression	Description
`chapter/para[1]`	Here the predicate «`[1]`» is being applied to the `Step` «`para`», which is short for «`./child::para`». It selects the first child **`<para>`** element of each child **`<chapter>`** element of the context node.
`(chapter/para)[1]`	This is a `FilterExpr` where the predicate «`[1]`» is being applied to the node-set selected by the path expression «`chapter/para`». The expression selects a single **`<para>`** element, the first child **`<para>`** of a **`<chapter>`** that is a child of the context node.

In effect, the predicate operator «`[ ]`» has higher precedence (it binds more tightly) than the path operator «`/`».

Another distinction between the two cases is that in the case of a `FilterExpr`, the nodes are always considered in document order when evaluating the predicate. In the case of a `Step`, the nodes are considered in the order of the relevant axis. This is explained in more detail below.

A predicate may be either a Boolean expression or a numeric expression. These are not distinguishable syntactically, because XPath is not a strongly-typed language; for example the predicate « `[$p]` » could be either. The distinction is only made at run-time. If the value of the predicate is a number, it is treated as a numeric predicate; if it is of any other type, it is converted to a Boolean using the **`boolean()`** function and is treated as a Boolean predicate. So for example the predicate « `[@sequence-number]` » is true if the context node has a sequence number attribute, and is false otherwise. The actual numeric value of the attribute **`sequence-number`** is immaterial: the value of «`@sequence-number`» is a node-set, so it is treated as « `[boolean(@sequence-number)]` ». If you want to use the sequence number attribute as a numeric predicate, write « `[number(@sequence-number)]` ».

A numeric predicate « `[P]` » is simply a shorthand for the Boolean predicate « `[position()=P]` », so you could also achieve the required effect by writing « `[position()=@sequence-number]` ».

As explained in Chapter 2, every expression is evaluated in a particular context. The context in which the predicate is evaluated is not the same as the context for the expression that it forms part of.

The predicate is applied to each node within a node-set separately. Each time it is evaluated:

- The context node (the node selected by « `.` ») is the node to which the predicate is being applied.
- The context position (the result of the **`position()`** function) is the position of that node within the node-set, *relative to some axis.*
- The context size (the result of the **`last()`** function) is the number of nodes in the node-set.

The significance of the phrase *relative to some axis* is that the position of a node in a `Step` depends on the direction of the axis used in that `Step`. Some axes (child, descendant, descendant-or-self, following, following-sibling) are forwards axes, so the **`position()`** function numbers the nodes in document order. Other axes (ancestor, ancestor-or-self, preceding, preceding-sibling) are reverse axes, so **`position()`** numbers them in reverse document order. The self and parent axes return a single node, so the order is irrelevant. The direction of the attribute and namespace axes is undefined.

Where a predicate is used as part of a `FilterExpr` (as distinct from a `Step`), the specification states that the context position is the position relative to the child axis. This is a rather obscure way of saying that for the purpose of evaluating the **`position()`** function within the predicate, the nodes are considered in document order, regardless of the order in which they were retrieved. It doesn't mean that the nodes have to be children of some common parent, or indeed children of anything at all. It's quite legitimate to write:

```
(document('a.xml') | document('b.xml'))[1]
```

Here we are forming a node-set consisting of two root nodes in different documents, and we are then filtering this node-set to take the one that comes first "in document order". Where nodes in a node-set come from different documents, document order is undefined, so you can't predict which of the two root nodes will be chosen. However, the order is stable, it won't change in the course of a single transformation.

In both contexts where predicates can be used, there can be a sequence of zero or more predicates. Curiously, the syntax is defined in different ways in the two cases: in the production rule for `Step` it is defined by iteration (`Step ⇒ AxisSpecifier NodeTest Predicate*`), while in the rule for `FilterExpr` it is defined by recursion (`FilterExpr ⇒ FilterExpr Predicate`). However, the effect is identical: there can be a sequence of zero or more predicates.

Specifying two separate predicates is not the same thing as combining the two predicates into one with an «`and`» operator. The reason is that the context for the second predicate is different from the context for the first. Specifically, in the second predicate, the context position (the value of the **`position()`** function) and the context size (the value of the **`last()`** function) consider only those nodes that successfully passed through the previous predicate. What this means in practice is shown in the examples below:

Expression	Description
`book[author="P. D. James"][1]`	The first book that was written by P. D. James.
`book[1][author="P. D. James"]`	The first book, provided that it was written by P. D. James.
`book[position()=1 and author="P. D. James"]`	The first book, provided that it was written by P. D. James. This is the same as the previous example, because in that example the second predicate is not dependant on the context position.

Examples in Context

Expression	Description
`para[1]`	The first **`<para>`** child element of the context node.
`para[last()]`	The last **`<para>`** child element of the context node.
`para[position()!=1]`	All **`<para>`** child elements of the context node, other than the first.
`para[@title]`	All **`<para>`** child elements of the context node that have a **`title`** attribute.

Expression	Description
`para[string(@title}]`	All <para> child elements of the context node that have a **title** attribute whose value is not the empty string.
`para[* or text()]`	All <para> child elements of the context node that have a child element or text node.

PredicateExpr

A `PredicateExpr` is an expression used within a `Predicate`.

Expression	Syntax
`PredicateExpr`	`Expr`

Defined in

XPath section 2.4, rule 9

Used in

`Predicate`

Usage

A `PredicateExpr` is syntactically just an `Expr`: in other words, any XPath expression can be used in a `Predicate`.

If the result of evaluating the `PredicateExpr` is a number, it is treated as a numeric predicate, which is true if the value is the same as the context position, and false otherwise.

In all other cases the `PredicateExpr` is treated as a Boolean value, converting it to a Boolean if necessary using the **`boolean()`** function.

Note that the rules for recognizing a predicate as a number are very strict. For example, the XSLT variable declared in the examples below is not a number, it is a node-set (or in XSLT 1.0, a result tree fragment: see the **<xsl:variable>** topic in Chapter 4, page 333, for further explanation):

```
<xsl:variable name="index">3</xsl:variable>
```

If you want to use this value as a predicate, either write it so the value of the variable is a number:

```
<xsl:variable name="index" select="3"/>
```

(but don't write «select="'3'"», because that would make it a string); or force it to a number in the predicate:

```
<xsl:value-of select="item[number($index)]"/>
```

or write the Boolean predicate in full:

```
<xsl:value-of select="item[position()=$index]"/>
```

Examples in Context

Any expression can be used as a predicate (the only exception is an expression whose value is an external object, because an external object cannot be converted to a Boolean). Here are some examples; the `PredicateExpr` is the section between the square brackets.

Expression	Description
`section[title]`	«`title`» is a `PathExpr`; the `PredicateExpr` is true if the relevant section has at least one child **`<title>`** element.
`section[ @title='Introduction']`	Here the predicate is a more conventional Boolean expression.
`title[ substring- before(.,':')]`	The `PredicateExpr` evaluates to true if the string-value of the title has one or more characters before its first colon: that is, if the **`substring-before()`** function returns a non-empty string.
`book[not(author= preceding-sibling ::author)]`	The `PredicateExpr` here is true if the author of the book is not the same as the author of some preceding book within the same parent element. The effect of this expression is to select the first book by each author.

PrimaryExpr

A `PrimaryExpr` is essentially an expression that contains no operators. It may also be a parenthesized sub-expression.

Expression	Syntax
`PrimaryExpr`	`VariableReference` | «`(`» `Expr` «`)`» | `Literal` | `Number` | `FunctionCall`

Defined in

XPath section 3.1, rule 15

Used in

`FilterExpr`

Usage

The production rule for `PrimaryExpr` covers an assortment of different kinds of expressions, which can be used as the basic building blocks of a more complex expression.

The only real thing that these different kinds of `PrimaryExpr` have in common is the context in which they can be used.

According to the syntax rules, any `PrimaryExpr` can be followed by a predicate to form a `FilterExpr`, so for example «`17[1]`» and «`'Berlin'[3]`» are both syntactically legal. The semantic rules, however, say that a predicate can only be applied to a value that is a node-set, so the only primaries that can sensibly be used with a predicate in a `FilterExpr` are a variable reference, a parenthesised expression, or a function call.

The notable omission from this production rule is `PathExpr`: a `PathExpr` is not a `PrimaryExpr`. This ensures that an expression such as «`para[1]`» is unambiguously a `PathExpr`, with the `Predicate` «`[1]`» taken as part of the `Step`, rather than being a `FilterExpr` consisting of a `PrimaryExpr` «`para`» followed by a `Predicate` «`[1]`». It is possible to turn a `PathExpr` into a `PrimaryExpr` by putting it in parentheses, so «`(para)[1]`» is a `FilterExpr`. In this case the meaning is the same, but this will not always be the case.

For example:

Expression	Description
`ancestor::*[1]`	Returns the first ancestor of the context node relative to the ancestor axis, in other words the parent of the context node.
`(ancestor::*)[1]`	Returns the first node in the node-set formed by «`ancestor::*`», taking the nodes in document order: that is, it returns the document element.
`//section/para[1]`	Returns all **`<para>`** elements that are the first **`<para>`** child of a **`<section>`** parent.
`(//section/para)[1]`	Returns the first element in the document that is a **`<para>`** child of a **`<section>`** parent.

Examples

Expression	Description
`23.5`	A `Number` is a `PrimaryExpr`
`'Columbus'`	A `Literal` is a `PrimaryExpr`

Expression	Description
`$var`	A `VariableReference` is a `PrimaryExpr`
`contains(@name, '#')`	A `FunctionCall` is a `PrimaryExpr`
`(position() + 1)`	A parenthesized expression is a `PrimaryExpr`

QName

A `QName` (qualified name) is a name optionally qualified by a namespace prefix.

Expression	Syntax
`QName`	`( Prefix «:» )? LocalPart`
`Prefix`	`NCName`
`LocalPart`	`NCName`

Defined in

XML Namespaces Recommendation

Used in

`NameTest`

`QNames` are also used in XSLT stylesheets in a number of other contexts, outside the scope of XPath expressions. They are used both to refer to elements in the source document (for example in **`<xsl:preserve-space>`** and **`<xsl:strip-space>`** and to name and refer to objects within the stylesheet itself, including variables, templates, modes, and attribute sets.

There are also some situations where `QNames` can be constructed dynamically as a result of evaluating an expression. They are used, for example, in **`<xsl:element>`** and **`<xsl:attribute>`** to generate names in the result document, and in the **`key()`** and **`format-number()`** functions to refer to objects (keys and decimal-formats respectively) defined in the stylesheet. `QNames` constructed at run-time are never used to match names in the source document, and they are never used to match template names, variable names, mode names, or attribute set names in the stylesheet; these references must all be fixed names.

Usage

A `QName` is used in XPath for matching the names of nodes in the source document.

If the name has a prefix, the prefix must be declared by a namespace declaration on some surrounding element in the stylesheet module.

For example:

```
<xsl:apply-templates select="math:formula" xmlns:math="http://math.org/"/>
```

Here the namespace is declared on the actual element that uses the prefix, but it could equally be any ancestor element.

The actual element in the source document does not need to have the tag «math:formula», it can use any prefix it likes (or even the default namespace) provided that in the source document the element name is in the namespace URI «http://math.org/».

If the QName does not have a prefix, then the name it matches must use the null namespace URI. This necessarily means the element in the source document will not have a prefix, since the XML Namespaces specification doesn't allow a non-null prefix to be paired with a null URI. However, the converse is not true: a name in the source document with no prefix may be in the default namespace, with a non-null URI, and in this case it will be necessary to use a prefix in the stylesheet to match this element.

A QName with no prefix appearing in an XPath expression uses the null namespace URI, not the default URI.

It's a common mistake to forget this. Your source document starts as follows:

```
<html xmlns="http://www.w3.org/1999/xhtml">
```

and your stylesheet starts:

```
<?xml version="1.0"?>
<xsl:stylesheet xmlns:xsl="http://www.w3.org/1999/XSL/Transform"
      xmlns="http://www.w3.org/1999/xhtml"
      version="1.0">

<xsl:template match="html">
```

Why doesn't the template rule for «match="html"» fire when the <html> element is encountered? The answer is that the default namespace (declared with «xmlns="..."») applies to unprefixed QNames in the source document, but it doesn't apply to unprefixed QNames appearing in expressions and match patterns in the stylesheet. You need to write:

```
<?xml version="1.0"?>
<xsl:stylesheet xmlns:xsl="http://www.w3.org/1999/XSL/Transform"
      xmlns:xhtml="http://www.w3.org/1999/xhtml"
      version="1.0">

<xsl:template match="xhtml:html">
```

Examples

Expression	Description
`TABLE`	Matches a node in the source document whose local name is `TABLE` and which is in the default namespace, provided the default namespace uses a null URI.
`HTML:TABLE`	Matches a node in the source document whose local name is `TABLE` and which is in a namespace whose URI matches the URI currently assigned to the prefix `HTML` in the stylesheet.

RelationalExpr

A non-trivial `RelationalExpr` compares the magnitude of two numbers. It provides the usual four operators: less-than, greater-than, less-than-or-equal to, and greater-than-or-equal to. When an operand is a node-set, the comparison applies to the numeric value of the individual nodes in the node-set.

<table>
<tr><th>Expression</th><th>Syntax</th></tr>
<tr><td>RelationalExpr</td><td>AdditiveExpr |
RelationalExpr «<» AdditiveExpr |
RelationalExpr «>» AdditiveExpr |
RelationalExpr «<=» AdditiveExpr |
RelationalExpr «>=» AdditiveExpr</td></tr>
</table>

Defined in

XPath section 3.4, rule 24

Used in

`EqualityExpr`

Usage

A non-trivial `RelationalExpr` in XPath consists of two or more `AdditiveExpr` operands separated by one of the operators «<» (less than), «>» (greater than), «<=» (less-than-or-equal to), or «>=» (greater-than-or-equal to).

A trivial `RelationalExpr` is one that consists of a single `AdditiveExpr` with no operator.

XPath defines an expression language that can be used in a number of environments. The main environment we are interested in is XSLT stylesheets, where the expression will always appear within an attribute of an XML element. An attribute value can't contain a «<» character, so it must be written either as a numeric character reference or as the entity reference «<». In practice most people choose to represent «>» as «>» as well, though it isn't strictly necessary.

These operators always perform a numeric comparison. There is no mechanism in XPath to compare string values according to their alphabetic sequence.

An expression such as «10 < $x < 30» is a syntactically valid RelationalExpr, but it probably does not have the expected meaning. The actual meaning is to evaluate «(10 < $x)», convert the Boolean result to a number, and then test whether this number is less than 30.

If neither of the operands is a node-set, both operands are converted to numbers by applying the **number()** function, and they are then compared numerically using the rules given in IEEE 754. For ordinary numbers, this gives the answer you would naturally expect, for example «1.0 < 3.5» is true, and «1.0 > 3.5» is false. If either of the numbers is plus or minus infinity, or negative zero, the result is still what you would expect intuitively, for example «1.0 < (2.0 div 0.0)» is true, because the result of «2.0 div 0.0» is positive infinity. If either or both of the numbers is NaN (not a number) , however, the result is always false. For example «'zero' <= 'one'» is false, because both operands when converted to numbers give NaN, and NaN <= NaN is false.

If one of the operands is a node-set, the result depends on the type of the other operand, as shown in the following table. In the text, I'll use the term "compares-correctly-with" to mean either "is less than", "is less than or equal to", "is greater than", or "is greater than or equal to", depending on which of the four operators <, <=, >, or >= was actually used. We'll assume first that the node-set is the first operand.

Data type of second operand	Result
Boolean	Testing whether a node-set is less than a Boolean is a singularly odd thing to do, but if you really want to know, the rules are as follows. Let P be the result of converting the node-set to a Boolean, and then to a number: the result is 0 if the node-set is empty, or 1 if it contains one or more nodes. Let Q be the result of converting the Boolean operand to a number: 0 if the Boolean is false, or 1 if it is true. The final result is true if P compares-correctly-with Q.
number	The result is true if there is a node in the node-set whose string-value, when converted to a number, compares-correctly-with the number operand. For example, «//price < 5.00» is true if there is a **<price>** element in the document whose string-value, when converted to a number, is less than 5.
string	The result is true if there is a node in the node-set whose string-value, when converted to a number, compares-correctly-with the result of converting the string operand to a number. For example, «//price < '5.00' » is true if there is a **<price>** element in the document whose string-value, when converted to a number, is less than 5. If the string cannot be converted to a number, the result will always be false.

If the node-set is the second operand, apply the rules in the table after inverting the expression, so for example «`$p < $q`» is rewritten as «`$q > $p`».

Finally, consider the situation if both operands are node-sets. In this case the result is true only if there is a node P in the first node-set and a node Q in the second node-set such that «`number(P)` compares-correctly-with `number(Q)`». Another way of defining this is according to the following table, where `max()` and `min()` represent the maximum and minimum numeric values of nodes in the node-set.

Expression	Result
`M < N`	True when min(M) < max(N)
`M <= N`	True when min(M) <= max(N)
`M > N`	True when max(M) > min(N)
`M >= N`	True when max(M) >= min(N)

In practice these comparisons defined on node-sets are most commonly used when the node-set consists of a single node. For example, the expression «`@price > 5.00`» is true if there is a **`price`** attribute, and its value is numeric, and its numeric value is greater than 5.00; it is false if there is no **`price`** attribute, or if the value of the attribute is not numeric, or if its value is 5.00 or less.

Where either or both operands are trees, the tree is considered as a node-set consisting of a single node, the root, in the normal way. Since there will always be exactly one node, the rules are similar to those for comparing strings or numbers, for example a tree-valued variable declared as:

```
<xsl:variable name="limit">142</xsl:variable>
```

can be used in a `RelationalExpr` just like one declared as a number:

```
<xsl:variable name="limit" select="142"/>
```

or as a string:

```
<xsl:variable name="limit" select="'142'"/>
```

Examples

Expression	Description
`count(*) > 10`	True if the context node has more than ten element children
`sum(SALES) < 10000`	True if the sum of the numeric values of the **`<SALES>`** children of the context node is less than ten thousand
`position() < last() div 2`	True if the context position is less than half the context size, that is, if the position of this node is less than half way down the list of nodes being processed
`not(//@temp <= 0.0)`	True if all values of the **`temp`** attribute in the document are numeric, and greater than zero

RelativeLocationPath

When used on its own as an expression, a `RelativeLocationPath` is a `LocationPath` that selects nodes by taking one or more steps starting at the context node.

A `RelativeLocationPath` can also be used within other constructs to represent a sequence of steps starting from some other baseline.

Expression	Syntax
`RelativeLocationPath`	`Step` | `RelativeLocationPath «/» Step` | `AbbreviatedRelativeLocationPath`

Defined in

XPath section 2, rule 3

Used in

```
LocationPath
AbsoluteLocationPath
AbbreviatedAbsoluteLocationPath
PathExpr
AbbreviatedRelativeLocationPath
```

Usage

A `RelativeLocationPath`, when used as an expression in its own right, represents a sequence of steps starting from the context node. When used as part of a `PathExpr` it represents a sequence of steps starting from the nodes in a given node-set, and when used as part of an `AbsoluteLocationPath` it represents a sequence of steps starting at the root node.

A `RelativeLocationPath` consists of one or more steps separated by the path operator «/» or the shorthand path operator «//». The production rule uses recursion to specify this; it could equally well have been written as:

```
RelativeLocationPath        Step ( ( «/» | «//» )  Step )*
```

The «//» can be thought of informally as selecting the descendants of a node. It is handled in a separate syntax rule, `AbbreviatedRelativeLocationPath`, because it is actually just shorthand. Specifically, if in a `RelativeLocationPath` one of the steps other than the first or last is «`descendant-or-self::node()`», then it may be omitted, so that «`A/descendant-or-self::node()/B`» may be replaced by «`A//B`». See `AbbreviatedRelativeLocationPath` on page 354 for more details and examples.

For a description of how the path operator «/» works, see `Step` on page 420.

Examples

Expression	Description
`ancestor::CHAPTER`	This is a `RelativeLocationPath` consisting of a single `Step`. It selects the ancestors of the context node that are elements with the name **<CHAPTER>**.
`TITLE`	This is a `RelativeLocationPath` consisting of a single `Step`: this time the `Step` is an `AbbreviatedStep`. It selects the children of the context node that are elements with the name **<TITLE>**.
`descendant::PARA/@style`	This is a `RelativeLocationPath` consisting of two `Steps`. The first `Step` selects the descendants of the context node that are **<PARA>** elements; the second `Step` is an `AbbreviatedStep` that selects the **style** attributes of these elements.
`section[1]/clause[3]`	This is a `RelativeLocationPath` consisting of two `Steps`, each of which includes a positional predicate. The first `Step` selects the first **<section>** element that is a child of the context node, the second `Step` selects the third **<clause>** element that is a child of the selected **<section>**.
`chapter/section/para/sentence`	This `RelativeLocationPath` selects every **<sentence>** element that is a child of a **<para>** element that is a child of a **<section>** element that is a child of a **<chapter>** element that is a child of the context node.
`.//sentence`	This `AbbreviatedRelativeLocationPath` selects every **<sentence>** element that is a descendant of the context node.

Step

A `Step` selects the set of nodes in the document which are related in a particular way to a supplied baseline; for example given a node-set A, a `Step` can find the nodes that are the children of the nodes in A, or the ancestors of the nodes in A, and so on.

Expression	Syntax
`Step`	`AxisSpecifier NodeTest Predicate* | AbbreviatedStep`

Defined in

XPath section 2.1, rule 4

Used in

RelativeLocationPath

Usage

There are two ways of defining a step: a long form and a short form. The short form, an AbbreviatedStep, can be used only to find the context node or the parent of the context node. The full form can be used to follow any axis and to find any kind of node.

A step is logically always the right-hand side of the «/» path operator. The left-hand side of the path operator evaluates to a node-set; the step defines for each of these nodes a set of related nodes found by navigating from that node in a given direction, and the result of the final expression is the result of applying the step to each node in the left-hand node-set. The left-hand side of the path operator is not always explicit; for example the step «TITLE» is a shorthand for the path «self::node()/child::TITLE», and the path expression «/descendant::FIGURE» can be regarded as shorthand for an imaginary expression «root()/descendant::FIGURE» where «root()» denotes the root node.

Although XPath defines the step operation in rather informal English, some readers may find a more mathematical definition helpful. A step *S* can be defined as a function *S(X)* ⇒ *N* that given a node X returns a set of nodes *N* in the same document. The path operator «/» can be defined as a function *map(A, F)* ⇒ *U* that takes a node-set *A* and a step function *F* as its inputs, and returns the node-set *U* that is the union of the results of applying the step function *F* to each of the nodes in its input node-set A.

For example, the step «ancestor::node()», given any node, finds all the ancestors of that node. When the step is used in a path expression such as «$n/ancestor::node()», it returns a node-set containing all the ancestors of all the nodes in $n.

The step itself is defined in terms of a simpler concept, the axis. Each axis returns a set of nodes relative to a specific origin node: for example, its previous siblings or its ancestors. The step returns a subset of the nodes on this axis, selected by node type, node name, and by the predicate expressions. The NodeTest supplies any restrictions on the node type and name of the selected nodes, and the predicate expressions provide arbitrary Boolean conditions that the nodes must satisfy, or positional filters that constrain their relative position.

Note that the step function is defined in terms of sets (which are unordered) and there is no concept of the result being ordered. To understand the meaning of positional predicates in the step it is often useful to think of the step as retrieving nodes in a particular order, but the formal definition doesn't require this. Instead these predicates are defined in terms of the proximity of the node to the origin of the axis. An axis does have direction; every axis that can be used in a step is either a forwards axis or a reverse axis, and the effect of positional predicates (such as «booklist/book[3]») is defined by considering the nodes in the node-set in either document order or reverse document order. If the axis is a forwards axis, the positional predicate «[3]» will return the third node in document order; if it is a reverse axis, the same predicate will return the third node in reverse document order.

So the evaluation of the step function, for a given context node, proceeds as follows:

1. All the nodes on the selected axis are found, starting at the context node.
2. Those that satisfy the node test (that is, those of the required node type and name) are selected.
3. The remaining nodes are numbered from 1 to n in document order if the axis is a forwards axis, or in reverse document order if it is a reverse axis.
4. The first (leftmost) predicate is applied to each node in turn. When evaluating the predicate, the context node (that is, the result of the «.» expression) is that node, the context position (the result of the **position()** function) is the number assigned to the node in stage 3, and the context size (the result of the **last()** function) is the largest number allocated in stage 3. A numeric predicate such as «[2]» or «[last()-1]» is interpreted as a shorthand for «[position()=2]» or «[position()=last()-1]» respectively.
5. Stages 3 and 4 are repeated for any further predicates.

Examples

Expression	Description
child::title	Selects child elements of the context node named **<title>**.
title	Short form of «child::title».
attribute::title	Selects attributes of the context node named **title**.
@title	Short form of «attribute::title».
ancestor::xyz:*	Selects ancestor elements of the context node whose names are in the namespace with prefix «xyz».
*[@width]	Selects all child elements of the context node that have a **width** attribute.
text()[starts-with(.,'The')]	Selects all text nodes that are a child of the context node and whose text content starts with the characters «The».
*[@code][position() < 10]	Selects the first nine child elements of the context node that have a **code** attribute.
*[position() < 10][@code]	Selects from the first nine child elements of the context node those that have a **code** attribute.
self::*[not(@code = preceding-sibling::*/@code)]	Selects the current element node provided that it does not have a **code** attribute with the same value as the **code** attribute of any preceding sibling element.
comment()	Selects all comment nodes that are children of the context node.
@comment()	Short for «attribute::comment()», this selects all comment nodes on the attribute axis. The attribute axis can only contain attribute nodes, so this will always return an empty node-set; nevertheless it is a legal *Step*.

UnaryExpr

A non-trivial `UnaryExpr` is used to change the sign of a number.

Expression	Syntax
`UnaryExpr`	`UnionExpr` | «-» `UnaryExpr`

Defined in

XPath section 3.5, rule 27

Used in

`MultiplicativeExpr`

Usage

A `UnaryExpr` consists of a `UnionExpr` preceded by an optional minus sign. In fact, for generality, the `UnionExpr` may be preceded by any number (zero or more) minus signs; each one changes the sign of the number.

The expression «`-0`» represents negative zero, a concept which is defined in the IEEE 754 model of floating-point arithmetic. This behaves in almost all respects just like positive zero (for example, it compares equal to positive zero, and it prints as «`0`»). One of the few differences is that if you divide +1 by it, you get negative infinity rather than positive infinity: but it's hard to find a practical stylesheet that needs to exploit this fact.

Intrinsically it may seem strange to be applying a numeric operator (unary minus) to a union, which is a node-set. However, this is simply an accident of the way operator priorities are defined. A `UnionExpr` does not actually need to contain a union operator, it merely has the potential to do so, and equally a `UnaryExpr` is not required to contain a minus sign.

In fact it is legal, if not very useful, to write an expression such as «`-$a | $b`». This forms the node-set that is the union of `$a` and `$b`, converts the result to a number, and then negates this number. A node-set is converted to a number by taking the string value of the first node in the node-set (in document order), and parsing that as a number.

Examples

Expression	Description
`-2`	The numeric value minus two. The minus sign is not part of the number; it is a separate token (and may therefore be separated from the number by whitespace).
`- @credit`	The negated numeric value of the **`credit`** attribute of the context element node. If the context node has no **`credit`** attribute, or if its value is not numeric, the result of the expression is `NaN` (not a number).

5 Expressions

Expression	Description
`1 - - - 1`	A not very useful but perfectly legal way of writing the value zero. The first minus sign is a binary subtraction operator; the next two are unary minus signs.

UnionExpr

A non-trivial `UnionExpr` forms the union between two node-sets; in other words, the result includes every node that is in either of the input node-sets.

Expression	Syntax
`UnionExpr`	`PathExpr` | `UnionExpr` «|» `PathExpr`

Defined in

XPath section 3.3, rule 18

Used in

`UnaryExpr`

Usage

A non-trivial `UnionExpr` consists of two or more `PathExpr` expressions separated by the union operator, «|». This operator forms the union of two or more node-sets: the resulting node-set contains all the nodes that are in any one of the node-sets, eliminating any duplicates.

A trivial `UnionExpr` consists of a single `PathExpr`, in which case its value is the value of the `PathExpr`.

Both operands to the union operator must be node-sets. The syntax doesn't enforce this; it not only allows expressions such as «`$a | $b`» where the variables might turn out at run-time to have the wrong type, but it also allows clearly nonsensical expressions such as « `2.0 | "London"` ». This is considered to be a semantic rather than a syntactic error.

Examples

Expression	Description
`*/figure | */table`	Returns a node-set containing all the grandchildren of the context node that are **`<figure>`** or **`<table>`** elements.

Expression	Description
`book[not(@publisher)] | book[@publisher='Wrox']`	Returns all the **<book>** children of the context node that either have no **publisher** attribute, or that have a **publisher** attribute equal to "Wrox". Note that the same result could be achieved, perhaps more efficiently, by using the «or» operator in the predicate.
`(.|..)/title`	Returns all the **<title>** elements that are immediate children of either the context node or the parent of the context node.
`sum((book|magazine)/@sales)`	Returns the total of the **sales** attribute values for all the **<book>** and **<magazine>** children of the context node.
`(//* | //@*)[.='nimbus2000']`	Returns a node-set containing all the element and attribute nodes in the document whose string value is «nimbus2000».

5

Expressions

There are no equivalent operators in XPath 1.0 to do other set operations such as intersection and difference. Some products supply extension functions to fill the gap; see the relevant appendices for details.

If you want to form the intersection between two node-sets `$p` and `$q`, the following rather tortuous expression achieves it:

```
$p [ count( . | $q) = count( $q ) ]
```

This selects the nodes in `$p` that are also in `$q`. They must be in `$q`, because their union with `$q` has the same number of nodes as `$q` itself.

Similarly, the following expression finds the nodes that are in `$p` and not in `$q`:

```
$p [ count( . | $q) != count( $q ) ]
```

VariableReference

A `VariableReference` is a reference to an XSLT variable or parameter.

Expression	Syntax
`VariableReference`	`«$» QName`

Defined in

XPath section 3.7 (Lexical Rules), rule 36

Used in

`PrimaryExpr`

Usage

The QName must match the name of a variable or parameter that is in scope at the point in the stylesheet where the expression containing the variable name appears. Normally this means the name will be exactly the same as the name attribute of the relevant **<xsl:variable>** or **<xsl:param>** element; however, if the name contains a namespace prefix, it is the namespace URI that must match, not necessarily the prefix.

A VariableReference is a lexical token, which means it may not contain whitespace between the $ sign and the QName.

The value of the variable reference is whatever value has been assigned to it by the matching **<xsl:variable>** or **<xsl:param>** declaration (in the case of **<xsl:param>**, this value may actually be derived from an **<xsl:with-param>** element in the calling template). The value may be of any type: a Boolean, a number, a string, or a node-set; or with XSLT 1.0, a result tree fragment. It may also be an external object, returned from an external function. If necessary, the value is converted to the data type required by the context: for example, if a variable holding a node-set is used in a context where a Boolean is required (such as the **test** attribute of **<xsl:if>**), it is converted to a Boolean – which means that it is treated as true if the node-set has one or more nodes in it, false if it is empty. In some cases, however, conversion is not possible, and in this case a run-time error will be reported. For example, it is not possible to use a Boolean value where a node-set is required, such as in the **select** attribute of **<xsl:apply-templates>** or **<xsl:for-each>**.

A variable reference can be used virtually anywhere in an XPath expression where a value is required: that is, an instance of one of the five data types: Boolean, number, string, node-set, or external object. It cannot be used to represent concepts of the language other than values, for example you can't use a variable in place of a name, a node type, or an axis. Nor can you use a variable to hold an entire expression.

A common mistake is to write:

```
<xsl:sort select="$expression"/>
```

where the variable $expression holds an XPath expression, represented as a string. This doesn't work because the sort key will be the expression itself, not its value, and of course the expression is the same for every node, so in effect you won't be sorting at all.

Provided the expression is nothing more than an element name, you can achieve the required effect by writing:

```
<xsl:sort select="*[name()=$element-name]"/>
```

If the possible sort keys are more complex than this, you can achieve the effect either by using the evaluate() extension function provided in several processors (including Saxon and Xalan). This function allows you to construct an XPath expression at run-time, from a string. Alternatively, you can modify the stylesheet before executing it, perhaps by applying another XSLT transformation to the stylesheet itself, or directly using DOM interfaces. In Appendix A (page 721) there is an example that shows how to do this with MSXML3.

Examples

```
$x
$lowest-common-
denominator
$ALPHA
$my-ns-prefix:param1
$
```

Summary

XPath expressions are used in XSLT to select data from the source document and to manipulate it to generate data to place in the result document. XPath expressions play the same role for XML as the SQL `SELECT` statement plays for relational databases – they allow us to select specific parts of the document for transformation, so that we can achieve the required output. However, their use is not restricted to XSLT stylesheets – they can also be used with XPointers to define hyperlinks between documents, and many DOM implementations allow XPath expressions to be used to find nodes within the DOM.

This chapter serves as a comprehensive reference guide for writing these expressions.

A subset of the XPath expression language can be used to write patterns in XSLT stylesheets that match specific nodes. Understanding patterns is the next step in understanding how XSLT works and Chapter 6 will examine them in detail.

6

Patterns

This chapter defines the syntax and meaning of **XSLT patterns**.

Patterns are used in just four places in an XSLT stylesheet:

- In the **`match`** attribute of **`<xsl:template>`**, to define to which nodes in the source document a template applies
- In the **`match`** attribute of **`<xsl:key>`**, to define to which nodes in the source document a key definition applies
- In the **`count`** and **`from`** attributes of **`<xsl:number>`**, to define which nodes are counted when generating numbers

In each case the purpose of a pattern is to define a condition that a node must satisfy in order to be selected. The most common use of patterns is in the **`match`** attribute of **`<xsl:template>`**, where the pattern says which nodes the template rule applies to. For example, `<xsl:template match="abstract">` introduces a template rule that matches every **`<abstract>`** element.

Most of the patterns found in stylesheets are simple and intuitive, for example:

Pattern	Meaning
`title`	Matches any **`<title>`** element
`chapter/title`	Matches any **`<title>`** element whose parent is a **`<chapter>`** element
`speech[speaker="Hamlet"]`	Matches any **`<speech>`** element that has a child **`<speaker>`** element whose string-value is «`Hamlet`»
`section/para[1]`	Matches any **`<para>`** element that is the first **`<para>`** child of a **`<section>`** element

The precise rules for the more complex patterns, however, are quite technical, so I'm afraid some of the explanations in this chapter are not going to be easy reading.

Patterns are defined in terms of the name, type, and string-value of a node, and its position relative to other nodes in the tree. To understand how patterns work you therefore need to understand the tree model, which I described in Chapter 2, and the different kinds of node.

Patterns look very similar to XPath expressions, which were described in the previous chapter, and it turns out that they are closely related; however, patterns and expressions are not quite the same thing. In terms of its syntax, every pattern is a valid XPath expression, but not every XPath expression is a valid pattern. It wouldn't make any sense to use the expression «`2+2`» as a pattern, for example – which nodes would it match?

I described the rules for expressions in the previous chapter. Expressions are defined in the XPath 1.0 Recommendation, which allows them to be used in contexts other than XSLT stylesheets. For example, XPath expressions are used in the XPointer specification to define hyperlinks between documents, and they are used in some DOM implementations as a way for applications to navigate around the DOM data structure. Patterns, however, are local to the XSLT Recommendation (the rules are defined in section 5.2 of the specification), and they are found only in stylesheets.

It would have been quite possible for XSLT to define both the syntax and the meaning of patterns quite independently of the XPath rules for expressions, but this would have created a risk of unnecessary inconsistency. What the XSLT language designers chose to do instead was to define the syntax of patterns in such a way that every pattern was sure to be a valid expression, and then to define the formal meaning of the pattern in terms of the meaning of the expression.

Look at the simplest pattern in the examples above, «`title`». If «`title`» is used as an expression, we saw in the previous chapter that it's an abbreviation for «`./child::title`», and it means "select all the **`<title>`** children of the current node". How do we get from that to a definition of the pattern «`title`» as something that matches all **`<title>`** elements?

In the next section, I'll explain how the formal definition of patterns in terms of expressions works. However, in practice it's easier to think of most patterns as following their own rules, rather like the intuitive examples listed above, and referring only to the formal definition in terms of expressions to resolve difficult cases. So I'll follow the formal explanation with an informal one.

The Formal Definition

The formal definition of how patterns are evaluated is expressed in terms of the XPath expression that is equivalent to the pattern. We've already seen that every pattern is a valid XPath expression. In fact, the rules are written so that the only XPath expressions that can be used as patterns are those that return a node-set, and the idea is that you should be able to decide whether a node matches a pattern by seeing whether the node is in the node-set returned by the corresponding expression.

This then raises the question of context. The result of the XPath expression «`title`» is all the **`<title>`** children of the context node. Does that include the particular **`<title>`** element we are trying to match, or not? It obviously depends on the context. Since we want the pattern «`title`» to match every **`<title>`** element, we could express the rule by saying that the node we are testing (let's call it *N*) matches the pattern «`title`» if we can find a node (*A*, say) anywhere in the document, which has the property that when we take *A* as the context node and evaluate the node-set expression «`title`», the node *N* will be selected as part of the result. In this example, we don't have to look very far to find node A; in fact, only as far as the parent node of *N*.

So the reason that a **`<title>`** element matches the pattern «`title`» is that it has a parent node, which when used as the context node for the expression «`./child::title`», returns a node-set that includes that **`<title>`** element. The pattern might be intuitive, but as you can see, the formal explanation is starting to get quite complex.

In an early draft of the XSLT specification, the rules allowed almost any node-set expression to be used as a pattern. For example, you could define a pattern «`ancestor::*[3]`», which would match any node that was the great-grandparent of some other node in the document. It turned out that this level of generality was neither needed nor possible to implement efficiently, and so a further restriction was imposed, that the only axes you could use in a pattern were the child and attribute axes (the various axes are explained on page 363 in Chapter 5). A consequence of this is that the only place where the XSLT processor has to look for node *A*, (the one to use as a context node for evaluating the expression) is among the ancestors of the node being matched (*N*), including *N* itself.

This brings us to the formal definition of the meaning of a pattern (read this slowly):

> **The node *N* matches a pattern *P* if and only if**
> **there is a node *A* that is an ancestor-or-self of *N*,**
> **such that evaluating *P* as an expression**
> **with *A* as the context node**
> **returns a node-set that contains *N*.**

In this rule, by saying that *A* must be an ancestor-or-self of *N*, I mean that *A* must either be *N* itself, or an ancestor of *N*.

The rule says that the expression is evaluated with *A* as the context node. It doesn't say what the context size and context position should be, because it makes no difference. Patterns cannot use the **`position()`** and **`last()`** function except within a predicate, so the question doesn't arise.

This means there is a theoretical algorithm for testing whether a given node *N* matches a pattern *P* as follows: for each node, starting from *N* and working through its ancestors up to the root node, evaluate *P* as an XPath expression with that node as the context node. If the result is a node-set containing *N*, the pattern matches; otherwise keep trying until you get to the root.

For example:

- A <title> element matches the pattern «title» because when the context node is the parent of the <title> element, the expression «title» (which is short for «./child::title») returns a node-set that includes that <title> element.
- The node with ID value 'n123' matches the pattern «id('n123')» because the expression «id('n123')» includes that node, regardless of what the context node is at the time.
- The pattern «chapter//figure» matches every <figure> element that is a descendant of a <chapter> element because, when the expression «chapter//figure» is evaluated with the parent node of a <chapter> element as the context node, every descendant <figure> of the <chapter> will be returned.
- The root node matches the pattern «/» because when the expression «/» is evaluated with the root node as context node, the root is included in the resulting node-set.
- An attribute **width** with value 100 matches the pattern «@width[.=100]» because when its parent element is taken as the context node, the expression «@width[.=100]» includes that attribute.

In practice XSLT processors won't usually use this algorithm, it's only there as a way of stating the formal rules. The processor will usually be able to find a faster way of doing the test – which is just as well, since pattern matching would otherwise be prohibitively expensive.

Although the formal rules usually give the answer you would expect intuitively, there can be surprises. For example, you might expect the pattern «node()» to match any node; but it doesn't. As an expression, «node()» is short for «./child::node()», and the only nodes that this can select are nodes that are children of something. Since root nodes, attribute nodes, and namespace nodes are never children of another node (see the description of the tree model on page 56, in Chapter 2), they will never be matched by the pattern «node()».

Patterns Containing Predicates

The formal equivalence of patterns and expressions becomes especially important when considering the meaning of predicates (conditions in square brackets), especially predicates that explicitly or implicitly use the **position()** and **last()** functions.

For example, the pattern «para[1]» corresponds to the expression «./para[position()=1]». This expression takes all the <para> children of the context node, and then filters this set to remove all but the first (in document order). So the pattern «para[1]» matches any <para> element that is the first <para> child of its parent. Similarly the pattern «*[1][self::para]» matches any element that is the first child of its parent and that is also a <para> element, while «para[last()!=1]» matches any <para> element that is a child of an element with two or more <para> children.

An Informal Definition

The formal rules for a pattern such as «book//para», because they are written in terms of expressions, encourage you to think of the pattern as being evaluated from left to right, which means finding a **<book>** element and searching for all its **<para>** descendants to see if one of them is the one you are looking for.

An alternative way of looking at the meaning of this expression, and the way in which most XSLT processors are likely to implement the pattern matching algorithm, is to start from the right. The actual logic for testing a node against the pattern «book//para» is likely to be along the lines:

- Test whether this is a **<para>** element. If not, then it doesn't match.
- Test whether there is a **<book>** ancestor. If not, then it doesn't match.
- Otherwise, it matches.

If there are predicates, these can be tested *en-route*, for example to evaluate the pattern «speech[speaker='Hamlet']», the logic is likely to be:

- Test whether this is a **<speech>** element. If not, then it doesn't match.
- Test whether this element has a **<speaker>** child whose string-value is «Hamlet». If not, then it doesn't match.
- Otherwise, it matches.

Most patterns can thus be tested by looking only at the node itself and possibly its ancestors, its attributes, and its children. The patterns that are likely to be the most expensive to test are those that involve looking further afield.

For example, consider the pattern «para[last() - 1]», which matches any **<para>** element that is the last but one **<para>** child of its parent. Most XSLT processors, unless they have an exceptionally good optimizer, are going to test whether a particular **<para>** element matches this pattern by counting how many children the parent element has, counting how many preceding **<para>** siblings the test **<para>** has, and comparing the two numbers. Doing this for every **<para>** element that is processed could get a little expensive, especially if there are hundreds of them with the same parent. With the patterns «para[1]» or «para[last()]» you've a slightly better chance that the processor will figure out a quicker way of doing the test, but I wouldn't rely on it.

If you write a stylesheet with a lot of template rules, then the time taken to find the particular rule to apply to a given node can make a significant difference. The exact way in which different XSLT processors do the matching may vary, but one thing you can be sure of is that patterns containing complex predicates will add to the cost.

Conflict Resolution

When a pattern is used in the definition of a template rule, it is possible that several patterns may match the same node. When this happens, there are rules for resolving this conflict. One of the factors these rules take into account is the default priority of the pattern, which is determined from the way it is written.

The conflict resolution rules, and the way in which the default priority of a pattern is determined, are described under **<xsl:template>** on page 312 in Chapter 4.

How to Read this Chapter

The overall structure of the rules is shown by the hierarchy below. Constructs marked with an asterisk are defined in Chapter 5, *Expressions*.

```
Pattern
   LocationPathPattern
      RelativePathPattern
         StepPattern
            ChildOrAttributeAxisSpecifier
               AbbreviatedAxisSpecifier *
            NodeTest *
            Predicate *
      IdKeyPattern
         Literal *
```

As this structure is relatively simple and regular, I decided that, unlike Chapter 5, I would present the rules in top-down order, starting with the `Pattern` construct itself. So you can find the rules on the following pages:

Construct	Page number
`Pattern`	434
`LocationPathPattern`	435
`RelativePathPattern`	437
`StepPattern`	439
`ChildOrAttributeAxisSpecifier`	445
`IdKeyPattern`	446

The production rules use the same syntax notation as in Chapter 5.

Pattern

This is the top-level construct for the XSLT Pattern syntax. A pattern defines a condition that is either true or false for any given node in the source document. The syntax for a `Pattern` is a subset of the syntax for a `UnionExpr` (and therefore for an `Expr`) in the Expression syntax.

Syntax

Expression	Syntax
`Pattern`	`LocationPathPattern |` `Pattern «|» LocationPathPattern`

A Pattern is either a LocationPathPattern or a sequence of LocationPathPatterns separated by the «|» (union) operator.

The syntax of a LocationPathPattern is given below.

Used in

match attribute of **<xsl:template>** (page 312)
match attribute of **<xsl:key>** (page 241)
from and **count** attributes of **<xsl:number>** (page 256)

Usage

Although «|» is technically a union operator, it is simpler to read it as "or"; a node matches the pattern «A | B» if it matches either A or B or both.

Examples

TITLE	«TITLE» is a LocationPathPattern, so it is also a Pattern
preface | chapter | appendix	A node matches this pattern if it is a **<preface>** element, a **<chapter>** element, or an **<appendix>** element
/ | *	A node matches this pattern if it is either the root node or an element node

LocationPathPattern

A LocationPathPattern states conditions that a node must satisfy based on its name, its node type, its position relative to other nodes, and/or its ID and key values.

This construct is a subset of the PathExpr construct in the Expression language (and not, as you might expect, of LocationPath).

Syntax

Expression	Syntax
LocationPathPattern	«/» RelativePathPattern ? | IdKeyPattern ((«/»|«//») RelativePathPattern) ? | «//» ? RelativePathPattern

The above production rule is the way the syntax is defined in the XSLT specification. However, the equivalent production rule below may be easier to understand, and corresponds with the description in the *Usage* section below.

Expression	Syntax
LocationPathPattern	«/» | RelativePathPattern | «/» RelativePathPattern | «//» RelativePathPattern | IdKeyPattern | IdKeyPattern «/» RelativePathPattern | IdKeyPattern «//» RelativePathPattern

The syntax of a RelativePathPattern is described on page 437, and the syntax of an IdKeyPattern on page 446.

Used in

Pattern (see page 434)

Usage

The syntax rule reproduced above from the XSLT specification can be better understood by listing the seven different kinds of LocationPathPattern, as follows:

«/»	Matches the root node.
RelativePathPattern	Matches a pattern that can appear anywhere in the document.
«/» RelativePathPattern	Matches a pattern defined relative to the immediate children of the root node.
«//» RelativePathPattern	Matches a pattern that can appear anywhere in the document. The inclusion of the leading «//» has no effect on the meaning of the pattern, though it does affect its default priority. The default priority of a pattern comes into play when two template rules match the same node: for details; see the description of **<xsl:template>** in Chapter 4, page 312.
IdKeyPattern	Matches a node with a given ID attribute or key value.
IdKeyPattern «/» RelativePathPattern	Matches a pattern defined relative to the children of a node with a given ID attribute or key value.
IdKeyPattern «//» RelativePathPattern	Matches a pattern defined relative to the descendants of a node with a given ID attribute or key value.

The pattern «/» matches the root node of any tree. In fact, it is the only pattern that will match a root node. This means that if you have several trees (which will be the case in a stylesheet that uses the **document()** function described on page 466, in Chapter 7), the pattern «/» will match the root nodes of each one. This means that you can't write different template rules to match the root nodes of different trees. The usual way around this is either to use different modes to process each tree (see the description of **<xsl:apply-templates>** on page 155 in Chapter 4), or to start the processing of secondary documents at the nodes immediately below the root.

A pattern such as «/item» will match an item element that is an immediate child of the root node. This kind of pattern is often useful when your stylesheet is dealing with multiple source documents, because it allows you to distinguish them by the name of the document element.

The pattern «/@width» is legal but meaningless; it would match a **width** attribute of the root node, but as the root node cannot have attributes, there is no such node.

For the other kinds of LocationPathPattern, see RelativePathPattern on page 437, and IdKeyPattern on page 445.

Examples

/	Matches the root node.
/*	Matches the outermost element node (the document element). In the case of a tree that is not well-formed (see page 56 Chapter 2), it matches any element whose parent is the root node.
/booklist	Matches a **<booklist>** element whose parent is the root node.
//book	Matches a **<book>** element that has the root node as an ancestor: in other words, any **<book>** element.
book	Matches any **<book>** element.
id('figure-1')	Matches an element with an **ID** attribute having the value 'figure-1'.
id('figure-1')//*	Matches any descendant element of an element with an **ID** attribute having the value 'figure-1'.
key('empnr', '624381')/@dob	Matches the **dob** attribute of an element having a value '624381' for the key named empnr.

RelativePathPattern

A RelativePathPattern consists of a StepPattern defining conditions a node must satisfy, optionally preceded by a RelativePathPattern that a parent or ancestor node must satisfy. The syntax for a RelativePathPattern is a subset of the syntax for a RelativeLocationPath in the XPath Expression language.

Syntax

Expression	Syntax

`RelativePathPattern`	`StepPattern |`
	`RelativePathPattern «/» StepPattern |`
	`RelativePathPattern «//» StepPattern`

A `RelativePathPattern` is thus a sequence of one or more `StepPatterns` separated by either of the operators «/» (is-parent-of) or «//» (is-ancestor-of).

The syntax of a `StepPattern` is described on page 439.

Used in

`LocationPathPattern`

Usage

With the first form, `StepPattern`, a node matches the pattern if it satisfies the conditions (node name, node type, and predicates) defined in the `StepPattern`. The simplest and most common form of `StepPattern` is simply an element name, for example «`title`».

With the second form, `RelativePathPattern «/» StepPattern`, a node matches the pattern if it satisfies the conditions (node name, node type, and predicates) defined in the `StepPattern`, and if its **parent node** matches the `RelativePathPattern`. This `RelativePathPattern` may in turn include conditions that the parent node's parent or ancestor nodes must satisfy.

With the third form, `RelativePathPattern «//» StepPattern`, a node matches the pattern if it satisfies the conditions (node name, node type, and predicates) defined in the `StepPattern`, and if it has an **ancestor** that matches the `RelativePathPattern`. This `RelativePathPattern` may in turn include conditions that the ancestor node's parent or ancestor nodes must satisfy.

Notice that although there is an equivalence between `RelativePathPattern` in the pattern language and `RelativeLocationPath` in the expression language, the meaning of a `RelativePathPattern` is most easily explained by examining the `StepPatterns` from right to left, starting at the node being tested and working up through its ancestors, if necessary; this is despite the fact that the meaning of a `RelativeLocationPath` is explained by considering the `Steps` from left to right, starting at the context node. It's likely that most implementations will adopt a strategy similar to the algorithm as I've explained it here.

In theory, everything you can do in a `RelativePathPattern` could be done in a single `StepPattern`, since the pattern «`A/B`» means exactly the same as «`B[parent::A]`», and the pattern «`A//B`» means exactly the same as «`B[ancestor::A]`». However, where several steps are present, the form using «/» and «//» operators is a lot easier to read.

Examples

`title`	This is a `StepPattern`, and therefore the simplest form of `RelativePathPattern`. It selects any **<title>** element.
`section/title`	This is a `RelativePathPattern` consisting of two `StepPatterns` joined by the «`/`» (is-parent-of) operator. It matches a **<title>** element whose parent is a **<section>** element.
`chapter//footnote`	This is a `RelativePathPattern` consisting of two `StepPatterns` joined by the «`//`» (is-ancestor-of) operator. It matches a **<footnote>** element that is a descendant of a **<chapter>** element.
`chapter/section//footnote`	A more complex `RelativePathPattern` that matches any **<footnote>** element that is a descendant of a **<section>** element that is a child of a **<chapter>** element.

StepPattern

A `StepPattern` defines conditions that an individual node must satisfy: typically the node name, node type, and optionally a set of Boolean predicates. The syntax for a `StepPattern` is a subset of the syntax for a `Step` in the XPath expression language.

Syntax

Expression	Syntax
`StepPattern`	`ChildOrAttributeAxisSpecifier NodeTest Predicate *`

The syntax of `ChildOrAttributeAxisSpecifier` is given on page 445. The constructs `NodeTest` (page 398) and `Predicate` (page 407) are constructs described in the XPath expression language in Chapter 5.

The `ChildOrAttributeAxisSpecifier` is mandatory, but if you look at its syntax on page 445 you will see that it may be empty, and in practice it usually is. So, unless you choose the long form of the syntax for an axis specifier, a `StepPattern` consists of an optional «`@`» sign to indicate the attribute axis, then a `NodeTest` which is generally either a node name or a node type such as «`text()`» or «`comment()`», followed by zero or more `Predicates`, which are Boolean expressions enclosed in square brackets.

Used in

`RelativePathPattern`

Usage

We'll look at the usage of each part of the StepPattern in turn.

The AxisSpecifier

The ChildOrAttributeAxisSpecifier may take the form «attribute::» (abbreviated «@») or «child::» (abbreviated to nothing: «»).

In the formal rules for evaluating a pattern, the steps in a RelativePathPattern are evaluated from left to right, and the choice of axis determines whether this step looks at the children or the attributes of the nodes found in the previous step.

Looking at it informally, it is simplest to think of the axis specifier as simply a way of saying what node type is required.

- If the child axis is used and the NodeTest is a NameTest (for example, «title», «*», or «svg:*», then we are looking for an element node.
- If the child axis is used and the NodeTest is a NodeType (for example, «comment()» or «text()»), then we are looking for that kind of node. If the NodeTest is «node()», then we are looking for any node on the child axis; elements, text nodes, comments, or processing instructions. Note that the pattern «node()», which is short for «child::node()» will not match root nodes, attributes, or namespace nodes, because these nodes never appear as the child of another node.
- If the attribute axis is used and the NodeTest is a NameTest (for example «@title», «@*», or «@svg:*», then we are looking for an attribute node.
- If the attribute axis is used and the NodeTest is a NodeType (for example, «@comment()» or «@text()»), then we are looking for that kind of node, but we are only looking for it on the attribute axis. The patterns «@comment()» and «@text()» are not illegal, but they are pointless, because the attribute axis cannot contain comments or text nodes. However, the NodeTest «@node()» looks for any node on the attribute axis, so it is equivalent to «@*».

The Node Test

The form of a NodeTest is defined in the XPath expression language; specifically it may be:

- A NameTest such as «title», «*», or «prefix:*». (The last form matches any element or attribute whose name is in a particular namespace.)
- A NodeType, one of «comment()», «text()», «processing-instruction()», or «node()».
- A named processing instruction, for example: «processing-instruction('pi-target')».

The Predicates

The form of a `Predicate` is defined in the XPath expression language (see Chapter 5, page 407): it is any expression enclosed in square brackets. For example «`[speaker='Hamlet']`», or «`[@width > 100]`», or «`[*]`», or «`[1]`».

If the predicate is numeric, it is interpreted as a test on the position of the node relative to its siblings. In all other cases, the expression is converted to a Boolean, and if the value is false then the pattern doesn't match.

There are three restrictions on predicates used in patterns:

- When a pattern is used in the **`match`** attribute of **`<xsl:template>`** or **`<xsl:key>`**, the predicate must not contain any references to variables. This is to prevent circular definitions; global variables can invoke keys and templates, so if keys and templates were allowed to be defined in terms of global variables, infinite recursion could happen. This restriction doesn't apply to patterns used in **`<xsl:number>`**.
- For the same reasons, when a pattern is used in the **`match`** attribute of **`<xsl:template>`** or **`<xsl:key>`**, the predicate must not use the **`key()`** function.
- Patterns must not use the **`current()`** function (described on page 463, in Chapter 7) within a predicate. This is to ensure that the decision as to whether a particular node matches a pattern is predictable and does not depend on the current state of processing. For example, considering the **`match`** attribute of the **`<xsl:key>`** element, this means that a node is either included in a key or excluded, it can't be included at some times and excluded at other times.

Predicates can be classified into two groups; those that depend on the node's position relative to its siblings, and those that don't. A positional predicate is one whose value is a number, or one that uses the functions **`position()`** or **`last()`**; all others are non-positional. For example, the predicates «`[1]`», «`[position()!=1]`», and «`[last()-1]`» are all positional predicates, whereas «`[@name='Tokyo']`» and «`[*]`» are non-positional.

For a non-positional predicate, its meaning is that the `StepPattern` fails to match a node if the predicate fails to match the node. For example, the predicate «`[@security='secret']`» is true when the node has a **`security`** attribute whose value is `'secret'`, so any `StepPattern` that uses this predicate will fail if the node has no **`security`** attribute or if the **`security`** attribute has any value other than `'secret'`.

For a positional predicate, the meaning of the predicate can be deduced from the formal rules given at the start of this chapter. However, it is easier to understand their meaning by using informal rules. A numeric predicate such as «`[1]`» or «`[last()-1]`» is equivalent to the Boolean predicate «`[position()=1]`» or «`[position()=last()-1]`». So to evaluate a positional predicate, we need to know what **`position()`** and **`last()`** are.

The use of positional predicates with the attribute axis doesn't make much sense, because the order of attributes is undefined. So in the following description, I'll assume that you're using the child axis.

If there is only one predicate in the `StepPattern`, or if this predicate is the first, then:

- **`last()`** is the number of siblings of the node being tested that satisfy the `NodeTest` (including the node itself). For example, if we are testing a **<para>** element against the pattern «`para[last()=1]`», then **`last()`** is the number of **<para>** elements that are children of the parent of the **<para>** element being tested. This pattern will match any **<para>** element that is the only **<para>** child of its parent.
- **`position()`** is the position of the node being tested among these siblings, taking them in document order and counting from one. So «`para[1]`», which means «`para[position()=1]`», will match any **<para>** element that is the first **<para>** child of its parent element, in document order.

Note that it is the position of the node relative to its siblings that counts, not the position in the sequence you are processing the nodes. For example, suppose you want to process all the **<glossary-entry>** elements in a document, in alphabetical order. You can write:

```
<xsl:apply-templates select="//glossary-entry">
    <xsl:sort/>
<xsl:apply-templates>
```

Then suppose you have the following two template rules:

```
<xsl:template match="glossary-entry[1]">
. . .
</xsl:template>

<xsl:template match="glossary-entry">
. . .
</xsl:template>
```

The first template rule will be used for any **<glossary-entry>** that is the first **<glossary-entry>** child of its parent. Not, as you might expect, the first **<glossary-entry>** in alphabetical order, nor even the first **<glossary-entry>** element in the document. If you want to apply different processing to the **<glossary-entry>** that is first in alphabetical order, the way to do it is:

```
<xsl:template match="glossary-entry">
<xsl:choose>
<xsl:when test="position()=1">
   . . .
</xsl:when>
<xsl:otherwise>
   . . .
</xsl:otherwise>
</xsl:template>
```

This is because the context position within the body of the template rule is the position of the node in the list of nodes being processed, whereas the result for deciding whether a node matches a pattern is the same regardless of the processing context.

If there are several predicates in the `StepPattern`, then **`position()`** and **`last()`** in predicates after the first apply to the nodes that survived the previous predicates. So «`speech[speaker='Hamlet'][1]`» matches a **<speech>** element that is the first **<speech>** element among its siblings, in which one of the **<speaker>**s is Hamlet.

The **position()** and **last()** functions relate to children of the same parent even when the «//» operator is used. For example, «chapter//footnote[1]» matches any **<footnote>** element that is a descendant of a **<chapter>** element and that is the first **<footnote>** child of its parent. There is no simple way to write a pattern that matches the first **<footnote>** element in a **<chapter>**, because the relevant expression «(chapter//footnote)[1]» is not a valid pattern. (Why not? No good reason, it's just that the spec doesn't allow it.)

Positional predicates in patterns need to be used with some attention to performance. Writing a template with the match pattern «para[last()-1]», for example, seems a sensible way to define the processing for the penultimate paragraph of a section. However, a simplistic XSLT processor will expand this predicate to «para[position()=last()-1]», and evaluate it by first determining the position of the current paragraph in its section, then finding the total number of paragraphs in the section, and comparing the two. If the number of paragraphs in a section is large, this could be a very expensive operation. An optimized XSLT processor will find a better strategy, but if performance is critical it would be worth doing some measurements.

Examples

child::title	Matches elements named **<title>**.
title	Short form of «child::title».
attribute::title	Matches attributes named **<title>**.
@title	Short form of «attribute::title».
*[@width]	Matches an element node that has an attribute named **width**.
text()[starts-with(.,'The')]	Matches a text node whose text content starts with the characters «The».
p[@code][position() < 10]	Matches a **<p>** element that is among the first nine **<p>** elements of its parent that have a **code** attribute.
p[position() < 10][@code]	Matches a **<p>** element that is among the first nine **<p>** elements of its parent and that has a **code** attribute.
[not(@code = preceding-sibling::/@code)]	Matches an element node provided that it does not have a **code** attribute with the same value as the **code** attribute of any preceding sibling element.
comment()	Matches any comment node.
@comment()	This matches comment nodes that are found on the attribute axis of their parent node. Since the attribute axis can only contain attribute nodes, this condition can never be satisfied; nevertheless, it is a legal StepPattern.

ChildOrAttributeAxisSpecifier

This construct is a subset of `AxisSpecifier` in the Expression syntax. The only two axes used directly in a pattern are the child axis and the attribute axis. Either can be written in its expanded form or its abbreviated form.

Syntax

Expression	Syntax
`ChildOrAttributeAxisSpecifier`	`AbbreviatedAxisSpecifier |` `( «child» | «attribute» ) «::»`

The construct `AbbreviatedAxisSpecifier` is part of the Expression syntax defined on page 353 in Chapter 5, and is either «`@`», denoting the attribute axis, or nothing, denoting the child axis.

As an `AbbreviatedAxisSpecifier` can be empty, so can a `ChildOrAttributeAxisSpecifier`. What this means in practice is that a `NodeTest` with no explicit axis specifier (for example, an element name or a node type such as «`text()`») implicitly uses the child axis.

A surprising consequence of this is that the pattern «`node()`» will only match a node that is the child of something, thus it will never match a root node, an attribute node, or a namespace node.

Used in

`StepPattern`

Usage

See `StepPattern` on page 439.

Unlike expressions, the only two axes that are available directly in a pattern are the child and attribute axes. However, testing for the presence of related nodes on a different axis can be done in the predicate of the `StepPattern`. Any expression can be used in the predicate, so all axes are available. For example:

```
caption[preceding-sibling::*[1][self::figure]]
```

matches a **<caption>** element whose immediately preceding sibling element is a **<figure>** element.

Examples

`child::`	Denotes the child axis
	(The box on the left is intentionally blank) Denotes the child axis: «`child::`» is the default axis specifier
`attribute::`	Denotes the attribute axis
`@`	Equivalent to «`attribute::`»

For examples showing a `ChildOrAttributeSpecifier` in context, see `StepPattern` on page 439.

IdKeyPattern

This construct allows a pattern to be matched only if the node being tested (or one of its ancestors) has a specified ID attribute or key value.

This construct is a subset of the `FunctionCall` construct in an Expression, described in Chapter 5, page 385. The only function calls that can be used in a pattern (except within predicates) are the **`id()`** and **`key()`** functions, and these can only be used with arguments that are literals.

The **`id()`** (page 496) and **`key()`** (page 499) functions are described in Chapter 7.

Syntax

Expression	Syntax
`IdKeyPattern`	`«id» «(» Literal «)» |` `«key» «(» Literal «,» Literal «)»`

Used in

`LocationPathPattern`

Usage

This facility provides an equivalent to the ability in CSS to define a style for a specific node in the source document.

There are a number of ways the facility can be used:

- If for a particular source document you want to use a general-purpose stylesheet, but want to override its behavior for certain selected nodes, you can write a stylesheet that imports the general-purpose one, and then write the overriding rules in the form of templates that match specific identified elements in the source document.
- Sometimes the source document is generated dynamically from a database. Perhaps there is something in the source document you want to highlight, say the search term that was used to locate this record. You could flag this item while generating the source document by giving it a special ID attribute value known to the stylesheet.

In practice this construct isn't as useful as it might seem, because the actual key value or ID has to be a literal constant; as we saw earlier, variables aren't allowed in match patterns.

In all cases, the **`id()`** and **`key()`** function could be spelled out in terms of a predicate on the ID attributes or the key value expression, so the facility can be seen simply as a shorthand. For example, if **`<book>`** elements are keyed on their ISBN property, and implemented as a child element, then the following declarations are equivalent:

(1) using a direct pattern match:

```
<xsl:template match="book[isbn='1-861002-68-8']">
```

(2) using a key definition:

```
<xsl:key name="isbn-key" match="book" use="isbn"/>
<xsl:template match="key('isbn-key', '1-861002-68-8')>
```

Of course there may be a performance difference between the two, but this depends on how the XSLT processor is implemented.

Examples

`id('figure1')`	Matches a node with an **`ID`** attribute equal to the string `'figure1'`. An attribute is an **`ID`** attribute if it is defined in the DTD as having type `ID` (the name of the attribute is irrelevant).
`key('empnr', '517541')`	Matches a node having a value of `'517541'` for the key named «`empnr`».

The following example shows how this feature can be used in a stylesheet:

Example: Using the key() Pattern to Format a Specific Node

In this example I will show how to use the **`key()`** pattern to format one selected node differently from the others.

Source

The source document, `itinerary.xml`, is a tour itinerary:

```
<itinerary>
<day number="1">Arrive in Cairo</day>
<day number="2">Visit the Pyramids at Gaza</day>
<day number="3">Archaelogical Museum at Cairo</day>
<day number="4">Flight to Luxor; coach to Aswan</day>
<day number="5">Visit Temple at Philae and Aswan High Dam</day>
<day number="6">Cruise to Edfu</day>
<day number="7">Cruise to Luxor; visit Temple at Karnak</day>
<day number="8">Valley of the Kings</day>
<day number="9">Return flight from Luxor</day>
</itinerary>
```

Stylesheet

We'll start with a straightforward stylesheet, `itinerary.xsl`, to display this itinerary:

```
<?xml version="1.0" encoding="iso-8859-1"?>
<xsl:stylesheet version="1.0"
       xmlns:xsl="">

<xsl:template match="/">
       <html>
       <head>
             <title>Itinerary</title>
       </head>
       <body><center>
             <xsl:apply-templates select="//day"/>
       </center></body>
       </html>
</xsl:template>

<xsl:template match="day">
    <h3>Day <xsl:value-of select="@number"/></h3>
    <p><xsl:apply-templates/></p>
</xsl:template>
</xsl:stylesheet>
```

Now we'll specialize this by importing it into another stylesheet, `today.xsl`, which displays the activities for day 5 in red:

```
<?xml version="1.0" encoding="iso-8859-1"?>
<xsl:stylesheet
      version="1.0"
      xmlns:xsl="http://www.w3.org/1999/XSL/Transform">

<xsl:import href="itinerary.xsl"/>
<xsl:key name="day-number" match="day" use="@number"/>

<xsl:template match="key('day-number','5')//text()">
    <font color="red"><xsl:value-of select="."/></font>
</xsl:template>

</xsl:stylesheet>
```

Output

The resulting output is as follows:

```
<html>
   <head>
      <META http-equiv="Content-Type" content="text/html; charset=utf-8">
      <title>Itinerary</title>
   </head>
   <body>
      <center>
         <h3>Day 1</h3>
         <p>Arrive in Cairo</p>
         <h3>Day 2</h3>
         <p>Visit the Pyramids at Gaza</p>
         <h3>Day 3</h3>
         <p>Archaelogical Museum at Cairo</p>
         <h3>Day 4</h3>
         <p>Flight to Luxor; coach to Aswan</p>
         <h3>Day 5</h3>
         <p><font
      color="red">Visit Temple at Philae and Aswan High
Dam</font></p>
```

```
<h3>Day 6</h3>
          <p>Cruise to Edfu</p>
          <h3>Day 7</h3>
          <p>Cruise to Luxor; visit Temple at Karnak</p>
          <h3>Day 8</h3>
          <p>Valley of the Kings</p>
          <h3>Day 9</h3>
          <p>Return flight from Luxor</p>
       </center>
    </body>
</html>
```

While this example shows one way of using this feature, I have to admit that it's not very convincing. You could achieve the same effect by writing the relevant pattern as «`day[@number=5]`», without the need to introduce a key at all. And in any practical situation I would want to decide which day's activities to display in red by means of a parameter to the stylesheet; unfortunately, there is no way of writing a pattern whose result depends on the value of a parameter, so the logic would have to be coded using **`<xsl:choose>`** instead.

Summary

In this chapter I described the syntax and meanings of patterns, whose main use in an XSLT stylesheet is to define which template rules apply to which nodes in the source document, but which are also used in the **`<xsl:key>`** and **`<xsl:number>`** elements.

Patterns, although their syntax is a subset of that for XPath expressions which we saw described in Chapter 5, are evaluated in a different way to expressions, though we saw that the formal rules express the meaning of a pattern in terms of the corresponding expression.

The next chapter describes the library of standard functions which can be used within XPath expressions in a stylesheet.

7

Functions

This chapter describes all the standard functions included in the XPath and XSLT specifications for use in expressions.

For each function, I give: its name, a brief description of its purpose, a reference to where in the XSLT or XPath specifications it is defined, a list of the arguments it expects and the value it returns, the formal rules defining what the function does, and finally usage advice and examples.

Some of these functions are defined in the XPath Recommendation, some in XSLT. If you are using them in an XSLT stylesheet, it doesn't matter where they were defined; but if you are using XPath in a context other than XSLT, you should be aware that only the XPath-defined functions (known as *core functions*) are guaranteed to be available. These are shown by a ✔ in the table below.

The syntax of a function call is described as part of the XPath expression syntax in Chapter 5. This describes where a function call can be used in an expression, and where it can't: the only significant restriction is that you can't use a function call on the right hand side of the path operator «`/`». Within a function call, the values supplied as arguments can be any XPath expression, subject only to the rules on data types (for example, some functions require an argument that is a node-set). So a function call such as «`count(..)`», though it looks strange, is perfectly legal: «`..`» is a valid XPath expression that returns the parent of the context node.

I've arranged the functions in alphabetical order so you can find them quickly if you know what you're looking for. However, in case you only know the general area you are interested in, you may find the following classification useful. In the table the core XPath functions are marked ✔ while the additional functions defined in XSLT are marked ✘. The difference is only important when you use XPath expressions in a context other than XSLT stylesheets.

Category	Function
Functions that convert values from one data type to another	✔ `boolean()` ✘ `format-number()` ✔ `number()` ✔ `string()`
Arithmetic functions	✔ `ceiling()` ✔ `floor()` ✔ `round()`
String manipulation	✔ `concat()` ✔ `contains()` ✔ `normalize-space()` ✔ `starts-with()` ✔ `string-length()` ✔ `substring()` ✔ `substring-before()` ✔ `substring-after()` ✔ `translate()`
Aggregation	✔ `count()` ✔ `sum()`
Getting node names and identifiers	✘ `generate-id()` ✘ `lang()` ✔ `local-name()` ✔ `name()` ✔ `namespace-uri()` ✘ `unparsed-entity-uri()`
Boolean functions	✔ `false()` ✔ `true()` ✔ `not()`
Functions that return information about the context	✘ `current()` ✔ `last()` ✔ `position()`
Functions that find nodes	✘ `document()` ✘ `key()` ✔ `id()`
Functions that provide information about the environment	✘ `element-available()` ✘ `function-available()` ✘ `system-property()`

All these functions are in the default namespace: their names do not need to be prefixed. In fact, they are the only functions in the default namespace – extension functions provided by vendors, users, or third parties should always be in a different namespace and will need to have a namespace prefix when called.

boolean

The **`boolean()`** function converts its argument to a Boolean value.

For example, the expression «`boolean(1)`» returns `true`.

Defined in

XPath section 4.3

Format

```
boolean(value) ⇒ boolean
```

Arguments

Argument	Data type	Meaning
value	any	The value that is to be converted to a Boolean

Result

A Boolean value; the result of converting the argument.

Rules

Any value may be converted to a Boolean. The rules for conversion are as follows:

Supplied data type	Conversion rules
Number	The number zero converts to `false`; anything else converts to `true`.
String	A zero-length string converts to `false`; anything else converts to `true`.
Boolean	The value is unchanged.
Node-set	An empty node-set converts to `false`; anything else converts to `true`. This means that a node-set representing a tree always converts to `true`, because it always has a root node.

Usage

In most cases conversion to a Boolean occurs automatically when the context requires it; it is only necessary to call the **`boolean()`** function explicitly in order to force a conversion.

Examples

The following example prints a message if the source document contains a **<header>** element and no **<footer>**, or if it contains a **<footer>** and no **<header>**.

```
<xsl:if test="boolean(//header) != boolean(//footer)">
   <xsl:message>Document must contain headers and footers,
                                   or neither</xsl:message>
</xsl:if>
```

The conversion of the two node-sets «`//header`» (true if there are any **<header>** elements in the document) and «`//footer`» (true if there are any **<footer>** elements) needs to be explicit here, because we want to do a Boolean comparison, not a node-set comparison.

The following example sets a variable to the Boolean value `true` or `false` depending on whether the document contains footnotes. In this case the explicit conversion is probably not necessary, since it could be done later when the variable is used, but it is probably more efficient to retain only a Boolean value in the variable rather than retaining the full set of footnote nodes. An intelligent XSLT processor will recognize that the expression «`//footnote`» occurs in a context where a Boolean is required, and scan the document only until the first footnote is found, rather than retrieving all of them.

```
<xsl:variable name="uses-footnotes" select="boolean(//footnote)"/>
```

See also

true() on page 562
false() on page 482

ceiling

The **ceiling()** function returns the smallest integer that is greater than or equal to the numeric value of the argument.

For example, the expression «`ceiling(33.9)`» returns `34`.

Defined in

XPath section 4.4

Format

```
ceiling(value)  ⇒  number
```

Arguments

Argument	Data type	Meaning
value	number	The input value. If it is not of type number, it is first converted to a number using the rules for the **number()** function.

Result

An integer value: the result of converting the first argument to a number and then rounding up, if necessary, to the next highest integer.

Rules

If the value is not numeric, it is first converted to a number. For the detailed rules, see the description of the **number()** function on page 531. If the value is a node-set, these rules mean that the function applies to the value of the first node in the node-set, in document order.

If the number is an integer, it is returned unchanged. Otherwise, it is rounded up to the next highest integer.

The number data type in XPath supports special values such as infinity, negative zero and NaN (not a number), which are described on page 89 in Chapter 2.

If the argument is NaN (not a number), which will happen if a string is supplied that cannot be converted to a number, the result will be NaN. Similarly when the argument is positive or negative infinity, the function will return the value of the argument unchanged.

If the argument value is greater than –1.0 but less than zero it will be rounded up to negative zero.

Usage and Examples

The result of this function is illustrated by the following examples:

```
ceiling(1.0) = 1.0
ceiling(1.6) = 2.0
ceiling(17 div 3) = 6.0
ceiling(-3.0) = -3.0
ceiling(-8.2) = -8.0
ceiling('xxx') = NaN
ceiling(-0.5) = -0
```

One situation where this function is useful is when calculating the size of a table. If you have a node-set `$ns` and you want to arrange the values in three columns, then the number of rows needed is: «`ceiling(count($ns) div 3)`».

See also

floor() on page 483
round() on page 537

concat

The **concat()** function takes two or more arguments. Each of the arguments is converted to a string, and the resulting strings are joined together end-to-end.

For example, the expression «`concat('Jane', ' ', 'Brown')`» returns the string «`Jane Brown`».

Defined in

XPath section 4.2

Format

```
concat(value1, value2, value3, …)  ⇒  string
```

Arguments

This function is unique in that it can take any number of arguments (two or more).

Argument	Data type	Meaning
value 1 … value n	string	An input value. If it is not of type string, it is first converted to a string using the rules for the **string()** function.

Result

A string value; the result of converting each of the arguments in turn to a string and concatenating the results.

Rules

Each of the arguments is converted to a string using the rules of the **string()** function, and each of the resulting strings is appended to the result string, in the order they appear.

Usage and Examples

The **concat()** function is often a convenient alternative to using multiple **<xsl:value-of>** elements to construct an output string. For example:

```
<xsl:value-of select="concat(first-name, ' ', last-name)"/>
```

is equivalent to:

```
<xsl:value-of select="first-name"/>
<xsl:text> </xsl:text>
<xsl:value-of select="last-name"/>
```

Another situation where **concat()** is useful is in defining a key (see **<xsl:key>** on page 241 in Chapter 4, and the description of the **key()** function on page 499). XSLT keys cannot be multi-part values, but you can get round this restriction by concatenating the parts of the key with an appropriate separator. For example:

```
<xsl:key name="full-name" match="person"
                          use="concat(first-name, ' ', last-name)"/>
```

This key can then be used to retrieve the person (or persons) with a given name using an expression such as:

```
<xsl:for-each select="key('full-name', 'Peter Jones')"/>
```

A more advanced usage of **concat()** is to build up a whitespace-separated list of names. As XSLT provides no complex data types for temporary results, a whitespace-separated list is often the best option available for maintaining what in other languages would be an array. You can use other separators, of course, but whitespace is generally the most convenient because it's then easy to separate the components using the functions **normalize-space()**, **substring-before()**, and **substring-after()**.

Example: Creating a Comma-separated List

The following example shows a template which, when supplied with a node-set containing **<city>** elements with a **country** attribute, builds a list of cities in the form *city, country*.

Source

The source file is `cities.xml`:

```
<cities>
   <city name="Paris" country="France"/>
   <city name="Roma" country="Italia"/>
   <city name="Nice" country="France"/>
   <city name="Madrid" country="Espana"/>
   <city name="Milano" country="Italia"/>
   <city name="Firenze" country="Italia"/>
   <city name="Napoli" country="Italia"/>
   <city name="Lyon" country="France"/>
   <city name="Barcelona" country="Espana"/>
</cities>
```

Stylesheet

The stylesheet `list-cities.xsl` iterates over all the **<city>** elements using the **concat()** function to output each one in the format *city, country*.

```
<xsl:transform
 xmlns:xsl="http://www.w3.org/1999/XSL/Transform"
 version="1.0"
>
<xsl:output indent="yes"/>
<xsl:template match="/">
  <out>
    <xsl:for-each select="//city">
      <city><xsl:value-of select="concat(@name, ', ',
@country)"/></city>
    </xsl:for-each>
  </out>
</xsl:template>
</xsl:transform>
```

Output

```
<?xml version="1.0" encoding="utf-8" ?>
<out>
   <city>Paris, France</city>
   <city>Roma, Italia</city>
   <city>Nice, France</city>
   <city>Madrid, Espana</city>
   <city>Milano, Italia</city>
   <city>Firenze, Italia</city>
   <city>Napoli, Italia</city>
   <city>Lyon, France</city>
   <city>Barcelona, Espana</city>
</out>
```

See also

contains() in the section immediately below
substring() on page 545

Format

`contains(value, substring) ⇒  boolean`

contains

The **contains()** function tests whether one string value contains another as a substring.

For example, the expression «`contains('Santorini', 'ant')`» returns true.

Defined in

XPath section 4.2

Arguments

Argument	Data type	Meaning
value	string	The containing string. If it is not of type string, it is first converted to a string using the rules for the **string()** function.
substring	string	The test string. If it is not of type string, it is first converted to a string using the rules for the **string()** function.

Result

A Boolean value: `true` if the containing string has a substring that is equal to the test string, `false` otherwise.

Rules

The result is `true` if the first string contains a consecutive sequence of characters where each character has the same Unicode value as the corresponding character of the second string.

If the second string is empty, the result is always `true`.

If the first string is empty, the result is `false` except when the second string is also empty.

Usage and Examples

The **contains()** function is often useful where a string has some internal syntax. For example the test:

```
<xsl:if test="contains($name, 'Michael') and contains($name, 'Kay')"/>
```

will succeed if the variable «`$name`» is the string value «`Michael Kay`» or «`Kay, Michael`» or «`Michael H. Kay`» or «`Michaelmas Kayaks, Inc.`».

Take care if you are using accented or other composite letter forms, as there may be more than one way of representing these in Unicode, and if the representations in the two strings are different, you may not get a match.

See also

substring() on page 545
substring-after() on page 549
substring-before() on page 550

count

The **count()** function takes a node-set as its parameter, and returns the number of nodes present in the node-set.

For example, the expression «`count(.)`» always returns 1.

Defined in

XPath section 4.1

Format

```
count(nodes)  ⇒  number
```

Arguments

Argument	Data type	Meaning
nodes	node-set	The input node-set. An error is reported if the argument is not a node-set.

Result

A number giving the number of distinct nodes in the input node-set.

Rules

The **count()** function takes a node-set as its parameter, and returns the number of nodes present in the node-set.

Only the nodes that are members of the node-set in their own right are counted. Nodes that are children or descendants of these nodes are not included in the count.

Usage

A node-set is a mathematical set, so all the nodes it contains are distinct (which means they are different nodes – it doesn't mean, of course, that they must have different string-values). If you form a node-set using the union operator «|», any nodes that are in both operands will only be included in the result once. This means, for example, that the result of «`count( . | / )`» will be 1 if, and only if, the context node is the root.

Since XPath provides no other way of comparing whether two node-sets contain the same node, this can be a useful programming trick. For example, to test whether the context node is one of the nodes in the node-set in variable «`$special`», write:

```
<xsl:if test="count($special | .) = count($special)"> . . . </xsl:if>
```

Avoid using **`count()`** to test whether a node-set is empty, for example by writing:

```
<xsl:if test="count(book[author='Hemingway']) != 0"> . . . </xsl:if>
```

This can be better expressed as:

```
<xsl:if test="book[author='Hemingway']"> . . . </xsl:if>
```

Both examples test whether the current node has any child **`<book>`** elements that have a child **`<author>`** element whose value is «`Hemingway`». However, the second example, as well as being more concise, is easier for the XSLT processor to optimize. Many implementations will be able to stop the scan of books as soon as a matching one is found.

The **`count()`** function is often an effective alternative to using **`<xsl:number>`**. For example, if the current node is a `<bullet>` element, then «`count(preceding-sibling::bullet)+1`» returns the same value as **`<xsl:number/>`** used with no attributes. The advantages of using `count()` are that it is rather more flexible in defining what you want to count, and it can be used directly in expressions. However, **`<xsl:number>`** gives a simple way of obtaining the sequence number, formatting it, and inserting it in the result tree in a single operation; it may also in some cases be easier for the processor to optimize.

Avoid using **`count()`** where **`last()`** would do the job just as well. This situation arises when you are processing a set of nodes using **`<xsl:apply-templates>`** or **`<xsl:for-each>`**; the number of nodes in that set is then available from the **`last()`** function. For example, it is probably inefficient to write:

```
<xsl:for-each select="book[author='Hemingway']">
   <h2>Book <xsl:value-of select="position()"/> of
            <xsl:value-of select="count(../book[author='Hemingway'])"/>
   </h2>
   . . .
</xsl:for-each>
```

because – unless the XSLT processor is rather clever – it will have to re-evaluate the expression «`../book[author='Hemingway']`» each time round the loop.

Instead, write:

```
<xsl:for-each select="book[author='Hemingway']">
   <h2>Book <xsl:value-of select="position()"/> of
            <xsl:value-of select="last()"/>
   </h2>
   . . .
</xsl:for-each>
```

An alternative is to assign the node-set to a variable, so it is only evaluated once.

Examples

The following example outputs the number of **<footnote>** elements in the source document:

```
<xsl:value-of select="count(//footnote)"/>
```

The following example assigns to a variable the number of attributes of the current node:

```
<xsl:variable name="num-atts" select="count(@*)"/>
```

Example: Counting Distinct Values

This example counts how many distinct values of the **country** attribute there are in a list of **<city>** elements.

Source

The source document is `cities.xml`:

```
<cities>
   <city name="Paris" country="France"/>
   <city name="Roma" country="Italia"/>
   <city name="Nice" country="France"/>
   <city name="Madrid" country="Espana"/>
   <city name="Milano" country="Italia"/>
   <city name="Firenze" country="Italia"/>
   <city name="Napoli" country="Italia"/>
   <city name="Lyon" country="France"/>
   <city name="Barcelona" country="Espana"/>
</cities>
```

Stylesheet

The stylesheet is `count-countries.xsl`. It is a complete stylesheet, written using the *Simplified Stylesheet* syntax described on page 113, in Chapter 3. It builds a node-set containing those **<city>** elements that have a different **country** attribute from any preceding **<city>**, and then counts the nodes in this node-set.

```
<count xsl:version="1.0"
      xmlns:xsl="http://www.w3.org/1999/XSL/Transform">
  <xsl:value-of

select="count(//city[not(@country=preceding::city/@country)])"/>
</count>
```

Output

```
<?xml version="1.0" encoding="utf-8"?>
<count>3</count>
```

current

The **current()** function returns a node-set containing a single node, the current node.

Defined in

XSLT section 12.4

Format

```
current() ⇒  node-set
```

Arguments

None

Result

A node-set containing a single node, the current node.

Rules

It is important to understand the difference between the current node and the context node.

The current node is established as follows:

- When evaluating a global variable, the current node is the root node of the source document.
- When **<xsl:apply-templates>** is used to process a selected set of nodes, each selected node in turn becomes the current node. So when a template rule is invoked, the current node is always the node that caused that template rule to be selected. On return from **<xsl:apply-templates>**, the current node reverts to its previous value.
- Similarly, when the system implicitly invokes a template to process the root node of the source document, the current node is the root node.
- When **<xsl:for-each>** is used to process a selected set of nodes, each selected node in turn becomes the current node. When the **<xsl:for-each>** loop completes, the current node reverts to its previous value.
- **<xsl:call-template>** and **<xsl:apply-imports>** leave the current node unchanged.
- The current node (unlike the context node) does not change when evaluating a predicate within a path expression.

The context node is the node returned by the XPath expression «`.`». When used as a freestanding XPath expression, «`current()`» and «`.`» return the same result. When used in a predicate, however, the values will generally be different.

The **`current()`** function cannot be used in a pattern. This is to ensure that the decision as to whether a node matches a pattern is context-free: it doesn't depend on the circumstances in which the pattern is evaluated.

Usage and Examples

The reason the **`current()`** function is provided is to allow you to determine the current node when it is different from the context node – specifically, inside a predicate. The context node can always be determined using the path expression «`.`» (or its longer form, «`self::node()`»).

The most common situation where **`current()`** is useful is when you want to follow a cross-reference from the current node to some other node. For example, suppose in a book catalog the **`<book>`** elements have an attribute **`category`**, whose value is a code such as "`CL`" or "`SF`", and that elsewhere there is a lookup table that gives the expansion of these codes, for example `CL` might be classical literature and `SF` might be science fiction.

Example: current()

This example lists the books in a catalog; in the description of each book, it also lists other books in the same category.

Source

The source document is `booklist.xml`:

```
<booklist>
<book category="S">
     <title>Number, the Language of Science</title>
     <author>Danzig</author>
</book>
<book category="FC">
     <title>The Young Visiters</title>
     <author>Daisy Ashford</author>
</book>
<book category="FC">
     <title>When We Were Very Young</title>
     <author>A. A. Milne</author>
</book>
<book category="CS">
     <title>Design Patterns</title>
     <author>Erich Gamma</author>
     <author>Richard Helm</author>
     <author>Ralph Johnson</author>
     <author>John Vlissides</author>
</book>
</booklist>
```

Stylesheet

The stylesheet is `list-books.xsl`. It processes all the books in an **`<xsl:for-each>`** loop, and for each one it displays the title and the first author. Then it looks for other books in the same category. Here it uses the predicate «`[./@category = current()/@category]`» which is true if the **`category`** attribute of the context element is the same as the **`category`** attribute of the current element. The context element is the one being tested, the current element is the one whose entry is being displayed. It also tests that these two elements have different identifiers produced by **`generate-id()`**, which is one way of testing that they are not the same element. Another way of doing this test would be to write «`count(.|current())=2`», since the union of the context node and the current node will contain one element if they are the same, and two if they are different. In this case you could also get away with writing «`.!=current()`», which tests whether the two nodes have a different string-value, but it can be a more expensive test, and it doesn't mean quite the same thing.

```
<xsl:transform
 xmlns:xsl="http://www.w3.org/1999/XSL/Transform"
 version="1.0"
>
<xsl:template match="/">
  <html><body>
    <xsl:variable name="all-books" select="//book"/>
    <xsl:for-each select="$all-books">
      <h1><xsl:value-of select="title"/></h1>
      <p><i>by </i><xsl:value-of select="author"/>
         <xsl:if test="count(author)!=1"> and others</xsl:if>
      </p>
      <xsl:variable name="others"
        select="$all-books[./@category=current()/@category and
                           generate-id(.)!=generate-id(current())]"/>
        <xsl:if test="$others">
          <p>Other books in this category:</p><ul>
          <xsl:for-each select="$others">
             <li><xsl:value-of select="title"/></li>
          </xsl:for-each>
          </ul>
        </xsl:if>
    </xsl:for-each>
  </body></html>
</xsl:template>

</xsl:transform>
```

Output

```
<html>
   <body>
      <h1>Number, the Language of Science</h1>
      <p><i>by </i>Danzig
      </p>
      <h1>The Young Visiters</h1><p><i>by </i>Daisy Ashford
      </p>
      <p>Other books in this category:</p>
      <ul>
```

```
    <li>When We Were Very Young</li>
          </ul>
          <h1>When We Were Very Young</h1>
          <p><i>by </i>A. A. Milne
          </p>
          <p>Other books in this category:</p>
          <ul>
             <li>The Young Visiters</li>
          </ul>
          <h1>Design Patterns</h1>
          <p><i>by </i>Erich Gamma and others
          </p>
       </body>
    </html>
```

See also

`AbbreviatedStep` on page 356, in Chapter 5.

document

The **`document()`** function finds an external XML document by resolving a URI reference, parses the XML into a tree structure, and returns its root node. It may also be used to find a set of external documents, and it may be used to find a node other than the root by using a fragment identifier in the URI.

For example, the expression «`document('data.xml')`» looks for the file `data.xml` in the same directory as the stylesheet, parses it, and returns the root node of the resulting tree.

Defined in

XSLT section 12.1

Format

```
document(uri) ⇒ number
document(uri, base-uri) ⇒ number
```

Arguments

Argument	Data type	Meaning
uri	any	Either: (a) a node-set identifying a set of nodes in the source document whose string-values are URI references, or (b) a value, which, when converted to a string, can be treated as a URI reference.
base-uri (optional)	node-set	If the argument is present, it must be a node-set. The base URI of the first node in this node-set is used for resolving any relative URI found in the first argument.

Result

The result is always a node-set.

Effect

I'll describe the rules, usage advice, and examples separately for each combination of supplied arguments.

In brief, the **document()** function locates an XML document using a URI. The resulting XML document is parsed and a tree is constructed. Whitespace-only nodes are stripped following the same rules as for the source document, based on the **<xsl:strip-space>** and **<xsl:preserve-space>** declarations in force. This is true even if the document happens to be a stylesheet. On completion, the result of the **document()** function is a node-set containing the root node of the new document.

However, first a word about URIs and URLs, which are terms I use rather freely throughout this section.

Establishing a Base URI

The XSLT specification always uses the term URI: Uniform Resource Identifier. The concept of a URI is a generalisation of the URLs (Uniform Resource Locators) that are widely used on the web today, and which are nowadays displayed on every cornflakes packet. The idea of a URI is to extend the URL mechanism, which is based on the established Domain Name System (with its hierarchic names such as www.ibm.com and www.cam.ac.uk), to allow other global naming and numbering schemes, including established ones such as ISBN book numbers and international telephone numbers. However, although URIs are a nice idea, the only ones that really work today are the familiar URLs. This is why the terms URI and URL seem to be used rather interchangeably in this section and indeed throughout the book. If you read carefully though, you'll see that I've tried to use both terms correctly.

The XSLT specification leaves it up to the implementation to decide which URI schemes it will support. In the short term, it is likely that most implementations will support conventional URLs only. However, some implementations (including any that support the TrAX API, described in Appendix F) may allow you to provide your own plug-in code to resolve other kinds of URI; in this case, the relationship between the URI supplied in the call and the document that is returned depends entirely on your own code.

A URI used as input to the **document()** function must identify an XML document. If the URI is invalid, or if it doesn't identify any resource, or if that resource is not an XML document, the specification leaves it up to the implementation to decidewhat to do: it can either report the error, or return an empty node-set.

The specification doesn't say whether the XML document must be valid, although most implementations will provide some way for the user to control whether a validating parser is used.

A URI can be relative rather than absolute. A typical example of a relative URI is `data.xml`. Such a URI is resolved (that is, converted to an absolute, globally unique URI) by interpreting it as relative to some base URI. By default, a relative URI that appears in the text of an XML document is interpreted relative to the URI of the document (or the external XML entity) that contains it, which in the case of the **`document()`** function is usually either the source document or the stylesheet. So if the relative URI `data.xml` appears in the source document, the system will try to find the file in the same directory as the source document, while if it appears in the stylesheet, the system will look in the directory containing the stylesheet. However, the **`document()`** function provides a second argument so that the base URI can be specified explicitly if required.

The expansion of relative URIs exploits the fact that in the XSLT tree model, which I described on page 56 in Chapter 2, every node has a base URI. (Don't confuse this with the namespace URI, which is quite unrelated.) By default the base URI of a node in the source document or the stylesheet will be the URI of the XML document or entity from which the node was constructed. In some cases, for example when the input comes from a DOM document, it may be difficult for the processor to determine the base URI (the concept does not exist in the DOM standard). What happens in this situation is implementor-defined. Microsoft, whose MSXML3 processor is built around their DOM implementation, have extended their DOM so it retains knowledge of the URI from which the document was loaded.

With XSLT 1.1 you can override the default rules for establishing the base URI of a node by using the **`xml:base`** attribute of an element. This attribute is defined in a W3C Recommendation called XML Base; it is intended to fulfil the same function as the **`<base>`** element in HTML. If an element has an **`xml:base`** attribute, the value of the attribute must be a URI, and this URI defines the base URI for the element itself and for all descendants of the element node, unless overridden by another **`xml:base`** attribute.

The URI specified in **`xml:base`** may itself be a relative URI, in which case it is resolved relative to the base URI of the parent of the element containing the **`xml:base`** attribute (that is, the URI that would have been the base URI of the element if it hadn't had an **`xml:base`** attribute).

With XSLT 1.1 it is also possible that the node used to establish the base URI for the **`document()`** function will be a node in a temporary tree created as the value of a variable. Normally the base URI for such a node will be the base URI of the **`<xsl:variable>`** (or **`<xsl:param>`**, or **`<xsl:with-param>`**) element that defines the temporary tree. Again, however, if an element has an **`xml:base`** attribute, that defines the base URI in the same way as for a source document.

If several calls on the **`document()`** function use the same URI (after expansion of a relative URI into an absolute URI), then the same root node is returned each time. You can tell that it's the same root node because the **`generate-id()`** function will return the same result, and because the **`count()`** function will treat the two nodes as duplicates. For example, «`count(document("a.xml") | document("a.xml"))`» should be 1.

A fragment identifier identifies a part of a resource: for example in the URL http://www.wrox.com/booklist#april2001, the fragment identifier is «april2001». In principle, a fragment identifier allows the URI to reference a node or set of nodes other than the root node of the target document; for example, the fragment identifier could be an XPointer expression containing a complex expression to select nodes within the target document. In practice though, this is all implementation-dependent. The interpretation of a fragment identifier depends on the media-type (often called MIME type) of the returned document. Implementations are not required to support any particular media types (which means they are not required to support fragment identifiers at all). The documentation of aconformant processor is supposed to say which fragment identifiers are supported, though this requirement appears to be widely neglected; I have seen little evidence of fragment identifiers being supported. (Saxon, however, supports a simple fragment identifier consisting of a name that must be the value of an `ID` attribute in the target document)..

The following sections describe the behavior of the **`document()`** function for each possible combination of arguments.

document(node-set)

Note that this includes the common case where the argument is an attribute reference, for *example* «`document(@href)`».

Rules

For a simple case such as «`document(@href)`» the result is a node-set containing one node, namely the root node of the document referenced by the **`href`** attribute.

More formally, the result is defined to be the union, for each node *N* in the supplied node-set, of the result of calling the **`document()`** function with two arguments: the first argument being the string-value of node *N*, and the second argument being a node-set with *N* as its only member. This is a recursive definition: to see what it means precisely, you'll have to read the section *document (string, node-set-2)* on page 476.

What it actually means, however, is that each of the nodes in the supplied node-set should contain a URI as its string-value. If this is a relative URI, it will be resolved relative to the base URI of that node. The base URI of a node is established using the rules given on page 467. In fact, each node in the supplied node-set could potentially have a different base URI.

This all sounds terribly complicated, but all it really means is that if the source document contains the link «`data.xml`», then the system will look for the file `data.xml` in the same directory as the source document.

In the most common case, with a call such as «`document(@href)`», the supplied node-set contains only a single node, so the result is a node-set containing a single node, namely the root node of the document whose URI is contained in the `href` attribute of the context node. If this is a relative URI it is resolved using the base URI of the element containing this attribute.

These rules also cover the case where the argument is a reference to a variable containing a temporary tree, for example:

```
<xsl:variable name="index">index.xml</xsl:variable>
<xsl:for-each select="document($index)">
. . .
</xsl:for-each>
```

In this case relative URI «index.xml» is resolved relative to the base URI of the <xsl:variable> element in the stylesheet.

Usage

The most common usage of the **document()** function is to access a document referenced from the source document, typically in an attribute such as **href**. For example, a book catalog might include links to reviews of each book, in a format such as:

```
<book>
   <review date="1999-12-28" publication="New York Times"
                             text="reviews/NYT/19991228/rev3.xml"/>
   <review date="2000-01-06" publication="Washington Post"
                             text="reviews/WPost/20000106/rev12.xml"/>
</book>
```

If you want to incorporate the text of these reviews in your output document, you can achieve this using the **document()** function. For example:

```
<xsl:template match="book">
   <xsl:for-each select="review">
      <h2>Review in <xsl:value-of select="@publication"/></h2>
      <xsl:apply-templates select="document(@text)"/>
   </xsl:for-each>
</xsl:template>
```

As the argument @text is a node-set, the result will be the root node of the document whose URI is the value of the **text** attribute, interpreted relative to the base URI of the **<review>** element, which (unless it comes from an external XML entity or is affected by an **xml:base** attribute on some ancestor node) will be the same as the URI of the source document itself.

Note that in processing the review document, exactly the same template rules are used as we used for the source document itself. There is no concept of particular template rules being tied to particular document types. If the review document uses the same element tags as the book catalog, but with different meanings, this can potentially create problems. There are two possible ways round this:

- Namespaces: use a different namespace for the book catalogue and for the review documents.

- Modes: use a different mode to process nodes in the review document, so that the **<xsl:apply-templates>** instruction above would become:

```
<xsl:apply-templates select="document(@text)" mode="review"/>
```

You might find that even if the element names are distinct, the use of modes is a good discipline for maintaining readability of your stylesheet. For more detail on modes, see **<xsl:apply-templates>** (on page 155) and **<xsl:template>** (on page 312) in Chapter 4.

Another useful approach, which helps to keep your stylesheet modular, is to include the templates for processing the review document in a separate stylesheet incorporated using **<xsl:include>**.

Example: Using the document() Function to Analyze a Stylesheet

A stylesheet is an XML document, so it can be used as the input to another stylesheet. This makes it very easy to write little tools that manipulate stylesheets. This example shows such a tool, designed to report on the hierarchic structure of the modules that make up a stylesheet.

This example uses the **document()** function to examine a stylesheet and see which stylesheet modules it incorporates using **<xsl:include>** or **<xsl:import>**. The modules referenced by **<xsl:include>** or **<xsl:import>** are fetched and processed recursively.

Source

Any stylesheet, preferably one that uses **<xsl:include>** or **<xsl:import>**. A file `dummy.xsl` is provided in the code download for the book for you to use as a sample.

Stylesheet

The stylesheet `list-includes.xsl` uses the **document()** function to access the document referenced in the **href** attribute of **<xsl:include>** or **<xsl:import>**. It then applies the same template rules to this document, recursively. Note that the root template is applied only to the initial source document, to create the HTML skeleton page.

```
<xsl:transform
 xmlns:xsl="http://www.w3.org/1999/XSL/Transform"
 version="1.0"
>

<xsl:template match="/">
  <html><body>
    <h1>Stylesheet Module Structure</h1>
    <ul>
    <xsl:apply-templates select="*/xsl:include | */xsl:import"/>
    </ul>
  </body></html>
</xsl:template>

<xsl:template match="xsl:include | xsl:import">
    <li><xsl:value-of select="concat(local-name(),'s ',@href)"/>
    <xsl:variable name="module" select="document(@href)"/>
    <ul>
    <xsl:apply-templates
        select="$module/*/xsl:include | $module/*/xsl:import"/>
    </ul>
    </li>
</xsl:template>

</xsl:transform>
```

Output

The output for the dummy.xsl stylesheet is as shown below:

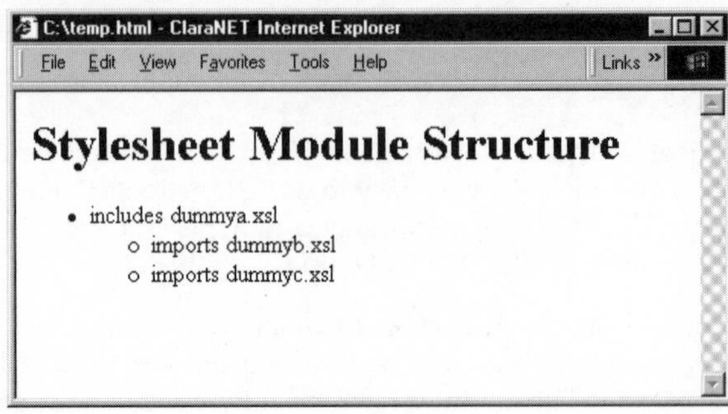

document(node-set-1, node-set-2)

This is the same as the previous case, except that instead of using the node itself as the base for resolving a relative URI, the base URI of the first node in node-set-2 is used. In other words, if a node in node-set-1 contains a relative URL such as «data.xml», the system will look for the file data.xml in the directory containing the XML document from which node-set-2 was derived.

Rules

Most commonly, node-set-2 will contain a single node. For example, the call «document(@href, /)» will use the root node of the source document as the base URI, even if the element containing the **href** attribute was found in an external entity with a different URI.

More formally, the result is defined to be the union, for each node *N* in the supplied node-set-1, of the result of calling the **document()** function with two arguments: the first argument being the string-value of node *N*, and the second argument being node-set-2. This of course is a recursive definition – to find out what it means, you have to read the section *document (string, node-set-2)* on page 476.

It is an error if node-set-2 is empty. The XSLT processor will either report this as a fatal error, or will recover by returning an empty node-set.

Usage

This option is not one you will need to use very often, but it is there for completeness.

If you want to interpret a URI relative to the stylesheet, you can write, for example:

```
document(@href, document(''))
```

This works because the second argument returns the root node of the stylesheet, which is then used as the base URI for the relative URI contained in the **href** attribute.

document(string)

This format is used when there is a single argument and it is not a node-set. The most common case is a URL hard-coded in the stylesheet, for example «`document('tax-rates.xml')`».

A common special case is «`document('')`», which refers to the stylesheet itself.

Rules

If the argument is not a string, it is converted to a string using the rules of the **`string()`** function – but since converting a Boolean or number is unlikely to yield a useful URL, the point is rather academic.

The string is treated as a URI reference. If it is a relative URI, it is treated as being relative to the base URI of the stylesheet element that contains the expression in which the function call was encountered. This will normally be the URI of the principal stylesheet document , but it may be different if **`<xsl:include>`** or **`<xsl:import>`** was used, or if pieces of the stylesheet are contained in external XML entities, or (with XSLT 1.1) if the base URI of any relevant element in the stylesheet has been set explicitly by using the **`xml:base`** attribute.

Again, all this really means is that relative URLs are handled just like relative URLs in HTML: if you write «`document('tax-rates.xml')`» in a particular stylesheet module, then the system looks for the file `tax-rates.xml` in the same directory as that stylesheet module.

If the string is an empty string, then the document referenced by the base URI is used. The XSLT specification states that «`document('')`» will return the root node of the stylesheet. Strictly speaking, however, this is only true if the base URI of the XSL element containing the call to the **`document()`** function is the same as the system identifier of the stylesheet module. If the base URI is different, perhaps because the stylesheet has been built up from a number of external entities, or because (with XSLT 1.1) the **`xml:base`** attribute has been used, the object loaded by «`document('')`» will not necessarily be the current stylesheet module; in fact, it might not be a well-formed document at all, in which case an error will be reported.

If the call is contained in a stylesheet brought in using **`<xsl:include>`** or **`<xsl:import>`**, it returns the root node of the included or imported stylesheet, not that of the principal stylesheet document.

Usage

With XSLT 1.0, this form of the **`document()`** function is very useful for handling data used by the stylesheet for reference information: for example, lookup tables to expand abbreviations, message files in different languages, or the text of the message of the day, to be displayed to users on the login screen. Such data can either be in the stylesheet itself (referenced as «`document('')`»), or in a separate file held in the same directory as the stylesheet (referenced as «`document('messages.xml')`») or a related directory (for example «`document('../data/messages.xml')`».

With XSLT 1.1 as currently defined, it is no longer necessary to use a secondary document for these purposes, because the data can be held in a tree-valued variable in the stylesheet and accessed directly. However, it may in some cases be more convenient to maintain the data in a separate file (for example, it makes it easier to generate the data periodically from a database), and in any case you may still want to write stylesheets that work with XSLT 1.0 processors, especially if you want the transformation to happen client-side. So I'll show the XSLT 1.0 technique first, and then show how the same problem can be tackled in XSLT 1.1.

XSLT allows data such as look-up tables to appear within any top-level stylesheet element, provided it belongs to a non-default namespace.

Example: a Lookup Table in the Stylesheet

Source

This is the `booklist.xml` file we saw earlier:

```
<booklist>
<book category="S">
     <title>Number, the Language of Science</title>
     <author>Danzig</author>
</book>
<book category="FC">
     <title>The Young Visiters</title>
     <author>Daisy Ashford</author>
</book>
<book category="FC">
     <title>When We Were Very Young</title>
     <author>A. A. Milne</author>
</book>
<book category="CS">
     <title>Design Patterns</title>
     <author>Erich Gamma</author>
     <author>Richard Helm</author>
     <author>Ralph Johnson</author>
     <author>John Vlissides</author>
</book>
</booklist>
```

Stylesheet

The stylesheet is `list-categories.xsl`. It processes each of the **<book>** elements in the source file and, for each one, finds the **<book:category>** element in the stylesheet whose code attribute matches the category attribute of the **<book>**. Note the use of **current()** to refer to the current book; it would be wrong to use «.» here, because «.» refers to the context node, which is the **<book:category>** element being tested.

```
<xsl:transform
 xmlns:xsl="http://www.w3.org/1999/XSL/Transform"
 version="1.0"
 xmlns:book="books.uri"
 exclude-result-prefixes="book"
>

<xsl:template match="/">
  <html><body>
    <xsl:for-each select="//book">
```

```
<h1><xsl:value-of select="title"/></h1>
      <p>Category: <xsl:value-of
                select="document('')/*/book:category
                [@code=current()/@category]/@desc"/>
      </p>
    </xsl:for-each>
  </body></html>
</xsl:template>

<book:category code="S" desc="Science"/>
<book:category code="CS" desc="Computing"/>
<book:category code="FC" desc="Children's Fiction"/>

</xsl:transform>
```

Output

```
<html>
   <body>
      <h1>Number, the Language of Science</h1>
      <p>Category: Science</p>
      <h1>The Young Visiters</h1>
      <p>Category: Children's Fiction</p>
      <h1>When We Were Very Young</h1>
      <p>Category: Children's Fiction</p>
      <h1>Design Patterns</h1>
      <p>Category: Computing</p>
   </body>
</html>
```


XSLT 1.1 Stylesheet

Now let's modify this stylesheet to take advantage of XSLT 1.1 facilities. It's renamed `list-categories1_1.xsl`. It isn't a big change; the lines that are different are shown with a shaded background.

```
<xsl:transform
 xmlns:xsl="http://www.w3.org/1999/XSL/Transform"
 version="1.1"
 xmlns:book="books.uri"
 exclude-result-prefixes="book"
>

<xsl:template match="/">
  <html><body>
    <xsl:for-each select="//book">
       <h1><xsl:value-of select="title"/></h1>
       <p>Category: <xsl:value-of
                 select="$categories/category

[@code=current()/@category]/@desc"/>
       </p>
    </xsl:for-each>
  </body></html>
</xsl:template>

<xsl:variable name="categories">
  <category code="S" desc="Science"/>
  <category code="CS" desc="Computing"/>
  <category code="FC" desc="Children's Fiction"/>
</xsl:variable>

</xsl:transform>
```

document(string, node-set-2)

This format is used when there are two arguments and the first argument is **not** a node-set. (For this purpose, a temporary tree counts as a node-set, even in XSLT 1.0.)

Rules

If the first argument is not a string, it is converted to a string using the rules of the **`string()`** function. But since the only other possibilities are a Boolean or a number, this is unlikely to be useful in practice.

The second argument will normally be a node-set containing a single node: if it contains more than one node, only the first node (in document order) is taken into account. It is not defined what happens if the node-set is empty.

The string is treated as a URI. If it is a relative URI, it is treated as being relative to the base URI of the first node in node-set-2.

Usage

You won't need to use this format very often, but it is there for completeness. With XSLT 1.1 it is just as convenient to specify the base URI using the **`xml:base`** attribute.

Note: Using keys and ids in Another Document

The functions **`key()`** and **`id()`** always return nodes in the same document as the context node. It is not possible to retrieve nodes in another document by using an expression such as:

```
<!-WRONG-->
<xsl:value-of select="document('a.xml')/key('k1', 'val1')"/>
<!-WRONG-->
```

Instead, the most convenient way to achieve the required effect is to change the context node using **<xsl:for-each>**, like this:

```
<xsl:for-each select="document('a.xml')">
   <xsl:value-of select="key('k1', 'val1')"/>
</xsl:for-each>
```

See also

`id()` on page 496
`key()` on page 499

element-available

This function is used to test whether a particular XSLT instruction or extension element is available for use.

For example, the expression «`element-available('xsl:text')`» returns `true`.

Defined in

XSLT section 15

Format

```
element-available(name) ⇒  boolean
```

Arguments

Argument	Data type	Meaning
name	string	The name of the element being tested. If the value is not a string, it will be converted to a string using the rules for the **string()** function. The resulting string must take the form of a QName.

Result

A Boolean value: true if the named element is available for use as an instruction in a template, false otherwise.

Rules

The first argument must take the form of a QName: that is, an XML name with an optional namespace prefix that corresponds to a namespace declaration that is in scope at the point in the stylesheet where the **element-available()** function is called.

If this namespace declaration identifies the XSLT namespace http://www.w3.org/1999/XSL/Transform, then the function returns true if the name is the name of an XSLT-defined *instruction*, and false otherwise. The instructions defined in XSLT version 1.0 are as follows:

```
<xsl:apply-imports>          <xsl:fallback>
<xsl:apply-templates>        <xsl:for-each>
<xsl:attribute>              <xsl:if>
<xsl:call-template>          <xsl:message>
<xsl:choose>                 <xsl:number>
<xsl:comment>                <xsl:processing-instruction>
<xsl:copy>                   <xsl:text>
<xsl:copy-of>                <xsl:value-of>
<xsl:element>                <xsl:variable>
```

In the XSLT 1.1 working draft, one new instruction is added to this list, namely **<xsl:document>**.

Instructions are XSLT elements that can appear directly within a template body. Top-level XSLT elements such as **<xsl:template>** and **<xsl:key>** are not instructions, so they should return false (but don't rely on it: at least one popular processor, Microsoft's MSXML3, seems to return true for all XSLT elements). The same applies to elements such as **<xsl:param>**, **<xsl:with-param>**, **<xsl:sort>**, **<xsl:when>**, and **<xsl:otherwise>**, that can only appear in specific contexts and not anywhere in a template body.

You can test to see whether the new XSLT 1.1 facility to produce multiple output documents is available by testing `element-available('xsl:document')`. If it isn't available, you can use an alternative approach: for example, you can use the proprietary syntax for this functionality offered by your chosen XSLT 1.0 processor.

It's best illustrated by an example.

Example: Creating Multiple Output Files

This example takes a poem as input, and outputs each stanza to a separate file. A more realistic example would be to split a book into its chapters, but I wanted to keep the files small. The example is written to work with the Saxon and also with any processor that conforms to the draft XSLT 1.1 specification.

Source

The source file is `poem.xml`. It starts:

```
<poem>
<author>Rupert Brooke</author>
<date>1912</date>
<title>Song</title>
<stanza>
<line>And suddenly the wind comes soft,</line>
<line>And Spring is here again;</line>
<line>And the hawthorn quickens with buds of green</line>
<line>And my heart with buds of pain.</line>
</stanza>
<stanza>
<line>My heart all Winter lay so numb,</line>
<line>The earth so dead and frore,</line>
. . .
```

Stylesheet

The stylesheet is in file `split.xsl`. The part to look at is the **`<xsl:choose>`** instruction, where each branch calls **`element-available()`** to test whether a particular instruction is available, before calling that instruction.

Note that «`saxon`» is defined as an extension element prefix, so the **`<saxon:output>`** element is recognised as an instruction. The **`<xsl:stylesheet>`** element specifies «`version="1.1"`» so that an XSLT 1.0 processor will not reject **`<xsl:document>`** as an error.

```
<?xml version="1.0"?>
<xsl:stylesheet xmlns:xsl="http://www.w3.org/1999/XSL/Transform"
    version="1.1">

<xsl:template match="poem">
    <poem>
        <xsl:copy-of select="title"/>
        <xsl:copy-of select="author"/>
        <xsl:copy-of select="date"/>
        <xsl:apply-templates select="stanza"/>
    </poem>
</xsl:template>
<xsl:template match="stanza">
    <xsl:variable name="file"
```

```
select="concat('verse', position(), '.xml')"/>
    <verse number="{position()}" href="{$file}"/>
    <xsl:choose>
    <xsl:when test="element-available('xsl:document')">
        <xsl:document href="{$file}">
            <xsl:copy-of select="."/>
        </xsl:document>
    </xsl:when>
    <xsl:when test="element-available('saxon:output')"
            xmlns:saxon="http://icl.com/saxon">
        <saxon:output file="{$file}"
            xsl:extension-element-prefixes="saxon">
            <xsl:copy-of select="."/>
        </saxon:output>
    </xsl:when>
    <xsl:otherwise>
        <xsl:message terminate="yes"
             >Cannot write to multiple output files</xsl:message>
    </xsl:otherwise>
    </xsl:choose>
</xsl:template>

</xsl:stylesheet>
```

Output

Provided the stylesheet is run with one of the processors that supports the required capability, the principal output file will contain the skeletal poem below (new lines added for legibility):

```
<?xml version="1.0" encoding="utf-8" ?>
<poem>
<title>Song</title>
<author>Rupert Brooke</author>
<date>1912</date>
<verse number="1" href="verse1.xml"/>
<verse number="2" href="verse2.xml"/>
<verse number="3" href="verse3.xml"/>
</poem>
```

Three further output files `verse1.xml`, `verse2.xml`, and `verse3.xml` are created in the current directory. Here is `verse1.xml`:

```
<?xml version="1.0" encoding="utf-8" ?>
<stanza>
<line>And suddenly the wind comes soft,</line>
<line>And Spring is here again;</line>
<line>And the hawthorn quickens with buds of green</line>
<line>And my heart with buds of pain.</line>
</stanza>
```

You can't use **`element-available()`** to test whether the XSLT 1.1 element **`<xsl:script>`** is available, because this is a top-level element, and a conformant XSLT 1.1 processor should therefore return `false`, the same result as an XSLT 1.0 processor. If you use this element in an XSLT 1.0 stylesheet, an error will be reported if you specify «`version="1.0"`» on the **`<xsl:stylesheet>`** element, but if you specify «`version="1.1"`» the **`<xsl:script>`** element will be ignored, under the rules for forwards-compatible processing. If you also invoke an alternative vendor-specified way of selecting extension functions, the stylesheet will probably work with both XSLT 1.0 and XSLT 1.1 processors.

If the prefix of the QName identifies any namespace other than the XSLT namespace, then the function returns true if and only if the XSLT processor has an implementation available for the named instruction: that is, if this element can be used as an instruction in a template, rather than being treated simply as a literal result element.

Note that the result of the **element-available()** function does not depend on whether the namespace has been designated an extension namespace by using the **[xsl:]extension-element-prefixes** attribute. If the XSLT processor has an implementation of the instruction available, the function should return true whether or not it is currently in a designated extension namespace.

If the QName has no prefix, the default namespace is used. This is one of the few cases where this happens, and the reason is that the name is always an element name: the default namespace applies only to elements.

However, if the QName expands to a name with a null namespace URI, the result of the function will always be false. This is because both XSLT instructions and extension elements will always have a non-null namespace URI.

Usage

There are two ways of using this function: it can be used to test for XSLT elements introduced in a later version of XSLT, and it can be used to test for the presence of vendor or third-party extensions.

Testing for Features Available in Later XSLT Versions

The ability to test whether a particular XSLT instruction is available was introduced in XSLT 1.0, but it only becomes useful now that version 1.1 of the specification is available. It was intended to come into its own when later versions of the specification introduced new instructions. As we've seen, the draft XSLT 1.1 specification only introduces one new instruction, **<xsl:document>**. (Recall that **<xsl:script>** is not an instruction, because it cannot be used in a template body.) If you want to use an instruction such as **<xsl:document>** that only became available in a particular version of XSLT, then you can test to see whether it is available with your chosen XSLT processor before using it. If it is not available, you can either use **<xsl:if>** to avoid executing it, or use the **<xsl:fallback>** mechanism to cope with its absence.

So why was the function specified as part of version 1.0? The answer is obvious when you think about it: you want to write a stylesheet that uses version 2.0 features, so you call **element-available()** in order to fail gracefully if you're running with an XSLT processor that only supports version 1.0 or 1.1 features. However, this will only work if the version 1.0 or 1.1 XSLT processor supports the **element-available()** function, which is why it was specified from the start. This is an unusually thoughtful piece of forward planning: the XSLT designers didn't want to get into the same kind of forwards-compatibility problems that have bedeviled HTML. Of course, it still means that if you want your stylesheet to run with XSLT processors that support different levels of the language you will have to write and test conditional code in your stylesheet but at least the capability is there.

In principle, you can test whether a version 1.0 instruction is available on the basis that there may be subset implementations around; unfortunately this will only work if the subset implementation includes the **element-available()** function, which is not guaranteed; it tends to be one of the things that implementors leave till last.

Note that if you write a stylesheet that uses features in XSLT version 2.0, say, and if you want to run it with an XSLT 1.0 processor, then you must specify «`version="2.0"`» on the **<xsl:stylesheet>** element, or «`xsl:version="2.0"`» on some literal result element, even if you write an **<xsl:if>** test using **element-available()** to avoid executing the relevant code. If you specify «`version="1.0"`», then any use of new XSLT 2.0 elements is flagged as an error even if the code is never executed.

Testing for Vendor Extensions

The second way of using the function is to test for vendor or third-party extensions. If you know that a particular extension element is present in some implementations and not others, you can use the **element-available()** test to see whether it is present at run-time, and again use either **<xsl:if>** or **<xsl:fallback>** to handle the situation when it isn't.

For example, the Saxon product provides an extension element to output an entity reference. If you're not using Saxon, you can achieve the same effect by using `disable-output-escaping`. So to output «` `» you could write:

```
<xsl:choose xmlns:saxon="http://icl.com/saxon">
<xsl:when test="element-available('saxon:entity-ref')">
    <saxon:entity-ref name="nbsp"
                          xsl:extension-element-prefixes="saxon"/>
</xsl:when>
<xsl:otherwise>
    <xsl:text disable-output-escaping="yes">&amp;nbsp;</xsl:text>
</xsl:otherwise>
</xsl:choose>
```

An alternative to using the **element-available()** function is to use the **<xsl:fallback>** mechanism described in Chapter 4, page 214: an **<xsl:fallback>** element allows you to define what processing should occur if its containing instruction isn't available. The two mechanisms are essentially equivalent, though a possible limitation of **<xsl:fallback>** is that it can only be used within an element that permits element children: it could not be used, for example, within **<xsl:copy-of>** as currently defined.

Examples

The following code defines a template that can be called to set a debugging breakpoint. It relies on a hypothetical **<xsl:breakpoint>** instruction introduced in XSLT version 37.1. If the stylesheet is executed with an XSLT processor that does not support this feature, it will ignore the request and continue.

```
<xsl:stylesheet
         xmlns:xsl="http://www.w3.org/1999/XSL/Transform"
         version="38.0">
<xsl:template name="set-breakpoint">
   <xsl:if test="element-available('xsl:breakpoint')">
      <xsl:breakpoint/>
   </xsl:if>

</xsl:template>
</xsl:stylesheet>
```

Note that if the **version** attribute on the **<xsl:stylesheet>** element were set to "1.0", this stylesheet would be rejected. With **version** set to any value other than "1.0", *forwards-compatible-mode* is enabled, and the implementation is not allowed to signal **<xsl:breakpoint>** as an error unless the instruction is actually instantiated. (With XSLT 1.1, forwards-compatible mode is activated if the version is a value other than "1.0" or "1.1".) Forwards-compatible mode is described in Chapter 3, on page 137.

See also

function-available() on page 487
<xsl:fallback> in Chapter 4, page 214

false

This function returns the Boolean value `false`.

Defined in

XPath section 4.3

Format

```
false() ⇒ boolean
```

Arguments

None

Result

The Boolean value `false`.

Usage

There are no Boolean constants available in XPath expressions, so the functions **true()** and **false()** can be used where a constant Boolean value is required.

In practice, constant Boolean values are not often required: perhaps the most common usage is when passing a parameter to a template.

Writing «`<xsl:if test="false()">`» can be useful as a temporary expedient to comment out a section of code in a stylesheet. XML comments are not ideal for this purpose because they cannot be nested.

Example

The following code calls a named template, setting the parameter «`verbose`» to `false`:

```
<xsl:call-template name="do-the-work">
   <xsl:with-param name="verbose" select="false()"/>
</xsl:call-template>
```

See also

`true()` on page 562

floor

The **`floor()`** function returns the largest integer that is less than or equal to the numeric value of the argument.

For example, the expression «`floor(11.3)`» returns 11.

Defined in

XPath section 4.4

Format

```
floor(value)      number
```

Arguments

Argument	Data type	Meaning
value	number	The input value. If it is not of type number, it is first converted to a number using the rules for the **`number()`** function.

Result

An integer value: the result of converting the first argument to a number and then rounding down, if necessary, to the integer below.

Rules

If the value is not numeric, it is first converted to a number. For the detailed rules, see the description of the **`number()`** function on page 531. If the value is a node-set, these rules mean that the function applies to the value of the first node in the node-set, in document order.

If the number is an integer, it is returned unchanged. Otherwise, it is rounded down to the integer below.

If the argument is NaN (not a number), which will happen if a string is supplied that cannot be converted to a number, the result is NaN. Similarly, when the argument is positive or negative infinity, the value of the argument is returned unchanged. Details of these special numeric values are given on page 89, in Chapter 2.

Usage and Examples

The result of this function is illustrated by the following examples:

```
floor(1.0) = 1.0
floor(1.6) = 1.0
floor(17 div 3) = 5.0
floor(-3.0) = -3.0
floor(-8.2) = -9.0
```

See also

ceiling() on page 454
round() on page 537

format-number

The **format-number()** function is used to convert numbers into strings for display to a human user. It is also useful when converting to legacy formats that require a number to occupy a fixed number of character positions. The format of the result is controlled using the **<xsl:decimal-format>** element.

For example, the expression «`format-number(12.5, '$#.00')`» returns the string «`$12.50`».

Defined in

XSLT section 12.3.

The effect of the function is defined by reference to the Java JDK 1.1 specifications; I have extracted the relevant information for ease of reference.

Format

```
format-number(value, format)  ⇒  string
format-number(value, format, name)  ⇒  number
```

Arguments

Argument	Data type	Meaning
value	number	The input value. If it is not of type number, it is first converted to a number using the rules for the **number()** function.
format	string	A format pattern. If it is not of type string, it is first converted to a string using the rules for the **string()** function.
name optional	string	The name (a `QName`) of a decimal format, established using the **<xsl:decimal-format>** element. If the argument is omitted, the default decimal format is used.

Result

A string value; the result of formatting the first argument using the format pattern supplied in the second argument, applying the rules defined in the decimal format named in the third argument if there is one, or the default decimal format otherwise.

Rules

The decimal-format Name

The third argument, if it is present, must take the form of a `QName`; that is, an XML name optionally prefixed with a namespace prefix that corresponds to a namespace declaration that is in scope at the point in the stylesheet where the **`format-number()`** function is called. There must be an **`<xsl:decimal-format>`** element in the stylesheet with the same expanded name, using the namespace URIs rather than prefixes in the comparison.

If the third argument is omitted, the default decimal format is used. A default decimal format can be established for a stylesheet by including an **`<xsl:decimal-format>`** element with no name. If there is no unnamed **`<xsl:decimal-format>`** element in the stylesheet, the system uses a built-in default format which is the same as specifying an **`<xsl:decimal-format>`** with no attributes.

The Format Pattern

The rules for the format pattern string are defined in XSLT by reference to the Java JDK 1.1 specification.

The structure of the format pattern is as follows, using the same syntax conventions as in Chapter 5, *Expressions*:

pattern	`subpattern ( pattern-separator subpattern )?`
subpattern	`prefix? integer ( decimal-point fraction )? suffix?`
prefix	`[#x0 - #xFFFD] - specialCharacters`
suffix	`[#x0 - #xFFFD] - specialCharacters`
integer	`digit* zero-digit* zero-digit` (but also allowing a `grouping-separator` to appear)
fraction	`zero-digit* digit*`
pattern-separator	«`;`» (by default)
decimal-point	«`.`» (by default)
grouping-separator	«`,`» (by default)
digit	«`#`» (by default)
zero-digit	«`0`» (by default)
specialCharacters	see table below

In these syntax rules, the characters shown as «;», «.», «,», «#», and «0» are the default representations of `pattern-separator`, `decimal-point`, `grouping-separator`, `digit`, and `zero-digit`. If the relevant **`<xsl:decimal-format>`** element nominates different characters in these roles, the nominated character is used in its place in the format pattern.

The first `subpattern` is for positive numbers. The second (optional) `subpattern` is for negative numbers.

The special characters used are as follows:

Special character	Meaning
`zero-digit` (default «0»)	A digit will always appear at this point in the result string.
`digit` (default «#»)	A digit will appear at this point in the result string unless it is a redundant leading or trailing zero.
`decimal-point` (default «.»)	Separates the integer and the fraction part of the number.
`grouping-separator` (default «,»)	Separates groups of digits.
`pattern-separator` (default «;»)	Separates the positive and negative format sub-patterns.
`minus-sign` (default «-»)	Minus sign.
`percent-sign` (default «%»)	Multiplies the number by 100 and show it as a percentage.
`per-mille` (default «‰»)	Multiplies by 1000 and show as per-mille.
`apostrophe` («'»)	Quotes any special characters used in the pattern to give them their ordinary meaning. For example, if you want to output «9» as «#9», set the format pattern to «'#'0».

If there is no explicit negative subpattern, «-» is prefixed to the positive form. That is, «0.00» alone is equivalent to «0.00;-0.00». If there is an explicit negative subpattern, it serves only to specify the negative prefix and suffix; the number of digits, minimal digits, and other characteristics are all the same as the positive pattern. That means that «#,##0.0#;(#)» has precisely the same result as «#,##0.0#;(#,##0.0#)».

The XSLT specification specifically references the JDK 1.1 specification for its definition of patterns. Some additional special characters were defined in decimal format patterns after the initial release of the JDK 1.1 specification: notably «¤» (the international currency sign #xA4), and «E», the exponent character, used for output in scientific notation. While the specification is clear that an XSLT processor isn't required to support these special characters, neither does it say that it must treat them as errors. If you're using a processor written in Java, it's actually quite likely that the way these characters are interpreted will vary depending on which specific Java VM you are using.

The grouping separator is commonly used for thousands, but in some countries for ten-thousands. The number of digits per group in the output string will be equal to the number of digits in the pattern between the last grouping separator and the end of the integer: any other grouping separators in the format pattern are ignored. For example, if you write «#,##,###,####» there will be a grouping separator every four digits.

It is not defined what happens if the format pattern is invalid. This means the implementation is free either to report an error or to display the number in some fallback representation.

Usage

Note that this facility for formatting numbers is completely separate from the facilities available through the **<xsl:number>** element. There is some overlapping functionality, but the syntax of the format patterns is quite unrelated. The **format-number()** function formats a single number, which need not be an integer. **<xsl:number>** is primarily designed to format a list of positive integers. For formatting a single positive integer, either facility can be used.

Examples

The following example shows the result of **format-number()** using the default decimal format. Examples with non-default decimal formats are shown under the **<xsl:decimal-format>** element in Chapter 4, page 199.

Number	Format Pattern	Result
1234.5	#,##0.00	1,234.50
123.456	#,##0.00	123.46
1000000	#,##0.00	1,000,000.00
-59	#,##0.00	-59.00
1 div 0	#,##0.00	Infinity
1234	###0.0###	1234.0
1234.5	###0.0###	1234.5
.00035	###0.0###	0.0004
0.25	#00%	25%
0.736	#00%	74%
1	#00%	100%
-42	#00%	-4200%
-3.12	#.00;(#.00)	(3.12)
-3.12	#.00;#.00CR	3.12CR

See also

<xsl:decimal-format> on page 199 in Chapter 4.

function-available

This function is used to test whether a particular function is available for use. It can be used to test the availability both of standard system functions and of extension functions.

For example, the expression «function-available('concat')» returns true.

Defined in

XSLT section 15

Format

```
function-available(name)  ⇒  boolean
```

Arguments

Argument	Data type	Meaning
name	string	The name of the function being tested. If the value is not a string, it will be converted to a string using the rules for the **`string()`** function. The resulting string must take the form of a `QName`.

Result

A Boolean value: `true` if the named function is available to be called, `false` otherwise.

Rules

The argument must take the form of a `QName`: that is, an XML name, with an optional namespace prefix that corresponds to a namespace declaration that is in scope at the point in the stylesheet where the **`function-available()`** function is called.

If there is no prefix, or if the namespace URI is null, the call tests whether there is a system function with the specified name. The system functions are those defined in the XPath and XSLT Recommendations (and thus in this chapter); vendors are not allowed to supply additional functions in this default namespace, nor are they allowed to omit any. So an XSLT processor that conforms to XSLT version 1.0 will return `true` if the name is one of the following, and `false` otherwise.

boolean	**generate-id**	**round**
ceiling	**id**	**starts-with**
concat	**key**	**string**
contains	**lang**	**string-length**
count	**last**	**substring**
current	**local-name**	**substring-after**
document	**name**	**substring-before**
element-available	**namespace-uri**	**sum**
false	**normalize-space**	**system-property**
floor	**not**	**translate**
format-number	**number**	**true**
function-available	**position**	**unparsed-entity-uri**

The draft XSLT 1.1 specification introduces no new functions. But suppose XSLT 2.0 introduced a function called **`distinct()`**. Then you could test whether this function is supported in your XSLT processor by writing:

```
<xsl:if test="function-available('distinct')">
```

If the QName includes a non-null namespace, the XSLT processor returns true if there is an extension function available with the given name. In general, if **function-available()** returns false then you are safe in assuming that a call on the function would fail, and if it returns true, then there will be some way of calling the function successfully. There is, however, no way of finding out at run-time how many arguments the function expects, or what their data types should be: it still relies on you calling the function with the right arguments.

Usage

There are two ways of using **function-available()**: it can be used to achieve backwards compatibility when using standard functions defined after version 1.0 of the specification, and it can be used to test for the presence of vendor or third-party extensions.

Testing for the Existence of System-defined Functions

The ability to test whether a particular system-defined function is available is not especially useful with version 1.0 of the specification. It was designed to come into its own when later versions of the specification were published. If you want to use a function that is newly defined in version 1.1 of XSLT, then you can test to see whether it is available with a particular XSLT processor before using it. If it is not available, you can use **<xsl:if>** to avoid executing it. Provided that you enable *forwards-compatible mode* by setting the **version** attribute on the **<xsl:stylesheet>** element to a value other than "1.0" (or "1.1" if you are using an XSLT 1.1 processor), the XSLT processor will not object to the presence of an expression in your stylesheet that calls an unknown function, unless the expression is actually executed.

For example, suppose that a function **schema-data-type()** becomes available at version 2.0 of the XSLT specification, allowing you to test the data type of a node, as defined in the schema for the source document. Then you could test for its existence by writing:

```
<xsl:if test="function-available('schema-data-type')>
```

For a fuller example, see the end of this section.

> *You can't always tell when an expression is going to be executed, for example if it is used as a predicate in a pattern or as the use expression in a key definition. You can, however, make sure that it* won't *be executed, by enclosing it inside an* **<xsl:if>** *statement that calls* **function-available()**.

Note that it is the XSLT version that is relevant, not the XPath version. XSLT 1.0 and XSLT 1.1 both reference XPath 1.0. It is reasonable to assume that when a new version of XPath is published, the XSLT specification will be updated to reference it, though this does not necessarily mean that the version numbers will always be synchronized.

In principle you can use **function-available()** to test whether a version 1.0 function is available, on the basis that there may be subset implementations around: unfortunately this only works if the **function-available()** function forms part of the subset that the vendor has chosen to implement.

Testing for Vendor or Third-party Extensions

The second way of using **function-available()** is to test for vendor or third-party extensions. If you know that a particular extension function is present in some implementations and not others, you can use the **function-available()** test to see whether it is present, and use **<xsl:if>** to handle the situation when it isn't.

Examples

The XSLT 1.1 working draft allows you to use a temporary tree (the value constructed when an **<xsl:variable>** element is not empty) in any context where a node-set can be used. This feature is not available in XSLT 1.0, which handles temporary trees as a distinct data type, known as a result tree fragment. Many vendors have filled the gap by allowing a temporary tree to be converted to a node-set using an extension function (for example **xt:node-set()** or **msxml:node-set()**). If you want to write a stylesheet that is as portable as possible, you therefore need to write code that discovers which of these facilities is available.

The following stylesheet contains a named template that takes a temporary tree as a parameter, and calls **<xsl:apply-templates>** to process its root node in a particular mode. When running with an XSLT 1.1 processor, it does this simply by passing the tree to **<xsl:apply-templates>** directly; in other cases, it tries to determine whether one of the proprietary **node-set()** extension functions is available, and uses that.

```
<xsl:stylesheet
         xmlns:xsl="http://www.w3.org/1999/XSL/Transform"
         version="1.1">
<xsl:template name="process-tree-fragment"
         xmlns:msxml="urn:schemas-microsoft-com:xslt"
         xmlns:xt="http://www.jclark.com/xt"
         xmlns:saxon=" http://icl.com/saxon">
   <xsl:param name="fragment"/>
   <xsl:choose>
   <xsl:when test="system-property('xsl:version') &gt; 1.0">
      <xsl:apply-templates mode="process-fragment"
                           select="$fragment"/>
   </xsl:when>

   <xsl:when test="function-available('msxml:node-set')">
      <xsl:apply-templates mode="process-fragment"
                           select="msxml:node-set($fragment)"/>
   </xsl:when>
   <xsl:when test="function-available('xt:node-set')">
     <xsl:apply-templates mode="process-fragment"
                           select="xt:node-set($fragment)"/>
   </xsl:when>
   <xsl:when test="function-available('saxon:node-set')">
     <xsl:apply-templates mode="process-fragment"
                           select="saxon:node-set($fragment)"/>
   </xsl:when>
   <xsl:otherwise>
   <xsl:message terminate="yes">
      Cannot convert result tree fragment to node-set
   </xsl:message>
   </xsl:otherwise>
   </xsl:choose>
</xsl:template>
</xsl:stylesheet>
```

This named template can be called as follows, to process all the nodes in the result tree fragment:

```
<xsl:variable name="the-node-set">
   <xsl:call-template name="process-tree-fragment">
      <xsl:with-param name="fragment" select="$supplied-fragment"/>
   </xsl:call-template>
</xsl:variable>
```

See also

element-available() on page 476

generate-id

The **generate-id()** function generates a string, in the form of an XML Name, that uniquely identifies a node. The only guarantee about the result is that it is different for every node.

For example, the expression «generate-id(..)» might return the string «N015732» when using one XSLT processor, and «b23a1c79» when using another.

Defined in

XSLT section 12.4

Format

```
generate-id()  ⇒  string
generate-id(node)  ⇒  string
```

Arguments

Argument	Data type	Meaning
node (optional)	node-set	The input node-set (only the first node in the document order is considered). If the argument is omitted, a node-set containing only the context node is used.

Result

A string value that uniquely identifies the node. This will consist only of ASCII alphanumeric characters, and the first character will be alphabetic. This makes the identifier suitable for use in many contexts, for example as an XML Name.

Rules

If the argument is an empty node-set, the function returns an empty string.

If the input node-set contains more than one node, the target node is the one that is first in document order.

If the argument is omitted, the target node is the context node.

The function returns an arbitrary string: the only constraints are that it will always return the same string for the same node, and that it will always return different strings for different nodes. This includes the case where the nodes are in different documents.

The generated identifiers are unique within a single execution of the stylesheet. If the same stylesheet is used several times, with the same or different source documents, it may generate the same identifiers in each run but is under no obligation to do so.

Usage and Examples

We'll look at two useful ways of exploiting the **`generate-id()`** function; using it to create links in the output document, and using it to compare nodes for identity.

Using generate-id() to Create Links

An important role of the **`generate-id()`** function is to create links in the output document. For example, it can be used to generate ID and IDREF attributes in an output XML document, or `<a name="X">` and `<a href="#X">` pairs in an output HTML document.

Example: Using generate-id() to Create Links

This example takes as input a file `resorts.xml` containing details of a collection of holiday resorts, each of which includes a list of hotels.

Source

```
<resorts>
   <resort>
      <name>Amsterdam</name>
      <details>A wordy description of Amsterdam</details>
      <hotel>
         <name>Grand Hotel</name>
         <stars>5</stars>
         <address> . . . </address>
      </hotel>
      <hotel>
         <name>Less Grand Hotel</name>
         <stars>2</stars>
         <address> . . . </address>
      </hotel>
   </resort>
   <resort>
      <name>Bruges</name>
      <details>An eloquent description of Bruges</details>
      <hotel>
         <name>Central Hotel</name>
         <stars>5</stars>
         <address> . . . </address>
      </hotel>
      <hotel>
         <name>Peripheral Hotel</name>
         <stars>2</stars>
         <address> . . . </address>
      </hotel>
   </resort>
</resorts>
```

Stylesheet

The stylesheet `resorts.xsl` constructs an output HTML page in which the hotels are listed first, followed by information about the resorts. Each hotel entry contains a hyperlink to the relevant resort details. The links for the resorts are generated using **`generate-id()`** applied to the **`<resort>`** element.

This is a complete stylesheet that uses the *Simplified Stylesheet* syntax introduced on page 113, in Chapter 3:

```
<html
 xmlns:xsl="http://www.w3.org/1999/XSL/Transform"
 xsl:version="1.0"
>

<body>
   <h1>Hotels</h1>
   <xsl:for-each select="//hotel">
   <xsl:sort select="stars"
                         order="descending" data-type="number"/>
      <h2><xsl:value-of select="name"/></h2>
      <p>Address: <xsl:value-of select="address"/></p>
      <p>Stars: <xsl:value-of select="stars"/></p>
      <p>Resort: <a href="#{generate-id(parent::resort)}">
            <xsl:value-of select="parent::resort/name"/></a></p>
   </xsl:for-each>

   <h1>Resorts</h1>
   <xsl:for-each select="//resort">
      <h2><a name="{generate-id()}">
         <xsl:value-of select="name"/>
      </a></h2>
      <p><xsl:value-of select="details"/></p>
   </xsl:for-each>
</body>
</html>
```

Notice how **`generate-id()`** is used twice, once to generate the identifier of the resort, the other to generate a link from the hotel.

Output

The output below was obtained using Saxon. I have added some extra indentation to show the structure. A different product will generate different identifiers in the **`<a>`** elements, but the links will work just as well.

```
<html>
   <body>
      <h1>Hotels</h1>
         <h2>Grand Hotel</h2>
            <p>Address:   . . . </p>
            <p>Stars: 5</p>
            <p>Resort: <a href="#b2b1b2">Amsterdam</a></p>
```

7

Functions

```
            <h2>Central Hotel</h2>
              <p>Address:   . . . </p>
              <p>Stars: 5</p>
              <p>Resort: <a href="#b2b1b4">Bruges</a></p>
            <h2>Less Grand Hotel</h2>
             <p>Address:   . . . </p>
              <p>Stars: 2</p>
              <p>Resort: <a href="#b2b1b2">Amsterdam</a></p>
            <h2>Peripheral Hotel</h2>
              <p>Address:   . . . </p>
              <p>Stars: 2</p>
              <p>Resort: <a href="#b2b1b4">Bruges</a></p>
          <h1>Resorts</h1>
            <h2><a name="b2ab1">Amsterdam</a></h2>
              <p>A wordy description of Amsterdam</p>
            <h2><a name="b2b1b4">Bruges</a></h2>
              <p>An eloquent description of Bruges</p>
      </body>
   </html>
```

There is no inverse function to **generate-id()**: specifically, there is no direct way to find a node if its generated id is known, other than the very inefficient:

```
//node()[generate-id()=$X]
```

If you need to do this, however, you can set up a key definition as follows:

```
<xsl:key name="gid-key" match="*" use="generate-id()"/>
```

and then find the element with a given id value using the expression:

```
key('gid-key', $X)
```

It is important to appreciate that the generated ids bear no resemblance to any ID attribute values in the source document, so the nodes cannot be found using the **id()** function.

Also, the ID values generated in one run of the processor may be different from those generated in a subsequent run. You need to bear this in mind if you are using the ID values as hyperlinks. If the transformation is likely to be run more than once, then it isn't safe to reference these ID values from another document, or even as a bookmark.

Using generate-id() to Compare Node Identity

The second common use of the **generate-id()** function is to compare whether two nodes are identical. Specifically, provided `$X` and `$Y` are node-sets each containing a single node, then

```
generate-id($x) = generate-id($Y)
```

will return true only if `$X` and `$Y` refer to the same node in the same document. Note that it's wrong to use «`$X = $Y`» to perform this test: this will return `true` for any pair of nodes that have the same string-value.

An example where such a test is useful is when grouping adjacent nodes together. For example, suppose your XML source document looks like this:

```
<plan>
<month>April</month>
<task>Sign contract</task>
<task>Recruit project manager</task>
<month>May</month>
<task>Place equipment orders</task>
<task>Hire laborers</task>
<task>Appoint PR agency</task>
<month>June</month>
<task>Get safety certification</task>
<task>Complete phase 1 construction</task>
<task>Arrange opening ceremony</task>
</plan>
```

and you want to display the results in an HTML bulleted list, as follows:

```
<h2>Tasks for April</h2>
    <ol>
       <li>Sign contract</li>
       <li>Recruit project manager</li>
    </ol>
<h2>Tasks for May</h2>
    <ol>
       <li>Place equipment orders</li>
       <li>Hire laborers</li>
       <li>Appoint PR agency</li>
    </ol>
<h2>Tasks for June</h2>
    <ol>
       <li>Get safety certification</li>
       <li>Complete phase 1 construction</li>
       <li>Arrange opening ceremony</li>
    </ol>
```

The job would be easier if the XML source wrapped the tasks for each month in an element; but we don't always get to influence the design of the XML input, so we have to work with what we're given.

Like all grouping problems, this one requires two nested loops, one to iterate over the groups and one to iterate over the items within the groups. In this case identifying the groups is straightforward:

```
<xsl:for-each select="month">
<h2>Tasks for <xsl:value-of select="."/></h2>
<ol>
. . .
</ol>
</xsl:for-each>
```

But what goes in the inner loop? We need to select all the sibling **<task>** elements for which the immediately preceding **<month>** is the current **<month>**. We can do this with **generate-id()**:

```
<xsl:for-each select="month">
<h2>Tasks for <xsl:value-of select="."/></h2>
<ol>
    <xsl:variable name="month-id" select="generate-id()"/>
    <xsl:for-each select="following-sibling::task[
                         generate-id(preceding-sibling::month[1])
                         = $month-id]">
             <li><xsl:value-of select="."/></li>
    </xsl:for-each>
</ol>
</xsl:for-each>
```

There are only two operations in XPath that are sensitive to node identity; one is the **generate-id()** function, the other is the union operator «|». So whenever you have the problem of deciding whether two variables or expressions refer to the same node, the solution will involve one of these constructs. In the simplest cases, you have a choice: when you know that `$x` and `$y` both refer to single nodes, then to test if they refer to the same node, you can write either:

```
<xsl:if test="generate-id($x) = generate-id($y)">
```

or equivalently,

```
<xsl:if test="count($x | $y ) = 1">
```

There's not really much to choose between these. Jeni Tennison has produced performance benchmarks that show the first is faster on some processors, the second on others; but optimizers are improving all the time anyway. On balance I would recommend using **generate-id()**, as I think it's clearer. Remember though that the two constructs are equivalent only when `$x` and `$y` each contain exactly one node.

See also

id() on page 496
key() on page 499

id

The **id()** function returns a node-set containing the node or nodes with a given ID attribute.

For example, if the **code** attribute is defined as an ID attribute, then the expression «`id('A321-780')`» might return a node-set containing the single element `<product code="A321-780">`.

Defined in

XPath section 4.1

Format

```
id(value)  ⇒  node-set
```

Arguments

Argument	Data type	Meaning
value	any	Specifies the required ID values, in a way that depends on the data type: see below for details

Result

A node-set containing the nodes with the required ID values.

Rules

If the argument is not a node-set, the argument is converted, if necessary, to a string using the rules for the **`string()`** function, and the resulting string is treated as a whitespace-separated list of tokens. Each token is used as a candidate ID value: if there is a node in the same document as the context node that has an ID attribute equal to this candidate ID value, this node is included in the result node-set.

If the argument is a node-set, this process is applied to each node in the node-set in turn: the node is converted to a string by taking its string-value, this string is treated as a whitespace-separated list of tokens, and each of these tokens is used as a candidate ID value. Note that this is different from simply converting the node-set to a string using the **`string()`** function, because it uses all the nodes in the node-set, not only the first.

An ID attribute in this context is any attribute declared in the DTD as having type ID.

It is not necessary for the nodes in the argument node-set to be attributes declared as type IDREF or IDREFS, though the function is designed to produce the expected result when they are: that is, it finds the nodes referenced by the IDREF or IDREFS values in the argument node-set.

It is not an error if there is no node with an ID equal to one of the candidate ID values. In this situation, there will simply be no node in the resulting node-set corresponding to this value. In the simplest case, where there is only one candidate ID value supplied, the resulting node-set will be empty if the ID is not present.

Notes

ID values only really work properly if the source document is valid (in the XML sense: meaning, loosely, that it obeys the rules in its own DTD). However, XSLT and XPath are designed to allow invalid documents as well as valid ones to be processed. One possible kind of validity error is that ID values are not unique within the document. This is explicitly covered in the specification – the first node with that ID value is located. Other validity errors are not discussed in the specification, for example what happens if an ID attribute contains embedded spaces. It is best to regard the behavior in such cases as undefined.

A non-validating XML parser isn't required to read attribute definitions from an external DTD. In this situation the XSLT processor will assume there are no ID attributes present, and the **id()** function will always return an empty result. If this appears to be happening, try a different XML parser. Most good parsers will report the attribute type, even though it isn't absolutely required by the XML standard.

Usage and Examples

The **id()** function provides an efficient means of locating nodes given the value of an ID attribute.

In a sense it is a convenience function, because if the attribute named **id** is always an ID attribute, then the expression:

```
id('B1234')
```

is equivalent to the path expression:

```
//*[@id='B1234']
```

However, the chances are that in most implementations, the **id()** function will be much more efficient than the straightforward path expression with a predicate, because the processor is likely to build an index rather than doing a sequential search.

It is also possible to use **key()** in place of **id()**. The main advantage of the **id()** function over using **key()** is that it handles a whitespace-separated list of IDs in one go. The **key()** function cannot do this, because there is nothing to stop a key value containing a space.

Note that the **id()** function always locates elements in the same document as the context node. To locate elements in a different document, use **<xsl:for-each>** to change the context node, for example:

```
<xsl:for-each select="document('a.xml')">
   <xsl:copy-of select="id('B1234')"/>
</xsl:for-each>
```

Where the source document includes an IDREFS attribute, it is possible to locate all the referenced elements at once. For example, if the **<book>** element has an attribute `authors` which is an IDREFS attribute containing a whitespace-separated list of author ids, the relevant **<author>** elements can be retrieved and processed using a construct such as:

```
<xsl:template match="book">
   . . .
by <xsl:for-each select="id(@authors)">
        <xsl:value-of select="surname"/>
        <xsl:if test="position()!=last()">, </xsl:if>
        <xsl:if test="position()=last()-1">and </xsl:if>
</xsl:for-each>
</xsl:template>
```

See also

`key()` on page 499

key

The **`key()`** function is used to find the nodes with a given value for a named key. It is used in conjunction with the **<xsl:key>** element described in Chapter 4, on page 241.

For example, if there is a key definition:

```
<xsl:key name="vreg" match="vehicle" use="@reg"/>
```

then the expression «`key('vreg', 'N498PAA')`» might return a node-set containing the single element `<vehicle reg="N498PAA">`.

Defined in

XSLT section 12.2

Format

```
key(name, value)  ⇒  node-set
```

Arguments

Argument	Data type	Meaning
name	string	Specifies the name of the key. If the argument is not a string, it is converted to a string using the rules of the **`string()`** function. The value of the string must be a `QName` that identifies a key declared using **<xsl:key>**.
value	any	Specifies the required value of the key, in a way that depends on the data type. See below.

7 Functions

Result

A node-set containing the nodes with the required key values.

Rules

The first argument must take the form of a `QName`: that is, an XML name optionally prefixed with a namespace prefix that corresponds to a namespace declaration that is in scope at the point in the stylesheet where the **`key()`** function is called. If there is no namespace prefix, the relevant namespace URI is null; the default namespace is not used. There must be an **`<xsl:key>`** element in the stylesheet with the same expanded name, using the namespace URIs rather than prefixes in the comparison. If there is more than one **`<xsl:key>`** element with this name, they are all used: a node is considered to match the key if it matches any of the key definitions with this name.

If the second argument is not a node-set, its value is converted, if necessary, to a string, using the rules of the **`string()`** function. All the nodes in the same document as the context node that have a value for the named key equal to this string are included in the result node-set. Note that one node may have several values for the same key, and there may also be many nodes with the same value for the key.

If the second argument is a node-set, this same process is applied to each node in the node-set. For each node *N* in this node-set, all the nodes in the same document as the context node that have a value for the named key equal to the string-value of *N* are added to the result node-set. This isn't the same as simply converting the node-set argument to a string using the **`string()`** function, because that would only use the string-value of the first node in the node-set.

Note that with multiple source documents, the resulting nodes will all be in the same document as the context node: but they will not necessarily be in the same document as the nodes from which the key values were obtained.

Usage and Examples

The **`key()`** function is provided to make associative access to nodes (finding the nodes given their content) more convenient and more efficient. Efficiency of course depends entirely on the implementation, but it is likely that most implementations will use some kind of index or hash-table data structure to make the **`key()`** function faster than the equivalent location path expression.

Another use for keys is that they provide an efficient way of grouping related nodes together.

We will examine these two ways of using keys in turn.

Using Keys to Find Nodes by Value

To start with a simple example, to locate the **`<book>`** elements having J. B. Priestley as the content of one of their **`<author>`** child elements, you could write:

```
<xsl:for-each select="//book[author='J. B. Priestley']">
```

However, it is probably more efficient, if this is done frequently in the stylesheet, to define the author name as a key:

```
<xsl:key name="book-author" match="book" use="author"/>
. . .
<xsl:for-each select="key('book-author', 'J. B. Priestley')"/>
```

The **key()** function always locates elements in the same document as the context node. To locate elements in a different document, use **<xsl:for-each>** to change the context node, for example:

```
<xsl:for-each select="document('a.xml')">
   <xsl:copy-of select="key('book-author', 'J. B. Priestley')"/>
</xsl:for-each>
```

The key value supplied can be either a string, or a node-set. In the former case, the key value can be calculated before use: for example it might be the concatenation of several values obtained from different places. In the second case, the key value must always be held as-is within the source document; but the advantage of this usage is that several key values can be supplied in the same call of the key function.

Example: Using keys as Cross-references

This example uses two source files: the principal source document is a file containing a list of books, and the secondary one (accessed using the **document()** function) contains biographies of authors. The author name held in the first file acts as a cross-reference to the author's biography in the second file, rather like a join in SQL.

Source

The principal source document is an abbreviated version of the `booklist.xml` file:

```
<booklist>
<book category="FC">
     <title>The Young Visiters</title>
     <author>Daisy Ashford</author>
</book>
<book category="FC">
     <title>When We Were Very Young</title>
     <author>A. A. Milne</author>
</book>
</booklist>
```

The secondary source document, `authors.xml`, reads like this. I've only included two authors to keep it short, but the **key()** function would really come into its own if there were hundreds of entries.

```
<authors>

<author name="A. A. Milne">
<born>1852</born>
<died>1956</died>
<biog>Alan Alexander Milne, educated at Westminster School and
Trinity College Cambridge, became a prolific author of plays,
novels, poetry, short stories, and essays, all of which have been
overshadowed by his children's books. </biog>
</author>
```

```
<author name="Daisy Ashford">
<born>1881</born>
<died>1972</died>
<biog>Daisy Ashford (Mrs George Norman) wrote <i>The Young
Visiters</i>, a small comic masterpiece, while still a young child
in Lewes. It was found in a drawer in 1919 and sent to Chatto and
Windus, who published it in the same year with an introduction by J.
M. Barrie, who had first insisted on meeting the author in order to
check that she was genuine.</biog>
</author>

</authors>
```

Stylesheet

The stylesheet is in the file `author-biogs.xsl`. It declares a key to match **`<author>`** elements by their name attribute. This is intended for use with the `authors.xml` file, though there is nothing in the key definition to say so.

Note the use of a global variable to reference the secondary source file. It would be possible to use the **`document()`** function each time the file is accessed, and any XSLT processor worthy of the name would only actually read and parse the file once, but using a variable in my view makes it easier to see what is going on.

The innermost **`<xsl:for-each>`** doesn't do any iteration, it is there merely to switch the context to the second document, because the **`key()`** function only looks in the document containing the context node. Switching the context means it is no longer possible to refer directly to nodes in the principal document, which is why the author's name is first extracted into a variable.

```
<xsl:transform
 xmlns:xsl="http://www.w3.org/1999/XSL/Transform"
 version="1.0"
>
<xsl:key name="biog" match="author" use="@name"/>
<xsl:variable name="biogs" select="document('authors.xml')"/>

<xsl:template match="/">
  <html><body>

<xsl:variable name="all-books" select="//book"/>
    <xsl:for-each select="$all-books">
                <!-- for each book in the booklist file -->
      <h1><xsl:value-of select="title"/></h1>
      <h2>Author<xsl:if test="count(author)!=1">s</xsl:if></h2>
      <xsl:for-each select="author">
                <!-- for each author of this book -->
         <xsl:variable name="name" select="."/>
         <h3><xsl:value-of select="$name"/></h3>
         <xsl:for-each select="$biogs">
                <!-- change the current node to be the authorsfile -->
                <!-- then retrieve the entry for this author -->
           <xsl:variable name="auth" select="key('biog', $name)"/>
           <p><xsl:value-of
                   select="concat($auth/born, ' - ',
```

```
$auth/died)"/></p>
            <p><xsl:value-of select="$auth/biog"/></p>
          </xsl:for-each>
       </xsl:for-each>
     </xsl:for-each>
   </body></html>
 </xsl:template>

 </xsl:transform>
```

Output

The output obtained if you run this stylesheet with the subset of the `booklist.xml` file shown above is as follows:

```
<html>
   <body>
      <h1>The Young Visiters</h1>
      <h2>Author</h2>
      <h3>Daisy Ashford</h3>
      <p>1881 - 1972</p>
      <p>Daisy Ashford (Mrs George Norman) wrote The Young
Visiters, a small comic masterpiece, while still a young child in
Lewes. It was found in a drawer in 1919 and sent to Chatto and
Windus, who published it in the same year with an introduction by J.
M. Barrie, who had first insisted on meeting the author in order to
check that she was genuine.</p>
      <h1>When We Were Very Young</h1>
      <h2>Author</h2>
      <h3>A. A. Milne</h3>
      <p>1852 - 1956</p>
      <p>Alan Alexander Milne, educated at Westminster School and
Trinity College Cambridge, became a prolific author of plays,
novels, poetry, short stories, and essays, all of which have been
overshadowed by his children's books.</p>
 </body>
 </html>
```

Using Keys for Grouping

Because keys provide an efficient way of retrieving all the nodes that share a common value, they are useful when you need to group nodes with common values in the output.

This technique is sometimes called the Muenchian grouping method, after Steve Muench of Oracle who introduced it.

To solve any grouping problem, you need two nested loops. The outer loop selects one node to act as a representative of each group, typically the first node in document order that is a member of the group. The processing associated with this node outputs information about the group as a whole, typically the common value used to group the nodes together, perhaps with counts or subtotals calculated over the members of the group, plus any necessary formatting. The inner loop then processes each member of the group in turn.

With the Muenchian method, a key is defined on the common value that determines group membership. For example, if all the cities in a country comprise one group, then the key definition will be:

```
<xsl:key name="country-group" match="city" use="@country"/>
```

The outer loop selects one city for each country. The way of doing this is to select all the cities, and then filter out those that are not the first in their country. You can tell that a city is the first one for its country by comparing it with the first node in the node-set returned by the **key()** function for that country:

```
<xsl:for-each select="//city[generate-id() =
                        generate-id(key('country-group', @country)[1])]">
```

The predicate here is using **generate-id()** to check that the city is the same node as the first one returned by the **key()** function for that key value. If we are confident that cities have a unique name we could compare the names instead:

```
<xsl:for-each select="//city[@name =
                              "key('country-group',
@country)[1]/@name]">
```

Within this loop the code can output any heading it needs, such as the name of the country. It can then start an inner loop to process all the cities in this country, which it can find by using the key once again:

```
<xsl:for-each select=key('country-group', @country)">
```

The following shows a complete example of this technique.

Example: Using keys for Grouping

Source

The source `cities.xml` is a list of cities:

```
<cities>
   <city name="Paris" country="France"/>
   <city name="Roma" country="Italia"/>
   <city name="Nice" country="France"/>
   <city name="Madrid" country="Espana"/>
   <city name="Milano" country="Italia"/>
   <city name="Firenze" country="Italia"/>
   <city name="Napoli" country="Italia"/>
   <city name="Lyon" country="France"/>
   <city name="Barcelona" country="Espana"/>
</cities>
```

Stylesheet

The stylesheet `citygroups.xsl` is as follows:

```
<xsl:transform
 xmlns:xsl="http://www.w3.org/1999/XSL/Transform"
 version="1.0"
>
<xsl:key name="country-group" match="city" use="@country"/>

<xsl:template match="/">
  <html><body>
   <xsl:for-each select="//city[generate-id()
              = generate-id(key('country-group', @country)[1])]">
      <h1><xsl:value-of select="@country"/></h1>
      <xsl:for-each select="key('country-group', @country)">
         <xsl:value-of select="@name"/><br/>
      </xsl:for-each>
   </xsl:for-each>
  </body></html>
</xsl:template>
</xsl:transform>
```

Output

Viewed in a browser, the output is as shown below:

See also

<xsl:key> on page 241 in Chapter 4
id() on page 496

lang

The **lang()** function tests whether the language of the context node, as defined by the **xml:lang** attribute, corresponds to the language supplied as an argument.

For example, if the context node is the element `<para lang="fr-CA">` (indicating Canadian French), then the expression «`lang('fr')`» would return `true`.

Defined in

XPath section 4.3

Format

```
lang(language)  ⇒  boolean
```

Arguments

Argument	Data type	Meaning
language	string	The language being tested. If the argument is not a string, it is converted to a string using the rules of the **string()** function.

Result

A Boolean: `true` if the language of the context node is the same as, or a sublanguage of, the language being tested.

Rules

The language of the context node is determined by the value of its **xml:lang** attribute, or if it has no such attribute, by the value of the **xml:lang** attribute on its nearest ancestor node that does have such an attribute. If there is no **xml:lang** attribute on any of these nodes, the **lang()** function returns `false`.

The **xml:lang** attribute is one of the small number of attributes that are given a predefined meaning in the XML specification (in fact, you could argue that it is the only thing in the XML specification that has anything to say about what the contents of the document might mean to its readers). The value of the attribute can take one of the following four forms:

- A two-letter language code defined in the international standard ISO 639. For example English is "en" and French is "fr". This can be given in either upper-case or lower-case, though lower-case is usual. The second edition of the XML specification also anticipates the introduction of three-letter language codes in a revision of Internet RFC 1766.
- A two letter language code as above, followed by one or more subcodes: each subcode is preceded by a hyphen «-». For example, US English is "en-US"; Canadian French is "fr-CA". The first subcode, if present, must be either a two-letter country code from the international standard ISO 3166, or a subcode for the language registered with IANA (Internet Assigned Numbers Authority). The ISO 3166 country codes are generally the same as Internet top-level domains, for example "DE" for Germany, "CZ" for the Czech Republic, but with the notable exception of the United Kingdom, whose ISO 3166 code (for some reason) is "GB" rather than "UK". These codes are generally written in upper case. The meaning of any subcodes after the first is not defined, but they must contain ASCII letters (a-z, A-Z) only.
- A language code registered with the IANA (see www.iana.org), prefixed "i-", for example "i-Navajo".
- A user-defined language code, prefixed "x-", for example "x-Java" if the element contains a Java program.

The **`xml:lang`** attribute defines the language of all text contained within the element it appears on, unless it is overridden by another **`xml:lang`** attribute in an inner element. So if a document is written in English but contains quotations in German, the **`xml:lang`** language code on the document element might say «`xml:lang="en"`», while an element containing a quotation specifies «`xml:lang="de"`».

The **`lang()`** function in XSLT allows you to test whether the language for the context node is the one you are expecting. For example «`lang('en')`» returns `true` if the language is English, while «`lang('jp')`» returns `true` if it is Japanese.

Specifically, the rules are as follows:

- If the value of **`xml:lang`** for the context node is equal to the string supplied in the argument, ignoring differences of case, the function returns `true`.
- If the value of **`xml:lang`** for the context node, ignoring any suffix starting with a hyphen «-», is equal to the string supplied in the argument, again ignoring differences of case, the function returns `true`.
- Otherwise, the function returns `false`.

Usage and Examples

This function provides a convenient way of testing the language used in the source document. Assuming that the source document has been properly marked up using the **`xml:lang`** attribute as defined in the XML specification, the **`lang()`** function allows you to do language-dependent processing of the data.

The example below shows another way of using **`lang()`**: to select language-dependent data from a lookup table held in the stylesheet.

Example: Using lang() for Localizing Dates

Source

The source file `issue-dates.xml` contains dates in ISO format (yyyymmdd). The dates below happen to be the dates of the various working drafts of the XSLT 1.0 specification.

```
<issues>
<iso-date>19991116</iso-date>
<iso-date>19991008</iso-date>
<iso-date>19990813</iso-date>
<iso-date>19990709</iso-date>
<iso-date>19990421</iso-date>
<iso-date>19981216</iso-date>
<iso-date>19980818</iso-date>
</issues>
```

Stylesheet

The stylesheet `format-dates.xsl` contains data and logic to output these dates using English, French, or German month names.

The stylesheet takes a global parameter which is the name of the required language for the output. The way you supply the parameter varies according to which product you are using. For Saxon, use the command line:

```
saxon issue-dates.xml format-dates.xsl language=fr
```

For xt, use:

```
xt issue-dates.xml format-dates.xsl language=fr
```

The language code should be «en», «de», or «`fr`».

```
<?xml version="1.0" encoding="iso-8859-1"?>
<xsl:transform
 xmlns:xsl="http://www.w3.org/1999/XSL/Transform"
 version="1.0"
>

<xsl:output encoding="iso-8859-1"/>

<data xmlns="data.uri">
<months xml:lang="en">
   <m>January</m><m>February</m><m>March</m><m>April</m>
<m>May</m><m>June</m><m>July</m><m>August</m>
   <m>September</m><m>October</m><m>November</m><m>December</m>
</months>
<months xml:lang="fr">
   <m>Janvier</m><m>Février</m><m>Mars</m><m>Avril</m>
   <m>Mai</m><m>Juin</m><m>Juillet</m><m>Août</m>
   <m>Septembre</m><m>Octobre</m><m>Novembre</m><m>Décembre</m>
</months>
```

```
<months xml:lang="de">
   <m>Januar</m><m>Februar</m><m>März</m><m>April</m>
   <m>Mai</m><m>Juni</m><m>Juli</m><m>August</m>
   <m>September</m><m>Oktober</m><m>November</m><m>Dezember</m>
</months>
</data>

<xsl:param name="language" select="'en'"/>

<xsl:template match="iso-date">
<date xmlns:data="data.uri" xsl:exclude-result-prefixes="data">
   <xsl:value-of select="substring(., 7, 2)"/>
   <xsl:text> </xsl:text>
   <xsl:variable name="month" select="number(substring(.,5,2))"/>
   <xsl:value-of select="document('')/*/

data:data/data:months[lang($language)]/data:m[$month]"/>
   <xsl:text> </xsl:text>
   <xsl:value-of select="substring(., 1, 4)"/>
</date>
</xsl:template>
</xsl:transform>
```


The crux of this is the lengthy path expression (starting with «`document('')`») that obtains the month name. This expression first locates the stylesheet document («`document('')`»), then its document element («`*`», giving the **`<xsl:stylesheet>`** or **`<xsl:transform>`** element), then the top-level **`<data>`** element (the actual element uses «`data.uri`» as a default namespace, but in the XPath expression it needs to be given an explicit namespace prefix), then the **`<months>`** element that matches the required language, and finally the **`<m>`** element for the required month. The «`[lang($language)]`» predicate will be true only for a <months> element whose language code matches the required language.

See the description of the **`document()`** function on page 466 for more details on how to use this function to get access to data held in the stylesheet.

With XSLT 1.1 you could simplify this stylesheet by placing the lookup tables in global tree-valued variables. You could replace the **`<data>`** element with `<xsl:variable name="data">` (getting rid of the extra namespace in the process), and then replace the statement that gets the required month name by:

```
<xsl:value-of select="$data/months[lang($language)]/m[$month]"/>
```

This technique doesn't work in XSLT 1.0 because you aren't allowed to address into a result tree fragment using the path operator «`/`».

I used iso-8859-1 encoding (the character set that Microsoft call Windows ANSI) for this example because that's what my text editor uses. If I had used the default encoding, UTF-8, my text editor wouldn't be able to cope with the accented letters, so it would be harder to see what's going on, though it would still work correctly.

Output

If you selected English, the output is:

```
<?xml version="1.0" encoding="iso-8859-1" ?>
<date>16 November 1999</date>
<date>08 October 1999</date>
<date>13 August 1999</date>
<date>09 July 1999</date>
<date>21 April 1999</date>
<date>16 December 1998</date>
<date>18 August 1998</date>
```

If you selected French, the output is:

```
<?xml version="1.0" encoding="iso-8859-1" ?>
<date>16 Novembre 1999</date>
<date>08 Octobre 1999</date>
<date>13 Août 1999</date>
<date>09 Juillet 1999</date>
<date>21 Avril 1999</date>
<date>16 Décembre 1998</date>
<date>18 Août 1998</date>
```

If you selected German, the output is:

```
<?xml version="1.0" encoding="iso-8859-1" ?>
<date>16 November 1999</date>
<date>08 Oktober 1999</date>
<date>13 August 1999</date>
<date>09 Juli 1999</date>
<date>21 April 1999</date>
<date>16 Dezember 1998</date>
<date>18 August 1998</date>
```

The **lang()** function only allows you to test whether the language is one of the languages you are expecting; if you want to find out the actual language, you will need to read the **xml:lang** attribute directly. You can find the relevant attribute using the expression «ancestor-or-self::*[@xml:lang][1]/@xml:lang».

last

The **last()** function returns the value of the context size. When processing a list of nodes, if the nodes are numbered from one, **last()** gives the number assigned to the last node in the list.

For example, if you are processing a set of nodes using **<xsl:for-each>**, then you can output a comma before each node other than the last one by writing:

```
<xsl:if test="position()!=last()">, </xsl:if>
```

Defined in

XPath section 4.1

Format

```
last()  ⇒  number
```

Arguments

None

Result

A number, the value of the context size. As the name implies, this is context dependent.

Rules

The XPath specification defines the value of the **last()** function in terms of the *context size*. The XSLT specification uses different terminology: it talks about the size of the *current node list*.

When a top-level expression is evaluated (that is, an XPath expression that is not part of another expression), the context size is set to the number of nodes in the current node list. This has three possible settings:

- When a global variable is being evaluated, or in certain other contexts such as evaluating the **use** expression in **<xsl:key>**, or evaluating the initial template that matches the root node, it is set to 1 (one).
- When **<xsl:apply-templates>** is called to process a set of nodes, the current node list is the list of nodes being processed, and the context size is therefore the number of nodes selected in the call of **<xsl:apply-templates>**.
- When **<xsl:for-each>** is called to process a set of nodes, the current node list is the list of nodes being processed, and the context size is therefore the number of nodes selected in the call of **<xsl:for-each>**.

When a predicate is evaluated, either in an expression or in a pattern, the context size is the number of nodes being tested in that step of the expression or pattern evaluation. For more details, see Chapter 5 *Expressions*, and Chapter 6 *Patterns*.

Usage and Examples

To understand the effect of calling **last()**, you need to know what the current node list is.

When **last()** is used as a top-level expression within an **<xsl:template>** (and not within **<xsl:for-each>**), it returns the number of nodes selected by the relevant **<xsl:apply-templates>** select expression. This is because **<xsl:apply-templates>** sets the current node list to be the set of nodes selected by the select expression, after sorting them into the order in which they are processed.

For example, the following code can be used to number all the figures in a document. The **last()** function prints the number of figure elements in the document.

```
<xsl:apply-templates select="//figure"/>
. . .
<xsl:template match="figure">
   <div align="center">
   <img src="{@href}"/>
   <p>Figure <xsl:value-of select="position()"/>
      <xsl:text/> of <xsl:value-of select="last()"/></p>
   </div>
</xsl:template>
```

Similarly, when **last()** is used as a top-level expression within **<xsl:for-each>**, it returns the number of nodes selected by the relevant **<xsl:for-each>** select expression. Again, this is because **<xsl:for-each>** sets the current node list to be the set of nodes selected by the select expression, after sorting into the correct order.

The **last()** function is often used to test whether the current node being processed is the last one in the list. This is illustrated in the following example:

Example: Formatting a List Using position() and last()

This example formats a list of names in the style «`Adam, Betsie, Charlie and Diana`».

Source

The source file is `booklist.xml`. A relevant subset is shown below:

```
<booklist>
<book category="CS">
     <title>Design Patterns</title>
     <author>Erich Gamma</author>
     <author>Richard Helm</author>
     <author>Ralph Johnson</author>
     <author>John Vlissides</author>
</book>
</booklist>
```

Stylesheet

The stylesheet `format-names.xsl` processes a book by formatting the list of authors into a single element:

```
<xsl:transform
   xmlns:xsl="http://www.w3.org/1999/XSL/Transform"
   version="1.0"
>

<xsl:template match="book">
<auth>
    <xsl:for-each select="author">
```

```
            <xsl:value-of select="."/>
            <xsl:choose>
                <xsl:when test="position() = last()"/> <!-- do nothing -->
                <xsl:when test="position() = last()-1"> and </xsl:when>
                <xsl:otherwise>, </xsl:otherwise>
            </xsl:choose>
        </xsl:for-each>
    </auth>
    </xsl:template>

    </xsl:transform>
```

Output

For the booklist.xml file, the output is:

```
    <auth>Danzig</auth>
    <auth>Daisy Ashford</auth>
    <auth>A. A. Milne</auth>
    <auth>Erich Gamma, Richard Helm, Ralph Johnson and John
Vlissides</auth>
```


<xsl:call-template> does not change the current node list, so **last()** will return the same value in the called template as in the calling template.

If the **last()** function is used within the select expression of an **<xsl:sort>** element, then it refers to the number of nodes being sorted. For example, specifying the following sort key:

```
  <xsl:sort select="position() mod (ceiling(last() div 3))"/>
```

will sort the nodes A, B, C, D, E, F, G, H into the sequence A, D, G, B, E, H, C, F, which might be useful if you want to arrange them in a table with three columns.

When **last()** is used within an expression used as a predicate applied to a node-set expression, the context size is the number of nodes selected by the current step of the expression, after applying any previous filters. For example, suppose the source document is as follows:

```
<countries>
 <country name="France" capital="Paris" continent="Europe"/>
<country name="Germany" capital="Berlin" continent="Europe"/>
<country name="Spain" capital="Madrid" continent="Europe"/>
<country name="Italy" capital="Rome" continent="Europe"/>
<country name="Poland" capital="Warsaw" continent="Europe"/>
<country name="Egypt" capital="Cairo" continent="Africa"/>
<country name="Libya" capital="Tripoli" continent="Africa"/>
<country name="Nigeria" capital="Lagos" continent="Africa"/>
</countries>
```

Then:

- The expression «`countries/country[last()]`» returns the country element for Nigeria
- The expression «`countries/country[@continent='Europe'][last()]`» returns the country element for Poland
- The expression «`countries/country[@continent='Europe'][last()-1]`» returns the country element for Italy
- The expression «`countries/country[@continent='Africa'] [position() != last()]`» returns the country elements for Egypt and Libya

The **`last()`** function can be used as a qualifier in a pattern when the last child of a given element is to be treated differently from the others. For example:

```
<xsl:template name="normal-p" match="p">
   <xsl:copy>
      <xsl:apply-templates/>
   </xsl:copy>
</xsl:template>

<xsl:template match="p[last()]">
   <xsl:call-template name="normal-p"/>
   <hr/>
</xsl:template>
```

However, this may not perform well, because each **`<p>`** element needs to be tested to see if it is the last one, which will probably involve looking at all the children of the parent of the **`<p>`** element. Using **`<xsl:if>`** will often achieve the same effect more economically:

```
<xsl:template match="p">
   <xsl:copy>
      <xsl:apply-templates/>
   </xsl:copy>
   <xsl:if test="position()=last()">
      <hr/>
   </xsl:if>
</xsl:template>
```

However, note that these two examples are not strictly equivalent. If the **`<p>`** elements are processed by a call on **`<xsl:apply-templates>`** with no **`<xsl:sort>`** specification, they will have the same effect; but if a sort key is specified, then the second template will output an **`<hr/>`** element after the last **`<p>`** element in the order of the output, whereas the first will output the **`<hr/>`** element after the last **`<p>`** element in document order.

An easy mistake is to think that `last()` returns a Boolean value. You can use `last()` in a predicate to match the last node, for example:

```
<xsl:value-of select="para[last()]"/>
```

This is a shorthand for the predicate «`[position()=last()]`», because in a predicate, a numeric value X is equivalent to a test for the condition «`position()=X`». However, this doesn't extend to other contexts, for example if you write:

```
<xsl:if test="last()"/>
```

then the numeric value of the `last()` function is simply converted to a Boolean as if the `boolean()` function were used. The result will always be true, because `last()` can never be zero.

See also

`position()` on page 533
`<xsl:number>` in Chapter 4, on page 256

local-name

The **`local-name()`** function returns the local part of the name of a node, that is, the part of the name after the colon if there is one, or the full name otherwise.

For example, if the context node is an element named **`<title>`** the expression «`local-name()`» returns «`title`»; for an element named **`<ms:schema>`** it returns «`schema`».

Defined in

XPath section 4.1

Format

```
local-name()  ⇒  string
local-name(node)  ⇒  string
```

Arguments

Argument	Data type	Meaning
node optional	node-set	Identifies the node whose local name is required. If the node-set contains more than one node, the target node is the one that comes first in document order. If the node-set is empty, the function returns an empty string. If the argument is omitted, the target node is the context node. It is an error if the argument supplied is not a node-set.

Result

A string value: the local part of the name of the target node.

Rules

The local name of a node depends on the node type, as follows:

Node type	Local name
root	None, an empty string is returned
element	The element name, after any colon
attribute	The attribute name, after any colon
text	None, an empty string is returned
processing instruction	The *target* used in the processing instruction to identify the application for which it is intended
comment	None, an empty string is returned
namespace	The namespace prefix; or the empty string if this is the default namespace

Usage

This function can be useful if you need to test the local name without also testing the namespace URI. For example if you want to select both **<title>** and **<html:title>** elements, you could do this by writing:

```
<xsl:apply-templates select="*[local-name()='title']"/>
```

Or you could define a template rule that matches both:

```
<xsl:template match="*[local-name()='title']">
```

In some ways this can be seen as a misuse of the XML Namespaces facility. The names in one namespace are supposed to bear no relation to the names in another, so any similarity between the names **<title>** and **<html:title>** is a pure coincidence.

In practice, this isn't always true. What often happens is that one namespace is adapted from another. For example the US Post Office might devise a schema (and associated namespace) for representing US names and addresses, and the Canadian Post Office might then create a variant of this, with a different namespace URI, for Canadian names and addresses. The two schemas will have many elements in common, and it's quite reasonable to try to write a stylesheet that can handle either. If you want to write template rules that match on both a **<us:address>** and a **<canada:address>**, there are two ways of doing it:

Either list both possibilities:

```
<xsl:template match="us:address | canada:address">
```

or match on the local name only:

```
<xsl:template match="*[local-name()='address']">
```

Examples

The following stylesheet fragment outputs an HTML table listing the attributes of the current element, sorted first by namespace and then by local name:

```
<xsl:template match="*" mode="tabulate">
   <table>
      <xsl:for-each select="attribute::node()">
      <xsl:sort select="namespace-uri()"/>
      <xsl:sort select="local-name()"/>
         <tr>
         <td><xsl:value-of select="namespace-uri()"/></td>
         <td><xsl:value-of select="local-name()"/></td>
         <td><xsl:value-of select="."/></td>
         </tr>
      </xsl:for-each>
   </table>
</xsl:template>
```


See also

name() in the section immediately below
namespace-uri() on page 523

name

The **name()** function returns a `QName` that represents the name of a node. Typically this will be the name of the node as written in the original XML source document.

For example, if the context node is an element named **<ms:schema>**, then the expression «`name()`» will normally return the string «`ms:schema`».

Defined in

XPath section 4.1

Format

```
name()  ⇒  string
name(node)  ⇒  string
```

Arguments

Argument	Data type	Meaning
node (optional)	node-set	Identifies the node whose name is required. If the node-set contains more than one node, the target node is the one that comes first in document order. If the node-set is empty, the function returns an empty string. If the argument is omitted, the target node is the context node. It is an error if the argument supplied is not a node-set.

Result

A string value: a QName representing the name of the target node.

Rules

The name of a node depends on the node type, as follows:

Node type	Name
root	None, an empty string is returned.
element	The element name (a QName), normally as it appears in the source XML, though a different prefix that maps to the same namespace URI may be substituted.
attribute	The attribute name (a QName), normally as it appears in the source XML, though a different prefix that maps to the same namespace URI may be substituted.
text	None, an empty string is returned.
processing instruction	The *target* used in the processing instruction to identify the application for which it is intended.
comment	None, an empty string is returned.
namespace	The namespace prefix; or the empty string if this is the default namespace. (This is **not** prefixed with «xmlns:» .)

Except for element and attribute nodes, **name()** returns the same value as **local-name()**.

The QName returned will normally use the same prefix as that which appeared in the original XML source. However, this is not guaranteed: the only guarantee is that it will use a prefix that maps to the same namespace URI. If the source document contains multiple prefixes that map to the same namespace URI the implementation can choose to normalize them.

With XSLT 1.1, it becomes possible to apply the **name()** function to a node in a temporary tree (created by using a non-empty **<xsl:variable>** element). The same considerations apply; the processor is free to choose any prefix that maps to the right namespace URI, including if necessary a prefix that it has invented itself. In this case, however, it is much more likely that there will be more than one prefix available.

Suppose your source document contains the following:

```
<items xmlns="http://acme.com/catalog">
       <item name="nut" stock="2300"/>
       <item name="bolt" stock="2500"/>
       <item name="washer" stock="500"/>
</items>
```

and suppose the stylesheet defines the following tree-valued variable:

```
<xsl:variable name="low-stock-items">
   <items xmlns:cat="http://acme.com/catalog">
      <xsl:copy-of select="//cat:item[@stock &lt; 1000"/>
   </items>
</xsl:variable>
```

What is the value of the expression «name($low-stock-items/items/item)»?

The <items> element on the tree, because it was created by copying a literal result element, will have a namespace node for every namespace declaration that was in scope for the literal result element in the stylesheet: in particular, it will have one that maps the prefix «cat» to the namespace URI «http://acme.com/catalog».

Within this element, the tree will contain a single **<item>** element (the one with «name="washer"»), copied from the source document. Under the rules for **<xsl:copy-of>**, this **<item>** element will have a namespace node for every namespace declaration that was in scope for the **<item>** element in the source document; in particular, it will have one that maps the empty prefix «» to the namespace URI «http://acme.com/catalog».

So in the tree-valued variable, there will be two namespace declarations with different prefixes («» and «cat») for the same namespace URI. This means that when you apply the **name()** function to the **<item>** element, the system has a choice of prefixes. The result will be either «item» or «cat:item»; it's up to the implementor to choose.

Usage

The **name()** function is useful when you want to display the element name, perhaps in an error message, because the form it takes is the same as the way in which users will generally write the element name.

So, for example, if your stylesheet requires every **<book>** to have an ISBN attribute, you might write:

```
<xsl:if test="not(@ISBN)">
<xsl:message>The <xsl:value-of select="name()"/> element
                has no ISBN attribute</xsl:message>
</xsl:if>
```

You can also use the **name()** function to test the name of a node against a string, for example «doc:title[name(..)='doc:section']». However, it's best to avoid this if you can:

- Firstly, this fails if the document uses a different prefix to refer to the namespace. There's nothing here to tell the system to treat «doc:section» as a QName, so if the writer of a particular document chose to use the prefix «DOC» instead of «doc» for this namespace, the test would fail, even though the names are equivalent.
- Secondly, there is usually a better way of doing it: this particular example can be written as «doc:title[parent::doc:section]». In fact, in most cases where you want to test whether a node has a particular name, you can do it using a predicate of this form. The «self» axis is particularly useful: for example, to test whether the current node is a **<figure>** element, write <xsl:if test="self::figure">.

There are some occasions when this won't work. For example, suppose your names are structured and you want to do a more complex test on the name; for example «*[starts-with(name(),'private.')]» to select elements whose name starts with the string «private.». This is poor document design, because XML names are not intended to carry hidden meaning by means of an internal syntax; if some elements have access restrictions, then rather than giving them names beginning with «private.», it would be better to indicate the restrictions using an attribute such as «private="yes"». However, you may sometimes have to deal with badly-designed documents, so the **name()** function provides a suitable mechanism. Take care, however, over the handling of namespace prefixes: unless you are certain that prefixes will be used consistently, it is better to test the local-name and the namespace URI rather than the value returned by **name()**. So the above example would be better written:

```
*[namespace-uri()='' and starts-with(local-name(),'private.')]
```

Another case where you need to use **name()** to test the name of a node is when you're comparing it against a variable or a parameter to the stylesheet. A common example is if you want to write a stylesheet to produce a sorted list of records, and you want the user to supply the sort key as a parameter. One user might want to sort books by author, another by publisher, and another by price. As the **select** expression in the **<xsl:sort>** element must be hard-coded in the stylesheet, the only way to achieve this is by writing:

```
<xsl:sort select="*[name()=$sort-key]"/>
```

where «$sort-key» is the stylesheet parameter containing the name of the field that the user wants to sort by.

Finally, another case where you can't use the «self» construct is when testing attribute nodes. This is because the principal node type for the self axis is elements. If you want to copy all attributes except the **description** attribute, you might be tempted to write:

```
<xsl:copy-of select="@*[not(self::description)]"/>
```

But this doesn't have the desired effect, because «self::description» is looking for elements named **<description>** on the self axis, and when the context node is an attribute, there aren't any.

In all these cases, the safest approach is not to write «name()='description'», but rather to write «local-name()="'description' and namespace-uri()=''"».

Avoid using **name()** to generate a name in the result document, for example by writing «<xsl:element name="{name()}">». The problem is that any prefix in **name()** is interpreted in the light of namespace declarations appearing in the stylesheet, not namespace declarations in the original source document. The correct tool for this job is **<xsl:copy>**. There are cases where **<xsl:copy>** won't do the job: for example you may want to use the name of an attribute in the input document to generate the name of an element in the output document. In this case use **local-name()** and **namespace-uri()** separately, for example:

```
<xsl:element name="{local-name()}" namespace="{namespace-uri()}">
```

Examples

The following stylesheet outputs an HTML table listing the elements that appear in the source document.

Example: Listing the Element Names that Appear in a Document

Source

This stylesheet can be applied to any source document. The output is more interesting if the source document uses namespaces. For example, try applying the stylesheet to itself as its own source document.

Stylesheet

The stylesheet `list-elements.xsl` is shown below. It processes all the element nodes in the document, sorted by namespace URI and then local name, and for each one it outputs the name, the prefix, the local name, and the namespace URI. There is no attempt to remove duplicate entries.

The only way to determine the namespace prefix is to call **name()** and extract the part of the string before the colon, if any.

```
<?xml version="1.0" encoding="iso-8859-1"?>
<xsl:transform
 xmlns:xsl="http://www.w3.org/1999/XSL/Transform"
 version="1.0"
>

<xsl:template match="/">
<html><body>
<h1>Table of elements</h1>
<table border="1" cellpadding="5">
<tr><td>Element</td><td>Prefix</td>
<td>Local name</td><td>Namespace URI</td></tr>
    <xsl:apply-templates select="//*">
          <xsl:sort select="namespace-uri()"/>
          <xsl:sort select="local-name()"/>
    </xsl:apply-templates>
</table></body></html>
</xsl:template>
```

```
<xsl:template match="*">
     <xsl:variable name="prefix">
        <xsl:choose>
        <xsl:when test="contains(name(), ':')">
           <xsl:value-of select="substring-before(name(),':')"/>
        </xsl:when>
        <xsl:otherwise/>
        </xsl:choose>
     </xsl:variable>
<tr>
     <td><xsl:value-of select="name()"/></td>
     <td><xsl:value-of select="$prefix"/></td>
     <td><xsl:value-of select="local-name()"/></td>
     <td><xsl:value-of select="namespace-uri()"/></td>
     </tr>
</xsl:template>

</xsl:transform>
```

Output

The illustration below shows the output when the stylesheet `list-cities.xsl` is used as the source document:

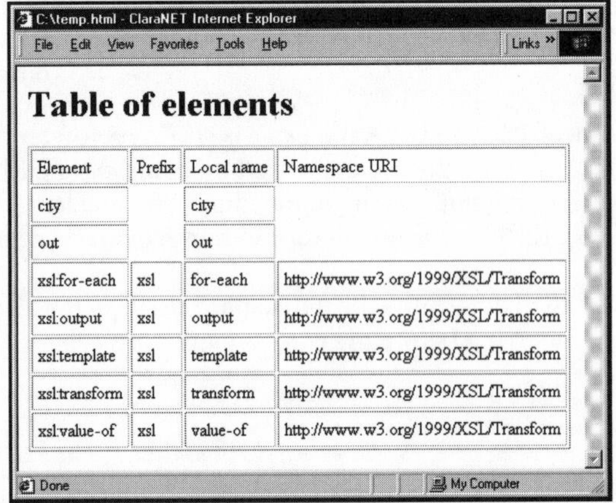

Table of elements

Element	Prefix	Local name	Namespace URI
city		city	
out		out	
xsl:for-each	xsl	for-each	http://www.w3.org/1999/XSL/Transform
xsl:output	xsl	output	http://www.w3.org/1999/XSL/Transform
xsl:template	xsl	template	http://www.w3.org/1999/XSL/Transform
xsl:transform	xsl	transform	http://www.w3.org/1999/XSL/Transform
xsl:value-of	xsl	value-of	http://www.w3.org/1999/XSL/Transform

See also

`local-name()` on page 515
`namespace-uri()` on page 523

namespace-uri

The **`namespace-uri()`** function returns a string that represents the URI of the namespace in the expanded name of a node. Typically this will be a URI used in a namespace declaration, that is, the value of an **`xmlns`** or **`xmlns:*`** attribute.

For example, if you apply this function to the outermost element of the stylesheet by writing the expression «`namespace-uri(document('')/*)`», the result will be the string «`http://www.w3.org/1999/XSL/Transform`».

Defined in

XPath section 4.1

Format

```
namespace-uri()  ⇒  string
namespace-uri(node)  ⇒  string
```

Arguments

Argument	Data type	Meaning
node (optional)	node-set	Identifies the node whose namespace URI is required. If the node-set contains more than one node, the target node is the one that comes first in document order. If the node-set is empty, the function returns an empty string. If the argument is omitted, the target node is the context node. It is an error if the argument supplied is not a node-set.

Result

A string value: the namespace URI of the expanded name of the target node.

Rules

The namespace URI of a node depends on the node type, as follows:

Node type	Namespace URI
root	None, an empty string is returned.
element	If the element name as given in the source XML contained a colon, the value will be the URI from the namespace declaration corresponding to the element's prefix. Otherwise, the value will be the URI of the default namespace. If this is null, the result will be an empty string.

Node type	Namespace URI
attribute	If the attribute name as given in the source XML contained a colon, the value will be the URI from the namespace declaration corresponding to the attribute's prefix. Otherwise, the namespace URI will be an empty string.
text	None, an empty string is returned.
processing instruction	None, an empty string is returned.
comment	None, an empty string is returned.
namespace	None, an empty string is returned.

Except for element and attribute nodes, **`namespace-uri()`** returns an empty string.

Usage

Let's start with some situations where you **don't** need this function.

If you want to test whether the current node belongs to a particular namespace, the best way to achieve this is using a `NameTest` of the form «`prefix:*`». For example, to test whether the current element belongs to the «`http://ibm.com/ebiz`» namespace, write:

```
<xsl:if test="self::ebiz:*" xmlns:ebiz="http://ibm.com/ebiz">
```

If you want to find the namespace URI corresponding to a given prefix the best solution is to use namespace nodes. You might need to do this if namespace prefixes are used in attribute values: the XSLT standard itself uses this technique in attributes such as `extension-element-prefixes`, and there is no reason why other XML document types should not do the same. If you have an attribute «`@value`» which you know takes the form of a namespace-qualified name (a `QName`), you can get the associated namespace URI by writing:

```
<xsl:variable name="prefix" select="substring-before(@value, ':')"/>
<xsl:variable name="ns-uri"  select="string(namespace::*[name()=$prefix])"/>
```

The **namespace-uri()** function, by contrast, is useful in display contexts, where you just want to display the namespace URI of the current node, and also if you want to do more elaborate tests. For example, you may know that there is a whole family of namespaces whose URIs all begin with `urn:schemas.biztalk`, and you may want to test whether the current node is in any one of these. You can achieve this by writing:

```
<xsl:if test="starts-with(namespace-uri(), 'urn:schemas.biztalk')>
```

Examples

The following stylesheet fragment determines the namespace URI of the current element, and then establishes the outermost ancestor on which that namespace is declared:

```
<xsl:template match="*">
   <xsl:variable name="uri" select="namespace-uri()"/>
   Namespace URI is <xsl:value-of select="$uri"/>
   Declared on element <xsl:value-of
        select="name(ancestor-or-self::*[namespace::*=$uri][last()])"/>
</xsl:template>
```


See also

local-name() on page 515
name() on page 517

normalize-space

The **normalize-space()** function removes leading and trailing whitespace from a string, and replaces internal sequences of whitespace with a single space character.

For example, the expression «`normalize-space(' x	 y ')`» returns the string «x y».

Defined in

XPath section 4.2

Format

```
normalize-space()  ⇒  string
normalize-space(value)  ⇒  string
```

Arguments

Argument	Data type	Meaning
value (optional)	string	The input string. If the argument is not a string, it is converted to a string using the rules of the **string()** function. If the argument is omitted, it defaults to the string-value of the context node.

Result

A string obtained by removing leading and trailing whitespace from the input string, and replacing internal sequences of whitespace by a single space character.

Rules

Whitespace is defined, as in the XML specification, as a sequence of space, tab, newline, and carriage return characters (`#x9`, `#xA`, `#xD`, and `#x20`).

Usage

It is often a good idea to apply the **normalize-space()** function to any string read from the source document before testing its contents, as many users will assume that leading and trailing whitespace has no significance and that within the string, multiple spaces or tabs are equivalent to a single space.

Don't imagine that **<xsl:strip-space>** does this for you. The only thing it does is to remove text nodes that contain whitespace only.

One situation where it isn't safe to use **normalize-space()** is where you are processing mixed element content containing character-level formatting attributes. For example, if you process the nodes that result from the element:

```
<p>Some <i>very</i> traditional HTML</p>
```

then the spaces after «`Some`» and before «`traditional`» are significant, even though they appear respectively at the end and the beginning of a text node.

Examples

The following key declaration indexes the titles of books with whitespace normalized:

```
<xsl:key name="book-title" match="book" use="normalize-space(title)"/>
```

This may then be used to locate books by title as follows:

```
<xsl:for-each select="key('book-title', normalize-space($title))">
```

The effect is that it will be possible, without knowing how many spaces and newlines there are, to retrieve a book appearing in the source document as:

```
<book>
   <title>Object Oriented Languages -
                Basic Principles and Programming Techniques</title>
</book>
```

The `normalize-space()` function can be particularly useful when processing a whitespace-separated list of values. Such lists are used in some document designs, and they may also be constructed at run-time because there is no other way in XSLT 1.0 of representing an array of computed values in a variable (with XSLT 1.1, of course, you can use a temporary tree for this purpose). Once the string has whitespace normalized, it is possible to use **`substring-before()`** to get the next token. To make this easier still, I usually add a space at the end of the string after normalization, so that every token is followed by a single space.

The following example shows how to use `normalize-space()` to obtain a count of the number of words in a string.

Example: Using normalize-space() to get a Word Count

This stylesheet contains a general-purpose template for counting the words in a string. It demonstrates this template by counting the words in the string-value of each element in the document in turn.

Source

This stylesheet can be used with any XML source document. For example, try it with the file `authors.xml` listed in the example on page 501.

Stylesheet

The stylesheet, called `word-count.xsl`, uses a named template «`word-count`» which counts the number of words in the parameter named «`text`». It does this by using **`normalize-space()`** to replace all whitespace sequences with a single space. If the string is now empty, it returns zero, otherwise it calls itself to process the string after the first space character and adds one to the result.

The template rule for the root node is simply a demonstration script that shows how to use the «`word-count`» template to count the words in every element in the document.

```
<xsl:transform
 xmlns:xsl="http://www.w3.org/1999/XSL/Transform"
 version="1.0"
>

<xsl:template name="word-count">
    <xsl:param name="text"/>
    <xsl:variable name="ntext" select="normalize-space($text)"/>
    <xsl:choose>
```

```
        <xsl:when test="$ntext">
            <xsl:variable name="remainder">
                <xsl:call-template name="word-count">
                    <xsl:with-param name="text"
                          select="substring-after($ntext, ' ')"/>
                </xsl:call-template>
            </xsl:variable>
            <xsl:value-of select="$remainder + 1"/>
        </xsl:when>
        <xsl:otherwise>0</xsl:otherwise>
        </xsl:choose>
    </xsl:template>

    <xsl:template match="/">
        <xsl:for-each select="//*">
            <xsl:variable name="length">
                <xsl:call-template name="word-count">
                    <xsl:with-param name="text" select="."/>
                </xsl:call-template>
            </xsl:variable>
            <element name="{name()}" words="{$length}"/>;
        </xsl:for-each>
    </xsl:template>

    </xsl:transform>
```

Output

If you apply this stylesheet to the file `authors.xml`, as suggested, the output is:

```
<element name="authors" words="101"/>;
<element name="author" words="35"/>;
<element name="born" words="1"/>;
<element name="died" words="1"/>;
<element name="biog" words="33"/>;
<element name="author" words="66"/>;
<element name="born" words="1"/>;
<element name="died" words="1"/>;
<element name="biog" words="64"/>;
<element name="i" words="3"/>;
```

See also

concat() on page 456
substring-after() on page 549
substring-before() on page 550

not

The **not()** function returns the Boolean negation of its argument: if the argument is true, it returns false, and vice versa.

For example, the expression «not(true())» returns false.

Defined in

XPath section 4.3

Format

```
not(condition)  ⇒  boolean
```

Arguments

Argument	Data type	Meaning
condition	Boolean	The input condition. If the argument is not a Boolean, it is converted to a Boolean using the rules of the **boolean()** function.

Result

The Boolean negation of the argument value: true if the argument is false, false if the argument is true.

Rules

If the argument is not a Boolean, it is converted to a Boolean using the rules of the **boolean()** function.

If the value (after any conversion) is true, **not()** returns false; if it is false, **not()** returns true.

Usage

Note that writing «not($A=2)» is not the same thing as writing «$A!=2». The difference arises when $A is a node-set: «not($A=2)» will be true if $A does not contain a node that is equal to 2, while «$A!=2» is true if A does contain a node that is not equal to 2. For example,. if $A is an empty node-set, «not($A=2)» will be true, while «$A!=2» will be false.

It is easy to forget this when testing attribute values: for example the following two examples behave the same way if the attribute **go** is present (they output «go» if the value is anything other than «no»), but they behave differently if the attribute is absent: the second one outputs «go», but the first one outputs nothing.

```
<xsl:if test="@go!='no'">go</xsl:if>
<xsl:if test="not(@go='no')">go</xsl:if>
```

When used with node-sets, the relational operators such as «=» and «!=» are subject to an implicit "if there exists" qualifier: «$X=$Y» means "if there exists a node x in $X and a node y in $Y such that x and y have the same string-value". If you want to achieve an "if all" qualifier, for example "if all nodes in the node-set have a **size** attribute equal to 0", then you can achieve this by negating both the condition and the expression as a whole: «not(@size!=0)».

Examples

The following test succeeds if the current node has no children:

```
<xsl:if test="not(node())">
```

The following test succeeds if the current node has no parent (that is, if it is a root node):

```
<xsl:if test="not(parent::node())">
```

The following **<xsl:for-each>** statement processes all the child elements of the current node except the **<notes>** elements:

```
<xsl:for-each select="*[not(self::notes)]">
```

The following test succeeds if the string-value of the current node is zero-length:

```
<xsl:if test="not(.)">
```

The following test succeeds if the **name** attribute of the current node is absent or is a zero-length string:

```
<xsl:if test="not(string(@name))">
```

The following test succeeds if the **name** attribute of the first node in node-set $ns is different from the **name** attribute of each subsequent node in the node-set (we assume that this attribute is present on all nodes in the node-set):

```
<xsl:if test="not($ns[1]/@name = $ns[position()!=1]/@name)">
```

See also

boolean() on page 452
false() on page 482
true() on page 562

number

The **`number()`** function converts its argument to a number.

For example, the expression «`number('  -17.3')`» returns the number –17.3.

Defined in

XPath section 4.4

Format

```
number()  ⇒  number
number(value)  ⇒  number
```

Arguments

Argument	Data type	Meaning
value optional	any	The value to be converted. If the argument is omitted, the string-value of the context node is used.

Result

A number: the value of the argument after conversion to a number.

Rules

The conversion rules depend on the data type of the value supplied, as defined in the following table.

Supplied data type	Conversion rules
Boolean	`False` becomes zero; `true` becomes one
number	The value is unchanged
string	Leading and trailing whitespace is removed; if the resulting string comprises an optional minus sign followed by an XPath `Number` it is evaluated as if it were an XPath expression; otherwise the result value is NaN (not a number)
node-set	The node-set is converted to a string using the rules for the **`string()`** function, and the resulting string is then converted to a number in the same way as a string argument is converted

Usage

In most circumstances, conversion to a number is implicit so it is not necessary to use the **`number()`** function explicitly.

There is one important situation where conversion needs to be explicit: this is in a predicate. The meaning of a predicate depends on the data type of the value, in particular, a numeric predicate is interpreted as a comparison with the context position. If the value is not numeric, it is converted to a Boolean.

So for example if a value held in an attribute or in a temporary tree is to be used as a numeric predicate, you should convert it explicitly to a number, thus:

```
<xsl:apply-templates select="$sales-figures[number(@month)]"/>
```

To test whether a value (for example, in an attribute) is numeric, use **`number()`** to convert it to a number and test the result against NaN (not a number). The most direct way to do this is:

```
<xsl:if test="string(number(@value))='NaN'"/>
```

Examples

Expression	Result
`number(12.3)`	12.3
`number("12.3")`	12.3
`number(true())`	1.0
`number("xyz")`	NaN
`number("")`	NaN

See also

`boolean()` on page 452
`format-number()` on page 484
`string()` on page 541
`<xsl:number>` on page 256, in Chapter 4

position

The **`position()`** function returns the value of the context position. When processing a list of nodes, **`position()`** gives the number assigned to the current node in the list, with the first node being numbered as 1.

Defined in

XPath section 4.1

Format

```
position()  ⇒  number
```

Arguments

None

Result

A number, the value of the context position. As the name implies, this is context dependant.

Rules

XPath specification defines the value of the **`position()`** function in terms of the *context position*. The XSLT specification uses different terminology: it talks about the *current node* and the *current node list*.

When a top-level expression is evaluated (that is, an expression that is not part of another expression), the context position is set to the position of the current node in the current node list. The nodes are numbered starting at 1. There are several possible settings:

- When a global variable is being evaluated, or in certain other contexts such as evaluating the **`use`** expression in **`<xsl:key>`**, the current node list contains a single node (the root), so the context position is always 1. This is also the case when the first template rule is invoked to process the root node.
- When **`<xsl:apply-templates>`** is called to process a set of nodes, the current node list is the list of nodes being processed, in the order in which they are processed, and the context position is therefore set successively to 1, 2, ... *n* as the nodes are processed. The position reflects the output order of the nodes, in other words the order after sorting, not necessarily the order in the source document.
- When **`<xsl:for-each>`** is called to process a set of nodes, the current node list is the list of nodes being processed, in the order in which they are processed, and the context position is therefore set successively to 1, 2, ... *n* as the nodes are processed. The position reflects the output order of the nodes, in other words the order after sorting, not necessarily the order in the source document.

- If the **position()** function is used within the **select** expression of an **<xsl:sort>** key, it refers to the position of the node before sorting. So, for example, if you want to sort nodes into reverse document order, you can do this by writing:

```
<xsl:sort select="position()" data-type="number"
order="descending">
```

  A more complex example, where the nodes are sorted into columns for display in a table, is given in the entry for the **last()** function on page 510.

When a predicate is evaluated, either in an expression or in a pattern, the context position is the relative position of the node currently being tested in that step of the expression or pattern evaluation, counting the nodes in document order if it is a forwards axis or in reverse document order if it is a reverse axis. For more details, see Chapter 5 *Expressions*, and Chapter 6 *Patterns*.

Usage and Examples

The two main uses of the **position()** function are to *display* the current position, and to *test* the current position.

Displaying the Current Position

In this role the **position()** function is an alternative to the **<xsl:number>** instruction, and can be used for simple numbering of paragraphs, sections, or figures.

There is much less flexibility to control how the numbering is done than when using **<xsl:number>**, but the **position()** function has two important advantages:

- It is generally faster
- It numbers items in the order they are output, whereas **<xsl:number>** can only allocate a number based on the position of a node in the source document. This means **<xsl:number>** is of little use when a list has been sorted using **<xsl:sort>**.

If you use **position()**, you can still exploit the formatting capabilities of **<xsl:number>** by writing for example:

```
<xsl:number value="position()" format="(a)"/>
```

This determines the position of the node and formats the result according to the given format pattern: the resulting sequence will be «(a)», «(b)», «(c)», and so on.

Testing the Current Position

It is possible to test the position of the current item either in a Boolean expression in an **<xsl:if>** or **<xsl:when>** element, or in a predicate within a node-set expression or pattern.

A common requirement is to treat the first or last item in a list differently from the rest. For example, to insert a horizontal rule after every item except the last, the following logic might be used:

```
<xsl:for-each select="item">
<xsl:sort select="@name"/>
   <p><xsl:value-of select="@name"/>:
      <xsl:value-of select="description"/></p>
   <xsl:if test="position() != last()">
      <hr/>
   </xsl:if>
</xsl:for-each>
```

Within a predicate in an expression or pattern, a numeric value represents an implicit test against the result of **`position()`**, for example «`item[1]`» is equivalent to «`item[position()=1]`», and «`item[last()]`» is equivalent to «`item[position()=last()]`».

> **You can only use this shorthand in a predicate; that is, within square brackets. If you use a numeric value in other contexts where a Boolean is expected, the number is converted to a Boolean on the basis that 0 is false; everything else is true. So `<xsl:if test="1">` does *not* mean `<xsl:if test="position()=1">`; it means the same as `<xsl:if test="true()">`.**

A common requirement when doing more complex processing is to separate the first node in a node-set from the set of nodes after the first.

Example: Using position() to Process a Node-set Recursively

Source

The source file `shapes.xml` represents a collection of shapes:

```
<shapes>
<rectangle width="10" height="30"/>
<square side="15"/>
<rectangle width="3" height="80"/>
<circle radius="10"/>
</shapes>
```

Stylesheet

The stylesheet `area.xsl` calculates the total area of these shapes. There is a separate rule for calculating the area of each kind of shape. The recursive template named «`total-area`» gets the area of the first shape by calling **`<xsl:apply-templates>`**, and adds the total area of the remaining shapes by calling itself with a list of shapes containing all the shapes except the first. When the set of shapes is empty, it returns zero.

```
<xsl:transform
 xmlns:xsl="http://www.w3.org/1999/XSL/Transform"
 version="1.0"
>

<xsl:template match="rectangle" mode="area">
    <xsl:value-of select="@width * @height"/>
</xsl:template>

<xsl:template match="square" mode="area">
    <xsl:value-of select="@side * @side"/>
</xsl:template>

<xsl:template match="circle" mode="area">
    <xsl:value-of select="3.14159 * @radius * @radius"/>
</xsl:template>

<xsl:template name="total-area">
    <xsl:param name="set-of-shapes"/>
    <xsl:choose>
    <xsl:when test="$set-of-shapes">
        <xsl:variable name="first">
            <xsl:apply-templates select="$set-of-shapes[1]"
                                 mode="area"/>
        </xsl:variable>
        <xsl:variable name="rest">
            <xsl:call-template name="total-area">
                <xsl:with-param name="set-of-shapes"
                    select="$set-of-shapes[position()!=1]"/>
            </xsl:call-template>
        </xsl:variable>
        <xsl:value-of select="$first + $rest"/>
    </xsl:when>
    <xsl:otherwise>0</xsl:otherwise>
    </xsl:choose>
</xsl:template>

<xsl:template match="shapes">
    <xsl:call-template name="total-area">
        <xsl:with-param name="set-of-shapes" select="*"/>
    </xsl:call-template>
</xsl:template>

</xsl:transform>
```

Output

Using Saxon, the output is:

```
1079.159
```

If you wanted to display this rounded to a single place after the decimal point, you could use **`format-number()`** with a format pattern of «0.0».

See also

last() on page 510
<xsl:number> in Chapter 4, on page 256

round

The **round()** function returns the closest integer to the numeric value of the argument.

For example, the expression «round(4.6)» returns 5.

Defined in

XPath section 4.4

Format

```
round(value)  ⇒  number
```

Arguments

Argument	Data type	Meaning
value	number	The input value. If it is not of type number, it is first converted to a number using the rules for the **number()** function.

Result

An integer value: the result of rounding the first argument to the nearest integer.

Rules

If the value is not numeric, it is first converted to a number. For the detailed rules, see the description of the **number()** function on page 531. If the value is a node-set, these rules mean that the function applies to the value of the first node in the node-set, in document order.

The XPath specification is very precise about the results of **round()**. The rules are given in the table below. The concepts of positive and negative zero, and positive and negative infinity, are explained in Chapter 2, starting on page 89.

If the argument is...	Then the result is...
An integer *N*	*N*
Between *N* and *N* + 0.5	*N*

If the argument is...	Then the result is...
Exactly $N + 0.5$	$N + 1$
Between $N + 0.5$ and $N + 1$	$N + 1$
Between –0.5 and zero	Negative zero
Positive zero	Positive zero
Negative zero	Negative zero
Positive infinity	Positive infinity
Negative infinity	Negative infinity
NaN (not a number)	NaN

Usage

The **`round()`** function is useful when you want the nearest integer, for example when calculating an average, or when deciding the geometric coordinates for an object to be displayed.

Examples

Example: Using round() to Arrange Data in a Table

The following example constructs an HTML table in which the number of columns is supplied as a parameter, with the first column taking half the available width, and the remaining columns being of equal width to each other.

Source

The source file is `sales.xml`:

```
<sales>
   <product>Windows 98
      <period name="Q1">82</period>
      <period name="Q2">64</period>
      <period name="Q3">58</period>
   </product>
   <product>Windows NT
      <period name="Q1">17</period>
      <period name="Q2">44</period>
      <period name="Q3">82</period>
   </product>
</sales>
```

Stylesheet

The stylesheet `sales-table.xsl` is shown below. It calculates the width of the rows in the table based on the number of columns needed:

```
<xsl:transform
 xmlns:xsl="http://www.w3.org/1999/XSL/Transform"
 version="1.0"
>

<xsl:template match="sales">
<html><body>
   <h1>Product sales by period</h1>
   <xsl:variable name="cols" select="count(product[1]/period)"/>
   <table border="1" cellpadding="5" width="100%">
      <tr>
      <th width="50%">Product</th>
      <xsl:for-each select="product[1]/period">
         <th width="{round(50 div $cols)}%">
            <xsl:value-of select="@name"/>
         </th>
      </xsl:for-each>
   </tr>
   <xsl:for-each select="product">
   <tr>
      <td><xsl:value-of select="text()"/></td>
      <xsl:for-each select="period">
         <td>
            <xsl:value-of select="."/>
         </td>
      </xsl:for-each>
   </tr>
   </xsl:for-each>
   </table>
</body></html>
</xsl:template>

</xsl:transform>
```

Output

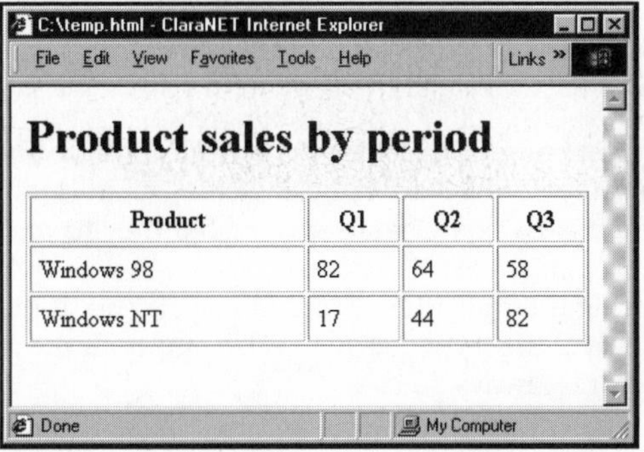

See also

ceiling() on page 454
floor() on page 483

starts-with

The **starts-with()** function tests whether one string starts with another string.

For example, the expression «starts-with('$17.30', '$')» returns true.

Defined in

XPath section 4.2

Format

```
starts-with(value, substring)  ⇒  boolean
```

Arguments

Argument	Data type	Meaning
value	string	The containing string. If the value is not a string, it is converted to a string using the rules of the **string()** function.
substring	string	The contained string. If the value is not a string, it is converted to a string using the rules of the **string()** function.

Result

A Boolean value; true if the first string starts with the second string, otherwise false.

Rules

The strings are compared, character by character, from the beginning. If the second string is exhausted before a pair of non-matching characters is found, the result is true; otherwise it is false. Characters match if they have the same Unicode value.

If the second string is empty, the result is always true. If the first string is empty, the result is true only if the second string is also empty. If the second string is longer than the first, the result is always false.

Usage and Examples

The **starts-with()** function is useful when the content of text values, or attributes, has some internal structure. For example, the following template rule matches all **<link>** elements that have an **href** attribute whose value starts with the character «#»:

```
<xsl:template match="link[starts-with(@href, '#')]">
. . .
</xsl:template>
```

Note

There is no **`ends-with()`** function. To test whether a string `$A` ends with a string `$B`, the simplest test is:

```
substring($A, string-length($A) - string-length($B) + 1) = $B
```

See also

`contains()` on page 458
`string-length()` on page 543

string

The **`string()`** function converts its argument to a string value.

For example, the expression «`string(4.00)`» returns the string «4».

Defined in

XPath section 4.2

Format

```
string()  ⇒  string
string(value)  ⇒  string
```

Arguments

Argument	Data type	Meaning
value optional	any	The value to be converted. If the argument is omitted, it defaults to a node-set containing only the context node.

Result

A string value: the result of converting the argument to a string.

Rules

Values of any data type can be converted to a string. The rules are as follows.

Data type	Conversion rules
Boolean	The Boolean value `false` is converted to the string «`false`». The value `true` is converted to the string «`true`».

Data type	Conversion rules
number	NaN is represented as «NaN». Positive and negative zero are both represented as «0». Positive infinity is represented as «Infinity». Negative infinity is represented as «-Infinity». An integer is represented in decimal form with no decimal point and no leading zeroes, preceded by a minus sign if it is negative. The result will be a valid XPath `Number`. Any other number is represented in decimal form with at least one digit before the decimal point and at least one digit after the decimal point, preceded by a minus sign if it is negative; there must be no leading zeros except immediately before the decimal point; after the decimal point there should be as many digits as are necessary to distinguish the number from other IEEE 754 numeric values. The result will be a valid XPath `Number`.
string	The value is unchanged.
node-set	If the node-set is empty, it is represented as the empty string. Otherwise, it is represented by the string-value of the node that is first in document order. The string-value of a text node is the text content. The string-value of a comment is the comment. The string-value of a processing instruction is the data part. The string-value of a namespace node is the namespace URI. The string value of an attribute node is the attribute value. The string-value of a root node or element node is the concatenation of the content of all its descendant text nodes, taken in document order.

A tree valued variable such as `<xsl:variable name="v">New York</xsl:variable>` is technically a node-set consisting of a root node, which has a single child text node. The string-value of this variable is the string-value of the root node: this is defined as the concatenation of the values of all its descendant text nodes, in document order. So in this case the string-value is «New York».

Here, although the variable is actually a node-set, it can be used to all intents and purposes as if it were a string with the value «New York». This is true both in XSLT 1.0 and 1.1; the XSLT 1.0 specifications explicitly states that a result tree fragment can be used anywhere that a string can be used.

Usage and Examples

It is not usually necessary to call the **string()** function explicitly, since it will normally be invoked automatically when a string is required and the supplied value is a different type.

An example of a situation where an explicit conversion is appropriate is when you want to force a string comparison of two values rather than a node-set comparison. For example, the following test succeeds if any **<author>** child of the current node has the value «`J. B. Priestley`».

```
<xsl:if test="author='J. B. Priestley'">
```

while the following succeeds only if the first **<author>** child, in document order, has this value:

```
<xsl:if test="string(author)='J. B. Priestley'">
```

However, it would be rather clearer in this case to write:

```
<xsl:if test="author[1]='J. B. Priestley'">
```


See also

boolean() on page 452
number() on page 531

string-length

The **string-length()** function returns the number of characters in a string value.

For example, the expression «`string-length('Beethoven')`» returns 9.

Defined in

XPath section 4.2

Format

```
string-length()  ⇒  number
string-length(value)  ⇒  number
```

Arguments

Argument	Data type	Meaning
value (optional)	string	The string whose length is required. If the value is not a string, it is converted to a string using the rules of the **`string()`** function. If the argument is omitted, the string-value of the context node is used.

Result

A number: the number of characters in the value of the argument.

Rules

Characters are counted as instances of the XML `Char` production. This means that a Unicode surrogate pair (a pair of 16-bit values used to represent a Unicode character in the range `#x10000` to `#x10FFFF`) is treated as a single character.

It is the number of characters in the string that matters, not the way they are written in the source document. A character written using a character reference such as «`ÿ`» or an entity reference such as «`&`» is still one character.

Unicode combining and non-spacing characters are counted individually, unless the implementation has normalized them. The implementation is allowed to turn strings into canonical form, but is not required to do so. In canonical form accents and diacriticals will typically be merged with the letter that they modify into a single character. This means that in such cases, the result of the **`string-length()`** function is not precisely defined.

Usage

The **`string-length()`** function can be useful when deciding how to allocate space on the output medium. For example, if a list is displayed in multiple columns then the number of columns may be determined by some algorithm based on the maximum length of the strings to be displayed.

It is **not** necessary to call **`string-length()`** to determine whether a string is empty (null), because converting the string to a Boolean, either explicitly using the **`boolean()`** function, or implicitly by using it in a Boolean context, returns `true` only if the string has a length of one or more. For the same reason, it is not usually necessary to call **`string-length()`** when processing the characters in a string using a recursive iteration, since the terminating condition when the string is empty can be tested by converting it to a Boolean.

Examples

The following table shows the result of the **string-length()** function for some example inputs:

Expression	Result
string-length('abc')	3
string-length('')	0
string-length('<>')	2
string-length('�')	1
string-length('𠀀')	1

See also

substring() in the section immediately below

substring

The **substring()** function returns part of a string value, determined by character positions within the string. Character positions are counted from one.

For example, the expression «substring('Goldfarb', 5, 3)» returns the string «far».

Defined in

XPath section 4.2

Format

```
substring(value, start)  ⇒  string
substring(value, start, length)  ⇒  string
```

Arguments

Argument	Data type	Meaning
value	string	The containing string. If the value is not a string, it is converted to a string using the rules of the **string()** function.
start	number	The position in the containing string of the first character to be included in the result string. If the value is not a number, it is converted to a number using the rules of the **number()** function.

Argument	Data type	Meaning
length optional	number	The number of characters to be included in the result string. If the value is not a number, it is converted to a number using the rules of the `number()` function. If the argument is omitted, characters are taken from the start position up to the end of the containing string.

Result

A string: the required substring of the containing string.

Rules

Informally, the function returns a string consisting of the characters in the *value* string starting at position *start*; if a *length* is given, the returned string contains this many characters, otherwise it contains all characters up to the end of the *value*.

Characters within a string are numbered 1, 2, 3 … *n*. This will be familiar to Visual Basic programmers but not to those accustomed to C or Java, where numbering starts at zero.

Characters are counted as instances of the XML `Char` production. This means that a Unicode surrogate pair (a pair of 16-bit values used to represent a Unicode character in the range #x10000 to #x10FFFF) is treated as a single character.

Combining and non-spacing characters are counted individually, unless the implementation has normalized them. The implementation is allowed to turn strings into canonical form, but is not required to do so. In canonical form accents and diacritics will typically be merged with the letter that they modify into a single character.

The formal rules are surprisingly complex, because they need to take into account conditions such as the start or length being negative, NaN, fractional, or infinite (for a description of the number data type, see Chapter 2, page 89). The rules are as follows:

Let start be the numeric value of the second argument.
Let length be the numeric value of the third argument, if specified.

If length was specified, the returned string contains those characters for which the position p of the character in the containing string satisfies: p >= round(start) and p < round(start) + round(length).

If length was omitted, the returned string contains those characters for which the position p of the character in the containing string satisfies: p >= round(start).

Rounding is done using the **round()** function, see page 537. The comparisons and arithmetic are done using IEEE 754 arithmetic, which has some interesting consequences if values such as infinity and NaN, or indeed any non-integer values are used. The rules for IEEE 754 arithmetic are summarized in Chapter 2.

The formal rule tells us that if the *start* argument is less than one, the result always starts at the first character of the supplied string, while if it is greater than the length of the string, the result will always be an empty string. If the *length* argument is less than zero, it is treated as zero, and again an empty string is returned. If the *length* argument is greater than the number of available characters, then characters will be returned up to the end of the containing string.

Usage and Examples

The **substring()** function is useful when processing a string character-by-character. One common usage is to determine the first character of a string:

```
<xsl:variable name="drive-letter">
   <xsl:if test="substring($filename,2,1)=':')">
      <xsl:value-of select="substring($filename,1,1)"/>
   </xsl:if>
</xsl:variable>
```


Or when manipulating personal names in the conventional American format of first name, middle initial, last name:

```
<xsl:variable name="display-name">
   <xsl:value-of select="first-name"/>
   <xsl:text> </xsl:text>
   <xsl:value-of select="substring(middle-name, 1, 1)"/>
   <xsl:text> </xsl:text>
   <xsl:value-of select="last-name"/>
</xsl:variable>
```

You can use the **substring()** function in conjunction with **string-length()** to test whether a string ends with a particular suffix. Remember that character positions are numbered from one:

```
<xsl:variable name="linked-document">
   <xsl:if test="substring(@href, string-length(@href)-3) = '.xml'">
      <xsl:value-of select="document(@href)"/>
   </xsl:if>
</xsl:variable>
```

The following example tests whether a supplied string contains the sequence «#x#» where «x» is any single character:

```
<xsl:if test="contains($s, '#') and
                     substring(substring-after($s, '#'), 2, 1)='#'">
```

The **substring()** function can be used as a kind of conditional expression. Suppose that $b is a Boolean value, and consider the following expression:

```
substring("xyz", 1, $b * string-length("xyz"))
```

Because `$b` is used in a numeric expression, it is converted to a number: `0` for false, `1` for true. So the value of the third argument is `0` if `$b` is false, `3` if `$b` is true. The final result of the `substring()` function is therefore an empty string if `$b` is false, or the string `"xyz"` if `$b` is true. The expression is equivalent to «`($b ? "xyz" : "")`» in Java or C.

In fact the third argument doesn't need to be exactly equal to the string length for this to work, it can be any value greater than the string length. So you could equally well write :

```
substring("xyz", 1, $b * 1000)
```

or even:

```
substring("xyz", 1, $b * (1 div 0))
```

exploiting the fact that «`1 div 0`» is infinity.

One situation where this kind of trick can be handy is in defining an HTML table. You often want to set up a table cell that contains a particular value (let's say «`item`») if it exists, or a non-breaking space (` `) if it doesn't. You can achieve this using **`<xsl:choose>`**; but a more concise way is:

```
concat(item, substring(' ', 1, not(item))
```

This construct can also be handy in contexts such as key definitions (**`<xsl:key>`**), or sort keys (**`<xsl:sort>`**), where you have to do a calculation entirely within XPath and don't get the chance to use XSLT for defining variables. Suppose you want to sort a set of prices, some of which are in pounds and some in dollars, for example:

```
<prices>
  <item currency="GBP" price="14.00"/>
  <item currency="GBP" price="18.00"/>
  <item currency="USD" price="23.50"/>
  <item currency="GBP" price="12.00"/>
  <item currency="USD" price="17.80"/>
</prices>
```

You can achieve this as follows:

```
<xsl:variable name="rate" select="1.53"/>
  <xsl:for-each select="item">
    <xsl:sort data-type="number"
         select="concat(
                substring(@price * $rate, 1, (@currency='USD') *
                          1000),
                substring(@price, 1, (@currency='GBP') * 1000))"/>
  </xsl:for-each>
</xsl:variable>
```

I'd suggest that if you attempt this, you include a detailed comment explaining how it works, and blame this book for making the idea respectable.

See also

substring-after() in the section immediately below
substring-before() on page 550
string-length() on page 543
contains() on page 458

substring-after

The **substring-after()** function returns that part of a string value that occurs after the first occurrence of some specified substring.

For example, the expression «substring-after('print=yes', '=')» returns «yes».

Defined in

XPath section 4.2

Format

```
substring-after(value, substring)  ⇒  string
```

Arguments

Argument	Data type	Meaning
value	string	The containing string. If the argument is not a string, it is converted to a string using the rules of the **string()** function.
substring	string	The test string. If the argument is not a string, it is converted to a string using the rules of the **string()** function.

Result

A string containing those characters that follow the first occurrence of the test substring within the containing string.

Rules

If the containing string does not contain the test substring, the function returns an empty string. Note that this could also mean that the containing string ends with the test substring; the two cases can be distinguished by calling the **contains()** function.

If the containing string does contain the test substring, the function returns a string made up of all the characters that appear in the containing string after the first occurrence of the test substring.

If the test substring is empty, the function returns the containing string.

If the containing string is empty, the function returns an empty string.

Usage and Examples

The **substring-after()** function is useful when splitting a string that contains delimiter characters. For example, when the string is a whitespace-separated list of tokens, the first token can be obtained using

```
substring-before($s, ' ')
```

and the rest of the string using

```
substring-after($s, ' ')
```

It is a good idea to use **normalize-space()** to make sure that each separator is a single space character, and it is also useful to use **concat()** to add an extra space character at the end so that these functions work properly when the list contains a single token.

The following example takes a whitespace-separated list and outputs each token separated by an empty **
** element.

```
<xsl:template name="output-tokens">
   <xsl:param name="list"/>
   <xsl:variable name="nlist"
      select="concat(normalize-space($list),' ')"/>
   <xsl:variable name="first" select="substring-before($nlist, ' ')"/>
   <xsl:variable name="rest" select="substring-after($nlist, ' ')"/>
   <xsl:value-of select="$first"/>
   <xsl:if test="$rest">
      <br/>
      <xsl:call-template name="output-tokens">
         <xsl:with-param name="list" select="$rest"/>
      </xsl:call-template>
   </xsl:if>
</xsl:template>
```

See also

contains() on page 458
substring() on page 545
substring-before() in the section immediately below

substring-before

The **substring-before()** function returns that part of a string value that occurs before the first occurrence of some specified substring.

For example, the value of «`substring-before('print=yes', '=')`» is the string «`print`».

Defined in

XPath section 4.2

Format

```
substring-before(value, substring)  ⇒  string
```

Arguments

Argument	Data type	Meaning
value	string	The containing string. If the argument is not a string, it is converted to a string using the rules of the **`string()`** function.
substring	string	The test substring. If the argument is not a string, it is converted to a string using the rules of the **`string()`** function.

Result

A string containing those characters that precede the first occurrence of the test substring within the containing string.

Rules

If the containing string does not contain the test substring, the function returns an empty string. Note that this could also mean that the containing string starts with the test string; the two cases can be distinguished by calling the **`starts-with()`** function.

If the containing string does contain the test substring, the function returns a string made up of all the characters that appear in the containing string before the first occurrence of the test substring.

If either the test substring or the containing string is empty, the function returns an empty string.

Usage and Examples

An example of the use of **`substring-after()`** and **`substring-before()`** to process a whitespace-separated list of tokens is given under **`substring-after()`** on page 549.

If the only reason for using **`substring-before()`** is to test whether the string has a given prefix, use **`starts-with()`** instead. You could write:

```
<xsl:if test="substring-before($url, ':')='https'">
```

but the following is simpler:

```
<xsl:if test="starts-with($url, 'https:')">
```

The **substring-before()** and **substring-after()** functions can be useful to replace a portion of a string. The **translate()** function cannot be used to substitute one word for another. For such processing, it is necessary to use a combination of **contains()**, **substring-before()**, **substring-after()**, and possibly **concat()**. This is illustrated in the example below.

Example: Replacing All Occurrences of a String

This stylesheet replaces all occurrences of a given string by another string, within any text node of the source document. The replaced string is given by the global parameter «replace», the replacement string by the parameter «by».

Source

This works with any source document. For example, try it with the file authors.xml, with parameters replace=author by=writer.

Stylesheet

The stylesheet replace.xsl copies all elements and attributes unchanged, but processes text nodes using the named template «do-replace» which replaces all occurrences of the «replace» string with the «by» string. It does the first replacement directly, then calls itself recursively to do the remainder.

To process this stylesheet you need to supply global parameters. The way you do this depends on the product: for example, with Saxon use the command line:

```
saxon source.xml replace.xsl replace=xxx by=yyy
```

With Xalan, write (all on one line):

```
java org.apache.xalan.xslt.Process -in source.xml -xsl
replace.xsl -param replace xxx -param by yyy
```

```
<xsl:transform
 xmlns:xsl="http://www.w3.org/1999/XSL/Transform"
 version="1.0"
>

<xsl:param name="replace"/>
<xsl:param name="by"/>

<xsl:template name="do-replace">
   <xsl:param name="text"/>
   <xsl:choose>
   <xsl:when test="contains($text, $replace)">
      <xsl:value-of select="substring-before($text, $replace)"/>
      <xsl:value-of select="$by"/>
      <xsl:call-template name="do-replace">
```

```
            <xsl:with-param name="text"
                        select="substring-after($text,
$replace)"/>
            </xsl:call-template>
        </xsl:when>
        <xsl:otherwise>
            <xsl:value-of select="$text"/>
        </xsl:otherwise>
        </xsl:choose>

    </xsl:template>

    <xsl:template match="*">
        <xsl:copy>
        <xsl:copy-of select="@*"/>
        <xsl:apply-templates/>
        </xsl:copy>
    </xsl:template>

    <xsl:template match="text()">
        <xsl:call-template name="do-replace">
            <xsl:with-param name="text" select="."/>
        </xsl:call-template>
    </xsl:template>

    </xsl:transform>
```

Output

The result of processing the file `authors.xml` with «`replace=author by=***`» is shown below:

```
   <authors>

   <author name="A. A. Milne">
   <born>1852</born>
   <died>1956</died>
   <biog>Alan Alexander Milne, educated at Westminster School and
Trinity College Cambridge, became a prolific *** of plays, novels,
poetry, short stories, and essays, all of which have been
overshadowed by his children's books.</biog>
   </author>

   <author name="Daisy Ashford">
   <born>1881</born>
   <died>1972</died>
   <biog>Daisy Ashford (Mrs George Norman) wrote <i>The Young
Visiters</i>, a small comic masterpiece, while still a young child
in Lewes. It was found in a drawer in 1919 and sent to Chatto and
Windus, who published it in the same year with an introduction by J.
M. Barrie, who had first insisted on meeting the *** in order to
check that she was genuine.</biog>
   </author>

   </authors>
```

See also

contains() on page 458
starts-with() on page 540
substring() on page 545
substring-after() on page 549

sum

The **sum()** function calculates the total of a set of numeric values contained in a node-set.

For example, if the context node is the element `<rect x="20" y="30"/>`, then the expression «`sum(@*)`» returns 50. (The expression «`@*`» is a node-set containing all the attributes of the context node.)

Defined in

XPath section 4.4

Format

```
sum(nodes)  ⇒  number
```

Arguments

Argument	Data type	Meaning
nodes	node-set	The set of nodes to be totaled. It is an error if the argument is not a node-set.

Result

A number: the result of taking the string-value of each node in the node-set, converting it to a number, and totaling these numeric values.

Rules

The conversion of the string-value of each node to a number follows the rules of the **number()** function.

The totaling of the numeric values follows the arithmetic rules defined in IEEE 754.

A consequence of these rules is that if there is any node in the node-set whose string-value cannot be converted to a number, the result of the **sum()** function will be NaN (not a number).

If the node-set is empty, the result is zero.

Usage

The **`sum()`** function can be used to create totals and subtotals in a report. It is also useful for calculating geometric dimensions on the output page.

A problem that sometimes arises is how to get a total over a set of values that aren't present directly in the source file, but are calculated from it. For example, if the source document contains **`<book>`** elements with attributes **`price`** and **`sales`**, how would you calculate the total sales revenue, which is obtained by multiplying **`price`** by **`sales`** for each book, and totaling the result over all books? Or how would you total a set of numbers if each one has a leading «$» sign which you need to strip off first? The short answer is that you can't use the **`sum()`** function to do this.

In fact, there are two limitations on the use of **`sum()`**:

- All the values to be totaled must be explicitly present as nodes in the source document, it is not possible to perform any preprocessing of the values, for example customized string-to-number conversion, before the calculation is done.
- If any value is non-numeric (this includes an absent value), the result will be NaN.

If the data doesn't satisfy these constraints, you'll need to use a different approach. One way is to process the node-set explicitly using a recursive template. There is an example that does this, calculating the total area of a set of shapes, on page 535. Another approach (which relies on XSLT 1.1, or the **`node-set()`** extension function provided with many XSLT 1.0 processors) is to do two passes over the data: the first pass constructs a temporary tree containing the calculated values to be totaled, and the second pass uses the **`sum()`** function on the nodes in this tree to get the final answer.

Examples

Example: A League Table

This example uses the **`count()`** and **`sum()`** functions to perform various calculations on the results of a set of soccer matches (the Group A matches from the 1998 World Cup Finals).

Source

The source file is `soccer.xml`:

```
<results group="A">
<match>
<date>10-Jun-98</date>
   <team score="2">Brazil</team>
   <team score="1">Scotland</team>
</match>
<match>
   <date>10-Jun-98</date>
   <team score="2">Morocco</team>
   <team score="2">Norway</team>
</match>
```

```
<match>
   <date>16-Jun-98</date>
   <team score="1">Scotland</team>
   <team score="1">Norway</team>
</match>
<match>
   <date>16-Jun-98</date>
   <team score="3">Brazil</team>
   <team score="0">Morocco</team>
</match>
<match>
   <date>23-Jun-98</date>
   <team score="1">Brazil</team>
   <team score="2">Norway</team>
</match>
<match>
<date>23-Jun-98</date>
   <team score="0">Scotland</team>
   <team score="3">Morocco</team>
</match>
</results>
```

Stylesheet

The stylesheet is in file `league.xsl`.

The stylesheet creates two global variables: «`teams`», which is the set of distinct **`<team>`** elements in the document (any **`<team>`** element that has the same string-value as a preceding **`<team>`** element is not included), and «`matches`» which is the set of all **`<match>`** elements.

For each team, the stylesheet calculates the number of matches played, won, drawn, lost, the total number of goals scored by that team, and the total number of goals scored by opposing teams.

```
<xsl:transform
 xmlns:xsl="http://www.w3.org/1999/XSL/Transform"
 version="1.0"
>

<xsl:variable name="teams" select="//team[not(.=preceding::team)]"/>
<xsl:variable name="matches" select="//match"/>

<xsl:template match="results">
<html><body>
   <h1>Results of Group <xsl:value-of select="@group"/></h1>

   <table cellpadding="5">
      <tr>
        <td>Team</td>
        <td>Played</td>
```

```
        <td>Won</td>
        <td>Drawn</td>
        <td>Lost</td>
        <td>For</td>
        <td>Against</td>
      </tr>
    <xsl:for-each select="$teams">
        <xsl:variable name="this" select="."/>
        <xsl:variable name="played" select="count($matches[team=$this])"/>
        <xsl:variable name="won"
           select="count($matches[team[.=$this]/@score &gt;
                                  team[.!=$this]/@score])"/>
        <xsl:variable name="lost"
           select="count($matches[team[.=$this]/@score &lt;
                              team[.!=$this]/@score])"/>
        <xsl:variable name="drawn"
           select="count($matches[team[.=$this]/@score =
                              team[.!=$this]/@score])"/>
        <xsl:variable name="for"
             select="sum($matches/team[.=current()]/@score)"/>
        <xsl:variable name="against"
             select="sum($matches[team=current()]/team/@score) - $for"/>
        <tr>
        <td><xsl:value-of select="."/></td>
        <td><xsl:value-of select="$played"/></td>
        <td><xsl:value-of select="$won"/></td>
        <td><xsl:value-of select="$drawn"/></td>
        <td><xsl:value-of select="$lost"/></td>
        <td><xsl:value-of select="$for"/></td>
        <td><xsl:value-of select="$against"/></td>
        </tr>
    </xsl:for-each>
    </table>
  </body></html>
  </xsl:template>
  </xsl:transform>
```

Output

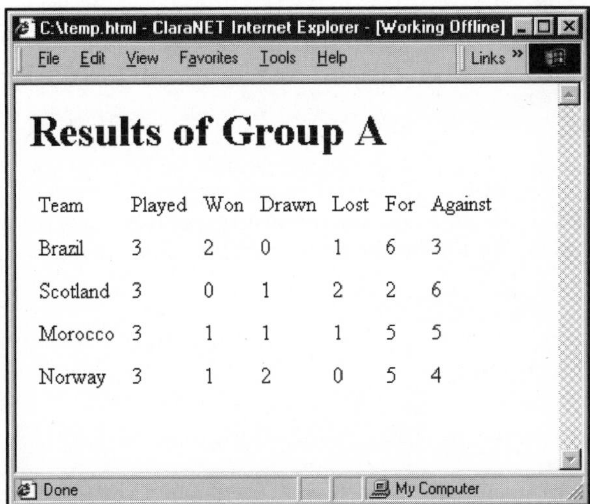

7 Functions

See also

count() on page 460

system-property

The **system-property()** function returns information about the processing environment.

For example, with a processor that implements XSLT version 1.1, the expression «system-property('xsl:version')» returns 1.1.

Defined in

XSLT section 12.4

Format

```
system-property(name)  ⇒  any
```

Arguments

Argument	Data type	Meaning
name	string	Specifies the name of the system property required. If the argument is not a string, it is converted to a string using the rules of the **string()** function. The value of the string should be a QName that identifies a system property. If there is no system property with this name, the function returns an empty string.

Result

The data type of the result, as well as its value, depends on the system property requested.

Rules

The supplied argument is converted into an expanded name using the namespace declarations in scope for the stylesheet element that contains the call on **system-property()**.

There are three system properties that every implementation must support: these are all in the XSLT namespace.

System Property Name	Value
xsl:version	A number giving the version of XSLT implemented by the processor. For current XSLT processors, this will be 1.0 or 1.1. Note that this is a number not a string, so if you display it using **<xsl:value-of>** it will be shown as «1» or «1.1».
xsl:vendor	A string identifying the vendor of the XSLT processor. In practice it will sometimes also identify the product name, but the actual value is implementor-defined. For Microsoft's MSXML3 product, the value is simply «Microsoft».
xsl:vendor-url	A string: the URL of the vendor's web site. For example, MSXML3 returns «http://www.microsoft.com»

Any additional system properties returned by this function are implementor-defined. Any implementor-defined properties would normally be in a namespace specific to the vendor.

An earlier draft of the XSLT specification stated that this function should give access to operating system environment variables. It would not be surprising to find implementations that provide this capability, but it is not mandatory.

Usage

The **system-property()** function can be used to determine details about the processor running the stylesheet, either for display purposes (for example, to produce a comment in the generated output), or to apply conditional logic.

Generally it is best to avoid using this function to test whether particular features are available. The functions **function-available()** and **element-available()** and the **<xsl:fallback>** instruction serve this need better, and the forwards-compatibility features described on page 137, in Chapter 3 can be used to ensure that a stylesheet can work with processors that implement an older dialect of XSLT.

However, there are some cases where testing «system-property('xsl:version')» is the only practical way of discovering whether a feature is available. For example, the XSLT 1.1 working draft introduces the ability to use a tree-valued variable (or a result tree fragment, as it is known in XSLT 1.0) as a node-set, in contexts such as **<xsl:for-each>** and **<xsl:apply-templates>**. Since this feature does not introduce any new functions or XSLT elements, the only practical way to test whether it is available is to check the XSLT version supported. Many XSLT 1.0 processors provide proprietary equivalents to this capability, usually through an extension function such as «msxml:node-set()», so you can write code such as:

```
<xsl:variable name="tree">
   ...
</xsl:variable>
<xsl:choose>
```

```
<xsl:when test="system-property('xsl:version') &gt;= 1.1">
   <xsl:apply-templates select="$tree"/>
</xsl:when>
<xsl:when test="function-available('msxml:node-set')">
   <xsl:apply-templates select="msxml:node-set($tree)"/>
</xsl:when>
<xsl:when test="function-available('xt:node-set')">
   <xsl:apply-templates select="xt:node-set($tree)"/>
</xsl:when>
<xsl:otherwise>
   <xsl:message terminate="yes">Cannot convert tree to node-set</xsl:message>
</xsl:otherwise>
</xsl:choose>
```

Examples

The following code outputs a documentary comment into the generated HTML:

```
<HTML>
   <xsl:comment>Generated using XSLT stylesheet abc.xsl
                using <xsl:value-of select="system-property('xsl:vendor')"/>
                at XSLT version
      <xsl:value-of select="system-property('xsl:version')"/>
   </xsl:comment>
. . .
```

See also

element-available() on page 476
function-available() on page 487
<xsl:fallback> on page 214, in Chapter 4

translate

The **translate()** function substitutes characters in a supplied string with nominated replacement characters. It can also be used to remove nominated characters from a string.

For example, the result of «translate('ABC-123', '-', '/')» is the string «ABC/123».

Defined in

XPath section 4.2

Format

```
translate(value, from, to)  ⇒  string
```

Arguments

Argument	Data type	Meaning
value	string	The supplied string. If the argument is not a string, it is converted to a string using the rules of the **`string()`** function.
from	string	The list of characters to be replaced. If the argument is not a string, it is converted to a string using the rules of the **`string()`** function.
to	string	The list of replacement characters. If the argument is not a string, it is converted to a string using the rules of the **`string()`** function.

Result

A string derived from the supplied string, but with those characters that appear in the second argument replaced by the corresponding characters from the third argument, or removed if there is no corresponding character.

Rules

For each character in the supplied string, one of three possible actions is taken:

- If the character is not present in the list of characters to be replaced, the character is copied to the result string unchanged
- If the character is present at position P in the list of characters to be replaced, and the list of replacement characters is of length P or greater, then the character at position P in the list of replacement characters is copied to the result string
- If the character is present at position P in the list of characters to be replaced, and the list of replacement characters is shorter than P, then no character is copied to the result string

Note that the third argument must be present, but it can be an empty string. In this case any character present in the second argument is removed from the supplied string.

If a character appears more than once in the list of characters to be replaced, the second and subsequent occurrences are ignored, as are the characters in the corresponding position in the third argument.

If the third argument is longer than the second, excess characters are ignored.

In these rules a *character* means an XML character, not a 16-bit Unicode code. This means that a Unicode surrogate pair (a pair of 16-bit values used to represent a Unicode character in the range `#x10000` to `#x10FFFF`) is treated as a single character, whichever of the three strings it appears in.

Usage and Examples

The **translate()** function can be used to perform simple case conversion where the alphabet is known and of modest size. For example, if the data uses only unaccented Latin letters, conversion to uppercase can be achieved by writing:

```
translate($X,
    'abcdefghijklmnopqrstuvwxyz',
    'ABCDEFGHIJKLMNOPQRSTUVWXYZ')
```

The **translate()** function is useful to remove extraneous punctuation or whitespace: for example to remove all whitespace, hyphens, and parentheses from a telephone number, write:

```
translate($X, '&#x20;&#x9;&#xA;&#xD;()-', '')
```

Another use for **translate()** is to test for the presence of a particular character or range of characters. For example, to test whether a string contains a sequence of three or more ASCII digits, write:

```
contains(translate($X, '0123456789', '9999999999'), '999')
```

Similarly, translate can be used to normalize delimiters before using **substring-after()** or **substring-before()** to extract part of the string. If a filename consists of a sequence of names separated by «/» or «\» characters, then the following expression will extract the part of the filename before the first separator:

```
substring-before(translate($X, '\', '/'), '/')
```

See also

contains() on page 458
substring() on page 545
substring-after() on page 549
substring-before() on page 550

true

This function returns the Boolean value `true`.

Defined in

XPath section 4.3

Format

```
true() ⇒ boolean
```

Arguments

None

Result

The Boolean value `true`.

Rules

There are no Boolean constants available in XPath expressions, so the functions **`true()`** and **`false()`** can be used where a constant Boolean value is required.

Usage

There are few occasions where constant Boolean values are required; the most common situation is in **`<xsl:with-param>`** when supplying a parameter to a template. See the example below.

Writing `<xsl:when test="true()">` can be useful as a temporary expedient to force execution down a particular path, perhaps because other paths are still under development.

Example

The following code calls a named template, setting the parameter «`verbose`» to `true`:

```
<xsl:call-template name="do-the-work">
   <xsl:with-param name="verbose" select="true()"/>
</xsl:call-template>
```

See also

`false()` on page 482

unparsed-entity-uri

The **`unparsed-entity-uri()`** function gives access to declarations of unparsed entities in the DTD of the source document.

For example, if the DTD contains the declaration:

```
<!ENTITY weather-map SYSTEM "weather.jpeg" NDATA JPEG>
```

then the expression «`unparsed-entity-uri('weather-map')`» returns the URI «`weather.jpeg`», expanded to an absolute URI by applying the base URI for the DTD.

Defined in

XSLT section 12.4

Format

```
unparsed-entity-uri(name)  ⇒  string
```

Arguments

Argument	Data type	Meaning
name	string	Specifies the name of the unparsed entity required. If the argument is not a string, it is converted to a string using the rules of the **`string()`** function. The value of the string should be an XML *Name*.

Result

A string containing the URI (the system identifier) of the unparsed entity with the given name, if there is one. Otherwise, an empty string.

Rules

If the document containing the context node includes an unparsed entity whose name is equal to the supplied string, a URI identifying that unparsed entity is returned. If there is no entity with this name, it returns an empty string.

If the system identifier is a relative URI, the XSLT processor should expand it into an absolute URI before returning it.

Usage

An unparsed entity is an entity defined in the DTD using a declaration of the form:

```
<!ENTITY weather-map SYSTEM "weather.jpeg" NDATA JPEG>
```

It's the NDATA (meaning "not XML data") that makes it an unparsed entity; and because it is an unparsed entity, it can't be referenced using a normal entity reference of the form «`&weather-map;`» but must instead be referenced by name in an attribute of type ENTITY or ENTITIES, for example `<forecastmap="weather-map">`.

As the author of the stylesheet, you are expected to know that the **`map`** attribute is of type ENTITY (there's no way within XSLT of finding out), and to pick up the attribute value in a call such as «`unparsed-entity-uri(@map)`». This call returns the absolute URI of the actual resource, that is, something like «`file:\c:\documents\forecasts\weather.jpeg`». You might use this, for example, to generate an HTML **`<IMG>`** element in the output file.

XSLT provides no way of finding out the notation name («`JPEG`» in our example) or the URI for the notation, nor can you determine the public identifier of the entity if there was one.

> *This is not exactly in the spirit of section 4.4.6 of the XML specification, which states: "When the name of an unparsed entity appears as a token in an attribute of declared type ENTITY or ENTITIES, a validating processor must inform the application of the system and public (if any) identifiers for both the entity and its associated notation." However, unparsed entities are hardly XML's most widely used feature, so it is unsurprising that XSLT support for them should be minimal.*

The rules in the XSLT specification don't explicitly permit this, but in practice, if you use a non-validating XML parser to process the source document, the parser isn't obliged to pass information to the XSLT processor about unparsed entities declared in the external subset of the DTD, and the **unparsed-entity-uri()** function is therefore likely to return an empty string. If this happens, try using a validating XML parser – assuming of course that the source document is valid.

Examples

Given the entity definition

```
<!ENTITY weather-map SYSTEM "weather.jpeg" NDATA JPEG>
```

and the entity reference

```
<FORECAST MAP="weather-map"/>
```

the following code will insert an **<IMG>** element into the HTML output:

```
<xsl:template match="FORECAST">
   <IMG HREF="{unparsed-entity-uri(@MAP)}"/>
</xsl:template>
```

See also

Trees, not Documents, in Chapter 2 (starting on page 52)

Summary

This exploration of the function library available to the XSLT programmer brings the reference part of this book to a close. You now have what I hope is a definitive reference guide to the XSLT language, including the embedded XPath query language. The following chapters are designed to help you put the language to work, developing real-world applications. In Chapter 8 we look at the rules for writing extension functions in Java and JavaScript.

8

Writing Extension Functions

In the previous four chapters we've covered all the facilities of the XSLT and XPath languages. Together, these provide most of the facilities you are likely to need when transforming XML documents. Sometimes, however, you will want to invoke code written in other languages from your stylesheet, and the purpose of this chapter is to explain how to achieve this.

The draft XSLT 1.1 specification defines a general mechanism for calling extension functions written in any language, and then defines detailed interfaces for Java and JavaScript (or ECMAScript, to give it its vendor-neutral name). Interfaces for other languages such as C++, Visual Basic, or Perl can be defined by vendors, but are not yet included in the standard.

Most XSLT 1.0 processors also provided facilities for calling extension functions. These are all slightly different – though not as different as you might expect, since the vendors all work together on the standards group and exchange ideas freely. These vendor-specific facilities in turn strongly influenced the design of the standard interface in XSLT 1.1. I'll give an outline of these vendor-defined mechanisms in the Appendix for each product.

XSLT 1.1 defines mechanisms for writing extension functions in Java and JavaScript. It doesn't require vendors to support either of these languages, so you won't find the facilities described in this chapter in every XSLT processor. It is likely, however, that any vendor who offers a Java or JavaScript interface will offer one that conforms to the specifications, which creates the prospect that it will be possible to write Java extension functions that can be used equally well with Saxon, Xalan, or Oracle XSL, or JavaScript extensions that are portable between Microsoft, Xalan, and Unicorn. This even creates the possibility that third-party developers will create libraries of external functions that can be used with any of these XSLT processors.

First, though, a word of warning about this chapter. At the time of writing, XSLT 1.1 is available only as a working draft, and there are no conformant products as yet. The specification could change in its final version. The whole question of defining external language bindings is inevitably an area of technical controversy, and there is also scope for commercial gamesmanship as each vendor will naturally have different views on the importance of different programming languages.

Also, because we are working here with a provisional specification that is not available yet in products, none of the examples in this Chapter are fully tested. They can all be easily adapted to work with one XSLT 1.0 processor or another, but that's different from saying they will work as written.

When are Extension Functions Needed?

There are a number of reasons you might want to call an extension function from your stylesheet:

- You might want to get data held externally, perhaps in a database or in an application.
- You may need to access system services that are not directly available in XSLT or XPath. For example, you might want to determine the current date, or access a random number generator, or append a record to a log file. If you are generating SVG graphics, you might need to use trigonometric functions such as `sin()` and `cos()`.
- You might want to perform a complex calculation that is cumbersome to express in XSLT, or that performs poorly. Common examples are string manipulation and date manipulation. XSLT enthusiasts will often write these calculations using recursive named templates, but if you're in a hurry, it's no crime to slip back into a more familiar language for these tasks.
- A more questionable use of external functions is to get around the "no side effects" rule in XSLT, for example to update a counter. Avoid this if you can; if you need such facilities, then you haven't yet learned to think about solving problems in the way that is natural for XSLT. More on this in the next chapter.

Although the title of this chapter says it is about *writing* extension functions, you will often find that the code you need has already been written by someone else. The interfaces for Java and JavaScript have been carefully designed so that the extensive class libraries available in both these languages will often be directly accessible to the stylesheet, with no further coding required. This is certainly true for mathematical functions, string manipulation, and date handling.

Which language you choose to use to write extension functions is a matter of personal choice. With a Java-based processor the natural choice is to write extension functions in Java. With Microsoft's MSXML3, the natural choice is a Microsoft scripting language. If you are using the 4XSLT processor, it is probably because your favorite language is Python. Processors written in C or C++ tend to require a more complex procedure for binding extension functions, if they are supported at all.

Calling Extension Functions

Extension functions are always called from within an XPath expression, and I explained the syntax for this in Chapter 6. A typical function call looks like this:

```
my:function($arg1, 23, string(title))
```

The name of an extension function will always contain a namespace prefix and a colon. The prefix («`my`» in this example) must be declared in a namespace declaration on some containing element in the stylesheet, in the usual way. The function may take any number of arguments (zero or more), and the parentheses are needed even if there are no arguments. The arguments can be any XPath expressions; in our example, the first argument is a variable reference, the second is a number, and the third is a function call. The arguments are passed to the function by value, which means that the function can never modify the values of the arguments. The function always returns a result.

We'll have a lot more to say about the data types of the arguments, and the data type of the result, in due course.

What Language is Best?

Many processors only offer one language for writing extension functions (if indeed it allows extension functions at all) so the choice may already be made for you. Some processors offer a choice, for example Xalan supports both Java and JavaScript, while Microsoft supports any of the usual scripting languages, for example JScript and VBScript.

Generally, I'd suggest using the "native" language for your chosen processor: for example Java for Oracle, Saxon, and Xalan, JScript for MSXML3, Python for 4XSLT. If you want to use your stylesheet with more than one processor, write one version of the extension function for each language.

Given a choice, JavaScript makes it very easy to write simple extension functions, because they can be written inline and the language, like XPath itself, is not statically typed. On the other hand, Java offers a rich library of pre-defined functions which you can easily call from a stylesheet.

Binding Extension Functions

When you call «`my:function()`» from within an XPath expression, the XSLT processor needs to find a suitable function to call. This process is called **binding**. There is a special top-level element, **`<xsl:script>`**, whose job is to tell the processor where to look. The detailed specifications for the **`<xsl:script>`** element are provided in Chapter 4, on page 293.

As always, the namespace prefix can be chosen arbitrarily; what really counts is the namespace URI. The system searches for an **`<xsl:script>`** element whose `implements-prefix` attribute maps to the same namespace URI as the prefix used in the function call. If there is no suitable **`<xsl:script>`** element, this isn't necessarily an error: the vendor is allowed to provide other mechanisms for binding extension functions beyond those defined in the standard.

If there are several **`<xsl:script>`** elements for this namespace and they specify different languages – for example, if one has «`language="java"`» and the other has «`language="javascript"`» — then these are regarded as alternative implementations of the same functions, and the system can choose whichever one it prefers. This potentially increases the portability of stylesheets, because it enables you to write a stylesheet that will work with one processor that only supports Java, and that also works with another processor that only supports JavaScript. Of course, it's entirely your responsibility to ensure that the two different implementations have the same effect.

In general, a namespace corresponds to a collection of related functions, and the local name of the function (the part after the colon) determines which of these functions is actually called. At this stage the details become language-dependant, since the rules for scoping of names are quite different in different languages. With Java, each namespace corresponds to a class, and the local name corresponds to a method defined in that class. With JavaScript, the namespace is more like a module (technically, it's a global object), and the local name identifies the function within that module.

We'll describe the details of the binding rules separately for each language. But before we divide into a Java section and a JavaScript section, there is one more area that is common between the two languages, namely the mapping of XPath trees to the DOM.

XPath Trees and the DOM

We haven't got space in this book for a detailed description of the DOM interface, but most readers will already have come across it in some form, and it is described in detail in most good books on XML. The DOM provides an object model (and therefore an API) for navigating and manipulating XML data in tree form.

If you want extension functions to access the XSLT source tree, or a secondary input tree that was loaded using the **`document()`** function, or even a temporary tree constructed during the course of the XSLT transformation, then you can do this by passing a node-set as one of the function arguments. The extension function can then manipulate these nodes as objects in a DOM structure. It is also possible for an extension function to construct a new tree, and return it (typically as a DOM Document object) to the calling XPath expression, where it can be manipulated as a secondary input tree in the same way as the result of the XSLT **`document()`** function.

The only problem with this approach, as we saw in Chapter 2, is that there are many small but significant differences between the tree model used by XSLT and XPath, and the tree model defined in the DOM specification. For example, the DOM model exposes entity references and CDATA sections, the XPath model doesn't.

This is exacerbated by the fact that there are two different implementation approaches adopted by XSLT vendors: both are perfectly valid and both need to be catered for. Some products, such as Microsoft's MSXML3, are DOM-oriented. Microsoft use a DOM as their internal tree model, and provide the XPath model as a virtual data structure (a view or wrapper) on top of this. This means, for example, that CDATA sections will be physically present on the tree, and XPath operations such as `following-sibling` will dynamically merge the CDATA contents with the surrounding text nodes. When an extension function is called, such a product will present the native underlying DOM to the called function, CDATA nodes and all. Other products, however, (Saxon is an example) use an internal data structure that is closely aligned to the XPath model described in Chapter 2. This data structure will have discarded any information that is not needed for XPath processing, such as CDATA sections and entity references. When an external function is called, the situation is now reversed; such a product will provide the DOM interface as a wrapper on top of the native XPath model.

It's impossible to hide all the differences between these two approaches. For example, where the XSLT specifications dictate that whitespace nodes must be stripped from the tree, a DOM-oriented product will probably not remove these nodes physically from the tree, but will simply hide them from XPath view. A product that uses a native XPath tree is likely to remove the unwanted whitespace nodes from the tree while building the tree. This means that with one approach, the stripped whitespace nodes will be present in the DOM as seen by extension functions, and with the other, they will be absent.

Another difference is that with a native XPath tree, adjacent text nodes will be merged (or normalized) into a single node, whereas with a native DOM tree, they may be unnormalized. (Actually, at the time of writing, MSXML3 doesn't always normalize text nodes correctly even in the XPath tree view.)

What all this means is that if you want your extension functions to be fully portable between different processors, you have to be aware of these possible differences, and work around them. The XSLT 1.1 specification lists the areas of potential differences between the DOM view and the XPath view as follows:

XPath node	DOM node	Correspondence
Root	Document	One to one.
Element	Element	One to one.
Attribute	Attr	The XPath tree never represents namespace declarations as attributes named `xmlns` or `xmlns:*`. The DOM might or might not have such `Attr` nodes. If the source document used entity references within the attribute value, these might or might not be preserved in the DOM model. The value of the `getSpecified` property in the DOM model is unpredictable.
Text	Text	The DOM text nodes might or might not be normalized. If CDATA sections were used in the original document, CDATA nodes might or might not be present in the DOM model. If the source document used entity references within the text value, these might or might not be preserved in the DOM model. Whitespace nodes that have been stripped as far as XSLT processing is concerned might or might not be present as text nodes in the DOM.
Processing Instruction	Processing Instruction	One to one.
Comment	Comment	One to one.

XPath node	DOM node	Correspondence
Namespace	N/A	There is no direct equivalent in the DOM to XPath's namespace nodes. It is possible in a DOM model for elements and attributes to use namespace URIs that are not declared anywhere on the tree.
N/A	CDATASection	CDATASection nodes may be present on the DOM tree if this is the native data structure used by the processor, but they are unlikely to be present if the processor constructs a DOM from the XPath tree.
N/A	Entity Reference	EntityReference nodes may be present on the DOM tree if this is the native data structure used by the processor, but they are unlikely to be present if the processor constructs a DOM from the XPath tree.

When you call methods defined in the DOM, the result will follow the DOM rules, not the XPath rules. For example, in XPath the string-value of an element node is the concatenation of all the text content within that element; but in the DOM, the apparently similar **`nodeValue()`** method returns null.

Extension functions that are passed references to nodes in a DOM should not attempt to update the DOM, and the effect of doing so is undefined. In practice there are three things that might happen:

- The attempt to update the DOM may cause an exception.
- If the DOM was constructed as a copy of the XPath tree, the updates may succeed, but have no effect on the tree as seen subsequently within the stylesheet.
- If the DOM and the XPath tree are different views of the same data, then updates may affect the subsequent XSLT processing. This might cause subsequent failures, for example if nodes have been deleted while the XSLT processor holds references to them.

It is possible for an extension function to construct a new tree, in the form of a DOM, and return this to the stylesheet as the result of the extension function.

If the returned value is a DOM Node or NodeList, then each of the nodes is handled as follows:

- First, the processor locates the root of the DOM tree containing the node, which must be either a **`Document`** or a **`DocumentFragment`** object.
- Then the processor decides whether this root node corresponds to the root of an existing XPath document that is already known to the stylesheet, either because the DOM in question was generated from an XPath document, or because it had already been returned by a previous call on an extension function.

- If the document is already known, the processor finds the XPath node in this document that corresponds to the **`Node`** object returned by the extension function.
- If the document is not already known to the stylesheet, it attempts to load the document as an additional input source, as if it had been loaded using the **`document()`** function. The processor is allowed to reject a document if it was constructed using an unsupported DOM implementation (for example, Oracle might reject a DOM constructed using Xerces). The way this rule is expressed is that the operation is only guaranteed to succeed if the root is a **`DocumentFragment`** whose **`ownerDocument`** identifies the same **`Document`** object as the **`ownerDocument`** property of the **`XSLTContext`** object.
- When a new document is imported in this way, namespace nodes are created corresponding to all the namespaces in use for element and attribute names, as well as any namespaces declared using **`xmlns:*`** attributes. Whitespace nodes are not stripped. The document, once passed to the XSLT processor, must not be updated, though the processor is not required to detect this error.

These rules for the mapping of XPath trees probably seem rather complicated, and there are certainly lots of potential pitfalls. My own advice would be to steer clear of this area if you possibly can. Navigating around the tree is something you can do perfectly well within XSLT and XPath, you don't need to escape into a different language for this. It's simpler, and usually quite adequate, to pass simple strings and numbers to your extension functions.

When calling JavaScript functions, whose arguments are untyped, it's a good idea to use XPath functions to convert the arguments in the function call to the required type. For example, if **`my:toUpperCase()`** expects a string, don't write «`my:toUpperCase(@desc)`», but rather, «`my:toUpperCase(string(@desc))`». This avoids bringing the rules on node-sets into force. In Java, though, the conversion to a string will happen automatically.

If you want to write an extension function that constructs and returns a new tree, you might well find that a simpler alternative is to call the **`document()`** function and implement a **`URIResolver`** that takes the URI provided in this call, and returns the relevant data source. The TrAX API described in Appendix F defines a standard way of doing this.

However, if you do want to do it in an extension function, you should create the DOM nodes using the **`ownerDocument`** property of the **`XSLTContext`** object. Create a **`DocumentFragment`** as the root of the tree, and then add further nodes to this. On completion, the most likely action is to return the new **`DocumentFragment`** itself, though if you prefer you can return any **`Node`** or **`NodeList`** made up of nodes from the new tree.

The Java Language Binding

This section describes the detailed interface between XPath function calls and Java classes and methods. This allows you to call Java methods from within your stylesheet.

The process of calling a Java method falls into four stages:

- Using the namespace prefix of the XPath function name to identify a Java class.

- Using the local part of the XPath function name, and if necessary the data types of the supplied arguments, to identify a method defined in that Java class.
- Converting the supplied arguments to Java objects.
- Handling the return value from the method, and any exceptions it throws.

We'll look at all these four stages in turn.

The Java language binding was designed to satisfy two slightly different objectives:

- Firstly, to make it easy to call methods available in the standard Java class library directly from your stylesheet. This allows you to perform common tasks such as obtaining the current date, getting a random number, performing trigonometric calculations, or testing whether a particular file exists.
- Secondly, to make it easy to write new Java methods to augment your stylesheet with application-specific logic, for example a method that is given a product code, and returns the product description by performing an SQL query on your product database.

The first objective resulted in an interface that makes it possible to call virtually any Java method. The main limitation is that if the method throws an exception, execution of the stylesheet will fail. The second objective resulted in facilities that allow your Java code to determine details of the XSLT and XPath processing context, which we will come back to on page 590.

Identifying the Java Class

As we've seen, a call on an extension function will always use a prefixed name, for example «`my:function()`». The prefix must be declared in a namespace declaration that is in scope at this point in the stylesheet, and the system uses this namespace declaration to determine the relevant namespace URI. For example, if the namespace declaration is «`xmlns:my="http://schmidt.de/functions"`», then this will be the namespace URI we are looking for.

> *I would normally recommend using a namespace URI that identifies the required class directly, for example* «`xmlns:math=java:java.lang.Math`». *However, the class and the namespace are distinct things, so giving them the same name would confuse this explanation. We can start overloading the names in this way once we've understood clearly what's going on.*

The processor then searches for an **`<xsl:script>`** element whose implements-prefix attribute identifies a prefix that maps to this same namespace URI. Often of course it will be the same prefix, but as always, it is the namespace URI that matters.

If the processor finds an **`<xsl:script>`** element for this namespace, and its `language` attribute is «`java`», then the **`src`** attribute of the **`<xsl:script>`** element identifies the fully-qualified Java class name, prefixed by «`java:`» to make it a valid URI.

For example, if the function call is

```
<xsl:value-of select="dt:new()"/>
```

then the **<xsl:script>** element might be

```
<xsl:script language="java" implements-prefix="dt"
src="java:java.util.Date"/>
```

This identifies the required Java class as `java.util.Date`. This class should normally be on the class path. Alternatively, it is possible to specify the path explicitly, using the `archive` attribute; this is especially useful when running the processor within a web browser, since it allows the classes to be downloaded from the server on demand.

If there are several **<xsl:script>** elements for the same namespace, the processor chooses the one with highest import precedence. It's an error if there are several **<xsl:script>** elements for the same language with the same precedence.

Choosing a Java Method

The local part of the name in the XPath function call is used to identify a method to be called.

If the name used in the call is «`new`», then the system looks for public constructors rather than public methods; in all other cases it looks for a method with a matching name. The matching is done as follows:

First of all, hyphens in the name are removed, and any character that immediately follows a hyphen is forced to upper case. For example, if the XPath function call is written as `acct:get-account-number()`, then the processor will look for a Java method called `getAccountNumber()`. This is purely a cosmetic process that allows both languages to use their normal naming conventions. If you know that you want to call the `getAccountNumber()` method, then you could equally well write the call as `acct:getAccountNumber()` if you prefer.

Next, the system identifies all the public methods in the chosen class that have this name. It is an error if there are none. Of course, a Java class can have several methods with the same name and different arguments (this capability is usually called method overloading), so when this happens the processor now needs to look at the arguments to the call.

The system next eliminates any method that has the wrong number of arguments. This doesn't necessarily mean it must have exactly the same number of arguments as the function call. There are two factors that complicate the calculation:

- If the first argument in the Java method signature is of class `org.w3c.xsl.XSLTContext`, then this argument doesn't contribute to the total. The processor will supply the value of this argument, as discussed on page 590, therefore it doesn't correspond to any argument in the XPath function call.

- If the Java method being considered is an instance-level method (as distinct from a static method or a constructor), then the XPath function call must have an extra first argument, which doesn't contribute to the total. This extra argument must be an external object, which is used as the target of the method call.

Any methods that have the wrong number of arguments, after taking these adjustments into account, are eliminated from consideration.

If this still leaves more than one candidate method, the selection now depends on the data types of the arguments to the XPath function call. Since XPath is a dynamically-typed language, the data types of the arguments can't always be determined in advance, so this final stage may have to be done at run-time. Potentially, the same XPath function call might cause different Java methods to be executed on different occasions.

The basic principle is to choose the method whose declared argument types are the best fit to the supplied argument types. The actual algorithm is similar to the one used by Java itself. Although it isn't the way the rules are described in the specification, the way I like to explain the algorithm is by showing that it chooses the method that requires minimum conversion effort for the arguments.

Between any XPath data type and any Java class there is a certain conversion effort: the effort is zero if the types correspond exactly, and it is infinite if the conversion is not allowed. So for each candidate method, it is possible to calculate the conversion effort for each argument (the actual "effort" values are given in the next section). If the XPath data type of the supplied argument is *A*, and the Java class of the required argument is *P*, then the conversion effort is a function of *A* and *P*: say *effort(A, P)*. The table starting on page 577 shows us, for example that *effort(number, double)*=0 and *effort(number, String)*=16.

Suppose that the XPath data types of the supplied arguments are A_1, A_2, and A_3, and that we are trying to choose between two Java methods, method *P* whose declared arguments are of Java classes P_1, P_2, and P_3, and method *Q* whose arguments are of Java classes Q_1, Q_2, and Q_3.

We don't simply work out the total effort by adding the conversion effort for each argument. Rather, we have to find a method where for each argument individually, the conversion effort for that argument is no worse than any other method.

If for each of the arguments *n*=1..3 (in our example), either P_n is the same class as Q_n, or $effort(A_n, P_n) < effort(A_n, Q_n)$, then method *P* is preferred to method *Q*. (There must be at least one argument where the two methods differ, otherwise Java would have rejected the methods as duplicates.) If there is one argument where $effort(A_n, P_n) < effort(A_n, Q_n)$, and another where $effort(A_m, P_m) > effort(A_m, Q_m)$, then neither *P* nor *Q* is preferred.

If, under these rules, one of the candidate methods is preferred to each one of the others, then that is the one chosen. If none of the methods is a clear winner, then an error is reported.

To put this in concrete terms, suppose that the function call is

```
date:compare('20010405', '20011011')
```

and that there are four candidate methods in the relevant class:

A	compare(int, int)
B	compare(int, String)
C	compare(String, int)
D	compare(String, String)

Intuitively, *D* is the best fit, because both the supplied arguments are strings. It turns out that it is also the winner when we do the calculation, because the conversion efforts for the two arguments (taken from the table on page 577 below) are as follows:

Method	Effort for converting argument 1	Effort for converting argument 2
A	4	4
B	4	0
C	0	4
D	0	0

Method *D*, and *D* alone, satisfies the rule that for each argument, the conversion effort is less than or equal to the conversion effort for the same argument in other methods. So method *D* is chosen.

If we only had methods *A*, *B*, and C to choose from, there would be no clear winner, because C is best when we consider the first argument, while *B* is best when we consider the second. So if method *D* were not available, the function call would be bounced as an error.

Conversion Effort Table

The table below is used to calculate the conversion effort for converting an XPath value to a Java object (or value). The XPath data type of the supplied argument is listed along the top of the table, the Java class of the required argument on the leftmost column. The numbers in this table, of course, are just relative indications of conversion cost. We are only interested in knowing that it is less effort to convert a boolean to a String than to a Float; the actual values are irrelevant.

	boolean	number	string	node-set	external
boolean	0	14	6	8	N/A
Boolean	0	15	7	9	N/A
byte	3	12	4	6	4
Byte	4	13	5	7	5
char	N/A	10	2	4	2
Character	N/A	11	3	5	3

	boolean	number	string	node-set	external
double	3	0	4	6	4
Double	4	1	5	7	5
float	3	2	4	6	4
Float	4	3	5	7	5
int	3	6	4	6	4
Integer	4	7	5	7	5
long	3	4	4	6	4
Long	4	5	5	7	5
Node (note 1)	N/A	N/A	N/A	1	N/A
NodeList	N/A	N/A	N/A	0	N/A
Object	1	17	1	3	0 (note 2)
short	3	8	4	6	4
Short	4	9	5	7	5
String	2	16	0	2	1

Note 1: This is the DOM class `org.w3c.dom.Node`, or any of its subclasses. In the row below, `NodeList` is the DOM class `org.w3c.dom.NodeList`.

Note 2: provided the class of the supplied object is assignment-compatible with the required class.

Where the table says "N/A", the conversion is not possible, so the conversion effort is, in effect, infinite.

Rules for Converting Arguments

We've given a table that shows the notional effort in performing each possible conversion, but now we need to explain exactly how the conversions are done. What does it mean, for example, to convert an XPath boolean to a Java byte?

The rules are given in the following sections, organised according to the XPath data type of the supplied argument value.

Converting from an XPath boolean

Target data type	Conversion rules
`boolean` or `Boolean`	No conversion required.
`Object`	The value supplied is a Java Boolean, either `Boolean.TRUE` or `Boolean.FALSE`.
`String`	The value supplied is the string «`true`» or «`false`».
`double`, `float`, `long`, `int`, `short`, `byte`, `Double`, `Float`, `Long`, `Integer`, `Short`, `Byte`.	False is supplied as `0`, true as `1`.

Converting from an XPath number

Target data type	Conversion rules
`double`, `Double`	No conversion required.
`float`, `Float`	The value is rounded to the precision that can be accommodated in a float value. Values that are out of range for a float are converted to plus or minus infinity.
`long`, `Long`, `int`, `Integer`, `short`, `Short`, `char`, `Character`, `byte`, `Byte`	The value is truncated to an integer (rounded towards zero) by removing its fractional part. If the value is out of range for the target data type, an error is reported. An error is also reported if the supplied value is NaN (not a number).
`boolean`, `Boolean`	The number is converted as if by the XPath **`boolean()`** function; zero becomes false, anything else becomes true.
`String`	The number is converted to a string as if by the XPath **`string()`** function.
`Object`	The number is supplied as a Java `Double` object.

Converting from an XPath string

Target data type	Conversion rules
`String`	No conversion required.
`Object`	The value is supplied as a Java String.
`char`, `Character`	If the string is one character long, this character is supplied as the value. If the string is zero-length or longer than one character, an error is reported.

Target data type	Conversion rules
double, float, long, int, short, byte, Double, Float, Long, Integer, Short, Byte	The XPath string is converted to an XPath number using the **number()** function, and the resulting XPath number is then converted to the required Java type following the rules given in the previous table.
boolean, Boolean	Zero-length strings are converted to false, anything else is converted to true.

Converting from an XPath node-set

Target data type	Conversion rules
org.w3c.dom.NodeList	The nodes in the node-set are presented in the form of a DOM NodeList. The list will be in document order. An error may be reported if the node-set contains any namespace nodes.
org.w3c.dom.Node org.w3c.dom.Attr org.w3c.dom.CDATASection org.w3c.dom.CharacterData org.w3c.dom.Comment org.w3c.dom.Document org.w3c.dom.Element org.w3c.dom.ProcessingInstruction org.w3c.dom.Text	If the node-set is empty, an error is reported. Otherwise the first node in document order is used, and the rest are ignored. If this node is of the wrong type, an error is reported (for example if the node is an Element and the method expects a Document).
String	The node-set is converted to a string following the rules of the XPath **string()** function. (This gets the string value of the first node if there is at least one, or an empty string if the node-set is empty.)
Object	The object supplied will be an org.w3.dom.NodeList
char, Character	The node-set is converted to a string using the XPath **string()** function. If this string contains exactly one character, that character is supplied; otherwise, an error is reported.
double, float, long, int, short, byte, Double, Float, Long, Integer, Short, Byte	The node-set is converted to a number using the XPath **number()** function, and this is then converted to the required Java type in the same way as if an XPath number had been supplied as the argument. This will cause an error if the value is not numeric.
boolean, Boolean	The value supplied will be false if the node-set is empty, true if it contains at least one node.

Converting from an external object

Target data type	Conversion rules
Any Java class C such that «OBJ instanceof C» is true, where OBJ is the wrapped external object	Unwrap the external object.
String	Call the wrapped object's **toString()** method.
char, Character	Call the wrapped object's **toString()** method. Use this value if it is exactly one character long, otherwise report an error.
double, float, long, int, short, byte, Double, Float, Long, Integer, Short, Byte	Call the wrapped object's **toString()** method, then convert this string to a number using the rules of the XPath **number()** function. Convert the resulting number to the required Java type as if an XPath number had been supplied in the function call.

Handling the Return Value

If the Java method throws an exception, an error is reported. It is not possible for the stylesheet to trap the error and continue processing. In practice this means that it's a bad idea to call Java methods that throw exceptions unless (a) you can prevent the exception occurring by making sure you get all the arguments right, or (b) the error would be fatal anyway.

If this is a problem, you can get round it by writing a wrapper method in Java that traps the exception and indicates the failure to the stylesheet within the return value, for example by returning a special value such as -1.

If the Java method returns void, the result of the XPath function is (arbitrarily) an empty node-set. (The only point in calling a method that returns void is to cause some side effects, so take care; see the notes on functions with side-effects on page 587.)

If the Java method returns null, the result of the XPath function is an external object that is null. Unfortunately there is no direct way to test an external object to see if it is null, except by passing it to another extension function. To confound matters further, Java doesn't have a simple method you can call to test if an object is null. I hunted around the Java API documentation and the best I could find was the static method `identityHashCode()` on class `java.lang.System`, which returns zero if the argument is null. So you can write:

```
<xsl:stylesheet...
  xmlns:sys="java:java.lang.System"
  xmlns:my="java:name.joe-programmer.ExtensionClass">
<xsl:script language="java" implements-prefix="sys"
            src="java:java.lang.System"/>
     . . .
```

```
<xsl:variable name="result" select="my:method($x)"/>
<xsl:if test="sys:identityHashCode($result) = 0">
   <xsl:message>my:method() returned null</xsl:message>
</xsl:if>
```

Simple return values are converted to XPath values as follows:

Value returned by Java method	Result of XPath function call
`String`	An equivalent string. The specification deliberately doesn't define what happens if the string contains characters that are valid in Java but not in XML, for example the ASCII control character NUL (`#x00`). It's an error if the string contains such characters, but the system isn't obliged to report it.
`double`, `float`, `long`, `int`, `short`, `byte`, `Double`, `Float`, `Long`, `Integer`, `Short`, `Byte`	The equivalent XPath number.
`boolean`, `Boolean`	The equivalent XPath boolean.

If the Java method returns a DOM NodeList, or a single Node, the rules can become quite complex, and at the time of writing they aren't very clearly defined. Some of the complications are:

- Many products will only be able to handle DOM data structures that were constructed using that particular vendor's product. In general, you can't expect to construct a DOM using, say, the Xerces XML parser, and then pass this DOM into the Oracle XSLT engine for processing: it will only accept a DOM constructed using its stable-mate Oracle parser.
- What happens if you call a sequence of extension functions, and several functions return the same DOM node? Will these each return the same XPath node (producing the same value for the **`generate-id()`** function), or to different XPath nodes? For a product that uses the DOM as its internal data structure, this probably isn't too much of a problem; you'll get the same node back each time. But for a product that performs a mapping or conversion between the DOM structure and its own internal tree representation, there are considerable difficulties in preserving node identity, especially as the Java DOM specification makes no guarantee that the same node in the DOM will always be represented by the same Java object – the DOM specification is deliberately written so that nodes can be materialized on demand, for example by fetching data from a database.

The XSLT specification does allow extension functions to return `NodeLists` or individual `Nodes`, but it doesn't really answer all these questions, so if you do this, you will probably find that your stylesheet is not fully portable.

Using Java Extension Functions

The simplest extension functions to write, and the kind to stick to whenever you can, are stateless methods, which get no external information from their environment and leave nothing behind when they have returned. These are best written as static methods, and we'll look at these first.

For more complex functions it may be necessary to maintain information between calls: for example if you want to generate a sequence of random numbers. This will normally require the use of an instance-level method, so we'll discuss those afterwards.

Calling Static Methods

To call a static method all you need to know is the class name, the method name, and the expected arguments.

A typical example is the method `max(a, b)` found in the class `java.lang.Math`. This takes two numbers as arguments and returns whichever of them is the greater.

You can call this function as follows:

```
<xsl:script implements-prefix="Math"
xmlns:math="java:java.lang.Math"
  language="java" src="java:java.lang.Math"/>
. . .
<xsl:template match="price">
   <xsl:value-of select="Math:max(number(@net-price), number(@gross-price))"
                 xmlns:Math="java:java.lang.Math"/>
</xsl:template>
```

I've now slipped into my usual convention of using the short form of the Java class name as the namespace prefix, and the long form (prefixed by «`java:`») as the namespace URI. Remember this is just a convention; you can use any prefix and URI you like.

Actually, in the `java.lang.Math` class there are four methods called `max()`, which are alternative versions that work on arguments of type `double`, `float`, `int`, and `long` respectively. The one that is called here will be the one that operates on `double` arguments and returns a `double`, because that is the one that minimizes the conversion effort.

Notice that both the arguments we supplied were XPath numbers. If we hadn't used the **`number()`** function to convert them to numbers, they would have been node-sets. Looking back at the table on page 577, the effort for converting an XPath node-set to a Java `double`, a `float`, a `long`, or an `int` is exactly the same. This means that none of the four methods would be preferred, and an error would be reported.

Static methods such as `max()` fit very cleanly into the XSLT processing model, because they have no side effects. It doesn't matter how often they are called, the same function with the same arguments will always produce the same results. So you don't need to worry about the order of execution of instructions in the stylesheet. As we'll see, the same can't be said of all external methods.

Calling Constructors and Instance-level Methods

You can call a Java constructor to create a new instance of a class as if it were a static method called `new()`.

The result of a constructor is a Java object, and this will be wrapped inside an XPath value with the special data type **external object**. The only thing you can do with an external object is to pass it to another extension function. You can either pass it as an argument to a method, or you can invoke its own instance-level (that is, non-static) methods. To invoke an instance-level method of an object, you supply that object as the first argument of the XPath function call, followed by the values of the ordinary arguments if there are any.

For example, suppose you want to output the current date. The Java class `java.util.Date` has a default constructor that creates a `Date` object representing the current date and time; and the `Date` object has an instance-level method `toString()` that outputs the date in the format «`Sat Jan 06 14:32:29 GMT 2001`». You can use the XPath **`substring()`** function to extract the parts of the date you actually want to display.

So, here's the stylesheet code to do this:

```
<xsl:script language="java" implements-prefix="Date"
   src="java:java.util.Date" xmlns:Date="java:java.util.Date"/>
...
<xsl:template match="/">
  <xsl:variable name="date" select="Date:toString(Date:new())"
                              xmlns:Date="java:java.util.Date"/>
  <xsl:comment>Output generated at <xsl:value-of select="
        concat(substring($date, 12, 5), ' on ',
               substring($date, 9, 2), ' ',
               substring($date, 5, 3), ' ',
               substring($date, 25, 4))"/></xsl:comment>
  . . .
</xsl:template>
```

This will insert into the output file a comment of the form:

```
<!-- Output generated at 14:32 on 06 Jan 2001-->
```

There are two external function calls here: a call to `Date:new()`, which calls the zero-argument constructor of the `java.util.Date` class to create a `Date` object, and a call to `Date:toString()`, which takes this object as its only argument. Because `Date:toString()` is identified as an instance-level (non-static) method, the first argument of the XPath function call must be a `Date` object, and this `Date` object is taken as the target of the method invocation.

The value returned by the first function call and passed to the second is not one of the standard XPath data types, it is an external object. In this example we used the external object immediately, by passing it directly to another function call, but we could equally well have stored it in a variable for use later, or passed it as a parameter to a template. If you do store an external object in a variable, however, take care not to attempt any XPath operations on it: apparently harmless operations such as comparing it with another value, or converting it to a string or a boolean, will all cause errors.

Although this example requires the set of XPath data types to be extended to incorporate the idea of an external object, it still fits very cleanly into the XSLT processing model, because both the function calls are free of side effects. In this particular case it's no longer true that we'd get the same result every time we called the function – the whole point of this particular function is that the results depend on when it was called. But we're still on pretty safe ground. The next example will tread into slightly more dangerous territory.

Calling External Functions within a Loop

In the next example we will use a Java `BufferedReader` object to read an external file, copying it to the output one line at a time, each line being followed by an empty `<br/>` element.

Example: Calling External Functions within a Loop

Source

This stylesheet doesn't access the primary source document, so any XML file will do. For example, you can use the stylesheet itself as the source document.

The real input is a serial file, which can be any text file. For example the following, `hiawatha.txt`:

```
Take your bow, O Hiawatha,
Take your arrows, jasper-headed,
Take your war-club, Puggawaugun,
And your mittens, Minjekahwan,
And your birch-canoe for sailing,
And the oil of Mishe-Nama.
```

Stylesheet

The stylesheet can be downloaded as `reader.xsl`.

First we declare the namespaces we will need. Since the namespaces are used both in the **`<xsl:script>`** element and in the XSL instruction that calls the external function, it's often easiest to declare these namespaces on the **`<xsl:stylesheet>`** element itself. I shall stick to my convention of using the same «`java:*`» URI both to identify the location of the Java class, and as its namespace URI, and I will also use the abbreviated class name as the namespace prefix. You won't usually want these namespaces appearing in the result document, so you can suppress them using `exclude-result-prefixes`.

```
<xsl:stylesheet
   xmlns:xsl="http://www.w3.org/1999/XSL/Transform"
   version="1.1"
   xmlns:FileReader="java:java.io.FileReader"
   xmlns:BufferedReader="java:java.io.BufferedReader"
```

```
xmlns:System="java:java.lang.System"
   exclude-result-prefixes="FileReader BufferedReader System">
<xsl:script language="java" implements-prefix="FileReader"
  src="java:java.io.FileReader"/>
<xsl:script language="java" implements-prefix="BufferedReader"
  src="java:java.io.BufferedReader"/>
<xsl:script language="java" implements-prefix="System"
  src="java:java.lang.System"/>
```

The name of the file we want to read from will be supplied as a parameter to the stylesheet:

```
<xsl:param name="filename"/>
```

When we are ready to read the file, we create the `BufferedReader` in a variable. Then we call a template to read the file, line by line:

```
<xsl:template match="/">
<out>
    <xsl:variable name="reader"
                  select="BufferedReader:new(
FileReader:new($filename))"/>
    <xsl:call-template name="read-lines">
        <xsl:with-param name="reader" select="$reader"/>
    </xsl:call-template>
</out>
</xsl:template>
```

The named template reads and outputs the first line of the file, and then calls itself recursively to process the remainder. The only problem is that the `readLine()` method of the `BufferedReader` class returns null to indicate that the end of file has been reached, and there is no easy way in XPath to test whether an external Java object is null. So we'll use the `System.identityHashCode()` trick that I mentioned earlier; this function returns zero if the argument is null.

```
<xsl:template name="read-lines">
    <xsl:param name="reader"/>
    <xsl:variable name="line"
select="BufferedReader:readLine($reader)"/>
    <xsl:if test="System:identityHashCode($line) != 0">
        <xsl:value-of select="$line"/><br/>
        <xsl:call-template name="read-lines">
            <xsl:with-param name="reader" select="$reader"/>
        </xsl:call-template>
    </xsl:if>
</xsl:template>
</xsl:stylesheet>
```

Output

When you run this stylesheet you need to supply a value for the filename parameter. For example:

```
xsltproc reader.xsl reader.xsl filename=hiawatha.xml
```

(I've left it vague which XSLT processor is being used, because at the time of writing, no XSLT processor had sufficient support for XSLT 1.1 to run this example: all needed some kind of modification.)

What the output should look like is:

```
<out>
Take your bow, O Hiawatha,<br/>
Take your arrows, jasper-headed,<br/>
Take your war-club, Puggawaugun,<br/>
And your mittens, Minjekahwan,<br/>
And your birch-canoe for sailing,<br/>
And the oil of Mishe-Nama.<br/>
</out>
```

In this example the function call does have side effects, because the `$reader` variable is an external Java object which holds information about the current position in the file being read, and advances this position each time a line is read from the file. In general, function calls with side effects are dangerous, because XSLT does not define the order in which statements are executed. But in this case, the logic of the stylesheet is such that an XSLT processor would have to be very devious indeed to execute the statements in any order other than the obvious one. The fact that the recursive call on the `read-lines` template is within an **<xsl:if>** instruction that tests the `$line` variable means that the processor is forced to read a line, test the result, and then, if necessary, make the recursive call to read further lines.

The next example uses side effects in a much less controlled way, and in this case causes results that will vary from one XSLT processor to another.

Functions with Uncontrolled Side Effects

Just to illustrate the dangers of using functions with side effects, we'll include an example where the effects are not predictable.

Example: A Function with Uncontrolled Side Effects

Source

Like the previous example, this stylesheet doesn't access the primary source document, so any XML file will do. For example, you can use the stylesheet itself as the source document.

In this example we'll read an input file containing names and addresses, for example addresses.txt. We'll assume this file is created by a legacy application and consists of groups of five lines. Each group contains a customer number on the first line, the customer's name on the second, an address on lines three and four, and a telephone number on line five. Because that's the way legacy data files often work, we'll assume that the last line of the file contains the string «****».

```
15668
Mary Cousens
15 Birch Drive
Wigan
01367-844355
17796
John Templeton
17 Spring Gardens
Wolverhampton
01666-932865
19433
Jane Arbuthnot
92 Mountain Avenue
Swansea
01775-952266
****
```

Stylesheet

We might be tempted to write the stylesheet as follows (addresses.xsl), modifying the previous example:

```
<xsl:stylesheet
   xmlns:xsl="http://www.w3.org/1999/XSL/Transform"
version="1.1"
   xmlns:FileReader="java:java.io.FileReader"
   xmlns:BufferedReader="java:java.io.BufferedReader"
   xmlns:System="java:java.lang.System"
   exclude-result-prefixes="FileReader BufferedReader System">

<xsl:script language="java" implements-prefix="FileReader"
  src="java:java.io.FileReader"/>
<xsl:script language="java" implements-prefix="BufferedReader"
  src="java:java.io.BufferedReader"/>
<xsl:script language="java" implements-prefix="System"
  src="java:java.lang.System"/>

<xsl:template match="/">
    <xsl:variable name="reader"
                  select="BufferedReader:new(
FileReader:new($filename))"/>
    <xsl:call-template name="read-addresses">
        <xsl:with-param name="reader" select="$reader"/>
    </xsl:call-template>
</xsl:template>
```

```
<xsl:template name="read-addresses">
   <xsl:param name="reader"/>
   <xsl:variable name="line1"
select="BufferedReader:readLine($reader)"/>
   <xsl:if test="$line1 != '****'">
     <xsl:variable name="line2"
select="BufferedReader:readLine($reader)"/>
     <xsl:variable name="line3"
select="BufferedReader:readLine($reader)"/>
     <xsl:variable name="line4"
select="BufferedReader:readLine($reader)"/>
     <xsl:variable name="line5"
select="BufferedReader:readLine($reader)"/>
     <label>
       <address>
         <xsl:value-of select="$line3"/><br/>
         <xsl:value-of select="$line4"/><br/>
       </address>
           <recipient>Attn: <xsl:value-of
select="$line2"/></recipient>
     </label>
     <xsl:call-template name="read-lines">
         <xsl:with-param name="reader" select="$reader"/>
     </xsl:call-template>
   </xsl:if>
</xsl:template>
</xsl:stylesheet>
```

What's the difference? This time we are making an assumption that the four variables `$line2`, `$line3`, `$line4`, and `$line5` will be evaluated in the order we've written them. **There is no guarantee of this**, and there are processors in existence for which this stylesheet will fail to produce the expected output. The processor is quite at liberty, for example, not to evaluate a variable until it is used, which means that `$line3` will be evaluated *before* `$line2`, and worse still, `$line5` (because it is never used) may not be evaluated at all, meaning that instead of reading a group of five lines from the file, the template will only read four lines each time it is invoked.

So this stylesheet may work on some XSLT processors but it will fail on others.

Output

The output depends entirely on the sequence of execution chosen by the particular XSLT processor.

As with the previous example, I couldn't find an XSLT processor that was capable of running this stylesheet at the time of writing.

In practice I would probably tackle this problem a completely different way. With a TrAX-based processor such as Saxon or Xalan, I would write a Java application to read the lines of the file and output them as a set of element nodes, as if the application were a SAX2 parser. I would specify a `URIResolver` that invokes this application if the URI takes a particular value, and then I would call the **`document()`** function from the stylesheet, with this URI as the argument value, to retrieve the contents of the data file as a secondary input document.

With MSXML3, I would probably adopt a similar approach, but using the DOM. I would write a JavaScript extension function that reads the file and populates a DOM, which it then returns to the stylesheet as a result of the extension function call.

Both these solutions are safer because they involve a single function call from the stylesheet to retrieve the entire file contents, so there is no dependency on the order of execution.

The XSLTContext Object

One of the aims of the XSLT language designers was to allow users to create libraries of extension functions that mirror the capability and calling conventions of the core functions provided in XPath and XSLT, so calling an extension function should feel the same as calling a built-in function. Many of the core functions need to know the XPath context; for example, functions such as **`name()`** and **`generate-id()`** operate on the context node if they are called with no arguments. So it was felt that extension functions should have access to information about the context. This is provided through an implicit extra parameter, which is supplied to a Java method if its signature is written to expect its first argument to be of class **`org.w3c.xsl.XSLTContext`**.

The `XSLTContext` object provides the following methods. None of them defines any specific exception conditions, though like any Java methods they are allowed to throw standard exceptions such as `java.lang.IllegalArgumentException` and `java.lang.NullPointerException`.

`org.w3c.dom.Node getContextNode()`

This method returns the XPath context node, represented as a DOM `Node`: the same node as retrieved by the XPath expression «`.`». You can use DOM methods to navigate from this node to other nodes in the tree. It isn't defined what happens in the unusual case where the context node is a namespace node (namespace nodes can't be represented directly in the DOM).

`int getContextPosition()`

This method returns the XPath context position, that is, the same value as the XPath **`position()`** function.

`int getContextSize()`

This method returns the XPath context size, that is, the same value as the XPath **`last()`** function.

`org.w3c.dom.Node getCurrentNode()`

This method returns the XSLT current node, represented as a DOM `Node`, which is the same node as that returned by the XPath **`current()`** function.

`org.w3c.dom.Document getOwnerDocument()`

This method returns a DOM `Document` object that can be used for creating new nodes. This is not necessarily related to any of the documents in use within the stylesheet. The methods that may be applied to this object are `createDocumentFragment`, `createElement`, `createElementNS`, `createAttribute`, `createAttributeNS`, `createTextNode`, `createComment`, `createProcessingInstruction`, and `importNode`. If you call any other methods, the effect is undefined.

`Object systemProperty(String namespaceURI, String localName)`

This method returns the same result as the XPath **`system-property()`** function. Instead of supplying the property name as a QName as you would do in XPath, the two components of the expanded name are supplied separately. The type of the result depends on the property that was requested.

`String stringValue(org.w3c.dom.Node node)`

This method returns the string-value of the specified node, following the XPath rules. This is a convenience method, made available because it is surprisingly difficult to write an equivalent function that uses DOM interfaces only.

Example

The following code shows a method used to implement an extension function that returns the type of the context node, for example `"root"`, `"element"`, `"text"`, etc. This can be determined in XPath, but it isn't at all easy.

```
package name.joe_programmer.xslt;
import org.w3c.dom.*;
import org.w3c.xsl.XSLTContext;

public abstract class Extensions {

    public static String nodeType(XSLTContext context) {
        Node node = context.getContextNode();
        if (node instanceof Document) return "root";
        if (node instanceof Element) return "element";
        if (node instanceof Attr) return "attribute";
        if (node instanceof ProcessingInstruction)
                                return "processing-instruction";
        if (node instanceof Comment) return "comment";
        if (node instanceof Text) return "text";
        return "unknown node type";
    }
}
```

This method can then be invoked from a stylesheet as follows:

```
<xsl:stylesheet. . .
    xmlns:my="http://joe-programmer.name/xslt">
<xsl:script implements-prefix="my" language="java"
            src="java:name.joe_programmer.xslt.Extensions"/>
. . .
<xsl:template name="a-template">
   <xsl:if test="my:node-type() = 'attribute'">
      <xsl:message terminate="yes">Context node is an attribute</xsl:message>
   </xsl:if>
   . . .
</xsl:template>
```

Of course each XSLT processor will provide its own implementation of the `XSLTContext` object. This will often provide additional information and services beyond those defined above, which you can access by casting the supplied `XSLTContext` object to the vendor-specific implementation class. In Saxon, for example, the context object provides information about the namespaces that are in scope for this expression in the stylesheet, which you need to know if your extension function (like **key()** or **format-number()**) takes a string-valued argument that is expected to contain a `QName`. The `XSLTContext` object thus frequently opens the door to a whole range of product-specific capabilities.

If you want to use such vendor-specific facilities, you can still keep your extension functions portable by using a structure such as:

```
public static String methodName(XSLTContext context) {
    if (context instanceof com.icl.saxon.Context) {
      com.icl.saxon.Context saxonContext =
(com.icl.saxon.Context)context;
      // logic for Saxon
    } else if (context instanceof

org.apache.xalan.extensions.ExpressionContext){
      org.apache.xalan.extensions.ExpressionContext  xalanContext =

(org.apache.xalan.extensions.ExpressionContext)context;
      // logic for Xalan
    } else {
        return "*** unknown XSLT processor: " +
                    context.systemProperty(
                        "http://www.w3.org/1999/XSL/Transform", "vendor");
    }
}
```

The JavaScript Language Binding

The draft XSLT 1.1 specification defines bindings for two languages, Java and JavaScript. So far we've concentrated on the Java binding, now is the time to look at JavaScript. Technically, the standard for this language uses the name ECMAScript, and this covers both Netscape's JavaScript product and Microsoft's JScript.

JavaScript is a much simpler language than Java, and it's not surprising to find, therefore, that the XSLT binding for JavaScript is also much simpler than the Java binding. It's simpler for three main reasons:

- JavaScript, like XSLT, is a dynamically-typed language, which means that values carry a run-time data type, but this is not constrained by variable declarations.
- Because JavaScript is interpreted, it is possible to include the source code within the stylesheet itself.
- JavaScript function names can have global scope, unlike Java where there are always two levels of naming, the class and the method.

One thing you need to be very clear about is the difference between JavaScript code that is called by the XSLT processor in the course of doing a transformation, and client-side JavaScript code that you want to form part of the HTML output that you are generating. To complicate things even further, if your XSLT transformation is running within a browser, then the transformation itself might be fired off by JavaScript within an HTML page. When you are debugging your web site late at night, these three kinds of JavaScript can easily start to get jumbled on the screen…

JavaScript used during the transformation is written either within the stylesheet, as the content of the **<xsl:script>** element, or in a separate file (typically with a «.js» extension) that is referenced from the `src` attribute of the **<xsl:script>** element. You can also, of course, use **<xsl:include>** or **<xsl:import>** to reference another stylesheet module that contains the required **<xsl:script>** element. This approach is useful when you want to use the same JavaScript functions in many stylesheets.

Because JavaScript function names can have global scope, it is possible to define all the JavaScript functions you need in a single **<xsl:script>** element, and use a single namespace prefix to refer to all of them. This contrasts with the Java binding, where you need one **<xsl:script>** element for each class that you reference.

A JavaScript Example

It's simplest to show how the JavaScript binding works by means of an example. Here is a stylesheet that uses a JavaScript function to test whether a string matches a regular expression, supplied as another string.

```
<xsl:stylesheet version="1.1"
   xmlns:xsl="http://www.w3.org/1999/XSL/Transform"
   xmlns:js="javascript:code">
```

```
<xsl:script language="javascript" implements-prefix="js">
   function matches(str, regexp) {
       return str.match(new RegExp(regexp));
   }
</xsl:script>

<xsl:template match="*[js:matches(name(), 'address$')]">
   . . .
</xsl:template>

</xsl:stylesheet>
```

The **<xsl:template>** element defines a template rule that will match any element whose name ends in «address», for example «billing-address» or «delivery-address».

Calling an extension function within the predicate of a match pattern is probably a rather expensive thing to do; but if this is the effect you want to achieve, it may be the best way of doing it.

I've used «js» as the namespace prefix here, and «javascript:code» as the namespace URI, but both of these choices are completely arbitrary. The only thing that matters is that the namespace URI for the namespace prefix used in the implements-prefix attribute of the **<xsl:script>** element is the same as the namespace URI for the namespace prefix used in the function call.

Selecting the Function to Execute

When the XSLT processing encounters a function call like js:matches(), the first thing it has to do is to find all the **<xsl:script>** elements that have an **implements-prefix** attribute identifying the correct namespace.

It then looks at the **language** attribute of these **<xsl:script>** elements. It is free to ignore any **<xsl:script>** elements for languages that are not supported by this processor, and if there are **<xsl:script>** elements for more than one language, it can choose arbitrarily which language it prefers. If two **<xsl:script>** elements have the same **implements-prefix** attribute, but different **language** attributes, then the assumption is that they provide alternative but equivalent implementations of the same extension functions.

So let's suppose that one or more **<xsl:script>** elements provide JavaScript implementations of the required extension function namespace, and that this is the implementation the processor chooses to use.

The local name used in the XPath function call is used to identify the required JavaScript function. If there are any hyphens in the name, they are removed, and the character immediately following the hyphen is forced to uppercase, so for example if the XPath function call is js:contains-same-nodes() then the processor will look for a JavaScript function called containsSameNodes().

The only functions considered are those that are properties of the global object. There is no equivalent to the mechanism in the Java binding for calling a function that is not global.

If there are several functions that match the required name then the one with highest import precedence is selected. The specification doesn't say what happens if there are several with the same import precedence, but the likely effect is that the one that is defined last is selected.

Unlike Java, there's no rule that says the number of arguments have to match. This is because it's not actually necessary in JavaScript to declare all the arguments that a function can handle, it can always access the actual supplied arguments using the `arguments` array.

Converting the Function Arguments

Because JavaScript function definitions do not have to declare the types of the arguments expected, the mapping rules are very simple, and are based only on the types of the XPath values supplied in the function call.

The various XPath data types are converted to JavaScript data types as follows:

XPath data type	JavaScript data type
string	`string`
number	`number`
boolean	`boolean`
node-set	DOM `NodeList`
external object	JavaScript object

If an external object is supplied as an argument, it must wrap a JavaScript object, and the wrapped JavaScript object is the object presented to the JavaScript function.

These rules mean that arguments supplied to JavaScript functions won't automatically be converted into the expected type in the way that they are for system-defined functions. For example, if a function expects a string, then you shouldn't supply a value that is a node-set; instead of calling «`my:func(@value)`», call `my:func(string(@value))`».

Getting XSLT and XPath Context Information

There is no special mechanism for passing context information as an extra function argument, as there is with the Java language binding. Instead the `XSLTContext` object is available as a property of the global object.

The `XSLTContext` object has the following properties :

Name	Type	Description
contextNode	Node	The XPath context node (the node returned by the expression «.»).
contextPosition	number	The XPath context position (the value of the position() function).
contextSize	number	The XPath context size (the value of the last() function).
currentNode	Node	The XSLT current node (the node returned by the current() function).
ownerDocument	Document	A DOM Document object that may be used for creating new nodes. This is not necessarily related to any Document used by the stylesheet. The methods that may be applied to this object are createDocumentFragment, createElement, createElementNS, createAttribute, createAttributeNS, createTextNode, createComment, createProcessingInstruction, and importNode. If you call any other methods, the effect is undefined.

The methods of the XSLTContext object are:

Name	Arguments	Result	Description
systemProperty	String namespaceURI String localName	Object	Equivalent to the XSLT **system-property()** function
stringValue	Node node	string	Returns the string-value of the given node, according to the XPath rules

Converting the Return Value

The rules for converting the JavaScript return value to an XPath value are rather more complex than the mappings for arguments, because of the complications of handling returned DOM nodes, discussed on page 582 above.

The rules are as follows:

JavaScript data type	XPath data type
string	string
number	number
boolean	boolean

JavaScript data type	XPath data type
`DocumentFragment, Document, Node, NodeList, Attr, Element, Text, Comment, CDATASection, EntityReference, ProcessingInstruction`	node-set
`null`	external object
undefined	empty node-set
any other object	external object

If a string is returned, it should not contain any characters that are illegal in XML, such as ASCII `NUL` (`#x00`); however, the XSLT processor is not required to report this error, because of the potential performance implications. The same applies to strings contained in any DOM nodes that are returned.

When a function returns null, there is no simple way of testing that the value is null from within XPath. You will need to provide another external function that can be called to do the test.

The function-available() Function

So long as the processor supports the calling of JavaScript external functions, the **`function-available()`** function will return true if, after executing all the scripts contained in (or referenced from) **`<xsl:script>`** elements, the global object for the namespace used in the function name has a function whose name matches the local part of the function name.

Summary

External functions are useful to extend the capabilities of XSLT stylesheets. They allow stylesheets to access external system services, and to perform calculations that are difficult or inefficient to achieve in "pure" XSLT and XPath.

The language bindings described in this chapter are those of the draft XSLT 1.1 Recommendation, which defines standard language bindings for external functions written in Java or JavaScript. At the time of writing, no XSLT processor fully implements this specification. However, many of them offer something quite similar, so if you understand the specifications given here, you shouldn't have much difficulty with the variations implemented in different XSLT 1.0 products. Even when XSLT 1.1 is finalized, vendors may well provide other language bindings, or alternative bindings for these two languages. In particular, many vendors are likely to offer continued support for the proprietary binding mechanisms available in their 1.0 products, which were developed before the standard binding mechanisms were defined. Details of some of these mechanisms are provided in the product appendices. When vendors do switch to the standard mechanisms described in this chapter, however, it will be a good idea to stick to these interfaces, because doing so will make your extension functions portable from one XSLT processor to another, so long as they both support your chosen language.

In the next chapter we'll move away from detailed specifications of interfaces, and look at how you can use the facilities of XSLT to create well-designed stylesheets.

Stylesheet Design Patterns

In this chapter we'll look at four common **design patterns** for XSLT stylesheets.

The concept of design patterns was introduced by Erich Gamma, Richard Helm, Ralph Johnson, and John Vlissides in their classic book *Design Patterns: Elements of Reusable Object-Oriented Software* (Addison-Wesley Professional Computing) ISBN: 0201633612. Their idea was that there was a repertoire of techniques which were useful again and again. They presented 23 different design patterns for object-oriented programming, claiming not that this was in some sense a complete list, but that the vast majority of programs written by experienced designers fell into one or more of these patterns.

For XSLT stylesheets, the vast majority of stylesheets I have seen fall into one of four design patterns. These are:

- ❑ Fill-in-the-blanks stylesheets
- ❑ Navigational stylesheets
- ❑ Rule-based stylesheets
- ❑ Computational stylesheets

Again, this doesn't mean that these are the only ways you can write stylesheets, nor does it mean that any stylesheet you write must follow one of these four patterns to the exclusion of the other three. It just means that a great many stylesheets actually written by experienced people follow one of these four patterns, and if you become familiar with these patterns, you will have a good repertoire of techniques that you can apply to solving any given problem.

I will describe the first three design patterns rather briefly, because they are not really very difficult. The fourth, the computational design pattern, is explored in much greater depth – not because it is encountered more often, but because it requires a different way of thinking about algorithms than you use with conventional procedural programming languages.

Fill-in-the-Blanks Stylesheets

Many proprietary templating languages have been built up around HTML. The template looks largely like a standard HTML file, but with the addition of extra tags used to retrieve variable data and insert it at a particular point in the HTML data page. The designers of XSLT took care to ensure that in spite of the power of XSLT as a full transformation language, it would still be possible to use it in this simple way, bringing it within the reach of non-programmers with HTML authoring skills.

Here's an example of such a stylesheet. It uses the **simplified stylesheet** syntax (or *literal result element as stylesheet* syntax as it is clumsily named in the standard), so the **`<xsl:stylesheet>`** element and the **`<xsl:template match="/">`** element are implicit.

Example: A "Fill-in-the-Blanks" Stylesheet

Input

This XML document, `orgchart.xml`, represents an organization chart showing the senior management of a certain company at a particular date. It is organized as a recursive structure that directly reflects the management hierarchy:

```
<orgchart date="28 March 2001">
<person>
<name>Tim Berners-Lee</name>
<title>Chief Executive Officer</title>
<reports>
       <person>
             <name>Sharon Adler</name>
             <title>Technical Director</title>
             <reports>
                   <person>
                       <name>Tim Bray</name>
                       <title>Chief Engineer</title>
                   </person>
                   <person>
                       <name>James Clark</name>
                       <title>Director of Research</title>
                   </person>
             </reports>
       </person>
       <person>
             <name>Henry Thompson</name>
             <title>Operations and Finance</title>
       </person>
       <person>
             <name>David Megginson</name>
             <title>Human Resources</title>
       </person>
       <person>
             <name>Steve Muench</name>
             <title>Marketing</title>
       </person>
       <person>
             <name>Scott Boag</name>
             <title>International</title>
       </person>
</reports>
</person>
</orgchart>
```

Stylesheet

There are many creative ways you could display this data; for example, you could use SVG graphics, explorer-style trees implemented in client-side JavaScript, or just indented lists. I'm not trying to teach you any clever HTML tricks, so in this stylesheet (`orgchart.xsl`) I'll show the data instead as a rather boring table, with one row per person, and three columns for the person's name, their title, and the name of their boss:

```
<html xmlns:xsl="http://www.w3.org/1999/XSL/Transform"
   xsl:version="1.0">
<head>
   <title>Management Structure</title>
</head>
<body>
   <h1>Management Structure</h1>
   <p>The following responsibilies were announced on
      <xsl:value-of select="/orgchart/@date"/>:</p>
   <table border="2" cellpadding="5">
   <tr>
<th>Name</th><th>Role</th><th>Reporting to</th>
   </tr>
   <xsl:for-each select="//person">
      <tr>
         <td><xsl:value-of select="name"/></td>
         <td><xsl:value-of select="title"/></td>
         <td><xsl:value-of select="ancestor::person[1]/name"/></td>
      </tr>
   </xsl:for-each>
   </table>
   <hr/>
</body>
</html>
```

The key to this design pattern is that the stylesheet has the same structure as the desired output. Fixed content is included directly in the stylesheet as text or as literal result elements, while variable content is included by means of **`<xsl:value-of>`** instructions that extract the relevant data from the source document. Repeated sections of output, typically rows in a table or items in a list, can be enclosed by **`<xsl:for-each>`**, and conditional sections by **`<xsl:if>`** or **`<xsl:choose>`**.

Output

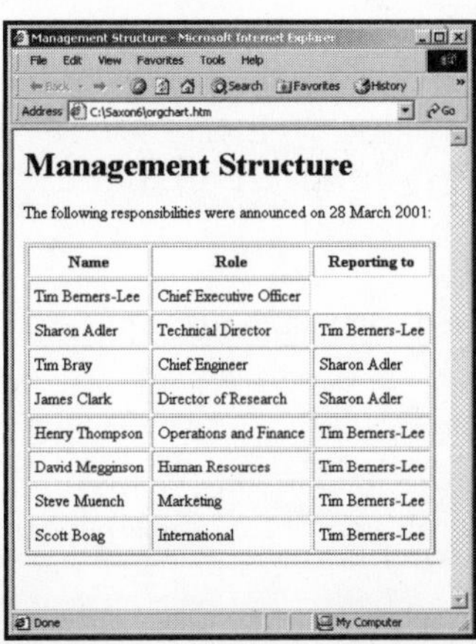

Management Structure

The following responsibilities were announced on 28 March 2001:

Name	Role	Reporting to
Tim Berners-Lee	Chief Executive Officer	
Sharon Adler	Technical Director	Tim Berners-Lee
Tim Bray	Chief Engineer	Sharon Adler
James Clark	Director of Research	Sharon Adler
Henry Thompson	Operations and Finance	Tim Berners-Lee
David Megginson	Human Resources	Tim Berners-Lee
Steve Muench	Marketing	Tim Berners-Lee
Scott Boag	International	Tim Berners-Lee

This kind of stylesheet makes very limited use of XSLT's power, but it is very similar to a wide variety of proprietary templating languages currently in use. Experience has shown that this kind of stylesheet is easy for experienced HTML authors to learn, even if they have no programming training. This is an important consideration, because on many larger web sites there is a constant need to introduce new page templates at very short notice, and this becomes much easier to achieve if content authors and editors can do the work themselves.

One restriction, of course, is that the input has to come from an XML document. This contrasts with most of the proprietary languages, where the input often comes directly from a relational database. The most elegant way around this restriction is to provide a way of extracting the required data into the tree format used by your chosen XSLT processor, without the need for an actual XML document as an intermediary format. Many XSLT processors accept input in the form of either a DOM tree, or a stream of SAX events, so you could write an interface module that does the database query and delivers the data in this form for use by the stylesheet authors. Another approach is to use the **`document()`** function (described in Chapter 7, page 466) with a URI that addresses a servlet with parameters to retrieve the required data. As you might expect, Oracle with their XSQL pages and XSQL servlet technology have probably gone further than most vendors in the direction of XML/XSLT/SQL integration: follow the links given in Appendix B.

Navigational Stylesheets

Navigational stylesheets are a natural progression from simple fill-in-the-blanks stylesheets.

Like fill-in-the-blanks stylesheets, a navigational stylesheet is still essentially output-oriented. However, it is now likely to use named templates as subroutines to perform commonly-needed tasks, it is likely to use variables to calculate values needed in more than one place, and it may use constructs such as keys, parameters, and sorting.

Whereas a fill-in-the-blanks stylesheet looks like HTML sprinkled with a few extra control statements, a navigational stylesheet (once you look beyond the angle-bracket syntax) looks very like a conventional procedural program with variables, conditional statements, for loops, and subroutine calls.

Navigational stylesheets are often used to produce reports on data-oriented XML documents, where the structure of the source document is regular and predictable.

Example: A Navigational Stylesheet

Input

Suppose the source document, `booklist.xml`, looks like this:

```
<booklist>
   <book>
      <title>Angela's Ashes</title>
      <author>Frank McCourt</author>
      <publisher>HarperCollins</publisher>
      <isbn>0 00 649840 X</isbn>
      <price>6.99</price>
      <sales>235</sales>
```

```
   </book>
   <book>
      <title>Sword of Honour</title>
      <author>Evelyn Waugh</author>
      <publisher>Penguin Books</publisher>
      <isbn>0 14 018967 X</isbn>
      <price>12.99</price>
      <sales>12</sales>
   </book>
</booklist>
```

Stylesheet

The following navigational stylesheet (booksales.xsl) produces a report on the total number of sales for each publisher.

Note the global variable «$publishers». This is a node-set containing one **<publisher>** element for each distinct publisher found in the source file. The way it works is that it selects only those publishers that are not the same as any previous publisher, in other words, it filters out the duplicates.

```
<xsl:stylesheet
   xmlns:xsl="http://www.w3.org/1999/XSL/Transform"
   version="1.0">

<xsl:key name="pub" match="book" use="publisher"/>

<xsl:variable name="publishers"
   select="//publisher[not(.=preceding::publisher)]"/>

<xsl:template match="/">
<html>
<head>
   <title>Sales volume by publisher</title>
</head>
<body>
   <h1>Sales volume by publisher</h1>
   <table>
      <tr>
      <th>Publisher</th><th>Total Sales Value</th>
      </tr>
   <xsl:for-each select="$publishers">
      <tr>
      <td><xsl:value-of select="."/></td>
      <td><xsl:call-template name="total-sales"/></td>
      </tr>
   </xsl:for-each>
   </table>
</body>
</html>
</xsl:template>

<!-- calculate total book sales for the current publisher -->
<xsl:template name="total-sales">
   <xsl:value-of select="sum(key('pub',string(.))/sales)"/>
</xsl:template>
</xsl:stylesheet>
```

This stylesheet is not very far removed from the fill-in-the-blanks example earlier in the chapter. But because it uses some top-level elements such as **<xsl:key>** and a named template, it now needs to use the full syntax with an **<xsl:stylesheet>** element.

Output

```
    <html>
       <head>
          <META http-equiv="Content-Type" content="text/html;
charset=utf-8">
          <title>Sales volume by publisher</title>
       </head>
       <body>
          <h1>Sales volume by publisher</h1>
          <table>
             <tr>
                <th>Publisher</th>
                <th>Total Sales Value</th>
             </tr>
             <tr>
                <td>HarperCollins</td>
                <td>235</td>
             </tr>
             <tr>
                <td>Penguin Books</td>
                <td>12</td>
             </tr>
          </table>
       </body>
    </html>
```

The obvious difference between a fill-in-the-blanks stylesheet and this navigational stylesheet is that the **<xsl:stylesheet>** and **<xsl:template>** elements are now explicit, which makes it possible to introduce other top-level elements such as **<xsl:key>** and a global **<xsl:variable>**. More subtly, the range of XSLT features used means that this stylesheet has crossed the boundary from being an HTML document with added control instructions, to being a real program. The boundary, though, is a rather fuzzy one, with no visa required to cross it, so many people who have learned to write simple fill-in-the-blanks stylesheets should be able, as they expand their knowledge, to progress to writing navigational stylesheets of this kind.

Although the use of flow-of-control instructions like **<xsl:if>**, **<xsl:call-template>** and **<xsl:for-each>** gives such a stylesheet a procedural feel, in fact it does not violate the original concept that XSLT should be a declarative language. This is because the instructions do not have to be executed in the order they are written – variables can't be updated, so the result of one instruction can't affect the next one. For example, it's easy to think of the **<xsl:for-each>** instruction in this example processing the selected nodes in document order and adding them one by one to the result tree; but it would be equally valid for an XSLT processor to process them in reverse order, or in parallel, so long as the nodes are added to the result tree in the right place. That's why I was careful to call this design pattern *navigational* rather than *procedural*. It's navigational in that you say exactly where to find the nodes in the source tree that you want to visit, but it's not procedural, because you don't define the order in which you will visit them.

Rule-Based Stylesheets

A rule-based stylesheet is one that consists primarily of rules describing how different features of the source document should be processed, such as, "if you find a **<species>** element, display it in italics".

Some would say that this rule-based approach is the essence of the XSLT language, the principal way that it is intended to be used. I would say that it's one way of writing stylesheets, often the best way, but not the only way, and not necessarily the best answer in every situation.

Unlike navigational stylesheets, a rule-based stylesheet is not structured according to the desired output layout. In fact, it makes minimal assumptions about the structure of either the source document or the result document. Rather, the structure reads like an inventory of components that might be encountered in the source document, arranged in arbitrary order.

Rule-based stylesheets are therefore at their most useful when processing source documents whose structure is flexible or unpredictable, or which may change a lot in the future. It is very useful when the same repertoire of elements can appear in many different document structures, so a rule like "display dates in the format *23 March 2000*" can be reused in many different contexts.

Rule-based stylesheets are a natural evolution of CSS and CSS2 stylesheets. In CSS, you can define rules of the form "for this set of elements, use this display rendition". In XSLT, the rules become much more flexible, in two directions: the pattern language for defining which elements you are talking about is much richer, and the actions you can define when the rule is fired are vastly more wide-ranging.

A simple rule-based stylesheet will consist of one rule for each element type. The typical rule matches a particular element type, outputs an HTML tag to define the rendition of that element, and calls **`<xsl:apply-templates>`** to process the child nodes of the template. This causes text nodes within the element to be copied to the output, and nested child elements to be processed each according to its own template rule.

Example: A Rule-Based Stylesheet

Input

The input `scene2.xml` is a scene from a play; Act I, Scene 2 of Shakespeare's *Othello*. It starts like this:

```
<?xml version="1.0" encoding="iso-8859-1" ?>
<SCENE>
   <TITLE>SCENE II.  Another street.</TITLE>
   <STAGEDIR>Enter OTHELLO, IAGO, and Attendants with
            torches</STAGEDIR>
   <SPEECH>
      <SPEAKER>IAGO</SPEAKER>
      <LINE>Though in the trade of war I have slain men,</LINE>
      <LINE>Yet do I hold it very stuff o' the conscience</LINE>
      <LINE>To do no contrived murder: I lack iniquity</LINE>
      <LINE>Sometimes to do me service: nine or ten times</LINE>
      <LINE>I had thought to have yerk'd him here under the
            ribs.</LINE>
   </SPEECH>
   <SPEECH>
      <SPEAKER>OTHELLO</SPEAKER>
      <LINE>'Tis better as it is.</LINE>
   </SPEECH>
</SCENE>
```

There are some complications that aren't shown in this sample, but which the stylesheet needs to take account of:

- The top-level element is not always a **<SCENE>**; it might also be a **<PROLOGUE>** or **<EPILOGUE>**. The **<STAGEDIR>** element can appear at any level of nesting, for example a stage directive can appear between two speeches, between two lines of a speech, or in the middle of a line.
- Several people can speak at the same time. In this case a single **<SPEECH>** element will have more than one **<SPEAKER>**. In general a **<SPEECH>** consists of one or more **<SPEAKER>** elements followed by any number of **<LINE>** and **<STAGEDIR>** elements in any order.

Stylesheet

The stylesheet `scene.xsl` consists of a number of template rules. It starts by declaring a global variable (used simply as a constant) and a rule for the document element:

```
<xsl:stylesheet
    xmlns:xsl="http://www.w3.org/1999/XSL/Transform"
    version="1.0"
>

<xsl:variable name="backcolor" select="'#FFFFCC'" />

<xsl:template match="SCENE|PROLOGUE|EPILOGUE">
   <HTML>
   <HEAD>
      <TITLE><xsl:value-of select="TITLE"/></TITLE>
   </HEAD>
   <BODY BGCOLOR='{$backcolor}'>
      <xsl:apply-templates/>
   </BODY>
   </HTML>
</xsl:template>
```

The appearance of **<xsl:value-of>** is a rare departure from the purely rule-based pattern, just to prove that none of the patterns have to be used to the exclusion of the others.

The template rule for the **<SPEECH>** element outputs a table containing one row and two columns: it puts the names of the speakers in the first column, and the lines of the speech, plus any stage directives, in the second, as follows:

```
<xsl:template match="SPEECH">
   <TABLE><TR>
   <TD WIDTH="160" VALIGN="TOP">
<xsl:apply-templates select="SPEAKER"/>
   </TD>
   <TD VALIGN="TOP">
   <xsl:apply-templates select="STAGEDIR|LINE"/>
   </TD>
   </TR></TABLE>
</xsl:template>
```

The remaining template rules are straightforward. Each of them simply outputs the text of the element using an appropriate HTML rendition. The only complication is that for some elements (**<STAGEDIR>** and **<SUBHEAD>**, which doesn't actually occur in this particular scene) the HTML rendition is different depending on the element's context, so there is more than one rule defined for these elements.

```
<xsl:template match="TITLE">
   <H1><CENTER>
   <xsl:apply-templates/>
   </CENTER></H1><HR/>
</xsl:template>

<xsl:template match="SPEAKER">
   <B>
      <xsl:apply-templates/>
      <xsl:if test="not(position()=last())"><BR/></xsl:if>
   </B>
</xsl:template>

<xsl:template match="SCENE/STAGEDIR">
    <CENTER><H3>
    <xsl:apply-templates/>
    </H3></CENTER>
</xsl:template>

<xsl:template match="SPEECH/STAGEDIR">
   <P><I>
   <xsl:apply-templates/>
   </I></P>
</xsl:template>

<xsl:template match="LINE/STAGEDIR">
   [ <I>
   <xsl:apply-templates/>
   </I> ]
</xsl:template>

<xsl:template match="SCENE/SUBHEAD">
   <CENTER><H3>
   <xsl:apply-templates/>
   </H3></CENTER>
</xsl:template>

<xsl:template match="SPEECH/SUBHEAD">
   <P><B>
   <xsl:apply-templates/>
   </B></P>
</xsl:template>

<xsl:template match="LINE">
   <xsl:apply-templates/>
   <BR/>
</xsl:template>

</xsl:stylesheet>
```

Output

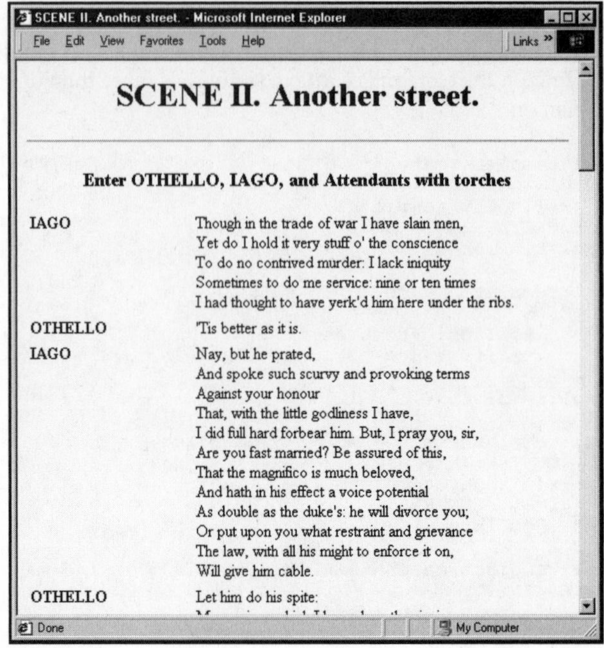

Most of the time a rule-based stylesheet creates a result tree that has quite a similar structure to the source tree, with most of the source text appearing in the same order in the result document, but often with different tags. The closer this describes the transformation you want to do, the closer your stylesheet will be to the example shown above. However, this doesn't mean that the processing has to be purely sequential. You can process chunks of the tree more than once using modes, you can reorder the nodes of the tree, and you can grab data from ancestor nodes, all without deviating from the rule-based design pattern.

The characteristic feature of a rule-based stylesheet is that there is generally one template rule for each type of object found in the source document. Of course it's possible to mix design patterns, particularly if your source document contains a mixture of "data-oriented" and "text-oriented" structures (an example might be a job application form). Then it's quite appropriate to use a navigational pattern for the regular structures and a rule-based pattern for the less regular. The larger and more complex your stylesheet, the more likely it is to contain examples of each of the design patterns.

Computational Stylesheets

Computational stylesheets are the most complex of the four design patterns. They arise when there is a need to generate nodes in the result tree that do not correspond directly to nodes in the source tree. This happens most commonly when there is structure in the source document that is not explicit in its markup. For example:

- A text field in the source might consist of a comma-separated list of items that are to be displayed as a bulleted list in the output.
- There might be a need to generate **`<section>`** elements in the output where a section is not explicit in the source, but is defined as comprising an **`<h1>`** element and all its following sibling elements up to the next **`<h1>`** element.

Other examples arise where you want to organize data into rows and columns when the input doesn't fall naturally into that structure, or if you need to do complex aggregation of the data, such as constructing a football league table when the source data contains the results of individual matches.

When you write computational stylesheets you will invariably run up against the fact that XSLT does not have an assignment statement, and that it is therefore not possible to write loops in the way you are probably used to in other languages. So you will need to understand some of the concepts of **functional programming**, which the following section tries to explain.

Programming without Assignment Statements

Back in 1968 the renowned computer scientist Edsger Dijkstra published a paper under the title *GoTo Statement Considered Harmful*. His thesis, that programs should be written without `goto` statements, shattered the world as most programmers saw it. Until then they had been familiar with early dialects of Fortran and Cobol in which the vast majority of decisions in a program were implemented by using a construct that mapped directly to the conditional jump instruction in the hardware: «`if` *`condition`* `goto` *`label`*». Even the design notation of the day, the ubiquitous flowchart drawn in pencil using a plastic template, represented control flow in this way.

Dijkstra argued that structured programs, written using `if-then-else` and `while-do` constructs instead of `goto` statements, were far less likely to contain bugs and were far more readable and therefore maintainable. The ideas were fiercely controversial at the time, especially among practising programmers, and for years afterwards the opponents of the idea would challenge the structured programming enthusiasts with arguments of the form, "OK, so how do you do *this* without a `goto` statement?".

Today, however, the battle is won, and the `goto` statement has been consigned to history. Modern languages like Java don't provide a `goto` statement, and we no longer miss it.

But, for just as long there has been another group of enthusiasts telling us that assignment statements are considered harmful. Unlike Dijkstra, these evangelists have yet to convince a skeptical world that they are right, though there has always been a significant band of disciples who have seen the benefits of the approach.

This style of coding, without assignment statements, is called *Functional Programming*. The earliest and most famous functional programming language was Lisp (sometimes ridiculed as "Lots of Irritating Superfluous Parentheses"), while more modern examples include ML and Scheme. (See, for example, *Simply Scheme: Introducing Computer Science* by Brian Harvey and Matthew Wright, MIT Press, 1999, ISBN 0-262082-81-0.)

XSLT is a language without assignment statements, and although its syntax is very different from these languages, its philosophy is based on the concepts of functional programming. It is not in fact a fully-fledged functional programming language, because you cannot manipulate functions in the same way as data; but in most other respects, it fits into this category of language. If you want to do anything at all complicated with it, you'll have to get used to programming without assignment statements. At first it probably won't be easy, because just as those early Fortran and Cobol programmers would instinctively reach for the `goto` statement as the solution to every problem, if your background is in languages like C or Visual Basic or even Java you will just as naturally cherish the assignment statement as your favorite all-purpose tool.

So what's wrong with assignment statements, and why aren't they available in XSLT?

The crux of the argument is that it's the assignment statements that impose a particular order of execution on a program. Without assignment statements, we can do things in any order, because the result of one statement can no longer depend on what state the system was left in by the previous statement. Just as the `goto` statement mirrors the "jump" instruction in the hardware, so the assignment statement mirrors the "store" instruction, and the reason we have assignment statements in our programming languages today is that they were designed to take advantage of sequential von Neumann computers with jump and store instructions. If we want to free ourselves from sequential thinking modeled on sequential hardware architecture, we should find a way of describing what effect we want to achieve, rather than saying what sequence of steps the machine should take in order to achieve it.

The idea of a functional program is to describe the output as a function of the input. XSLT is a transformation language; it is designed to transform an input document into an output document. So, we can regard a stylesheet as a function that defines this transformation: a stylesheet is a function *O=S(I)* where *I* is the input document, *S* is the stylesheet, and *O* is the output document. Recall the statement made by James Clark at the 1995 Paris workshop, which I quoted in Chapter 1, page 33:

> *A DSSSL stylesheet very precisely describes a function from SGML to a flow object tree.*

This concept clearly remained a key part of the XSLT vision throughout the development of the language. (And, indeed, the flow objects of DSSSL eventually became the Formatting Objects of XSL-FO.)

We're using the word **function** here in something close to its mathematical sense. Languages like Fortran and Visual Basic have borrowed the word to mean a subroutine that returns a result, but the mathematical concept of a function is not that of an algorithm or sequence of steps to be performed, rather it is a statement of a relationship. The square root function defines a relationship between 3 and 9, namely `3=sqrt(9)`. The essence of a function is that it is a fixed, constant, reliable relationship, and evaluating it doesn't change the world. When you ask me "what's the square root of 9 if you work it out?" I can honestly reply "exactly the same as if I don't". I can say this because square root is a **pure** function, it gives the same answer whoever calls it and however often they call it, and calling it once doesn't change the answer it gives next time; in fact, it doesn't change anything.

The nice property of pure functions is that they can be called any number of times, in any order, and produce the same result every time. If I want to calculate the square root of every integer between zero and a thousand, it doesn't matter whether I start at zero and work up, or start at a thousand and work down, or whether I buy a thousand and one computers and do them all at the same time, I know I will get the same answer. Pure functions have no side effects.

An assignment statement isn't like that. The effect of an assignment statement "if you work it out" is **not** the same as if you don't. When you write «`x = x+1;`», the effect depends very much on how often the statement is executed. When you write several assignment statements, for example

```
temp = x;
x = y;
y = temp;
```

then the effect depends on executing them in the right order.

This means, of course, that a pure function can't update external variables. As soon as we allow assignment, we become dependent on doing things in sequence, one step at a time in the right order.

Don't object-oriented languages achieve the same thing, by preventing one object updating data held in another? No, because although they prevent direct writing to private data, they allow the same effect to be achieved by **`get()`** and **`set()`** methods. An update to a variable achieved indirectly through a defined interface creates exactly the same dependence on sequence of execution as an update done directly with an assignment statement. A pure function must have no side effects; its only output is the result it returns.

The main reason that functional languages are considered ideal for a stylesheet language (or a tree transformation language if you prefer) is not so much the ability to do things in parallel or in any order, but rather the ability to do them incrementally. We want to get away from static pages; if you're showing a map of the traffic congestion hotspots in your area, then when the data for a particular road junction changes, you want the map updated in real time, and it should be possible to do this without recalculating and redrawing the whole map. This is only possible if there's a direct relationship – a function – between what's shown at a particular place on the map display and a particular data item in the underlying database. So if we can decompose our top-level stylesheet function, $O=S(I)$, into a set of smaller, independent functions, each relating one piece of the output to one piece of the input, then we have the potential to do this on-the-fly updating.

Another benefit of this incremental approach is that when a large page of XML is downloaded from the network, the browser can start displaying parts of the output as soon as the relevant parts of the input are available. That's the theory, at any rate. There aren't any XSLT processors that can do this yet, because it requires some quite complex analysis of the stylesheet to work out when and to what extent it's possible in any given case – but if the stylesheet were a conventional program with side effects, it wouldn't ever be possible, because the last bit of input to arrive could change everything.

This is where XSLT template rules come in. They act as the small, independent functions relating one piece of the output to one piece of the input. A template rule has no side effects, its output is a pure function of its inputs. The inputs are (idealizing slightly) the current position in the input document plus any supplied parameters. It doesn't matter in what order the template rules are executed, so long as we assemble their individual outputs together in the right way to form the result tree. If part of the input changes, then we only need to re-evaluate those template rules that depend on that part of the input, slotting their outputs into the appropriate place in the output tree. In practice, of course, it's not as easy as that, and no-one has yet implemented an incremental stylesheet processor that works like this. However, it will almost certainly come, and the reason assignment statements were left out of the language was to make it possible.

Meanwhile, while the researchers and product developers work out how to implement an incremental stylesheet processor, you as a user are left with a different problem: learning how to program without assignment statements. After this rather lengthy digression into Computer Science theory, in the next section I shall get my feet back on the ground and show you some examples of how to do this.

However, first let's try and separate this from another programming challenge that arises with XSLT, which is the limited number of data types available. In terms of language design principles, the lack of assignment statements and the absence of a rich type system are quite separate matters. With XSLT 1.0, you often hit the two issues together:

- The only effect a template can have is via the output it produces (because of the ban on side effects).
- And the only output it can produce, if you want to process it further, is a character string (because of the limited range of data types available).

However, in XSLT 1.1 it becomes possible for a template to construct a tree, which can be used as input to further stages of processing. The tree is about as versatile a data structure as you can get, so the second problem is really a thing of the past. With XSLT 1.0 you could often get around the problem by representing complex data in the form of character strings, but the introduction of temporary trees in XSLT 1.1 greatly reduces the contortions that are necessary to implement complex algorithms in your transformations.

So Why Are They Called Variables?

XSLT, as we have seen, does have variables that can hold values. You can initialize a variable to a value, but what you can't do is change the value of an existing variable once it has been initialized.

So some people have asked, why call it a variable if you can't vary it? The answer lies in the traditional mathematical use of the word variable: a variable is a symbol that can be used to denote different values on different occasions. When I say "area = length × breadth", then **area**, **length**, and **breadth** are names or symbols used to denote values: here they denote properties of a rectangle. They are variables because these values are different every time I apply the formula, not because a given rectangle is changing size as I watch.

Cheating

Just occasionally, you may feel that programming without assignment statements is too mind-boggling, or too slow. In these cases you may be tempted to cheat.

Most XSLT processors actually allow user-written extension functions to have side effects, and some have gone to considerable lengths in their documentation to describe how to exploit this feature to implement a substitute for updateable variables.

The Saxon product goes one step further, and provides an extension element **`<saxon:assign>`** that allows you to update a variable directly.

> *Since I've just spent several pages explaining why side-effect-free languages are a "Good Thing", you might find it surprising that I should put a feature in my own product that destroys the principle at a stroke. I have several excuses:*
>
> *(a) At the time I did it, XSLT was far less advanced as a functional programming language than it finally became.*
>
> *(b) I thought that although side-effect-free programming is a good thing in theory, many users wouldn't be ready for it.*
>
> *(c) I wanted to experiment to see whether the costs (in performance and usability) of the pure functional approach exceeded the benefits, and the best way to do this was to launch a genetically modified variant of the language into the wild and see whether the mutation thrived.*

These features are a last resort. Most XSLT processors actually do their processing in a predictable way, so you can usually get away with such cheating. If you use a processor that does more optimization, however, then using such extensions might have different side effects from the ones you wanted. You can find yourself, for example, closing a file before you've written to it, because the order of execution of different instructions is not predictable. These facilities are like the `PEEK` and `POKE` of early Basic dialects, a messy escape into a lower level of programming, that you should use only if you are desperate. Having said that, there are situations where they can give a dramatic boost to the speed of a stylesheet with performance problems.

Avoiding Assignment Statements

In the following sections I'll look at some of the common situations where assignment statements appear to be needed, and show how to achieve the required effect without them.

Conditional Initialization

This problem has an easy solution, so I shall get it out of the way quickly.

In conventional languages you might want to initialize a variable to zero in some circumstances and to a value of one in others. You might write:

```
int x;
if (zeroBased) {
   x=0;
} else {
   x=1;
}
```

How can you do the equivalent in XSLT without an assignment statement?

The answer is simple: think of the equivalent:

```
int x = (zeroBased ? 0 : 1 );
```

which has its parallel in XSLT as:

```
<xsl:variable name="x">
   <xsl:choose>
      <xsl:when test="$zeroBased">0</xsl:when>
      <xsl:otherwise>1</xsl:otherwise>
   </xsl:choose>
</xsl:variable>
```

The only slight hitch is that when you use the content of **`<xsl:variable>`** to set its value, rather than the **`select`** attribute, the value of the variable will always be a tree. This doesn't matter if, as here, you want a string or number, because a tree can easily be converted to a string or number, but it's a problem when what you want is a set of nodes from the source document.

Suppose you want the variable `$transactions` to be all the credits or all the debits depending on the value of the Boolean variable `$getCredits`. Here's one way to achieve the desired result:

```
<xsl:variable name="transactions"
        select="//credits[$getCredits] |
//debits[not($getCredits)]"/>
```

What this does is to form the union of two node-sets, one of which is always empty. Notice the union operator, «|». If `$getCredits` is true, the first predicate «`[$getCredits]`» is always true and the second predicate «`[not($getCredits)]`» is always false, so the expression is equivalent to «`//credits`»; while if `$getCredits` is false, the situation is reversed, and the expression is equivalent to «`//debits`».

Don't Iterate, Recurse

One of the most common uses of variables in conventional programming is to keep track of where you are in a loop. Whether this is done using an integer counter in a `for` loop, or using an `Iterator` or `Enumerator` object to process a list, the principle is the same: we have a variable that represents how far we have got and that tells us when we are finished.

In a functional program you can't do this, because you can't update variables. So instead of writing a loop, you need to write a recursive function.

In a conventional program a common way to process a list of items is as follows:

```
iterator = list.getIterator();
while (iterator.hasMoreItems()) {
   item = iterator.getNextItem();
   item.doSomething();
}
```

The killer assignment statement is «`item = iterator.getNextItem()`». This assigns a different value to the `item` each time, and what's more, it relies on the `iterator` containing some sort of updateable variable that keeps track of how far it's got.

In a functional program we handle this by recursion rather than iteration. The pseudo-code becomes:

```
function process(list) {
   if (!isEmpty(list)) {
      doSomething(getFirst(list));
      process(getRemainder(list));
   }
}
```

This function is called to process a list of objects. It does whatever is necessary with the first object in the list, and then calls itself to handle the rest of the list. (I'm assuming that **`getFirst()`** gets the first item in the list and **`getRemainder()`** gets a list containing all items except the first). The list gets smaller each time the function is called, and when it finally becomes empty, the function exits, and unwinds through all the recursive calls.

It's important to make sure there is a terminating condition such as the list becoming empty. Otherwise the function will keep calling itself forever – the recursive equivalent of an infinite loop.

So the first lesson in programming without variables is to use recursion rather than iteration to process a list. With XSLT this isn't necessary to handle every kind of loop, because XSLT provides built-in facilities such as **`<xsl:apply-templates>`** and **`<xsl:for-each>`** that process all the members of a node-set without requiring an explicit control variable, as well as functions like **`sum()`** and **`count()`** to do some common operations on node-sets; but whenever you need to process a set of things that can't be handled with these constructs, you need to use recursion.

Is recursion expensive? The answer is, not necessarily. It's quite possible for a reasonably smart compiler to generate exactly the same code for a recursive procedure as for an iterative one. For example a common compiler technique with functional programming languages is that of *tail recursion*, which recognizes that when a function calls itself as the last thing it does, there's no need to allocate a new stack frame or new variables, you can just loop back to the beginning.

The following example uses a recursive template to process a whitespace-separated list of numbers which, for some reason, have not been marked up as separate elements.

Example: Totaling a List of Numbers

Input

Suppose you have a string that holds a whitespace-separated list of numbers, for example `"12 34.5 18.2 –35"` and you want to find the total. (Don't ask why; when someone else designs your XML documents for you, these things happen.)

For the sake of an example, this is the entire content of the document, `number-list.xml`:

```
<numbers>12  34.5  18.2  -35</numbers>
```

Stylesheet

We need to use some of the string-handling functions provided in the XPath expression language. These are described in Chapter 7; the ones we will use are:

- **`normalize-space()`**, which removes leading and trailing spaces and replaces internal whitespace with a single space character (see page 524).
- **`concat()`**, which concatenates two strings. I shall use this to add a space at the end of the string, so that it works correctly even when there is only one number in the string (see page 456).
- **`substring-before()`**, which I will use to find the part of a string that comes before the first space (see page 549).
- **`substring-after()`**, which I will use to find the part of a string that comes after the first space (see page 548).
- **`number()`**, which converts a string to a number. Actually this would happen automatically, but I will do it explicitly for clarity (see page 530).

Here's the recursive template (in file `number-total.xsl`):

```
<xsl:template name="total-numbers">
   <xsl:param name="list"/>
   <xsl:variable name="wlist"
      select="concat(normalize-space($list), ' ')"/>
   <xsl:choose>
      <xsl:when test="$wlist!=' '">
         <xsl:variable name="first"
            select="substring-before($wlist, ' ')"/>
         <xsl:variable name="rest"
            select="substring-after($wlist, ' ')"/>
```

```
            <xsl:variable name="total">
               <xsl:call-template name="total-numbers">
                  <xsl:with-param name="list" select="$rest"/>
               </xsl:call-template>
            </xsl:variable>
            <xsl:value-of select="number($first) + number($total)"/>
         </xsl:when>
         <xsl:otherwise>0</xsl:otherwise>
      </xsl:choose>
   </xsl:template>
```

Notice how closely this mirrors the pseudo-code structure given earlier.

- First, to make tests on the whitespace-separated list easier, it normalizes the supplied list. It uses the **normalize-space()** function to remove leading and trailing spaces and replace all intermediate whitespace with a single space character; then it uses **concat()** to add an extra space at the end, so that the first number in the list will always have a space after it even if it is the only number in the list. (It's actually unnecessary to do this when the template calls itself recursively, because the list will already be in the right format. If you want to write a bit more code to make it go a little faster, there's room for optimization here.)
- If the supplied list is empty, the template returns the value zero. The test in the **<xsl:when>** instruction returns false (after normalization, a string containing no numbers will have turned into a single space). So the **<xsl:otherwise>** branch is taken and the template returns, thus terminating the recursion.
- Otherwise it extracts the first number from the list into the variable `$first` by **substring-before()**, and extracts the remainder of the list into the variable `$rest` by **substring-after()**. The template then calls itself recursively to process the remainder of the list, and adds the value of the first number to the total obtained from the other numbers. The **<xsl:with-param>** element sets the parameter for the called template, so that next time around the list it is processing will be the "rest" of the list – the remainder after removing the first element. The **<xsl:value-of>** element writes the result to the current output tree, which may be a variable or the final result tree.

To test this, add the template rule below, and run the stylesheet against the above source document:

```
<xsl:template match="/">
   <xsl:call-template name="total-numbers">
      <xsl:with-param name="list" select="."/>
   </xsl:call-template>
</xsl:template>
```

Output

```
29.7
```

Another example similar to this one was given under **<xsl:call-template>** in Chapter 4, page 178.

Here's another example, this time processing a node-set. XPath provides built-in functions for counting nodes and for totaling their values, but they aren't always flexible enough: sometimes you need to walk round the nodes yourself.

Example: Finding the Total Sales Value

The requirement is to find the total sales value of a list of books, using the book list example on page 602. To find the total sales value, you need to multiply the number of sales of each book by its price, which you cannot do using the **sum()** function provided in XSLT.

Input

This example uses the `booklist.xml` file introduced earlier in this chapter. It records sales figures for a number of books, as follows:

```
<booklist>
   <book>
      <title>Angela's Ashes</title>
      <author>Frank McCourt</author>
      <publisher>HarperCollins</publisher>
      <isbn>0 00 649840 X</isbn>
      <price>6.99</price>
      <sales>235</sales>
   </book>
   <book>
      <title>Sword of Honour</title>
      <author>Evelyn Waugh</author>
      <publisher>Penguin Books</publisher>
      <isbn>0 14 018967 X</isbn>
      <price>12.99</price>
      <sales>12</sales>
   </book>
</booklist>
```

Stylesheet

The stylesheet `total-sales.xsl` is as follows. Once again it defines a recursive template, named «`total-sales-value`». This is called to process a set of **`<book>`** elements passed in the parameter «`list`». The recursion terminates, returning zero, when the list is empty.

When the list isn't empty, the template multiplies the number of sales by the price for the first book in the list, and adds the total sales value of all the books after the first, which it obtains by calling itself with this shorter list as a parameter. As we're dealing with node-sets this time rather than strings, we use the XPath syntax for manipulating node-sets: in particular, the predicate « `[1]` » to find the first node in the set, and « `[position()!=1]` » to find the remainder.

```
<xsl:stylesheet
   xmlns:xsl="http://www.w3.org/1999/XSL/Transform"
   version="1.0">

<xsl:template name="total-sales-value">
   <xsl:param name="list"/>
   <xsl:choose>
      <xsl:when test="$list">
         <xsl:variable name="first" select="$list[1]"/>
         <xsl:variable name="total-of-rest">
            <xsl:call-template name="total-sales-value">
               <xsl:with-param name="list"
                          select="$list[position()!=1]"/>
            </xsl:call-template>
         </xsl:variable>
         <xsl:value-of select="$first/sales * $first/price +
                                              $total-of-rest"/>
      </xsl:when>
      <xsl:otherwise>0</xsl:otherwise>
   </xsl:choose>
</xsl:template>
```

The root template simply calls the recursive template to process the set of all books in the input file, and displays the result in a suitable format by calling the **`format-number()`** function, which was described in Chapter 7, page 484.

```
<xsl:template match="/">
   <xsl:variable name="total">
       <xsl:call-template name="total-sales-value">
          <xsl:with-param name="list" select="//book"/>
       </xsl:call-template>
   </xsl:variable>
Total sales value is: <xsl:value-of select="format-number($total,
                      '$#.00')"/>
   </xsl:template>

</xsl:stylesheet>
```

Output

```
Total sales value is: $1798.53
```

Recursion: Summary

By now the principle should be clear. Whenever you need to find something out by processing a list of items, write a recursive template that is given the entire list as a parameter. If the list isn't empty, deal with the first item, and make a recursive call to deal with the rest of the list after the first item.

As I mentioned, with XSLT 1.0 there was another problem when doing this, which was nothing to do with the lack of an assignment statement, but is a consequence of the limited range of data types available. The result of a template is always a temporary tree, and with XSLT 1.0 there are only two things you can do with the tree: you can copy it to the final result tree, or you can convert it to a string. What this means is that if you want to do any more processing on the result of your recursive function, you have to find some way of expressing the result as a string.

With XSLT 1.1 this becomes much easier because you can manipulate a temporary tree in any way you like, treating it just like another source document. In fact this facility is so useful that it has been provided in several XSLT 1.0 processors as a vendor extension, for example MSXML3 has an **`msxml:node-set()`** function to convert a tree to a node-set. Although you will probably want to avoid relying too much on vendor extensions, this one is reasonably safe: it doesn't get you locked in, because equivalent facilities are available from several vendors, and you know that when you move forward to the next version of the standard, the facility will become available in a portable way.

For an example that takes advantage of this, see the Knight's Tour in Chapter 10.

Avoid Doing Two Things at Once

Another common requirement for variables arises when you are trying to do two things at once. For example, you are trying to copy text to the output destination, and at the same time to keep a note of how much text you have copied. You might feel that the natural way of doing this is to keep the running total in a variable, and update it as a side-effect of the template that does the copying. Similarly, you might want to maintain a counter as you output nodes, so that you can start a new table row after every ten.

Or perhaps you want to scan a set of numbers calculating both the minimum and the maximum value; or while outputting a list of employees, to set a flag for later use if any salary greater than $100,000 was found.

You have to think differently about these problems in XSLT. Think about each part of the output you want to produce separately, and write a function (or template rule) that generates this piece of the output from the input data it needs. Don't think about calculating other things at the same time.

So you need to write one function to produce the output, and another to calculate the total. Write one template to find the minimum, and another to find the maximum.

This might mean writing a little more code, and it might take a little longer, because work is being repeated, but it is usually the right approach. The problem of repeated processing can often be solved by using variables for the node-sets used in both calculations: if you need to use a particular node-set as input to more than one process, save that node-set in a variable which can then be supplied as a parameter to the two separate templates.

An alternative that may occasionally give better performance is to write a template that returns a composite result. With standard XSLT 1.0 the only practical way to do this is to write the result as a whitespace-separated string. With XSLT 1.1, however (or with an XSLT 1.0 processor that offers the **node-set()** extension function), it is possible to return a composite result structured as a tree. The calling code is then able to access the individual nodes of this tree using an XPath expression. For example, the following recursive template, when supplied with a node-set as a parameter, constructs a tree containing two elements, `<min>` and `<max>`, set to the minimum and maximum value of the nodes respectively. A working stylesheet based on this example can be found in the download file as `minimax.xsl`: it acts as its own source document.

```
<xsl:template name="get-min-and-max">
  <xsl:param name="nodes"/>
  <xsl:param name="best-so-far">
    <min><xsl:value-of select="999999999"/></min>
    <max><xsl:value-of select="-999999999"/></max>
  </xsl:param>
  <xsl:choose>
    <xsl:when test="$nodes">
      <xsl:variable name="new-best-so-far">
      <min>
        <xsl:choose>
          <xsl:when test="$nodes[1] &lt; $best-so-far/min">
            <xsl:value-of select="$nodes[1]"/>
          </xsl:when>
          <xsl:otherwise>
            <xsl:value-of select="$best-so-far/min"/>
          </xsl:otherwise>
        </xsl:choose>
      </min>
       <max>
        <xsl:choose>
          <xsl:when test="$nodes[1] &gt; $best-so-far/max">
            <xsl:value-of select="$nodes[1]"/>
          </xsl:when>
          <xsl:otherwise>
            <xsl:value-of select="$best-so-far/max"/>
          </xsl:otherwise>
        </xsl:choose>
      </max>
      </xsl:variable>
      <xsl:call-template name="get-min-and-max">
        <xsl:with-param name="nodes" select="$nodes[position() &gt; 1]"/>
        <xsl:with-param name="best-so-far" select="$new-best-so-far"/>
      </xsl:call-template>
    </xsl:when>
    <xsl:otherwise>
      <xsl:copy-of select="$best-so-far"/>
    </xsl:otherwise>
  </xsl:choose>
</xsl:template>
```

When you call this template you can let the second parameter, `$best-so-far`, take its default value:

```
<xsl:variable name="min-and-max">
  <xsl:call-template name="get-min-and-max">
    <xsl:with-param name="nodes" select="//item/price"/>
  </xsl:call-template>
</xsl:variable>
Minimum price is: <xsl:value-of select="$min-and-max/min"/>.
Maximum price is: <xsl:value-of select="$min-and-max/max"/>.
```

One particular situation where it is a good idea to save intermediate results in a tree-valued variable, and then use them as input to more than one process, is where the intermediate results are sorted. If you've got a large set of nodes to sort, the last thing you want to do is to sort it more than once. The answer to this is to do the transformation in two passes: the first pass creates a sorted tree, the second does a transformation on this sorted tree. There are actually two ways you can achieve a multi-stage transformation in XSLT:

- Create a temporary tree in which the nodes appear in sorted order. Then use **<xsl:for-each>** or **<xsl:apply-templates>** to process the nodes on this tree in their sorted order. This is similar to the max-and-min example above; it relies on having either XSLT 1.1, or an XSLT 1.0 processor with the **node-set()** extension function.
- Use a sequence (or **chain**) of stylesheets: the first stylesheet creates a document in which the nodes are sorted in the right order, and subsequent stylesheets take this document as their input. Such a chain of stylesheets can be conveniently manipulated using the TrAX interface described in Appendix F.

Note that neither of these techniques violates the XSLT design principle of "no side effects".

Grouping

A common processing task that appears at first sight to need updateable variables is the splitting of data into groups.

Suppose that your source logged cities and their respective countries in the following format:

```
<cities>
   <city name="CityName" country="CountryName"/>
...etc...
</cities>
```

However, you want to list together all cities found in a particular country:

```
<countries>
   <country name="CountryName">
      <city>CityName1</city>
      <city>CityName2</city>
   </country
...etc...
</countries>
```

In other languages we've probably all written code that achieved similar effects using pseudo-code such as this:

```
sortedCities = cities.sortBy("country");
previousCountry = null;
write("<country>")
for each city in sortedCities {
   thisCountry = city.getAttribute("country");
   if (thisCountry != previousCountry) {
      write("</country>\n<country>");
   }
   write("<city>" + city.getAttribute("city") + "</city>");
   previousCountry = thisCountry;
}
write("</country>")
```

In XSLT, of course, this is a non-starter, for two reasons. Firstly, you need to output a tree, not a text file containing markup tags: this means you can't write the end tag for an element as a separate operation from writing the start tag. Secondly, you can't use assignment statements to spot the change of country as you go through the data.

The best way to tackle this problem in XSLT is to first build a list of unique countries, and then process each one in turn. Let's have a look at an example.

Example: Splitting Data into Groups

Input

This example uses the `cities.xml` file. It logs cities and their respective countries as follows:

```
<cities>
   <city name="Paris" country="France"/>
   <city name="Roma" country="Italia"/>
   <city name="Nice" country="France"/>
   <city name="Madrid" country="Espana"/>
   <city name="Milano" country="Italia"/>
   <city name="Firenze" country="Italia"/>
   <city name="Napoli" country="Italia"/>
   <city name="Lyon" country="France"/>
   <city name="Barcelona" country="Espana"/>
</cities>
```

Stylesheet

You can get a list of unique countries (as a node-set containing the relevant attribute nodes) as follows. The stylesheet is in `unique-cities.xsl`

```
<xsl:template match="/">
<xsl:variable name="unique-countries"
   select="/cities
           /city[not(@country=preceding-sibling::city/@country)]
           /@country"
/>
```

The predicate on the **<city>** element rejects any **<city>** whose **country** attribute is the same as the **country** attribute of a preceding sibling, if there is one. In other words, it includes every city that is the first one in its country. Variations on this predicate are possible:

- If you know that the cities are sorted by country, you can replace the predicate `preceding-sibling::city` by `preceding-sibling::city[1]`. This means the country would only be compared with that of the immediately preceding city. This might improve performance.
- If the **<city>** elements were not all siblings of each other, you could use the `preceding` axis instead of `preceding-sibling`. This, however, would lengthen the search.

Having built a list of unique countries, you can then generate the **<city>** elements for each one. Here goes:

```
<xsl:template match="/">
<xsl:variable name="unique-countries"
   select="/cities
         /city[not(@country=preceding-sibling::city/@country)]
         /@country"
/>
<countries>
   <xsl:for-each select="$unique-countries">
      <country name="{.}">
         <xsl:for-each select="//city[@country=current()]">
            <city><xsl:value-of select="@name"/></city>
         </xsl:for-each>
      </country>
   </xsl:for-each>
</countries>
</xsl:template>
```

Output

```
<countries>
   <country name="France">
      <city>Paris</city>
      <city>Nice</city>
      <city>Lyon</city>
   </country>
   <country name="Italia">
      <city>Roma</city>
      <city>Milano</city>
      <city>Firenze</city>
      <city>Napoli</city>
   </country>
   <country name="Espana">
      <city>Madrid</city>
      <city>Barcelona</city>
   </country>
</countries>
```

A performance improvement

The main problem with such algorithms is that if there are N nodes to be grouped, then each one may need to be compared with all the previous ones, which gives a total of $N \times (N - 1) / 2$ comparisons in total. Double the number of nodes, and it will take about four times as long. The result may be acceptable if there are ten cities, but you will have to be very patient if there are several thousand. Of course a clever XSLT processor might optimize the query and find a more efficient way of doing it, but you can't rely on this. The technology of XSLT processors is still young, and techniques for query optimization have a long way to go.

One answer to this is to sort the nodes first, and then group them; during the grouping stage, each node needs to be compared only to its immediate predecessor, as shown in our example. This requires a two-stage transformation, as discussed earlier: this first stage creates a temporary tree on which the nodes are sorted, and the second stage processes this tree.

Here's a revised stylesheet `sorted-cities.xsl` that uses this approach. It relies on XSLT 1.1, which allows the temporary tree `$sorted-cities` to be processed as a node-set.

```
<xsl:stylesheet
   xmlns:xsl="http://www.w3.org/1999/XSL/Transform"
   version="1.1">

<xsl:output indent="yes"/>

<xsl:template match="/">
<xsl:variable name="sorted-cities">
  <xsl:for-each select="//city">
    <xsl:sort select="@country"/>
    <xsl:copy-of select="."/>
  </xsl:for-each>
</xsl:variable>
<xsl:variable name="unique-countries"
   select="$sorted-cities
          /city[not(@country=preceding-
sibling::city[1]/@country)]
          /@country"
/>
<countries>
   <xsl:for-each select="$unique-countries">
      <country name="{.}">
         <xsl:for-each select="$sorted-
cities/city[@country=current()]">
            <city><xsl:value-of select="@name"/></city>
         </xsl:for-each>
      </country>
   </xsl:for-each>
</countries>
</xsl:template>

</xsl:stylesheet>
```

This will only give a performance improvement if the XSLT processor is clever enough to notice that it can evaluate «`preceding-sibling::city[1]`» by looking at the immediately preceding element, rather than finding all the preceding siblings and testing each one to see if its `position()` on the axis equals `1`. However, this is a very straightforward optimization, so any self-respecting XSLT processor should implement it.

Of course, with the tiny source data file we are using for illustration,the difference is not significant: but it will become so if there are thousands of cities.

The Muenchian Grouping Technique

There's another even better way to solve this kind of grouping problem, known as the Muenchian grouping technique, after Steve Muench of Oracle who invented it. This relies on keys. The following example shows how it works.

Example: Muenchian Grouping

Input

This example uses the same `cities.xml` file as the previous example.

Stylesheet

This stylesheet is in `muenchian-cities.xsl`.

We want to group cities according to the country they are in, so the first step is to define the grouping value as a key:

```
<xsl:stylesheet
   xmlns:xsl="http://www.w3.org/1999/XSL/Transform"
   version="1.0">

<xsl:output indent="yes"/>

<xsl:key name="country-key" match="city" use="@country"/>
```

This means that we can use a function call «`key('country-key', 'France')`» to find all the `<city>` elements whose `@country` attribute is «`France`».

This also means that «`key('country-key', 'France')[1]`» will find the first city whose country is France.

And this means that the following expression will be true only for a city that is the first city in its country (in document order):

```
generate-id(.)=generate-id(key('country-key', @country)[1])
```

In fact the predicate «`[1]`» here is redundant, because the **`generate-id()`** function only looks at the first node in the supplied node-set.

Another way of writing this test is:

```
count(. | key('country-key', @country)[1]) = 1
```

We can use either expression in place of the test «`city[not(@country=preceding-sibling::city/@country)]`» which we used in the previous example. So the stylesheet becomes:

```
<xsl:key name="country-key" match="city" use="@country"/>

<xsl:template match="/">
<xsl:variable name="unique-countries"
   select="/cities
           /city[generate-id(.)=
                 generate-id(key('country-key', @country))]
           /@country"
/>
<countries>
   <xsl:for-each select="$unique-countries">
      <country name="{.}">
         <xsl:for-each select="key('country-key', .)">
            <city><xsl:value-of select="@name"/></city>
         </xsl:for-each>
      </country>
   </xsl:for-each>
</countries>
</xsl:template>
```

Output

The output is the same as the previous example.

Muenchian grouping is typically faster than the straightforward approach using the preceding-sibling axis to test whether a node is the first one in its group, because keys will generally be implemented using some kind of index or hash-table that makes it fast to find all the nodes with the same key value. Another advantage is that it can be used where the grouping expression (the common value that determines whether two nodes belong in the same group) is something other than the string-value of a node, as it was in the above example. A typical example is where you want to create alphabetical groups, one for each letter of the alphabet. For example if you wanted to list the cities alphabetically, with a heading for each initial letter of the alphabet, you could simply use the following key definition:

```
<key name="alpha-group" match="city" use="substring(@name, 1, 1)"/>
```

and apart from this change, the logic of the stylesheet would be much the same.

Grouping problems are very frequently encountered in XSLT stylesheet programming, and they can be quite tricky to solve: they certainly require you to get your mind around programming without assignment statements. With practice, they can always be solved, though in some cases you will need to write recursive templates to tackle them.

The W3C working group responsible for development of the language has acknowledged that extensions to the language in this area are required, to make grouping as easy to specify as, say, sorting or numbering. What these new facilities will look like is anyone's guess, though you can get a feel for the way the working group is currently thinking from the XSLT 2.0 requirements document published at http://www.w3.org/TR/xslt20req. One possibility is that they will be something like the **<saxon:group>** extension element provided by the Saxon product, or the similar extension in the Unicorn XSLT processor. The Saxon stylesheet to group our list of cities by country would look like this:

```
<countries>
<saxon:group select="//city" group-by="@country">
   <xsl:sort select="@country"/>
   <country name="{@country}">
      <saxon:item>
         <city><xsl:value-of select="@name"/></city>
      </saxon:item>
   </country>
</saxon:group>
</countries>
```

For more details of this feature, see Appendix C.

Summary

This chapter described four design patterns for writing XSLT stylesheets:

- Fill-in-the-blanks
- Navigational
- Rule-based
- Computational

In the last category I described how we need to approach many problems in a way that might seem unfamiliar, because XSLT is a pure functional programming language, with no assignment statements or other side effects that constrain the order of execution. The result of this is that many of the more complex algorithms need to be written using recursive named templates.

10

Worked Examples

This chapter aims to show how all the facilities of the XSLT language can work together to solve some real XML processing problems of significant complexity. I have chosen three example applications, and give complete stylesheets for handling them. The code is presented incrementally in this chapter, but the complete stylesheets, and specimen data files, can be downloaded from the Wrox web site at http://www.wrox.com/.

As I described in the previous chapter, XSLT has a broad range of applications, and in this chapter I have tried to cover a representative selection of problems. The three examples presented in this chapter are as follows:

- The first example is a stylesheet for rendering sequential documents: specifically, the stylesheet used for rendering W3C specifications such as the XML and XSLT Recommendations. This is a classic example of the *rule-based* design pattern described on page 604 in Chapter 9.
- The second example is concerned with presenting structured data. I have chosen a complex data structure with many cross-references to illustrate how a navigational stylesheet can find its way around the source tree: the chosen example is a data file containing the family tree of the Kennedys.
- The final example stylesheet is quite unrealistic, but fun. It shows how XSLT can be used to calculate a knight's tour of the chessboard, in which the knight visits every square without ever landing on the same square twice. This is not the sort of problem XSLT was designed to solve, but by showing that it can be done I hope it will convince you that XSLT has the computational power and flexibility to deal with the many more modest algorithmic challenges that arise in routine day-to-day formatting applications.

Formatting the XML Specification

In this worked example we'll study the stylesheet used for formatting the XML specifications themselves. You may have noticed that on the W3C web site, you can get the specifications for standards such as XML, XSLT, and XPath either in XML format or in HTML. We'll look at a stylesheet for converting the XML Recommendation from its XML form to its HTML form, shown below:

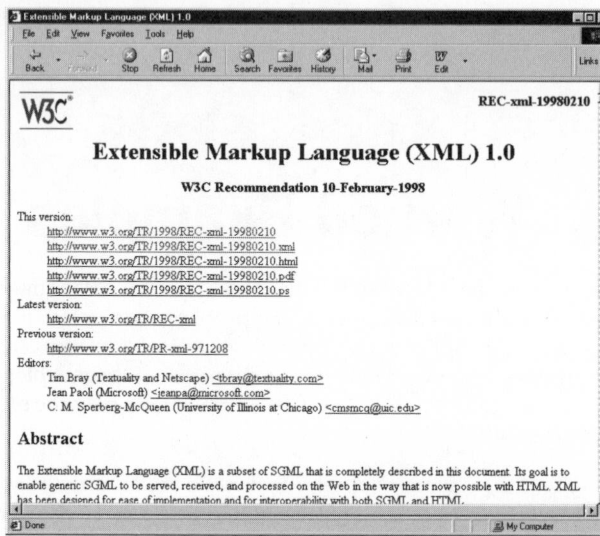

The stylesheets used for the XSLT and XPath specifications are adapted from the version used for the XML specification, and we'll take a quick look at the adaptations too.

This stylesheet was originally written by Eduardo Gutentag and subsequently modified by James Clark. I am grateful to James Clark for placing it in the public domain. I have made changes to the layout and ordering of the rules for the sake of clarity, and I have removed some duplicate rules that caused warning messages from an XSLT processor that does careful checking; but I haven't altered the logic. The download file for this chapter on http://www.wrox.com/ contains the original stylesheet from James Clark.

This stylesheet is a classic example of the *rule-based* design pattern, which was introduced on page 604 in Chapter 9. It makes minimal assumptions about where all the different elements in the XML source document appear relative to each other, and it allows new rules to be added freely as the document structure evolves.

You'll probably find it helpful while reading this stylesheet to have the XML source document readily accessible. The official version is on the web at http://www.w3.org/TR/1998/REC-xml-19980210.xml, but you may have problems with that version. You might expect that, since the XML specification was written by XML experts, it would be a perfect example of how to write good XML. Unfortunately this isn't the case, and it uses constructs which some parsers aren't happy with. Specifically:

- It contains the entity declaration `<!ENTITY lt "<">` which violates the rule that the replacement text of a parsed entity must be well-formed. This declaration causes IE5 to throw up its hands in horror and refuse to display the document. The declaration is in any case quite unnecessary except for compatibility with SGML.

- More subtly, the DTD (called `spec.dtd`) contains references to parameter entities that don't exist, or whose declaration comes after the reference. It happens that these references are all contained within comments in the DTD. In the original XML specification, the rules for parameter entities occurring in comments were unclear. They were clarified in later errata, but there are still some parsers around that adopted a different interpretation of the spec.

So to make your life easier, I've created a modified version of the source document and DTD that avoids these problems, and included them in the download for this book. The source file is called `REC-xml-19980210.xml` and the DTD is called `spec.dtd`. You can view the source either in a text editor, or using the default XML viewer in IE5.

The XML versions of the XSLT and XPath specifications don't suffer from the same problems, and you can view these directly on the W3C web site using the IE5 browser, although copies are included on the Wrox web site for convenience. They don't contain references to a stylesheet, so IE5 will use its default stylesheet, which displays the XML as a collapsible tree. Then you can use View Source to display the source XML, and save it locally on your hard disk if you wish.

Now let's look at the stylesheet, `xmlspec.xsl`.

Preface

Let's start at the beginning:

```
<?xml version="1.0" encoding="ISO-8859-1" ?>

<!-- 1999/01/11 SMI; Style Sheet for the XML and XSL
     Recommendations and Working Drafts;
     written by Eduardo Gutentag -->
<!-- v 1.28 1999/11/15 12:58:16 by James Clark -->

<!DOCTYPE xsl:stylesheet [
<!ENTITY copy   "&#169;">
<!ENTITY nbsp   " ">
]>

<xsl:stylesheet
   version="1.0"
   xmlns:xsl="http://www.w3.org/1999/XSL/Transform">
```

```
<xsl:output method="html"
      doctype-public="-//W3C//DTD HTML 4.0 Transitional//EN"/>

<xsl:param name="w3">http://www.w3.org/</xsl:param>
```

The stylesheet is an XML document, so it starts with an XML declaration; the chosen encoding is iso-8859-1 because with most editing tools that's easier to edit than UTF–8. Actually, all the characters are ASCII, so specifying UTF-8 would work just as well.

There's then a couple of comments indicating the change history and authorship.

The <!DOCTYPE> declaration doesn't reference an external DTD; this is normal practice for stylesheets because a DTD would restrict your ability to include any element you like in a template and have it treated as a literal result element. What the <!DOCTYPE> does do is to declare a couple of entities for special characters. These allow us to write the copyright symbol as «©» and the non-breaking-space character as « » – if we hadn't declared these entities, we would have to write them each time they appear as «©» and « » respectively.

> *The fact that we've used entity references rather than numeric character references for these characters in the stylesheet doesn't mean that this is how they will appear in the HTML output. The way the XSLT processor represents these characters in the output is entirely up to the implementor; but whatever representation it chooses, they will display correctly in the browser.*

The **<xsl:stylesheet>** element should be familiar by now. The **<xsl:output>** element defines the output method as `html`, and indicates the public identifier of the version of HTML that is being generated, which will be copied into the generated output file. This is good practice. It isn't essential, but of course the W3C want to produce HTML that conforms to their own recommended practice.

The **<xsl:param>** statement declares a global parameter named `w3`, and gives it a default value which is the URL for the W3C web site. Making this a global parameter rather than a global variable allows a different value to be supplied during testing, perhaps the URL of a staging server.

Creating the HTML Outline

Now we start with the main template rules for the document. The order is arbitrary, and I've changed the order used by the original authors to present similar rules together.

```
<xsl:template match="spec">
   <html>
      <head>
         <title>
            <xsl:value-of select="header/title"/>
         </title>
```

```
        <link rel="stylesheet" type="text/css"
              href="{$w3}StyleSheets/TR/W3C-{
                    substring-before(header/w3c-designation,'-')}"/>

        <!-- This stops Netscape 4.5 from messing up. -->
        <style type="text/css">
           <xsl:apply-templates select="." mode="css"/>
        </style>
     </head>
     <body>
        <xsl:apply-templates/>
     </body>
  </html>
</xsl:template>
```

This is the top-level template rule that generates the HTML outline. There isn't a rule that matches the root node, so the built-in root template kicks in and finds a rule that matches the outermost element, which happens to be **<spec>**.

Apart from producing the HTML outline, this template does three things: it extracts the document title, it outputs a reference to the CSS stylesheet to be used (in two different formats so it works with different browsers), and within the HTML **<body>** element it calls **<xsl:apply-templates>** to process the child elements of the **<spec>** in the source document.

The call on `<xsl:apply-templates mode="css"/>` invokes the following little template rule which just outputs some standard content for the **<style>** element. Note that this could equally well have been done using **<xsl:call-template>**, or written inline. I don't know why the authors chose to do it this way instead – one possibility is that they wanted to override this rule in another stylesheet module that imports this one. It's also likely that at the time this stylesheet was first written, some XSLT features such as named templates were not yet available in products.


```
<xsl:template match="spec" mode="css">
   <xsl:text>code { font-family: monospace }</xsl:text>
</xsl:template>
```

Formatting the Document Header

We generated the title of the HTML document by accessing the title element within the header element of the source XML file. To understand such queries, you need to take a look at the structure of the **<header>** element in the source document. In abbreviated form, the structure of the XML specification starts like this:

```
<spec>
   <header>
      <title>Extensible Markup Language (XML) 1.0</title>
      <version></version>
      <w3c-designation>REC-xml-&iso6.doc.date;</w3c-designation>
      <w3c-doctype>W3C Recommendation</w3c-doctype>
      <pubdate>
```

```
        <day>&draft.day;</day>
        <month>&draft.month;</month>
        <year>&draft.year;</year>
     </pubdate>

     <publoc>
        <loc  href="url">url</loc>
        <loc  href="url">url</loc>
     </publoc>
     <latestloc>
        <loc  href="url">url</loc>
     </latestloc>
     <prevlocs>
        <loc  href="url">url</loc>
     </prevlocs>

     <authlist>
        <author>
           <name>Tim Bray</name>
           <affiliation>Textuality and Netscape</affiliation>
           <email href="mailto:tbray@textuality.com">
                        tbray@textuality.com</email>
     </author>
        more authors
     </authlist>

     <abstract>
        <p>The Extensible Markup Language (XML) is a subset of SGML
                    that is completely described in this document...
        </p>
     </abstract>

     <status>
     <p>This document has been reviewed by W3C Members and
                           other interested parties ...</p>

     <p>This document specifies a syntax… It is a product of the W3C
              XML Activity, details of which can be found at <loc
              href='url'>url</loc>.  A list of current W3C
              Recommendations … can be found at <loc
              href='url'>url</loc>.</p>

     <p>This specification uses the term URI, which is defined by
           <bibref ref="Berners-Lee"/>, a work in progress expected
            to update
           <bibref ref="RFC1738"/> and <bibref ref="RFC1808"/>. </p>
     </status>
  </header>
  <body>
     main section of document
  </body>
  <back>
     appendices
  </back>
</spec>
```

Note that some of the tags are structural elements with predictable nesting, while others such as **<loc>** can appear in all sorts of places, including inline within the text.

The next few template rules are all concerned with processing this header:

```
<xsl:template match="header">
   <div class="head">

      <!-- output clickable W3C logo -->

      <a href="http://www.w3.org/">
         <img src="{$w3}Icons/WWW/w3c_home"
               alt="W3C" height="48" width="72"/>
      </a>

      <!-- output title and version of document -->

      <h1><xsl:value-of select="title"/><br/>
          <xsl:value-of select="version"/>
      </h1>

      <!-- output publication type and date -->

      <h2>
         <xsl:value-of select="w3c-doctype"/>
         <xsl:text> </xsl:text>
         <xsl:value-of select="pubdate/day"/>
         <xsl:text> </xsl:text>
         <xsl:value-of select="pubdate/month"/>
         <xsl:text> </xsl:text>
         <xsl:value-of select="pubdate/year"/>
      </h2>

      <!-- output URLs of successive versions, and authors -->

      <dl>
         <xsl:apply-templates select="publoc"/>
         <xsl:apply-templates select="latestloc"/>
         <xsl:apply-templates select="prevlocs"/>
         <xsl:apply-templates select="authlist"/>
      </dl>

      <!-- output standard copyright statement -->

      <xsl:call-template name="copyright"/>
      <hr title="Separator for header"/>
   </div>

   <!-- output abstract and status sections -->

   <xsl:apply-templates select="abstract"/>
   <xsl:apply-templates select="status"/>
```

```
</xsl:template>

<!-- template rules for document locations -->

<xsl:template match="publoc">
   <dt>This version:</dt>
   <dd><xsl:apply-templates/></dd>
</xsl:template>

<xsl:template match="latestloc">
   <dt>Latest version:</dt>
   <dd><xsl:apply-templates/></dd>
</xsl:template>

<xsl:template match="prevlocs">
   <dt>
      <xsl:text>Previous version</xsl:text>
      <xsl:if test="count(loc)>1">s</xsl:if>
      <xsl:text>:</xsl:text>
   </dt>
   <dd><xsl:apply-templates/></dd>
</xsl:template>

<xsl:template match="publoc/loc | latestloc/loc | prevlocs/loc">
   <a href="{@href}"><xsl:apply-templates/></a>
   <br/>
</xsl:template>

<!-- template rules for authors and affiliations -->

<xsl:template match="authlist">
   <dt>
      <xsl:text>Editor</xsl:text>
      <xsl:if test="count(author)>1">s</xsl:if>
      <xsl:text>:</xsl:text>
   </dt>
   <dd><xsl:apply-templates/></dd>
</xsl:template>

<xsl:template match="author">
   <xsl:apply-templates/><br/>
</xsl:template>

<xsl:template match="author/name">
   <xsl:apply-templates/>
</xsl:template>

<xsl:template match="author/affiliation">
   <xsl:text> (</xsl:text>
      <xsl:apply-templates/>
   <xsl:text>) </xsl:text>
</xsl:template>
```

```
<xsl:template match="author/email">
   <a href="{@href}">
      <xsl:text>&lt;</xsl:text>
      <xsl:apply-templates/>
      <xsl:text>&gt;</xsl:text>
   </a>
</xsl:template>

<!-- templates to display abstract and status paragraphs -->

<xsl:template match="abstract">
   <h2><a name="abstract">Abstract</a></h2>
   <xsl:apply-templates/>
</xsl:template>

<xsl:template match="status">
   <h2><a name="status">Status of this document</a></h2>
   <xsl:apply-templates/>
</xsl:template>
```

So much for the header. There's nothing very complicated here, though the techniques used to produce a plural label for "previous versions" and "editors" are worth noting, as is the use of **<xsl:text>** to avoid copying whitespace to the output where it isn't wanted.

The Table of Contents

The next part of the stylesheet deals with the body of the document, and at the same time with the "back" of the document, which has a similar structure. The **<back>** element contains appendices, bibliography, and so on.

```
<xsl:template match="body">
   <h2><a name="contents">Table of contents</a></h2>
   <xsl:call-template name="toc"/>
   <hr/>
   <xsl:apply-templates/>
</xsl:template>

<xsl:template match="back">
   <hr title="Separator from footer"/>
   <xsl:apply-templates/>
</xsl:template>
```

The **<body>** template rule follows a common pattern: it first calls a template to generate the table of contents, then it uses **<xsl:apply-templates>** to process its own children.

Let's see how the table of contents is produced. The structure of the **<body>** element, and also of **<back>**, consists of a sequence of **<div1>** elements representing top-level sections, like this:

```
<div1>
   <head>First-level heading</head>
   <p>Some text</p>
   <div2>
      <head>Second-level heading</head>
      <p>Some more text</p>
      <div3>
         <head>Third-level heading</head>
         <p>Lots more text</p>
      </div3>
   </div2>
</div1>
```

Each **<div1>** element contains a **<head>** element giving its heading, paragraphs of immediate content, and zero or more **<div2>** elements containing level-2 subsections. The **<div2>** elements similarly contain a **<head>** and zero or more **<div3>** elements for level-3 subsections, and so on.

In the **<back>** section, a non-normative appendix is represented by an **<inform-div1>** element instead of the usual **<div1>**, but otherwise the structure is the same.

> *Non-normative is jargon meaning "for information only, not part of the specification".*

So the named template to generate the table of contents looks like this. It first works its way through the nested sections in the **<body>**, and then does the same again for the sections in the **<back>**. The work of actually producing the cross-reference is delegated to another named template, «makeref»:

```
<xsl:template name="toc">
   <xsl:for-each select="/spec/body/div1">
      <xsl:call-template name="makeref"/><br/>
      <xsl:for-each select="div2">
         <xsl:text>    </xsl:text>
         <xsl:call-template name="makeref"/><br/>
         <xsl:for-each select="div3">
            <xsl:text>    </xsl:text>
            <xsl:text>    </xsl:text>
            <xsl:call-template name="makeref"/><br/>
         </xsl:for-each>
      </xsl:for-each>
   </xsl:for-each>

   <h3>Appendices</h3>
```

```
    <xsl:for-each select="/spec/back/div1 | /spec/back/inform-div1">
        <xsl:call-template name="makeref"/><br/>
        <xsl:for-each select="div2">
            <xsl:text>    </xsl:text>
            <xsl:call-template name="makeref"/><br/>
            <xsl:for-each select="div3">
                <xsl:text>    </xsl:text>
                <xsl:text>    </xsl:text>
                <xsl:call-template name="makeref"/><br/>
            </xsl:for-each>
        </xsl:for-each>
    </xsl:for-each>
</xsl:template>

<xsl:template name="makeref">
    <xsl:apply-templates select="." mode="number"/>
    <xsl:choose>
        <xsl:when test="@id">
            <a href="#{@id}">
                <xsl:value-of select="head"/>
            </a>
        </xsl:when>
        <xsl:otherwise>
            <a href="#section-{translate(head,' ','-')}">
                <xsl:value-of select="head"/>
            </a>
        </xsl:otherwise>
    </xsl:choose>
   <xsl:for-each select="head">
        <xsl:call-template name="inform"/>
   </xsl:for-each>
</xsl:template>

<xsl:template name="inform">
    <xsl:if test="parent::inform-div1">
        <xsl:text> (Non-Normative)</xsl:text>
    </xsl:if>
</xsl:template>
```

The «makeref» template first generates a sequence number for the section, then creates a hyperlink to it, using the section's **id** attribute if it has one, or a name derived from its heading otherwise (spaces are replaced by hyphens). This isn't a particularly brilliant idea, it means that any non-unique headings like "Example" have to be allocated an **id** manually: presumably the authors would have used the **generate-id()** function if it had been around at the time. Then if the section is a non-normative one (an **<inform-div1>** element) it outputs the string "(Non-Normative)".

> *The way in which this is done is not particularly elegant, though it works. I suspect the template named* «inform» *was written initially to display the actual section heading in situ, and then reused for the table of contents. A more natural approach would be to include an* `<xsl:if self::inform-div1>` *test in the* «makeref» *template.*

The «makeref» template delegates the work of generating a sequence number to a template rule associated with the section being numbered. This uses a special mode, to avoid conflict with the template rule for expanding the content of this section. There are two versions of the rule, one for sections in the body of the document, and one for appendices. There is no need to have different rules for different section levels, because the way the number formatting works is sufficiently flexible to give the right answer at each level.

```
<xsl:template mode="number" match="*">
   <xsl:number    level="multiple"
                  count="inform-div1 | div1 | div2 | div3 | div4"
                  format="1.1 "/>
</xsl:template>

<xsl:template mode="number" match="back//*">
   <xsl:number    level="multiple"
                  count="inform-div1 | div1 | div2 | div3 | div4"
                  format="A.1 "/>
</xsl:template>
```

This use of a list of alternatives in the **count** attribute is a common way of doing multi-level numbering. It means, in effect, outputting a sequence number for each ancestor element that is either an **<inform-div1>**, or a **<div1>**, or a **<div2>**, etc. Like most template rules in a rule-based stylesheet, it doesn't attempt to do any validation: if the input structure is wrong, it will produce some sort of output regardless, and it's up to the document author to work out what the problem is. This raises an interesting question that you need to consider when designing your own stylesheets: is it the job of the stylesheet to detect and report on errors in the source document?

Creating Section Headers

The next section of the stylesheet is concerned with formatting the section headers. These all have some common logic, concerned with generating the section number and creating a text anchor (<a name="xyz">...</a>) as the target for hyperlinks, so they all call a common named template to do this work. If the section has an **id** attribute, this is used as the anchor; otherwise an anchor is generated from the section's title. This logic must match the logic used earlier when creating hyperlinks in the table of contents.

Numbers are generated by reusing the template rule we saw while producing the table of contents.

```
<xsl:template match="div1/head | inform-div1/head">
   <h2><xsl:call-template name="head"/></h2>
</xsl:template>

<xsl:template match="div2/head">
   <h3><xsl:call-template name="head"/></h3>
</xsl:template>
```

```
<xsl:template match="div3/head">
   <h4><xsl:call-template name="head"/></h4>
</xsl:template>

<xsl:template match="div4/head">
   <h5><xsl:call-template name="head"/></h5>
</xsl:template>

<xsl:template name="head">
   <xsl:for-each select="..">
      <xsl:call-template name="insertID"/>
      <xsl:apply-templates select="." mode="number"/>
  </xsl:for-each>
   <xsl:apply-templates/>
   <xsl:call-template name="inform"/>
</xsl:template>

<xsl:template name="insertID">
   <xsl:choose>
      <xsl:when test="@id">
         <a name="{@id}"/>
      </xsl:when>
      <xsl:otherwise>
         <a name="section-{translate(head,' ','-')}"/>
      </xsl:otherwise>
   </xsl:choose>
</xsl:template>
```

Note the use of `<xsl:for-each select="..">`. This doesn't do an iteration (a node only has one parent), rather it is there to change the current node from the **<head>** element to its parent **<divX>** element, because that is where the `insertID` template expects to be positioned.

Within the «`head`» template, the call on the «`inform`» template simply produces the phrase "(Non-normative)" on appropriate appendices, as before.

Formatting the Text

We now find a number of template rules to process simple textual markup within the body of the document. These are very straightforward, though if you want to understand exactly why they take the form they do, it is worth looking at the source document to understand its structure. In fact, not all the elements mentioned here are used in the XML specification: it's likely that these were present in earlier drafts.

```
<xsl:template match="item/p" priority="1">
   <p><xsl:apply-templates/></p>
</xsl:template>
                     <!-- this template appears to be redundant,
                          it was probably at some time different
                          from the following template -->
```

```
<xsl:template match="p">
   <p><xsl:apply-templates/></p>
</xsl:template>
```

This innocent-looking rule for processing <p> elements is actually incorrect! If you study the DTD for the source XML document, you will see that it is more liberal than the HTML specification about the nesting of lists within paragraphs. As a result, this stylesheet can produce invalid HTML from a valid source document. Later versions of this stylesheet, used for subsequent W3C standards, have corrected this error — something that actually requires the solution of a rather interesting grouping problem. But we'll resist the temptation to fix it here.

```
<xsl:template match="term">
   <b><xsl:apply-templates/></b>
</xsl:template>

<xsl:template match="code">
   <code><xsl:apply-templates/></code>
</xsl:template>

<xsl:template match="emph">
   <i><xsl:apply-templates/></i>
</xsl:template>

<xsl:template match="blist">
   <dl><xsl:apply-templates/></dl>
</xsl:template>

<xsl:template match="slist">
   <ul><xsl:apply-templates/></ul>
</xsl:template>

<xsl:template match="sitem">
   <li><xsl:apply-templates/></li>
</xsl:template>

<xsl:template match="olist">
   <ol><xsl:apply-templates/></ol>
</xsl:template>

<xsl:template match="ulist">
   <ul><xsl:apply-templates/></ul>
</xsl:template>

<xsl:template match="glist">
   <dl><xsl:apply-templates/></dl>
</xsl:template>

<xsl:template match="olist">
   <ol><xsl:apply-templates/></ol>
</xsl:template>

<xsl:template match="item">
   <li><xsl:apply-templates/></li>
</xsl:template>

<xsl:template match="label">
   <dt><b><xsl:apply-templates/></b></dt>
</xsl:template>
```

```
<xsl:template match="def">
   <dd><xsl:apply-templates/></dd>
</xsl:template>

<xsl:template match="quote">
   <xsl:text>"</xsl:text>
   <xsl:apply-templates/>
   <xsl:text>"</xsl:text>
</xsl:template>

<!-- examples -->

<xsl:template match="eg">
   <pre>
      <xsl:if test="@role='error'">
          <xsl:attribute name="style">color: red</xsl:attribute>
      </xsl:if>
      <xsl:apply-templates/>
   </pre>
</xsl:template>

<!-- general-purpose tables -->

<xsl:template match="htable">
   <table border="{@border}"
            cellpadding="{@cellpadding}"
            align="{@align}">
      <xsl:apply-templates/>
   </table>
</xsl:template>
```

An observation here is that «`border="{@border}"`» will generate the output «`border=""`» if the element in the source document has no **`border`** attribute. It might have been better to write:

```
<table>
   <xsl:copy-of select="@align | @border | @cellpadding"/>
   <xsl:apply-templates/>
</table>
```

The stylesheet continues:

```
<xsl:template match="htbody">
   <tbody><xsl:apply-templates/></tbody>
</xsl:template>

<xsl:template match="tr">
   <tr align="{@align}" valign="{@valign}">
      <xsl:apply-templates/>
   </tr>
</xsl:template>
```

```
<xsl:template match="td">
   <td bgcolor="{@bgcolor}"
         rowspan="{@rowspan}"   colspan="{@colspan}"
         align="{@align}"   valign="{@valign}">
      <xsl:apply-templates/>
   </td>
</xsl:template>

<!-- notes -->

<xsl:template match="ednote">
   <blockquote>
      <p><b>Ed. Note: </b><xsl:apply-templates/></p>
   </blockquote>
</xsl:template>

<xsl:template match="edtext">
   <xsl:apply-templates/>
</xsl:template>

<xsl:template match="issue">
   <xsl:call-template name="insertID"/>
   <blockquote>
      <p><b>Issue (<xsl:text/>
         <xsl:value-of   select="substring-after(@id,'-')"/>
         <xsl:text/>): </b>
         <xsl:apply-templates/>
      </p>
   </blockquote>
</xsl:template>

<xsl:template match="note">
   <blockquote>
      <b>NOTE: </b><xsl:apply-templates/>
   </blockquote>
</xsl:template>

<xsl:template match="issue/p | note/p">
   <xsl:apply-templates/>
</xsl:template>
```

Setting out the Production Rules

Now we get to a more interesting area. The XML Recommendation contains syntax production rules, and these are marked up in some detail. A sequence of production rules is contained within a **<scrap>** element, and each rule is a **<prod>** element. Here is an example of a scrap that contains a single production rule:

```
<scrap lang='ebnf' id='document'>
   <head>Document</head>
   <prod id='NT-document'>
      <lhs>document</lhs>
```

```
        <rhs>
            <nt def='NT-prolog'>prolog</nt>
            <nt def='NT-element'>element</nt>
            <nt def='NT-Misc'>Misc</nt>*
        </rhs>
    </prod>
</scrap>
```

This is of course the XML production rule, which appears in the spec as:

Document			
[1]	document	::=	prolog element Misc*

In some cases the production rules within a **<scrap>** are grouped into **<prodgroup>** elements, but this grouping is ignored in the output.

Here are the top-level template rules:

```
<xsl:template match="scrap">
   <xsl:if test="string(head)">
      <h5><xsl:value-of select="head"/></h5>
   </xsl:if>
   <table class="scrap">
      <tbody>
         <xsl:apply-templates select="prodgroup | prod"/>
      </tbody>
   </table>
</xsl:template>

<xsl:template match="prodgroup">
   <xsl:apply-templates/>
</xsl:template>

<xsl:template match="prod">
  <!-- select elements that start a row -->
   <xsl:apply-templates
      select="*[self::lhs
                 or (self::rhs
                     and not(preceding-sibling::*[1][self::lhs]))
                  or ((self::vc or self::wfc or self::com)
                     and not(preceding-sibling::*[1][self::rhs]))]
            "/>
</xsl:template>
```

What is this horrendous **select** expression doing? A production rule (**<prod>**) has one left-hand side (**<lhs>**), one or more right-hand sides (**<rhs>**), and one or more annotations (**<vc>**, **<wfc>**, or **<com>**). A **<vc>** element is used to refer to a validation constraint, a **<wfc>** element to refer to a well-formedness constraint, and a **<com>** element to refer to a comment. A rule with one **<lhs>** element, two **<rhs>** elements, and three **<wfc>** annotations would be laid out in an HTML table like this:

[17]	lhs1	::=	rhs1	
			rhs2	wfc1
				wfc2
				wfc3

As the comment says, the **`select`** expression is processing the children of the **`<prod>`** element that start a new row: here `lhs1`, `rhs2`, `wfc2`, and `wfc3`. More precisely, the selected elements include any **`<lhs>`** element, any **`<rhs>`** element that is not immediately preceded by an **`<lhs>`** element, and any **`<vc>`**, **`<wfc>`** or **`<com>`** element that is not immediately preceded by an **`<rhs>`** element. So, this template selects the elements that will start a new row, and calls **`<xsl:apply-templates>`** to process them.

We'll now look at the template rules that will match these elements. First the **`<lhs>`**:

```
<xsl:template match="lhs">
   <tr valign="baseline">
   <td><a name="{../@id}"/>
      <xsl:number from="body" level="any"
                  format="[1]   "/>
   </td>
   <td><xsl:apply-templates/></td>
   <td>
      <xsl:text>   ::=   </xsl:text>
   </td>
   <xsl:for-each select="following-sibling::*[1]">
      <td><xsl:apply-templates mode="cell" select="."/></td>
      <td><xsl:apply-templates mode="cell"
            select="following-sibling::*[1]
                   [self::vc or self::wfc or self::com]"/>
      </td>
   </xsl:for-each>
   </tr>
</xsl:template>
```

The call on **`<xsl:number>`** here is a good example of how to generate a sequence of numbers that runs through the document. It creates a sequential number for each **`<lhs>`** element, that is, for each production rule.

The template then calls **`<xsl:apply-templates/>`** to process the contents of the **`<lhs>`** element, which will generally just be the name of the syntactic term being defined, and outputs the «   `::=`   » that separates the term from its definition.

The **`<xsl:for-each>`** that follows does not do any iteration, it merely moves the current position along to the next sibling. This is because the **`select`** expression, with its « `[1]` » predicate, can only ever select a single node.

This node will be the first **<rhs>** element. It calls **<xsl:apply-templates>** to process this first **<rhs>** element with «mode="cell"»; and then, if the element after this is a **<vc>**, **<wfc>** or **<com>** element, it processes that one with «mode="cell"» too. This logic must match the logic used earlier for deciding which elements should start a new row: we must only process those that go on the same row as the **<lhs>** element at this stage.

The next two template rules are used respectively for **<rhs>** elements that start a new row, and for **<vc>**, **<wfc>**, and **<com>** elements that start a new row: that is, `rhs2`, `wfc2`, and `wfc3` in our example. In each case the template has to generate a number of empty table cells to get the horizontal alignment right.

```
<xsl:template match="rhs">
   <tr valign="baseline">
      <td></td>
      <td></td>
      <td></td>
      <td><xsl:apply-templates mode="cell" select="."/></td>
      <td><xsl:apply-templates mode="cell"
           select="following-sibling::*[1]
                   [self::vc or self::wfc or self::com]"/>
      </td>
   </tr>
</xsl:template>

<xsl:template match="vc | wfc | com">
   <tr valign="baseline">
      <td></td>
      <td></td>
      <td></td>
      <td></td>
      <td><xsl:apply-templates mode="cell" select="."/></td>
   </tr>
</xsl:template>
```

Some people prefer to avoid empty table cells by writing «`<td> </td>`», but that's only really necessary if the table has borders or a background color.

The **<rhs>** rule uses the same kind of logic as the **<lhs>** rule to process any following **<vc>**, **<wfc>**, and **<com>** elements that belong in the same row.

Now we need to write template rules for elements that go in the same row as a previous element, like `rhs1` and `wfc1` in the example. These will always be invoked with «mode="cell"». The first two are very simple, because the surrounding **<td>** elements have already been generated.

```
<xsl:template match="rhs" mode="cell">
   <xsl:apply-templates/>
</xsl:template>

<xsl:template match="com" mode="cell">
   <xsl:text>/*</xsl:text>
   <xsl:apply-templates/>
   <xsl:text>*/</xsl:text>
</xsl:template>
```

For **<vc>** and **<wfc>** elements, we need some logic to generate a hyperlink to the paragraph that describes the validation constraint or well-formedness constraint. The link is represented in the XML by a **def** attribute, and this is used directly to construct the HTML internal hyperlink. The displayed text of the link is formed by retrieving the element whose `ID` is equal to this def attribute, and displaying its text.

For example, if the **<vc>** element has the form `<vc def="vc-roottype"/>`, this points to the following element in the source file:

```
<vcnote id="vc-roottype">
    <head>Root Element Type</head>
<p>The Name in the document type declaration must match the element type
        of the root element.</p>
</vcnote>
```

so the generated HTML is:

```
<a href="#vc-roottype">Root Element Type</a>
```

Back to the stylesheet:

```
<xsl:template match="vc" mode="cell">
   <xsl:text>[ VC: </xsl:text>
   <a href="#{@def}">
      <xsl:value-of select="id(@def)/head"/>
   </a>
   <xsl:text> ]</xsl:text>
   <xsl:apply-templates/>
</xsl:template>

<xsl:template match="wfc" mode="cell">
   <xsl:text>[ WFC: </xsl:text>
   <a href="#{@def}">
      <xsl:value-of select="id(@def)/head"/>
   </a>
   <xsl:text> ]</xsl:text>
   <xsl:apply-templates/>
</xsl:template>
```

So much for formatting the production rules! This was by far the most complicated part of this stylesheet, the rest should be plain sailing.

Making Cross-references

The next section of the stylesheet is concerned with formatting cross-references. First we'll show the template rules for creating anchors that we can link to – these all generate an element of the form `<a name="xyz">...</a>`. They are used for bibliography items, definitions of terms, and descriptions of validity and well-formedness constraints.

```
<xsl:template match="blist/bibl">
   <dt>
      <a name="{@id}"><xsl:value-of select="@key"/></a>
   </dt>
   <dd>
      <xsl:apply-templates/>
   </dd>
</xsl:template>
```

```
<xsl:template match="termdef">
   <a name="{@id}"/><xsl:apply-templates/>
</xsl:template>

<xsl:template match="vcnote">
   <a name="{@id}"/>
   <p><b>Validity Constraint: <xsl:text/>
      <xsl:value-of select="head"/></b></p>
   <xsl:apply-templates/>
</xsl:template>

<xsl:template match="wfcnote">
   <a name="{@id}"></a>
   <p><b>Well Formedness Constraint: <xsl:text/>
      <xsl:value-of   select="head"/></b></p>
   <xsl:apply-templates/>
</xsl:template>
```

And now the template rules that generate the hyperlinks. These all generate an element of the form `<a href="xyz">...</a>` for an external reference or `<a href="#xyz">...</a>` for an internal one.

```
<!-- external references -->

<xsl:template match="p/loc" priority="1">
   <a href="{@href}"><xsl:apply-templates/></a>
</xsl:template>

<xsl:template match="loc">
   <a href="{@href}"><xsl:apply-templates/></a>
</xsl:template>
```

The **`priority`** attribute on the first template rule is not really necessary; the default priorities would automatically give it higher priority than the rule that follows. In fact it's doubly unnecessary here because the two rules are identical! However, some people prefer to make priorities explicit in such cases, for documentation if nothing else.

```
<xsl:template match="xspecref | xtermref">
   <a href="{@href}"><xsl:apply-templates/></a>
</xsl:template>

<xsl:template match="xnt">
   <a href="{@href}"><xsl:apply-templates/></a>
</xsl:template>

<!-- internal cross-references -->

<xsl:template match="titleref">
   <a href="#{@href}"><xsl:apply-templates/>   </a>
</xsl:template>

<xsl:template match="nt">
   <a href="#{@def}"><xsl:apply-templates/></a>
</xsl:template>

<xsl:template match="termref">
   <a href="#{@def}"><xsl:apply-templates/></a>
</xsl:template>
```

```
<xsl:template match="bibref">
   <a href="#{@ref}">
      <xsl:text>[</xsl:text>
      <xsl:value-of select="id(@ref)/@key"/>
      <xsl:apply-templates/>
      <xsl:text>]</xsl:text>
   </a>
</xsl:template>

<xsl:template match="specref">
   <a href="#{@ref}">
      <xsl:text>[</xsl:text>
      <b>
         <!-- Add the section number and heading of the target -->
         <xsl:for-each select="id(@ref)/head">
         <xsl:apply-templates select=".." mode="number"/>
         <xsl:apply-templates/>
         </xsl:for-each>
      </b>
      <xsl:apply-templates/>
      <xsl:text>]</xsl:text>
   </a>
</xsl:template>
```

Nothing very complicated here. The last template rule is a bit more complicated than the others: it's creating a reference to a section that incorporates its section number, which it obtains by calling **<xsl:apply-templates>** to process the referenced element with «mode="number"».

Filtering Out What We Don't Want

We now have some template rules for elements in the XML source document that we don't want to include in the HTML output at all. An empty **<xsl:template>** element is a "no-op", it says that when this pattern is matched, no output should be produced. If these template rules weren't included, the built-in template rule would kick in for these elements, which would output the text of the element without any markup.

```
<xsl:template match="w3c-designation"/>
<xsl:template match="w3c-doctype"/>
<xsl:template match="header/pubdate"/>
<xsl:template match="spec/header/title"/>
<xsl:template match="revisiondesc"/>
<xsl:template match="pubstmt"/>
<xsl:template match="sourcedesc"/>
<xsl:template match="langusage"/>
<xsl:template match="version"/>
```

These elements are mainly meta data, of interest to the authors but not to the readers. (Actually, the revision history is fascinating if you are interested in that sort of thing. It acts as a reminder that using a stylesheet to filter out confidential information is not the world's most effective security technique.)

Boilerplate Text

There is now a template that generates fixed boilerplate text:

```
<xsl:template name="copyright">
   <xsl:variable name="legal"
         select="'http://www.w3.org/Consortium/Legal/'"/>
```

```
    <p class="copyright">
       <a href="{$legal}ipr-notice.html#Copyright">Copyright</a>
           &copy;  1999
        <a href="http://www.w3.org">W3C</a>
       (<a href="http://www.lcs.mit.edu">MIT</a>,
       <a href="http://www.inria.fr/">INRIA</a>,
       <a href="http://www.keio.ac.jp/">Keio</a>),
          All Rights Reserved. W3C
       <a href="{$legal}ipr-notice.html#Legal_Disclaimer"
          >liability</a>,
       <a href="{$legal}ipr-notice.html#W3C_Trademarks"
          >trademark</a>,
       <a href="{$legal}copyright-documents.html">document use</a>
          and
       <a href="{$legal}copyright-software.html"
          >software licensing</a> rules apply.
    </p>
</xsl:template>
```

List of Contributors

The last four template rules format the list of contributors at the end of the document. There are two rules that match «`orglist/member`», the effect is that a semicolon is placed before the name of every member except the first. The **`priority`** attribute is necessary this time, because the default priority for both rules would be the same.

```
<xsl:template match="orglist">
   <xsl:apply-templates select="*"/>
</xsl:template>

<xsl:template match="orglist/member[1]" priority="2">
   <xsl:apply-templates select="*"/>
</xsl:template>

<xsl:template match="orglist/member">
   <xsl:text>; </xsl:text>
   <xsl:apply-templates select="*"/>
</xsl:template>

<xsl:template match="orglist/member/affiliation">
   <xsl:text>, </xsl:text>
   <xsl:apply-templates/>
</xsl:template>

<xsl:template match="orglist/member/role">
   <xsl:text> (</xsl:text>
   <xsl:apply-templates/>
   <xsl:text>)</xsl:text>
</xsl:template>
```

And that brings us to the end:

```
</xsl:stylesheet>
```

Variant Stylesheets for the XSLT and XPath Specs

The stylesheet just presented is the one used for the XML specification. The stylesheets used for the XPath and XSLT specifications are slightly different, because these documents use additional element types beyond those used in the XML specification. In each case the XML source document has an internal DTD subset which supplements the base DTD with some additional element types. For example, the XPath document uses special tags to mark up function templates, and the XSLT document has special tags to mark up the pro formas used to summarize the syntax of each XSL element.

The stylesheets used for XPath and XSLT therefore consist of a small module that uses **<xsl:import>** to import the baseline XML stylesheet, and which then defines the extra rules needed for these additional constructs. All three stylesheets are included in the download files for this chapter.

Summary

The example presented here was a real stylesheet, used for a real application, and not just for teaching purposes. It's perhaps slightly atypical in that much of it was written before the XSLT specifications stabilised, so it sometimes does things in a roundabout way. However, it's probably not that dissimilar from many other stylesheets used in document formatting applications.

The phrase "document formatting" is key. The main tasks performed in this stylesheet were applying HTML display styles to different elements, generating hyperlinks, and formatting tables. These are all tasks that lend themselves to using the *rule-based* design pattern.

The next example will be a very different kind of application – one that uses highly-structured data, and displays it in a very different form from the way it arrives in the source document.

A Family Tree

XML is often used for representing information that is a mixture of structured data and text. Rather than taking a simple example of structured data (like the book catalog found in so many XML examples) we will take a look at how to process something rather more complex – a family tree.

I could have used an example with invoices and requisitions and purchase orders. I believe that the techniques used in this worked example are equally applicable to many practical commercial problems, but that you will find a little excursion into the world of genealogy a pleasant relief from the day job.

One caveat, though. Throughout this book I have been talking about tree models of XML, and I have been using words like parent and child, ancestor and descendant, in the context of these data trees. Don't imagine, though, that we can use this tree structure to represent a family tree directly. In fact, a family tree is not really a tree at all, because everyone has two parents but in XML trees one parent is considered sufficient.

The structure of the family tree is actually quite different from the document tree used to represent it. And in this section, words like parent and child have their everyday meaning!

The Data Model and its XML Representation

The established standard for representing genealogical data is known as GEDCOM, and data in this format is routinely exchanged between software packages and posted on the Internet. The main objects found in a GEDCOM file are records representing individuals (called INDI records), and records representing couples (called FAM records).

An INDI record looks like this:

```
0 @I1@ INDI
1 NAME John Fitzgerald/Kennedy/
1 SEX M
1 BIRT
2 DATE 29 MAY 1917
2 PLAC Brookline, MA, USA
1 DEAT
2 DATE 22 NOV 1963
2 PLAC Dallas, TX, USA
2 NOTE Assassinated by Lee Harvey Oswald.
1 NOTE Educated at Harvard University.
2 CONT Elected Congressman in 1945
2 CONT aged 29; served three terms in the House of Representatives.
2 CONT Elected Senator in 1952. Elected President in 1960, the
2 CONT youngest ever President of the United States.
1 FAMS @F1@
1 FAMC @F2@
```

This is not XML, of course, but we can mechanically convert it to XML, so that it looks like this:

```
<INDI ID="I1">
   <NAME>John Fitzgerald<S>Kennedy</S></NAME>
   <SEX>M</SEX>
   <BIRT>
      <DATE>29 MAY 1917</DATE>
      <PLAC>Brookline, MA, USA</PLAC>
   </BIRT>
   <DEAT>
      <DATE>22 NOV 1963</DATE>
      <PLAC>Dallas, TX, USA</PLAC>
      <NOTE>Assassinated by Lee Harvey Oswald.<BR/></NOTE>
   </DEAT>
   <NOTE>Educated at Harvard University.<BR/>
Elected Congressman in 1945<BR/>
aged 29; served three terms in the House of Representatives.<BR/>
Elected Senator in 1952. Elected President in 1960, the<BR/>
youngest ever President of the United States.<BR/>
   </NOTE>
   <FAMS REF="F1"/>
   <FAMC REF="F2"/>
</INDI>
```

I'll come back later on (page 676) to show how we actually do the conversion into XML.

Each record in a GEDCOM file has a unique identifier (in this case `I1` – that's letter I, digit one), which is used to construct cross-references between records. Most of the information in this record is self-explanatory, except the **<FAMS>** and **<FAMC>** fields: **<FAMS>** is a reference to a **<FAM>** record representing a family in which this person is a parent, and **<FAMC>** is a reference to a family in which this person is a child.

Note how the fields may be nested to indicate the structure. The GEDCOM specification (which is developed by the Church of Jesus Christ of Latter-day Saints) defines a strict schema saying how the tags can be nested, very much like an XML DTD.

> *An HTML version of the GEDCOM specification can be found at* *http://www.gendex.com/gedcom55/55gcint.htm.*

However, although the schema is strict, it still allows very varied information to be entered. For example, any number of events or attributes relating to an individual, with full or partial dates, textual notes at any level, and references to sources of information. Examples of events might be birth, death, adoption, or retirement; examples of attributes might be occupation, religion, or health: but the list is open-ended.

The <INDI> record contains information about the events and attributes for a person, while the <FAM> record defines events for a couple and their family (a "couple" here represents two people who either were married, or had children, or both: either partner may be unknown or unrecorded). A <FAM> record, like an <INDI> record, has an arbitrary unique identifier. After conversion to XML, it might look like this:

```
<FAM ID="F1">
   <HUSB REF="I1"/>
   <WIFE REF="I2"/>
   <CHIL REF="I5"/>
   <CHIL REF="I6"/>
   <CHIL REF="I7"/>
   <MARR>
      <DATE>12 SEP 1953</DATE>
      <PLAC>Newport, RI, USA</PLAC>
   </MARR>
</FAM>
```

The <FAM> element contains links to all the individuals making up the family. These are technically redundant in the sense that they could be deduced by finding links in the opposite direction; but redundancy is not always a bad thing. The element also contains information about events affecting both partners, the most common being their marriage.

To make this clearer, here is a diagram showing how the family relationships are represented.

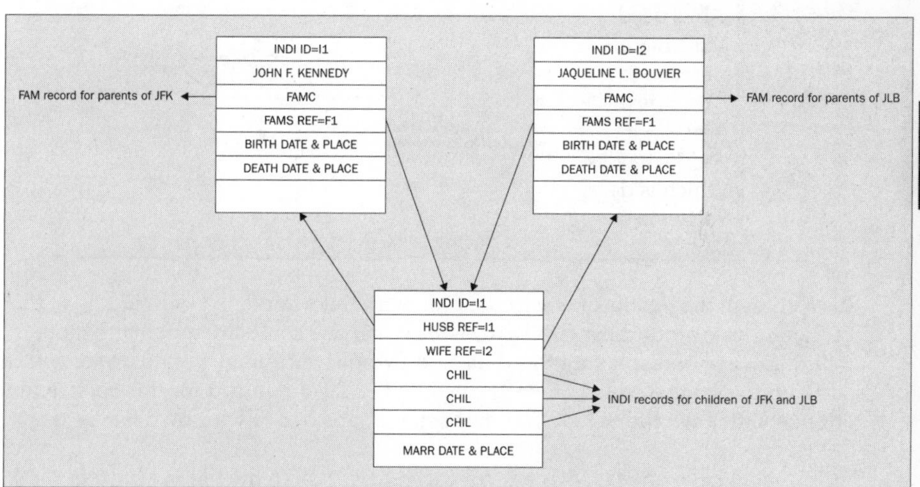

I'm not going to spend time discussing whether this is a good way of representing genealogical information or not. Many people have criticized the data model, either on technical grounds or from the point of view of political correctness, but like the QWERTY keyboard, GEDCOM persists despite its faults simply because so many people are using it.

In GEDCOM, there is no formal way of linking one file to another. XML, of course, creates wonderful opportunities to define how your family tree links to someone else's. But the linking isn't as easy as it sounds (nothing is, in genealogy) because of the problems of maintaining version integrity between two datasets that are changing independently. So I'll avoid getting into that area, and stick to the model that the whole family tree is in one XML document.

Displaying the Family Tree Data

What we want to do is to write a stylesheet that displays the data in a GEDCOM file in HTML format. We'll assume for the moment that the conversion to XML syntax has already been done (I'll discuss how it's done later in the chapter, on page 676). We want the display to look something like the screenshot below:

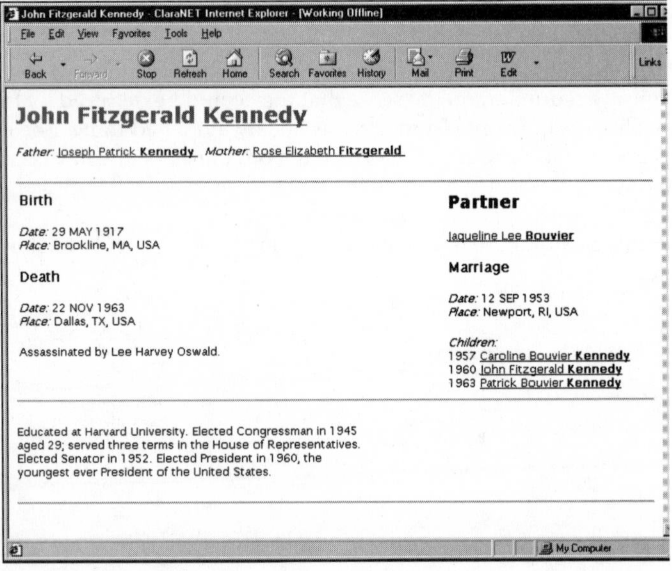

This shows all the details of one individual, with links to related individuals so that you can browse around the family tree. Of course one could attempt many more ambitious ways of displaying this data, and I would encourage you to do so: you can start with the small Kennedy data set included in the download for this book, and then continue with any other GEDCOM data set, perhaps one of your own family tree.

Since we will have one HTML page for each individual in the file, we have to think about how to create multiple HTML pages from a single XML input document. There are at least three ways of doing this:

- A bulk publishing process, in which you convert the XML input document into a set of HTML pages, and then publish these as static pages on the web server. This has the benefit that you only incur the cost of transformation once. It minimizes your dependence on the facilities available from your Internet Service Provider, and it will work with any browser.

- Generating HTML pages on demand in the server, using Java servlets or ASP pages. Again this will work with any browser, but this time you need to find an Internet Service Provider who allows you to run servlets or ASP pages.

- Downloading the entire XML file to the client, and generating the display there. This has the advantage that the data is only downloaded once, and the user can then browse it at leisure, with no further interaction with the server. However, this will only work if the user has an XML-capable browser, which today means Internet Explorer 5 or above.

  The Netscape 6 / Mozilla browser will support XML and CSS but XSLT support (using the Transformiix engine) is still work-in-progress. Watch out for news on http://www.mozilla.org/projects/xslt/.

  Another disadvantage is security; you have no way of filtering the data, for example to remove details of living persons, and you have no way to stop your entire XML file being copied by the user (for example, the user can View Source, or can poke around in the browser cache).

The only real difference between the three cases, as far as the stylesheet is concerned, is that the hyperlinks will be generated differently.

We'll handle the differences by writing a generic stylesheet module containing all the common code for the three cases, and then importing this into stylesheets that handle the variations.

The Stylesheet

We're ready to write a stylesheet, `person.xsl` that generates an HTML page showing the information relevant to a particular individual. This stylesheet will need to accept the ID of the required individual as a global parameter. If no value is supplied, we'll choose the first **`<INDI>`** record in the file. Here's the top-level structure:

```
<xsl:transform
   xmlns:xsl="http://www.w3.org/1999/XSL/Transform"
   version="1.0" >

<xsl:param name="id" select="/*/INDI[1]/@ID"/>

<!-- define keys to allow records to be found by their id -->

<xsl:key name="indi" match="INDI" use="@ID"/>
<xsl:key name="fam" match="FAM" use="@ID"/>
```

```
<xsl:template match="/">
   <xsl:variable name="person" select="key('indi', $id)"/>
   <xsl:apply-templates select="$person"/>
</xsl:template>

. . .

</xsl:transform>
```

I've decided to define two keys to give immediate access to **<INDI>** and **<FAM>** elements if their **ID** attributes are known. I could have relied on the **id()** function, but that would only work if the **ID** attribute is defined in the DTD as being an attribute of type ID. This makes the stylesheet dependent on the document having a DTD, so on balance I decided that using the **key()** function is safer.

The initial template (the one that matches the root node) then calls **<xsl:apply-templates>** to process the **<INDI>** element representing the selected person.

The template rule for an **<INDI>** element creates the shell of the HTML page:

```
<xsl:template match="INDI">
   <html>
      <head>
         <xsl:call-template name="css-style"/>
         <xsl:variable name="name">
            <xsl:apply-templates select="NAME"/>
         </xsl:variable>
         <title><xsl:value-of select="$name"/></title>
      </head>

      <!-- choose background color based on gender -->

      <xsl:variable name="color">
         <xsl:choose>
            <xsl:when test="SEX='M'">cyan</xsl:when>
            <xsl:otherwise>pink</xsl:otherwise>
         </xsl:choose>
      </xsl:variable>

      <body bgcolor="{$color}">

         <!-- Show name and parentage -->

         <h1><xsl:apply-templates select="NAME"/></h1>
         <xsl:call-template name="show-parents"/>
         <hr/>

         <table>
         <tr>
```

```
        <!-- Show events and attributes -->

        <td width="50%" valign="top">
           <xsl:call-template name="show-events"/>
        </td>
        <td width="20%"/>

        <!-- Show partners, marriages, and children -->

        <td width="30%" valign="top">
           <xsl:call-template name="show-partners"/>
        </td>
     </tr>
     </table>

     <hr/>

     <!-- Show notes -->

     <xsl:for-each select="NOTE">
        <p class="text"><xsl:apply-templates/></p>
        <xsl:if test="position()=last()"><hr/></xsl:if>
     </xsl:for-each>

   </body>
 </html>
</xsl:template>
```

This template rule works through the process of generating the output page. Some observations:

- The title in the HTML header is generated by first creating a variable, and then copying the value of the variable to the **<title>** element. This is deliberate, it takes advantage of the standard template rules for generating a personal name, but the **<xsl:value-of>** instruction then removes the tags such as **<b>** that appear in the generated name, because these clutter the displayed title in some browsers.
- The background color of the page depends on the value of the person's **SEX** attribute. You might consider this to be rather childish, in which case you are welcome to change it, but I left it in because it illustrates another XSLT technique.
- The main task of generating the content of the page is split up and delegated to separate named templates, simply for reasons of modularity.
- There is no attempt to display all the data that GEDCOM allows to be included in, or referenced from, an **<INDI>** record, for example citations of sources, multimedia objects such as photographs, etc. Any such data will simply be skipped.

I've chosen to use an internal CSS stylesheet to define font sizes and the like, and the task of generating this is delegated to the template named `css-style`. This generates fixed output, as follows:

```
<xsl:template name="css-style">
   <style type="text/css">

   H1 {
      font-family: Verdana, Helvetica, sans-serif;
      font-size: 18pt;
      font-weight: bold;
      color: "#FF0080"
   }

   H2 {
      font-family: Verdana, Helvetica, sans-serif;
      font-size: 14pt;
      font-weight: bold;
      color: black;
   }

   H3 {
      font-family: Lucida Sans, Helvetica, sans-serif;
      font-size: 11pt;
      font-weight: bold;
      color: black;
   }

   SPAN.label {
      font-family: Lucida Sans, Helvetica, sans-serif;
      font-size: 10pt;
      font-weight: normal;
      font-style: italic;
      color: black;
   }

   P,LI,TD {
      font-family: Lucida Sans, Helvetica, sans-serif;
      font-size: 10pt;
      font-weight: normal;
      color: black;
   }

   P.text {
      font-family: Comic Sans MS, Helvetica, sans-serif;
      font-size: 10pt;
      font-weight: normal;
      color: black;
   }

   </style>
</xsl:template>
```

It would have been quite possible, of course, to attach these attributes to the various HTML elements individually, or to incorporate them using XSLT attribute sets, but this way seems cleaner, and shows how XSLT and CSS can complement each other. In fact, it might have been even better to use an external CSS stylesheet, since a user displaying many of these HTML pages would then get more benefit from caching.

The next template displays the parents of the current individual, as hyperlinks. Here it is:

```
<xsl:template name="show-parents">

    <xsl:variable name="parents" select="key('fam', FAMC/@REF)"/>
    <xsl:variable name="father" select="key('indi',
    $parents/HUSB/@REF)"/>
    <xsl:variable name="mother" select="key('indi',
    $parents/WIFE/@REF)"/>

    <p>
    <xsl:if test="$father">
       <span class="label">Father: </span>
       <xsl:apply-templates select="$father/NAME" mode="link"/> 
    </xsl:if>
    <xsl:if test="$mother">
       <span class="label">Mother: </span>
       <xsl:apply-templates select="$mother/NAME" mode="link"/> 
    </xsl:if>
    </p>
</xsl:template>
```

The template starts by locating the **<FAM>** record referenced by the **<FAMC>** field of the current **<INDI>** record. It does this using the «`fam`» key defined earlier. Then it selects the **<INDI>** records for the father and mother, these being the records pointed to by the **<HUSB>** and **<WIFE>** fields of the **<FAM>** record: this time the «`indi`» key is used.

If the data is not all present, for example if there is no **<FAMC>** field, or if the **<FAM>** has no **<HUSB>** or **<WIFE>** (no ancestry goes back to infinity), then the «`$father`» and or «`$mother`» variables will simply identify an empty node-set. The subsequent **<xsl:if>** instructions ensure that when this happens, the relevant label is omitted from the output.

The actual hyperlinks are generated by using **<xsl:apply-templates>** with «`mode="link"`»: this gets reused for all the other links on the page, and we'll see later how it works. The «` `» character reference outputs a non-breaking space. It's actually simpler to do this than to output an ordinary space, which would require an **<xsl:text>** element. If you don't like numeric character references you can define an entity called «`nbsp`» in the `<!DOCTYPE>` declaration and then use «` `» in place of «` `».

The next named template is used to display the list of events for an individual, such as birth and death. We will also use it later to display all the events for a couple (such as marriage and divorce).

```
<xsl:template name="show-events">
   <xsl:for-each select="*">
      <xsl:sort select="substring(DATE, string-length(DATE) - 3)"/>

      <xsl:variable name="event-name">
         <xsl:apply-templates select="." mode="expand"/>
      </xsl:variable>

      <xsl:if test="string($event-name)">
         <h3><xsl:value-of select="$event-name"/></h3>
         <p>
         <xsl:if test="DATE">
            <span class="label">Date: </span>
            <xsl:value-of select="DATE"/><br/>
         </xsl:if>
         <xsl:if test="PLAC">
            <span class="label">Place: </span>
            <xsl:value-of select="PLAC"/><br/>
         </xsl:if>
         </p>
         <xsl:for-each select="NOTE">
            <p class="text"><xsl:apply-templates/></p>
         </xsl:for-each>
      </xsl:if>
   </xsl:for-each>
</xsl:template>
```

The events are presented in an attempt at date order. The logic in **`<xsl:sort>`** to extract the last four characters of the **`<DATE>`** field is pragmatic, but in the vast majority of cases it gives the year of the event. Simple dates in GEDCOM are in the format «`21 APR 1862`». The pragmatic approach works even where the date has a form such as «`BETWEEN 1865 AND 1868`». It fails with a date of «`55 BC`», but fortunately the Kennedy data doesn't go that far back. A nice enhancement to the stylesheet would be to take the month and day into account when sorting (it is common for two events to occur in the same year, for example death and burial). The best way to achieve this would probably be to use an extension function which converts the GEDCOM date into an ISO date in the form YYYYMMDD.

It's not immediately obvious which elements in the source data relate to events. The GEDCOM standard lists dozens of possible events, and we don't really want to use a union expression of the form «`select="BIRT | DEAT | BAPM | BURI"`» that lists them all. Also, we need some kind of translation from the abbreviated tag name (such as `BURI`) to a more meaningful name or description of the event, such as "Burial". We can kill two birds with one stone by applying another template to the element, in mode «`expand`»: where the element is recognized as an event, this will return the meaningful name of the event, and where it isn't, it will return an empty string. So we only process those where the returned `$event-name` is a non-empty string. This is one of the few cases where the type conversion needs to be explicit. If we just wrote `<xsl:if test="$event-name"/>`, we would be converting a tree to a boolean, and this always yields true. It's the string value we want to test, so we use the **`string()`** function to convert it explicitly.

So there should now be a long list of templates to expand the tags of individual event types. I won't list them all, just those used most commonly:

```
<xsl:template match="BIRT" mode="expand">Birth</xsl:template>
<xsl:template match="DEAT" mode="expand">Death</xsl:template>
<xsl:template match="BURI" mode="expand">Burial</xsl:template>
<xsl:template match="BAPM" mode="expand">Baptism</xsl:template>
<xsl:template match="MARR" mode="expand">Marriage</xsl:template>
<xsl:template match="EVEN" mode="expand">
   <xsl:value-of select="TYPE"/>
</xsl:template>
<xsl:template match="*" mode="expand"/>
```

The template rule for **<EVEN>** catches GEDCOM's all-purpose event, which has a **<TYPE>** child element to give a description of the event. This is used for non-standard events such as "won the jackpot in the National Lottery" that have no explicit tag allocated in the GEDCOM standard. And the final rule ensures that non-event elements return an empty string, and are thus recognized as non-events.

The only part of the HTML display that remains is the right-hand panel, where we show information about a person's partner(s) and marriage(s). If multiple partners or marriages are recorded for an individual, there will be multiple **<FAMS>** fields within the **<INDI>** element. If there are several, we use headings such as "Partner 1", "Partner 2"; if there is only one, we omit the number.

So the first thing we do is to find all the **<FAM>** records in which the individual is a spouse: we assign this node-set to the variable `$partnerships`.

For a woman, to find the name of her partner we need to follow the **<HUSB>** link, while for a man we need to follow the **<WIFE>** link. Since the sex may not be recorded, the safest strategy is to look at both partners and list whichever is different from the starting individual. That is also tolerant to situations such as same-sex marriages: when handling genealogical data it's best to be flexible, not only because such things may actually happen whether you approve of it or not, but more importantly, because errors in historical source data are part of life.

The template looks like this:

```
<xsl:template name="show-partners">
   <xsl:variable name="subject" select="."/>
   <xsl:variable name="partnerships"
                    select="key('fam', FAMS/@REF)"/>
   <xsl:for-each select="$partnerships">
      <xsl:sort select="substring(MARR/DATE,
                                string-length(MARR/DATE) - 3)"/>

      <xsl:variable name="partner"
         select="key('indi',
                 (HUSB/@REF | WIFE/@REF)[.!=$subject/@ID])"/>
```

```
      <xsl:variable name="partner-seq">
         <xsl:choose>
            <xsl:when test="count($subject/FAMS)=1"></xsl:when>
            <xsl:otherwise>
               <xsl:value-of select="position()"/>
            </xsl:otherwise>
         </xsl:choose>
      </xsl:variable>

      <xsl:if test="$partner">
         <h2>Partner <xsl:value-of select="$partner-seq"/></h2>
         <p>
         <xsl:apply-templates select="$partner/NAME" mode="link"/>
         </p>
      </xsl:if>

      <xsl:call-template name="show-events"/>

      <xsl:variable name="children" select="key('indi', CHIL/@REF)"/>
      <xsl:if test="$children">
         <p><span class="label">Children:</span><br/>
         <xsl:for-each select="$children">
            <xsl:sort select="substring(BIRT/DATE,
                              string-length(BIRT/DATE) - 3)"/>
            <xsl:value-of select="substring(BIRT/DATE,
                              string-length(BIRT/DATE) - 3)"/>
            <xsl:text> </xsl:text>
            <xsl:apply-templates select="NAME" mode="link"/><br/>
         </xsl:for-each>
         </p>
      </xsl:if>
   </xsl:for-each>
</xsl:template>
```

As before, we try to list the partners in chronological order, based on the year of marriage. If this isn't known, there's not much we can do about it. For each partnership, we list the partner's name, as a hyperlink, then the events associated with the partnership (typically just the marriage), and finally the children's names, again as hyperlinks. The children are found from the **<CHIL>** fields of the **<FAM>** record, and are listed in order of year of birth where this is known.

The next group of template rules is used to create the HTML hyperlinks:

```
<xsl:template match="NAME" mode="link">
   <a>
      <xsl:attribute name="href">
         <xsl:call-template name="make-href"/>
      </xsl:attribute>
      <xsl:apply-templates/>
   </a>
</xsl:template>
```

```
<xsl:template match="S">
   <xsl:text> </xsl:text>
   <b><u><xsl:apply-templates/></u></b>
   <xsl:text> </xsl:text>
</xsl:template>

<xsl:template name="make-href">
   <xsl:value-of select="concat(../@ID, '.html')"/>
</xsl:template>
```

The «`make-href`» template is the only place where the form of a link is defined: in this case it consists of a relative URL reference to another HTML file, with a filename based on the individual's **ID** attribute, for example `I27.html`.

The stylesheet ends with a trivial rule for **
** elements, which are used to separate lines of text:

```
<xsl:template match="BR"><BR/></xsl:template>

</xsl:transform>
```

Putting it Together

We've now got a stylesheet that can generate an HTML page for a single chosen individual. We don't yet have a working web site!

As I suggested earlier, there are three ways you can work. You can do a batch conversion of the entire data file into a collection of linked static HTML pages held on the web server, you can generate each page on demand from the server, or you can generate pages dynamically at the client. I'll show how to do all three.

Publishing Static HTML

To generate HTML files for all the individuals in the data file, we need some kind of script that processes each individual in turn and produces a separate output file for each one. Here we can take advantage of the XSLT 1.1 capability to produce multiple output files from one input file. Many XSLT 1.0 products have a similar capability, but unfortunately each product uses different syntax.

We'll need a new template for processing the root element, and because this must override the template defined in `person.xsl`, we'll need to use **`<xsl:import>`** to give the new template higher precedence.

Here is the complete stylesheet, `publish.xsl`, to do the bulk conversion. As well as generating an HTML page for each individual, it also creates an index page listing all the individuals sorted first by surname, then by the rest of the name.

```
<xsl:transform
 xmlns:xsl="http://www.w3.org/1999/XSL/Transform"
version="1.1" >

<xsl:import href="person.xsl"/>

<xsl:param name="dir" select="'.'"/>

<xsl:template match="/">
   <xsl:for-each select="*/INDI">
      <xsl:document href="{$dir}/{@ID}.html">
         <xsl:apply-templates select="."/>
      </xsl:document>
   </xsl:for-each>
   <xsl:document href="{$dir}/index.html">
      <xsl:call-template name="make-index"/>
   </xsl:document>
</xsl:template>

<xsl:template name="make-index">
   <html>
   <head>
      <title>Index of names</title>
   </head>
   <body>
   <h1>Index of names</h1>
   <p>
      <xsl:for-each select="/*/INDI/NAME">
         <xsl:sort select="S"/>
         <xsl:sort select="text()"/>
         <a>
            <xsl:attribute name="href">
               <xsl:call-template name="make-href"/>
            </xsl:attribute>
            <xsl:value-of select="S"/>,
            <xsl:for-each select="text()">
               <xsl:value-of select="concat(' ', ., ' ')"/>
            </xsl:for-each>
         </a>
         <br/>
      </xsl:for-each>
   </p>
   </body>
   </html>
</xsl:template>

</xsl:transform>
```

You can run this stylesheet using any XSLT processor that supports the XSLT 1.1 **<xsl:document>** instruction, or you can modify it to run with any XSLT 1.0 processor that has an extension to produce multiple output files. At the time of writing, the only processor that will run this stylesheet as written is Saxon. So you will first need to install the Saxon product, which can be found at http://users.iclway.co.uk/mhkay/saxon/. If you are using a Windows platform, it is simplest to install Instant Saxon; the latest version can be found via the same URL.

You will also need to download the example files from the Wrox web site. Create a new directory, copy the stylesheets and the XML data file into it, make this the current directory, and then run the command:

```
saxon kennedy.xml publish.xsl
```

This assumes that you've added saxon.exe to your PATH; if not, change the command to (say) `c:\saxondir\saxon` if you installed the product into `c:\saxondir`.

If you want to generate the HTML files in a different directory, you can specify this on the command line, for example:

```
saxon kennedy.xml publish.xsl dir=d:\jfk
```

The new directory should fill with HTML files. Double-click on the `index.html` file, and you should see an index of names. Click on any of the names to see the screen shown on page 658, in glorious color. Then browse the data by following the relationships.

Generating HTML Pages from a Servlet

An alternative to bulk-converting the XML data into static HTML pages is to generate each HTML page on request. This requires execution of a stylesheet on the server, which in principle can be controlled using ASP pages, Java servlets, or even raw CGI programs. However, as many of the available XSLT processors are written in Java, it turns out to be convenient to use servlets.

If you aren't familiar with servlet programming, it's probably best to skip this section, because there isn't space here to start from first principles. If you're keen, check out *Professional Java Server Programming* (1-861002-77-7), also published by Wrox Press.

If you are using Saxon or Xalan, you can write your servlet to use the TrAX API described in Appendix F; other Java processors such as Oracle are expected to implement this in due course. This means you can write a servlet that works with any processor. In fact, most of the processors come with some kind of packaged servlet interface, though it's often best to customize it to suit the particular requirements of the application. As there are a lot of variations depending on the environment you are working in, I won't try to give a complete working solution for this situation, but will just sketch out the design.

A particular feature of this application is that there are lots of requests to get data from the same source document, using the same stylesheet, but with different parameters. So ideally we want to hold both the source document and the stylesheet in memory on the server: we don't want to incur the overhead of parsing the full XML document to display each individual.

We would like to accept incoming requests from the browser in the form:

```
http://www.myserver.com/examples/servlet/GedServlet?tree=kennedy&id=I1
```

The parameters included in the URL are firstly, the name of the data set to use (we'd like the server to be able to handle several concurrently), and secondly, the identifier of the individual to display.

> **When the above URL is included in an XML document, the «`&`» must be represented as «`&`». Most HTML browsers will accept either «`&`» or «`&`». But strictly, «`&`» is correct according to the HTML specification, and that is what our stylesheet will actually generate.**

So the first thing that we need to do is to generate hyperlinks in this format. We can do this by writing a new stylesheet module that imports `person.xsl` and overrides the template that generated the hyperlinks. We'll call this `ged-servlet.xsl`.

The `ged-servlet.xsl` stylesheet module looks like this. It has an extra parameter, which is the name of the tree we are interested in, because the same servlet ought to be able to handle requests for data from different family trees. And it overrides the «`make-href`» template with one that generates hyperlinks in the required format:

```
<xsl:transform
   xmlns:xsl="http://www.w3.org/1999/XSL/Transform"
   version="1.0" >

<xsl:import href="person.xsl"/>
<xsl:param name="tree"/>

<xsl:template name="make-href">
   <xsl:value-of select="concat('/examples/servlet/GedServlet?tree=',
                 $tree, '&amp;id=', ../@ID)"/>
</xsl:template>

</xsl:transform>
```

If you configure the servlet in a different location from this, you will need to modify this stylesheet to use a different URL.

The stylesheet and the servlet interface could also be extended to generate an index of names, as in the previous example, but as that's a simple task I'll leave you to work that out for yourself.

More tricky is writing the servlet. The code below uses the TrAX interface described in Appendix F, and should work with any XSLT processor that supports this API. At the time of writing, Xalan implements both the `javax.xml.transform` and the `javax.xml.parsers` packages, while Saxon implements only `javax.xml.transform`. To use this with Saxon, you will need a separate parser that provides the `javax.xml.parsers` classes: for example, Crimson from http://xml.apache.org/.

```
import javax.servlet.*;
import javax.servlet.http.*;
import java.util.Hashtable;

import org.w3c.dom.Document;

import javax.xml.parsers.*;
import javax.xml.transform.*;
import javax.xml.transform.stream.*;
import javax.xml.transform.dom.*;
import org.xml.sax.SAXException;

public class GedServlet extends HttpServlet {

    /**
    * Respond to an HTTP request
    */

    public void service(HttpServletRequest req, HttpServletResponse
    res)
       throws ServletException, IOException
    {
        res.setContentType("text/html");

        try {
            String clear = req.getParameter("clear");
            if (clear!=null && clear.equals("yes")) {
                resetData();
            }
            String family = req.getParameter("tree");
            Document doc = getSourceDocument(family);
            Source source = new DOMSource(doc);

            Result result = new StreamResult(res.getOutputStream());

            Templates style = getStyleSheet();
            Transformer transformer = style.newTransformer();
            transformer.setParameter("id", req.getParameter("id"));
            transformer.setParameter("tree", family);
            transformer.transform(source, result);

        } catch (TransformerException err) {
            res.getOutputStream().
                  println("Error applying stylesheet: " +
                                                  err.getMessage());
        }
    }

    /**
    * Get the prepared stylesheet from memory; prepare it if necessary
    */

    private synchronized Templates getStyleSheet()
    throws TransformerConfigurationException {
        if (stylesheet == null) {
            File sheet =
                  new File(getServletContext().getRealPath("/ged-
                                                       servlet.xsl"));
            stylesheet = TransformerFactory.newInstance().
                           newTemplates(new StreamSource(sheet));
        }
        return stylesheet;
    }

    /**
    * Load the source document
    */
```

10

Worked Examples

```
    private synchronized Document getSourceDocument(String tree)
    throws ParserConfigurationException, SAXException {
        Document doc = (Document)trees.get(tree);
        if (doc==null) {
            File source =
       new File(getServletContext().getRealPath("/" + tree + ".xml"));
            doc = DocumentBuilderFactory.newInstance().

            newDocumentBuilder().parse(source);
        }
        return doc;
    }

    /**
    * Reset data held in memory
    */

    private synchronized void resetData() {
        trees = new Hashtable();
        stylesheet = null;
    }

    private Hashtable trees = new Hashtable();
    private Templates stylesheet = null;
}
```

The XML file holding the family tree data must be in a file *`tree`*`.xml` where *`tree`* identifies the specific family tree, in our case `kennedy.xml`. This must be in the home directory for the web application containing the servlet, as defined by the configuration parameters for your web server. The two stylesheet modules `person.xsl` and `ged-servlet.xsl` must also be in this directory.

The servlet keeps in memory a copy of the compiled stylesheet (the TrAX `Templates` object): it makes this copy the first time it is needed. It also keeps in memory a DOM `Document` object representing each family tree. The various documents are indexed using a hash table. Note that all accesses to these variables must be in synchronized methods to avoid concurrency conflicts, because in a servlet several threads can be running the same code at once.

The servlet then allocates a new instance or activation of the stylesheet – a TrAX `Transformer` object – which is not shared with any other thread, and which is used only once. The servlet passes this object details of the parameters (extracted from the URL) and the required output destination, before calling on it to process the source document by calling its **`renderDocument()`** method.

Generating HTML Using ASP Pages

If you work in a Microsoft environment, an alternative to writing Java servlets to perform server-side transformation is to control the process using an ASP page. In this case you will probably be using Microsoft's MSXML3 parser and XSLT processor. While MSXML3 is best known for its ability to do client-side transformations, it is equally effective as a server-side engine. The product uses COM interfaces so it can be called from an ASP page in the same way as any other COM object. The API to control transformation using MSXML3 is described in Appendix A.

We will need to modify the hyperlinks in the HTML pages we generate, so that this time they call on the ASP page to generate the output for another individual. This modification to the stylesheet can again be achieved by writing a new stylesheet that imports the original one, changing only the template that produces the hyperlink. This is `ged-asp.xsl`:

```
<xsl:transform
   xmlns:xsl="http://www.w3.org/1999/XSL/Transform"
   version="1.0"
>

<xsl:import href="person.xsl"/>
<xsl:param name="tree"/>

<xsl:template name="make-href">
<xsl:value-of select="concat('GedAsp.asp?tree=', $tree, '&amp;id=', ../@ID)"/>
</xsl:template>

</xsl:transform>
```

To keep the ASP code simple we will reload the source document and stylesheet each time. If you want to do this for real, it would be better to hold these as application- or session-level objects. Here is the complete ASP page (I've kept it short by doing no error handling):

```
<%@ LANGUAGE = JScript %>
<%


  // Read the query parameters from the URL
 var family = Request.QueryString("tree") + "";
 var indi = Request.QueryString("id") + "";
  // Set the source and style sheet locations
  var sourceFile = Server.MapPath("kennedy.xml");
  var styleFile = Server.MapPath("ged-asp.xsl");

  // Load the XML
  var source = new ActiveXObject("MSXML2.DOMDocument");
  source.async = false;
  source.load(sourceFile);

  // Load the XSLT
  var style = new ActiveXObject("MSXML2.FreeThreadedDOMDocument");
  style.async = false;
  style.load(styleFile);

  var transformer = new ActiveXObject("MSXML2.XSLTemplate");
  transformer.stylesheet = style.documentElement;

  var xslproc = transformer.createProcessor();
  xslproc.input = source;

  // Set the parameters for the transformation
  xslproc.addParameter("id", indi, "");
    xslproc.addParameter("tree", family, "");

  // run the transformation
  xslproc.transform();
  Response.Write(xslproc.output);

%>
```

Generating HTML in the Browser

Finally, let's look at another way to display the family tree: namely, to download the whole XML file to the browser as a single chunk, and then use client-side scripts to invoke stylesheet processing whenever the user clicks on a hyperlink. This particular example runs only in Internet Explorer 5, and only with the MSXML3 version of Microsoft's XML parser installed (hopefully it will also work with later versions). Information about installing this product is included in Appendix A.

If the XML file is large (family trees produced by serious genealogists often run to several megabytes) then this approach means the user is going to have to wait rather longer to see the first page of data. But the advantage is that once it's downloaded, browsing around the file can be done offline: there is no need to go back to the server to follow each link from one individual to another. This gives the user a lightning-fast response to navigation requests, and reduces the processing load and the number of hits on the server. Another benefit, given that many genealogists only have access to the limited web space provided by a commercial ISP, is that no special code needs to be installed on the server. Until XSLT support in the browser becomes universal, however, the disadvantage is that the only users able to view the data will be those who have taken the trouble to install the MSXML3 parser.

This time, the transformation is controlled from JavaScript code on an HTML page `famtree.html`. The page itself reads as follows. The **`<script>`** elements contain client-side Javascript code.

```
<html>
<head>
   <title>Family Tree</title>
   <style type="text/css">
      ... as before ...
   </style>
   <script>
      var source = null;
      var style = null;
      var transformer = null;

      function init() {
         source =
            new ActiveXObject("MSXML2.DOMDocument");
         source.async = false;
         source.load('kennedy.xml');

         style =
            new ActiveXObject("MSXML2.FreeThreadedDOMDocument");
         style.async = false;
         style.load('ms-person.xsl');

         transformer = new ActiveXObject("MSXML2.XSLTemplate");
         transformer.stylesheet = style.documentElement;
         refresh("I1");
      }

      function refresh(indi) {
         var xslproc = transformer.createProcessor();
         xslproc.input = source;
         xslproc.addParameter("id", indi, "");
         xslproc.transform();
         displayarea.innerHTML = xslproc.output;
      }
   </script>
```

```
    <script for="window" event="onload">
       init();
    </script>
</head>
<body>
    <div id="displayarea"></div>
</body>
</html>
```

The CSS style definitions have moved from the XSLT stylesheet to the HTML page, but they are otherwise unchanged.

The **`init()`** function on this page is called when the page is loaded. It creates two DOM objects, one for the source XML and one for the stylesheet, and loads these using the relative URLs `kennedy.xml` and `ms-person.xsl`. It then compiles the stylesheet into an object which is rather confusingly called an `XSLTemplate;` this corresponds directly with the TrAX `Templates` object. Finally it calls the **`refresh()`** function to display the individual with identifier `I1`.

> *I've taken a bit of a short cut here. There's no guarantee that a GEDCOM file will contain an individual with this identifier. A more carefully constructed application would display the first individual in the file, or an index of people.*

The **`refresh()`** function creates an executable instance of the stylesheet by calling the **`createProcessor()`** method on the `XSLTemplate` object. It then sets the value of the global `id` parameter in the stylesheet, and applies the stylesheet to the source document by calling the **`transform()`** method. The HTML constructed by processing the stylesheet is then written to the contents of the `<div id="displayarea">` element in the body of the HTML page.

We can use the same stylesheet as before, again with modifications to the form of the hyperlinks. This time we want a hyperlink to another individual, `I2` say, to take the form:

```
<a href="Javascript:refresh('I2')">Jaqueline Lee Bouvier</a>
```

When the user clicks on this hyperlink, the **`refresh()`** function is executed, which causes a new execution of the compiled stylesheet, against the same source document, but with a different value for the `id` parameter. The effect is that the contents of the page switches to display a different individual.

The `ms-person.xsl` stylesheet is again written by importing the standard `person.xsl` stylesheet presented earlier, and then overriding the aspects we want to change. This time there are two changes: we want to change the form of the hyperlink, and we want to leave out the generation of the CSS style, because the necessary definitions are already present on the HTML page. Here is the stylesheet:

```
<xsl:transform
 xmlns:xsl="http://www.w3.org/1999/XSL/Transform"
 version="1.0"
>

<xsl:import href="person.xsl"/>

<!-- Change the way hyperlinks are generated -->
```

```
<xsl:template name="make-href">
     <xsl:variable name="apos">'</xsl:variable>
        <xsl:value-of
          select="concat('Javascript:refresh(', $apos, ../@ID, $apos,
')')"/>
</xsl:template>

<!-- Suppress the generation of a CSS stylesheet -->

<xsl:template name="css-style"/>

</xsl:transform>
```

One slight infelicity in the resulting stylesheet is that it generates a full HTML page, complete with `<html>`, `<head>`, and `<body>` elements, and then inserts this as the content of a `<div>` element within an existing HTML page. Fortunately Internet Explorer tolerates this abuse of the HTML specification rather well, though it does ignore the background color requested in the generated (inner) HTML page. You might regard this as an aesthetic improvement on the original. If you do want to set the background color based on the results of the transformation (or other properties such as the page title) you will need some additional JavaScript code to copy the relevant information from the transformation output into the appropriate place in the HTML page.

If the «`match="INDI"`» template in the original `person.xsl` stylesheet were split into multiple named templates, it would be possible to override it to avoid generating the unnecessary HTML page skeleton. But it works as written, so we'll resist the temptation to make further improvements.

Converting GEDCOM Files to XML

At the start of this exercise I explained that the GEDCOM format widely used by genealogical software packages is not an XML format, but it can easily be translated into XML. Having got these examples working, you may well want to use them to display your own family tree. There's a wide range of genealogy packages on the market, and any respectable one can do GEDCOM export. For a list of packages, go to http://www.cyndislist.com/software.htm. A good one to start with, which also happens to be free, is Personal Ancestral File or PAF.

The obvious way to translate GEDCOM to XML is to write a program that takes a GEDCOM file as input and produces an XML file as output. However, there's a smarter way: why not write a GEDCOM parser which looks just like a SAX-compliant XML parser, so that any program that can handle SAX input can read GEDCOM directly, just by switching parsers? In particular, many XSLT processors can take input from a SAX-compliant parser, so this enables you to feed GEDCOM straight into a stylesheet.

Equally, many XSLT processors can send the result tree to a user-specified `DocumentHandler` in the form of a stream of SAX events, so if we write a SAX2-compatible `ContentHandler`, our XSLT processor can also output GEDCOM files. This suddenly means we can write stylesheets to transform one GEDCOM file into another, without the hassle of creating an XML file as an intermediate form. As an example, I've included on the web site a stylesheet called `nonliving.xsl` which removes all living individuals from the data set, which is a sensible courtesy to your relatives if you are publishing your data on the web, quite apart from being a legal requirement in some countries.

A SAX2 parser for GEDCOM is supplied with the sample files for this chapter on the Wrox web site; it is named `GedcomParser`. GEDCOM uses an archaic character set called ANSEL, so along with `GedcomParser` is another class, `AnselInputStreamReader` to translate the ANSEL characters into Unicode.

Similarly, on the output side, there is a SAX2 `ContentHandler` called `GedcomOutputter`, which in turn translates Unicode to ANSEL using an `AnselOutputStreamWriter`.

This structure is shown in the diagram below:

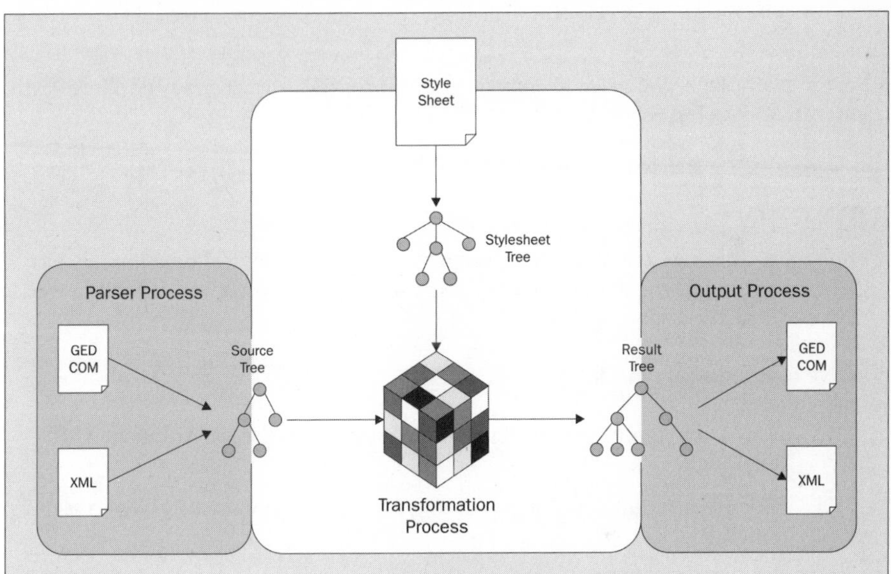

If you do want to see the XML, you can always feed the GEDCOM into a stylesheet that does an identity transformation, the simplest being:

```
<xsl:transform
   xmlns:xsl="http://www.w3.org/1999/XSL/Transform"
   version="1.0" >

<xsl:template match="/">
   <xsl:copy-of select="."/>
</xsl:template>

</xsl:transform>
```

In fact, to create the `kennedy.xml` data file which I used as the input to these example stylesheets, I used a slightly more elaborate stylesheet than this to post-process the output of the GEDCOM parser.

This is called `normalize.xsl`, and it turns various structures found in GEDCOM into a more natural XML representation. Specifically:

- A name is represented in GEDCOM in the form «`Michael /Kay/`», but in XML it is easier to handle it if the surname is tagged as «`Michael <S>Kay</S>`».
- GEDCOM uses the tags `CONT` and `CONC` to represent continuation lines: with `CONT` the continuation is assumed to represent a new line, with `CONC` it represents a concatenation of the previous line. The `normalize.xsl` stylesheet removes the `CONC` tag, and precedes a `CONT` line with an empty **
** tag as in HTML.

So, for example, if you want to convert your GEDCOM file `mytree.ged` into XML, you can do it using Saxon by entering the command

```
saxon -x GedcomParser mytree.ged normalize.xsl >mytree.xml
```

Summary

I hope this little excursion into the strange world of genealogical data models has given you some flavor of the power of XSLT as a manipulation and reporting tool for complex structured data.

We've covered a lot of ground:

- How to navigate your way around complex linked data within an XML document.
- Several different ways of generating an interactive view of a large XML data set:
  - Generating lots of static HTML pages in one go at publication time.
  - Generating HTML pages dynamically using either a Java servlet or a Microsoft ASP page.
  - Generating HTML incrementally within the browser.
- Using XSLT to transform structured data that wasn't originally in XML format.

The next worked example will venture into even stranger territory, using XSLT to solve a chess problem.

Knight's Tour Stylesheet

This example stylesheet is rather far-fetched, but it does illustrate some advanced use of XSLT features, which you are likely to encounter if you want to do any complex data manipulation.

The purpose of the stylesheet is to produce a knight's tour of the chessboard, in which each square is visited exactly once, as shown in the illustration opposite. A knight can move to any square that is at the opposite corner of a 3×2 rectangle.

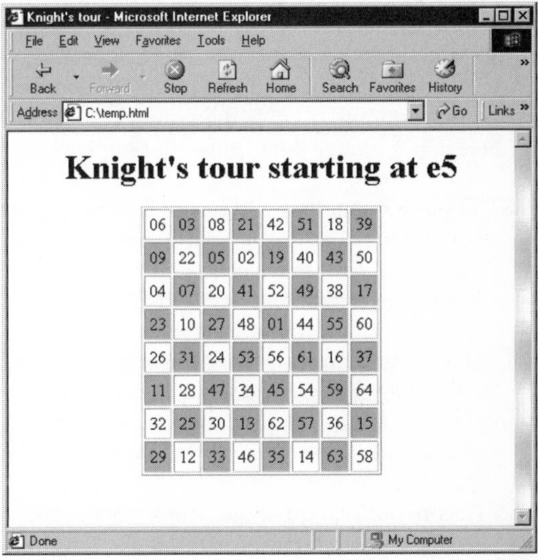

The only input to the stylesheet is an indication of the starting square: in modern chess notation, the columns are denoted by the letters a–h starting from the left, and the rows by the numbers 1–8, starting at the bottom. We'll supply the starting square as a parameter to the stylesheet. The stylesheet doesn't need to get anything from the source document. To meet the requirements of the language, there must be a source document present, but there is nothing that says the stylesheet has to read it.

We'll build up the stylesheet piece by piece: you can find the complete stylesheet, `tour.xsl`, on the Wrox web site.

The version described here uses the new XSLT 1.1 feature to access a tree-valued variable as a node-set. So you will see constructs such as «`$board/square`», which an XSLT 1.0 processor will reject as errors. The stylesheet will run as written with Saxon. If your XSLT 1.0 processor supports a **`node-set()`** extension function, you can get the stylesheet to run by rewriting these expressions, for example «`$board/square`» becomes «`xx:node-set($board)/square`». I have produced a version of the stylesheet adapted in this way for Microsoft's MSXML3, which you can find as `ms-tour.xsl` in the code download. There is also a version of the stylesheet designed to use only standard XSLT 1.0 facilities. This is achieved by representing all the working data structures as strings rather than trees. I won't try to explain how this works, but you can study it yourself: the file is `tour10.xsl`.

The inspiration for this stylesheet came from Oren Ben-Kiki, who published a stylesheet for solving the eight-queens problem. The concept here is very similar, though the details are quite different.

The Algorithm

The strategy for getting the knight round the board is based on the observation that if a square hasn't been visited yet, it had better have at least two unvisited squares that are a knight's move away from it, because there needs to be a way of getting in and another way of getting out. That means that if we can get to a square that's only got one exit left, we'd better go there now or we never will.

This suggests an approach where at each move, we look at all the squares we can jump to next, and choose the one that has fewest possible exits. It turns out that this strategy works, and always gets the knight round the board. I don't know a way of proving it, and if any reader does, please let me know: I just know that it seems to work.

The place I usually start design is with the data structures. Here the main data structure we need is the board itself. We need to know which squares the knight has visited, and so that we can print out the board at the end, we need to know the sequence in which they were visited. In XSLT 1.0 we don't have a great deal of choice about how to represent data structures, so the only practical option is a string; but in XSLT 1.1 we can use a temporary tree, which is much easier to manipulate. We'll use a tree containing 64 **`<square>`** elements, each representing one square of the board; the value will be an integer between «`1`» and «`64`» if the square has been visited (with the number indicating when it was visited), and will be empty if not.

In a conventional program this data structure would probably be held in a global variable and updated every time the knight moves. We can't do this in XSLT, because variables can't be updated. Instead, every time a template is called, it passes the current state of the board as a parameter, and when the knight moves, a new copy of the board is created, that differs from the previous one only in the details of one square.

It doesn't really matter which way the squares are numbered, but for the sake of convention we'll number them as shown below:

0	1	2	3	4	5	6	7
8	9	10	11	12	13	14	15
16	17	18	19	20	21	22	23
24	25	26	27	28	29	30	31
32	33	34	35	36	37	38	39
40	41	42	43	44	45	46	47
48	49	50	51	52	53	54	55
56	57	58	59	60	61	62	63

So if we number the rows 0 – 7, and the columns 0 – 7, the square number is given as «`row * 8 + column`».

Having decided on the principal data structure we can decide the broad structure of the program. There are three stages:

- Prepare the initial data structures (the empty board with a knight placed on it, somewhere)
- Calculate the tour
- Display the final state of the board

Calculating the tour involves 63 steps, each one taking the form:

- Find all the unvisited squares that the knight can move to from the current position
- For each one of these, count the number of exits (that is, the number of unvisited squares that can be reached from there)
- Choose the square with the fewest exits, and move the knight there

We're ready to start coding. The tricky bit, as you've probably already guessed, is that all the loops have to be coded using recursion. That takes a bit of getting used to at first, but it quickly becomes a habit.

The Root Template

Let's start with the framework of top-level elements:

```
<xsl:transform
 xmlns:xsl="http://www.w3.org/1999/XSL/Transform"
 version="1.1"
>

<xsl:param name="start" select="'a1'"/>

<!-- start-column is an integer in the range 0-7 -->

<xsl:variable name="start-column"
   select="number(translate(substring($start, 1, 1),
         'abcdefgh', '01234567'))"/>

<!-- start-row is an integer in the range 0-7, with zero at the top -->

<xsl:variable name="start-row"
   select="8 - number(substring($start, 2, 1))"/>

. . .

</xsl:transform>
```

All I'm doing here is declaring the global parameter, `start`, which defines the starting square, and deriving from it two global variables: a row number and column number.

Some observations:

- The parameter `start` has the default value `a1`. As this is a string-value, it needs to be in quotes; these quotes are additional to the quotes that surround the XML attribute. If I had written «`select="a1"`», the default value would be the string-value of the **<a1>** element child of the document root.
- The simplest way of converting the alphabetic column identifier (a-h) into a number (0–7) is to use the **`translate()`** function, which is described in Chapter 7, on page 559.
- The row number is subtracted from 8 so that the lowest-numbered row is at the top, and so that row numbers start from zero. Numbering from zero makes it easier to convert between row and column numbers and a number for each square on the board in the range 0–63.
- I haven't yet checked that the supplied start square is valid. I'll do that in the root template.

Now we can move on to the root template. This is invoked when the root node of the source document is matched, but it doesn't actually do anything with the source document.

The root template defines the stages of processing, as follows:

- Validate the supplied parameter
- Set up the empty board and place the knight on it at the specified starting square
- Compute the knight's tour
- Print out the tour in HTML format

These tasks are all delegated to other templates, so the root template itself is quite simple:

```
<xsl:template match="/">

   <!-- Validate the input parameter -->

   <xsl:if test="not(string-length($start)=2) or
     not(translate(substring($start,1,1), 'abcdefgh', 'aaaaaaaa')='a') or
     not(translate(substring($start,2,1), '12345678', '11111111')='1')">
      <xsl:message terminate="yes"
         >Invalid start parameter: try (say) 'a1' or 'f6'</xsl:message>
   </xsl:if>

   <!-- Set up the empty board -->

   <xsl:variable name="empty-board">
      <xsl:call-template name="make-board"/>
   </xsl:variable>

   <!-- Place knight on the board at the chosen starting position -->
```

```
    <xsl:variable name="initial-board">
       <xsl:call-template name="place-knight">
          <xsl:with-param name="move" select="1"/>
          <xsl:with-param name="board" select="$empty-board"/>
          <xsl:with-param name="square"
                select="$start-row * 8 + $start-column"/>
       </xsl:call-template>
    </xsl:variable>

    <!-- Evaluate the knight's tour -->

    <xsl:variable name="final-board">
       <xsl:call-template name="make-moves">
          <xsl:with-param name="move" select="2"/>
          <xsl:with-param name="board" select="$initial-board"/>
          <xsl:with-param name="square"
                select="$start-row * 8 + $start-column"/>
       </xsl:call-template>
    </xsl:variable>

    <!-- produce the HTML output -->

    <xsl:call-template name="print-board">
       <xsl:with-param name="board" select="$final-board"/>
    </xsl:call-template>

 </xsl:template>
```

Notice how most of the calls to **<xsl:call-template>** are nested within an **<xsl:variable>**. This is the only way of returning a result from a called template. The **<xsl:variable>** creates a new temporary tree, and any output produced by the called template is directed to that tree. The resulting value of the variable is a node-set containing a single node, namely the root node of the temporary tree.

The code for validating the `start` parameter is worth examining. It performs three tests: that the length of the supplied string is two characters, that the first character is one of the letters a–h, and that the second is one of the digits 1–8. The simplest way to perform these checks is to use the **`translate()`** function in the way shown. If any of the tests fail, the stylesheet outputs a message using **<xsl:message>**, and terminates.

Several of the variables (`empty-board`, `initial-board`, and `final-board`) represent a chessboard containing all or part of a knight's tour. These variables are all trees, and they all have the same structure: a root node owning 64 `<square>` element nodes. Remember that XPath trees do not have to represent well-formed XML documents, so there is no need for an outer element that contains all the **<square>**s.

If the square has been visited, it contains a sequence number representing the order of visiting (1 for the start square, 2 for the next square visited, and so on). If the square has not been visited, the element is empty.

Squares on the board are represented by an integer in the range 0–63, which is calculated as `$row * 8 + $column`.

Setting Up the Board

It's time to look at how the called templates work. I'll start with `make-board`, whose task is to initialize an empty board. I could have written this out as 64 empty **<square/>** elements in the stylesheet, but I was too lazy, so I computed it instead:

```
<xsl:template name="make-board">
   <xsl:param name="size" select="64"/>
   <xsl:if test="$size!=0">
      <square/>
      <xsl:call-template name="make-board">
         <xsl:with-param name="size" select="$size - 1"/>
      </xsl:call-template>
   </xsl:if>
</xsl:template>
```

When this template is called from the root template, the parameter `$size` takes its default value of 64. The template creates one unvisited square (denoted by **<square/>**) and then calls itself to create the other 63. After 64 recursive calls are complete, the `$size` parameter reaches zero: at this stage 64 unvisited squares will have been written, and the empty board is complete.

The next step is to place the knight in its initial position using the «`place-knight`» template. Here it is:

```
<xsl:template name="place-knight">
   <xsl:param name="move"/>
   <xsl:param name="board"/>
   <xsl:param name="square"/>
   <xsl:copy-of select="$board/square[position()-1 &lt; $square]"/>
   <square><xsl:value-of select="$move"/></square>
   <xsl:copy-of select="$board/square[position()-1 &gt; $square]"/>
</xsl:template>
```

This template takes three parameters: the number of this move, the current state of the chessboard, and the square on which the knight is to be placed. When I call it from the root template, the move number is always one, and the board is always empty, but I will use the same template again later with different parameters.

What the template does is to copy the whole supplied chessboard before and after the square where the knight is to be placed. This square itself is replaced by a new **<square>** element whose content is the move number. For example, the fifth move is written as `<square>5</square>`.

I can't, of course, modify the supplied chessboard in situ. All variables in XSLT are immutable. Instead I create a new board as a modified copy of the original. The result of the template (the value written to its current output destination) is a tree representing the new state of the chessboard after placing the knight.

Displaying the Final Board

I'll skip the template that computes the knight's tour for the moment, and describe the relatively easy task of outputting the final result as HTML. This actually requires three named templates. The first produces the HTML outline and calls «`print-rows`» to print the rows:

```
<xsl:template name="print-board">
   <xsl:param name="board"/>
   <html>
      <head>
         <title>Knight's tour</title>
   </head>
   <body>
      <div align="center">
      <h1>Knight's tour starting at <xsl:value-of select="$start"/></h1>
      <table border="1" cellpadding="4">
```

```
            <xsl:call-template name="print-rows">
               <xsl:with-param name="board" select="$board"/>
            </xsl:call-template>
         </table>
         </div>
      </body>
      </html>
   </xsl:template>
```

The second template prints the rows. Actually it just prints the first row (by calling the «print-columns» template), and then calls itself recursively to print the remaining rows, stopping when it has printed all eight:

```
   <xsl:template name="print-rows">
      <xsl:param name="board"/>
      <xsl:param name="row" select="0"/>
      <xsl:if test="$row &lt; 8">
         <tr>
            <xsl:call-template name="print-columns">
               <xsl:with-param name="board" select="$board"/>
               <xsl:with-param name="row" select="$row"/>

            </xsl:call-template>
         </tr>

         <xsl:call-template name="print-rows">
             <xsl:with-param name="board" select="$board"/>
             <xsl:with-param name="row" select="$row + 1"/>
          </xsl:call-template>
      </xsl:if>
   </xsl:template>
```

The «print-columns» template is very similar. It prints the first column, and calls itself to print the remaining columns.

```
   <xsl:template name="print-columns">
      <xsl:param name="board"/>
      <xsl:param name="row"/>
      <xsl:param name="column" select="0"/>
      <xsl:if test="$column &lt; 8">
         <xsl:variable name="color">
            <xsl:choose>
               <xsl:when test="($row + $column) mod 2">xffff44</xsl:when>
               <xsl:otherwise>white</xsl:otherwise>
            </xsl:choose>
         </xsl:variable>
         <td align="center" bgcolor="{$color}">
            <xsl:value-of select="$board/square[$row*8 + $column + 1]"/>
         </td>

         <xsl:call-template name="print-columns">
            <xsl:with-param name="board" select="$board"/>
            <xsl:with-param name="row" select="$row"/>
            <xsl:with-param name="column" select="$column + 1"/>
         </xsl:call-template>
      </xsl:if>
   </xsl:template>
```

The template contains a little bit of logic to achieve the traditional checkerboard coloring of the squares, using the «mod» operator to test whether the sum of the row number and the column number is a multiple of 2, and handling the two cases with an **<xsl:choose>** instruction.

The actual content of each square is the move number, extracted from the relevant <square> in the temporary tree representing the board.

Finding the Route

So much for the input and output of the stylesheet, now for the substance: the algorithm to calculate the knight's tour.

The basic algorithm we use is that at each move, we consider all the squares we could go to, and choose the one with the fewest exits. For example, if we are on c2 then we could move to a1, e1, a3, e3, b4, or d4, assuming they are all unvisited. Of these, the corner square a1 has only one exit, namely b3, and if we don't visit the corner square now, then we'll never get another chance later. It turns out that this strategy of always visiting the square with least exits always succeeds in generating a complete knight's tour, though just in case it doesn't, the algorithm is actually resilient enough to backtrack and try a different route if the first one fails.

The root template makes a call on the template named «`make-moves`». This template, starting from any given start position, works out all the moves needed to complete the knight's tour. Of course, it does this by recursion: but unlike previous templates which called themselves directly, this one does so indirectly, via another template named «`try-possible-moves`».

The first thing the «`make-moves`» template does is to call the template «`list-possible-moves`» to construct a list of moves that are legal in the current situation. The result of this template, a list of moves, uses a very similar data structure to that of the chessboard itself. The list is represented as a temporary tree, and each move is represented by a `<move>` element whose value is the number of the square to which the knight travels.

Having established the list of possible moves, the template then calls «`try-possible-moves`» to select one of these moves and execute it.

Here is the template. Its parameters are the number of this move (starting at move 2, because the knight's initial position is numbered 1), the state of the board before this move, and the number of the square on which the knight is currently sitting.

```
<xsl:template name="make-moves">
   <xsl:param name="move"/>
   <xsl:param name="board"/>
   <xsl:param name="square"/>

   <!-- determine the possible moves that the knight can make -->

   <xsl:variable name="possible-move-list">
       <xsl:call-template name="list-possible-moves">
          <xsl:with-param name="board" select="$board"/>
          <xsl:with-param name="square" select="$square"/>
      </xsl:call-template>
   </xsl:variable>
   <!-- try these moves in turn until one is found that works -->
```

```
      <xsl:call-template name="try-possible-moves">
         <xsl:with-param name="board" select="$board"/>
         <xsl:with-param name="square" select="$square"/>
         <xsl:with-param name="move" select="$move"/>
         <xsl:with-param name="possible-moves" select="$possible-move-
         list/move"/>
      </xsl:call-template>

   </xsl:template>
```

The next template to examine is «`list-possible-moves`». This takes as input the current state of the board and the position of the knight, and it produces a list of squares that the knight can move to. For a knight in the center of the board there are eight possible squares it can move to, being those squares that are either two columns and one row, or two rows and one column, removed from the current row, as shown below.

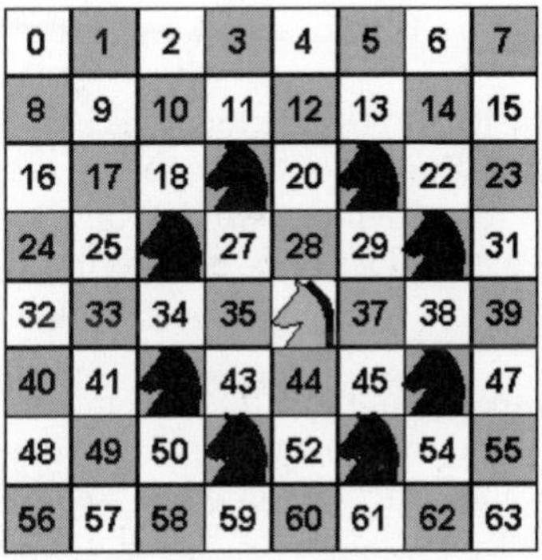

0	1	2	3	4	5	6	7
8	9	10	11	12	13	14	15
16	17	18		20		22	23
24	25		27	28	29		31
32	33	34	35		37	38	39
40	41		43	44	45		47
48	49	50		52		54	55
56	57	58	59	60	61	62	63

However, we have to consider the case where some of these squares are unavailable because they are off the edge of the board, and we also have to eliminate any squares that have already been visited. The logic I have used is simple, if verbose; it simply examines each of the eight candidate squares in turn:

```
   <xsl:template name="list-possible-moves">
      <xsl:param name="board"/>
      <xsl:param name="square"/>
      <xsl:variable name="row" select="$square div 8"/>
      <xsl:variable name="column" select="$square mod 8"/>
       <xsl:if test="$row &gt; 1 and $column &gt; 0
                    and $board/square[($square - 17) + 1]=''">
           <move><xsl:value-of select="$square - 17"/></move>
       </xsl:if>
       <xsl:if test="$row &gt; 1 and $column &lt; 7
                    and $board/square[($square - 15) + 1]=''">
           <move><xsl:value-of select="$square - 15"/></move>
       </xsl:if>
       <xsl:if test="$row &gt; 0 and $column &gt; 1
                    and $board/square[($square - 10) + 1]=''">
           <move><xsl:value-of select="$square - 10"/></move>
       </xsl:if>
       <xsl:if test="$row &gt; 0 and $column &lt; 6
                    and $board/square[($square - 6) + 1]=''">
           <move><xsl:value-of select="$square - 6"/></move>
       </xsl:if>
       <xsl:if test="$row &lt; 6 and $column &gt; 0
                    and $board/square[($square + 15) + 1]=''">
           <move><xsl:value-of select="$square + 15"/></move>
```

```
      <xsl:if test="$row &lt; 6 and $column &lt; 7
                    and $board/square[($square + 17) + 1]=''">
          <move><xsl:value-of select="$square + 17"/></move>
      </xsl:if>
      <xsl:if test="$row &lt; 7 and $column &gt; 1
                    and $board/square[($square + 6) + 1]=''">
          <move><xsl:value-of select="$square + 6"/></move>
      </xsl:if>
      <xsl:if test="$row &lt; 7 and $column &lt; 6
                    and $board/square[($square + 10) + 1]=''">
          <move><xsl:value-of select="$square + 10"/></move>
      </xsl:if>

  </xsl:template>
```

So having found the possible moves we can make, we need to select one of them and make it. This is the job of the `try-possible-moves` template.

This template is quite complex. It's worth looking at it carefully.

First, it checks whether the list of possible moves is empty. If it is, it takes the **<xsl:otherwise>** route at the end of the template body, which returns the special value «##» indicating that this attempt to find a route through the chessboard failed. As I've mentioned, my "least number of exits" algorithm in fact never does fail, but it's as well to be sure.

In the normal case, there are one or more possible moves, and we call the template `find-best-move` to find the best one (that is, the one with fewest exits). Just in case we need to backtrack, we also form a list of other possible moves, containing all the moves except the chosen one, so that we can use these later if we need to.

Now we execute the chosen move, which is simply a case of calling the `place-knight` template, which I described earlier, to place the knight on the chosen square and generate a new board.

And now we can repeat the process: except that as usual in XSLT, when we want to repeat, we recurse. If the board still has unvisited squares (recognized by an empty `<square/>` element), we call the «`make-moves`» template, described above, to calculate the rest of the tour. If not, we output the value of the final board. This output value is passed right down through all 64 levels of recursion to the «`$final-board`» variable in the root template, which is then passed to the «`print-board`» template to create the final display.

```
  <xsl:template name="try-possible-moves">

     <xsl:param name="move"/>
     <xsl:param name="board"/>
     <xsl:param name="square"/>
     <xsl:param name="possible-moves"/>

     <xsl:choose>
     <xsl:when test="$possible-moves">

        <!-- if at least one move is possible, find the best one -->
```

```
      <xsl:variable name="best-move">
         <xsl:call-template name="find-best-move">
            <xsl:with-param name="board" select="$board"/>
            <xsl:with-param name="possible-moves"
                                        select="$possible-moves"/>
         </xsl:call-template>
      </xsl:variable>

      <!-- find the list of possible moves excluding the best one -->

      <xsl:variable name="other-possible-moves"
                    select="$possible-moves[. != $best-move]"/>

      <!-- update the board to make the move chosen as the best one -->

      <xsl:variable name="next-board">
         <xsl:call-template name="place-knight">
            <xsl:with-param name="move" select="$move"/>
            <xsl:with-param name="board" select="$board"/>
            <xsl:with-param name="square" select="$best-move"/>
          </xsl:call-template>
      </xsl:variable>

      <!-- now make further moves, until the board is complete -->

      <xsl:variable name="final-board">
         <xsl:choose>
         <xsl:when test="$next-board/square = ''">
                    <!-- if there is an empty square -->
            <xsl:call-template name="make-moves">
               <xsl:with-param name="move" select="$move + 1"/>
               <xsl:with-param name="board" select="$next-board"/>
               <xsl:with-param name="square" select="$best-move"/>
            </xsl:call-template>
         </xsl:when>
         <xsl:otherwise>
             <xsl:copy-of select="$next-board"/>
         </xsl:otherwise>
         </xsl:choose>
      </xsl:variable>

       <!-- if the final board has the special value '##', we got stuck,
            and have to choose the next best of the possible moves.
            This is done by a recursive call. In practice,
            we never do get stuck, so this path is not taken. -->

      <xsl:choose>
      <xsl:when test="$final-board='##'">
         <xsl:call-template name="try-possible-moves">
            <xsl:with-param name="board" select="$board"/>
            <xsl:with-param name="square" select="$square"/>
            <xsl:with-param name="move" select="$move"/>
            <xsl:with-param name="possible-moves"
                                     select="$other-possible-moves"/>
         </xsl:call-template>
      </xsl:when>
      <xsl:otherwise>
         <xsl:copy-of select="$final-board"/>
      </xsl:otherwise>
   </xsl:choose>
   </xsl:when>

   <xsl:otherwise>
      <!-- if there is no possible move, we return the special value '##'
         as the final state of the board, to indicate that we got stuck -->
      <xsl:value-of select="'##'"/>
   </xsl:otherwise>
   </xsl:choose>
</xsl:template>
```

The one thing remaining is to look at the template «find-best-move», which from a set of possible moves chooses the best one, namely the move to the square with fewest exits.

As always, the logic is recursive. We keep track of the best move so far, and the number of exits that the best move so far possesses. If the first move in the list (the *trial move*) is better than the best move so far, it replaces the previous best, and we then call the template to process the other moves in the list. The final output is the best move after examining the whole list.

To find the number of exits for a given move, we create a trial board, and make that move by calling the «place-knight» template described earlier. Using this board, we then call the «list-possible-moves» template, also described earlier, to see what moves would be available after the trial move. We aren't interested in the details of these moves, only in how many there are, which we can find out simply by examining the length of the list.

We can now calculate two variables: the best move so far, and the least number of exits, based on whether the trial move is better than the previous best. If the move is the best one so far, it is output. Finally, the «find-best-move» template calls itself recursively to process the remaining moves in the list. On completion, the value returned by the template is the best move, that is, the square to which the knight should move next.

```
<xsl:template name="find-best-move">
   <xsl:param name="board"/>
   <xsl:param name="possible-moves"/>
   <xsl:param name="fewest-exits" select="9"/>
   <xsl:param name="best-so-far" select="'XX'"/>

   <xsl:variable name="trial-move"
                 select="number($possible-moves[1])"/>

   <xsl:variable name="other-possible-moves"
                 select="$possible-moves[position() &gt; 1]"/>

   <!-- try making the first move -->

   <xsl:variable name="trial-board">
      <xsl:call-template name="place-knight">
         <xsl:with-param name="board" select="$board"/>
            <xsl:with-param name="move" select="99"/>
            <xsl:with-param name="square" select="$trial-move"/>
         </xsl:call-template>
   </xsl:variable>

   <!-- see how many moves would be possible the next time -->

   <xsl:variable name="trial-move-exit-list">
      <xsl:call-template name="list-possible-moves">
         <xsl:with-param name="board" select="$trial-board"/>
         <xsl:with-param name="square" select="$trial-move"/>
      </xsl:call-template>
   </xsl:variable>

   <xsl:variable name="number-of-exits"
                    select="count($trial-move-exit-list/move)"/>
   <!-- determine whether this trial move is the best so far -->
```

```
    <xsl:variable name="minimum-exits">
       <xsl:choose>
       <xsl:when test="$number-of-exits &lt; $fewest-exits">
          <xsl:value-of select="$number-of-exits"/>
       </xsl:when>
       <xsl:otherwise>
          <xsl:value-of select="$fewest-exits"/>
       </xsl:otherwise>
       </xsl:choose>
    </xsl:variable>

    <!-- determine the best move (the one with fewest exits) so far -->

    <xsl:variable name="new-best-so-far">
       <xsl:choose>
       <xsl:when test="$number-of-exits &lt; $fewest-exits">
          <xsl:value-of select="$trial-move"/>
       </xsl:when>
       <xsl:otherwise>
          <xsl:value-of select="$best-so-far"/>
       </xsl:otherwise>
       </xsl:choose>
    </xsl:variable>

    <!-- if there are other possible moves, consider them too, using a recursive
         call. Otherwise return the best move found. -->

    <xsl:choose>
    <xsl:when test="$other-possible-moves">
       <xsl:call-template name="find-best-move">
          <xsl:with-param name="board" select="$board"/>
          <xsl:with-param name="possible-moves"
                                 select="$other-possible-moves"/>
          <xsl:with-param name="fewest-exits" select="$minimum-exits"/>
          <xsl:with-param name="best-so-far" select="$new-best-so-far"/>
       </xsl:call-template>
    </xsl:when>
    <xsl:otherwise>
       <xsl:value-of select="$new-best-so-far"/>
    </xsl:otherwise>
    </xsl:choose>

</xsl:template>
```

And that's it.

Running the Stylesheet

To run the stylesheet, download it from the Wrox web site, and execute it against an arbitrary source document (for example, against itself). With Saxon, for example, try:

```
saxon tour.xsl tour.xsl start=b6 >tour.html
```

and then display `tour.html` in your browser. The details of how to supply a global parameter vary for each XSLT implementation: if you don't supply one, the tour will start at the a1 square.

As written, this stylesheet requires an XSLT 1.1 processor. It can be adapted to work with any XSLT 1.0 processor that allows conversion of a tree to a node-set. A version of the stylesheet that works with MSXML3, by using the `msxsl:node-set()` function, is included in the download file under the name `ms-tour.xsl`. This includes a self-referential `<?xml-stylesheet?>` processing instruction, so you can execute the knight's tour (with default parameters) simply by double-clicking on this file in Windows Explorer.

Observations

The knight's tour not a very typical stylesheet, but it's one that illustrates the computational power of the XSLT language, and in particular the essential part that recursion plays in any stylesheet that needs to do any non-trivial calculation or handle non-trivial data structures. And although you will never need to use XSLT to solve chess problems, you may just find yourself doing complex calculations to work out where best to place a set of images on a page, or how many columns to use to display a list of telephone numbers, or which of today's news stories should be featured most prominently given your knowledge of the user's preferences.

So if you're wondering why I selected this example, there are two answers: firstly, I enjoyed writing it, and secondly, I hope it will have persuaded you that there are no algorithms too complex to be written in XSLT.

Summary

In this chapter I've presented three complete stylesheets, all similar in complexity to many of those you will have to write for real applications. I tried to choose three that were very different in character, reflecting three of the design patterns introduced in the previous chapter, namely:

- A rule-based stylesheet for converting a document containing semantic markup into HTML. In this stylesheet, most of the logic was concerned with generating the right HTML display style for each XML element, and with establishing tables of contents, section numbering, and internal hyperlinks, with some interesting logic for laying data out in a table.
- A navigational stylesheet for presenting selected information from a hierarchical data structure. This stylesheet was primarily concerned with following links with the XML data structure, and it was able to use the full power of XPath expression to achieve this. This stylesheet also gave us the opportunity to explore some of the systems issues surrounding XSLT; when and where to do the XML-to-HTML conversion, and how to handle data in non-XML legacy formats.
- A computational stylesheet for calculating the result of a moderately complex algorithm. This stylesheet demonstrated that even quite complex algorithms are quite possible to code in XSLT once you have mastered recursion. Such algorithms are much easier to implement in XSLT 1.1 than in XSLT 1.0, because of the ability to use temporary trees to hold working data.

To get the second stylesheet to work, I had to use some non-standard interfaces provided by the various XSLT implementations. In the appendices of the book we'll take a more detailed look at some of the more widely-used XSLT processors available.

Microsoft MSXML3

This appendix contains information about using Microsoft's MSXML3 product, which includes an XSLT 1.0 processor integrated with an XML parser and other tools.

MSXML3 is the latest version of Microsoft's XML and XSLT technology. It contains an XML parser supporting a DOM interface that is an extended implementation of the W3C DOM Recommendation, an XSLT processor which implements the W3C XSLT 1.0 Recommendation, and an XPath 1.0 processor which can be used either in conjunction with XSLT stylesheets or directly against the DOM document. It also contains a schema processor which implements Microsoft's own version of XML schemas (which is significantly different from the almost-finalized W3C definition of an XML schema).

This appendix is **not** designed to cover the original 1998 versions of MSXML, which shipped with IE4 and later with IE5 and IE5.5. These implemented a version of XSL based on the draft specifications as they existed at the time, with many Microsoft extensions. This 1998 dialect of XSLT is recognizably similar to XSLT 1.0 and XSLT 1.1 as described in this book, but there are so many differences of detail that it is best regarded as a separate language. I refer to it in this book as **WD-xsl** (read this as "working draft XSL"), because stylesheets using this dialect use the namespace declaration «`xmlns:xsl="http://www.w3.org/TR/WD-xsl"`», rather than the XSLT namespace «`xmlns:xsl="http://www.w3.org/1999/XSL/Transform"`»

> **In Microsoft documentation, a reference to XSL generally means the WD-xsl dialect. When they want to refer to XSLT, they call it XSLT.**

At the time of writing, MSXML3 is a production release, and is fully supported, but it is not yet shipped as a standard component of other products such as Internet Explorer, Windows 2000, or SQL Server. These products are still delivered with older versions of the MSXML product that only support the WD-xsl dialect. The only way of getting MSXML3 is to download it from Microsoft's web site. You can find it by following the download links at http://msdn.microsoft.com/xml/.

I'll start this appendix by looking at the contents of an MSXML3 stylesheet: that won't take long, because the conformance to XSLT 1.0 is very close. Then I'll explain the various different ways of installing and running the product for use within the Internet Explorer browser, which will form the bulk of the chapter. After this, I'll briefly cover how to run MSXML3 on the server, typically from an ASP page. The appendix ends with a summary of the main classes and methods used in the MSXML API.

MSXML Versions

At the time of writing, Microsoft has released several versions of the MSXML product. The original beta version 1.0 was quickly superseded by version 2.0, which is supplied with the final release of Internet Explorer 5 and 5.5, and with Windows 2000. There is also a full SDK for it, supplied as part of the Internet Explorer and Windows 2000 SDKs. MSXML as a software package includes both an XML parser and an XSLT processor, and although our interest in this book is in the XSLT processor, the product is frequently referred to simply as "the MSXML parser". The version 2.0 product, as we've seen, implemented something close to the December 1998 XSL working draft from the W3C, together with some Microsoft extensions designed to simplify common operations and handle non-W3C-specified activities like loading and saving XML documents.

Version 3, MSXML3, was first released in March 2000 and then reissued in a rapid series of releases with increasing functionality until the production release in October 2000. It is generally expected that it will be included as a standard part of Internet Explorer 6. As we've mentioned, it is now a fully-supported Microsoft product, but can only be obtained by downloading from the web.

MSXML3 continues to support WD-xsl syntax as well as XSLT syntax. However, you must use one or the other, you can't mix them. They are distinguished by the namespace URI of the `<xsl:stylesheet>` element:

- WD-xsl stylesheets use the namespace URI `http://www.w3.org/TR/WD-xsl`
- XSLT stylesheets use the namespace URI `http://www.w3.org/1999/XSL/Transform`

If you use the WD-xsl namespace, you can't use XSLT syntax, and if you use the XSLT namespace, you can't use WD-xsl syntax. XSLT features missing from WD-xsl include variables, named templates, attribute value templates, keys, `<xsl:import>`, and several of the XPath axes. There are also numerous differences of syntax and notation.

It's possible that for practical reasons, because all your users have IE5 installed, you have no choice but to write stylesheets using the WD-xsl dialect. If you do this, you need to be aware that very many of the constructs described in this book will not work. You should also be aware that you are using an obsolescent technology. The documentation for WD-xsl is no longer included with the MSXML3 download; you can find it on the Microsoft web site, but it is well hidden, because the company is now promoting the XSLT syntax instead.

MSXML3 Stylesheets

MSXML3 offers a very good level of conformance to XSLT 1.0. But it doesn't currently support any of the new XSLT 1.1 syntax described in this book. However, it does provide its own alternatives, for example:

- You can't directly use a temporary tree (or result tree fragment in XSLT 1.0 parlance) as a node-set. You can use a variable that refers to a temporary tree in any context where you could use a string, but you cannot use it in contexts that require a node-set. For example, you cannot write «`$tree/element`», or `<xsl:apply-templates select="$tree">`, or `<xsl:for-each select="$tree">`. What you can do in these contexts, however, is to use the **`msxsl:node-set()`** extension function to convert the tree explicitly to a node-set.
- You can't produce multiple output files using the **`<xsl:document>`** element. Perhaps because MSXML3 is designed very much with the browser environment in mind, it does not support any mechanism for producing multiple output files. You can get around this by running multiple transformations on the same source document, using a parameter to control which part of the output you want to produce on each run. Alternatively, it is quite easy to write a JScript extension function, to be called from the stylesheet, which takes a result tree fragment as a parameter, and serializes it as XML in a file.
- You can't use the **`<xsl:script>`** element for declaring external functions. However, MSXML3 does support an **`<msxsl:script>`** element with almost identical functionality. Microsoft's processor can call external functions written in any of the typical Microsoft scripting languages such as JScript and VBScript, but it cannot directly call Java methods. Of course, you can call any COM object by writing a simple JScript wrapper function.

Microsoft's implementation of XSLT is very close to the XSLT 1.0 standard, so we don't need to say very much more about it in this Appendix. But in this section we'll look at some of the restrictions and extensions, and areas where Microsoft have used the discretion that the standard gives to implementors.

Extensibility

There is no support in MSXML3 for extension elements.

Extension functions can be implemented by coding VBScript or JScript modules inside a top-level **`<msxsl:script>`** element. This is very similar to the **`<xsl:script>`** element described in the current working draft of XSLT 1.1.

Here is an example stylesheet that uses such an extension:

Example: Using VBScript in an MSXML3 Stylesheet

This example shows a stylesheet that converts dimensions in inches to the equivalent in millimeters.

Source

The source file is `inches.xml`. Double-click on it in Windows Explorer to invoke the stylesheet.

```
<?xml version="1.0" encoding="iso-8859-1"?>
<?xml-stylesheet type="text/xsl" href="to-mm.xsl"?>
<dimensions>
The size of the picture is <inches>5</inches> by
<inches>12</inches>.
</dimensions>
```

Stylesheet

The stylesheet is `to-mm.xsl`

It contains a simple VBScript function within an **`<msxsl:script>`** element, and invokes this as an extension function from the template rule for the **`<inches>`** element.

```
<xsl:stylesheet
      xmlns:xsl="http://www.w3.org/1999/XSL/Transform"
      version="1.0"
      xmlns:extra="urn:extra-functions"
>
<msxsl:script xmlns:msxsl="urn:schemas-microsoft-com:xslt"
       language="VBScript"
       implements-prefix="extra"
>

Function ToMillimetres(inches)
   ToMillimetres = inches * 25.4
End Function

</msxsl:script>

<xsl:output method="html"/>

<xsl:template match="/" >
<html><body><p>
   <xsl:apply-templates/>
</p></body></html>
</xsl:template>
```

```
<xsl:template match="inches">
   <xsl:text> </xsl:text>
   <xsl:value-of select="format-number(extra:ToMillimetres(number(.)),
                           '0.00')"/>
   <xsl:text>mm </xsl:text>
</xsl:template>

</xsl:stylesheet>
```

Output

The following text is displayed in the browser:

```
The size of the picture is 127.00mm by 304.80mm.
```

These scripts can call COM objects named in the system registry in the usual way. However, if the stylesheet is running in the browser, the user's security settings may prevent your script from instantiating a client-side object.

Don't confuse script that is invoked by the stylesheet with script that is part of the HTML page that invokes the stylesheet, or with script that is part of the HTML generated by the stylesheet. If you use all three, you will need to keep a very clear head to remember which is which. You should only use **<msxsl:script>** for functions that are to be called from within XPath expressions written in the stylesheet. Conversely, if the stylesheet contains **<script>** literal result elements, these contain code that is to form part of the generated HTML page: this code is not available to be executed as part of the transformation process.

The msxsl:node-set() Function

MSXML3 conforms to XSLT 1.0, and it therefore enforces the restrictions defined in XSLT 1.0 on the use of tree-valued variables (result tree fragments). These restrictions apply to a variable whose value is defined by a construct such as the following:

```
<xsl:variable name="tree">
   <tag>value</tag>
</xsl:variable>
```

In particular, a tree-valued variable cannot be used:

- In a path expression such as «$tree/tag»
- In the select expression of **<xsl:for-each>**
- In the select expression of **<xsl:apply-templates>**.

To get round these restrictions, MSXML3, like many other XSLT 1.0 processors, provides an extension function that converts a tree to a node-set. The resulting node-set holds a single node, the root of the tree. So you can write:

- `<xsl:value-of select="count(msxsl:node-set($tree)/tag)"/>`
- `<xsl:for-each select="msxsl:node-set($tree)">`
- `<xsl:apply-templates select="msxsl:node-set($tree)"/>`

The namespace URI for the **node-set()** extension function (as for the **<msxsl:script>** element) is `xmlns:msxsl="urn:schemas-microsoft-com:xslt"`. Of course, you can use any namespace prefix you like so long as you use the correct namespace URI.

System Properties

MSXML3 currently returns the following values for the **system-property()** function:

System property name	Value
xsl:version	1
xsl:vendor	Microsoft
xsl:vendor-url	http://www.microsoft.com
msxsl:version	3

Restrictions

Microsoft claims full compliance with XSLT 1.0 and XPath 1.0. At present there is no independent conformance testing of XSLT processors, so you can only take a vendor's claims to conformance on trust. But the fact that they claim conformance means that in theory any non-conformances found are bugs, and are therefore likely to be fixed.

There are one or two gray areas where conformance is not quite as strict as some people would like. These include:

- Handling of whitespace nodes. The normal way of supplying input to Microsoft's XSLT processor is in the form of a DOM, and the default option in MSXML3 for building a DOM is to remove whitespace text nodes as the text is parsed. The result is that **<xsl:preserve-space>** in the stylesheet appears to have no effect, because by the time the XSLT processor gets to see the data, there are no whitespace text nodes left to preserve. If you want conformant behavior in this area, set the `preserveWhitespace` property of the `DOMDocument` object to `True`, before loading the document. The same applies to the stylesheet; if you want to use **<xsl:text>** to control output of whitespace, particularly when generating output in a space-sensitive format such as comma-separated values, then load the stylesheet with `preserveWhitespace` set to `True`.
- Normalization of text nodes. XSLT and XPath specify that adjacent text nodes in the tree are always merged into a single node. MSXML3 uses a DOM as its internal data structure, and the DOM does not impose the same rule. Although MSXML3 does a good job at creating a correct XPath view of the underlying DOM tree, this is one area where the mapping is incomplete. The two common cases where adjacent text nodes are not merged are firstly, when one of the text nodes represents the contents of a `CDATA` section in the source XML, and secondly, when one of them represents the expanded text of an entity reference (other than the built-in entity references such as «`<`»). This makes it dangerous to use a construct such as `<xsl:value-of select="text()"/>` because MSXML3 will return only the first of the text nodes, that is, the text up to the start of an entity or `CDATA` boundary. It's safer to output the value of an element by writing `<xsl:value-of select="."/>`.
- The **<xsl:message>** instruction has no effect, unless you specify «`terminate="yes"`».

Installing the MSXML3 Product

The current release of the MSXML product is available from the XML download page at Microsoft's web site. To download it, go to :

http://msdn.microsoft.com/downloads/webtechnology/xml/msxml.asp

After the file `msxml3.exe` has been downloaded to your machine, simply double-click on it to install the software.

You will almost certainly want to install the SDK (software development kit) as well, if only to get the documentation. This is available from the same web page. It comes in the form of an executable `xmlsdk.exe`, which again you can install simply by downloading it to your machine and then double-clicking on it. The documentation is in the form of a compiled HTML Help file `xmlsdk.chm` which the default installation places in `c:\Program Files\Microsoft XML Parser SDK\Docs` – open it by double-clicking on it in Explorer.

By default, MSXML3 runs in **side-by-side** mode with the older version of MSXML that will already be installed on your machine if you have IE5 or IE5.5. This means it will only be invoked by applications that specifically request it; and in particular, it will not be used by default by Internet Explorer. As an XSLT user, you probably want to install MSXML3 in **replace** mode, in which case all calls to the standard parser from applications such as Internet Explorer, are redirected to MSXML3. To install MSXML3 in replace mode, you'll need to run a little utility called `xmlinst.exe`, which is available as a separate download from the Microsoft MSDN download site.

> **Don't attempt to run MSXML3 in replace mode on a production server where products such as SQL Server or Biztalk Server are in use. These products rely on the default processor being MSXML2.**

Also on the web site is a page full of useful information about Microsoft's XML initiative and strategy at http://msdn.microsoft.com/xml/default.asp. This includes samples, demos, and articles about XML and related technologies.

The download page also provides links to several tools that you may find useful:

- Internet Explorer Tools for Validating XML and Viewing XSLT Output. These provide a plug-in to Internet Explorer allowing you to perform two functions by clicking the right mouse button: validating the source XML, and viewing the output of the XSLT transformation. I'll say a little bit more about the viewing tool in a later section.

- Microsoft XSL ISAPI Extension. This web server-based extension makes it easier to perform server-side XML/XSL transformations. It can automatically execute an XSL style sheet on the server, allowing you to choose alternative stylesheets based on browser type. It manages stylesheet caching for improved server performance, has the capability to specify the output encoding, and provides customizable error messages. Unfortunately, though, it doesn't distinguish whether the browser has MSXML2 or MSXML3 installed.

- XSL Stylesheet for XML Schemas. This stylesheet (which uses WD-xsl) can be used to generate documentation for XML schemas based on the syntax. I haven't discussed XML schemas much in this book. The XSLT specification doesn't use them yet, because the standard isn't completely finished (it's currently a Candidate Recommendation). But Microsoft implemented their own version of XML schemas, and MSXML takes advantage of these as an alternative to using DTDs.
- XSL to XSLT Converter. This stylesheet updates WD-xsl stylesheets to the XSLT-compliant syntax, making them suitable for use with the MSXML3 product and others. It doesn't do a 100% job of the conversion, but it looks after all of the most common differences.

Note that you must install Internet Explorer (IE5, or IE5.5) in order for MSXML3 to be fully functional. This is true even if you only want to use MSXML3 on a server.

MSXML ProgID and ClassID Information

Rather than use the same file name, ProgID and ClassID for the three versions, Microsoft has given each one different values so that they can be installed and run in parallel:

Parser Version	DLL Name	ProgID and ClassID
MSXML 2.0	`msxml.dll`	**ProgID:** `Microsoft.XMLDOM` or `MSXML.DOMDocument` **ClassID:** {2933bf90-7b36-11d2-b20e-00c04f983e60}
MSXML 2.6	`msxml2.dll`	**ProgID:** `MSXML2.DOMDocument` **ClassID:** {f6d90f11-9c73-11d3-b32e-00c04f990bb4}
MSXML 3.0	`msxml3.dll`	**ProgID:** `MSXML2.DOMDocument.3.0` **ClassID:** {f5078f32-c551-11d3-89b9-0000f81fe221}

The terminology here may be confusing. These objects use the name "`DOMDocument`" because when you create an instance, it will hold an in-memory representation of an XML document, conforming to Microsoft's version of the W3C Document Object Model (DOM). The `Document` object has a method `load` which allows this in-memory document to be built from a source XML file. To do this, of course, the XML has to be parsed. There is no separate `Parser` object, rather the XML parser is part of the functionality of the `Document` object. Microsoft has followed the policy of naming objects according to what information they contain (nouns), not according to what functions they perform (verbs).

The above table shows the `ProgID` and `ClassID` for running the parser in normal apartment-threaded mode. You can also run the parser in free-threaded mode by using an alternative `ProgID` or `ClassID` when you instantiate the component (note that the `ClassID`s vary only on the eighth character). You will probably want to do this when running MSXML3 on the server because frequently used stylesheets can then be cached in the `Application` object.

Parser Version	Free-threaded ProgID and ClassID
MSXML 2.0	**`ProgID:`** `Microsoft.FreeThreadedXMLDOM` or `MSXML.FreeThreadedDOMDocument` **`ClassID:`** {2933bf91-7b36-11d2-b20e-00c04f983e60}
MSXML 2.6	**`ProgID:`** `MSXML2.FreeThreadedDOMDocument` **`ClassID:`** {f6d90f12-9c73-11d3-b32e-00c04f990bb4}

MSXML 3.0	**`ProgID:`**
	`MSXML2.FreeThreadedDOMDocument.3.0`
	
	`ClassID:`
	`{f5078f33-c551-11d3-89b9-0000f81fe221}`

See the topic *GUID and ProgID Information* in the MSXML3 SDK help file (you can reach it via *XML Developer's Guide*, then *XML DOM User Guide*) for a full list of the `ProgID`s and `ClassID`s for the other objects that are implemented by the product – such as the `XMLHTTP` object, the `XSLTemplate` object, and the XMLDSO data-binding control.

Because the different versions of MSXML cause so much confusion, I have included in the download file for this appendix an HTML page `msxml-version.html`. This page tells you, when you display it in Internet Explorer, which version of MSXML is the default version on your system. It is based on a JScript routine written by Jarno Elovirta. You can run a more advanced version, which tells you about all the versions of the parser installed on your machine, at http://www.vbxml.com/parsers/sniffer/default.asp

Running MSXML in Replace Mode

I have already mentioned the utility program `xmlinst.exe`. This program can be used to change the settings in the system registry to specify how the parser versions are used. Running this program with no parameters (just download it into any folder and double-click on it) changes the registry entries on that machine so that the default ProgID «`MSXML.DOMDocument`» will actually instantiate the latest version of the parser, rather than the version 2.0 parser. This can be useful if your applications have this original ProgID string hard-coded in. See the topic *Running MSXML3 in Replace Mode* in the help file (you can reach it via *XML Developer's Guide*, then *XML DOM User Guide*) for a list of the command-line arguments that can be used with `xmlinst.exe` to make other changes to the registry settings.

If you don't run `xmlinst.exe`, then Internet Explorer will continue to use the old MSXML parser, unless you run scripts that explicitly tell it to load the new one. The effect of this is that if (as described on page 706) you double-click on an XML document whose **`<?xml-stylesheet?>`** processing instruction refers to an XSLT stylesheet, the old parser will not recognize the stylesheet, and you won't get any useful output. This is a common source of confusion, and as a general piece of advice, if you're using XSLT on a client machine I would advise running `xmlinst.exe` to make MSXML3 the default parser. The machine will still be able to execute WD-xsl stylesheets, because MSXML3 supports both.

Of course, if you use XSLT stylesheets on your web site you will also want to make sure that all your users have MSXML3 installed. The techniques to achieve this are beyond the scope of this book, but you will find some information about redistribution of the product on the Microsoft web site.

On the other hand, making MSXML3 the default parser isn't the right thing to do on a server, particularly if you have software such as SQL Server or Biztalk Server running on the machine. That's because these products assume the presence of the MSXML2 product. On the server, it's best to run MSXML3 in side-by-side mode (which means it can co-exist with earlier versions of the product), and to invoke it explicitly when required by using the ProgID «`MSXML2.DOMDocument.3.0`» or «`MSXML2.FreeThreadedDOMDocument.3.0`».

Using the Default Stylesheet

When you double-click on an XML document that has no associated stylesheet, Internet Explorer 5 will display an XML document directly, as a collapsible tree structure. This makes it easy to examine the document and see the element structure:

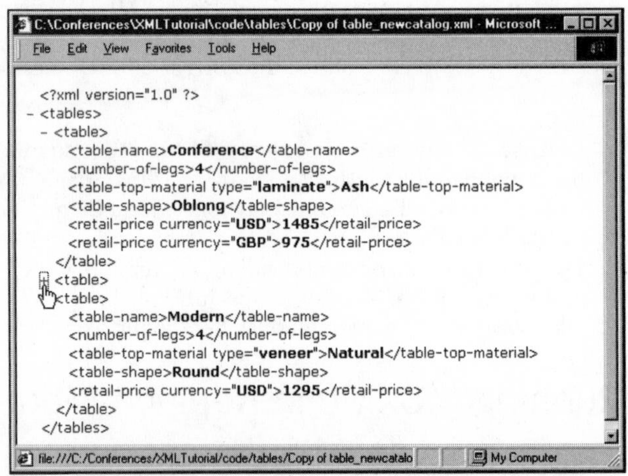

It does this by applying a default stylesheet to the document when it is loaded, and what you see is the result of the transformation specified by this stylesheet. This stylesheet is only used if you don't specify any other. In the next section, I'll show how to specify your own XSLT stylesheet to be used for the transformation.

If you load a document that is not well-formed, an error message is displayed instead:

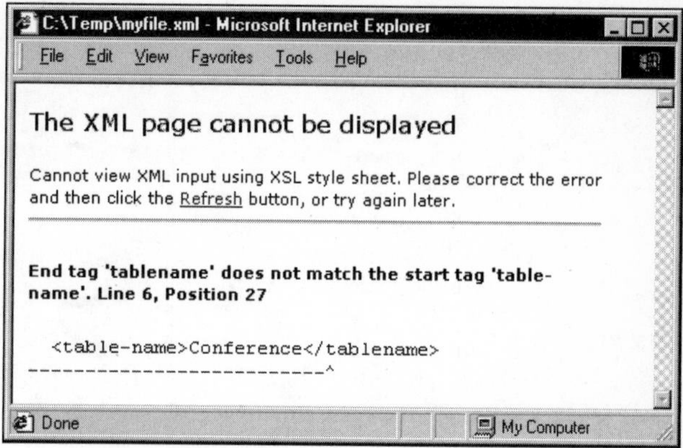

If you want to see the contents of the default stylesheet, type the URL `res://msxml.dll/DEFAULTSS.XSL` into your browser's address bar (the same stylesheet is produced by the URL `res://msxml3.dll/DEFAULTSS.XSL` from the MSXML3 parser).

This default stylesheet is currently written in the WD-xsl dialect. You can spot this because it uses the old namespace URI «`http://www.w3.org/TR/WD-xsl`», and because it uses obsolete XSL elements such as **`<xsl:entity-ref>`** and **`<xsl:node-name>`**.

Attaching an XSLT Stylesheet to a Document

The easiest way to display the result of an XSLT transformation is to attach the specific stylesheet to the XML document using an XML processing instruction. The simplest syntax is:

```
<?xml-stylesheet type="text/xsl" href="url_of_stylesheet"?>
```

For example, if you have a suitable stylesheet named `tablecatalog.xsl` in the same folder as the XML document, you can write:

```
<?xml-stylesheet type="text/xsl" href="tablecatalog.xsl"?>
```

This should be written after the **`<?xml version="1.0"?>`** XML declaration and any **`<!DOCTYPE>`** declaration, but before the start tag of the document element. For example:

```
<?xml version="1.0" ?>
<!DOCTYPE tables SYSTEM "tables.dtd">
<?xml-stylesheet type="text/xsl" href="tablecatalog.xsl"?>
<tables>
. . .
</tables>
```

The result could look like this:

MSXML3 only takes any notice of the first **<?xml-stylesheet?>** processing instruction in an XML document that specifies «`type="text/xsl"`», indicating an XSLT or WD-xsl stylesheet. However, it is possible to display XML documents using Cascading Stylesheets (CSS), and there can be any number of **<?xml-stylesheet?>** processing instructions in an XML document that specify CSS stylesheets (that is, have «`type="text/css"`»). Internet Explorer will choose the XSL stylesheet if it is present, otherwise it will merge the CSS stylesheets together in the same way as it would with multiple HTML **<LINK>** elements that specify CSS stylesheets.

The full list of attributes that can be used in the **<?xml-stylesheet?>** processing instruction is given in Chapter 3, page 107 but for XSLT stylesheets, Internet Explorer appears to ignore all except `type` and `href`. The `type` attribute must be «`text/xsl`», even though this is not the MIME type recommended by the W3C.

Debugging the stylesheet

If the stylesheet isn't well-formed XML, Internet Explorer will display an error message as shown in the example on page 705. These error messages usually identify the line where the error occurred, and so long as you understand XML terminology reasonably well, they are usually easy to fix.

If the stylesheet is well-formed at the XML level, but isn't valid according to the XSLT rules, you'll still get an error message, but this time it isn't always so explicit. For example, if you misspell the name of an XSLT instruction, you might get an error message like this:

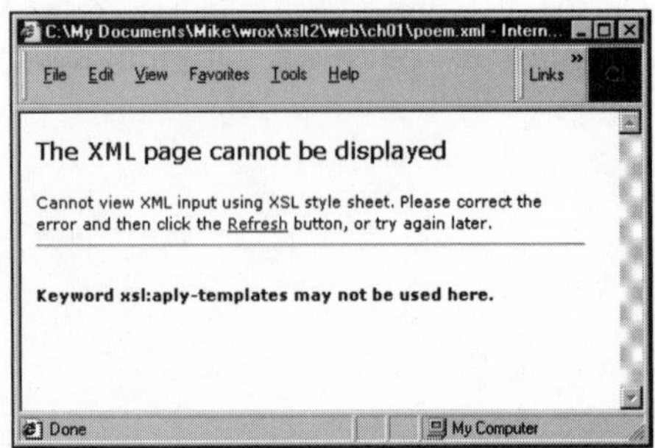

In this case there is no line number, so you are going to have to search the stylesheet to find the error. Frankly, as your stylesheets get longer, this can become a pain. You might well find it useful at this stage to install another XSLT processor, such as Saxon or Xalan, just because they make debugging much easier. If nothing else, every processor will occasionally produce error messages that seem obscure, and getting a second opinion in such cases will often be the quickest way to see what's wrong.

Also, there will be times when you are convinced that MSXML3 is producing the wrong output. At these times, running your code through another processor will usually confirm that the output, however unexpected, is actually correct. And very occasionally, of course, you may find that two processors produce different results, in which case your original suspicions might be confirmed.

Another tool you might find useful is Microsoft's `msxsl.exe` interface, which allows transformations to be run from the command line. This can be downloaded from the MSDN site; it's a very small download, less than 60Kb, so it's well worth the effort. This allows you to run a transformation using a command such as

```
MSXML source.xml style.xsl -o out.xml param=value
```

Unfortunately, though, the diagnostics are still very primitive, the following being a fairly typical example (which I encountered somewhere in a 400-line stylesheet):

```
Error occurred while compiling stylesheet 'test75.xsl'.
Code:   0x80004005
Expected token 'eof' found 'NUMBER'.
1.2-->.2<--
```

Eventually, you will get to the point where your stylesheet is syntactically correct. But that's not the end of the story; at your first attempt, it probably won't produce the output you intended. This is particularly true because XSLT is a very tolerant language: if you write «`select="title"`» when you meant «`select="Title"`» or «`select="'title'"`», the result will simply be that nothing is output, because no **`<title>`** element was found.

Your instinct at this point is probably to click on View Source in Internet Explorer. Unfortunately this is no use at all, as it only shows you the orginal XML. What you want to see is the HTML output from the stylesheet.

At this point Microsoft's tool for displaying XSLT output comes in handy. I mentioned this previously; it's one of the tools you can download from the MSDN download site. Installation is rather quirky (you have to right-click on the `.inf` file and select install) but if you follow the instructions to the letter, it works. Once you've installed this tool, you will be able to right-click in Internet Explorer and see the menu option View XSL Output. Selecting this option gives you a listing of the HTML that the stylesheet has produced, and which the browser is trying to display.

If seeing the HTML output isn't enough to help you find a problem, a useful technique is to insert diagnostic output in the form of comments. For example, add an instruction such as the following to the start of each template rule:

```
<xsl:comment>Entering template rule for xyz element</xsl:comment>
```

These comments won't show up in the browser display, but they will be visible with the View XSL Output tool. (With other XSLT processors you can use **<xsl:message>**, but this has no effect with MSXML3 under Internet Explorer, unless you use the draconian «`terminate="yes"`» option).

If this tool isn't enough to reveal what's wrong, then I really would suggest installing some extra software. MSXML3 is great for production running of client-side stylesheets, but it's not yet the world's most wonderful development environment. One of the great benefits of the XSLT scene is that there are so many free products around, so make use of them. Xalan, for example, has an interactive debugger, and Saxon has a useful option for tracing the complete stylesheet execution.

Controlling XSLT Processing with Client-side Script

Using the **<?xml-stylesheet?>** processing instruction is just one of the ways that an XSL stylesheet can be applied to an XML document. An alternative approach is to write script code in an HTML page which explicitly loads the XML document and the stylesheets, and invokes the transformation. This is where the `ProgID` and `ClassID` strings for the objects that I showed earlier come into play.

Creating an Instance of an MSXML Document

To create an instance of a DOM Document that will use the version 3.0 MSXML parser, you can use several approaches.

In VBScript:

```
Dim doc
Set doc = CreateObject("MSXML2.DOMDocument.3.0")
```

In JScript:

```
var doc = new ActiveXObject('MSXML2.DOMDocument.3.0');
```

In Visual Basic, you will first need to add a reference to the component DLL using the Project | References dialog. You can see the three versions of the parser listed in the screenshot here:

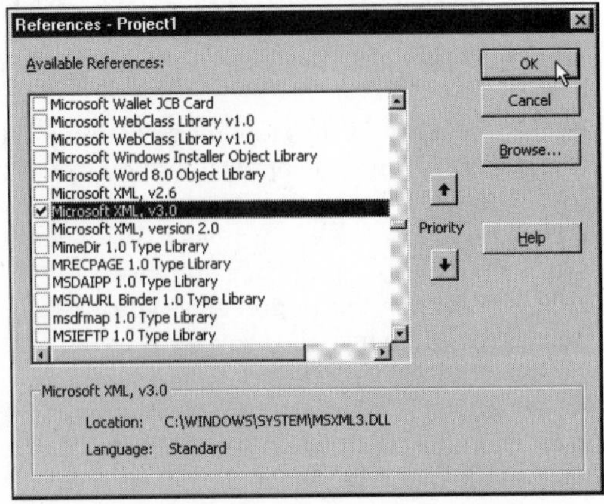

Then you can use the `CreateObject` method:

```
Dim doc
Set doc = CreateObject("MSXML2.DOMDocument.3.0")
```

However, the more usual technique is to use the `New` keyword, which then allows the development environment to display pop-up syntax help and member-lists:

```
Dim doc As New DOMDocument3.0
```

Loading XML and XSLT Documents

Once you've created an instance of a `Document` object, you can use the Microsoft-specific methods to load the content. To load an XML file, use the `load` method:

```
'in VBScript or Visual Basic
doc.Load "c:\temp\myfile.xml"
```

```
//in JScript
doc.load('c:\temp\myfile.xml');
```

If the XML is held in a string rather than in a file (which can arise, for example, because you have read the XML out of a relational database using SQL or ADO) you can use the `loadXML` method:

```
'in VBScript or Visual Basic:
Dim strXML
strXML = "<?xml version='1.0'?><test><testitem/></test>"
doc.LoadXML strXML
```

```
//in JScript
var strXML = '<?xml version="1.0"?><test><testitem/></test>';
doc.loadXML(strXML);
```

You can then set any other properties you need for the MSXML3 parser. For example, it is usually a good idea to set the `async` property to `False` so that parsing of the document is completed before the transformation starts. However, for maximum performance you can load the source document and the stylesheet concurrently, by leaving this at the default value of `True`. This also allows you to give the user feedback on progress as the document is loaded. There's an example of how to use asynchronous loading on page 712 below.

You can also turn on validation in the parser. By default, the parser only checks that the XML is well-formed as it loads and parses documents. By setting the `validateOnParse` property to `True`, you can force the parser to validate the structure of the document against any DTD or Schema that it specifies:

```
'in VBScript or Visual Basic
doc.ValidateOnParse = True
```

```
//in JScript
doc.validateOnParse = true;
```

Checking for Load Errors, Well-Formedness and Validity

After the parser has attempted to load a document, you can check if there was an error by examining the properties of the `parseError` object that the `DOMDocument` object exposes. The `parseError` object provides seven properties that reflect the most recent load error:

Property	Description
`errorCode`	The standard error number of the error that occurred.
`filepos`	The character position within the entire file where the error was discovered.
`line`	The number of the line where the error was discovered.
`linepos`	The character position within this line where the error was discovered.
`reason`	A text description of the error.
`srcText`	The source code (text) of the line where the error was discovered.
`url`	The URL or path of the file that was loaded.

By checking the `errorCode` property, you can tell if an error occurred. The value will be non-zero if the parser has detected an error. The following code samples show how the error details can be retrieved and displayed:

In VBScript or Visual Basic:

```
'check if there was an error while loading
If doc.parseError.errorCode <> 0 Then
  'create the error message
  Dim strError
  strError = "Invalid XML file !" & vbCrlf _
           & "File URL: " & doc.parseError.url & vbCrlf _
           & "Line No.: " & doc.parseError.line & vbCrlf _
           & "Character: " & doc.parseError.linepos & vbCrlf _
           & "File Position: " & doc.parseError.filepos & vbCrlf _
           & "Source Text: " & doc.parseError.srcText & vbCrlf _
           & "Error Code: " & doc.parseError.errorCode & vbCrlf _
           & "Description: " & doc.parseError.reason
  MsgBox strError  'display error message
Else
  'loaded OK so continue processing
  ...
End If
```

In JScript:

```
...
// check if there was an error while loading
if (doc.parseError.errorCode != 0) {
   // create the error message
   var strError = new String;
   strError = 'Invalid XML file !\n'
         + 'File URL: ' + doc.parseError.url + '\n '
```

```
            + 'Line No.: ' + doc.parseError.line + '\n '
            + 'Character: ' + doc.parseError.linepos + '\n '
            + 'File Position: ' + doc.parseError.filepos + '\n '
            + 'Source Text: ' + doc.parseError.srcText + '\n '
            + 'Error Code: ' + doc.parseError.errorCode + '\n '
            + 'Description: ' + doc.parseError.reason;
      alert(strError);  // display error message
      }
   else {
      // loaded OK so continue processing
      ...
   }
```

Both produce a similar result, here showing the effect when a document that is not well-formed is loaded:

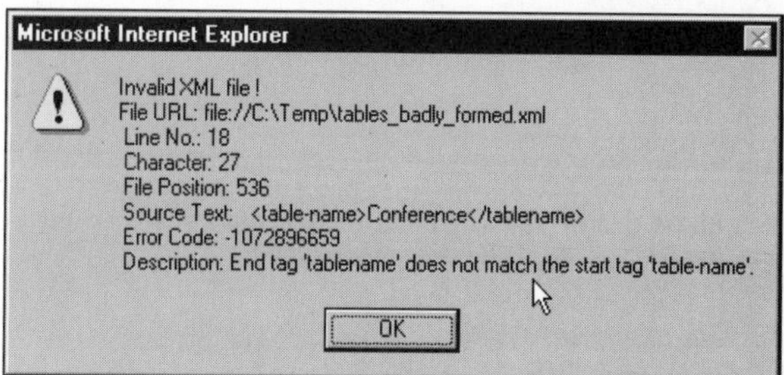

If you have set the `validateOnParse` property to `True`, and load an XML document that is invalid against its DTD or Schema, the error message shows the details of where the file is invalid (usually: it's not very good at reporting the position of errors found in external entities). This screenshot shows the VBScript `MsgBox dialog` version:

However, not all the properties will always have a value. For example, if you attempt to load an XML document that doesn't exist, you can't expect to get values for the error position or the source text:

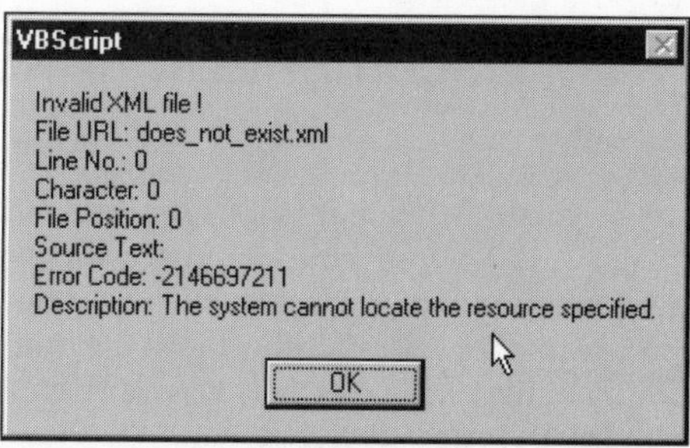

Loading Documents Asynchronously

Asynchronous loading may give a faster response to the user when there are several documents to be loaded, especially if you can show something useful to the user before they are all available, or if you want to load several documents in parallel.

To start the load process, set the `async` property to `true`, and specify a function to be called when loading is complete:

In JScript:

```
var doc;
function loadDocument() {
     doc = new ActiveXObject('MSXML2.DOMDocument.3.0');
     doc.onDataAvailable = processDocument;
     doc.async = true;
     doc.load("source.xml");
}
```

When the data is all available, your `processDocument()` function will be called. You could then, for example, carry out a transformation:

```
function processDocument() {
     if (doc.parseError.errorCode != 0) {
          showError();
     } else {
          transformDocument();
     }
}
```

We've already seen how to display the error messages; in the next section we'll see how to run the transformation.

If you load both the source document and the stylesheet asynchronously, you'll need to be careful in your coding, because either might complete first. One simple approach is to use the same **`onDataAvailable`** method for both documents, and within this method check the **`readyState`** property of both documents. If both are set to the value `4` (completed), the transformation can proceed.

If you really want the ultimate in response time, you can actually fire off the transformation before the source document is fully available. In this case you may need to call the **`transform()`** method repeatedly until it returns the value `true`; you can check the progress of the transformation using the **`readyState`** property of the **`IXSLProcessor`** object.

Transforming XML Documents with XSLT Using Script

You can load any well-formed XML document using the MSXML3 parser. This includes XSLT stylesheets and XML schemas, both of which are documents in XML format. If you create two instances of the `DOMDocument` object, and load an XML source document into one and an XSL stylesheet into the other, you can then perform a transformation by calling either of the methods **`transformNode()`** or **`transformNodeToObject()`**, described below.

This provides an alternative technique to specifying the stylesheet for an XML document by using the **`<?xml-stylesheet?>`** processing instruction. This allows you to select the stylesheet from your own code, and has the advantage that different stylesheets can be used to process the same source document at different times.

The transformNode Method

This method is probably the most useful, as it returns a string-value containing the result of the transformation.

```
strResult = objXMLNode.transformNode(objStylesheet)
```

The `objXMLNode` parameter will usually be a DOM `Document` object, but the method is often called on the document element instead. In fact it can be called on any node in the document. The stylesheet still has visibility of the whole source document, but the first template rule that fires is not the «`match="/"`» rule as normal, but the rule that matches the selected node. This is useful in cases where you only want to produce output from a small section of the XML file.

The `objStylesheet` parameter must also be a DOM object, either a `Document` instance containing a valid XSLT stylesheet or a `Node` within a document that represents an embedded XSLT stylesheet (embedded stylesheets were described in Chapter 3, page 110).

The return value is a string that represents the result of the transformation. Usually it will contain a chunk of HTML which you can then insert into the HTML page to display it. Typically your HTML page will contain a body like this:

```
<body>
<div id="divResults"></div>
</body>
```

and your script will place the transformation results in this place:

```
var objResults = document.all['divResults'];
objResults.innerHTML = objXML.transformNode(objXSL);
```

An example that does this is shown with the Kennedy family tree stylesheet in Chapter 10, page 655; another example can be found on the web site for this book in the file `msxml_transform\default.htm`.

> **The View XSL Output tool doesn't work when you run the transformation from script: it complains with the error message "Not XML Document". So debug your stylesheets first, by running them in a different environment.**

The transformNodeToObject Method

This method is useful when you want to send the result to another object, such as another DOM `Document` or a `Stream` object:

```
objXMLNode.transformNodeToObject(objStylesheet, objOutput)
```

The `objXMLNode` parameter must be a DOM object, either a `Document` object itself or a Node within an XML document (in which case this node and its descendants are treated as a single standalone XML document).

The `objStylesheet` parameter must also be a DOM object, either a `Document` object containing a valid XSLT stylesheet or a `Node` within a `Document` representing an embedded XSLT stylesheet.

The `objOutput` object will usually be another DOM `Document`, which will then hold the result of the transformation. For this to work, the transformation must produce a well-formed XML document. You can of course use this `Document` as the input to another transformation.

Remember that if you capture the result of a transformation as a DOM `Document`, the XSLT processor will not be doing any serialization, and the **`<xsl:output>`** element will therefore have no effect. If you subsequently serialize the document using the **`save`** method or the **`xml`** property on a DOM object, the DOM will do its own serialization, taking no account of anything you specified in the stylesheet.

Example: Using Client-side JScript to Transform a Document

This example demonstrates the way that you can load, parse and transform an XML document using client-side JScript in Internet Explorer 5 or higher. The files are in a folder named `msxml_transform`.

The example shows an HTML page with two buttons on it. The user can click on either of the buttons to select how the data should be displayed. The effect of clicking either button is to apply the corresponding stylesheet to the source XML document.

XML Source

The XML source file for this example is `tables_data.xml`. It defines several tables (real tables, the kind you sit at to eat your dinner), each looking like this:

```
<tables>
<table>
   <table-name>Conference</table-name>
   <number-of-legs>4</number-of-legs>
   <table-top-material type="laminate">Ash</table-top-material>
   <table-shape>Oblong</table-shape>
   <retail-price currency="USD">1485</retail-price>
</table>
...
</tables>
```

Stylesheet

There are two stylesheets, `tables_list.xsl` and `tables_catalog.xsl`. Since this example is designed to show the JScript used to control the transformation rather than the XSLT transformation code itself, I won't list them here.

HTML page

The page `default.htm` contains some simple styling information for the HTML page, then the JScript code that loads the XML and XSL documents, checks for errors, and performs the transformation. Notice that the `transformFiles` function takes the name of a stylesheet as a parameter, which allows you to specify the stylesheet you want to use at run-time:

```
<html>
<head>
<style type="text/css">
     body {font-family:Tahoma,Verdana,Arial,sans-serif; font-
     size:14px}
       .head {font-family:Tahoma,Verdana,Arial,sans-serif;
                      font-size:18px; font- weight:bold}
</style>

<script language="JScript">
function transformFiles(strStylesheetName) {

  // get a reference to the results DIV element
  var objResults = document.all['divResults'];

   // create two new document instances
   var objXML = new ActiveXObject('MSXML2.DOMDocument.3.0');
   var objXSL = new ActiveXObject('MSXML2.DOMDocument.3.0');

   // set the parser properties
   objXML.validateOnParse = true;
   objXSL.validateOnParse = true;

   // load the XML document and check for errors
   objXML.load('tables_data.xml');
   if (objXML.parseError.errorCode != 0) {
      // error found so show error message and stop
      objResults.innerHTML = showError(objXML)
      return false;
   }

  // load the XSL stylesheet and check for errors
  objXSL.load(strStylesheetName);
  if (objXSL.parseError.errorCode != 0) {
    // error found so show error message and stop
    objResults.innerHTML = showError(objXSL)
    return false;
  }

   // all must be OK, so perform transformation
   strResult = objXML.transformNode(objXSL);

   // and display the results in the DIV element
   objResults.innerHTML = strResult;
   return true;
}
```

Providing that there are no errors, the function performs the transformation using the XML file `tables_data.xml` and the stylesheet whose name is specified as the `strStylesheetName` parameter when the function is called. The result of the transformation is inserted into the **`<div>`** element that has the **`id`** attribute value «`divResults`». You'll see where this is defined in the HTML later on.

A

Microsoft MSXML3

If either of the `load` calls fail, perhaps due to a badly-formed document, a function named `showError` is called. This function takes a reference to the document where the error was found, and returns a string describing the nature of the error. This error message is then displayed in the page instead of the result of the transformation:

```
function showError(objDocument) {
   // create the error message
   var strError = new String;
   strError = 'Invalid XML file !<BR />'
         + 'File URL: ' + objDocument.parseError.url + '<BR />'
         + 'Line No.: ' + objDocument.parseError.line + '<BR />'
         + 'Character: ' + objDocument.parseError.linepos + '<BR />'
         + 'File Position: ' + objDocument.parseError.filepos + '<BR />'
         + 'Source Text: ' + objDocument.parseError.srcText + '<BR />'
         + 'Error Code: ' + objDocument.parseError.errorCode + '<BR />'
         + 'Description: ' + objDocument.parseError.reason
   return strError;
}

//-->
</script>
```

The remainder of the page is the HTML that creates the visible section. The opening **<body>** element specifies an **onload** attribute that causes the `transformFiles()` function in our script section to run once the page has finished loading:

```
...
</head>
<body onload="transformFiles('tables_list.xsl')">
<p><span class="head">Transforming an XML Document using
      the client-side code</span></p>
...
```

Because it uses the value «`tables_list.xsl`» for the parameter to the function, this stylesheet is used for the initial display. This shows the data in tabular form.

The next thing in the page is the code that creates the two HTML **<button>** elements, marked Catalog and Simple List. The **onclick** attributes of each one simply executes the `transformFiles()` function again, each time specifying the appropriate stylesheet name:

```
   ...
   View the tables as a  
   <button
onclick="transformFiles('tables_catalog.xsl')">Catalog</button>
     or as a  
   <button onclick="transformFiles('tables_list.xsl')">Simple
List</button>
   <hr />
```

Finally, at the end of the code, you can see the definition of the **<div>** element into which the function inserts the results of the transformation.

```
<!-- to insert the results of parsing the object model -->
<div id="divResults"></div>

</body>
</html>
```

Output

When the page is first displayed, it looks like this:

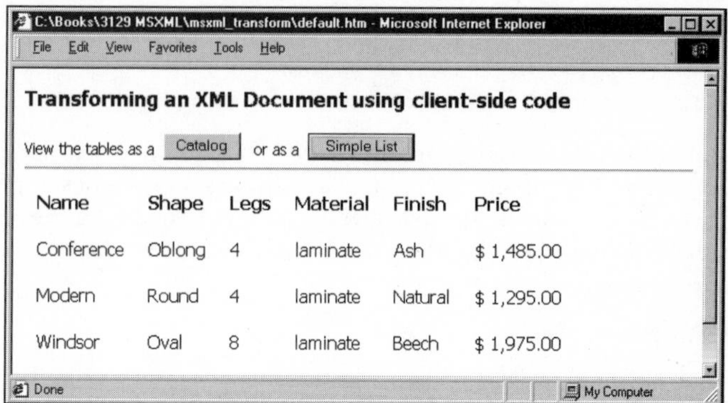

Click on the Catalog button, and you will see an alternative graphical presentation of the same data, achieved by applying the other stylesheet.

Using the XSLTemplate Object

In the example above, I created one `Document` object for the source XML file, and another for the stylesheet, and used the `transformNode` method on the source document to apply the stylesheet and create the resulting HTML.

If you need to use the same stylesheet repeatedly this can be inefficient, particularly on a server, because all the work of analyzing and validating the stylesheet has to be repeated each time it is used. You can avoid this overhead by compiling the stylesheet into another object, which is rather confusingly called an **`XSLTemplate`**. The `XSLTemplate` object can then be used repeatedly to do many transformations. I showed an example of this with the Kennedy family tree in Chapter 10, page 655, where each transformation was applied to the same source document, but using different parameter settings to control which part of the XML data would be displayed.

To compile a stylesheet, you create the `XSLTemplate` object and set its `stylesheet` property to the DOM Node (typically the document itself) containing the **`<xsl:stylesheet>`** element:

```
objStyle = new ActiveXObject("MSXML2.FreeThreadedDOMDocument");
objStyle.async = false;
objStyle.load('stylesheet.xsl');

objTemplates = new ActiveXObject("MSXML2.XSLTemplate");
objTemplates.stylesheet = objStyle.documentElement;
```

The `XSLTemplate` object can be used as often as you like to perform transformations. To perform a transformation, you first need to create an `XSLProcessor` object, which you can regard as holding the information to control one particular transformation. You'll normally create a new one of these each time you want to apply the stylesheet to another source document. You don't need to create the `XSLProcessor` object yourself, the `XSLTemplate` object will do it for you:

```
var objTransformer = objTemplates.createProcessor();
```

You can then perform a transformation by telling the `XSLProcessor` what source document to use, supplying any parameters (these set the values of global **`<xsl:param>`** elements in the stylesheet), and invoking the **`transform()`** method. The result of the transformation can then be retrieved from the `XSLProcessor`'s `output` property:

```
objTransformer.input = source;
objTransformer.addParameter("name1", "value1", "");
objTransformer.addParameter("name2", "value2", "");
objTransformer.transform();
objResults.innerHTML = objTransformer.output;
```

The third argument to `addParameter()` is the namespace URI of the parameter's name, which will usually be an empty string.

Using <object>s and XML Data Islands

Instead of creating an instance of the MSXML `Document` object using script, you can use an **`<object>`** element in the HTML page. You can also create a data island within an HTML page using the **`<xml>`** element. Both **`<object>`** and **`<xml>`** are HTML elements, not XML.

Creating Document Instances with an <object> Element

You can create instances of the MSXML `Document` object using an HTML **`<object>`** element, specifying the appropriate `ClassID`, depending on which version of the parser you want to use. In the following code, I'm creating documents that use the version 3.0 MSXML parser, and setting the `async` and `validateOnParse` properties to false:

```
<object id="XMLDocument" width="0" height="0"
  classid="clsid:f5078f32-c551-11d3-89b9-0000f81fe221">
  <param name="async" value="false">
  <param name="validateOnParse" value="false">
</object>

<object id="XSLDocument" width="0" height="0"
  classid="clsid:f5078f32-c551-11d3-89b9-0000f81fe221">
  <param name="async" value="false">
  <param name="validateOnParse" value="false">
</object>
```

The only change required to the code that I used earlier is to get a reference to the two `Document` objects, rather than creating them directly with script code:

```
// get a reference to the XML document parser
var objXML = document.all['XMLDocument'];

// get a reference to the XSL stylesheet parser
var objXSL = document.all['XSLDocument'];

// load the XML document and check for errors
objXML.load('tables_data.xml');
if (objXML.parseError.errorCode != 0) {
   // error found so show error message and stop
   objResults.innerHTML = showError(objXML)
   return false;
}

// load the XSL stylesheet and check for errors
objXSL.load(strStylesheetName);
if (objXSL.parseError.errorCode != 0) {
   // error found so show error message and stop
   objResults.innerHTML = showError(objXSL)
   return false;
}

// all must be OK, so perform transformation
strResult = objXML.transformNode(objXSL);
```

Using XML Data Islands

Internet Explorer 5 introduced a new HTML element named **<xml>**, which automatically creates an XML document within an HTML page, as a data island. These documents will use the default version of the MSXML parser. Note that the **<xml>** element is part of the HTML syntax – it is not an XML element. The following HTML creates two data islands, one containing the source XML document and one containing the XSL stylesheet:

```
<xml id="Source" src="tables_data.xml"></xml>
<xml id="Stylesheet" src="tables_list.xsl"></xml>
```

You can then perform a transformation using similar script code to that shown earlier:

```
function transformFiles() {

   // get a reference to the results DIV element
   var objResults = document.all['divResults'];

   // get a reference to the XML document
   var objXML = document.all['Source'].XMLDocument;

   // get a reference to the XSL stylesheet
   var objXSL = document.all['Stylesheet'].XMLDocument;
```

```
    // perform transformation
    strResult = objXML.transformNode(objXSL);

    // and display the results in the DIV element
    objResults.innerHTML = strResult;
}
```

However, notice that you have to specify that you want the `XMLDocument` property of the data islands. Unlike the `DOMDocument` objects created directly with script code or an **`<object>`** element, the data island created by the **`<xml>`** element is itself just a wrapper for the XML Document. It is an HTML object, and so the XML it contains must be accessed through the **`XMLDocument`** property of the **`<xml>`** element object.

Using an **`<xml>`** data island is simpler than creating `Document` objects in other ways, but is less flexible as you usually specify the source document in the **`<xml>`** element through the **`src`** attribute. However, you can set the **`src`** attribute value dynamically instead if you wish:

```
    // get a reference to the XSL stylesheet parser
    var objDI = document.all['XSLParser'];
    objDI.src = 'tables_list.xsl';
    var objXSL = objDI.XMLDocument;
```

This gives the same flexibility as using any of the methods described previously.

Finally, as if you weren't spoilt for choice already, you can also create an identical XML data island using the **`<script>`** element rather than the **`<xml>`** element:

```
  <script language="XML" src="tables_data.xml"></script>
```

Modifying XML Documents Dynamically

As well as providing the ability to transform XML documents using XSLT, the MSXML parser also implements full support for the W3C Document Object Model (DOM), with many Microsoft extensions. This includes a whole range of properties and methods that can be used to access and manipulate an XML document when it is loaded into memory.

For example, you can load an XML document, modify particular values, and then apply a stylesheet to perform a transformation. Or you may wish to use the DOM methods to extract certain sections of an XML document into another document and then apply a transformation to that new document. You might even consider loading an XML document and an XSLT stylesheet, then modifying values in both to meet some specific criteria before performing the transformation to obtain the result.

An alternative approach might be to simply create an empty `Document` instance for either the XML document or the XSLT stylesheet, and then populate it directly using the DOM methods. This is obviously more long-winded than just loading a previously created XML file or document string. But it may prove a useful technique in some cases – especially for small documents where the actual transformation operations required vary widely, and are easier to build from scratch than as a series of different XSLT files on disk.

Modifying an XSLT Stylesheet Dynamically

In many cases you can vary the behavior of an XSLT stylesheet by supplying parameters, in the way I described earlier. There are some things in a stylesheet, however, that have to be hard-coded, and one example is the expression used in the **<xsl:sort>** element to define the sort order. If you're feeling adventurous, however, you can get round this limitation by modifying the stylesheet in memory after it's been loaded.

One way to do this modification, of course, is by applying a stylesheet! But if you just want to make a small change, it's probably more efficient to use the DOM interfaces directly, and make the change in situ.

To give you an idea of what's possible, the next example loads an XML document and an XSLT stylesheet and displays the transformation in the HTML page. However, it also provides a set of buttons that can be used to sort the results into different orders.

Example: Varying the Sort Order

The files for this example can be found in the folder `msxml_dynamic`.

XML Source

The XML source file for this example is `tables.data.xml`. It defines several **<table>** elements representing pieces of furniture, each looking like this:

```
<tables>
<table>
  <table-name>Conference</table-name>
  <number-of-legs>4</number-of-legs>
  <table-top-material type="laminate">Ash</table-top-material>
  <table-shape>Oblong</table-shape>
  <retail-price currency="USD">1485</retail-price>
</table>
...
</tables>
```

Stylesheet

The stylesheet is `tables_list.xsl` You can find it in the folder mentioned above; since this example is designed to show the JScript used to control the transformation rather than the XSLT transformation code itself, I won't list it in full here.

The important part of the stylesheet for this example is the **<xsl:apply-templates>** instruction that controls sorting, which looks like this:

```
<xsl:template match="/">
   <html>
     . . .
     <xsl:apply-templates select="/tables/table">
         <xsl:sort select="table-name" order="ascending"/>
     </xsl:apply-templates>
     . . .
   </html>
</xsl:template>
```

The script in the HTML page will modify the attributes of the **<xsl:sort>** element to vary the field on which the data is sorted, and the direction of sorting.

HTML page

The HTML code to create the visible part of the page is shown below. It's in file `default.htm`.

The **<body>** element's **onload** attribute has the value «`if (preparePage()) sort('table-name', 'ascending')`». This executes a function named `preparePage()` as soon as the HTML page has loaded. If the result of this function is true (that is, the process succeeds), it then calls the `sort()` function to display the data sorted in ascending order of the «`table-name`» field.

```
. . .
<body onload="if (preparePage()) sort('table-name', 'ascending')">
<p><span class="head">Modifying an XSLT Stylesheet
                                       using client-side code</span></p>
```

The HTML code then displays a set of buttons allowing the user to change the sort order. Notice that each of the **<button>** elements executes the `sort` function when clicked, but with different values for the parameters. These values will be used to modify the **select** and **order** attributes of the **<xsl:sort>** element in the stylesheet.

```
Sort by:  
<button onclick="sort('table-name', 'ascending')">Name</button>
<button onclick="sort('table-shape', 'ascending')">Shape</button>
<button onclick="sort('number-of-legs', 'ascending')">Nr of Legs</button>
<button onclick="sort('table-top-material/@type',
                                       'ascending')">Material</button>
<button onclick="sort('table-top-material', 'ascending')">Finish</button>
<button onclick="sort('retail-price', 'ascending')">Price +</button>
<button onclick="sort('retail-price', 'descending')">Price -</button>
<hr/>
```

The HTML page then defines the objects to hold the source document, stylesheet document, and the output HTML:

```
<object id="XMLDocument" width="0" height="0"
   classid="clsid:f5078f32-c551-11d3-89b9-0000f81fe221">
   <param name="async" value="false">
   <param name="validateOnParse" value="false">
</object>

<object id="XSLDocument" width="0" height="0"
   classid="clsid:f5078f32-c551-11d3-89b9-0000f81fe221">
   <param name="async" value="false">
   <param name="validateOnParse" value="false">
</object>

<!-- to insert the results of parsing the object model -->
<div id="divResults"></div>

</body>
</html>
```

The JScript code that implements the functions is shown next. First the `preparePage()` function, which creates some global variables to reference the output **<div>** element and the two `Document` objects, and then loads the XML and XSL files into these documents:

```
// global variables to hold references to objects
var gobjResults;
var gobjXML;
var gobjXSL;

function preparePage() {

   // get the reference to the results DIV element
   gobjResults = document.all['divResults'];

   // get the reference to the XML document parser
   gobjXML = document.all['XMLDocument'];

   // get the reference to the XSL stylesheet parser
   gobjXSL = document.all['XSLDocument'];

   // load the XML document and check for errors
   gobjXML.load('tables_data.xml');
   if (gobjXML.parseError.errorCode != 0) {
      // error found so show error message and stop
      gobjResults.innerHTML = showError(gobjXML)
      return false;
   }
```

```
// load the XSL stylesheet and check for errors
   gobjXSL.load('tables_list.xsl');
   if (gobjXSL.parseError.errorCode != 0) {
      // error found so show error message and stop
      gobjResults.innerHTML = showError(gobjXSL)
      return false;
   }

   // all OK, so return true
   return true;
}
```

If either of the `load()` calls should fail, the function `showError()` (the same as the one used in the earlier examples) is used to display the error, and the function returns false. If all is well, it returns true and the `sort()` function can then be executed.

We're now ready to write the `sort()` function which changes the value of the **`select`** and **`order`** attributes of the **`<xsl:sort>`** element. Because the stylesheet is loaded as a DOM `Document` in memory, we can do this by using the DOM interfaces. It's particularly convenient to use an XPath expression to locate the two attributes directly.

The Microsoft-specific `selectSingleNode()` method takes an XPath expression, and returns the first selected node from the document. Conveniently, our stylesheet contains only one **`<xsl:sort>`** element.

> *Technically,* `selectSingleNode()` *expects the expression to be in Microsoft WD-xsl syntax unless the* `selectionLanguage` *property of the* `DOMDocument` *is set to* «`XPath`». *But for a simple expression like this one, the syntax is the same in both cases.*

So we can write the **`sort()`** function as follows:

```
function sort(strSortBy, strOrder) {

   // get a reference to the 'select' and 'order' attributes from
   // the 'xsl:sort element' in the root template
   var objSelect =
   gobjXSL.selectSingleNode("//xsl:sort/@select");
   var objOrder = gobjXSL.selectSingleNode("//xsl:sort/@order");

   // change the attribute value to the specified XPath value
   objSelect.nodeValue = strSortBy;
   objOrder.nodeValue = strOrder;

   // perform the transformation
   strResult = gobjXML.transformNode(gobjXSL);

   // and update the contents of the DIV element
   gobjResults.innerHTML = strResult;
}
```

Output

There is a button for each column in the results table. There are two buttons for the Price column, allowing it to be sorted in ascending or descending order.

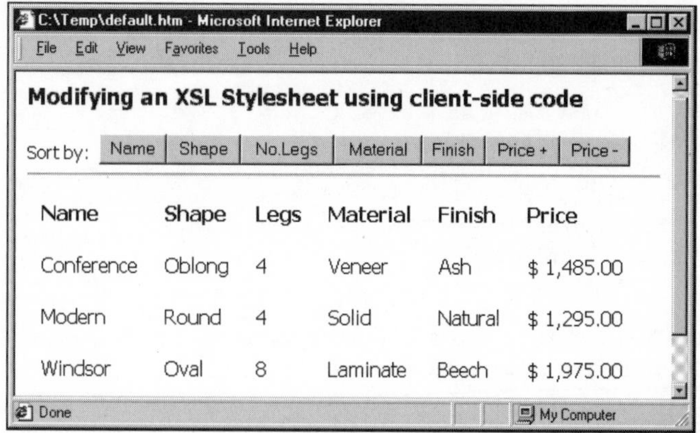

Clicking any of the buttons changes the display without reloading the page, sorting the results into the appropriate order as seen in the next screenshot:

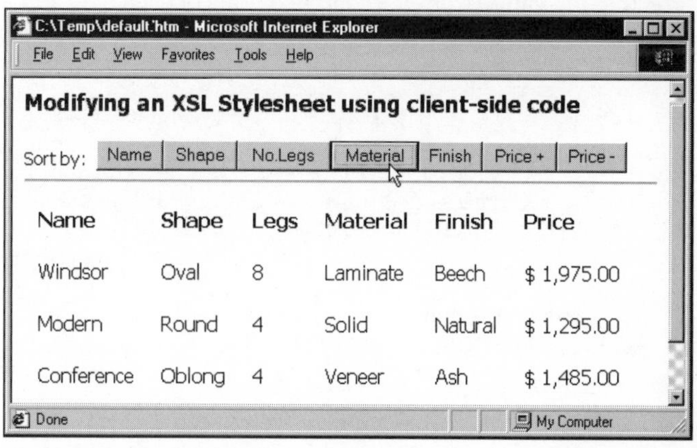

Using XPath with the DOM

In the previous example I used the method `selectSingleNode()` to select a node from the DOM document by supplying an XPath expression. This works because MSXML allows you to use XPath expressions independently of an XSLT stylesheet. If you only want to extract a few simple pieces of information from a document, this provides a convenient alternative to running an XSLT transformation.

The following function creates a DOM document and populates it by loading an XML file into it. It then calls the XPath expression «`//table/table-name`» in the XML DOM's `selectNodes` function, which returns a `NodeList` object containing all the **`<table-name>`** elements from the document:

```
function getTableNames() {

   // get the reference to the results DIV element
   var objResults = document.all['divResults'];

   // create an XML document instance
   var objXML = new ActiveXObject('MSXML2.DOMDocument.3.0');

   // load the XML document and check for errors
   objXML.load('tables_data.xml');
   if (objXML.parseError.errorCode != 0) {
      // error found so show error message and stop
      objResults.innerHTML = showError(objXML)
      return false;
   }

   var strResult = new String;   // to hold the result
   strResult = 'The table names are: ';

   // get a NodeList containing all the <table> elements
   var objTableNodeList = objXML.selectNodes('//table/table-name');
```

Having got a list of the **<table-name>** elements, it's a simple task to iterate through them extracting the value (from the child text node of each one) and adding it to a string that is then placed into the **<div>** element elsewhere on the page:

```
   // iterate through all the <table-name> nodes
   for (var i = 0; i < objTableNodeList.length; i++) {

      // get the value of this node from the child text node
      strName = objTableNodeList(i).childNodes(0).nodeValue;
      strResult += '"<b>' + strName + '</b>" ';
   }

   // and update the contents of the DIV element
   objResults.innerHTML = strResult;
}
```

Here's the result using the XML document we've seen earlier:

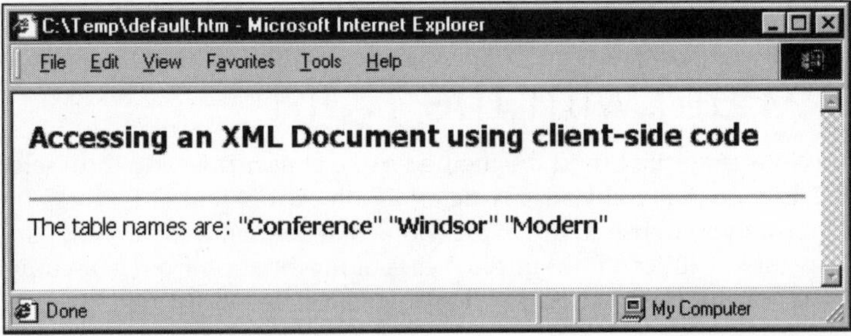

Using the MSXML3 Parser on the Server

So far in this appendix we've been using MSXML3 to perform XSLT transformations on the client. This is great, but it will obviously only work where the client supports the use of the MSXML3 parser. Even if all browsers offered XSLT support, the scripts we've been writing in our HTML pages will only work with Microsoft's proprietary APIs.

If you have to develop a web site to serve users with a wide variety of browsers installed, or if you want to avoid shipping the XML data to the client, perhaps for security reasons, then your only real option is to perform the XML-to-HTML transformation on the server, and then send the resulting HTML to the client. In the other appendices of this book I describe a number of XSLT processors that can be used on the server, but so long as it's a Windows server, the MSXML3 product can also be used in this role.

The MSXML3 parser is a standard COM object, so you can instantiate and use it from any COM-enabled language. This includes VBScript and JScript running in an Active Server Pages file on the server, as well as server-based applications built using Visual Basic, C++, Java, Delphi, and so on.

Using MSXML3 with Active Server Pages

To create an instance of the parser on the server in ASP, we use almost the same techniques as we did on the client. However, to instantiate it in the correct context of the ASP page, we must use the `Server` object's `CreateObject` method:

In VBScript:

```
Dim objDocument
Set objDocument = Server.CreateObject("MSXML2.DOMDocument.3.0")
```

In JScript:

```
var objDocument = Server.CreateObject('MSXML2.DOMDocument.3.0');
```

Of course, you can also use the **`<object>`** element to create the document instance, as we did earlier on the client. You need to set the attribute **`runat:server`**. This has the advantage that the instance is not actually created until first referenced, whereas the `Server.CreateObject` method will create the instance immediately. Of course, any advantage depends on how you structure your code (that is, on when you execute the `Server.CreateObject` method).

> **If you create an instance of the document in ASP within your `global.asa` file, so that it is available for the entire user's session or for the life of the application, be sure to specify the Free-Threaded version of the parser, by using the object names specified on page 703**

Once the document has been created, the techniques for using it are almost identical. Of course, you can't use message boxes or alert dialogs, and you have to write the output to the client using the `Response.Write` method instead of inserting it into an element on the page dynamically as we did in our earlier examples.

Example: A Server-Side XSLT Transformation

This ASP page, together with the support files it requires, is provided in a folder named `msxml_asp`. It demonstrates a simple server-side XSLT transformation that sends the result to the client as an HTML page.

Source XML

The source XML file is the same furniture catalog as we used in previous examples in this chapter, which starts:

```
<tables>
<table>
  <table-name>Conference</table-name>
  <number-of-legs>4</number-of-legs>
  <table-top-material type="Veneer">Ash</table-top-material>
  <table-shape>Oblong</table-shape>
  <retail-price currency="USD">1485</retail-price>
</table>
```

Stylesheet

The stylesheet is file `tables_style.xsl` in the same folder. We're not really concerned with the contents of the stylesheet here; it's much the same as in previous examples. The only important thing is that it generates HTML output.

ASP Page

The ASP page reads as follows. It is called `simple_transform.asp`:

```
<%@LANGUAGE="VBScript"%>

<%
' tell client that we're sending an HTML page
Response.ContentType = "text/html"

' error handling subroutine
Sub ShowError(objDoc)
   'create and display error message
   Dim strError
   strError = "Invalid XML file !<BR />" _
      & "File URL: " & objDoc.parseError.url & "<BR />" _
      & "Line No.: " & objDoc.parseError.line & "<BR />" _
      & "Character: " & objDoc.parseError.linepos & "<BR />" _
      & "File Position: " & objDoc.parseError.filepos & "<BR />" _
      & "Source Text: " & objDoc.parseError.srcText & "<BR />" _
      & "Error Code: " & objDoc.parseError.errorCode & "<BR />" _
      & "Description: " & objDoc.parseError.reason
   Response.Write strError
End Sub
```

```
Dim objXML
Dim objXSL

' create two document instances
Set objXML = Server.CreateObject("MSXML2.DOMDocument.3.0")
Set objXSL = Server.CreateObject("MSXML2.DOMDocument.3.0")

' set the parser properties
objXML.ValidateOnParse = True
objXSL.ValidateOnParse = True

' load the source XML document and check for errors
objXML.load Server.MapPath("tables_data.xml")
If objXML.parseError.errorCode <> 0 Then
   'error found so show error message and stop
   ShowError objXML
   Response.End
End If
```

Notice that we have to use the `Server.MapPath` method to convert the XML and XSLT document names to a full valid physical path when running under ASP. If not, the `load` method will fail to find the file and report an error.

```
' load the XSL stylesheet and check for errors
objXSL.load Server.MapPath("tables_style.xsl")
If objXSL.parseError.errorCode <> 0 Then
   'error found so show error message and stop
   ShowError objXSL
   Response.End
End If

' all must be OK, so perform transformation
strResult = objXML.transformNode(objXSL)

' and insert the results into the page
Response.Write strResult
%>
```

Output

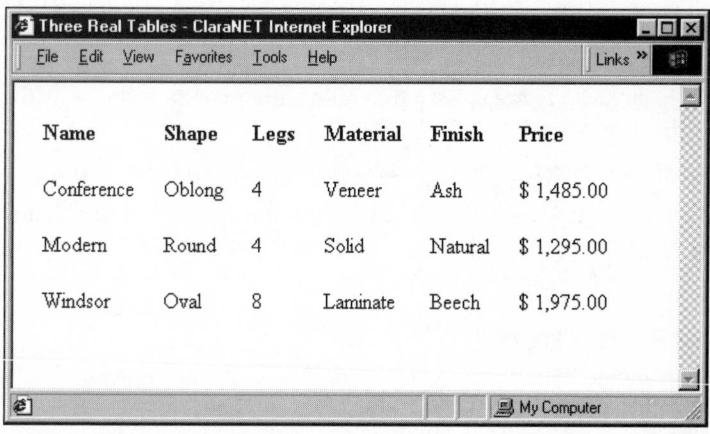

A

Microsoft MSXML3

You could, of course, select the XML document and the XSLT stylesheet dynamically when the page is executed, rather than hard-coding the names into the script. For example, a **<FORM>** section on another page could reference this page and provide a value for the stylesheet name in an HTML control – perhaps named "stylesheet_name". The ASP code then just needs to use this value in the load method:

```
objXSL.load Server.MapPath(Request.Form("stylesheet_name"))
```

Setting the Appropriate Content Type Header

Notice that the previous example uses the ASP statement

```
Response.ContentType = "text/html"
```

to set the HTTP content type header so that the client knows that the data is to be treated as an HTML page. This is because we are creating HTML as the result of our server-side transformation. In this case, if you didn't include this statement, the page would still work because a web browser will default to «text/html» if no other content type is specified.

The content type is specified as one of the standard MIME types, and you should always specify this using the Response.ContentType statement. It is particularly important if you are creating something other than an HTML page. For example, if your XSLT transformation or other ASP code creates XML-format output, you should use:

```
Response.ContentType = "text/xml"
```

If you are creating an XSLT stylesheet to send to the client, use «text/xml». Internet Explorer will also accept «text/xsl», but other browsers might not, because it is not a standard MIME type. For a pure text file, use «text/plain». Remember, however, that it is the client itself (or rather the operating system environment in which it is running) that actually decides what to do with the output you send, based on the content type you specify. You can only tell the client what type of output you are creating, and it will decide how to handle it when it arrives.

In fact Internet Explorer tries to second-guess the MIME type in the HTTP header. In particular, it attaches significance to the final part of the URL: if this ends in «.html», for example, it expects to receive an HTML file, and if it ends in «.xml», it expects the output to be XML. I once spent a frustrating afternoon puzzling why the response to the URL:

```
http://www.company.com/transform.asp?style=my.xsl&source=my.xml
```

was being displayed as if it were XML, when the code was clearly setting the HTTP content type to «text/html». The answer turned out to be the «.xml» at the end of the URL. Adding a dummy parameter «&x=y» fixed the problem.

Setting Parameters

A very common requirement when using ASP pages to control a transformation is to set stylesheet parameters based on the parameters supplied in the URL. For example if the URL is

```
http://www.company.com/transform.asp?employee=517541
```

then you might want to invoke a transformation setting the value of the employee parameter in the stylesheet to the value 517541. Fortunately, this is quite easy.

If you want to supply parameters, you cannot use the short-cut method of calling `transformNode()` on the `DOMDocument` directly. Instead, you need to create an `XSLTemplate` object representing the compiled stylesheet; you need to generate an `XSLTProcessor` from this by calling the `XSLTemplate`'s `createProcessor()` method; and then you need to call the `XSLTProcessor`'s `addParameter()` method to set the parameter value. In the previous example we wrote:

```
strResult = objXML.transformNode(objXSL)
```

but now we need to expand this:

```
Dim templates
Dim transformer

templates = Server.CreateObject("MSXML2.XSLTemplate")
templates.stylesheet = objXSL.documentElement
transformer = templates.createProcessor()
transformer.input = objXML
transformer.addParameter("employee", Request.QueryString("employee"),
"")
strResult = transformer.transform()
```

Actually, you wouldn't really want to do all this in the same ASP page. The whole point about compiling a stylesheet into an `XSLTemplate` object is that you can use the same stylesheet again and again. So in a production application you would want to build the `XSLTemplate` once, holding a reference to it at application level in the `global.asa` file. Note that if you do this, it is important to use the `FreeThreaded` version of the `DOMDocument` object.

Creating Links to Other ASP Pages

One other point to watch: when you generate HTML pages in this kind of application, the HTML pages will often contain links to further ASP pages. People often have problems with the «`&`» character in these URLs: when you try to generate a URL such as

```
«http://www.company.com/transform.asp?emp=517541&loc=bracknell»,
```

the «`&`» will be generated as «`&`». Don't worry about this: in an HTML page, this is the correct way of writing the URL, and the browser will be perfectly happy with it. In fact, writing the «`&`» without escaping it is technically an error, though many HTML authors do it all the time.

Deciding Where To Do XSLT Transformation

Given that some browsers support client-side XSLT transformation and others don't, a natural thing to do is to perform the transformation on the client if it is supported there, or on the server if not. In principle you can do this with an ASP script that detects the browser version (from the HTTP header sent with every message) and sends back the appropriate content. In fact, Microsoft supply an ISAPI extension to their web server that does just this. But as far as XSLT is concerned, there is a snag; knowing the browser version doesn't tell you whether the user has installed MSXML3.

Detecting the browser version is easy enough with some simple script code – this example sets a Boolean variable named `blnIsIE5` to `True` if the browser is Internet Explorer 5 or later:

```
blnIsIE5 = False
strUA = Request.ServerVariables("HTTP_USER_AGENT")
If InStr(strUA, "MSIE") Then
  intVersion = CInt(Mid(strUA, InStr(strUA, "MSIE") + 5, 1))
  If intVersion > 4 Then blnIsIE5 = True  'this is IE5 or later
End If
```

The only problem now is determining which version of the MSXML3 parser is available.

In principle you could write two stylesheets, one in XSLT and one in WD-xsl, and you could send to the client an HTML page containing script that determines what software is installed, and loads the appropriate stylesheet. This technique has been demonstrated earlier in the example *Using Client-side JScript to Transform a Document* on page 714. All you need to do is to add logic similar to the script by Jarno Elovirta included on our `msxml-version.html` sample page before deciding which stylesheet to load.

In practice, few projects can afford the luxury of writing every stylesheet twice! A more reasonable approach is to tell the users that they can either download and install MSXML3, or use the server-based version of the site. This is rather like asking the user to select between a version of the site that uses frames and one that doesn't: it's not a great hardship, especially if you remember the user preference as part of your site membership information or in a cookie.

Once the application knows whether to do the transformation server-side or client-side, it's not too difficult to arrange. The great thing is that both can be based on the same XML source documents, and can use almost the same stylesheets; we saw with the Kennedy family tree example on page 655 in Chapter 10 how to make the small modifications needed using **`<xsl:import>`**.

If you're generating the XML on the server (for example, building it from a database) you can easily add the `<?xml-stylesheet?>` processing instruction while you do so. This has the advantage that you don't need a skeletal HTML page on the client to control the transformation. On the server you can select a different stylesheet programmatically: the `<?xml-stylesheet?>` processing instruction will simply be ignored.

If the XML is stored on the server, it's probably not a good idea to add the `<?xml-stylesheet?>` processing instruction before sending it to the client. This could undo many of the performance advantages you gained by doing the transformation on the client: ideally you don't want to touch the data on the server at all. Instead, it's better to control the transformation from the HTML page in the way we have seen.

When you get this right, you can present exactly the same visual image to the user regardless of whether the transformation is done on the server or the client, as illustrated below:

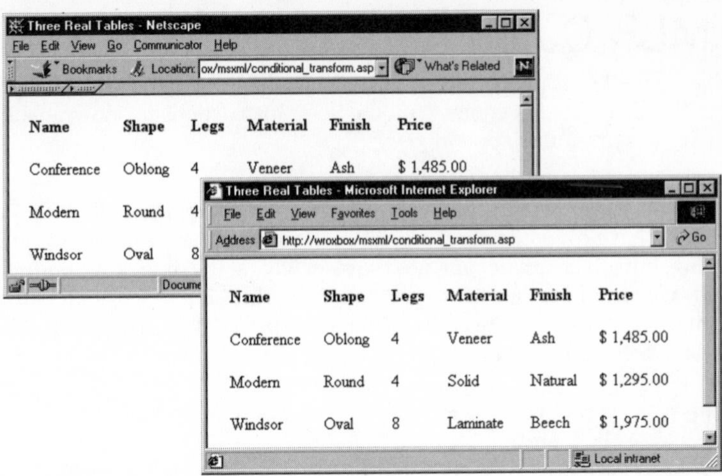

The result is that Internet Explorer 5 and higher will receive the XML source document containing the **<xsl:stylesheet>** instruction, and retrieve this stylesheet for use in a client-side XSLT transformation. However, other browsers will receive just the HTML result of performing the transformation on the server.

The only difference will be performance: if successive pages navigate around the same source XML dataset, as in our family tree example in Chapter 10, following the links will be far faster if it doesn't involve another request to the server.

Performing Bulk Transformations

If you use server-based transformations to create output for clients, you do place an extra load on your server. Web servers are optimized to serve pages from disk to the client on demand, rather than carrying out intermediate processing each time. If the XML content of the site is relatively static, then one way to reduce the load is to perform the transformations at the time the data is published, and write the results to the server's disk as a series of files. The client can then access and download the appropriate file, rather than having the translation performed in real time.

You can easily write the results of a transformation to the server's disk using the `FileSystemObject`:

```
...
'all must be OK, so perform transformation
strResult = objXML.transformNode(objXSL)

'and write the results to the server's disk
Set objFSO = Server.CreateObject("Scripting.FileSystemObject")
Set objFile = objFSO.CreateTextFile("resultpage.htm", True)
                                        'overwrite any existing file
objFile.Write strResult
objFile.Close
```

Alternatively, you might like to look at the `XSLTransform` product from StoneBroom that uses a batch file to automatically perform multiple transformations to disk files. See http://www.stonebroom.com for more details.

MSXML3 Quick Reference

The objects, methods, properties and events available with the MSXML3 parser are listed in the Help file that comes with the SDK. Instructions for downloading this appear at the start of this appendix.

I have only included here the parts of the interface that are relevant to XSLT and XPath processing. I have covered only the basic interfaces, and have omitted some that look interesting, but which are documented so sketchily (at the time of writing) that a fair bit of trial and error would be needed to get them to work. A full description of the Microsoft DOM interface (excluding the new additions in MSXML3) can be found in the Wrox book *Professional XML* - ISBN 1-861003-11-0.

Objects

The objects of particular interest to XSLT and XPath processing are listed below:

Object	Description
`IXMLDOMDocument`	The root of an XML document
`IXMLDOMNode`	Any node in the DOM
`IXMLDOMNodeList`	A collection of `Node` objects
`IXMLDOMParseError`	Details of the last parse error that occurred
`IXMLDOMSelection`	A selection of nodes
`IXSLProcessor`	An execution of an XSLT stylesheet
`IXSLTemplate`	A compiled XSLT stylesheet in memory

These objects are described in the sections that follow.

IXMLDOMDocument and IXMLDOMDocument2

The `IXMLDOMDocument` class inherits all the properties and methods of `IXMLDOMNode`. `IXMLDOMDocument2` is a later version of the interface, introducing a few extra properties and methods. This section lists the additional methods and properties of relevance to XSLT and XPath processing, in other words, all the methods and properties that are not also present on `IXMLDOMNode`, which is described on page 737.

Additional methods

The methods particularly relevent to XPath and XSLT processing are described in detail below.

The `validate()` and `setProperty()` methods actually belong to the `IXMLDOMDocument2` interface, which is an extension to `IXMLDOMDocument` introduced with the MSXML2 product.

Name	Returns	Description
abort	(Nothing)	Aborts download
load	Boolean	Loads document from the specified XML source
loadXML	Boolean	Loads the document from a string
save	(Nothing)	Saves the document to a specified destination
setProperty	(Nothing)	Sets various system properties
validate	(Nothing)	Validates the document, using the current DTD or schema

abort() ⇒ Nothing

When a document is being loaded asynchronously, `abort()` can be called at any time to abandon the process.

load(url) ⇒ Boolean

The argument is normally a string containing a URL; this URL should identify an XML document. The effect of this method is to clear out any existing content of the `Document` object, and replace it with the result of parsing the XML source from the specified URL. The method returns `True` if successful, `False` otherwise.

The URL can of course be a relative URL such as «`../article.xml`»; when the code is running within an HTML page such a URL is interpreted relative to the URL of the HTML page itself. On the server you will normally want to use a URL obtained using the `mapPath()` function.

loadXML(string) ⇒ Boolean

The string contains the text of an XML document. The effect of this method is to clear out any existing content of the `Document` object, and replace it with the result of parsing the XML string. The method returns `True` if successful, `False` otherwise.

save(destination) ⇒ Nothing

The destination is usually a filename, given as a string. The effect is to serialize the Document in XML format as a file. It is also possible to specify various other objects as a destination, for example, it can be another `Document` object, in which case the document is duplicated. You can also save directly to the `Response` object.

setProperty(name, value) ⇒ Nothing

This method is used to set the values of various system properties that affect the behavior of other methods, especially the **`selectNodes()`** and **`selectSingleNode()`** methods. There is also a corresponding **`getProperty()`** method. The three most important properties are:

- **SelectionLanguage**. This takes the value «XPath» or «XSLPattern». The default is «XSLPattern». This affects the syntax used in the expression passed to the **selectNodes()** and **selectSingleNode()** methods. If you want to use XPath 1.0 syntax in these expressions, you must set this property to «XPath». The default value, «XSLPattern», refers to the Microsoft-specific WD-xsl dialect.
- **SelectionNamespaces**. The value of this property should be a space-separated list of namespace declarations, for example

  «xmlns:a='http://company-a.com/' xmlns:b='http://company-b.com/'»

  These define the namespace prefixes that can be used within any expression passed to the **selectNodes()** and **selectSingleNode()** methods.
- **ServerHTTPRequest**. This takes the Boolean values True or False; the default is False. The value should be set to True when you are executing script on the server and where there is likely to be a significant level of concurrent activity. If this property is set to True, then the async property should be set to False. This property was introduced to prevent problems that were encountered by some users of the beta versions of MSXML3 on heavily loaded servers. **Note:** if you use this property on an intranet, you will also need to configure WinHTTP's proxy settings. This requires a configuration utility, which you can download separately. Instructions are included in the SDK help file.

validate() ⇒ Nothing

This method checks that the document is valid, that is, that it conforms to its DTD or schema. If it is valid, the call returns normally, otherwise it raises an error condition.

This is an alternative to validating while the document is being parsed. It can be useful, for example, to ensure that the document created as the output of an XSLT transformation is valid.

A typical call sequence in JScript is:

```
try {
   xmldoc.validate();
} catch(e) {
   alert("Validation error: " + e.description);
}
```

Additional properties

Name	Returns	Description
async	Boolean	True if the document is to be loaded asynchronously
parseError	IXMLDOMParseError	The last parser error
readyState	Long	Current state of readiness for use
validateOnParse	Boolean	Requests validation

async ⇒ Boolean

If this property is set to its default value of `True`, processing can continue while the document is being parsed and loaded. When using stylesheets, `async` is normally set to `False` so that as soon as control returns from the `load()` method, transformation can proceed.

parseError ⇒ IXMLDomParseError

This property returns an `IXMLDOMParseError` object. To determine if a parsing error occurred, test whether the `errorCode` of the returned object is non-zero.

readyState ⇒ Long

When loading a document asynchronously, this property takes one of the values:

0	UNINITIALIZED The `load()` method has not yet been called
1	LOADING The `load()` method is executing
2	LOADED The document has been loaded and is being parsed
3	INTERACTIVE Some data has been read and it is now possible to access the DOM data structure in read-only mode
4	COMPLETED The data is fully available

You can nominate a function to be called when the state changes, using the `onReadyStateChange` event, or a function to be called when the state switches to `COMPLETED`, using the `onDataAvailable` event.

validateOnParse ⇒Boolean

If this property is set to `True`, the document will be validated (against its DTD or schema) as it is loaded.

IXMLDOMNode

This object represents a node in the document tree. Note that the tree conforms to the DOM model, which is not always the same as the XPath model described in Chapter 2: for example, the way namespaces are modeled is different, and text nodes are not necessarily normalized.

There are subclasses of `IXMLDOMNode` for all the different kinds of node found in the tree. I have not included descriptions of all these, since they are not directly relevant to XSLT and XPath processing. The only subclass I have included is `IXMLDOMDocument`, which can be regarded as representing either the whole document or its root node, depending on your point of view.

Methods

The methods available on `IXMLDOMNode` that are relevant to XSLT and XPath processing are listed below. Most often, these methods will be applied to the root node (the DOM `Document` object) but they can be applied to any node.

Name	Returns	Description
`selectNodes`	IXMLDOMNodeList	Executes an XPath expression and returns a list of matching nodes
`selectSingleNode`	IXMLDOMNode	Executes an XPath expression and returns the first matching node
`transformNode`	String	Applies a stylesheet to the subtree rooted at this node, returning the result as a string
`transformNode ToObject`	(Nothing)	Applies the stylesheet to the subtree, placing the result into a supplied document or stream

selectNodes(String expression) ⇒ IXMLDOMNodeList

This method takes an XPath expression as its argument, and returns the list of nodes selected by that expression.

If you want to use XPath 1.0 syntax in the expression, rather than Microsoft's WD-xsl variant, you must set the `selectionLanguage` property of the document object to «`XPath`». For many simple expressions the syntax of the two dialects is the same, but if the expression uses XPath functions or predicates, or axes other than the default child axis, the syntax can be very different.

Microsoft's documentation on this method is very limited. It seems that the XPath expression must be one that returns a node-set, and that the node to which the expression is applied is used as the context node. Any namespace prefixes in the expression are interpreted using the namespace declarations supplied in the `selectionNamespaces` property of the `DOMDocument` object.

If no nodes are selected, the method returns an empty list.

The documentation makes no guarantee that the nodes are returned in any particular order.

If the target document supports the `IXMLDOMDocument2` interface, which is an extension of the basic `IXMLDOMDocument` interface, then the `IXMLDOMNodeList` returned will also implement the `IXMLDOMSelection` interface.

selectSingleNode(String expression) ⇒ IXMLDOMNode

This method is the same as `selectNodes()` above, except that it only returns the first selected node in document order.

As with `selectNodes()`, if you want to use XPath 1.0 syntax in the expression, rather than Microsoft's WD-xsl variant, you must set the `selectionLanguage` property of the document object to «`XPath`».

If no nodes are selected, the method returns null.

transformNode(IXMLDOMNode stylesheet) ⇒ String

This method applies a stylesheet to the document containing this node. The target node is used as the initial context for the stylesheet (that is, it starts by looking for a template rule that matches this node), but the stylesheet has access to the entire document.

The argument identifies the XSLT stylesheet. This will usually be a `Document`, but it may be a `Node` representing an embedded stylesheet within a `Document`.

The result of the transformation is serialized and returned as a string. Note that this is a string of characters conforming to the `BSTR` data type, which means that the encoding specified using **`<xsl:output>`** is ignored.

transformNodeToObject(IXMLDOMNode stylesheet, Variant result) ⇒ Nothing

This method applies a stylesheet to the document containing this node. The target node is used as the initial context for the stylesheet, but the stylesheet has access to the entire document.

The argument identifies the XSLT stylesheet. This will usually be a `Document`, but it may be a `Node` representing an embedded stylesheet within a `Document`.

The result of the transformation is written to the object identified in the second argument. This will usually be a `Document`. It may also be a `Stream`.

Properties

The most useful properties are listed below. Properties whose main purpose is to navigate through the document are not listed here, because navigation can be achieved more easily using XPath expressions.

Name	Returns	Description
`baseName`	String	The local name of the node, excluding any namespace prefix.
`namespaceURI`	String	The namespace URI.
`nodeName`	String	The name of the node, including its namespace prefix if any. Note that unlike the XPath model, unnamed nodes are given conventional names such as `"#document"`, `"#text"`, and `"#comment"`.
`nodeTypeString`	String	Returns the type of node in string form. For example, `"element"`, `"attribute"`, or `"comment"`.

Name	Returns	Description
nodeValue	Variant	The value stored in the node. This is not the same as the XPath string-value; for elements, it is always null.
prefix	String	The prefix for the namespace applying to the node.
text	String	Text contained by this node (like the XPath string-value).
xml	String	XML representation of the node and its descendants.

IXMLDOMNodeList

This object represents a list of nodes. For our present purposes, we are interested in this object because it is the result of the `selectNodes()` method.

An `IXMLDOMNodeList` is returned as a result of the `selectNodes()` method: it contains the list of nodes selected by the supplied XPath expression. You can process all the nodes in the list either by using the `nextNode()` method or by direct indexing using the `item` property. There is nothing in the documentation that says the nodes will be returned in any particular order.

If the document from which the nodes were selected implements the `IXMLDOMDocument2` interface introduced in MSXML2, then the node list returned by `selectNodes()` will also implement the `IXMLDOMSelection` interface, described on page 741.

Methods

Name	Returns	Description
item	IXMLDOMNode	Gets the collection of nodes
nextNode	IXMLDOMNode	Gets the next node
reset	(Nothing)	Resets the current position

item(Long *position*) ⇒ IXMLDOMNode

Returns the node at the given position. This is the default collection, so the node at position `n` in a `NodeList nodes` can also be referenced as `nodes[n]`.

nextNode() ⇒ IXMLDOMNode

Returns the next node, or null when all the nodes have been processed.

reset() ⇒ Nothing

Resets the node list so that the next node returned by `nextNode()` will be the first one.

Properties

Name	Returns	Description
length	Long	Identifies the number of nodes in the collection

IXMLDOMParseError

This object is accessible through the `parseError` property of the `IXMLDOMDocument` interface. Examples of how to use this object to generate diagnostics are given earlier in this appendix on page 710.

Properties

Name	Returns	Description
errorCode	Long	The error code
filepos	Long	The character position of the error within the XML document
line	Long	The line number of the error
linepos	Long	The character position in the line containing the error
reason	String	Explanation of the error
srcText	String	The XML text in error
url	String	The URL of the offending document

IXMLDOMSelection

This object represents a selection of nodes. It is returned as the result of the `selectNodes()` method when the target document implements the `IXMLDOMDocument2` interface.

It's simplest to think of this object as a stored expression that returns a list of nodes on demand. It's rather like a relational view: you don't need to know whether the results are actually stored, or whether they are obtained as required.

This interface extends the `IXMLDOMNodeList` interface.

Methods

Name	Returns	Description
clone	IXMLDOMSelection	Produces a copy of this `IXMLDOMSelection`.
getProperty	String	Returns the value of a named property.
item	IXMLDOMNode	Get the collection of nodes.

Name	Returns	Description
`matches`	`IXMLDOMNode`	Tests whether the given node is a member of the set of nodes
`nextNode`	`IXMLDOMNode`	Gets the next node
`reset`	(Nothing)	Resets the current position

clone() ⇒ IXMLDOMSelection

Produces a copy of this `IXMLDOMSelection`.

getProperty(String *name*) ⇒ String

Returns the value of a named property. The only property currently defined is `SelectionLanguage`, which mirrors the `SelectionLanguage` property of the owning `IXMLDOMDocument`.

item(Long *position*) ⇒ IXMLDOMNode

Returns the node at the given position. This is the default collection, so the node at position `n` in a `NodeList nodes` can also be referenced as `nodes[n]`.

matches(IXMLDOMNode *node*) ⇒ Boolean

Determines whether the given node is a member of the set of nodes returned by this selection expression. (In effect, this is using the XPath expression as a match pattern, in much the same way that XSLT does.)

nextNode() ⇒ IXMLDOMNode

Returns the next node, or null when all the nodes have been processed.

reset() ⇒ Nothing

Resets the node list so that the next node returned by `nextNode()` will be the first one.

Properties

Name	Returns	Description
`expr`	String	The XPath expression that determines the nodes selected. This can be changed at any time; doing so implicitly resets the current list of nodes, replacing it with a new list.
`context`	`IXMLDOMNode`	Establishes the context node for evaluating the expression. Changing the context node implicitly resets the current list of nodes, replacing it with a new list.
`length`	Long	Identifies the number of nodes in the collection.

IXSLProcessor

An `IXSLProcessor` object represents a single execution of a stylesheet to transform a source document.

The object is normally created by calling the `createProcessor()` method of an `IXSLTemplate` object.

The transformation is achieved by calling the `transform()` method.

Methods

Name	Returns	Description
`addParameter`	(Nothing)	Sets **`<xsl:param>`** value
`reset`	(Nothing)	Resets state of processor and abort current transform
`setStartMode`	(Nothing)	Sets XSLT mode and its namespace
`transform`	Boolean	Starts or resume the XSLT transformation process

addParameter(String localName, Variant value, String namespaceURI) ⇒ Nothing

This method supplies a value for a global parameter declared within the stylesheet using a top-level **`<xsl:param>`** element. The `localName` identifies the local name of the parameter, and the namespaceURI its namespace. In the common case that the parameter name has a null namespace URI, the third argument should be an empty string.

The value of the parameter is passed in the second argument. It can be a Boolean, a number, or a string; or a `Node` or `NodeList`. The last two cases will both be treated within the stylesheet as a node-set value. (Supplying a `Document` node as a parameter to a stylesheet is a convenient alternative to using the XSLT **`document()`** function, espiecally if the document is already in memory.)

reset() ⇒ Nothing

If a transformation is in progress, this aborts the transformation and resets the processor so it can be used again. It does **not** clear any parameters that have been added, or the `startMode`.

setStartMode(String mode, String namespaceURI) ⇒ Nothing

Normally when a stylesheet is used, processing starts by looking for a template rule that matches the root node and that is defined with no **`mode`** attribute. Sometimes it is useful to be able to use the same stylesheet in different ways on different occasions, so MSXML3 allows processing to start in a different mode from the default. Modes are described in Chapter 4, page 162: see the descriptions of the **`<xsl:apply-templates>`** and **`<xsl:template>`** elements.

Modes are identified by a QName (a namespace-qualified name), so this method allows both the local name and the namespace URI to be specified. Most commonly the second parameter will be an empty string.

transform() ⇒ Boolean

This method applies the stylesheet (from which this XSLProcessor was derived) to the source document identified in the input property. The result of the transformation is accessible through the output property.

If the transformation is completed, the return value is True. If the source document is being loaded asynchronously, it is possible for the transform() method to return False, meaning that it needs to wait until more input is available. In this case, it is possible to resume the transformation by calling transform() again later. The current state of the transformation can be determined from the readyState property.

Properties

Name	Returns	Description
input	Variant	XML source document to transform. This is normally supplied as a DOM Document, but it may also be a Node. The input can also be supplied as an IStream.
output	Variant	Output of the transformation. If you don't supply an output object, the processor will create a String to hold the output, which you can read using this property. If you prefer, you can supply an object such as a DOM Document, a DOM Node, or an IStream to receive the output.
ownerTemplate	IXSLTemplate	The XSLTemplate object used to create this processor object.
readyState	Long	The current state of the transformation. This will be READYSTATE_COMPLETE (3) when the transformation is finished.
startMode	String	Name of starting XSLT mode. See setStartMode() method above.
startModeURI	String	Namespace of starting XSLT mode. See setStartMode() method above.
stylesheet	IXMLDOMNode	The current stylesheet being used.

IXSLTemplate

An `IXSLTemplate` object represents a compiled stylesheet in memory. If you want to use the same stylesheet more than once, then creating an `IXSLTemplate` and using it repeatedly is more efficient than using the raw stylesheet repeatedly using `transformNode()`.

Methods

Name	Returns	Description
`createProcessor`	`IXSLProcessor`	Create an `IXSLProcessor` object

createProcessor() ⇒ IXSLProcessor

This method should only be called after the stylesheet property has been set to associate the `IXSLTemplate` object with a stylesheet.

It creates an `IXSLProcessor` object which can then be used to initiate a transformation of a given source document.

Properties

Name	Returns	Description
`stylesheet`	`IXMLDOMNode`	Identifies the stylesheet from which this `IXSLTemplate` is derived

Setting this property causes the specified stylesheet to be compiled; this `IXSLTemplate` object is the reusable representation of the compiled stylesheet.

The DOM `Node` representing the stylesheet will normally be a DOM `Document` object, but it may be an Element representing an embedded stylesheet. (Embedded stylesheets are described in Chapter 3, page 106.)

The document identified by the stylesheet property must be a free-threaded document object.

Summary

This appendix summarized the techniques and application programming interfaces available for using Microsoft's MSXML3 product, with a particular focus on its XSLT transformation capabilities.

We saw how to view XML directly in the IE5 browser, either with the default stylesheet or with one identified through the `<?xml-stylesheet?>` processing instruction. Then we saw how to use client-side scripting to control the transformation process, even seeing how it is possible to modify the stylesheet each time it is used.

Then we looked at the use of MSXML3 as a server-side technology, performing transformations controlled from an ASP page, or doing transformations either on the server or on the client, depending on the capabilities of the user's browser.

We finished with a summary of the classes and methods used to control XSLT transformation in the Microsoft API.

Microsoft are sometimes criticized as the bad guys when it comes to standards conformance. Certainly, they caused an immense amount of confusion in the market by shipping their own WD-xsl dialect in Internet Explorer before the standards had stabilized. Indeed this is still causing confusion, because at the time of writing, the XSL processor being shipped with Microsoft general release software still only supports WD-xsl and not XSLT 1.0 (let alone XSLT 1.1).

However, MSXML3 as it has finally emerged delivers a very high level of conformance to the standards, and appears destined to become a robust and high-performance XSLT engine. Its unique claim to fame at present (until Netscape catches up, which can't be far away) is the ability to integrate XSLT processing into the client, something that has great potential to revolutionize the way we distribute processing load between the client and the server, while at the same time creating opportunities for a much more interactive and responsive experience for the user.

Oracle

Oracle's XML technology is loosely coupled under the name Oracle XML Developer's Kit (XDK) . This consists of a number of components which can be installed separately from each other. One of these components is the Oracle XML parser for Java; another is the Oracle parser for C++. Both these parsers, despite their name, actually include XSLT processors as an integral part.

In this appendix we'll take a quick look at the overall structure of the XDK, and then home in quickly on the XSLT processor. It's important to understand the context in which the Oracle parsers have been developed. Oracle are not really trying to develop their XML technology as a stand-alone product, and if you evaluated each component on its own there would be few convincing reasons to choose them in preference to the many open source alternatives available. The main reason for using Oracle's XML components, apart from the fact that you may value Oracle's technical support, is that they integrate well with the rest of the Oracle platform.

The Oracle XML Development Kit

For a full treatment of the Oracle XML Development Kit (XDK), see the Wrox Press book *Professional Oracle 8i Application Programming* (ISBN 1861004842) . In this book we only have space for a quick overview, so you can assess what is there before looking elsewhere for the detail.

These components can all be downloaded from the Oracle technet web site at http://technet.oracle.com/tech/xml. They are free to play with, but for production use you need to get a proper license and support agreement. Before you can download the software you need to go through a rather lengthy registration process giving lots of information about you and your company, and ticking a number of checkboxes asking whether you are a convicted terrorist, a narcotics dealer, or a resident of Libya (if you answer yes, they helpfully advise you to change your answer before continuing).

No source code is provided, even if you aren't a terrorist.

Parsers

Oracle has parsers available for Java, C++ (also supporting C), and PL/SQL.

The Java and C++ parsers include XSLT processors. They both support DOM and SAX interfaces. At the time of writing the released parsers support SAX 1.0 and DOM 1.0, but there is a beta release of the Java parser (version 2.1) that supports SAX 2.0 and DOM 2.0 available from the same web site. All work either in validating or non-validating mode.

The bulk of this appendix is devoted to the XSLT processor included with the Java parser. I haven't made any attempt to describe the C++ XSLT processor, for the simple reason that I wasn't able to discover from Oracle's documentation how to install it and make it work. You can probably get over the installation hurdles if you are completely familiar with the procedures for building and installing C++ applications on your chosen platform, but even then, you will find the documentation for actually using the product extremely sparse. When I downloaded it, for example, the file `XSLProcessor.html` was empty. Unless you're a hobbyist who sees this as an intellectual challenge, or have a friendly Oracle consultant on hand with privileged sources of knowledge, I'd advise you to wait until the technology is rather better packaged.

There are two PL/SQL parsers that can be invoked from Oracle stored procedures. One is simply a wrapper around the Java parser. The second is a pure PL/SQL parser, supporting a DOM interface, which is compatible with Oracle 7.3.4 and above, but this has much more limited functionality. I won't say any more about the PL/SQL products, as they aren't directly relevant to the use of XSLT.

XML Schema Support

Oracle have introduced one of the first implementations of the W3C XML Schema specification, currently a Candidate Recommendation, which is widely tipped to replace DTDs as the preferred way of defining and validating document structures. The processor is currently described as a beta release.

The schema processor is a separate download, but it has no API of its own: it is invoked automatically by the Java XML parser if the source document contains a reference to a schema. All you need to do is to put the schema processor (the `xschema.jar` file) on the class path, the parser will do the rest.

XSQL Pages

Unlike the other components of the XDK, which implement recognized W3C standards, XSQL is a technology peculiar to Oracle. As one might expect from a company that specializes in database technology, it is part of an ambitious attempt to integrate the relational world of SQL with the hierarchical world of XML.

An XSQL page is essentially an XML document containing SQL queries. For example:

```
<?xml version 1.0?>
<xsql:query xmlns="urn:oracle-xsql" connection="productdb">
   SELECT description FROM product WHERE code='PZ662431'
</xsql:query>
```

The connection name (`productdb`) refers to an entry in a configuration file defining the actual connection parameters to the database.

An XSQL page sits on the server rather like an ASP page or a JSP page. When a user requests the page by specifying its URL in a browser, then instead of returning the page itself, the web server executes the logic on the page and returns the result. The XSQL page is executed by a servlet, and the release notes for the product explain how to configure the XSQL engine to run with a variety of popular web servers that support the servlet API. There is also a freestanding Web-to-Go server included with the Windows 2000 version.

Executing the example page above performs a database query, and the result of the query is returned to the browser in the form of an XML document:

```
<?xml version="1.0"?>
<ROWSET>
  <ROW num="1">
    <description>High-speed electric drill</description>
  </ROW>
</ROWSET>
```

There are of course many additional elements and attributes you can use in the query page to affect the layout of the result, but this trivial example illustrates the basic idea.

An XSQL page can directly reference the parameters included in the requesting URL, so if the URL takes the form

```
http://www.megacorp.com/xsql/catalog.xsql?prodcode=PZ87453
```

then the SQL query can be parameterized to read

```
<xsql:query xmlns="urn:oracle-xsql" connection="productdb">
   SELECT description FROM product WHERE code='{@prodcode}'
</xsql:query>
```

Of course, the XML form of the query results can be converted to HTML using an XSLT stylesheet. To do this, simply add an **<?xml-stylesheet?>** processing instruction to the XSQL page. In fact, you can add several such processing instructions, specifying different stylesheets to use depending on the requested media (which in effect means the combination of client device and browser). For example:

```
<?xml version 1.0?>
<?xml-stylesheet type="text/xsl" media="Mozilla"
href="navigator.xsl"?>
<?xml-stylesheet type="text/xsl" media="Spyglass" href="mosaic.xsl"?>
<?xml-stylesheet type="text/xsl" href="default.xsl"?>
<xsql:query xmlns="urn:oracle-xsql" connection="productdb">
   SELECT description FROM product WHERE code='{@prodcode}'
</xsql:query>
```

An alternative is to pass the name of the required stylesheet as a parameter in the URL. The URL can also specify whether the transformation is to be carried out on the server or on the client. For example, the following URL (all on one line) nominates the stylesheet `iexplorer.xsl` and indicates that the transformation will take place in the browser:

```
http://www.megacorp.com/xsql/catalog.xsql?prodcode=PZ87453&
    xml-stylesheet=iexplorer&transform=client
```

Remember that when you write such a URL in an HTML page or an XSLT stylesheet, the «`&`» character should be written as «`&`». HTML browsers will happily accept «`&`», though it is technically incorrect, but the rules in XML are more strict.

The Oracle XML SQL Utility

The servlet code that implements XSQL pages, described in the previous section, is in fact nothing more than a thin layer above a subsystem called the Oracle XML SQL utility. This subsystem can also be accessed from the command line, or via a Java API.

The main two functions of this subsystem are represented by the Java classes `OracleXMLQuery`, which generates an XML document as the result of an SQL query, and `OracleXMLSave`, which does the opposite: it loads data into the database from an XML document.

Oracle defines a standard XML representation of relational data: the simplest way to see how your own tables will be represented in this form is to put a simple «`SELECT * FROM products`» query into an XSQL page and view the results directly in Internet Explorer, without any XSLT stylesheet. It is essentially a three-level structure: a `<ROWSET>` element to define the table, a `<ROW>` element to define each row, and an element, whose name is derived from the SQL column name, to define each column value within the row. You can set various options to change the names of the elements and attributes used in this representation, or you can simply use it as it is, and rely on an XSLT stylesheet to do the work of transforming it into something else.

Once you understand the format of the XML data that the `OracleXMLQuery` tool generates, you can write XSLT stylesheets that convert data into this format from other sources. The resulting XML files can then be used to load data into the database using the `OracleXMLSave` tool.

The XML Class Generators

Whereas the OracleXML utility performs a mapping between relational data structures and XML data structures, the Oracle Class Generators perform a mapping between XML structures and Java or C++ class definitions.

At present the class generators are driven from a DTD rather than an XML Schema. The tool takes the DTD as input, and generates a Java or C++ class for each element definition in the DTD.

The idea of this tool is to allow Java or C++ applications to be written in terms of the actual business objects relevant to the application (for example, Customer, Account, and Invoice), instead of using abstract objects such as `Element`, `Attribute`, and `Document` as defined in the DOM. It should be possible to take the class definitions generated by the Oracle class generator and add business logic to make them active: instead of being static data objects reflecting the XML structure, they can start to have methods that reflect the application behavior.

But I won't say any more about this, because I don't want to distract you from writing this logic in an even higher-level language, namely XSLT!

The Java XSLT Processor

Oracle's XSLT processor is bundled with their XML parser software. It is available from http://technet.oracle.com/tech/xml/. The Java XSLT processor is part of the **XML: Parser for Java v2** product. It is still described as early adopter software, though it has in fact been around for a while now, but a new version that is fully integrated with Oracle 9i can be expected later this year (2001) – check the Oracle web site for details. The free license is for internal data processing operations only but permits distribution to third parties under specified conditions. Source code is not provided, and formal support is only available if you have a separate support agreement with Oracle. However, there is an active discussion forum where the development team (including the chief architect, Steve Muench) regularly answer users' questions.

As well as an XSLT processor, Oracle's product includes an XML parser supporting DOM and SAX interfaces, with support for the XML Namespaces Recommendation. The parser operates in both validating and non-validating modes. The current production release, 2.0, supports DOM 1.0 and SAX 1.0. But there is also a beta version, 2.1, which supports DOM 2.0 and SAX 2.0.

Oracle claim that their XSLT implementation is fully conformant with the final (November 1999) XSLT 1.0 and XPath 1.0 Recommendations. As with other vendors, you have to take this on trust because there are no independent conformance tests available yet.

Oracle don't say very much about their coverage of features that the standard leaves optional or implementation-defined, so in these areas you may need to do some trial and error. In fact, the documentation for this product is surprisingly weak: it feels much more like the kind of documentation produced by a one-man startup than by the world's second largest software company. Be prepared to explore the `javadoc` API documentation for clues, or to browse around the discussion forum for answers to questions raised by other users. No doubt this will all improve as the technology reaches product status.

The Command Line Interface

The Oracle XSLT processor may be invoked through a simple command line interface. Once you have installed the Java Virtual Machine and the Oracle software, and set up the `PATH` and `CLASSPATH` environment variables, you can run the processor from the command line as follows:

```
java oracle.xml.parser.v2.oraxsl source.xml stylesheet.xsl result.xml
```

The `java` command typically invokes Sun's Java Virtual Machine. If you prefer to use Microsoft's Java VM (which will already be installed on your machine if you are running a recent version of Internet Explorer), use the command `jview` instead.

The following options are available:

Option	Meaning
`-d directory`	Name of directory containing source files to transform
`-e error-log`	Name of file to which error messages will be written
`-i source-extension`	Extensions of source files to include
`-l xml-file-list`	List of source files to transform
`-o directory`	Name of directory where result files will be written
`-p parameter-list`	List of stylesheet parameters, in name=value notation (see below)
`-r result-extension`	Extension to use for result files
`-s stylesheet`	Name of stylesheet file
`-t number-of-threads`	Number of threads to use
`-v`	Verbose mode
`-w`	Show warnings
`-x source-extension`	Extensions of source files to exclude

Stylesheet parameters can be specified using the `-p` option. I couldn't find any documentation saying how to use this, but discovered by trial and error that the following works (for running the knight's tour stylesheet in Chapter 10, with the knight starting on square d3):

```
  java oracle.xml.parser.v2.oraxsl -p start='d3' dummy.xml tour10.xsl
out.html
```

As with the other products, the command-line interface is really only intended as a development tool. For serious production use, you should write an application that invokes the Java API directly. This is described in the following section.

The Transformation API

The Oracle XSLT processor does not as yet implement the TrAX API described in Appendix F, or other parts of JAXP 1.1, though Steve Muench has stated in response to questions on the discussion forum that an implementation is planned as part of a forthcoming new release of the parser with Oracle 9i. The information in this section is therefore temporary: watch the Oracle web site for news of the new API. Quite apart from the benefits of making your applications portable between different XSLT processors, the TrAX API will be easier to use because it is much better documented than the current Oracle API.

You can find the details of the current API within the `javadoc` documentation for the product, and there are several sample applications to get you started. The two key classes are `XSLStylesheet`, which represents a pre-processed (or compiled) stylesheet which you can use as often as you like, and `XSLProcessor`, which you use to apply a stylesheet to a source document. `XSLStylesheet` is the Oracle equivalent of the TrAX `Templates` object, while `XSLProcessor` is the Oracle equivalent of a TrAX `Transformer`.

You start the process by creating an `XSLStylesheet` object. There are four constructors you can use. In each case the first argument indicates the source of the stylesheet, and the second is a URL that will be used as the base URI for resolving relative URIs in **`<xsl:include>`** and **`<xsl:import>`** elements.

The first argument can be any one of:

- An `XMLDocument` (that is, a DOM built using the Oracle parser)
- A URL identifying the location of the source stylesheet
- An `InputStream` from which the stylesheet can be read
- A `Reader` from which the stylesheet can be read

The `XSLStylesheet` represents the compiled form of the stylesheet. This can be used as often as you like to transform different source documents. These transformations can be done serially or in parallel, in multiple threads. Each transformation requires its own `XSLProcessor`.

(That's the theory, anyway. Unfortunately if the transformation requires parameters, the parameter values must be supplied to the `XSLStylesheet` object, not to the `XSLProcessor`. This means you can only do parallel transformations using the same compiled stylesheet if they all use the same parameter values.)

You create an `XSLProcessor` using a constructor with no arguments: it is not initially tied to any particular stylesheet. You can then perform a transformation using any one of a large number of `processXSL()` methods, listed in the table below:

<table>
<tr><th>Method</th><th>Effect</th></tr>
<tr><td><code>XMLDocumentFragment
processXSL(
      XSLStylesheet xsl,
      java.io.InputStream xml,
      java.net.URL baseURI)</code></td><td>Transform an input XML document using a given stylesheet. The input document is read from the <code>InputStream</code> using the supplied base URI to resolve any relative URIs in the document. The result is returned as a DOM <code>DocumentFragment</code> object.</td></tr>
<tr><td><code>XMLDocumentFragment
processXSL(
      XSLStylesheet xsl,
      java.io.Reader xml,
      java.net.URL baseURI)</code></td><td>Transform an input XML document using a given stylesheet. The input document is read from the <code>Reader</code> using the supplied base URI to resolve any relative URIs in the document. The result is returned as a DOM <code>DocumentFragment</code> object.</td></tr>
</table>

Method	Effect
`XMLDocumentFragment processXSL( XSLStylesheet xsl, java.net.URL xml, java.net.URL baseURI)`	Transform an input XML document using a given stylesheet. The input document is read from the location given by the first URL, using the supplied base URI to resolve any relative URIs in the document. The result is returned as a DOM `DocumentFragment` object.
`XMLDocumentFragment processXSL( XSLStylesheet xsl, XMLDocument xml)`	Transform an input XML document using a given stylesheet. The input document is supplied as a DOM. The result is returned as a DOM `DocumentFragment` object.
`void processXSL( XSLStylesheet xsl, XMLDocument xml, ContentHandler handler)`	Transform an input XML document using a given stylesheet. The input document is supplied as a DOM. The result tree is streamed into the supplied SAX2 `ContentHandler`.
`XMLDocumentFragment processXSL( XSLStylesheet xsl, XMLDocumentFragment inp)`	Transform an input XML document using a given stylesheet. The input document is supplied as a DOM `DocumentFragment`. The result is returned as a DOM `DocumentFragment` object.
`void processXSL( XSLStylesheet xsl, XMLDocumentFragment xml, java.io.OutputStream os)`	Transform an input XML document using a given stylesheet. The input document is supplied as a DOM `DocumentFragment`. The result is written to the supplied `OutputStream`.
`void processXSL( XSLStylesheet xsl, XMLDocumentFragment xml, java.io.PrintWriter pw)`	Transform an input XML document using a given stylesheet. The input document is supplied as a DOM `DocumentFragment`. The result is written to the supplied `PrintWriter`.
`void processXSL( XSLStylesheet xsl, XMLDocumentFragment inp, XMLDocumentHandler handler)`	Transform an input XML document using a given stylesheet. The input document is supplied as a DOM `DocumentFragment`. The result tree is streamed into the supplied SAX1 `DocumentHandler`.
`void processXSL( XSLStylesheet xsl, XMLDocument xml, java.io.OutputStream os)`	Transform an input XML document using a given stylesheet. The input document is supplied as a DOM `Document`. The result is written to the supplied `OutputStream`.
`void processXSL( XSLStylesheet xsl, XMLDocument xml, java.io.PrintWriter pw)`	Transform an input XML document using a given stylesheet. The input document is supplied as a DOM `Document`. The result is written to the supplied `PrintWriter`.
`void processXSL( XSLStylesheet xsl, XMLDocument xml, XMLDocumentHandler handler)`	Transform an input XML document using a given stylesheet. The input document is supplied as a DOM `Document`. The result tree is streamed into the supplied SAX1 `DocumentHandler`.

Note that while the Oracle XSLT engine can take its input from a source tree supplied in the form of a DOM `Document` or `DocumentFragment`, this must be a `Document` or `DocumentFragment` that was created using the Oracle tools.

The typical sequence for performing a transformation is given by the example code below.

```
// create a parser and configure it

parser = new DOMParser();
parser.setPreserveWhitespace(true);

// parse the input XSLT file into a DOM Document
xslURL = createURL(args[0]);
parser.parse(xslURL);
xsldoc = parser.getDocument();

// parse the source XML file into a DOM Document
xmlURL = createURL(args[1]);
parser.parse(xmlURL);
xmldoc = parser.getDocument();

// instantiate a stylesheet
XSLStylesheet xsl = new XSLStylesheet(xsldoc, xslURL);

// create an XSL processor and configure it
XSLProcessor processor = new XSLProcessor();
processor.showWarnings(true);
processor.setErrorStream(System.err);

// perform the transformation
DocumentFragment result = processor.processXSL(xsl, xmldoc);

// create an output document to hold the result
out = new XMLDocument();

// create a dummy document element for the output document
Element root = out.createElement("root");
out.appendChild(root);

// append the transformed tree to the dummy document element
root.appendChild(result);

// print the transformed document
out.print(System.out);
```

An alternative way to perform a transformation is to call the **`transformNode()`** method on an `XMLNode` object (Oracle's implementation of `org.w3c.dom.Node`). This method takes an `XSLStylesheet` object as its parameter, and returns a `DocumentFragment`.

Vendor extensions

Oracle supply two vendor extensions to XSLT 1.0; a function to convert a result tree fragment to a node-set, and an extension element to create multiple output files.

These are not well-documented; in fact the only reference I could find was in one-liners buried among long lists of cleared bugs in the readme file.

The oracle:node-set() Extension Function

This function has the same purpose as the **node-set()** function in other popular XSLT 1.0 products: it accepts a result tree fragment as an argument, and returns a node-set containing a single node, the root of the tree.

This function greatly increases the power of the language, because it means you can do a transformation in a sequence of stages; the output of the first stage is a result tree fragment, and this can then be converted to a node-set to provide input for subsequent stages. The function will become obsolete with XSLT 1.1, which allows implicit conversion of a result tree fragment to a node-set when required.

You can use any namespace prefix for the function, so long as it is declared with the namespace URI http://www.oracle.com/XSL/Transform/java.

Example: Using the oracle:node-set() Function

Here is an example stylesheet that uses the **oracle:node-set()** function. It doesn't do anything very useful, but illustrates the functionality.

Source

You can run this stylesheet against any source document. (For example, you can use the stylesheet itself as the source document.)

Stylesheet

The stylesheet is in file `oracle-nodeset.xsl`:

```
<xsl:stylesheet
    xmlns:xsl="http://www.w3.org/1999/XSL/Transform"
    version="1.0">

<xsl:template match="/">
  <xsl:variable name="tree">
    <table><tr><td val="85"/></tr></table>
  </xsl:variable>
  <xsl:variable name="ns" select="oracle:node-set($tree)"
      xmlns:oracle="http://www.oracle.com/XSL/Transform/java"/>
  <out><xsl:value-of select="$ns//td/@val"/></out>
</xsl:template>

</xsl:stylesheet>
```

Output

The output from the stylesheet is:

```
<?xml version = '1.0' encoding = 'UTF-8'?>
<out>85</out>
```

The oracle:output Extension Element

This extension element is provided to allow a stylesheet to generate multiple output files. It thus corresponds to the **<xsl:document>** element introduced in XSLT 1.1.

Oracle have chosen to separate this function into two parts: one is an instruction (used within a template body) that switches the output destination, the other is a top-level element that describes the format of the output file. Both of these functions are performed by elements called **<oracle:output>**, but the **<oracle:output>** instruction has a **use** attribute that refers to the **name** attribute of a top-level **<oracle:output>** element. The top-level element may contain any of the attributes allowed on **<xsl:output>**, for example method, encoding, and indent. The name of the output file is defined by the **href** attribute of the **<oracle:output>** instruction.

The following example shows how it works. It performs the same function as the example given in the **<xsl:document>** entry in Chapter 4 (on page 204), of splitting a poem into its stanzas, but adapted to use the Oracle syntax.

Example: Using the oracle:output Extension Element

Here is an example stylesheet that uses the **oracle:output** extension element to split a poem into one file for each stanza.

Source

The source file is the Rupert Brooke poem `poem.xml` (which if you've read this far in the book, you will now know by heart). It contains a <poem> element which acts as the parent of a number of <stanza> elements, among other things.

Stylesheet

The stylesheet is in file `oracle-split.xsl`. Each stanza in the original poem is output to a separate file, and the main output file contains hyperlinks to the stanza files.

```
<?xml version="1.0"?>
<xsl:stylesheet xmlns:xsl="http://www.w3.org/1999/XSL/Transform"
    version="1.0"
    xmlns:oracle="http://www.oracle.com/XSL/Transform/java"
    extension-element-prefixes="oracle">

<xsl:template match="poem">
    <poem>
        <xsl:copy-of select="title"/>
        <xsl:copy-of select="author"/>
        <xsl:copy-of select="date"/>
        <xsl:apply-templates select="stanza"/>
    </poem>
</xsl:template>

<xsl:template match="stanza">
    <xsl:variable name="file"
                  select="concat('verse', position(), '.xml')"/>
    <verse number="{position()}" href="{$file}"/>
    <oracle:output href="{$file}" use="stanza-format">
            <xsl:copy-of select="."/>
    </oracle:output>
</xsl:template>

<oracle:output name="stanza-format" method="xml" encoding="iso-
8859-1"/>

</xsl:stylesheet>
```

B

Oracle

Output

The principal output from the stylesheet is (indented for readability):

```
<?xml version = '1.0' encoding = 'UTF-8'?>
<poem xmlns:oracle="http://www.oracle.com/XSL/Transform/java">
  <title>Song</title>
  <author>Rupert Brooke</author>
  <date>1912</date>
  <verse number="1" href="verse1.xml"/>
  <verse number="2" href="verse2.xml"/>
  <verse number="3" href="verse3.xml"/>
</poem>
```

There will also be one output file produced for each stanza, for example `verse1.xml` looks like this:

```
<?xml version = '1.0' encoding = 'iso-8859-1'?>
<stanza>
<line>And suddenly the wind comes soft,</line>
<line>And Spring is here again;</line>
<line>And the hawthorn quickens with buds of green</line>
<line>And my heart with buds of pain.</line>
</stanza>
```

Extensibility

The Java version of the Oracle XSLT processor allows the use of user-defined extension functions written in Java. As yet there is no mechanism for creating user-defined extension elements.

An extension function can be called from an XPath expression using the syntax `prefix:method(arguments)`. Here `prefix` must be a namespace prefix that has been declared using a namespace declaration of the form

```
xmlns:prefix="http://www.oracle.com/XSL/Transform/java/package.name.Cl
assname"
```

For example, to call methods defined in the Java class `java.util.Date`, you could declare the namespace as:

```
xmlns:Date="http://www.oracle.com/XSL/Transform/java/java.util.Date"
```

The local part of the name used in the XPath function call must be the name of a method defined in the chosen class, or **new**, indicating a constructor.

For a constructor, or for static methods, the arguments supplied in the XPath function call must correspond one-to-one with the arguments declared in the Java method signature.

If an external function returns a Java object that cannot be converted to one of the XPath data types, it can be held in the stylesheet as an external object. An external object can be stored in an XPath variable or parameter, and passed as an argument to other external method calls.

For an instance-level (non-static) method, the XPath function call will contain an additional first argument that is not present in the Java method signature: this argument identifies the external Java object that acts as the target of the method invocation.

The supplied XPath arguments will be converted automatically to the required Java types. The following data types are considered to map directly:

Java data type	XPath data type
`java.lang.String`	string
`int, double, float`	number
`boolean`	boolean
`org.w3c.dom.NodeList` (see note)	node-set
`org.w3c.dom.DocumentFragment`	result tree fragment

Note: the documentation says `XMLNodeList`, whch is Oracle's implementation of this interface; but the class `XMLNodeList` isn't public, so you can't use it. I tried using the DOM `NodeList` interface directly, and it worked fine. Similarly the documentation lists the implementation class `XMLDocumentFragment`, but the DOM interface `DocumentFragment` works happily.

If the types of the arguments do not correspond directly, then conversion is attempted using the XPath rules. For example, if a `String` is expected and a node-set is supplied, then the node-set is converted to a string following the rules of the XPath **`string()`** function.

Method overloading is permitted, to a limited extent. The class can contain several methods with the same name (or several constructors) if they have different numbers of arguments. It can also have several methods with the same name (or constructors) with the same number of arguments, provided that no conversion is permitted between the relevant data types. For example, the class `java.lang.Math` has four `max()` methods each expecting two arguments, specifically `max(int, int)`, `max(double, double)`, `max(long, long)`, and `max(float, float)`. It is not possible to call any of these methods directly from the stylesheet, because it is ambiguous as to which of the methods is intended.

The return value can be any Java object or value. If it can be converted to one of the XSLT 1.0 data types (string, number, boolean, node-set, or result tree fragment) then the return value will be of this type; otherwise, the return value is held as an external object.

Examples

The following code sets a variable to a random number between 0.0 and 1.0. This example calls a static method on the class `java.lang.Math`.

```
<xsl:variable name="random" select="Math:random()"
    xmlns:Math=="http://www.oracle.com/XSL/Transform/java/java.lang.Math"/>
```

The following code outputs the current date and time, in the default Java format. This example calls the default constructor for the class `java.util.Date`. The resulting `Date` object is treated by XPath as an external object. It is immediately passed as an argument to another external function, the `toString()` method of `java.util.Date`, which creates a printable representation of the date. This instance-level method expects no arguments, so the external object supplied in the function call is used as the target instance of the method invocation.

```
  <xsl:value-of select="Date:toString(Date:new())"

xmlns:Date="http://www.oracle.com/XSL/Transform/java/java.util.Date"/>
```

Finally, here's an extension function I wrote before I discovered the documentation of **`oracle:node-set()`** buried in the readme file. It doesn't work exactly like the **`oracle:node-set()`** function which returns a single node, the root of the tree: this **`children()`** function returns a node-set containing all the children of the root of the tree.

Here's the Java code, which you can find in `OracleChildren.java`. Yes, this powerful function turns out to be a one-liner:

```
import org.w3c.dom.*;

public class OracleChildren {
    public static NodeList children(DocumentFragment tree) {
        return tree.getChildNodes();
    }
}
```

And here is a stylesheet that uses it, in `oracle-children.xsl`. You can run this stylesheet against any source document, once the `OracleChildren` class is on your class path. The output is `<out>85</out>`

```
<xsl:stylesheet xmlns:xsl="http://www.w3.org/1999/XSL/Transform" version="1.0">

<xsl:template match="/">
  <xsl:variable name="tree">
    <table><tr><td val="85"/></tr></table>
  </xsl:variable>
  <xsl:variable name="ns" select="my:children($tree)"
      xmlns:my="http://www.oracle.com/XSL/Transform/java/OracleChildren"/>
  <out><xsl:value-of select="$ns//td/@val"/></out>
</xsl:template>

</xsl:stylesheet>
```

XPath Support

Buried deep within the `javadoc` documentation for the product, you will find that the class `XMLNode`, which is Oracle's implementation of the standard `org.w3c.dom.Node` interface, supports methods to select nodes within the DOM using XPath expressions, independently of the XSLT processor.

The four methods are:

Method	Effect
`selectNodes( String expression)`	Evaluates the given expression, returning the result as a DOM `NodeList`
`selectNodes( String expression, NSResolver resolver)`	Evaluates the given expression, using the supplied `NSResolver` to resolve any namespace prefixes, and returning the result as a DOM `NodeList`
`selectSingleNode( String expression)`	Evaluates the given expression, returning the result as a DOM `Node`
`selectSingleNode( String expression, NSResolver resolver)`	Evaluates the given expression, using the supplied `NSResolver` to resolve any namespace prefixes, and returning the result as a DOM Node

An `NSResolver` is an object that can turn a namespace prefix into a namespace URI. Conveniently, any `XMLElement` or `XMLDocument` (Oracle's implementations of the DOM `Element` and `Document` nodes) is capable of acting as an `NSResolver`.

As so often happens with documentation derived from comments in the source code, the published `javadoc` descriptions of these methods are sadly inaccurate. The documentation says that the first argument is an XSL pattern, and that the method returns all nodes that match this pattern. This isn't what actually happens; if the argument supplied is `"author"`, then the documentation would imply that all the `<author>` elements in the document are returned. A little trial and error shows that the method actually returns the `<author>` children of the context node (that is, the node to which the method is applied). In other words, the system is interpreting the argument as an XPath expression with the target node acting as the context node – which is exactly what you would expect if you are familiar with the Microsoft methods of the same name.

Some further experimentation also shows that entering an XPath expression that does not return a node-set may either throw an `XSLException` or return null, so you should cater for both possibilities.

The following little application (which I took from the Wrox book *Developing Oracle 8i Applications*, and improved slightly) uses the `selectNodes()` method to allow you to enter XPath expressions from the console, and see the selected nodes displayed. The expression is always interpreted with the root of the document as the context node. You will find the application (in both source and compiled forms) among the download files for this appendix.


```
import java.io.*;
import oracle.xml.parser.v2.*;
import org.xml.sax.*;
import org.w3c.dom.*;

public class XPathToy {
    private  XMLDocument document;
    private  String query;
public XPathToy(String filename) {
    try {
```

```
            document = loadXMLDocument(filename);
            BufferedReader in =
               new BufferedReader(new InputStreamReader(System.in));
            do {
                System.out.print("XPath> ");
                query = in.readLine();
                try {
                    NodeList nodes = ((XMLNode)document).selectNodes(
                                   query,
                                  (NSResolver)document.getDocumentElement());
                    if (nodes==null) {
                        System.out.println("XPath query must return a node-set");
                    } else {
                        for (int i = 0; i < nodes.getLength(); i++) {
                            System.out.println(
                                "Name:  " + nodes.item(i).getNodeName());
                            System.out.println(
                                "Value: " + nodes.item(i).getNodeValue());
                        }
                    }
                } catch (XSLException e) {
                    System.out.println("Invalid XPath query: " + query);
                }
            } while (!(query.equals("quit")));
        } catch (IOException e) {
            System.err.println(
                "Could not load '" + filename + "': " + e.toString());
        } catch (SAXException e) {
            System.err.println("Could not parse XML: " + e.toString());
        }
    }

    private XMLDocument loadXMLDocument(String filename)
    throws  IOException, SAXException {
        File file = new File(filename);
        FileReader reader = new FileReader(file);

        DOMParser parser = new DOMParser();
        parser.parse(reader);

        return parser.getDocument();
    }


    public static void main(String[] args) {
        if (args.length == 1)
            new XPathToy(args[0]);
        else
            System.err.println("Usage: java XPathToy <filename>");
    }

    }  // end of class XPathToy
```

To run this application, make sure that both the directory holding the `XPathToy` class and the `xmlparserv2.jar` file are on your class path, and from the command line, type

```
java XPathToy poem.xml
```

The application prompts you to enter an XPath expression. For example, type:

```
XPath>//stanza[1]/line[2]/text()
```

and the system responds:

```
Name:  #text
Value: And Spring is here again;
```

To exit the application, type «quit».

The names and values that are output by this toy application are those returned by the DOM methods getNodeName() and getValue(). These are not the same as the XPath name and value, for example the value of an element node is always null. To get the text within an element node, you have to use «text()» as part of the path expression, as shown.

Character Encodings

The Oracle parser currently supports the following encodings, for both input and output.

BIG 5
EBCDIC-CP-*
EUC-JP
EUC-KR
GB2312
ISO-10646-UCS-2
ISO-10646-UCS-4
ISO-2022-JP
ISO-2022-KR
ISO-8859-1to -9
KOI8-R
Shift_JIS
US-ASCII
UTF-16
UTF-8

Any other ASCII or EBCDIC based encodings that are supported by the Java Virtual Machine in use may be used. However, they must be specified using the Java name for the encoding, which is not always the same as the official character set names defined by IANA.

Summary

I want to avoid making value judgements on the different products that are available, but at the end of writing this appendix, I have to say that I feel Oracle's XSLT technology is badly let down by the poor quality of documentation available. It seems a shame to make the substantial investment needed to write a complex piece of software and then not tell people how to use it. Certainly, the current impression is that Oracle intend the software only to be used by fairly dedicated enthusiasts. But keep your eyes on it: once they decide that the technology is ready for mass exposure, the white papers will no doubt be flowing thick and fast.

If you're running a site that is heavily based around an Oracle database, then the XSQL Pages technology looks like a very attractive way of getting information out of the database and on to the web, without any procedural coding. Combine this with XSLT transformations on the extracted data, and you have all the components you need for rapid application development – and in this scenario, the lack of detailed programming documentation is perhaps not such a handicap after all.

Saxon

Saxon is an open source implementation of XSLT produced by the author of this book, Michael Kay. The development was sponsored initially by ICL, the IT services company, and more recently by Software AG, but it remains essentially a one-man effort rather than a corporate product.

Saxon is available at http://users.iclway.co.uk/mhkay/saxon/.

The product is available under the Mozilla Public License, which in effect allows you to use it free, for any purpose. The source code is available, and can be modified and enhanced subject to the terms of the license. There is no formal warranty or support, though there is a mailing list at `http://saxon.xsl.listbot.com/` where problems can be raised. The product is written in Java and runs on any Java 1.1 or Java 2 platform.

The product comes in two flavors: full Saxon, which contains the full Java source code, binaries, API documentation, and sample applications; and Instant Saxon, which is a no-frills command-line executable for the Windows platform. Both are built from the same source code and have identical functionality.

The current release, version 6.2, implements the whole of the W3C XSLT 1.0 and XPath 1.0 Recommendations and a major part of the new features in the XSLT 1.1 working draft of 5 December 2000. This includes most of the features that are optional or implementor-defined (the XSLT specification is very open-ended in aspects such as which character encodings and collating sequences should be supported). Detailed documentation is available with the product.

Installation

Instant Saxon comes in the form of a `.zip` file, `instant-saxon.zip`. Simply download this to any convenient location and open it with WinZip or any other suitable unzipper. Within it you will find a file `saxon.exe` which is the executable XSLT processor. Extract this file to any suitable directory, and for convenience, add this directory to your `PATH` in `autoexec.bat`.

The full Saxon product is a rather larger download, because it includes source files, full javadoc API documentation, and a selection of sample applications. It again comes as a `.zip` file, `saxon.zip`. Within this the important component is `saxon.jar`, which you should extract into a suitable directory. You need to add `saxon.jar` (**not** the directory containing it) to your `CLASSPATH`. On Windows 98 you do this by defining the `CLASSPATH` variable in your `autoexec.bat` file; on Windows NT and Windows 2000 you set it via the `System` icon on the control panel. If you use any other operating system, then I'll leave you to read the manual!

Saxon doesn't need any other software, beyond a Java VM. It will work with any SAX2-conformant XML parser, but by default it uses its own bundled parser, which is a slightly-modified version of David Megginson's Ælfred parser (this is a bug-fixed version of the original which can be found at http://www.opentext.com/microstar; it also adds a SAX2 driver written by David Brownell). There is an interface to the FOP implementation of XSL Formatting Objects, which you can get from http://xml.apache.org/, but this is optional.

Invoking the Saxon Processor

Saxon is written in Java, and implements the TrAX API defined in JAXP 1.1, which is described in detail in Appendix F. This allows it to be invoked from a Java application. There is also a command line interface. In addition, Saxon provides a servlet wrapper allowing a stylesheet to be invoked directly from a URL entered at a browser; however this is more in the nature of a demonstration application than a real part of the product.

There is no graphical user interface; however Saxon can be used with visual tools such as XMLSpy (http://www.xmlspy.com) to provide a friendlier front-end.

Using Saxon from the Command Line

If you just want to run the product on a Windows platform, and don't need access to API specifications, source code, or sample applications, it is simplest to download *Instant Saxon*, which is a packaged version designed to run as an executable under Microsoft's Java VM. You can then run a stylesheet using the command:

```
saxon source.xml style.xsl >output.html
```

You can do this from the standard MS-DOS console that comes with Windows, but I wouldn't recommend it because it's too difficult to correct your typing mistakes and to stop output scrolling off the screen. Far better is to install a text editor that includes a Windows-friendly command line capability. The two that I use are Programmer's File Editor and UltraEdit.

> *If the directory containing the* `saxon.exe` *file isn't the current directory, and isn't on your* `PATH`*, then you'll need to use the full name of the file, for example* `C:\saxon-dir\saxon`.

On other platforms, or with the full Saxon product, you invoke Saxon as a Java application. The command line becomes

```
java com.icl.saxon.StyleSheet source.xml style.xsl >output.html
```

if you use the Sun Java Virtual Machine, or

```
jview com.icl.saxon.StyleSheet source.xml style.xsl >output.html
```

if you prefer the Microsoft JVM. For production use, Sun JDK 1.3 is considerably faster than the current Microsoft JVM, though for single short runs from the command line, Instant Saxon (which uses the Microsoft JVM) often wins because the start-up costs are lower.

There are a number of options you can use on the command line. With Instant Saxon these are written immediately after the `saxon` keyword, before the name of the source file, thus:

```
saxon -t -w2 source.xml style.xsl >out.html
```

With full Saxon, they are written after the class name, for example:

```
java com.icl.saxon.StyleSheet -t -w2 source.xml style.xsl >out.html
```

The command line options are as follows:

Option	Description
`-a`	Use the `<?xml-stylesheet?>` processing instruction in the source document to identify the stylesheet to be used. The stylesheet argument should then be omitted.
`-ds` `-dt`	Selects the implementation of the internal tree model. `-dt` selects the "tinytree" model (the default). `-ds` selects the traditional tree model. This is a performance tuning option: the tinytree model is faster to build, and occupies less memory, but is sometimes slower to navigate. The default is `-dt`.
`-l`	Switches line numbering on for the source document. Line numbers are accessible through the extension function **`saxon:line-number()`**, or from a trace listener. Line numbering will be switched on automatically if the `-T` option is used.
`-m classname`	Specifies the full name of a Java class used to process the output of **`<xsl:message>`** instructions in the stylesheet. The class must extend the Saxon class `com.icl.saxon.output.Emitter`, whose design is based on the SAX2 `ContentHandler` interface. If this argument is omitted, the output of **`<xsl:message>`** is written to `System.err`
`-o filename`	Defines a filename to contain the output of the transformation. If the source file is a directory, the output must also be a directory: this allows all the files in a directory to be transformed using the same stylesheet, or each file using its own associated stylesheet if the `-a` option is also used. If this argument is omitted, the output is written to `System.out` (which may be redirected to a file by using the `>filename` construct).

Table continued on following page

`-r classname`	Specifies the full name of a Java class used to resolve URIs appearing in the **`document()`** function or the **`<xsl:include>`** or **`<xsl:import>`** elements in the stylesheet. It is also used to resolve the URIs identifying the source file and stylesheet on the command line. This class must implement the TrAX-defined interface **`javax.xml.transform.URIResolver`**.
`-t`	This option causes Saxon to display information about the Saxon and Java versions in use, and progress messages indicating which files are being processed and how long the key stages of processing took.
`-T`	Traces execution of the stylesheet. Each instruction is traced as it is executed, identifying the instruction and the current location in the source document by line number. The trace is written to `System.err`. It is written in the form of an XML document, so if you want to analyze the trace, you can write a stylesheet to do it!
`-TL classname`	Traces execution with a user-defined trace routine. The classname names a user-defined class, which must implement `com.icl.saxon.trace.TraceListener`. This interface is provided to allow the integration of third-party debuggers, for example **tbug**, written by Edwin Glaser and available at http://tbug.sourceforge.net.
`-u`	Indicates that the names of the source document and stylesheet given on the command line are to be interpreted as URLs rather than file names. (If the names start with «`http:`» or «`file:`», this will be assumed automatically.)
`-w0`	Indicates that where recovery from a stylesheet error is possible, Saxon should recover silently, taking the recovery action defined in the XSLT specification. For example, if a node matches two template rules with the same precedence and priority, it will choose the last.
`-w1`	Indicates that where recovery from a stylesheet error is possible, Saxon should recover with a warning message, taking the recovery action defined in the XSLT specification. For example, if a node matches two template rules with the same precedence and priority, it will choose the last, but will first output a message to indicate that the rules are ambiguous.
`-w2`	Indicates that when a stylesheet error occurs, Saxon should report the error and terminate execution even if recovery is possible.
`-x classname`	Defines the XML parser to be used for the source document, and for any additional document loaded using the **`document()`** function. The classname must be the name of a parser that implements the SAX1 `org.xml.sax.Parser` interface, or the SAX2 `org.xml.sax.XMLReader` interface.

-y classname	Defines the XML parser to be used for the stylesheet document, and for any additional stylesheet module loaded using **<xsl:include>** or **<xsl:import>**. The classname must be the name of a parser that implements the SAX1 org.xml.sax.Parser interface, or the SAX2 org.xml.sax.XMLReader interface.

(Why would you want to use different parsers for the source document and the stylesheet? One reason is that the source document might not really be XML; see the GEDCOM example in Chapter 10. Another reason is that you might want to use a validating parser for the source document, but not for the stylesheet.)

You can specify values for global parameters defined in the stylesheet using a keyword=value notation; for example:

```
saxon source.xml style.xsl param1=value1 param2=value2
```

or with full Saxon:

```
java com.icl.saxon.StyleSheet source.xml style.xsl param1=value1
param2=value2
```

If the parameter names have a non-null namespace, you can use the TrAX syntax for expanded names, for example «{namespace-uri}local-name». The parameter values are interpreted as strings. If the string contains a space, you should enclose it in quotes, for example «param1="John Brown"».

Using Saxon from a Java Application

Saxon can also be invoked from a Java application by using the TrAX API, which is described in Appendix F. This allows you to compile a stylesheet into a Templates object, which can then be used repeatedly (in series or in multiple threads) to process different source documents through the same stylesheet. This can greatly improve throughput on a web server. A sample application to achieve this, in the form of a Java servlet, is provided with the product.

Saxon implements the whole of the javax.xml.transform package, including the dom, sax, and stream sub-packages, both for input and output. It also implements the SAXTransformerFactory which allows you to do the transformation as part of a SAX pipeline.

The saxon.jar package includes a file that has the effect of causing the TrAX TransformerFactory to choose Saxon as the default XSLT processor. This means that if Saxon is the only TrAX implementation on your classpath, calling TransformerFactory.newInstance() will automatically give you an instance of Saxon's TrAX implementation. If however you have multiple TrAX implementations on the classpath, perhaps Xalan as well as Saxon, then the one that is loaded by default will depend on the ordering of entries on your classpath. The safest policy in such cases is to choose one of the implementations explicitly. There are several ways this can be achieved:

- You can choose Saxon by setting the Java system property named `javax.xml.transform.TransformerFactory` to the value `com.icl.saxon.TransformerFactoryImpl`. Use the `-D` option on the java command when you invoke your application. Note that this goes before the name of the class to be executed:

  ```
  java -Djavax.xml.transform.TransformerFactory=
         com.icl.saxon.TransformerFactoryImpl com.my-com.appl.Program
  ```

  This all goes on one line. In practice of course you won't want to type this more than once, so create a batch file or shell script using your text editor, and invoke that instead.

- Create a file called `jaxp.properties` within the directory `$JAVA_HOME/lib` (where `$JAVA_HOME` is the directory containing your Java installation), and include in this file a line of the form `key=value`, where `key` is the property key `javax.xml.transform.TransformerFactory` and `value` is the Saxon class `com.icl.saxon.TransformerFactoryImpl`.

- Put the call

  ```
  System.setProperty ("javax.xml.transform.TransformerFactory",
                      "com.icl.saxon.TransformerFactoryImpl")
  ```

  in your application, to be executed at run-time. This is the only technique that works if you want to run several different TrAX processors from the same application, perhaps in order to compare their results or to benchmark their performance.

Saxon, at the time of writing, does not implement the other half of the JAXP 1.1 specification, the `javax.xml.parsers` package, which is used to select SAX and DOM parsers. Nor does it currently use these interfaces when deciding which parser to load. To specify the SAX2 `XMLReader` or SAX1 `Parser` to be used to parse source documents and stylesheet modules (they can be different), call the `setAttribute()` method of the `TransformerFactory` as follows:

```
import com.icl.saxon.FeatureKeys;

TransformerFactory factory = TransformerFactory.newInstance();
factory.setAttribute(
     FeatureKeys.SOURCE_PARSER_CLASS,
     "org.apache.xerces.parsers.SAXParser");
factory.setAttribute(
     FeatureKeys.STYLE_PARSER_CLASS,
     " com.icl.saxon.aelfred.SAXDriver");
```

If these attributes are not set, Saxon will use its built-in version of the Ælfred parser.

There is no direct way of setting configuration options for the chosen parser, for example telling it to do XML validation, or telling it to use a particular SAX `EntityResolver`. If you want to do this, the best way is to write a Java class that subclasses your chosen parser, and set the options from the initialization code of this subclass. You can then nominate the subclass as the parser for Saxon to use.

For example, you could define the following class:

```
import org.xml.sax.*;
import com.icl.saxon.aelfred.*;

public class CustomizedParser extends SAXDriver implements EntityResolver {
```

```
    public CustomizedParser () {
      setEntityResolver(this);
    }

    public InputSource resolveEntity(String publicId, String systemId)
        throws org.xml.sax.SAXException, java.io.IOException {
      if (systemId.equals("http://www.acme.com/standard.dtd")) {
        return new InputSource("file://e:/dtds/standard.dtd");
      } else {
        return null;
      }
    }
  }
```

And then nominate this as your source parser:

```
factory.setAttribute(
     FeatureKeys.SOURCE_PARSER_CLASS,
     "CustomizedParser");
```

The only special action your customized parser takes is to redirect references to a particular DTD to use a local copy. (When **resolveEntity()** returns null, this indicates that the entity reference should be resolved by the parser in its normal way.)

Other Saxon configuration properties that you can set via the `setAttribute()` interface include the following. The names given are the constants defined in the class `com.icl.saxon.FeatureKeys`, rather than the actual strings passed across at run-time.

Attribute name	Value
`TIMING`	Boolean. Equivalent to the `-t` option on the command line.
`TREE_MODEL`	Integer, one of `Builder.STANDARD_TREE` or `Builder.TINY_TREE`. Defines the internal tree implementation to be used. (Despite the names, `TINY_TREE` is the default.)
`TRACE_LISTENER`	An instance of a class that implements the `com.icl.saxon.trace.TraceListener` interface.
`LINE_NUMBERING`	Boolean. Equilvalent to the `-l` option on the command line.
`RECOVERY_POLICY`	Integer. One of `Controller.RECOVER_SILENTLY`, `Controller.RECOVER_WITH_WARNINGS`, `Controller.DO_NOT_RECOVER`. Equivalent to the options `-w0`, `-w1`, or `-w2` on the command line.
`MESSAGE_EMITTER_CLASS`	A string containing the name of a class to be instantiated to handle output from **<xsl:message>**. The class must extend `com.icl.saxon.output.Emitter`.

Table continued on following page

Attribute name	Value
SOURCE_PARSER_CLASS	A string containing the name of the class to be used for parsing source documents, including documents read using the **document()** function. The class must be a SAX Parser or SAX2 XMLReader.
STYLE_PARSER_CLASS	A string containing the name of the class to be used for parsing stylesheet modules, including modules read using the **<xsl:include>** or **<xsl:import>** elements. The class must be a SAX Parser or SAX2 XMLReader.

The TransformerFactory can be further configured by calling the standard setURIResolver() and setErrorListener() methods.

Saxon and the DOM

Saxon has two internal tree representations, the standard tree and the tiny tree, which both implement the same internal Java interface. This interface is an extension of the core DOM level 1 interface defined by W3C. However, it is a read-only implementation. All the methods that attempt to update the DOM will throw exceptions.

The reason for this is that XSLT processing never needs to make in-situ changes to a tree; the nodes can always be added to the tree in document order. This fact allows the internal tree structure to be optimized for XSLT and XPath processing. For example, an element that has no attributes or namespace declarations does not need to leave space in case these are added later; and it is possible to support the all-important function of sorting nodes into document order by including a simple serial number within each node of the tree, which would not be possible if more nodes could be added later. Also, multi-threading is far easier to arrange when update is severely restricted in this way.

While this is good for performance, it all makes for a slightly uneasy relationship between Saxon and the DOM.

- You can supply a DOM as input to a transformation, using the TrAX DOMSource class, but it is not the most efficient way of supplying input, because Saxon will first make a copy of the document using its own internal tree representation. If the data originates as an XML file, it is much more efficient to supply it as a SAXSource. In this respect Saxon is quite different from MSXML3, which uses the supplied DOM as its internal tree representation.
- You can ask for the result tree to be delivered as a DOM, but if you want this to be a fully updateable DOM, you must supply the Document object yourself. If you leave Saxon to create the result Document, it will use its own non-updateable DOM implementation.

- When Saxon calls external Java functions that expect DOM nodes or node-lists as their arguments, it will provide references to its own non-updateable tree structure. This will include only information that is relevant to the XPath tree model, for example it will include no CDATA or entity reference nodes, and it will not contain any whitespace text nodes that have been stripped from the tree. Returning DOM nodes as the result of a function is currently allowed only if they use Saxon's own restricted DOM implementation.

Using XPath Expressions in Saxon

Using Saxon's Java API, you can execute XPath expressions against the internal tree representation of the source document, independently of any stylesheet. This can be useful either outside the scope of an XSLT transformation, or as something done within a Java extension function.

The key to this is the class `com.icl.saxon.expr.Expression`. This has a static method `make()`, which is used to compile an XPath expression written as a string. This acts as a factory method, returning an instance of the `Expression` class which represents the compiled expression. To evaluate the expression you call its `evaluate()` method. In the case of an expression that returns a node-set, you can also get the result in the form of an enumeration of nodes by calling its `enumerate()` method.

`Expression.make()` takes two arguments; the first is the XPath expression, as a string, the second is a `StaticContext` object which supplies information that would normally depend on the position of the expression in the stylesheet. This includes things such as the bindings of namespace prefixes, variables, and extension functions. For a simple expression that doesn't use namespaces, variables, or functions, you can make a simple call like:

```
Expression exp = Expression.make("//item[@code='c']", new StandaloneContext());
```

`StandaloneContext` is an implementation of `StaticContext` that provides a minimal set of context information.

The call to evaluate an expression also takes an additional argument; this time it is a `Context` object representing the run-time context. This gives information about the context node, position, and size, the current values of variables, and so on. Saxon's `Context` object implements the `org.w3.xsl.XSLTContext` interface defined in the draft XSLT 1.1 specifications. You can get a `Context` object from the TrAX `Transformer` by calling

```
Context context = ((Controller)transformer).newContext();
```

You will then typically want to initialize the context, for example:

```
context.setContextNode(node);
context.setPosition(1);
context.setLast(1);
```

Finally you can evaluate the expression:

```
Value val = exp.evaluate(context);
```

The `Value` returned may be a `BooleanValue`, a `StringValue`, a `NumericValue`, or a `NodeSetValue`, depending on the result of the XPath expression. If you want the result converted to a particular type, say a `String`, there are short-cut methods to achieve this:

```
String s = exp.evaluateAsString(context);
```

For a full description, see Saxon's javadoc API documentation.

Extensibility

In this section I will describe the facilities Saxon provides for user-written extension functions and extension elements, and other interfaces for extending the functionality of the product. Following that, I'll look at the extension functions and elements that come ready-supplied with the Saxon product.

Saxon supports a range of extensibility mechanisms, described below.

Writing Extension Functions

Extension functions may be written in Java, using the interface defined in the draft XSLT 1.1 specifications, as described in Chapter 8. At the time of writing (version 6.2) Saxon does not implement these specifications in full, but most of the features are there. Saxon supports Java external functions only, there is no support for JavaScript or other languages. There is, however, a mechanism to write extension functions in XSLT itself, see the description of the **<saxon:function>** element on page 791.

An external Java class may be defined using the **<xsl:script>** element, described in Chapter 4 on page 293. Saxon ignores any **<xsl:script>** element that does not have the attribute «`language="java"`». So, if you want to use methods in the class `java.util.Date`, you can define:

```
<xsl:script language="java" implements-prefix="Date" src="java:java.util.Date"/>
```

and then call a method or constructor such as:

```
<xsl:variable name="today" select="Date:new()"/>
```

There is also a short-cut way of defining the binding. If the namespace prefix `Date` is bound to a namespace URI such as `java:java.util.Date`, then the **<xsl:script>** element above is implicit. This means that you can make a call such as:

```
<xsl:variable name="today" select="Date:new()"
                           xmlns:Date="java:java.util.Date"/>
```

with no further declaration of the external class.

The current release, Saxon 6.2, does not implement the full XSLT 1.1 rules for finding a method within the selected class. It looks for methods that have the right name and the right number of arguments, but if there is more than one, it reports an error, rather than trying to find the one that is the best fit to the arguments supplied.

As defined in the XSLT 1.1 draft, Saxon allows an external Java method to have an extra first argument: this may be declared with class `org.w3c.xsl.XSLTContext` or, for compatibility with previous releases, with class `com.icl.saxon.Context`. This argument, if it is present, is not supplied by the calling XPath code, but by Saxon itself. This is the same `Context` object that Saxon uses to evaluate free-standing XPath expressions, so you can use the supplied `Context` object within an extension function if you need to evaluate such expressions. The `Context` object allows the method to access contextual information such as the current node and current node list; it also gives access to Saxon's implementation of the TrAX `Transformer` class (called `com.icl.saxon.Controller`) which in turn gives access to the error listener, the tracing routines, the factory configuration, and a host of other things which only the determined systems programmer will ever need.

Writing Extension Elements

Saxon implements the XSLT element extensibility feature. This feature allows you to define your own instruction types for use in the stylesheet.

If a namespace prefix is to be used to denote extension elements, it must be declared in the **`extension-element-prefixes`** attribute on the **`<xsl:stylesheet>`** element, or the **`xsl:extension-element-prefixes`** attribute on any enclosing literal result element.

Implementing extension elements is rather more complex than implementing simple extension functions. You need to be a fairly dedicated systems programmer to attempt it, especially as the documentation in this area is limited. Saxon supplies a sample set of extension elements that allow the stylesheet to write data to a relational database, and the documentation recommends that you use these as an example for writing your own extension elements.

There's no space here for a full description of this interface, but its outline is as follows.

First, corresponding to each extension element namespace there must be a factory class that implements the interface `com.icl.saxon.style.ExtensionElementFactory`.

The namespace URI for the extension elements must be of the form `xmlns:xxx="http://icl.com/saxon/extensions/full.class.Name"`, where `full.class.Name` is the relevant factory class.

For each extension element defined in this namespace, there must be a class that extends `com.icl.saxon.style.StyleElement`. The mapping of extension element names to class names is the job of the `ExtensionElementFactory` for the namespace. This defines a single method, `getExtensionClass()`, that takes the local name of the element as a parameter, and returns the relevant class.

The `StyleElement` class for the extension element can implement a number of methods, but the most important ones are:

Method	Effect
`isInstruction()`	Should always return true for an extension element.
`mayContainTemplateBody()`	Return true if this element may contain further instructions. It is good practice to return true, because otherwise an **<xsl:fallback>** element will not be allowed.
`prepareAttributes()`	This is called at compile time to allow the class to do local validation, and to parse any information supplied in its attributes.
`validate()`	This is also called at compile time. It is called as soon as every element in the stylesheet has performed its own local validation; its purpose is to allow cross-validation, for example checking that this element has the required parents and/or children.
`process(Context c)`	This is called at run-time, to execute the instruction. The code is able to take advantage of many supporting services, either inherited from the `StyleElement` superclass, or accessible via the `Context` object. It is important for multi-threading integrity that this method makes no modifications to the contents of the stylesheet tree.

Writing Filters

Saxon takes its input as a stream of SAX2 events. Normally these will come directly from a SAX2-compliant XMLReader. (If you supply the input as a DOM, Saxon simply navigates this DOM to generate the SAX events from it.) Instead, however, you can generate these events from an application.

Equally, Saxon generates its output as a stream of SAX2 events. Actually, it uses a slightly modified interface internally, called the `Emitter`, but there is a class, the `ContentHandlerProxy`, that converts `Emitter` events into standard SAX2 `ContentHandler` events. So, you can write a post-processor for the output of the transformation. You can specify a `ContentHandler` to receive Saxon's output either in the **<xsl:output>** element in the stylesheet, or via the TrAX API.

There are many ways you can exploit this capability:

- You can write an application that acts as a filter between the XML parser and the stylesheet, performing functions such as normalizing data values and supplying defaulted attributes. The TrAX interface makes it easy to insert an XSLT transformation into a pipeline consisting of a number of filters, some of which may be defined in XSLT and others in Java. An example of such a filter is given in Appendix F. A filter could also split an incoming document into multiple input documents to be processed separately, reducing the size of the tree to be held in memory. For information on writing SAX filters, see the Wrox book *Professional XML*, ISBN 1-861003-11-0.

- Your application could also supply data from a source that is not originally XML at all. I showed an example of that in Chapter 10, where the Kennedy family tree came from a non-XML data source in GEDCOM format. The application could also be fetching the data from a relational database. In effect, your application is pretending to be an XML parser, so the stylesheet thinks it is getting input from an XML parser when it is actually coming from somewhere else.
- You can pass the output of the transformation to another application designed to accept SAX2 input; for example the Apache FOP processor, which is a partial implementation of the XSL Formatting Objects specification. This only works, of course, if the stylesheet generates XML elements and attributes that conform to this specification.

As an alternative to writing an output filter in Java, Saxon also allows you to process the output through another XSL stylesheet. You can do this using the TrAX interface, or you can do it simply by naming the next stylesheet in the **`saxon:next-in-chain`** attribute of **`<xsl:output>`**. This can be useful if you want to do things such as numbering the elements in the result tree: the **`<xsl:number>`** instruction always generates numbers that relate to the position of a node in the source tree, which is not very useful if your stylesheet is sorting the data. So you can do sorting with one stylesheet, and then put the data through another stylesheet to add section numbers and a table of contents.

Implementing Collating and Numbering Sequences

Saxon allows you to implement a collating sequence for use by **`<xsl:sort>`**. This is controlled through the **`lang`** attribute of the **`<xsl:sort>`** element. The feature is primarily intended to provide language-dependent collating, but in fact it can be used to provide arbitrary collating sequences: for example, if you want to sort the names of the months January, February, March, etc. in the conventional sequence you could do this by writing and providing a collating sequence for language «`x-months`».

Similarly, you can define a numbering sequence for use by **`<xsl:number>`**. For example, if you have a sequence of items which you want to label as "January", "February", "March", etc. you could implement a special numbering class, and invoke it by specifying `<xsl:number format="January" lang="x-months"/>`.

Built-in Saxon Extensions

As well as supporting user-defined extensions through the above extensibility mechanisms, Saxon also comes with a rich collection of built-in extensions, described in the following sections.

Extension Functions

Saxon comes with a powerful library of extension functions (that is, functions not defined in the XSLT standard), listed in the table below. These must be used with a prefix that maps to the namespace URI `http://icl.com/saxon`.

Some of these functions use what is in effect an additional XPath data type, the **stored expression**. This concept, which is analagous to stored procedures in SQL, or first-class functions in functional programming languages, is a powerful addition to the language. In standard XSLT, there is no way of constructing an XPath expression from a string. This makes it difficult to do things that are very familiar to SQL programmers, for example building a query from the values of parameters read from a form, or sorting a table on a column selected by the user. It also makes it impossible to interpret XPath expressions held as part of the text of the source document, perhaps implementing a subset of the XPointer specification for defining links between documents. The Saxon stored expression concept fills this gap: you can use the **`saxon:expression()`** extension function to create a stored expression from a string, and **`saxon:eval()`** to evaluate the stored expression; or you can combine these two operations into one using the **`saxon:evaluate()`** function, which we'll look at in a little more detail in the next section.

Here is a list of the extension functions that Saxon currently supports.

Function	Explanation
`after(ns1, ns2)`	This function is based on the **`AFTER`** operator defined in the draft W3C XQuery proposal (http://www.w3.org/XML/Group/xmlquery/xquery). It selects all those nodes in `ns1` that come after the first node in `ns2`, in document order.
`base-uri()`	This returns the base URI of the context node. This is the same as the result of **`system-id()`**, unless the **`xml:base`** attribute has been used to choose a base URI that is different from the system identifier of the containing entity.

`before(ns1, ns2)`	This function is based on the **`BEFORE`** operator defined in the draft W3C XQuery proposal. It selects all those nodes in `ns1` that come before the last node in `ns2`, in document order. For example, if the context node is an `<h1>` element, then to select all the `<h2>` elements that come before the next `<h1>`, you can write:
	`saxon:before(`
	`   following-sibling::h2, following-sibling::h1[1])`

`difference (ns1, ns2)`	This returns a node-set that is the difference of the two supplied node-sets; that is, it contains all the nodes that are in `ns1` that are not also in `ns2`. The function call «`saxon:difference($a, $b)`» is equivalent to the standard XPath expression «`$a[count(.│$b) != count($b)]`»:

Function	Explanation

distinct(ns1)	This returns a node-set containing all the nodes in `ns1` that have distinct string-values. Nodes with duplicate string-values are discarded. For example:
	`<xsl:variable name="cities"`
	`select="saxon:distinct(//city)"/>`
	creates a node-set containing one element for each uniquely named **<city>** in the source document. If there were several **<city>** elements with the same name, it keeps the one that is first in document order. The next step will often be to process them all as a group:
	`<xsl:for-each select="$cities">`
	`  <h2>City name is: <xsl:value-of select="."/></h2>`
	`    <xsl:for-each select="//city[.=current()]">`
	`        . . .`
	If the nodes in `$a` are sibling elements (but only if!), then `saxon:distinct($a)` has the same effect as the standard XPath expression «`$a[not(. = preceding-sibling::*]`».

distinct(ns1, expression)	This returns a node-set containing all the nodes in ns1 that have distinct values for the stored expression supplied in the second argument. For example, if you want to group all the <city> elements according to their initial letter (to build an index), you can write:
	`<xsl:variable name="cities"`
	`   select="saxon:distinct(//city,`
	`        saxon:expression('substring(., 1, 1)'))"/>`
	`This will return a node-set containing one`
	`city for each initial letter. You can use this`
	`to find the others:`
	
	`<xsl:for-each select="$cities">`
	`  <xsl:variable name="initial"`
	`                  select="substring(., 1, 1)"/>`
	`  <h2><xsl:value-of select="$initial"/></h2>`
	`  <xsl:for-each`
	`      select="//city[substring(., 1, 1)=$initial]">`
	`    <p><xsl:value-of select="."/></p>`
	`  </xsl:for-each>`
	`</xsl:for-each>`

eval(expression)	This function evaluates a stored expression supplied in the argument. The stored expression will have been constructed using the **`saxon:expression()`** function. The context for evaluation (for example, the context node) is the context in which **`saxon:eval()`** is called.

Table continued on following page

Function	Explanation

`evaluate(string)`	This function allows an XPath expression to be constructed at run-time, as a string, and immediately evaluated. This is useful if a query is not known in advance, but must be constructed based on information supplied by the user in parameters, or read from the source document. For example the following code constructs a node-set consisting of all **`<book>`** elements that satisfy a predicate passed to the stylesheet as a parameter:
	
	`<xsl:param name="predicate"/>`
	`<xsl:variable name="selectedBooks" select=`
	`"saxon:evaluate(concat('//book[',`
	`$predicate,`
	`']'))"/>`

`exists(ns1, expression)`	This function returns true if the node-set `ns1` contains at least one node for which the stored expression is true. The function is not really necessary, since the function call «`saxon:exists($a, `*`expr`*`)`» is equivalent to the XPath construct «`boolean($a[`*`expr`*`])`», but it is provided for completeness.
`expression (string)`	This function constructs a stored expression from the XPath expression contained in the supplied string. The stored expression can be evaluated later using the **`saxon:eval()`** function, or it can be passed to any other function that takes a stored expression as one of its arguments, for example **`saxon:distinct()`** or **`saxon:sum()`**. If the XPath expression contains namespace prefixes or variable references, these are resolved at the time the stored expression is created, not at the time it is subsequently evaluated. The context node, position, and size, however, are determined when the expression is evaluated.
`for-all(ns1, expression)`	This function returns true if every node in the node-set `ns1` is such that the stored expression evaluates to true. The function is not really necessary, since the function call «`saxon:for-all($a, `*`expr`*`)`» is equivalent to the XPath construct «`not($a[not(`*`expr`*`)])`», but it is provided for completeness.
`get-user-data(string)`	Gets a value that was saved earlier using **`saxon:set-user-data()`**. The string names this item of user data. User data is associated with a particular node in the tree, so you will only be able to retrieve the data if the context node is the same as when it was saved. It is often sensible to store user data with the root of the tree. User data is also associated with a particular TrAX Transformer: the data will only be accessible within the same transformation.

Function	Explanation
`has-same-nodes (ns1, ns2)`	This returns a Boolean that is true if and only if `ns1` and `ns2` contain exactly the same set of nodes. Note this is quite different from the «`=`» operator, which tests whether there is a pair of nodes with the same string-value. The function call «`saxon:has-same-nodes($a, $b)`» is equivalent in standard XSLT to «`count($a)=count($b) and count($a)=count($a\|$b)`».

`highest(ns1, expression?)`	This function finds the maximum numeric value among the nodes in the supplied node-set `ns1`, and returns a node-set containing all the nodes that have this highest value (there may be more than one). The value in question is the string-value of the nodes if the function is called with one argument, or the value of the supplied stored expression if it is called with two. For example, to find the `<sale>` with the highest value of «`@qty * @price`», use:
	
	`<xsl:variable name="top-sales"`
	`select="saxon:highest(//sale,`
	`saxon:expression('@qty * @price'))"/>`

`if(condition, v1, v2)`	The first argument is evaluated as a Boolean; if it is true, the function returns the value `v1`, if it is false, it returns `v2`. The value may be of any type. Note that both `v1` and `v2` are evaluated and then one of the values is discarded, so you can't use this function to mask an error in evaluating one of the arguments.

`intersection (ns1,ns2)`	This returns a node-set that is the intersection of the two supplied node-sets; that is, it contains all the nodes that are in both `ns1` and `ns2`.
	
	This function can be useful in conjunction with keys, for example to list all programmers based in Denver, write:
	
	`<xsl:for-each select="saxon:intersection(`
	`key('job', 'Programmer'),`
	`key('location', 'Denver'))">`
	
	The function call «`saxon:intersection($a, $b)`» is equivalent to the standard XPath expression «`$a[count(.|$b) = count($b)]`».

`is-null(object)`	This functions tests whether an external object is null. Any extension function may return a Java object as its result; the only thing the stylesheet can do with this is to pass it to another extension function as an argument. Since a common requirement is to test whether the returned object is null, this extension function is provided for the purpose.
`leading(ns1, expression)`	This function considers the nodes in `ns1` in document order, and returns each of them that returns true for the supplied stored expression, up to and excluding the first node that returns false for this expression.

Table continued on following page

Function	Explanation

leading(ns1, expression) *(continued)*	For example, suppose a <section> element has a sequence of children of the form:
	`<h1/><p/><p/><h1/><p/><p/><p/>`
	Then with an <h1> as the context node you can process its immediately following <p> elements (up to the next <h1>) by writing:
	`<xsl:apply-templates`
	`    select="saxon:leading(`
	`            following-sibling::*,`
	`            saxon:expression('self::p'))"/>`
	An alternative is to use the **saxon:before()** function, described above.

line-number()	This returns the line number of the current node in the source document within the entity that contains it. There are no arguments. This is useful for constructing error messages and for debugging. The line number is only available if the tree was built with line numbering information retained: use the -l option on the command line.

lowest(ns1, expression?)	This function finds the minimum numeric value among the nodes in the supplied node-set ns1, and returns a node-set containing all the nodes that have this lowest value (there may be more than one). The value in question is the string-value of the nodes if the function is called with one argument, or the value of the supplied stored expression if it is called with two. For example, to find the <sale> with the lowest value of «@qty * @price», use:
	`<xsl:variable name="worst-sales"`
	`select="saxon:lowest(//sale,`
	`      saxon:expression('@qty * @price'))"/>`

max(ns1, expression?)	This function finds the maximum numeric value among the nodes in the supplied node-set ns1, and returns this value. (Unlike **saxon:highest()**, which returns the node itself.) The value in question is the string-value of the nodes if the function is called with one argument, or the value of the supplied stored expression if it is called with two. For example, to find the highest value of «@qty * @price» in any <sale> element, use:
	`<xsl:variable name="max-sales"`
	`select="saxon:max(//sale,`
	`      saxon:expression('@qty * @price'))"/>`

min(ns1, expression?)	This function finds the minimum numeric value among the nodes in the supplied node-set ns1, and returns this value. (Unlike **saxon:lowest()**, which returns the node itself.) The value in question is the string-value of the nodes if the function is called with one argument, or the value of the supplied stored expression if it is called with two. For example, to find the lowest value of «@qty * @price» in any <sale> element, use:

Function	Explanation
min(ns1, expression?) *(continued)*	`<xsl:variable name="min-sales" select="saxon:min(//sale, saxon:expression('@qty * @price'))"/>`
node-set (tree)	This function is a hangover from XSLT 1.0, which does not allow conversion of a tree to a node-set. It performs the conversion explicitly. This function is no longer needed because Saxon (following the draft XSLT 1.1 specification) will do the conversion automatically when required.
path()	This function returns, as a string, an XPath expression that is an absolute location path to reach the context node. (Note, if you want to use this expression to locate the node again later, you must ensure that all the required namespace prefixes are in scope.)

range(n1, n2)	This constructs a new node-set whose nodes have numeric values in the range `n1` to `n2`. It is designed to provide an equivalent to a conventional for-loop. The following example will create five table cells containing the numbers 1 to 5:
	`<xsl:for-each select="saxon:range(1,5)">`
	`<td><xsl:value-of select="."/></td>`
	`</xsl:for-each>`

set-user-data(string, value)	Saves a value that can be retrieved later using **saxon:get-user-data()**. The string names this item of user data. User data is associated with a particular node in the tree, so you will only be able to retrieve the data if the context node is the same as when it was saved. It is often sensible to store user data with the root of the tree. User data is also associated with a particular TrAX Transformer: the data will only be accessible within the same transformation. Note that **saxon:set-user-data()** is a function with side effects, so the result depends on the order in which different instructions are executed, which is not always predictable.
system-id()	This returns the system identifier of the entity containing the current node in the source document. There are no arguments. This is useful for constructing error messages.
tokenize(string, delimiter?)	This function constructs a new node-set whose nodes result from splitting the supplied string into tokens, separated either the supplied delimiter, or by whitespace. It is designed for operations such as replacing newline characters in the source by ** ** elements in the output, or searching for a particular word in the text content of an element.

Using saxon:evaluate()

Many of the extension functions listed above rely on the idea of being able to construct an XPath expression dynamically as a string, and then evaluate it: the simplest form of this is the **evaluate()** function.

In standard XSLT 1.0 (and 1.1) XPath expressions are always written statically in the stylesheet. This can be a significant limitation, as you will be well aware if you are familiar with the use of SQL within ASP or JSP pages, where dynamic construction of SQL queries is the norm.

Saxon allows you to do this by means of the **`saxon:evaluate()`** extension function. (The same capability is now offered by several other XSLT processors: see the relevant product descriptions for details.)

Allowing XPath queries to be constructed dynamically gives a number of benefits:

- You can construct a query (such as «`author="Kay" and publisher="Wrox"`», from the values of stylesheet parameters supplied at run-time.
- You can easily change the sort order used in an **`<xsl:sort>`** element based on parameters supplied at run-time.
- You can allow XPath expressions to be used within the source document, for example to define hyperlinks between documents, and you can write code in your stylesheet to follow these links.
- You can use XPath expressions to define business rules in a separate document.

The following example demonstrates the last of these techniques.

Example: Using saxon:evaluate() to Apply Business Rules

In this example, we imagine a call center that is charging customers for the calls they make. We want to prepare the account for a period, listing all the calls and calculating the total charge.

Source

The list of calls is in the file `calls.xml`, as follows:

```
<calls>
<call date="2001-01-15" time="08.15" duration="17"/>
<call date="2001-01-16" time="10.42" duration="8"/>
<call date="2001-01-18" time="17.42" duration="5"/>
<call date="2001-01-18" time="22.10" duration="06"/>
<call date="2001-01-24" time="12:19" duration="41"/>
<call date="2001-01-25" time="06.40" duration="13"/>
<call date="2001-01-27" time="11.15" duration="26"/>
</calls>
```

We want to put the business rules for calculating the charges in a separate document. Of course, these rules could go in the stylesheet, but that isn't very good practice; mixing business rules and presentation rules in one place doesn't give the right separation of responsibilities. Instead, we'll put the relevant formula in a separate document `tariff.xml`, in the form of an XPath expression. This calculates the total charge, with different rates per minute during the working day and outside office hours:

```
<tariff>
sum(call[@time &gt;= 08.00 and @time &lt; 18.00]/@duration) *
1.50 +
sum(call[@time &lt; 08.00 or @time &gt;= 18.00]/@duration) *
2.50
</tariff>
```

Stylesheet

Most of the stylesheet (`account.xsl`) is conventional, and is concerned with displaying the information. When it comes to calculating the total charges, however, the stylesheet reads the XPath expression containing the relevant formula from the `tariff.xml` document, and evaluates it (using **`saxon:evaluate()`**) in the context of the source document.

```
<?xml version="1.0"?>
<xsl:stylesheet xmlns:xsl="http://www.w3.org/1999/XSL/Transform"
                xmlns:saxon="http://icl.com/saxon"
                version="1.0">

<xsl:template match="/">
  <html>
    <head>
      <title>Account for period ending
           <xsl:value-of select="(//@date)[last()]"/></title>
    </head>
    <body>
      <h1>Account for period ending
           <xsl:value-of select="(//@date)[last()]"/></h1>
      <xsl:apply-templates/>
    </body>
  </html>
</xsl:template>

<xsl:template match="calls">
   <table>
      <tr>
         <th width="100">Date</th>
         <th width="100">Time</th>
         <th width="100">Duration</th>
      </tr>
      <xsl:apply-templates/>
   </table>
   <xsl:variable name="total"
                select="saxon:evaluate(document('tariff.xml'))"/>
   <p>Total charges for the period:
      <xsl:value-of select="format-number($total, '$###0.00')"/>
   </p>
</xsl:template>

<xsl:template match="call">
   <tr>
     <td><xsl:value-of select="@date"/></td>
     <td><xsl:value-of select="@time"/></td>
     <td><xsl:value-of select="@duration"/></td>
   </tr>
</xsl:template>

</xsl:stylesheet>
```

Output

The output of this stylesheet appears in the browser as shown below:

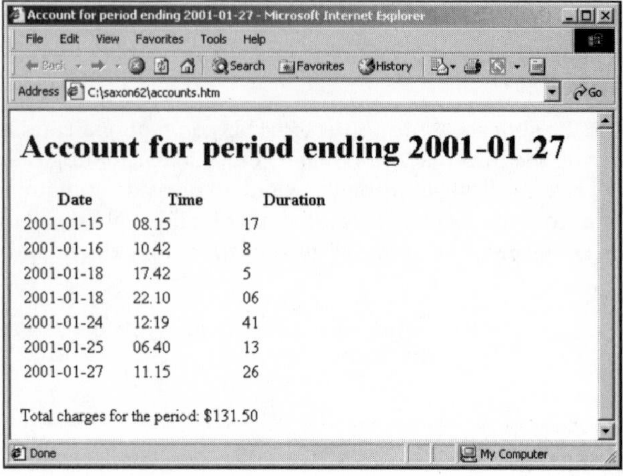

Saxon Extension Elements

Saxon-supplied extension elements are available only if:

- They are used with a namespace prefix that identifies the namespace `http://icl.com/saxon`, and (except for top-level elements)
- A prefix for that namespace is listed in the **`extension-element-prefixes`** attribute of the enclosing **`<xsl:stylesheet>`** element, or in the **`xsl:extension-element-prefixes`** attribute of an enclosing literal result element

The prefix `saxon` is used here as a conventional namespace prefix only: as with the `xsl` prefix, you can use any prefix you like so long as it maps to the proper namespace URI.

The Saxon extension elements are:

Element	Description
`<saxon:assign>`	This element is used to change the value of a local or global variable that has previously been declared using **`<xsl:variable>`** (or **`<xsl:param>`**). For example: **`<saxon:assign name="n" select="$n+1"/>`** Providing an explicit assignment statement like this blows a gaping hole in the design principle that XSLT is a language where side effects are not allowed. In Chapter 9, I call this "cheating". Use it only when all other options have been exhausted.

Element	Description
<saxon:assign> (continued)	The variable that is updated must carry the extra attribute «`saxon:assignable="yes"`» to signal that its value may change, which prevents the processor from performing optimizations that rely on the value not changing. Despite this, there are algorithms such as finding a path through a network where using **<saxon:assign>** can simplify coding and give a significant performance saving.

<saxon:doctype>

This element allows a DOCTYPE declaration containing an internal DTD subset to be generated within the target XML document. The **<saxon:doctype>** instruction contains a representation of the DTD, transcribed into XML syntax. For example:

```
<saxon:doctype xsl:extension-element-prefixes="saxon">
  <dtd:doctype name="booklist"
       xmlns:dtd="http://icl.com/saxon/dtd"
       xsl:exclude-result-prefixes="dtd">
    <dtd:element name="booklist" content="(book)*"/>
    <dtd:element name="book" content="EMPTY"/>
    <dtd:attlist element="book">
       <dtd:attribute name="isbn" type="ID"
                      value="#REQUIRED"/>
       <dtd:attribute name="title" type="CDATA"
                      value="#IMPLIED"/>
    </dtd:attlist>
    <dtd:entity name="blurb">'A <i>cool</i> book with
                   &gt; 200
    pictures!'</dtd:entity>
    <dtd:entity name="cover" system="cover.gif"
                   notation="GIF"/>
    <dtd:notation name="GIF"
                   system="http://gif.org/"/>
  </dtd:doctype>
  </saxon:doctype>
```

The elements in the «`dtd`» namespace are not themselves extension elements, they act merely as data interpreted by the containing **<saxon:doctype>** instruction.

<saxon:entity-ref>

This element is useful to generate entities such as «` `» in HTML output. For example:

```
<saxon:entity-ref name="nbsp"/>
```

You can achieve the same effect within the standard by writing:

```
<xsl:text disable-output-escaping="yes">&amp;nbsp;
   </xsl:text>
```

(But this is not a very good example, because if you generate a non-breaking space in the output, e.g. by writing «` `», then by default Saxon will serialize this as «` `» in HTML output.)

Table continued on following page

<saxon:function> and <saxon:return>

The **<saxon:function>** element is not technically an extension element, because it is a top-level element in the stylesheet rather than an instruction. This element allows an extension function to be written within the stylesheet, using XSLT syntax. It is called exactly like an external function written in Java or JavaScript. The **<saxon:return>** element is used within **<saxon:function>** to exit from the function and return a result.

An example showing how to use **<saxon:function>** is provided in the next section.

<saxon:group> and <saxon:item>

These elements together provide grouping of items that share a common value. The **<saxon:group>** element operates like **<xsl:for-each>**, but with an additional attribute **group-by** which defines the grouping key.

The **<saxon:group>** element must contain somewhere within it an **<saxon:item>** element. The XSL instructions outside the **<saxon:item>** element are executed only once for each group of consecutive elements with the same value for the grouping key; the instructions within the **<saxon:item>** are executed once for each individual item in the **<saxon:group>** selection.

For example, to list a collection of books sorted and grouped by author, write:

```
   <saxon:group select="book" group-
by="author">
      <xsl:sort select="author"/>
      Books by <xsl:value-of select="author"/>:
      <ul>
      <saxon:item>
         <li><xsl:value-of
select="title"/></li>
      </saxon:item>
      </ul>
   </saxon:group>
```

<saxon:preview>791

This feature is useful for processing very large input documents. Normally XSLT processing requires that the entire source document be constructed as a tree in memory. With very large documents, this may be infeasible. The **<saxon:preview>** extension allows an element to be nominated that acts as a document in its own right; as soon as such an element has been read, it is processed by the stylesheet and is then discarded from the tree, together with all its descendants.

`<saxon:preview>` (*continued*)	The **<saxon:preview>** element has two attributes: **mode**, which must match the mode of the template rule used to process the element, and **elements**, which gives a space-separated list of element names that are to be processed in this way. Typically, if your large XML document consists of a large number of **<item>** elements, you will specify «elements="item"».

`<saxon:while>`	This element is used to iterate while some condition is true. The condition is given as a Boolean expression in the mandatory **test** attribute. Because the value of the condition can only change if something causes a side-effect, it is generally used either with **<saxon:assign>** or with an extension function, such as one that reads the next record from a file. For example:
	`<xsl:variable name="n" select="10"/>`
	`<saxon:while test="$n != 0">`
	`   <xsl:value-of select="$n"/>`
	`   <saxon:assign name="n" select="$n - 1"/>`
	`</saxon:while>`

Using <saxon:function>

The **<saxon:function>** element adds a powerful feature to the XSLT language, so it is worth dwelling on it in a little more detail.

XSLT allows you to write expressions containing function calls. These can either be calls to the functions defined in the XPath and XSLT specifications (for example **not()** and **key()**), or they can be calls to user-defined functions (called extension functions). XSLT 1.0, however, doesn't provide any standardized way of writing a user-defined function. XSLT 1.1, as we saw in Chapter 8, defines mechanisms for writing them in Java or JavaScript. But this involves complex rules on how XPath values should be mapped to Java or JavaScript values. It also makes it very difficult for the XSLT processor to do any optimization, because it has no idea whether the external function will have any side effects. In providing **saxon:function**, I reckoned that many simple and useful functions could be written within the XSLT language itself, and that it shouldn't be necessary to switch languages purely in order to perform a simple calculation.

The following example shows how a simple function can be invoked from a sort key.

Example: Using saxon:function for Sorting

Source

We'll use unsorted-calls.xml, which is a very similar source file to our previous example, relating a list of calls made to a call center. But this time we'll assume that the source file contains the calls in no particular order, and that they aren't conveniently in ISO format:

```
<calls>
<call date="27 Jan 2001" time="11.15" duration="26"/>
<call date="18 Jan 2001" time="17.42" duration="5"/>
<call date="18 Feb 2001" time="22.10" duration="06"/>
<call date="25 Jan 2001" time="06.40" duration="13"/>
<call date="15 Mar 2001" time="08.15" duration="17"/>
<call date="24 Jan 2001" time="12:19" duration="41"/>
<call date="16 Jan 2001" time="10.42" duration="8"/>
</calls>
```

Stylesheet

We want to list these calls sorted by date and time. (We'll leave out the calculation of the total charge this time, because that's not relevant to this example.) The following stylesheet, `sorted-account.xsl`, achieves this.

The stylesheet first creates a sorted copy of the source document, in a global tree-valued variable; then it does the rest of the processing using this sorted tree, exploiting the XSLT 1.1 capability to process a temporary tree as a node-set.

The interesting feature, however, is the calculation of the sort key. This is done by calling a function, `f:iso-date()`, which reformats the date into a format that collates correctly. The function is implemented at the end of the stylesheet, using a **`<saxon:function>`** element.

```
<?xml version="1.0"?>
<xsl:stylesheet xmlns:xsl="http://www.w3.org/1999/XSL/Transform"
                xmlns:saxon="http://icl.com/saxon"
                xmlns:f="http://pricey-call-
centres.com/namespace"
                extension-element-prefixes="saxon"
                exclude-result-prefixes="f"
                version="1.1">

<xsl:variable name="sorted-calls">
  <xsl:for-each select="//call">
     <xsl:sort select="f:iso-date(@date)"/>
     <xsl:sort select="@time"/>
     <xsl:copy-of select="."/>
  </xsl:for-each>
</xsl:variable>

<xsl:variable name="period-end"
   select="($sorted-calls//@date)[last()]"/>

<xsl:template match="/">
  <html>
    <head>
      <title>Account for period ending
             <xsl:value-of select="$period-end"/></title>
    </head>
    <body>
      <h1>Account for period ending
             <xsl:value-of select="$period-end"/></h1>
      <table>
         <tr>
            <th width="100">Date</th>
            <th width="100">Time</th>
            <th width="100">Duration</th>
         </tr>
         <xsl:apply-templates select="$sorted-calls/call"/>
      </table>
    </body>
  </html>
</xsl:template/>

<xsl:template match="call">
   <tr>
     <td><xsl:value-of select="@date"/></td>
     <td><xsl:value-of select="@time"/></td>
     <td><xsl:value-of select="@duration"/></td>
   </tr>
</xsl:template>
```

```
<saxon:function name="f:iso-date">
<!--
   Converts a date from the form "21 Jan 1998" to the form "19980121"
-->
  <xsl:param name="date"/>
  <xsl:variable name="months"
                select="'JanFebMarAprMayJunJulAugSepOctNovDec'"/>
  <xsl:variable name="dd"
                select="substring($date, 1, 2)"/>
  <xsl:variable name="mon"
                select="substring($date, 4, 3)"/>
  <xsl:variable name="yyyy"
                select="substring($date, 8, 4)"/>
  <xsl:variable name="mm"
                select="(string-length(
                substring-before($months, $mon)) div 3) +1"/>

<saxon:return select="concat($yyyy, format-number($mm, '00'),$dd)"/>
</saxon:function>


</xsl:stylesheet>
```

Output

The output appears in the browser as:

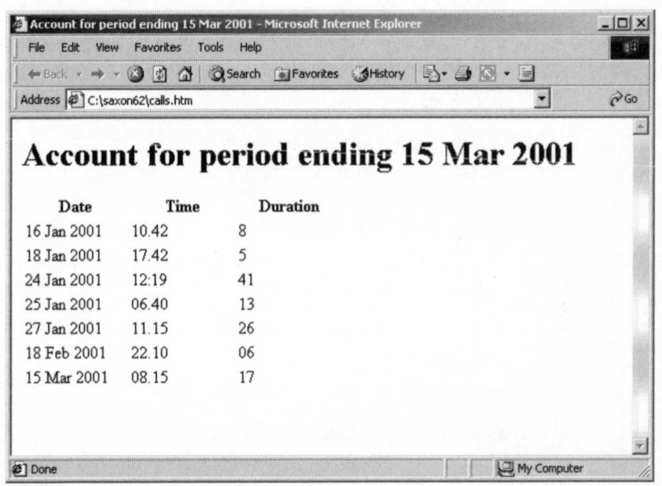

Note that a function defined by **<saxon:function>** must have no side effects: in particular, it must not write to the result tree. Its only action is to return a value, which can be a number, a Boolean, a string, a node-set, or a temporary tree. Note also that **<saxon:return>** is an extension element, so the Saxon namespace must be declared as an extension element namespace; if you don't do this, **<saxon:return>** will be treated as a literal result element to be copied to the result tree, which will cause an error because a **<saxon:function>** is not allowed to write to the result tree.

The Saxon Serializer

Saxon supports the standard output methods (xml, html, and text), and all the attributes of the **<xsl:output>** and **<xsl:document>** elements as defined in the XSLT 1.1 draft specification.

The output attributes can be specified either in the **<xsl:output>** or **<xsl:document>** element, or via the **setOutputProperties()** method in the TrAX API, as described in Appendix F.

Saxon also supports some additional attributes, or attribute values, to give more precise control over the form of the output. These are all in the Saxon namespace (`http://icl.com/saxon`) so any other processor should ignore them.

These attributes are as follows:

method	This attribute supports some additional values: **saxon:fop** Directs output to the Apache FOP processor for XSL Formatting Objects. **saxon:xhtml** Formats output according to XHTML conventions, designed for legacy browsers. For example ` ` is output as ` ` (with a space). **saxon:*class-name*** Directs output to the specified Java class, which should implement either the SAX2 `ContentHandler` interface or the Saxon `Emitter` interface.
saxon:indent-spaces	An integer defining the number of spaces used in indented output when «`indent="yes"`».
saxon:character-representation	A string defining the preferred way of outputting special characters. With «`method="xml"`» this only affects characters outside the selected character encoding. The value may be **decimal**, causing output as a decimal character reference (for example «`&2345;`» or **hex**, which causes ouput as a hexadecimal character reference (such as «`&x20a4;`»). With «`method="html"`» the value may consist of two keywords, separated by a semicolon. The first keyword indicates how non-ASCII characters that are within the character encoding should be represented, the second how characters outside the encoding are written. There are four permitted keywords: **native**, **entity**, **decimal**, and **hex**. The values **decimal** and **hex** have the same meaning as with XML output. In addition, **native** means output the character as itself, in the selected encoding (which is only meaningful for the first keyword), while **entity** asks the system to use one of the predefined HTML entity names such as «`Á`» if possible. The default is «`entity;decimal`».

saxon:omit-meta-tag	This attribute may be set to **yes** or **no**; the default is **no**. The XSLT specification states that with HTML output, the processor should output a **<meta>** element as part of the document header. Sometimes this is a nuisance, for example if you are transforming an XHTML document that already contains this element. The **saxon:omit-meta-tag** attribute is therefore provided so it can be suppressed.
saxon:next-in-chain	The value is the URL of another XSLT stylesheet. This causes the output of this stylesheet to be directed as input to the second stylesheet. The result destination specified for this stylesheet (for example, the file named in the **href** attribute of **<xsl:document>**) is passed on to act as the final destination for the output of the second stylesheet.

Saxon supports a number of character encodings for the output file, specifically:

ascii, us-ascii, utf-8, utf8, iso-8859-1, iso-8859-2, ko18-r, cp1250, windows-1250, cp1251, windows-1251

The names may be written in either uppercase or lowercase. However, the encoding only works if it is also supported by your particular Java VM. This is because the work of producing output in the chosen encoding is split between Saxon and the JVM. Saxon is responsible for deciding which Unicode characters can be represented directly and which need to be represented as symbolic character references. The JVM is then responsible for translating the Unicode character into its target encoding.

It is possible to add your own character encodings to Saxon, but only if the JVM supports the encoding. For details, see the product documentation.

Summary

As the author of the Saxon product it would be difficult for me to give an objective assessment of its strengths and weaknesses relative to other products, and in any case, that is not the purpose of this book.

However, it has certainly established itself as one of the leading processors available, certainly among the Java contingent:

- It is strong on conformance to the XSLT 1.0 and draft XSLT 1.1 standards, as well as JAXP 1.1.
- It also offers an exceptionally rich library of extensions (which you might quite rightly choose to ignore, in the interests of keeping your stylesheets portable).
- It offers good performance compared with other Java processors.

There are perhaps two main potential drawbacks: the lack of any corporate support or warranty, which makes it difficult for project managers to take seriously, and the fact that it is very much an XSLT processor only, rather than being part of a full XML development kit that also comes with support for DOM, XML Schemas, XLink and XPointer, and all the rest.

D

Xalan

Xalan is an open source XSLT processor produced by the Apache organization. The various Xalan products are all available by following the relevant links from http://xml.apache.org/.

> *Xalan originally derived from an earlier product called LotusXSL which was developed by a team under Scott Boag of IBM's Lotus subsidiary before being handed over to the Apache Software Foundation. LotusXSL as currently available from the IBM site (*http://www.alphaworks.ibm.com/*) is merely a wrapper around the Xalan product. Since the transfer to Apache, however, a great deal of further development has taken place, involving people from a number of organizations, though Scott Boag remains the lead architect. According to the Apache web site, the name Xalan refers to a rare musical instrument. If that's so, then it must be very rare – it is unknown to both the Oxford English Dictionary and the Encyclopædia Britannica.*

Xalan is available both in Java and C++ versions. I shall devote most of this chapter to describing the Java version, which appears to be more mature, more widely used, and better documented. There have also been reports that the Java version is faster, though I'm told that this may have been due to errors in the benchmarking methodology. Generally, I refrain from making performance comparisons in this book partly because benchmark results are so unreliable, and partly because they tend to be short-lived; version 1.1 of the C++ product, featuring major performance enhancements, was announced shortly before we went to press.

The Xalan-Java product has received a good level of user exposure. Recently the product has been restructured to create Xalan-Java 2, the major innovation being support of the TrAX transformation API described in Appendix F. This version also brings the product up to date with the DOM2 and SAX2 specifications. Xalan-Java 2 is the product that we will be mainly describing in this appendix. Version 1 remains available, and is probably rather more stable and reliable at the time of writing, but if you are using the product for the first time, I would recommend going straight to version 2.

The software is free, and is distributed under the Apache Software License, which essentially allows any kind of use, redistribution, or modification, but disclaims any liability. There is no formal warranty or support, though there are active mailing lists and bug submission procedures. Source code is included with the product, including full instructions and scripts for building the product if you want to change the source.

Xalan uses the Apache XML parser, Xerces; the Java product works with the Java version of Xerces Java, and the C++ product with the C++ version of Xerces. Xalan-Java 2 will also work with any other parser that conforms to the JAXP 1.1 parser interface. Xalan will output to a SAX2 `ContentHandler` or to a DOM2 tree as well as supporting the standard output methods of XML, HTML, and text.

Xalan claims complete support for mandatory XSLT 1.0 and XPath 1.0 features. There are no independent conformance tests yet for XSLT, so as with other vendors, you have to take this statement on trust; but Xalan has a good reputation and probably comes at least as close to one hundred percent conformance as any product.

Xalan-Java 2

Installation

Follow the links at http://xml.apache.org/ to download a suitable version of Xalan. The software is available either as a `.zip` file (suitable for Windows platforms) or in `.tar.gz` format which is better suited to Unix platforms, but it is the same software either way.

You will need to install a Java Virtual Machine. Xalan explicitly supports the IBM and SUN Java implementations at version 1.1.8, 1.2.2, or 1.3. The Microsoft JVM is not in the list of supported Java Virtual Machines. I found it worked for me, but there may well be limitations I didn't discover.

Xalan contains the necessary components of the Xerces parser, so you don't need to install an XML parser separately.

Download the Xalan `.zip` or `.tar.gz` file and uncompress it to a suitable directory. Then locate the subdirectory containing the `xalan.jar` and `xerces.jar` files, and add these files to your Java classpath. That's all!

> *I actually find it convenient to copy the* `.jar` *files to a single directory such as* `c:\apache`. *One advantage of this is that I don't have to change my classpath every time I install a new version, I just have to replace the old* `.jar` *files with the new ones.*
>
> *Remember to put the* `.jar` *files themselves on the classpath, not the directories containing them. The classpath is a list of directories and* `.jar` *files that will be searched when the Java VM needs to load a class. With Windows 98, it is best to set it up by adding a line to your* `autoexec.bat` *file, for example:*
>
> *SET CLASSPATH=.;c:\apache\xerces.jar;c:\apache\xalan.jar;*
> *With Windows NT or Windows 2000, you can set this environment variable from the Control Panel, System icon. If you use a different operating system, you probably know what you're doing!*

Invoking Xalan-Java from the Command Line

The Xalan XSLT processor may be run from the command line, or by calling its Java API. There are also wrappers provided to allow it to be run within an applet or within a servlet.

A typical call from the command line is:

```
java org.apache.xalan.xslt.Process -in a.xml -xsl b.xsl -out c.html
```

The `java` command invokes the Java Virtual Machine. If it complains that it can't find the class `org.apache.xalan.xslt.Process`, then you haven't succeeding in putting `xalan.jar` on your classpath. If the complaint relates to the class `org.apache.xerces.jaxp.SAXParserFactoryImpl`, this means that `xerces.jar` isn't on your classpath.

The full list of options that may be specified on the command line is as follows. The options may be specified either in lowercase or uppercase.

Option	Effect
`-DIAG`	Requests output of timing diagnostics.
`-EDUMP`	Requests output of a stack trace if an error occurs.
`-HTML`	Requests the serializer to use the `html` output method, overriding anything specified using **`<xsl:output>`**.
`-IN url`	Specifies the URL of the source XML document. If this is a relative URL, it is taken as a filename relative to the current directory.
`-INDENT n`	Specifies the number of spaces to be used at each level when producing indented output.
`-MEDIA`	(Undocumented option: may not be fully supported.) Specifies the media type, used to select an **`<?xml-stylesheet?>`** processing instruction when there is more than one. The value should match the value of the media pseudo-attribute of the **`<?xml-stylesheet?>`** processing instruction to be selected.
`-OUT filename`	Names the file that is to contain the serialized output of the transformation. If this argument is omitted, output is directed to `System.out`.
`-PARAM name value`	Sets the value of a global stylesheet parameter. If the namespace URI of the parameter is not null, the TrAX format «`{namespace-uri}local-name`» can be used. The value will always be a string. Note: in previous Xalan releases, the value was an XPath expression, so a string-value had to be supplied in nested quotes, for example: `-PARAM city "'London'"`

Table continued on following page

Option	Effect

`-PARAM name value` *(continued)*	This is no longer the case with Xalan-Java 2; to pass a string, just write:
	`-PARAM city London`
	If there are several parameters, the `-PARAM` keyword should be repeated, for example:
	`-PARAM city London -PARAM country UK`

`-Q`	Quiet mode: suppresses progress messages.
`-QC`	Switches off warnings about ambiguous template rules (that is, situations where two template rules with the same precedence and priority both match the same node).
`-TEXT`	Requests the serializer to use the `text` output method, overriding anything specified using **`<xsl:output>`**.
`-TG`	Requests tracing of each event that writes a node to the result tree.
`-TS`	Requests tracing of each event that selects nodes from the source tree.
`-TT`	Requests trace information that identifies which template rules are instantiated.
`-TTC`	Requests tracing of individual instructions within a template.
`-V`	Requests output of Xalan version information.
`-XML`	Requests the serializer to use the `xml` output method, overriding anything specified using **`<xsl:output>`**.
`-XSL url`	Specifies the URL of the stylesheet document. If this is a relative URL, it is taken as a filename relative to the current directory. If this option is omitted, Xalan tries to identify the stylesheet by looking for an **`<?xml-stylesheet?>`** processing instruction in the source document.

For example, to run the knight's tour stylesheet described in Chapter 10, the command would be (all on one line):

```
java org.apache.xalan.xslt.Process -param start e5 -in dummy.xml
    -xsl tour10.xsl -out tour.html
```

This assumes you have changed directory to the directory containing the `tour10.xsl` stylesheet, which is available in the code download for the book. This particular stylesheet works with any source document so the only requirements on `dummy.xml` are that is exists and is XML. The file `tour10.xsl` holds a version of the stylesheet that works with XSLT 1.0, and is different from the version described in Chapter 10, which exploits features of the draft XSLT 1.1 standard.

In fact `tour10.xsl` can be used as its own source document, so for convenience it contains an **`<?xml-stylesheet?>`** processing instruction referring to itself. This allows you to run it with the simpler command:

```
java org.apache.xalan.xslt.Process -param start e5 -in tour10.xsl -out
tour.html
```

Invoking Xalan from a Java Application

Xalan also has a Java API, allowing it to be invoked from an application, an applet, or a servlet.

Xalan-Java 2 uses the TrAX API defined as part of JAXP 1.1. The TrAX API is fully described in Appendix F. This differs from the proprietary API used in Xalan-Java 1. Xalan-Java 2 includes a compatibility wrapper providing support for much of the Xalan-Java 1 API, but I shall concentrate on the newer TrAX interface in this appendix.

Xalan implements the whole of the `javax.xml.transform` package, including the `dom`, `sax`, and `stream` sub-packages, both for input and output. It also implements the `SAXTransformerFactory` which allows you to do the transformation as part of a SAX pipeline.

The `xalan.jar` package includes a version of the top-level `java.xml.transform.TransformerFactory` class and is configured so that it chooses Xalan as the platform-default XSLT processor. This means that if Xalan is the only TrAX implementation on your classpath, calling `TransformerFactory.newInstance()` will automatically give you an instance of Xalan's TrAX implementation. If however you have multiple TrAX implementations on the classpath, perhaps Saxon as well as Xalan, then the one that is loaded by default will depend on the ordering of entries on your classpath. The safest policy in such cases is to choose one of the implementations explicitly. There are several ways this can be achieved:

- You can choose Xalan by setting the Java system property named `javax.xml.transform.TransformerFactory` to the value `org.apache.xalan.processor.TransformerFactoryImpl`. Use the `-D` option on the java command when you invoke your application. Note that this goes before the name of the class to be executed:

  ```
  java -Djavax.xml.transform.TransformerFactory=
       org.apache.xalan.processor.TransformerFactoryImpl
       com.my-com.appl.Program
  ```

  This all goes on one line. In practice of course you won't want to type this more than once: create a batch file or shell script using your text editor, and invoke that instead.

- Create a file called `jaxp.properties` within the directory `$JAVA_HOME/lib` (where `$JAVA_HOME` is the directory containing your Java installation), and include in this file a line of the form `key=value`, where `key` is the property key `javax.xml.transform.TransformerFactory` and `value` is the Xalan class `org.apache.xalan.processor.TransformerFactoryImpl`.

- Put the call `System.setProperty ("javax.xml.transform.TransformerFactory", "org.apache.xalan.processor.TransformerFactoryImpl")` in your application, to be executed at run-time. This is the only technique that works if you want to run several different TrAX processors from the same application, perhaps in order to compare their results or to benchmark their performance.

Xalan selects a SAX2 parser by using the mechanism defined in JAXP 1.1, specifically the `javax.xml.parsers.ParserFactory` interface. The default parser for JAXP 1.1 is Crimson (`org.apache.crimson.jaxp.SAXParserFactoryImpl`) a new lightweight Java XML parser from Apache based on the original Sun Project X parser. The `META-INF/services/javax.xml.parsers.SAXParserFactory` file in `xalan.jar`, however, overrides this by specifying `org.apache.xerces.jaxp.SAXParserFactoryImpl` as the default parser. This will be loaded provided that the Xerces parser is also on the classpath. A suitable version of `xerces.jar` is included in the Xalan distribution.

If you want to use a different parser, you can achieve this by setting the system property `javax.xml.parsers.SAXParserFactory`. Alternatively, you can load a parser explicitly as part of a `javax.xml.transform.sax.SAXSource` object that you supply as the input to the transformation; this is particularly useful if you want to use different parsers for the source document and the stylesheet, perhaps one validating and one not.

Similarly, when Xalan needs to create a DOM Document, it again uses the JAXP 1.1 mechanism: this time the `javax.xml.parsers.DocumentBuilderFactory` interface. Once again the default in JAXP 1.1 is the new `crimson` parser, but the `META_INF` file in `xalan.jar` nominates the tried-and-trusted Xerces DOM, specifically the class `org.apache.xerces.jaxp.DocumentBuilderFactoryImpl`.

The TrAX API splits transformation into two stages, the preparation of a `Templates` object from the source stylesheet, and the use of this `Templates` object to control a transformation. The benefit of this architecture is that the `Templates` object can be re-used as often as required: it's often the case on a web server that the same stylesheet us used again and again to transform many different source documents. The `Templates` object can not only be used repeatedly, but since it is thread-safe, it can also be used to run multiple transformations in parallel. Xalan exploits this architecture to the full: the `Templates` object is in effect a compiled version of the source stylesheet. Xalan also ensures that the `Templates` object is serializable (in the Java sense), allowing it to be moved freely between memory and disk, or to be relocated or replicated between servers in an EJB (Enterprise JavaBeans) environment.

The capability in Xalan-Java 1 to write the compiled stylesheet directly to disk from the command line is no longer present in Xalan-Java 2, but the concept of reusability remains as important as ever. For good performance it is essential to exploit this: keep the compiled stylesheet around in a cache, don't keep recompiling it every time it's needed.

Xalan and the DOM

Xalan can use any DOM2-conformant DOM implementation as its input, and it can also attach its result tree to any DOM2-conformant document. If you supply a DOM as the source tree, Xalan will use this as its internal tree representation. If you supply input in the form of a SAX stream or a source XML file, however, Xalan will use its own internal tree representation, called an STree. This replaces the DTM tree used in earlier versions. The STree is more efficent than a general-purpose DOM, notably because each node contains a sequence number which can be used for rapid sorting of nodes into document order. Determining document order is notoriously difficult and slow when done using standard DOM2 interfaces alone. The STree does implement all the required DOM2 interfaces, but it will bounce many of the updating methods with an exception, because it is designed to allow appending of nodes only in document order.

A particular feature of the STree implementation is that it allows the parser thread that builds the tree to operate in parallel with the transformer thread that reads it. If the transformer thread needs access to nodes that have not yet been parsed, it waits until the parser catches up. For a significant number of transformations, this means that the user will start seeing results on the screen before the whole source document has been parsed. An aspiration that the Xalan designers have in mind for a future release is to detect, by analysing the source code of the stylesheet, when access to a particular node in the source tree is no longer required; the idea is that it will then be possible to delete that node from memory, in the same way as a Java garbage collector deletes objects that are no longer referenced. This creates the potential to process large XML documents that are too big to fit in memory, provided that the transformation process is written to work its way serially through the document. If they can find a way of achieving this, the effect will be similar to the **`<saxon:preview>`** mechanism offered by the Saxon XSLT processor (see Appendix C, page 790), except that it will be completely automatic.

Using XPath Expressions in Xalan

Using Xalan's Java API, you can execute XPath expressions against the tree representation of the source document, independently of any stylesheet. The XPath processor is written so it will operate against any DOM: it is not dependent on the rest of Xalan or on any particular tree implementation (though at present it shares some utility classes with the rest of Xalan).

This has two benefits: it allows DOM-based Java applications to navigate the tree using XPath expressions, and it allows other software subsystems, for example XPointer, to reuse the XPath library.

Most of the XPath functionality you are likely to need is provided by a set of static methods in the class `org.apache.xpath.XPathAPI`. This provides a wrapper around the lower-level XPath routines elsewhere in the package.

The methods are summarized in the table below:

Method	Explanation
`eval( Node contextNode, String xPath)` → `XObject`	The `xPath` argument contains the XPath expression; the `contextNode` identifies the context node. The context position and context size will both be 1. The namespace prefixes that can be used are those in scope for the context node. The result of evaluating the expression is an `XObject`: this represents an XPath value, typically `XBoolean`, `XNumber`, `XString`, `XNodeSet`, or `XRTreeFrag`, depending on the data type.
`eval( Node contextNode, String xPath, Node nsNode)` → `XObject`	This is the same as the previous method, except that the namespace prefixes that can be used are those in scope for `nsNode`.
`eval( Node contextNode, String xPath, PrefixResolver p)` → `XObject`	This is the same as the previous method, except that any namespace prefixes are resolved using a user-supplied `PrefixResolver` class.

Table continued on following page

Method	Explanation

`selectNodeIterator(`
`Node contextNode,`
`String xPath)`
→ `NodeIterator`
	This method can be called to evaluate an XPath expression whose result is a node-set. As before, the `contextNode` argument is used both as context node for the XPath evaluation and as the reference point for resolving namespace prefixes. The result is returned in the form of a DOM2 `NodeIterator` (part of the `org.w3c.dom.traversal` package). This means that the evaluation can be pipelined: it is not necessary for the system to find all the nodes first, and save them in memory, rather it can fetch each node as it is needed.

`selectNodeIterator(`
`Node contextNode,`
`String xPath,`
`Node nsNode)`
→ `NodeIterator`
	This is the same as the previous method, except that the namespace prefixes that can be used are those in scope for `nsNode`.

`selectNodeList(`
`Node contextNode,`
`String xPath)`
→ `NodeList`
	This method is the same as the corresponding `selectNodeIterator()` method, except that the result is returned in the form of a DOM `NodeList`. Normally this will mean that all the nodes have been found before the method returns.

`selectNodeList(`
`Node contextNode,`
`String xPath,`
`Node nsNode)`
→ `NodeIterator`
	This is the same as the previous method, except that the namespace prefixes that can be used are those in scope for `nsNode`.

`selectSingleNode(`
`Node contextNode,`
`String xPath)`
→ `Node`
	This method is the same as the corresponding `selectNodeIterator()` method, except that the result is returned in the form of a DOM `Node`. Use this method only if you know that the XPath expression will return at most one node (if no nodes are selected, it returns null).

`selectSingleNode(`
`Node contextNode,`
`String xPath,`
`Node nsNode)`
→ `Node`
	This is the same as the previous method, except that the namespace prefixes that can be used are those in scope for `nsNode`.

The class `XObject` provides methods corresponding to most of the common XPath operations on values, for example `equals()` to compare two values according to the XPath rules, `str()` to convert the value to a string, and so on.

Xalan also comes with a demonstration application that uses this capability to allow XPath expressions to be executed from the command line. This provides a convenient way of learning about XPath and testing complex XPath expressions. You can run it as:

```
java ApplyXPath XMLFile XPathExpression
```

where *XMLFile* is an XML source file and *XPathExpression* is an XPath expression to apply to that file. Use quotes if the expression contains spaces. For example:

```
java ApplyXPath books.xml "//author[starts-with(., 'B')]"
```

With this utility, the context node will always be the root node. The XPath expression must be one that returns a node-set.

Running Xalan-Java as an Applet

Xalan includes a class `org.apache.xalan.client.XSLTProcessorApplet` which provides all the functionality you need to run Xalan transformations within the browser, as an applet. The product also includes a sample HTML page, in `samples/AppletXMLtoHTML/appletXMLtoHTML.html`, which shows how to build this functionality into your own applications. Your browser, of course, must be configured to allow Java applets to run. The sample application shows three frames side-by-side, containing the original XML, the stylesheet, and the generated HTML:

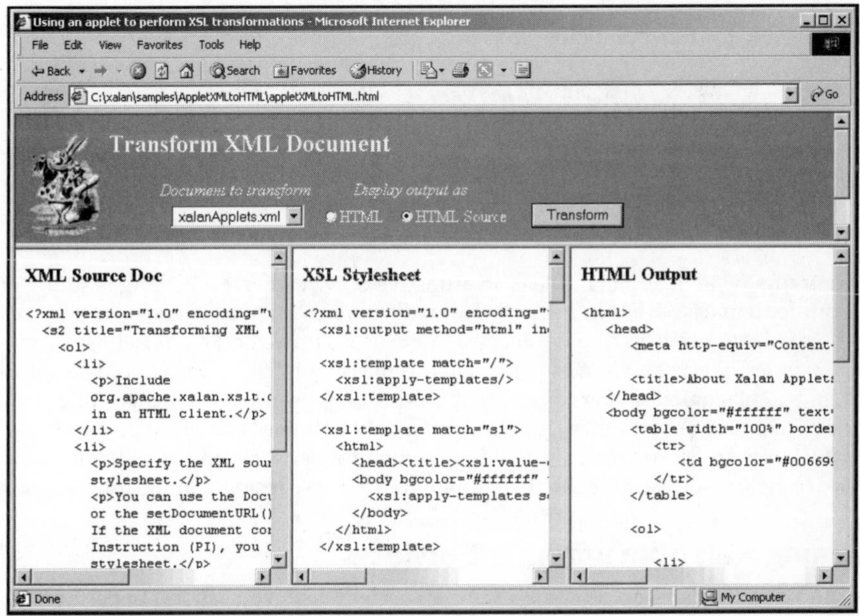

The key piece of HTML you need to include in your page is:

```
<applet
  name="xslControl"
  code="org.apache.xalan.client.XSLTProcessorApplet.class"
  archive="../../bin/xalan.jar,../../bin/xerces.jar"
  height="0"
  width"0">
  <param name="documentURL" value="default.xml"/>
  <param name="styleURL" value="stylesheet.xsl"/>
</applet>
```

The `archive` attribute must point to the location on the server, relative to the HTML page itself, where the `xalan.jar` and `xerces.jar` files are to be found: the example here will work only with the directory structure used by the sample application. The filenames of the source document and stylesheet are supplied as parameters to the applet. They don't have to have fixed values, of course, you can set them dynamically from JavaScript code on the page as follows:

```
document.xslControl.setDocumentURL(xmlFileName)
document.xslControl.setStyleURL(xslFileName)
```

You don't need to set the stylesheet if the source document contains an **`<?xml-stylesheet?>`** processing instruction: this will act as the default stylesheet for this source document.

You can also set stylesheet parameters, with calls such as:

```
document.xslControl.setStylesheetParam("start-record", "1")
document.xslControl.setStylesheetParam("last-record", "5")
```

To execute the transformation, call:

```
var outputHTML = document.xslControl.getHtmlText();
```

You can then insert this HTML into the target page in the normal way: for example if the page contains the tag `<div id="resultArea">` you can write:

```
resultArea.innerHTML = outputHTML;
```

Running Xalan in applet mode is an attractive option when everything is sitting on your local machine, but in the real world, of course, you need to consider the size of the code that needs to be downloaded to the user's browser. Xalan itself is currently just under 700Kb, and Xerces weighs in at a massive 1450Kb. You should be able to achieve substantial savings by using the Crimson parser instead, a mere 185Kb. But even with this improvement, downloading only becomes a practical proposition if your users are all connected via a high-bandwidth network, and even then only if they are using the software frequently enough for it to stay resident in the browser cache.

Running Xalan-Java from a Servlet

The Xalan distribution contains a sample servlet which you can use to perform server-side transformations, responding to requests from the browser. The code is in the `samples/servlet` directory, the main servlet class being called `ApplyXSLT.java`.

You can either use the servlet code directly as supplied, or more likely, you can adapt it to the needs of your own application.

In fact the sample servlet is written almost entirely using the TrAX interface, so it could be used to drive any TrAX processor. The only dependencies on Xalan are that it uses an error handler derived from the standard Xalan error handler, and that it sets configuration parameters which processors other than Xalan will not recognize.

First you must set up your web server and servlet engine, and ensure that `xalan.jar` and `xerces.jar` are on the classpath that the servlet engine uses. Make sure you are using an up-to-date version of Xerces, or another parser that supports the SAX2 interface. The servlet engine also needs to be able to find the classes and property files included in source form in the `samples/servlet` directory, or in compiled form in `bin/xalanservlet.jar`. Remember that the servlet engine will not necessarily load classes from the same places as when you run Java applications from the command line as a common mistake is to leave old versions of parsers lying around in directories used by the servlet engine.

You can compile the sample servlet into the servlets directory provided by the web server. You can then call it using a URL such as:

```
http://my.company.com/servlet/ApplyXSLT?URL=/source.xml&xslURL=/style.xsl
```

This assumes that the source XML document `source.xml` and the stylesheet `style.xsl` are in the home directory of the web site.

There are considerable variations possible on this theme. You can also supply the source file as part of the URL, rather than as a parameter:

```
http://my.company.com/servlet/ApplyXSLT/source.xml?xslURL=/style.xsl
```

If you are confident about configuring your servlet engine, you can arrange for it to map the data file to the servlet automatically, so the URL can be shortened to:

```
http://my.company.com/servlet/source.xml?xslURL=/style.xsl
```

You can omit the `xslURL` parameter if the data file includes an **`<?xml-stylesheet?>`** processing instruction (though of course there is a potential performance penalty as soon as the server has to look inside the data file rather than simply sending it to the client). You can even use the `media.properties` file to arrange that different stylesheets are used, depending on the media type contained in the HTTP request, so that different processing is carried out depending on the capabilities of the client device.

Alternatively, of course, you can write a subclass of the standard `ApplyXSLT` servlet, and you can then decide which stylesheet to use based on your own knowledge of the application structure. For example, there might be one stylesheet for each directory holding source documents.

For a more comprehensive solution to managing XSLT transformation in a Java server environment, take a look at Xalan's stable mate product, Cocoon, which I describe briefly on page 827 in Appendix E. Cocoon is a complex product to understand, but that's because the task it's tackling is a complex one, going well beyond the simple job of transforming one source document using one stylesheet to look at the overall complexities of web publishing with many different document types presented in many different ways to different audiences. Cocoon has until now always used Xalan-Java as its transformation engine, though with the emergence of the TrAX API, in future it is likely to offer users a choice.

Extensibility

Xalan allows you to define both extension functions and extension elements.

At the time of writing, Xalan does not yet implement these bindings according to the draft XSLT 1.1 specification; rather it has defined its own mechanisms. However, they are not too dissimilar.

In Xalan's extensibility model, a collection of extension elements and functions is bundled together into a **component**, and each component is identified by a namespace URI. The elements and functions available in this component are defined by a **<xalan:component>** element at the top level of the stylesheet. But before looking at the **<xalan:component>** element, we'll look at the short-cut syntax for calling Java methods.

The Short-Cut Syntax for Calling Java Methods

For Java extension functions, there is a short-cut syntax, in which the namespace URI of the extension function tells Xalan the name of the Java class where the relevant method will be found. In fact there are three variants on this short-cut syntax:

- Use the namespace to identify a class. You can call a Java external function using a call such as:

  ```
  <xsl:variable name="today" select="Date:new()"
            xmlns:Date="xalan://java.util.Date"/>
  ```

  Here the namespace URI directly identifies the required class. The «xalan://» prefix in the namespace URI is conventional, but Xalan only actually uses the part of the URI after the final «/». (This is convenient, because Saxon and xt adopt similar conventions, which makes it possible to write code that will work on a number of different processors.)

- Use the namespace to identify the Java language. With this technique you can include the full class name in the local name of the function call, using the prefix only to indicate that it is a Java class. In this notation, you would write:

  ```
  <xsl:variable name="today" select="java:java.util.Date.new()"
            xmlns:java="http://xml.apache.org/xslt/java"/>
  ```

  In this case the namespace URI must be exactly as shown. The advantage of this approach is that you only need one namespace declaration to cover all your Java extension function calls: you would normally attach it to the **<xsl:stylesheet>** element, rather than putting it with the function call as in our example. This also means there is only one namespace you will need to exclude from the result document using the **exclude-result-prefixes** attribute.

- Use the namespace to identify a Java package, and use the local name of the function to identify the class and method within this package. In this format, you would write:

  ```
  <xsl:variable name="today" select="util:Date.new()"
              xmlns:util="xalan://java.util"/>
  ```

This format is useful when you want to use many classes within the same Java package. It can be a good choice when that package contains your own application.

The <xalan:component> Element

The **<xalan:component>** element is a top-level element that defines a bundle of extension functions and extension elements.

Format

```
<xalan:component
     prefix    = namespace prefix
     functions = list-of-NCNames
     elements  = list-of-NCNames  >
   <xalan:script>...</xalan:script>
</xalan:component>
```

Position

<xalan:component> element is a top-level element, it must appear as a child of the **<xsl:stylesheet>** or **<xsl:transform>** element.

You can have any number of **<xalan:component>** elements in a stylesheet but they must implement components with different namespaces.

Because it is a top-level element rather than an instruction appearing within a template body, **<xalan:component>** is not technically an extension element, and therefore doesn't require the Xalan namespace to be declared using the **extension-element-prefixes** on the **<xsl:stylesheet>** element. However, it does no harm to do so.

Attributes

Name	Value	Meaning
prefix *mandatory*	A namespace prefix that is in scope at this point in the stylesheet	Identifies the namespace used with the extension functions and extension elements that make up this component
functions *optional*	Space-separated list of names (without a namespace prefix)	Identifies the extension functions within this component
elements *optional*	Space-separated list of names (without a namespace prefix)	Identifies the extension elements within this component

Contents

The **<xalan:component>** element contains exactly one **<xalan:script>** element and no other elements.

Usage

A component defines a package of related extension functions and extension elements: for example, you might have such a package that provides access to a relational database, or a package that provides date and time handling.

The reason why two elements, **<xalan:component>** and **<xalan:script>** are necessary is not obvious, but presumably it was done this way to accommodate future enhancements.

The <xalan:script> Element

The **<xalan:script>** element defines the implementation of a set of extension functions or extension elements.

Format

```
<xalan:script
    lang  = "javaclass" | "javascript" | other-language
    src   = see below
</xalan:script>
```

Position

<xalan:script> always appears as the only child of a **<xalan:component>** element.

Attributes

Name	Value	Meaning
lang *mandatory*	«javaclass» (meaning Java), «javascript», or the name of another language supported by the Bean Scripting Framework	Identifies the language in which the component is implemented.
src *optional*	Used only where «lang="javaclass"». As with the short-cut technique, there are three permitted formats: xalan://java.util.Date identifies a specific Java class http://xml.apache.org/xslt/java indicates that the function call itself will identify the full Java class name xalan://java.util identifies a Java package	Identifies where to find the Java class or package

Contents

The **`<xalan:script>`** element will be empty in the case of a Java extension function, and will contain the code implementing the functions in the case of JavaScript or other scripting languages. In this case it is often convenient to write the code within a `CDATA` section to avoid problems with special characters.

Usage: Java

For Java extension functions the **`lang`** attribute is always «`javaclass`». The **`src`** attribute is always present and will be in one of the three formats shown above. In conjunction with the local name used in the function call itself, this is enough to identify both the Java class and the method to be called.

When the **`src`** attribute uses the class format (for example `xalan://java.util.Date`), the function call is of the form «`prefix:function(args)`». The function name must be one of:

- **`new`**, indicating a constructor
- the name of a static method
- the name of an instance-level method in which the target instance is specified as the first argument
- the name of an instance-level method in which the target instance will be specially created, using the default constructor

When the **`src`** attribute has the value `http://xml.apache.org/xslt/java`, the function name must be one of the following, where `full.class.Name` represents a Java class name qualified by its package name:

- `full.class.Name.new`, indicating a constructor
- `full.class.Name.method` where `method` is the name of a static method on the class
- `full.class.Name.method` where `method` is the name of an instance-level `method` in which the target instance is specified as the first argument

Finally, when the **`src`** attribute takes the form `xalan://package.name`, the function name must be one of the following, where `Class` is the name of the class without its package name:

- `Class.new`, indicating a constructor
- `Class.method` where `method` is the name of a static method on the class
- `Class.method` where `method` is the name of an instance-level `method` in which the target instance is specified as the first argument

A Java class may have several methods with the same name. In choosing a method, Xalan tries to identify the one that has the best fit between the data types of the XPath values supplied in the function call, and the Java classes defined for the arguments in the method signature. In finding the best fit, it uses rules that are similar to, but not quite the same as, those defined in the draft XSLT 1.1 specification.

In mapping the arguments supplied in the XPath function call to Java objects and values, the permitted mappings between XPath data types and Java data types are shown in the table below, in order of preference (bracketed types are equally preferred).

XPath Type	Java Types
Node-Set	`org.w3c.dom.traversal.NodeIterator`, `org.w3c.dom.NodeList`, `org.w3c.dom.Node` or its subclasses, `java.lang.String`, `java.lang.Object`, `char`, `[double, float, long, int, short, byte]`, `boolean`
String	`java.lang.String, java.lang.Object, char, [double, float, long, int, short, byte], boolean`
Boolean	`boolean, java.lang.Boolean, java.lang.Object, java.lang.String`
Number	`double, java.lang.Double, float, long, int, short,char, byte, boolean, java.lang.String, java.lang.Object`
Result Tree Fragment	`org.w3c.dom.traversal.NodeIterator`, `org.w3c.dom.DocumentFragment`, `org.w3c.dom.Node` or its subclasses, `java.lang.String`, `java.lang.Object`, `char`, `[double, float, long, int, short, byte]`, `boolean`
External Object	the native type or any of its superclasses, `double, float, long, int, short, char, byte, java.lang.String`

Where there are several methods with the same name, all having the correct number of arguments, Xalan assigns each of them a score based on the position of the declared data types in the above lists, and then chooses the one with the best score. If there is a tie, an error is reported.

Any Java extension function can have an extra first parameter of type `org.apache.xalan.extensions.ExpressionContext`. This is similar to the `w3c.org.xsl.XSLTContext` object defined in the draft XSLT 1.1 specification, though the details are slightly different. The `ExpressionContext` object is supplied automatically by the system, and does not need to be included in the explicit arguments of the XPath function call.

Usage: JavaScript

Xalan extension functions may be implemented in Java or JavaScript, or in other languages supported by the Bean Scripting Framework, such as Perl and Python. However, documentation on scripting languages other than JavaScript is thin on the ground, so you will be flying blind if you try to use them.

JavaScript extensions are always embedded directly within the stylesheet itself, in the **`<xalan:script>`** element within the **`<xalan:component>`** element. This is illustrated in the example below, which implements an extension function **`user:datePlus()`** and an extension element **`<user:trace>`**.

Example: Using JavaScript Extension Functions with Xalan

Source

This stylesheet can be run with any source document.

Stylesheet

This stylesheet is `xalan-script.xsl`.

The stylesheet creates a Xalan component which is identified by the namespace URI associated with the prefix «`user`». This component defines an extension element **`<user:trace>`** and an extension function **`user:datePlus()`**.

The template rule for the root node shows how this extension element and extension function can be invoked.

```
<xsl:stylesheet xmlns:xsl="http://www.w3.org/1999/XSL/Transform"
                       version="1.0"
                       xmlns:xalan="http://xml.apache.org/xslt"

xmlns:user="http://any.user.com/xslt/extension1"
                       extension-element-prefixes="user">

<xalan:component prefix="user" elements="trace"
functions="datePlus">
   <xalan:script lang="javascript">
      function trace (xslProcessorContext, extensionElement) {
         return "trace called, message=" +
            extensionElement.getAttribute("message");
      }
      function datePlus (days) {
         var d = new Date();
         d.setDate(d.getDate() + parseInt(days));
         return d.toLocaleString();
      }
   </xalan:script>
</xalan:component>

<xsl:template match="/">
    <html><body>
    <p><user:trace message="starting"/></p>
    <p>In 5 days time it will be <xsl:value-of
      select="user:datePlus(5)"/></p>
    <p><user:trace message="finished"/></p>
    </body></html>
</xsl:template>

</xsl:stylesheet>
```

Output

```
   <html>
   <body>
   <p>trace called, message=starting</p>
   <p>In 5 days time it will be February 25, 2001 11:36:25 AM GMT
+00:00</p>
   <p>trace called, message=finished</p>
   </body>
   </html>
```

D

Xalan

Getting scripted extension functions to work properly requires some careful assembly of all the right software. There are five software products that need to be correctly installed and configured to get this example to run:

- the Java Virtual Machine
- the Xerces XML Parser
- the Xalan XSLT Processor
- the Bean Scripting Framework
- the Rhino JavaScript interpreter

As we have seen, Xalan is downloaded from http://xml.apache.org, and comes with a basic copy of Xerces. The Bean Scripting Framework is also bundled with Xalan. Rhino Javascript is a separate download from http://www.mozilla.org/rhino/. Xalan-Java 2 is designed to work with version 1.5 of Rhino. I got this to work with the following command:

```
java -cp XXX org.apache.xalan.xslt.Process -in dummy.xml -xsl xalan-script.xsl
```

where XXX is the Java classpath, as follows, all on one line, with no spaces. The actual filenames will depend, of course, on where you installed the software.

```
D:\JavaLib\xerces\xerces-j_1_2_3\xerces.jar;
D:\JavaLib\xalan\xalan-j_2_0_0\xalan.jar;
D:\JavaLib\rhino\js.jar;
D:\JavaLib\xalan\xalan-j_2_0_0\bsf.jar
```

Usage: Implementing Extension Elements

Implementing extension elements is very similar to implementing extension functions. Essentially it works on the basis that if your extension function implements a particular Java signature, it can be used directly as an extension element.

The Java method name should match the local name of the extension element, and it should take two arguments:

- The first argument is an `org.apache.xalan.extensions.XSLProcessorContext`. This argument gives full access to the source document, the stylesheet, the current node and current node list, and other internal information.
- The second argument is an `org.apache.xalan.templates.ElemExtensionCall`. This argument represents the node in the stylesheet tree corresponding to the extension element. It provides services that the extension code can call on, for example expanding attribute value templates.

(This information is correct for Xalan-Java 2. For Xalan-Java 1, the class names and definitions are slightly different.)

Xalan's internal tree structure conforms to the DOM specification , so standard DOM interfaces can be used to find related nodes in the tree. The result of the function, if any, is copied to the result tree.

Extensions

Xalan has a useful library of built-in extension functions and extension elements, which I will describe in the following sections. These functions and elements are conventionally prefixed xalan:xxx, where the namespace prefix is declared as

```
xmlns:xalan="http://xml.apache.org/xalan"
```

Built-in Extension Functions

The following extension functions are provided:

difference (ns1, ns2)	This returns a node-set that is the difference of the two supplied node-sets; that is, it contains all the nodes that are in `ns1` that are not also in `ns2`.

distinct(ns1)	This returns a node-set containing all the nodes in `ns1` that have distinct string-values. Nodes with duplicate string-values are discarded. For example:
	`<xsl:variable name="cities" select="xalan:distinct(//city)"/>`
	creates a node-set containing one element for each uniquely named **<city>** in the source document. If there were several **<city>** elements with the same name, the one that is first in document order will be retained, though it generally doesn't matter, because the next step will usually be to process them all as a group:
	`<xsl:for-each select="$cities">`
	`<h2>City name is: <xsl:value-of select="."/></h2>`
	`<xsl:for-each select="//city[.=current()]">`
	`. . .`

evaluate (string)	This function allows an XPath expression to be constructed at run-time, as a string, and immediately evaluated. This is useful if a query is not known in advance, but must be constructed based on information supplied by the user in parameters, or read from the source document. For example the following code constructs a node-set consisting of all **<book>** elements that satisfy a predicate passed to the stylesheet as a parameter:
	`<xsl:param name="predicate"/>`
	`<xsl:variable name="selectedBooks" select=`
	`"xalan:evaluate(concat('//book[', $predicate, ']'))"/>`

hasSameNodes (ns1, ns2)	This returns a Boolean that is true if and only if `ns1` and `ns2` contain exactly the same set of nodes. Note this is quite different from the «=» operator, which tests whether there is a pair of nodes with the same string-value. The equivalent test in standard XSLT is: `<xsl:if test="count(ns1)=count(ns2) and count(ns1)=count(ns1|ns2)">`

intersection (ns1,ns2)	This returns a node-set that is the intersection of the two supplied node-sets; that is, it contains all the nodes that are in both `ns1` and `ns2`. This function can be useful in conjunction with keys, for example to list all programmers based in Denver, write: `<xsl:for-each select="xalan:intersection( key('job', 'Programmer'), key('location', 'Denver'))">`
nodeset(tree)	This function allows a result tree fragment to be converted to a node-set, allowing it to be processed further. This allows you to get round the XSLT 1.0 restrictions (lifted in the XSLT 1.1 draft) on the use of result tree fragments in contexts such as path expressions.
tokenize (string, delimiter?)	This function constructs a new node-set whose nodes result from splitting the supplied string into tokens, separated either by the supplied delimiter, or by whitespace. It is designed for operations such as replacing newline characters in the source by ** ** elements in the output, or searching for a particular word in the text content of an element.

SQL Extension Functions

Xalan provides a set of extension functions for connecting to a JDBC database, executing a query, and processing the recordset resulting from a query.

There are three extension functions that you can use in your stylesheet. These assume the namespace declaration `xmlns:sql="org.apache.xalan.lib.sql.XConnection"`.

- `sql:new()` establishes a database connection. The resulting connection object will normally be assigned to a variable. The first argument is the name of the JDBC driver required; the second is the URL identifying the database, and you can optionally supply the username and password as the third and fourth arguments.
- `sql:query(connection, selectStatement)` performs a query. The first argument is the connection object returned by `sql:new()`, the second is the SQL select statement, as a string. The function returns the root node of a new document containing the results of the query in a fixed format defined by Xalan. If you want to see what this format is, the simplest way to find out is to display it by writing:

```
<xsl:copy-of select="sql:query($connection, 'SELECT * FROM EMP')"/>
```

- `sql:close(connection)` terminates the database connection.

We wanted to show you an example of how to use these facilities, but to be honest, we found the code rather fragile. It worked fine with some JDBC drivers, but crashed with others (notably the JDBC:ODBC bridge). No doubt the facility will become more robust in future releases, but for the moment, Wrox prefer not to publish examples that only work sometimes!

Multiple Output Files

The only extension element currently supplied in Xalan is a facility to produce multiple output files, using an element called **<xalan:redirect>**. This has similar functionality to the **<xsl:document>** instruction introduced in the XSLT 1.1 draft specification, described on page 204 in Chapter 4, but with differences of detail.

This extension element allows an XSLT transformation to redirect its output to multiple output destinations. You must declare a namespace for the extension prefix (say `xmlns:redirect="org.apache.xalan.xslt.extensions.Redirect"`) and you must declare this namespace as an extension (`extension-element-prefixes="redirect"`).

You can either just use **<xalan:write>**, as in my example below, in which case the file will be opened and immediately closed after the write, or you can bracket the write calls by **<xalan:open>** and **<xalan:close>**, in which case the file will be kept open for multiple writes until the close call is encountered. Calls can be nested. Calls can take a **file** attribute and/or a **select** attribute in order to get the filename. If a `select` attribute is encountered, it will evaluate that expression to construct a string that indicates the filename. If the string evaluates to empty, it will attempt to use the **file** attribute as a default. The element can also have a **mkdirs** attribute, which, if set to true, will cause any non-existent directories to be created.

It's best illustrated by an example.

Example: Creating Multiple Output Files

This example takes a poem as input, and outputs each stanza to a separate file. A more realistic example would be to split a book into its chapters, but I wanted to keep the files small.

Source

The source file is `poem.xml`. It starts:

```
<poem>
<author>Rupert Brooke</author>
<date>1912</date>
<title>Song</title>
<stanza>
<line>And suddenly the wind comes soft,</line>
<line>And Spring is here again;</line>
<line>And the hawthorn quickens with buds of green</line>
<line>And my heart with buds of pain.</line>
</stanza>
<stanza>
<line>My heart all Winter lay so numb,</line>
<line>The earth so dead and frore,</line>
. . .
```

Stylesheet

The stylesheet is xalan-split.xsl.

Note that «xalan» is defined as an extension element prefix, so the **<xalan:write>** element is recognised as an instruction. Its effect is to switch all output produced by its template body to a different output file. In fact, it's very similar to the effect of an **<xsl:variable>** element that creates a tree, except that the tree, instead of becoming a fragment of the principal result tree, is serialized directly to an output file of its own.

```
<?xml version="1.0"?>
<xsl:stylesheet xmlns:xsl="http://www.w3.org/1999/XSL/Transform"
xmlns:xalan="org.apache.xalan.xslt.extensions.Redirect"
                extension-element-prefixes="xalan" version="1.0">
<xsl:template match="poem">
   <poem>
      <xsl:copy-of select="title"/>
      <xsl:copy-of select="author"/>
      <xsl:copy-of select="date"/>
      <xsl:apply-templates select="stanza"/>
   </poem>
</xsl:template>

<xsl:template match="stanza">
   <xsl:variable name="file" select="concat('verse', position(),
'.xml')"/>
   <verse number="{position()}" href="{$file}"/>
   <xalan:write select="$file">
        <xsl:copy-of select="."/>
   </xalan:write>
</xsl:template>
</xsl:stylesheet>
```

Output

The principal output file contains the skeletal poem below (new lines added for legibility):

```
<?xml version="1.0" encoding="utf-8" ?>
<poem>
<title>Song</title>
<author>Rupert Brooke</author>
<date>1912</date>
<verse number="1" href="verse1.xml"/>
<verse number="2" href="verse2.xml"/>
<verse number="3" href="verse3.xml"/>
</poem>
```

Three further output files verse1.xml, verse2.xml, and verse3.xml are created in the current directory. Here is verse1.xml:

```
<?xml version="1.0" encoding="utf-8" ?>
<stanza>
<line>And suddenly the wind comes soft,</line>
<line>And Spring is here again;</line>
<line>And the hawthorn quickens with buds of green</line>
<line>And my heart with buds of pain.</line>
</stanza>
```

The Xalan Serializer

Although the Xalan serializer appears as an integral component of the product when you run an XSLT transformation, it is actually engineered as a free-standing piece of software that can also be used in other contexts, for example to serialize a document held in a DOM. It interfaces with the rest of Xalan using the SAX2 `ContentHandler` interface.

Xalan supports the standard output methods (xml, html, and text), and all the attributes of the **`<xsl:output>`** element as defined in the XSLT 1.0 specification.

One minor surprise – not strictly a non-conformance – is that «`indent="yes"`» appears to have no effect. In fact, it causes Xalan to inject new lines into the output but not to add any spacing. You can correct this by setting the «`xalan:indent-amount`» property to a value other than its default of zero.

The output attributes can be specified either in the **`<xsl:output>`** element, or via the **`setOutputProperties()`** method in the TrAX API, as described in Appendix F.

Xalan also supports some additional attributes, or attribute values, to give more precise control over the form of the output. These are all in the Xalan namespace (`http://xml.apache.org/xslt`) so any other processor should ignore them.

For example, you can set the depth of indentation by writing

```
<xsl:output method="xml" indent="yes" xalan:indent-amount="5"
            xmlns:xalan="http://xml.apache.org/xslt"/>
```

You can make changes to the built-in defaults for all output properties by editing the property files in the directory `src/org/apache/xalan/templates`, and rebuilding the `xalan.jar` file using the tools provided. The property files containing the default output properties are called `output_xxx.properties`, where xxx is `html`, `text`, or `xml`.

The Xalan-defined output properties are as follows:

Property name	Applies to	Meaning
`xalan:indent-amount`	XML, HTML	The number of spaces to indent. Default is 0, which means no indentation.
`xalan:content-handler`	XML, HTML, TEXT	The name of a SAX2 `ContentHandler` to process the output. The default is to use a `ContentHandler` within the Xalan package.

Property name	Applies to	Meaning
xalan:entities	XML, HTML	The name of a resource file holding the definitions of HTML entities such as «é». The default is HTMLEntities.res.
xalan:use-url-escaping	HTML	Indicates whether URLs contained in HTML attributes are to be escaped using the %HH convention. The default is «yes»; set the value to «no» to suppress this behavior.

You can use the xalan:entities property to change the representation of characters by named entities. For example you can specify:

```
<xsl:output xalan:entities="myEntities.txt"/>
```

where the file myEntities.txt looks like this:

```
quot 34
amp 38
lt 60
gt 62
nbsp 160
```

The effect of this is that as well as the standard entities such as «<», the output will also represent any non-breaking-space character (Unicode value #160 or #xA0) as the entity reference « » (which unlike a non-breaking space, is visible in the output).

Xalan essentially supports any character encoding for the output file that is supported by the underlying Java VM. For well-known encodings such as ISO 8859/1 it translates the ISO name of the encoding (iso-8859-1), which you use in XML, to the Java name of the encoding (ISO8859_1). For each encoding, it outputs characters up to some threshold Unicode value as themselves, and characters above this threshold using numeric character references such as «ࠈ». The threshold is different for different encodings: for example, for US-ASCII it is 127; for encodings in the ISO 8859 family it is 255; for EBCDIC encodings it is 255; but for Chinese, Japanese, and Korean encodings, as well as utf-8 and utf-16, it is 65535.

Xalan-C++

As I promised at the start, I have devoted most of this appendix to the Java version of Xalan, but there is also a C++ version that deserves mention, although the product is not used as widely and is not as rich in functionality. There have been independent benchmarks that suggest it is slower than the Java product, but as often happens with benchmarks, others have reported the opposite: performance is notoriously sensitive to the precise conditions of measurement. In any case, the latest release (version 1.1) appears to have made substantial performance improvements.

You can download the Xalan-C++ product from `http://xml.apache.org`, in formats that are packaged for particular platforms, or you can build it yourself for your own machine. Assuming a Windows environment, it will install itself as a number of separate DLLs, plus an executable that provides a command-line interface. It is a good idea to include the directory containing this executable on the `PATH` defined in your `autoexec.bat` file.

The Command Line Interface

The executable is called `TestXSLT` and it has similar arguments and options to the Xalan-Java product.

For a basic transformation you can call it as follows:

```
TestXSLT -IN source.xml -XSL style.xsl -OUT output.html
```

The full list of options and arguments is shown in the table below. They are all case insensitive.

Option	Meaning
-DOM	Produces the output as a DOM, which is then serialized. This provides a test that the output is well-formed XML
-EER	Indicates whether entity references in the source file should be expanded: the default is **not** to expand them.
-ESCAPE	List of characters to be escaped in the output (the default is «`<>&"'\r\n`»).
-ESCAPECDATA	Removes the brackets around a CDATA section, and escapes the contents.
-HTML	Requests output method HTML.
-IN	URL of source file.
-INDENT n	Indicates the number of spaces by which output should be indented (default is zero).
-NH	Suppresses output of the XML declaration.
-OUT	File name to hold the output.
-PARAM name expr	Sets the value of a parameter to the transformation. Name gives the name of the parameter, and expr is an XPath expression that gives its value. Note if this is simply a string, it is necessary to enclose it in one pair of quotes to indicate that it is a string literal, and another pair of quotes to tell the command-line interpreter that the inner quotes are part of the expression. For example. `-PARAM city "'London'"`
-Q	Suppresses warnings and progress messages
-QC	Suppresses warnings of ambiguous matches on template rules.

Table continued on following page

Option	Meaning
-STRIPCDATA	Removes the brackets around a CDATA section, but without escaping the contents.
-TEXT	Requests output method TEXT.
-TG	Causes tracing of events that write nodes to the result tree.
-TS	Causes tracing of events that select nodes from the source tree.
-TT	Causes tracing of templates as they are called.
-TTC	Causes tracing of instructions within templates as they are executed.
-V	Requests output of version information.
-VALIDATE	Indicates that the source file and stylesheet should be validated by the XML parser.
-XML	Requests output method XML.
-XSL	URL of stylesheet.

Unicode Support

Unlike Java, the C++ language does not have built-in support for Unicode. Instead, Xalan-C++ provides an option to integrate the International Components for Unicode (ICU) available from IBM's DeveloperWorks site. Incorporating these components requires a re-build of the product; but without them, features such as the **`format-number()`** function and the **`<xsl:sort>`** element will not be fully Unicode-enabled.

Similarly, to enable support for Unicode in the Xerces-C++ parser, Xerces must also be rebuilt with these extensions.

Extensibility

Xalan-C++ allows you to write extension functions in C or C++. It does not currently allow you to write extension elements.

Each extension function must be written as a subclass of the **`Function`** class. As a minumum, it should provide an **`execute()`** method which will be called to evaluate the function, and a **`clone()`** method which allows Xalan to create a new instance.

Binding the function to the Xalan-C++ processor is rather trickier than with Java. It isn't possible to declare the function in the stylesheet and have it picked up by name; rather you need to make calls from your application to nominate your extension functions at the time you invoke the processor. Specifically, you need to instantiate an `XSLTProcessorEnvSupportDefault` object, and call its methods `installExternalFunctionGlobal()` or `installExtensionFunctionLocal()`. These methods take as arguments the namespace URI and local name of the function as it will be known within the stylesheet, and a pointer to the `Function` object itself.

Summary

Xalan is a mature open source product with a wide level of industry support, channeled through the Apache organisation. Although the reliance on a distributed team of developers means that progress is not always predictable, the product appears to combine comprehensive functionality, a high level of technical innovation, and good reliability and conformance. At present it isn't the fastest processor available, but it isn't far behind, and it has some excellent architectural features that suggest the gap may narrow in the future.

I would recommend using the Java product in preference to the C++ product unless you have some strong reasons for not using Java. But that, of course, is a decision you'll have to make for yourself.

E

Other Products

In the previous four appendices we looked at four XSLT processors in detail (MSXML3, Saxon, Oracle, and Xalan). We chose these because they probably account for 90% of current XSLT usage. But there are other products around that also deserve a mention, either because they have distinctive features that make them credible alternatives to these four, or because they appear to have sufficient promise to make them worth watching.

Most of the products listed in this appendix are XSLT processors, but I have also included a few tools such as XSLT development environments and editors. What I haven't done is to list XML tools that have no direct relationship to XSLT, because there are simply too many of them to cover.

This is a rapidly changing field, and it's only possible here to present a snapshot of the current situation. Inevitably there will be products I have missed, either because I didn't know about them, or because I haven't had time to research them properly. For comprehensive information on XSLT products as well as other XML software, a good place to look is http://www.xmlsoftware.com/.

The products covered in this chapter are as follows; they are listed in alphabical order.

4XSLT

This is an open source implementation of XSLT written in the Python language. The vendor is the FourThought company of Boulder, Colorado, and the lead designer is Uche Ogbuji. Information on the company is on http://www.fourthought.com/, and the open source tools can be downloaded from http://4suite.org/index.epy.

4XSLT forms one component of a suite of XML software which is remarkable in its scope, given the small size of the company producing it. As well as the XSLT processor, it includes an XML parser with DOM and SAX interfaces, an implementation of XLink and XPointer, an RDF implementation, and an object database. The main distinguishing feature of these tools is that they are all written in Python.

4XSLT is (as far as I can tell) a complete implementation of the XSLT 1.0 and XPath 1.0 Recommendations. The XPath implementation is freestanding, and can also be used directly in conjunction with the DOM implementation.

The XSLT processor can be run either from the command line, or from a Python application program. It also allows extension elements and extension functions to be written in Python.

The product contains a few built-in extension elements, including:

- **ft:apply-templates**
  A variation on `xsl:apply-templates` that allows the mode to be selected dynamically at run-time
- **ft:write-file**
  Produces multiple output documents (similar to the XSLT 1.1 `<xsl:document>` instruction)
- **ft:message-output**
  Defines the destination for output from the `<xsl:message>` instruction

4XSLT also contains a useful library of extension functions, many of them familiar from other processors, but some of them unique to 4XSLT:

- **ft:node-set()**
  Converts a result tree fragment to a node-set
- **ft:match()**
  Determines whether a string matches a regular expression
- **ft:escape-url()**
  Escapes special characters appearing in a URL
- **ft:iso-time()**
  Returns the current date and time in ISO 8601 format
- **ft:evaluate()**
  Evaluates an XPath expression supplied as a string
- **ft:distinct()**
  Removes duplicate nodes from a node-set
- **ft:split()**
  Splits a string into a set of text nodes, using a specified delimiter

- **ft:range()**
  Constructs a set of text nodes whose values are consecutive numbers
- **ft:if()**
  Acts as a conditional expression
- **ft:find()**
  Finds the position of a string within a containing string

In the weeks before we went to press, Uche Ogbuji was championing the creation of a vendor-neutral library of specifications for extension functions, being prepared under the editorship of Jeni Tennison; for details see http://www.exsit.org The thinking behind this initiative is that there is already so much overlap between different vendors' sets of extension functions, it makes sense for those provided by multiple vendors to use the same namespace, so that portable stylesheets can be written. It seems likely that 4XSLT will be in the lead in implementing this library, so watch out for news on this.

I haven't actually tried to install the 4XSLT product; it's probably very easy if you know Python and are familiar with its conventions, but a bit daunting if you don't. Having said that, Python seems to be one of those languages that people fall in love with once they've discovered it, so it might well be a skill worth acquiring. Find out more at http://www.python.org.

Cocoon

Cocoon is not an XSLT processor, though you will often hear people speak of it as if it were. It is a framework for XML-based publishing on the web, and as such it makes use of an XSLT processor as a key component. Cocoon is one of the open source XML technologies being developed under the auspices of the Apache organization, and you can find it at http://xml.apache.org/. As such, it is normally used with the Xalan XSLT processor described in Appendix D, and indeed Xalan is delivered as an intrinsic part of Cocoon.

Cocoon addresses the wider concerns of a publishing application. XSLT is a focused technology that does one job, XML transformation, while Cocoon tries to address the whole architecture needed for web-based publishing. It is particularly concerned with the separation of the tasks of creating information (XML authoring), processing information, and rendering information for output.

Cocoon provides facilities to control the delivery and rendition of documents, by selecting XSLT transformations or other processing steps to be performed, based on factors such as the type of client device and browser in use. It is essentially a web server plug-in technology. Cocoon also provides interfaces to SQL databases and LDAP directories.

The main vehicle for controlling what Cocoon does is the XSP page. XSPs (eXtensible Server Pages) are XML documents defining processing carried out on the server. Architecturally they play a similar role to ASP or JSP pages (as you might guess from the name), but they are less procedural in form. They can, however, define procedural logic steps, either by embedding Java code as script in the page, or by getting and setting the properties of Enterprise Java Beans.

That's a quick overview of what Cocoon is; it's a complex product, and I can't hope to do it justice in a small space. Remember, though, that if you ask someone what XSLT processor they are using and the answer that they give is Cocoon, then the chances are they are really using Xalan, they just haven't noticed the fact.

EZ/X

This product can be found at http://www.activated.com/products/products.html.

This is another Java product, containing an XML parser and XSLT processor. I mentioned it in the previous edition of this book as a product to watch, but unfortunately it seems to have made no progress over the last year. Indeed it still only claims conformance to the October 1999 XSLT draft rather than the finished XSLT 1.0 specification.

The documentation makes aggressive claims for performance, but these appear to be way out of date.

There is no detailed statement available of which features are implemented, though reports from some users suggest the coverage is rather incomplete.

iXSLT

The iXSLT product is available from the Japanese company Infoteria (http://www.infoteria.com).

This product looks like a serious attempt to produce a commercial quality Windows-based XSLT processor. By contrast with most of the open source products, the web site has a very professional image, and this is sustained by the install scripts and the Windows front-end to the product: a welcome relief from typing on the command line and editing environment variables by hand. You can download a free trial version of the product, or pay for a properly shrink-wrapped version that comes nicely packaged with a CD-ROM and arrangements for technical support. The version I tried was version 2.0c, dated November 2000.

The iXSLT engine is packaged as a Windows DLL, allowing transformations to be controlled via COM or C++ programming interfaces.

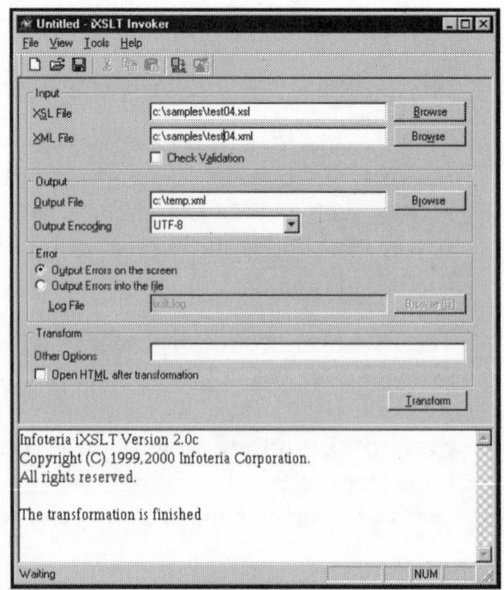

There is a simple Windows-based user interface as shown on the right. If you really want you can also run the product from the command line.

There is also a stylesheet generation wizard, which attempts to take the hard work out of creating an initial stylesheet. This appears to be designed primarily to handle tabular data, such as you might get from a relational database.

The downloaded evaluation copy comes with a manual in PDF format. This tells you everything you need to know about how to drive the product, but says very little about what you can actually write in a stylesheet. I would have assumed therefore that the language supported is XSLT 1.0, nothing more and nothing less, but unfortunately several of my test stylesheets were rejected or incorrectly processed, so there may be some undocumented limitations.

The `readme` file gives some information about the extensions that are implemented. These include extension elements to create multiple output files and to invoke an external command, and extension functions to convert a result tree fragment to a node-set, and to evaluate an XPath expression supplied as a string.

jd:xslt

This product is a new open source Java XSLT engine, announced on 5 March 2001 by Johannes Döbler of Munich, Germany, just before we went to press. This means we haven't had time to do a full evaluation. Unlike most open source developers who follow the "release early, release often" philosophy, and thus hit the world with products that are unreliable and unfinished, Döbler seems to have decided to keep his code to himself until he had a functionally complete implementation. Indeed, this product is the first that claims to be a complete implementation of the draft XSLT 1.1 specification, which should make it very useful for testing out some of the new features described in this book.

One likely drawback of the release strategy is that the product won't have benefited from the amount of field testing that comes from wide exposure to users, and it's no surprise to find that the initial release 1.0 product has a few bugs. However, the engineering seems to be very solid and I would expect these to be ironed out quickly. The initial indications of the product's performance are also encouraging, though it's too early to make any firm judgements on this.

This appears to be a one-man effort, with no evidence of corporate sponsorship. The product can be downloaded from http://www.aztecrider.com/xslt/jd.zip. Full source code is available, under the conditions of the Mozilla Public License.

jd:xslt is designed to work with the Crimson XML parser from Apache. It has its own internal tree representation, which conforms to the DOM. It currently supports its own Java API, and not the TrAX API described in Appendix F. No extension functions or extension elements are described (but by supporting XSLT 1.1, the biggest gaps are filled anyway). User-written extension functions can be implemented in Java or JavaScript.

For what it's worth, the table below compares the source code size of four open source XSLT engines written in Java. There is no implication that big is beautiful, or indeed the converse; the only reason I include this table is that it provides some evidence that although jd.xslt is a new kid on the block, it is definitely a product to be taken seriously.

	Total source lines	Non-comment lines
jd:xslt	37K	19K
Saxon	63K	31K
Xalan	118K	46K
xt	15K	13K

Sablotron

Sablotron is an XSLT processor produced by the oddly-named Ginger Alliance, a company based in Prague in the Czech Republic, that specializes in application integration using XML data interchange. Details are at http://www.gingerall.com/.

The Ginger Alliance's main product is the equally-oddly-named Charlie, a piece of distributed middleware allowing applications to communicate with each other using XML. Sablotron, which is written in C++ and available as an open source product, comes over as something of a sideline: the company's explanation is that they wrote it because they needed a fast, compact, and portable XSLT processor for use within the Charlie framework, and couldn't find an existing one that was suitable. Sablotron is specifically designed to be as compact as possible, to allow it to run on hand-held devices, TV set-top boxes, and the like, and it has already developed an excellent reputation for performance.

At the time of writing, Sablotron is an incomplete implementation of XSLT 1.0. Features that are not yet available include attribute sets, the **<xsl:import>**, **<xsl:key>**, **<xsl:number>**, and **<xsl:fallback>** elements, the preceding, following, and namespace axes in XPath, and the **format-number()**, **id()**, and **unparsed-entity-uri()** functions.

Sablotron is available under Windows NT, Linux, Solaris, and various other Unix derivatives. The lead developer is Tomas Kaiser. The product relies on expat, the open source XML parser written by James Clark.

Stylus Studio

The Excelon corporation, based in Burlington (near Boston, USA), markets the well-known ObjectStore object database as well as a range of XML server products targeted at the e-commerce marketplace. Its XML development tools are branded under the name Stylus Studio. For details see http://www.exceloncorp.com/products/excelon_stylus.html.

This was one of the first products that went beyond being a simple batch-mode XSLT interpreter to provide a visual development environment. I was rather unimpressed with earlier versions of the product, but the latest (Stylus 3.0) looks very impressive. The graphical tools work either with Microsoft's MSXML3 XSLT engine, or with Excelon's own XSLT processor. However, the latter is an incomplete implementation of the XSLT 1.0 standard, so the indications are that Excelon is concentrating on its development environment rather than the XSLT processor itself.

Stylus Studio is a commercial product. The web site invites you to "download an evaluation copy today", but I couldn't find any download button. Instead, you have to sign up for the Stylus 3.0 beta evaluation programme, which involves a rather complex process of registration, getting a password by e-mail, then downloading and installing. It was only after completing this process that I discovered the product requires Windows NT or 2000 – a rather surprising restriction for a desktop tool (but perhaps this is only true for the beta release; check the web site for the latest information). When I did get past these hurdles I found that it was a massive download (with no warning of how long it would take), but an hour later I found myself with some 40Mb of software successfully installed.

Stylus Studio offers a rich collection of tools for editing, viewing, and validating XML documents, and creating and debugging stylesheets. I shall concentrate here on the XSLT tools. The product does not try to relieve you of the burden of understanding the XSLT language, but it does take a lot of the tedium out of typing it correctly and debugging it.

There are several ways you can create an XSLT stylesheet, and I found they all worked well; moreover, the different techniques can be readily mixed.

One approach is simply to use Stylus as a syntax-driven editor. This is probably what you will choose to do once you have established the basic structure of the stylesheet. The product offers the usual typing short-cuts, and when you get used to using these it reduces the number of keystrokes considerably, as well as eliminating many of the silly mistakes.

To create a stylesheet in the first place, I found it useful to use the Templates view. Stylus starts with an example XML document and from this produces a model of its structure in DTD or schema format. This then allows you to work your way through the structure, defining a template rule for each element type. Since many template rules are very simple, and Stylus gives you a default rule to start from, this can be a very quick process.

Another useful technique is to import an HTML file that is typical of the output you want to produce. Stylus will insert the structure of the HTML into the root template of the stylesheet, and you can then edit it to indicate the points at which you want to fetch data from the source document, or you can cut-and-paste sections of the HTML into other template rules if you wish. If you want to write complex XPath expressions to insert into the logic, Stylus has an XPath query tool that allows you to enter XPath expressions and view their results; once you have got the expression right, you can copy it into the stylesheet.

Yet another approach is to create your initial stylesheet using the Mapper tool, illustrated below. To use this tool you first load exemplars of the source document and the destination document, and then define the relationship between them by dragging lines from one to the other. You can define various properties of the mapping by right-clicking on the lines. I suspect this only really works well when the structure of the source and destination documents are quite closely related, but in these cases, it certainly gives you a quick start. I did find, though, that the stylesheet it generated was not one I particularly wanted to start from; it made very heavy use of nested `<xsl:for-each>` statements rather than template rules.

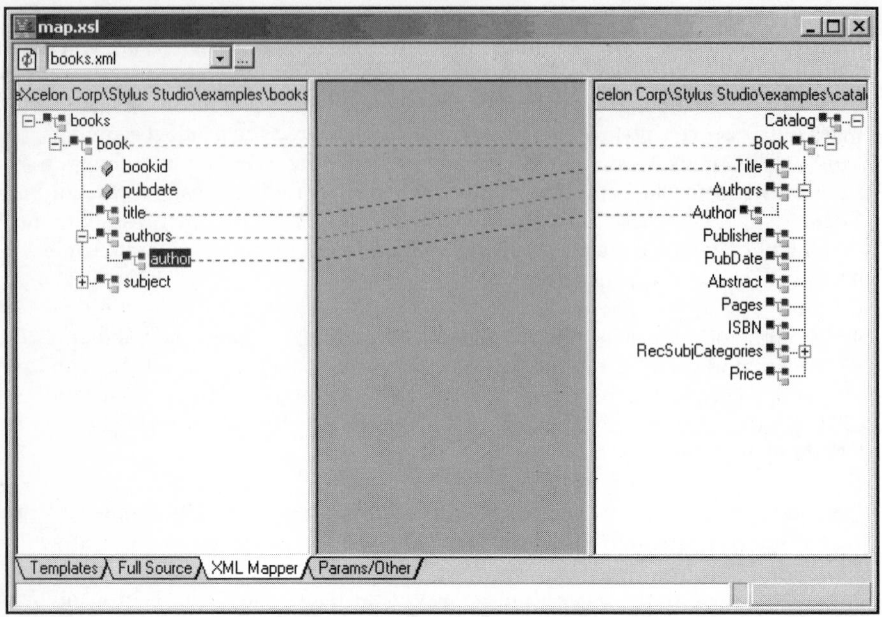

Whichever way you generate your initial stylesheet, you can always revert to manual syntax-driven editing for the final touches. And at any stage, you can press F5 to apply the stylesheet to the source document and view the result, either in raw source layout, XML tree view, or as it will be seen in the HTML browser. Not only that, but when you click on part of the result document, the stylesheet display automatically switches to show you the template rule that produced that part of the output.

I didn't get as far as using the stylesheet debugging tools in anger, but they appear to be comprehensive. You can set breakpoints, set a watch on particular variables, and display the state of the stack. Moreover, you can do this for your own Java extension functions as well as for instructions in the stylesheet.

The weakest part of the Stylus Studio product is the XSLT processor itself. Although the documentation claims that the processor is XSLT 1.0 compliant, the small print reveals that it isn't: the most significant omission is that there is no support for namespaces. Also, when handling documents of any size (say 250Kb), the processor appears to be very slow.

In summary: as a development environment, Stylus Studio is the best I have seen; but as an XSLT processor, it leaves a lot to be desired.

TransforMiix

TransforMiix is an open source XSLT processor being developed under the umbrella of the Mozilla organization. It is intended to play the same role in the Mozilla browser as MSXML3 plays in the Internet Explorer world. Details are at http://www.mozilla.org/projects/xslt/. The lead developers are Keith Visco and Peter van der Becken.

At present, entering the TransforMiix web site has very much the feel of trespassing on a busy construction site. Don't enter it without a hard hat! You will find the site full of talk of unimplemented features, restrictions, memory leaks, and test coverage. You'll be pleased to discover that you can download a binary for Windows or Linux, and that there is a form that automatically detects the right version for your platform; but then you will be quickly brought down to earth by reading that this is designed to work "with your recent Mozilla nightlies".

If you're a Netscape/Mozilla fan and want to join an energetic community of like-minded developers, TransforMiix is for you. If you just want a working XSLT processor that you can use off-the-shelf, I would steer clear for the time being, but working versions of the product are starting to appear in Linux and Mozilla binaries, so this situation could change quite soon.

Unicorn

The Unicorn XML Toolkit is centred around an XSLT processor written in C++. The product runs only under Microsoft Windows. It is produced by Unicorn Enterprises, a company based in Schwyz, Switzerland, who provide software development and consulting services in the area of document processing. Details can be found at http://www.unicorn-enterprises.com/.

The product is available on commercial licensing terms, including source code as well as a standard support contract, but several of the components including the binary XSLT processor can also be downloaded for free. I found it easy to download and install, with no irritating registration procedures. Simply extract the `.zip` file into a suitable directory, say `c:\unicorn`, and with this as your current directory, run the processor:

```
uxt  demo\demo.xml  demo\demo.xsl  c:\output.html
```

The commercial product is packaged to give you a choice of three options:

- The standard edition contains a version of the XSLT processor that can be run from the command line. It contains a library of extension functions supporting input from a variety of text-based formats, and report writer capabilities.
- The database edition adds a library of extension functions supporting relational database access.
- The professional edition contains object extensions, providing integration via Microsoft's ActiveX architecture.

The product includes a non-validating XML parser conforming to the C++ version of SAX2, a DOM1 implementation, a free-standing XPath implementation, and of course an XSLT 1.0 processor. There is also an ECMAScript interpreter and a regular expression library. More unusually, there is also an implementation of XSL Formatting Objects.

The supplier claims full conformance with the XSLT 1.0 and XPath 1.0 standards. The product failed some of my tests (including some of the examples in this book), but only in fairly obscure areas of the specification.

As well as the command-line interface, the transformation engine can be invoked from C++ or from ECMAScript (that is, JavaScript to you and me). Extension functions can be written in ECMAScript, and the object integration facilities in the professional edition also allow access to arbitrary COM objects.

Database Access

Unicorn includes a comprehensive and well-documented package of extension elements and extension functions enabling access to relational databases, typically via ODBC. This is perhaps best illustrated with a couple of examples.

The following stylesheet takes data from the source document and writes it to a database. The output of the stylesheet is an empty tree.

```
<xsl:template match='/'>
  <root>
    <sql:connect
        source="{$source}"
        user="{$user}"
        authentication="{$authentication}"
        type="odbc"
        connection-id="dbc1"/>
    <sql:prepare
        connection-id="dbc1"
        sql="INSERT INTO PRODUCT (CODE, CATEGORY, NAME)
                 VALUES (?, ?, ?)"
        statement-id="stmt1">
      <sql:param type="CHAR" precision="64"/>
      <sql:param type="CHAR" precision="64"/>
      <sql:param type="CHAR" precision="64"/>
    </sql:prepare>
    <xsl:apply-templates/>
  </root>
</xsl:template>

<xsl:template match="product">
  <sql:execute statement-id="stmt1">
    <sql:with-param value="{code}"/>
    <sql:with-param value="{category}"/>
    <sql:with-param value="{name}"/>
  </sql:execute>
</xsl:template>
```

A stylesheet can also read data from the database. The following stylesheet reads all the PRODUCTs in a particular category (supplied as a parameter to the stylesheet), and writes an XML representation of the product information to the result tree. In this case the contents of the input document are ignored.

```
<xsl:param name="category" select="'Desktop'"/>

<xsl:template match='/'>
  <root>
    <sql:connect
        source="{$source}"
        user="{$user}"
        authentication="{$authentication}"
        type="odbc"
        connection-id="dbc1"/>
    <sql:prepare
        connection-id="dbc1"
        sql="SELECT CODE, CATEGORY, NAME FROM PRODUCT
```

```
                WHERE CATEGORY=? ORDER BY CODE"
        statement-id="stmt1">
      <sql:param type="CHAR" precision="50"/>
    </sql:prepare>
    <sql:for-each statement-id="stmt1">
      <sql:with-param value="{$category}"/>
      <product>
        <code><xsl:value-of select="sql:fetch('CODE')"/></code>
        <category><xsl:value-of select="sql:fetch('CATEGORY')"/></category>
        <name><xsl:value-of select="sql:fetch('NAME')"/></name>
      </product>
    </sql:for-each>
  </root>
</xsl:template>
```

Report Generation

The extensions that Unicorn XSLT provides for report generation essentially fall into two categories: support for named counters, and support for grouping.

Named counters can be declared, initialized, incremented, and accessed using different forms of the **<rpt:counter>** element. Like Saxon's **<saxon:assign>** instruction, this blatantly ignores the "no-side-effects" philosophy of XSLT, and allows you to revert to a more traditional procedural style of programming.

Grouping is achieved using a **<rpt:group>** element. An outer **<rpt-group>** is used to define an iteration that is executed once for each group of nodes sharing a common value for some grouping expression; an inner **<rpt:group>** instruction is used to iterate over the nodes in each group. For example:

```
<rpt:group select="city" key="@country">
  <country name="{@country}">
    <rpt:group>
      <xsl:copy-of select="city"/>
    </rpt:group>
  </country>
</rpt:group>
```

The groups can be sorted using an **<rpt:sort>** element with similar syntax to **<xsl:sort>**.

Reading Formatted Text Files

Unicorn provides a package of extension elements and extension functions for reading the contents of text files written in either fixed-width column layouts, or delimited formats such as comma-separated values.

The **<txt:format>** element, which contains **<txt:field>** elements, defines the format of the input records. This may either be fixed-width format:

```
<txt:format name="TEXT01">
      <txt:field name="CODE" width="10"/>
      <txt:field name="CATEGORY" width="15"/>
      <txt:field name="NAME" width="50"/>
</txt:format>
```

or delimited:

```
<txt:format name="TEXT02" separator=",">
      <txt:field name="CODE"/>
      <txt:field name="CATEGORY"/>
      <txt:field name="NAME"/>
</txt:format>
```

The records are read from the input file using a **<txt:read>** instruction, and the individual fields are accessed using the extension function **txt:field-value()**:

```
<txt:read href="text02.txt" format="TEXT02">
   <product>
      <code><xsl:value-of select="txt:field-value('CODE')"/></code>
      <category><xsl:value-of select="txt:field-value('CATEGORY')"/></category>
      <name><xsl:value-of select="txt:field-value('NAME')"/></name>
   </product>
</txt:read>
```

XESALT

XESALT is a a relatively little-known XSLT processor from the German company Inlogix, a startup based in Leipzig, Germany. So far this appears to be their only product. Details are at http://www.inlogix.de/xesalt.html.

The software is configured for three different environments:

- as a command line processor
- as a web server module
- as a Netscape Communicator 4.X plugin for client-side transformation

The processor is currently described as pre-release software that is "likely to have a number of deficiencies". So at least you know you are dealing with a company that believes in honesty. The web site offers a free download for evaluation, but I was dissuaded firstly because (in February 2001) it said that the evaluation license expired in September 2000; and secondly because I couldn't actually find the download button.

For the moment, I'll categorize this as a product to keep an eye on, rather than one to spend time on now.

XML Spy

XML Spy is produced by Altova GmbH of Vienna, Austria. The company was founded in 1992, and recently changed its name from Icon Information Systems. But it doesn't seem to be particularly fond of its new name either; all searches under either the old or new company name take you straight to the XML Spy web site, which you will find at http://www.xmlspy.com/. The product is sold commercially at $200 for an individual user license. You can download a free 30-day evaluation copy.

XML Spy is not an XSLT processor as such; rather it is an interactive XML editor and development environment. One of the many jobs you can do with it is to edit stylesheets and examine their effects.

XML Spy offers a display of the hierarchic structure of a document in terms of nested boxes, a display it calls the grid view. An example is shown below. You can use this view directly for editing, by selecting particular elements with the right mouse button and choosing options such as Insert, Append, or Add Child to create additional nodes relative to the selected node. In all cases you are only offered options that are structurally valid, taking into account the constraints imposed by the DTD or schema if there is one.

The diagram below shows how the XML version of Shakespeare's *Othello* looks using the grid view:

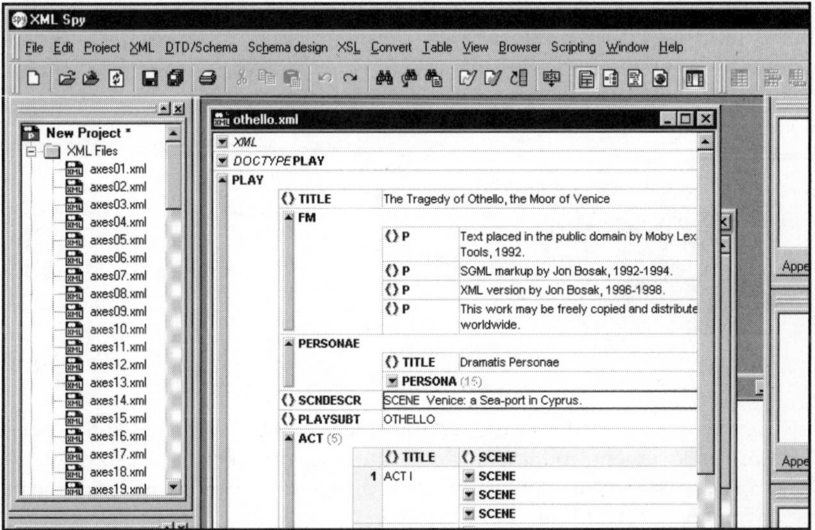

You can use XML Spy in the same way to edit stylesheets, viewing them either in grid view or in text view, as shown below:

A stylesheet in grid view:

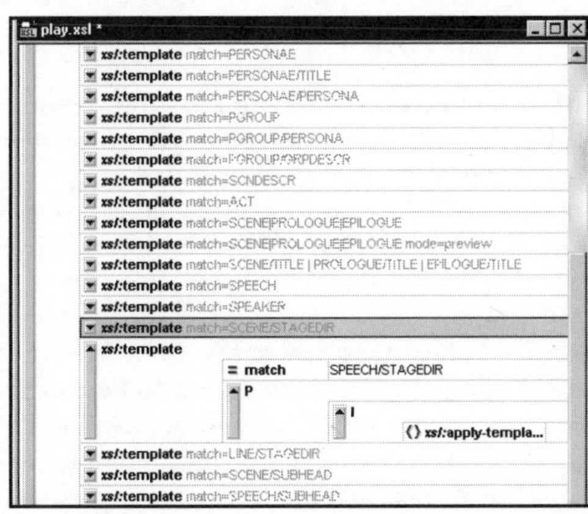

The same stylesheet in text view:

```
play.xsl *
        <TABLE>
            <TR>
                <TD WIDTH="160" VALIGN="TOP">
                    <xsl:apply-templates select="SPEAKER"/>
                </TD>
                <TD VALIGN="TOP">
                    <xsl:apply-templates select="STAGEDIR|LINE"/>
                </TD>
            </TR>
        </TABLE>
    </xsl:template>
    <xsl:template match="SPEAKER">
        <B>
            <xsl:apply-templates/>
            <xsl:if test="not(position()=last())">
                <BR/>
            </xsl:if>
        </B>
    </xsl:template>
    <xsl:template match="SCENE/STAGEDIR">
        <CENTER>
            <H3>
                <xsl:apply-templates/>
            </H3>
        </CENTER>
    </xsl:template>
    <xsl:template match="SPEECH/STAGEDIR">
```

XML Spy allows you to define the stylesheet that is to be associated with a particular XML source document, and then to apply the transformation. You can view the output of the transformation, again in a number of different views. This includes the option of displaying XML or HTML output directly in the browser.

One omission is that there seems to be no direct way of setting stylesheet parameters when running a transformation. You can set options for the XSLT processor, but only by editing the command line used to invoke the processor. Another drawback is that to transform a given source document with a stylesheet, you have to update the document's `<?xml-stylesheet?>` processing instruction, which is not necessarily what you want to do.

The product works with a number of different XSLT processors: MSXML3, Saxon, and Infoteria iXSLT are offered, and you can integrate your own choice of processor through the processor's command line interface if you prefer. If a transformation fails, the error output from the XSLT processor is displayed in a pop-up message box, and XML Spy allows you to move to the line number in the stylesheet where the error was detected.

As well as stylesheet processing, XML Spy has features for creating and editing DTDs and XML Schemas (in a number of different flavors, reflecting the slow development of this standard). It includes some handy tools for generating DTDs and schemas from instance documents, and for converting between different kinds of schema. But these facilities are outside our present scope.

XSL Composer

This is a commercial product available from Whitehill Technologies at http://www.whitehill.com/. It is not an XSLT processor, and I wouldn't even describe it primarily as a tool for creating XSLT stylesheets; rather, I would characterize it as a tool for defining the way you want XML documents rendered in HTML, that happens to use XSLT as a vehicle for the transformation.

This is a tool for web designers and HTML authors, not a tool for XSLT developers. If you already know XSLT, you will probably find it frustrating, because you can only tell the tool what output you want, not what transformation logic you want to use to achieve it.

The principal *modus operandi* when using this tool is to select individual elements of an XML document, and then describe the rules for how you want them presented in HTML. The rules available fall basically into two categories: paragraph style, and table style.

Paragraph style is very straightforward: you are basically presented with a set of tabbed forms that allow you to select all the possible variations of font color, size, alignment, and anything else you might wish to apply to the text.

Creating tables I found much more difficult. I got it to work reasonably where the XML data was a very simple structure of rows and columns, but when it was anything more complex, I found it hard to control what was happening. I never found a way, for example, of using HTML tables to produce a side-by-side display of the speakers and speeches in a play. I strongly suspect it can be done, but if so, you probably need to go on a training course to find out how.

One limitation with the design approach is that it starts with an XML document instance, not with a schema or DTD. So there is no way that the tool can know whether the fact that your `<annual-sales>` element contains twelve `<monthly-sales>` elements is something that will be true of all source documents processed with this stylesheet, or an accident of this particular source document.

The product includes a visual XPath Builder which you might find useful when you are new to the concepts.

Generally, I think most programmers, especially those with any XSLT knowledge, would find this tool frustrating. It is designed for non-programmers and for those to whom XSLT is a black art. These people, of course, far outnumber the readers of this book. But whether the product will actually appeal to people in that category is something I am not in a position to judge.

XSLTC

Details of this product, which is currently described as an alpha release, are at http://www.sun.com/xml/developers/xsltc/.

Sun's XSLTC is unlike all the other XSLT processors described in this book, in that it is a compiler that takes a stylesheet as input and generates executable code as its output. Not machine code, in fact, but Java bytecode. The bytecode is exactly the same as the output of a Java compiler; it is produced in `.class` files that can be executed by the Java Virtual Machine. The `.class` file that is output by XSLTC is known (rather unnecessarily, I feel) as a translet, and it can be executed by the Java VM in exactly the same way as a class compiled from Java source code.

The claim is that the translets are both small and fast, and that this technique is therefore ideal for running transformations on "thin client" devices such as hand-held computers or mobile phones.

The claim that the files are small certainly seems valid: when I compiled a 750-line stylesheet (the one for formatting the XML specification, described in Chapter 10) the result was a set of 9 class files occupying a total of 30Kb. When I asked the compiler to produce the output as a `.jar` file, this was reduced to 13Kb: considerably smaller than the original stylesheet. Of course, to execute these translets you also need to load a run-time library: this consists of the two files `xml.jar` (the XML parser) at 127 Kb and `xsltrc.jar` (the run-time support library for XSLT processing) at 109Kb. This is substantially smaller than Saxon at 555Kb or Xalan at 687Kb – though the margin over xt (at 345Kb) is narrower.

As for speed, I ran some very simple benchmarks and found the run-time transformation performance to be about the same as xt or Saxon. Given that this is an alpha release, that may indicate that it will eventually be significantly faster; but I shall wait and see. For simple transformations, performance is dominated by the cost of parsing the input, building the tree, and formatting the output, and since these tasks are largely independent of anything in the stylesheet, there's no reason to believe that generating compiled code will speed them up. It also won't help much with time-consuming tasks such as sorting.

I find it a little paradoxical that it should be Sun who are pursuing this particular technology avenue, since in the area of Java performance, it is Sun themselves who have shown that a good interpreter using techniques such as just-in-time compilation (for example HotSpot) can be just as fast as traditional compiled code. This may explain why Sun are now emphasizing size rather than speed in their claims for this technology.

But there are other potential advantages in compiling a stylesheet into executable code. For example, compiling hides the source code, which may be useful if you want to build significant parts of a commercial application in XSLT. Also, compiled code is easily relocated; many products such as Saxon which produce a "compiled" stylesheet in memory don't allow you to move the compiled stylesheet between machines or to download it to run in the browser, and even those such as Xalan which make the stylesheet serializable still incur a significant cost in serializing and deserializing it. So the technology definitely has a place alongside the traditional interpretive approach.

The current version of XSLTC, at the time of writing, does not support the full XSLT 1.0 specification, but the restrictions are very minor. I did find a few bugs, both with the actual transformation logic, and with the environment (for example, the Windows versions of the command-line scripts cause error messages to be suppressed). But for something that only claims to be an alpha release, the problems were minor.

xt

The **xt** product is an open source implementation of XSLT produced by the editor of the specification, James Clark. It was the first implementation available, and is still one of the fastest; however, it is an incomplete implementation of the XSLT 1.0 specification, and is not being developed any further (which is why I decided not to give it an appendix of its own). The latest version, referenced as version 19991105, is still described as a beta release.

Like Saxon, xt is a one-man effort rather than a corporate product. It is available under a very flexible license that essentially allows you to do anything you like with the software, but protects the author from any claims. There is no warranty or support. The product is written in Java, and source code is provided.

xt is available at http://www.jclark.com/xml/xt.html.

The following features of the XSLT 1.0 and XPath 1.0 Recommendations are not implemented:

- The element extension mechanism (the **`extension-element-prefixes`** and **`xsl:extension-element-prefixes`** attributes, the **`<xsl:fallback>`** element, and the **`element-available()`** function)
- Keys (the **`<xsl:key>`** element, and the **`key()`** function)
- The **`<xsl:decimal-format>`** element and the optional third argument on the **`format-number()`** function, which references an **`<xsl:decimal-format>`** element
- The namespace axis
- Forwards-compatible processing
- The **`xsl:exclude-result-prefixes`** attribute on literal result elements (however, the **`exclude-result-prefixes`** attribute on **`<xsl:stylesheet>`** is implemented)

Another restriction is that errors are not always reported when they should be, which means that an incorrect stylesheet may sometimes appear to work on xt when a strictly- conforming XSLT processor would reject it. For example, xt allows a local variable to be declared when another variable of the same name is in scope.

Invoking the xt Processor

The xt processor may be run from the command line, via a Java API, or as a servlet.

With the full product, the typical command line is

```
java com.jclark.xsl.sax.Driver source.xml style.xsl out.html param1=value1...
```

The product also comes packaged as a Windows executable, in which case you can type:

```
xt source.xml style.xsl out.html param1=value1...
```

If you are running on Windows, this version is simplicity itself to install and get working.

As the name of the Java class suggests, xt is structured as a SAX filter, taking a stream of SAX events from the XML parser as input, and delivering the result tree to the final formatting process as another stream of SAX events.

xt works with any SAX1-compliant XML parser, and the selected parser can be specified by means of a system property. However, the recommended parser is James Clark's xp, which has a specially-extended SAX1 interface allowing comments to be passed to the application.

The `param1=value1` parameters supply values for any global parameters in the stylesheet; the values must be strings.

The xt product also has a Java API, which can be used to run it in a servlet environment. Unfortunately the speed of James Clark's code is matched only by the brevity of his documentation, so if you want to use this API, be prepared to explore the product structure in some depth. There are, however, some example source files (in `xt.jar`, which you can open using WinZip or any other ZIP file extractor) showing how to use the SAX and DOM interfaces provided by xt, and how to run the processor from a servlet.

Extensibility

The xt product allows user-defined extension functions to be written in Java.

The Java class is identified directly from the namespace URI used in the function call. You can make a call such as:

```
<xsl:variable name="today" select="Date:new()"
              xmlns:Date="http://www.jclark.com/xt/java.util.Date"/>
```

with no further declaration of the external class. The class is taken as the part of the namespace URI after the «`http://www.jclark.com/xt/`».

xt allows static methods to be called in this way, as well as constructors. To call instance methods, you need to supply an additional first argument to the call: this will be an external object obtained by first calling a static method or constructor that returns a Java object.

Details of the mappings from XPath data types to Java classes can be found in the documentation that comes with the product.

xt does not currently support element extensibility, though it implements a subset of the syntax for use with its own extension elements, described below.

Extensions

xt supports several extensions, including multiple output documents, non-XML output, user-defined output handlers, and a number of extension functions. These are described in the following sections.

Multiple Output Documents

xt supports an extension element **`<xt:document>`** that allows the stylesheet to create multiple output documents. The prefix `xt` (or whatever other prefix you choose to use) must be bound to the namespace URI `http://www.jclark.com/xt`. The **`<xt:document>`** element has a very similar effect to the **`<xsl:document>`** instruction introduced in the XSLT 1.1 working draft, which is described in Chapter 4 on page 204.

The **<xt:document>** element has a required **href** attribute, which must be a relative URL. The value of the **href** attribute is interpreted as an attribute value template. The content of the **<xt:document>** element is a template body for the result tree to be stored in the location specified by the **href** attribute. The base URL for resolving the **href** relative URL is the URL of the parent output document: either the URL of the main output document or the URL in which the parent **<xt:document>** element was stored. Thus, the same relative URL specified by the **href** attribute can be used in the parent document to reference the document created by the **<xt:document>** element.

The **<xt:document>** element can also have all the same attributes as the **<xsl:output>** element. These attributes are merged with attributes specified on top-level **<xsl:output>** elements to determine the output method for this document. The attributes on the **<xt:document>** element take precedence over the attributes specified on top-level **<xsl:output>** elements.

Non-XML output

It is possible to produce text output using `<xsl:output method="text">`; however this has limitations. For example, it is not possible to output control characters outside the XML character set.

xt therefore provides an alternative method for text output using an output method of «`xt:nxml`» where the prefix `xt` is bound to the namespace URI `http://www.jclark.com/xt`. This produces an XML tree in which certain elements have special meanings:

- The **<char>** element allows the output of a character that is not allowed by XML, for example most of the ASCII control characters below `#x20`.
- The **<data>** element contains data. Within a **<data>** element special characters get escaped.
- The **<escape>** element defines a special character and says how it should be escaped.
- The **<control>** element contains characters to be output directly without escaping.

Example: Producing Text Output with xt

Source

This stylesheet can be run with any source document.

Stylesheet

This stylesheet is `xt-text.xsl`.

```
<xsl:stylesheet xmlns:xsl="http://www.w3.org/1999/XSL/Transform"
                                version="1.0">
<xsl:output method="xt:nxml" xmlns:xt="http://www.jclark.com/xt"/>
<xsl:template match="/">
   <nxml>
      <escape char="\">\\</escape>
      <data>&amp;&lt;&gt;\</data>
      <control>&amp;&lt;&gt;\</control>
   </nxml>
</xsl:template>
</xsl:stylesheet>
```

Output

```
&<>\\&<>\
```

User-defined Output Handlers

The method attribute of `<xsl:output>` or `<xt:document>` can take the form «java:package.name.class» where the prefix «java» is bound to the namespace URI http://www.jclark.com/xt/java and «package.name.class» is the full name of a Java class that implements the com.jclark.xsl.sax.OutputDocumentHandler interface (which extends the SAX1 interface org.xml.sax.DocumentHandler).

This will cause the nodes of the result tree to be streamed to the user-specified document handler.

Extension Functions

xt provides the following extension functions. The namespace URI for these is http://www.jclark.com/xt.

xt:node-set (frag)	Converts a result tree fragment to the equivalent node-set. The argument must be a node-set or a result tree fragment; the result will be a node-set.
xt:intersection (ns1, ns2)	Returns the intersection of two node-sets (the nodes that are present in both the supplied node-sets).
xt:difference (ns1, ns2)	Returns the difference of two node-sets (the nodes in the first node-set that are not in the second node-set).

Summary

In this appendix I've given brief overviews of over a dozen XSLT-related products. They include some solid corporate products that you can use today, some technologies that are still under construction and perhaps have an exciting future, and some products where development seems to have stalled.

The overall conclusion is that this is a pretty vibrant scene. There's a lot going on, and I can't hope to cover everything. Nor can I hope, in a few paragraphs, to give a fair treatment to fourteen very different software products that each represent years of hard work by extremely talented engineers. Do remember that what I write about the products early in 2001 may no longer be true if you are reading this six or twelve months later; and do remember that your requirements in a product may be quite different from the things I regard as strengths and weaknesses. I just hope you'll find my summaries useful as a guide to doing your own research and evaluation to find the products that meet your own particular needs.

TrAX: The Transformation API for XML

TrAX is a Java API for controlling XSLT transformations.

One of the successes of XSLT was that within months of the publication of the first stable version of the standard, XSLT 1.0, a number of implementations were available showing a high level of conformance to the specifications. Several of these were written in Java. Users, therefore, wanted to write applications that could run with any of these XSLT processors, allowing them to compare performance and protect the application from bugs in one processor or another.

Unfortunately, though, each of these processors provided a different Java API, so an application that wanted to run with any processor had to write a separate driver module for each processor.

The vendors got together informally, under the leadership of Scott Boag of Lotus, to see whether it was possible to agree on a common API, and the result was **TrAX**, the transformation API for XML. Progress initially was slow, but eventually Sun took the initiative and decided to publish an interface based on the TrAX proposals as part of JAXP, the Java API for XML Processing. JAXP Version 1.1 Final Release was published on February 6, 2001. Details are at:

http://java.sun.com/xml/download.html

The information in this appendix is based on this final release of JAXP 1.1. It should now be stable, though there is always the possibility that minor bugs will be corrected. At the time of writing, there are reasonably complete implementations of TrAX in the Saxon and Xalan products. Others can be expected to follow.

Notation

To save space, I've used an abbreviated notation in this appendix to indicate the exceptions thrown by each method. A list such as «[SAXE, IOE]» indicates the exceptions that may be thrown, using the following codes:

FCE	javax.xml.parsers.FactoryConfigurationError
IAE	java.lang.IllegalArgumentException
IOE	java.io.IOException
PCE	javax.xml.parsers.ParserConfigurationException
SAXE	org.xml.sax.SAXException
SAXNRE	org.xml.sax.SAXNotRecognizedException
SAXNSE	org.xml.sax.SAXNotSupportedException
TCE	javax.xml.transform.TransformerConfigurationException
TE	javax.xml.transform.TransformerException
TFCE	javax.xml.transform.TransformerFactoryConfigurationError

The JAXP 1.1 Parser API

JAXP actually defines two sets of interfaces: interfaces for XML parsing, in package `javax.xml.parsers`, and interfaces for XML transformation (that is, TrAX) in package `javax.xml.transform` and its subsidiary packages. Although the parser APIs could be regarded as being out of scope for this book, applications will often use both together, so I shall start by quickly reviewing the two parser APIs, covering SAX parsing and DOM parsing.

These interfaces do not supersede the SAX and DOM interfaces, which are described in many XML reference books. Rather, they supplement them with facilities that are lacking in both SAX and DOM, namely the ability to select a SAX or DOM parser to do the processing, and to set options like specifying whether you want a validating or non-validating parser, and whether you want namespace processing to be performed.

I'll look at the two parts of the interface, SAX and DOM, separately.

JAXP Support for SAX

JAXP 1.0 supported SAX1 interfaces; JAXP 1.1 has moved forwards to SAX2, but remains backwards compatible with JAXP 1.0. In the interests of brevity, I will leave out the features that are relevant only to SAX1.

javax.xml.parsers.SAXParserFactory

The first thing an application must do is to obtain a **`SAXParserFactory`**, which it can do by calling the static method `SAXParserFactory.newInstance()`. Different vendors of SAX parsers will each implement their own subclass of `SAXParserFactory`, and this call determines which vendor's parser your application will end up using. If there are several available, the one that is used is based on the following decision process:

- Use the value of the system property `javax.xml.parsers.SAXParserFactory` if it is available. You can typically set system properties using the `-D` option on the java command line, or by calling `System.setProperty()` from your application.

- Look for a properties file `$JAVA_HOME/lib/jaxp.properties`, and within this file, for the property named `javax.xml.parsers.SAXParserFactory`.
- Use the services API, which is part of the JAR specification.

It is likely that when you install a particular SAX parser, it will contain a file within its `.jar` archive that causes that particular parser to be the default, so if you don't do anything to select a specific parser, the one chosen will depend on the order of files and directories on your class path.

Once you have got a `SAXParserFactory`, you can use a number of methods to configure it. Finally, you can call the `newSAXParser()` method to return a `SAXParser`. The methods available are as follows. The codes in square brackets indicate the exceptions thrown, according to the table at the start of this appendix.

Method	Description
`boolean getFeature(String)` `[SAXNRE, SAXNSE, PCE]`	Determines whether the parser factory is configured to support a particular feature. The names of features correspond to those defined in SAX2 for the `XMLReader` class.
`boolean isNamespaceAware()`	Determines whether parsers produced using this factory will be namespace aware.
`boolean isValidating()`	Determines whether parsers produced using this factory will perform XML validation.
`static SAXParserFactory newInstance()` `[FCE]`	Produces a `SAXParserFactory` for a specific vendor's parser, decided according to the rules given above.
`SAXParser newSAXParser()` `[PCE]`	Returns a `SAXParser` that can be used to perform parsing. This is a wrapper around the SAX2 `XMLReader` object.
`void setFeature(String, boolean)` `[SAXNRE, SAXNSE, PCE]`	Sets a particular feature on or off. The names of features correspond to those defined in SAX2 for the XMLReader class.
`void setNamespaceAware(boolean)`	Indicates whether parsers produced using this factory are required to be namespace aware.
`void setValidating(boolean)`	Indicates whether parsers produced using this factory are required to perform XML validation.

javax.xml.parsers.SAXParser

A **`SAXParser`** is obtained using the `newSAXParser()` method of a `SAXParserFactory`. A `SAXParser` is a wrapper around a SAX2 `XMLReader`. The `XMLReader` may itself be a wrapper around a SAX1 Parser. You can use the `getXMLReader()` method to get the underlying `XMLReader`, but in simple cases you won't need to, since you can perform a parse and nominate a handler for all the parsing events using this class alone.

The methods relevant to SAX2 parsers are:

Method	Description
`Object getProperty(String)` `[SAXNRE, SAXNSE]`	Gets the named property of the underlying SAX2 `XMLReader`.
`XMLReader getXMLReader()` `[SAXE]`	Gets the underlying SAX2 `XMLReader`.
`boolean isNamespaceAware()`	Determines whether the underlying SAX2 `XMLReader` is namespace aware.
`boolean isValidating()`	Determines whether the underlying SAX2 `XMLReader` performs XML validation.
`void parse(File, DefaultHandler)` `[IOE, IAE, SAXE]`	Parses the contents of the specified File, passing all parsing events to the specified event handler. Normally of course this will not actually be a SAX2 `DefaultHandler`, but a user-defined subclass of `DefaultHandler` written to process selected events.
`void parse(InputSource, DefaultHandler)` `[IOE, IAE, SAXE]`	Parses the contents of the specified SAX `InputSource`, passing all parsing events to the specified event handler.
`void parse(InputStream, DefaultHandler)` `[IOE, IAE, SAXE]`	Parses the contents of the specified `InputStream`, passing all parsing events to the specified event handler. Note that in this case the System ID of the input is unknown, so the parser has no way of resolving relative URIs contained in the XML source.
`void parse(InputStream, DefaultHandler, String)` `[IOE, IAE, SAXE]`	Parses the contents of the specified `InputStream`, passing all parsing events to the specified event handler. The third argument contains a System ID that will be used for resolving relative URIs.
`void parse(String, DefaultHandler)` `[IOE, IAE, SAXE]`	Parses the XML document identified by the URI in the first argument, passing all parsing events to the specified event handler.
`void setProperty(String, Object)` `[SAXNSE, SAXNRE]`	Sets a property of the underlying SAX2 `XMLReader`.

JAXP Support for DOM

While JAXP 1.0 supported the original DOM level 1 specification, JAXP 1.1 is aligned with DOM level 2. There are a number of features in DOM level 2 to make navigation easier, but the main advance (and source of complications) is support for XML namespaces.

The DOM interface itself defines methods for constructing a tree programmatically, and methods for navigating around a tree, but it does not define any way of constructing a DOM tree by parsing a source XML document. JAXP 1.1 is designed to plug this gap.

The architecture of the interface is very similar to the SAX case:

- First call the static method `DocumentBuilderFactory.newInstance()` to get a `DocumentBuilderFactory` representing one particular vendor's DOM implementation.
- Then use the `newDocumentBuilder()` method on this `DocumentBuilderFactory` to obtain a `DocumentBuilder`.
- Finally, call one of the various `parse()` methods on the `DocumentBuilder` to obtain a DOM Document object.

javax.xml.parsers.DocumentBuilderFactory

The first thing an application must do is to obtain a **`DocumentBuilderFactory`**, which it can do by calling the static method `DocumentBuilderFactory.newInstance()`. Different vendors of DOM implementations will each implement their own subclass of `DocumentBuilderFactory`, and this call determines which implementation your application will end up using. If there are several available, the one that is used is based on the following decision process:

- Use the value of the system property `javax.xml.parsers.DocumentBuilderFactory` if it is available. You can typically set system properties using the `-D` option on the java command line, or by calling `System.setProperty()` from your application.
- Look for a properties file `$JAVA_HOME/lib/jaxp.properties`, and within this file, for the property named `javax.xml.parsers. DocumentBuilderFactory`.
- Use the services API, which is part of the JAR specification.

It is likely that when you install a particular DOM implementation, it will contain a file in its `.jar` archive that makes that particular implementation the default, so if you don't do anything to select a specific implementation, the one chosen will depend on the order of files and directories on your class path.

Once you have got a `DocumentBuilderFactory`, you can use a number of methods to configure it. Finally, you can call the `newDocumentBuilder()` method to return a **`DocumentBuilder`**. The methods available are:

Method	Description
`Object getAttribute(String)` `[IAE]`	Gets information about the properties of the underlying implementation.
`boolean isCoalescing()`	Determines whether the resulting `DocumentBuilder` will merge CDATA nodes into their adjacent text nodes.
`boolean isExpandEntityReferences()`	Determines whether the resulting `DocumentBuilder` will expand entity references and merge their content into the adjacent text nodes.
`boolean isIgnoringComments()`	Determines whether the resulting `DocumentBuilder` will ignore comments in the source XML.
`boolean isIgnoringElementContent Whitespace()`	Determines whether the resulting `DocumentBuilder` will ignore whitespace in element content.
`boolean isNamespaceAware()`	Determines whether the resulting `DocumentBuilder` is namespace aware.
`boolean isValidating()`	Determines whether the resulting `DocumentBuilder` will validate the XML source.
`DocumentBuilder newDocumentBuilder()` `[PCE]`	Returns a new `DocumentBuilder` configured as specified by previous calls.
`static DocumentBuilderFactory newInstance()` `[FCE]`	Returns a vendor-specific `DocumentBuilderFactory` selected according to the rules given above.
`setAttribute(String, Object)` `[IAE]`	Sets vendor-specific properties on the underlying implementation.
`void setCoalescing(boolean)`	Determines whether the resulting `DocumentBuilder` will merge CDATA nodes into their adjacent text nodes.
`void setExpandEntityReferences (boolean)`	Determines whether the resulting `DocumentBuilder` will expand entity references and merge their content into the adjacent text nodes.
`void setIgnoringComments(boolean)`	Determines whether the resulting `DocumentBuilder` will ignore comments in the source XML.
`void setIgnoringElementContent Whitespace(boolean)`	Determines whether the resulting `DocumentBuilder` will ignore whitespace in element content.
`void setNamespaceAware(boolean)`	Determines whether the resulting `DocumentBuilder` is namespace aware.
`void setValidating(boolean)`	Determines whether the resulting `DocumentBuilder` will validate the XML source.

javax.xml.parsers.DocumentBuilder

A **`DocumentBuilder`** is always obtained by calling the `newDocumentBuilder()` method of a `DocumentBuilderFactory`.

A `DocumentBuilder` performs the task of parsing a source XML document and returning the resulting instance of `org.w3.dom.Document`, containing the root of a tree representation of the document in memory.

The source document is specified in similar ways to the input for a SAX parser. This doesn't mean that a `DocumentBuilder` has to use a SAX parser to do the actual parsing: some will work this way and others won't. It's defined this way to avoid unnecessary differences between the SAX and DOM approaches.

> *You might be aware that in the Microsoft DOM implementation, the* Document *class has a method* `load()` *that parses a source XML file and constructs a* Document *object. This is a Microsoft extension, there is no corresponding method in the W3C DOM definition. This* DocumentBuilder *class fills the gap.*

The methods available are:

Method	Description
`boolean isNamespaceAware()`	Indicates whether the parser understands XML namespaces.
`boolean isValidating()`	Indicates whether the parser validates the XML source.
`Document newDocument()`	Returns a new `Document` object with no content. The returned Document can be populated using DOM methods such as `createElement()`.
`Document parse(File)` `[IOE, SAXE, IAE]`	Parses the XML in the supplied file, and returns the resulting `Document` object.
`Document parse(InputSource)` `[IOE, SAXE, IAE]`	Parses the XML in the supplied SAX `InputSource`, and returns the resulting `Document` object.
`Document parse(InputStream)` `[IOE, SAXE, IAE]`	Parses the XML in the supplied `InputStream`, and returns the resulting `Document` object. Note that the System ID of the source document will be unknown, so it will not be possible to resolve any relative URIs contained in the document.

Table continued on following page

Method	Description
`Document parse(InputStream, String) [IOE, SAXE, IAE]`	Parses the XML in the supplied `InputStream`, and returns the resulting `Document` object. The second argument supplies the System ID of the source document, which will be used to resolve any relative URIs contained in the document.
`Document parse(String) [IOE, SAXE, IAE]`	Parses the XML in the document identifed by the supplied URI, and returns the resulting `Document` object.
`void setEntityResolver(EntityResolver)`	Supplies a SAX `EntityResolver` to be used during the parsing.
`void setErrorHandler(ErrorHandler)`	Supplies a SAX `ErrorHandler` to be used during the parsing.

The JAXP 1.1 Transformation API

The previous sections provided a summary of the classes and methods defined in JAXP 1.1 to control XML parsing. Now we'll look at the classes and methods used to control XSLT transformation, collectively known as TrAX.

In fact, these classes are designed so they could be used with transformation mechanisms other than XSLT, for example they could be used to drive a transformation defined using the new W3C XQuery specification. However, XSLT is the initial target and is the one we will concentrate on.

There is one other kind of transformation that's worth mentioning, however, and that is an identity transformation in which the result represents a copy of the source. TrAX provides explicit support for identity transformations. These are more useful than they might appear, because TrAX defines three ways of supplying the source document (SAX, DOM, or serial XML) and three ways of capturing the result document (SAX, DOM, or serial XML), so an identity transformation can be used to convert any of these inputs to any of the outputs. For example, it can take SAX input and produce a serial XML file as output, or it can take DOM input and produce a stream of SAX events as output.

TrAX is also designed to control a composite transformation consisting of a sequence of transformation steps, each defined by an XSLT stylesheet in its own right. To do this, it builds on the SAX2 concept of an `XMLFilter`, which takes an input document as a stream of SAX events and produces its output as another stream of SAX events. Any number of such filters can be arranged end to end in a pipeline to define a composite transformation.

As with the JAXP `SAXParser` and `DocumentBuilder` interfaces, TrAX allows the specific XSLT implementation to be selected using a `TransformerFactory` object. Typically each XSLT vendor will provide their own subclass of `TransformerFactory`.

For performance reasons, the API separates the process of compiling a stylesheet from the process of executing it. A stylesheet can be compiled once and executed many times against different source documents, perhaps concurrently in different threads. The compiled stylesheet, following Microsoft's MSXML3 nomenclature, is known as a `Templates` object. To keep simple things simple, however, there are also methods that combine the two processes of compilation and execution into a single call.

The classes defined in the `javax.xml.transform` package fall into several categories:

Category	Class or Interface	Description
Principal classes	`TransformerFactory`	Selects and configures a vendor's implementation.
	`Templates`	Represents a compiled stylesheet in memory.
	`Transformer`	Represents a single execution of a stylesheet to transform a source document into a result.
	`SAXTransformer-Factory`	Allows a transformation to be packaged as a SAX `XMLFilter`.
	`Source`	Represents the input to a transformation.
	`Result`	Represents the output of a transformation
Source classes	`SAXSource`	Transformation input in the form of a SAX event stream.
	`DOMSource`	Transformation input in the form of a DOM `Document`.
	`StreamSource`	Transformation input in the form of a serial XML document.
Result classes	`SAXResult`	Transformation output in the form of a SAX event stream.
	`DOMResult`	Transformation output in the form of a DOM `Document`
	`StreamResult`	Transformation output in the form of a serial XML document (or HTML, or a plain text file).
Helper classes	`URIResolver`	User-supplied object that takes a URI contained in the stylesheet (for example, in the `document()` function) and fetches the relevant document as a `Source` object.
	`ErrorListener`	User-supplied object that is notified of warnings and errors. The `ErrorListener` notifies these conditions to the user and decides whether to continue processing.
	`SourceLocator`	Used primarily to identify where in the stylesheet an error occurred.
	`DOMLocator`	Subclass of `SourceLocator`, used when the source was a DOM.

Table continued on following page

Category	Class or Interface	Description
Helper classes (continued)	`OutputKeys`	A collection of constants defining the names of properties for serial output files.
Error classes	`Transformer-Configuration-Exception`	Generally denotes an error in the stylesheet that is detected at compile time.
	`Transformer-Exception`	A failure occuring in the course of executing a transformation.
	`Transformer-Factory-ConfigurationError`	A failure to configure the Transformer.

In the following sections I will describe each of these classes, in alphabetical order of the class name (ignoring the name of the package).

javax.xml.transform.dom.DOMLocator

A **`DOMLocator`** is used to identify the location of an error when the document is supplied in the form of a DOM. This object will normally be created by the processor when an error occurs, and can be accessed using the `getLocator()` method of the relevant `Exception` object. It specializes `SourceLocator`, providing one additional method:

Method	Description
`org.w3c.dom.Node getOriginatingNode()`	Returns the node at which the error or other event is located

javax.xml.transform.dom.DOMResult

Supplying a `DOMResult` as the result of a transformation indicates that the output is to be written to a DOM in memory. This object will normally be created by the application, and supplied to the processor as the second argument of the `Transformer.transform()` method.

The `DOMResult` identifies a `Node` (which will generally be a `Document` or an `Element`, or possibly a `DocumentFragment`) to hold the results of the transformation. The children of the root in the result tree will become children of this `Node` in the DOM. If no `Node` is supplied by the application, the system will create a `Document` node, which can be retrieved using `getNode()`.

Many XSLT processors will support DOM output, but it is not mandatory. If the processor does support it, then `getFeature(DOMResult.FEATURE)` will return true.

If the XSLT stylesheet outputs text using «`disable-output-escaping="yes"`», then this text will be preceded in the tree by a processing instruction named by the constant `Result.PI_DISABLE_OUTPUT_ESCAPING`, and followed by another processing instruction named by the constant `Result.PI_ENABLE_OUTPUT_ESCAPING`.

The DOMResult object holds a reference to the destination Node, and also to a String containing a system identifier.

The class has two constructors:

```
DOMResult()
DOMResult(org.w3c.xml.Node)
```

and the following methods:

Method	Description
org.w3c.dom.Node getNode()	Gets the node that will contain the result tree.
String getSystemId()	Gets the system identifier.
void setNode(org.w3c.dom.Node)	Sets the node that will contain the result tree. It must be a Document, an Element, or a DocumentFragment.
void setSystemId(String)	Sets the system identifier.

javax.xml.transform.dom.DOMSource

A **DOMSource** packages a DOM Document as a Source, so it can be supplied as input to a transformation.

The DOMSource object will normally be created by the application, and supplied to the processor as the first argument of the Transformer.transform() method. It can also be used to identify the stylesheet document, in which case it will be supplied as a parameter to TransformerFactory.newTemplates().

It is a good idea to call **setSystemId()** to supply a URI for the document, so that relative URIs (for example, those used in the **document()** function) can be resolved. The DOM itself does not hold this information, so it must be supplied extraneously.

The DOMSource can identify any node in the DOM, it does not have to be the Document node. For example, when you use a DOMSource to identify a stylesheet, this might be a stylesheet embedded within another document, in which case the DOMSource would identify the **<xsl:stylesheet>** element node. When you supply a node other than the Document node as input to the **transform()** method, the effect is not specified very clearly, but it is probably intended that it should behave like the **transformNode()** method in MSXML3. This means that the entire document containing the identified node forms the input to the transformation, but the transformation starts by looking for a template rule that matches the specified node, rather than the one that matches the root node.

Note that there are two different ways XSLT processors might handle the supplied document. They might create the XPath tree model as a view or wrapper around the DOM tree, or they might make a copy. The difference between these approaches will become apparent if the stylesheet makes calls to external Java functions which attempt to manipulate the tree as a DOM. It will also, of course, affect performance. Generally, it is best to supply input as a stream or SAX source if you can. Don't construct a DOM specially in order to supply it as input to a transformation, as you might do if you are used to the Microsoft MSXML API.

Not every XSLT processor will support DOM input. If the processor does so, then `getFeature(DOMSource.FEATURE)` will return true.

The class has three constructors:

```
DOMSource()
DOMSource(Node)
DOMSource(Node, String)
```

Its methods are listed below:

Method	Description
`Node getNode()`	Gets the starting node of this `DOMSource`
`String getSystemId()`	Gets the system ID for resolving relative URIs
`void setNode(Node)`	Sets the starting node of this `DOMSource`
`setSystemId(String)`	Gets the system ID for resolving relative URIs

javax.xml.transform.ErrorListener

`ErrorListener` is an interface; if you want to do your own error handling you can write a class that implements this interface and supply it to the `setErrorListener()` methods of the `TransformerFactory` or `Transformer` classes. The `ErrorListener` will be notified of both compile-time and run-time errors.

The class is modeled on the SAX `ErrorHandler` interface, and recognizes three categories of error: warnings, errors, and fatal errors. After a warning, the transformation can proceed to a successful conclusion; after an error, the processor can continue for the purpose of finding further errors, but in the end it will fail; and after a fatal error, it will stop immediately.

Each method can throw an exception to cause processing to stop immediately, even where the processor is prepared to continue.

If no `ErrorListener` is supplied, errors will be reported on the standard `System.err` output stream.

The methods are listed below. The « `[TE]` » after each method shows that each of them can throw a `TransformerException`, to terminate processing.

Method	Description
`void error(TransformerException) [TE]`	Handles an error
`void fatalError(TransformerException) [TE]`	Handles a fatal error
`void warning(TransformerException) [TE]`	Handles a warning

javax.xml.transform.OutputKeys

This class defines a set of constant strings used to represent the standard output properties defined in the **<xsl:output>** and **<xsl:document>** elements.

The names of these constants are:

```
CDATA_SECTION_ELEMENTS
DOCTYPE_PUBLIC
DOCTYPE_SYSTEM
ENCODING
INDENT
MEDIA_TYPE
METHOD
OMIT_XML_DECLARATION
STANDALONE
VERSION
```

They correspond in the obvious way to the attributes of the **<xsl:output>** element.

These constants are useful when you call methods such as `getOutputProperty()` and `setOutputProperty()` on the `Transformer` object.

javax.xml.transform.Result

`Result` is an interface; it exists as an abstraction of the three classes **`SAXResult`**, **`DOMResult`**, and **`StreamResult`**, which are different ways of representing an XML output destination. This allows any of these different kinds of destination to be supplied as the second argument to the `Transformer.transform()` method.

This class defines the two static constants `PI_DISABLE_OUTPUT_ESCAPING` and `PI_ENABLE_OUTPUT_ESCAPING` which are the names of the processing instructions generated as a result of setting «`disable-output-escaping="yes"`» on the **<xsl:text>** or **<xsl:value-of>** instructions in the stylesheet.

The interface defines two methods, allowing any of the different types of Result to have a system identifier:

Method	Description
`String getSystemId()`	Gets the system identifier
`void setSystemId()`	Sets the system identifier

javax.xml.transform.sax.SAXResult

Specifying a `SAXResult` as the output of the transformation causes the result tree produced by the transformation to be fed to a user-supplied SAX2 `ContentHandler` as a sequence of SAX events, just as if the events came from an XML parser. The `SAXResult` object holds a reference to this `ContentHandler`, and also to a `String` containing a system identifier. (This system identifier might be made available to the `ContentHandler` code as part of the `Locator` object, though the spec doesn't make it clear that this is what should happen.)

Many XSLT processors will support SAX output, but it is not mandatory. If the processor does support it, then `getFeature(SAXResult.FEATURE)` will return `true`.

There are several potential difficulties with supplying XSLT output to a `ContentHandler`:

- What happens about **`disable-output-escaping`**? The TrAX spec solves this by saying that any text output using `disable-output-escaping="yes"` will be preceded by a processing instruction named by the constant `Result.PI_DISABLE_OUTPUT_ESCAPING`, and followed by another processing instruction named by the constant `Result.PI_ENABLE_OUTPUT_ESCAPING`.
- What happens to comments in the result tree? The TrAX spec solves this by allowing the `SAXResult` to hold a `LexicalHandler` as well as a `ContentHandler`. Comments can then be notified to the `LexicalHandler`.
- What happens if the result tree is not a well-formed document? The SAX `ContentHandler` interface is designed to receive a stream of events representing a well-formed document, and many `ContentHandlers` will fail (gracefully or otherwise) if they are sent anything else. However, as we saw in Chapter 2, the output of an XSLT transformation needs only to be well-balanced. Unfortunately, the TrAX spec doesn't answer this question. (The solution in Saxon is to send the content handler a special processing instruction indicating that the output will be truncated because it is not well-formed, and only if the `ContentHandler` **rejects** this processing instruction with a `SAXException` are the subsequent events sent.)

The class has two constructors:

```
SAXResult()
SAXResult(org.xml.sax.ContentHandler)
```

and the following methods:

Method	Description
`org.xml.sax.ContentHandler getHandler()`	Gets the `ContentHandler`
`org.xml.sax.ext.LexicalHandler getLexicalHandler()`	Gets the `LexicalHandler`
`String getSystemId()`	Gets the system identifier
`void setHandler(org.xml.sax.ContentHandler)`	Sets the `ContentHandler` that is to receive events representing the result tree
`void setHandler(org.xml.sax.ext.LexicalHandler)`	Sets the `LexicalHandler` that is to receive lexical events (notably, comments) representing the result tree
`void setSystemId()`	Sets the system identifier

javax.xml.transform.sax.SAXSource

A SAXSource is a Source, so it is one of the possible inputs you can supply to the Transformer.transform() method (when it represents a source XML document) or to the TransformerFactory.newTemplates() method (when it represents a stylesheet).

Essentially, a SAXSource is the combination of a SAX parser (XMLReader) with a SAX InputSource, which can be either a URL, a binary input stream, or a character input stream. A SAXSource delivers the source document in the form of a stream of SAX events. Usually it will achieve this by parsing XML held in a file or somewhere in memory; but by defining your own implementations of XMLReader and/or InputSource you can supply the SAX events from anywhere, for example you can generate them as the result of an SQL query or an LDAP directory search.

If no XMLReader is supplied, the system will use a default one. It may do this using the rules for the javax.xml.parsers.SAXParserFactory class described earlier in this appendix, but this is not guaranteed.

Not every XSLT processor will support SAX input. If the processor does so, then getFeature(SAXSource.FEATURE) will return true.

There are three constructors:

```
SAXSource()
SAXSource(InputSource)
SAXSource(XMLReader, InputSource)
```

plus the following methods:

Method	Description
InputSource getInputSource()	Gets the SAX InputSource.
String getSystemId()	Gets the System Identifier used for resolving relative URIs.
XMLReader getXMLReader()	Gets the XMLReader (the parser) if one has been set.
void setInputSource(org.xml.sax .InputSource)	Sets the SAX InputSource.
void setSystemId(String)	Sets a System Identifier that can be used to resolve relative URIs.
void setXMLReader(XMLReader)	Sets the XMLReader (the parser) to be used.
static org.xml.sax.InputSource sourceToInputSource(Source source)	This static method attempts to construct a SAX InputSource from any kind of TrAX Source object. It will return null if this isn't possible.

javax.xml.transform.sax.SAXTransformerFactory

This class is a subclass of `TransformerFactory` that provides three additional facilities:

- The ability to construct a SAX `ContentHandler` (called a `TemplatesHandler`) which will accept a stream of SAX events representing a stylesheet, and on completion return a `Templates` object for that stylesheet.
- The ability to construct a SAX `ContentHandler` (called a `TransformerHandler`) that will accept a stream of SAX events representing a source document, and on completion automatically apply a given stylesheet to that source document.
- The ability to construct a SAX `XMLFilter` based on a particular stylesheet: the `XMLFilter` performs the same SAX-to-SAX transformation as the equivalent `Transformer` would perform, but using the interfaces defined for an `XMLFilter`. This makes it possible to insert this transformation filter into a pipeline of filters.

These are advanced facilities, and they are optional, so not every TrAX processor will support them.

- If `getFeature(SAXTransformerFactory.FEATURE)` returns `true`, then the implementation's `TransformerFactory` will be a `SAXTransformerFactory`.
- If `getFeature(SAXTransformerFactory.FEATURE_XMLFILTER)` returns `true`, then the two `newXMLFilter()` methods can be used.

If a `SAXTransformerFactory` is available at all, then it will always be produced as a result of calling `TransformerFactory.newInstance()`.

The class has the following methods, in addition to those of `TransformerFactory`:

Method	Description
`TemplatesHandler newTemplatesHandler()` [TCE]	Creates and returns a `TemplatesHandler`. The `TemplatesHandler` can be supplied with a stream of SAX events representing the contents of a stylesheet.
`TransformerHandler newTransformerHandler()` [TCE]	Creates and returns a `TransformerHandler`. The `TransformerHandler` will perform an identity transformation on the XML source document that is supplied to it in the form of a stream of SAX events.
`TransformerHandler newTransformerHandler (Source)` [TCE]	Creates and returns a `TransformerHandler`. The `Source` identifies a document containing a stylesheet. The `TransformerHandler` will perform the transformation defined by this stylesheet, on the XML source document that is supplied to it in the form of a stream of SAX events.

Method	Description
TransformerHandler newTransformerHandler (Templates) [TCE]	Creates and returns a TransformerHandler. The Templates argument identifies a compiled stylesheet. The TransformerHandler will perform the transformation defined by this stylesheet, on the XML source document that is supplied to it in the form of a stream of SAX events.
org.sax.xml.XMLFilter newXMLFilter(Source) [TCE]	Creates and returns an XMLFilter. The Source identifies a document containing a stylesheet. The resulting XMLFilter will perform the transformation defined by this stylesheet.
org.sax.xml.XMLFilter newXMLFilter(Templates) [TCE]	Creates and returns an XMLFilter. The Templates argument identifies a compiled stylesheet. The resulting XMLFilter will perform the transformation defined by this stylesheet.

javax.xml.transform.Source

Source is an interface; it exists as an abstraction of the three classes **SAXSource**, **DOMSource**, and **StreamSource**, which are different ways of representing an XML document. This allows any of these different kinds of object to be supplied as the source document to the Transformer.transform() method, or as the stylesheet to the TransformerFactory.newTemplates() method.

The interface defines two methods, allowing any of the different types of Source to have a system identifier:

Method	Description
String getSystemId()	Gets the system identifier
void setSystemId()	Sets the system identifier

javax.xml.transform.SourceLocator

SourceLocator is an interface modeled on the SAX Locator interface. A SourceLocator is used to indicate where in the stylesheet an error occurred. Normally a SourceLocator will be produced by the XSLT processor, and the application will access it using the TransformerException.getLocator() method.

The methods available are:

Method	Description
int getColumnNumber()	Returns the column number of the location if known, or -1 if not
int getLineNumber()	Returns the line number of the location if known, or -1 if not

Table continued on following page

Method	Description
String getPublicId()	Returns the public identifier of the document, if available, or null if not
String getSystemId()	Returns the system identifier of the document, if available, or null if not

javax.xml.transform.stream.StreamSource

A StreamSource represents XML input in the form of a character or byte stream. It is modeled on the SAX InputSource class; the only reason StreamSource is necessary is that InputSource does not implement the Source interface, so it cannot be supplied directly as the input to methods such as Transformer.transform(Source, Result).

Most XSLT processors will support stream input, but it is not mandatory. If the processor does support it, then getFeature(StreamSource.FEATURE) will return true.

If input is from a byte stream (InputStream) or character stream (Reader) it is a good idea to call **setSystemId()** to supply a URI for the document, so that relative URIs (for example, those used in the **document()** function) can be resolved. The stream itself does not hold this information, so it must be supplied extraneously.

The constructors are as follows:

```
StreamSource()
StreamSource(java.io.File)
StreamSource(java.io.InputStream)
StreamSource(java.io.InputStream, String)
StreamSource(java.io.Reader)
StreamSource(java.io.Reader, String)
StreamSource(String)
```

In each case the effect is the same as using the default constructor followed by the relevant setXXX() method. The String argument is always a System ID for the document.

The methods are straightforward:

Method	Description
java.io.InputStream getInputStream()	Gets the supplied InputStream
String getPublicId()	Gets the supplied Public Identifier
java.io.Reader getReader()	Gets the supplied Reader
String getSystemId()	Gets the system identifier
void setInputStream(java.io.InputStream)	Supplies an InputStream
void setPublicId(String)	Supplies a Public Identifier
void setReader(java.io.Reader)	Supplies a Reader
void setSystemId(java.io.File)	Supplies a File from which a system identifier can be obtained
void setSystemId(String)	Supplies a system identifier (a URL)

javax.xml.transform.stream.StreamResult

You can supply a **StreamResult** as the result of a transformation if you want the result tree to be serialized. The format of the resulting file will be XML, HTML, or plain text, depending on the output method defined using **<xsl:output>** or the Transformer methods setOutputProperty() and setOutputProperties().

StreamResult is defined analagously to StreamSource, which in turn is based on the SAX InputSource class. A StreamResult may be either a file (represented by a URL or a Java File object), or a character stream (Writer), or a byte stream (OutputStream).

Most XSLT processors will support stream output, but it is not mandatory. If the processor does support it, then getFeature(StreamResult.FEATURE) will return true.

Although the output destination can be expressed as a URI, this must be a writable destination. In practice this usually means it should be a URI that uses the «file:» prefix, but it could potentially be an ftp or WebDAV destination. If you're running the processor in an applet, writing the output to a file is probably not feasible. The spec doesn't say what happens if you supply a relative URI, but since relative URIs are not allowed in a SAX InputSource, on which this class is modeled, it's best to avoid them. Some processors might interpret a relative URI as being relative to the current directory.

The class has constructors for each of the possible output destinations. The constructor for a String expects the string to contain a system identifier (URL).

```
StreamResult()
StreamResult(File)
StreamResult(java.io.OutputStream)
StreamResult(String)
StreamResult(java.io.Writer)
```

The methods are straightforward:

Method	Description
java.io.OutputStream getOutputStream()	Gets the binary output stream
String getSystemId()	Gets the system identifier
java.io.Writer getWriter()	Gets the Writer (character output stream)
void setOutputStream(java.io.OutputStream)	Sets the binary output stream
void setSystemId(java.io.File)	Sets output to go to the specified file, by setting the system identifier to the URL of this file
void setSystemId(String)	Specifies the system identifier of the output, as a URL
void setWriter(java.io.Writer)	Specifies the Writer (character output stream) to receive the output

javax.xml.transform.Templates

A **`Templates`** object represents a compiled stylesheet. Compiled stylesheets cannot be saved on disk, but they are held in memory and can be used as often as required. To use a `Templates` object to perform a transformation, first create a **`Transformer`** by calling its `newTransformer()` method, then configure the `Transformer` as required (for example, setting its parameters and output properties), then run the transformation using the `Transformer.transform()` method.

The methods available on the `Templates` object are:

Method	Description
`java.util.Properties getOutputProperties()`	Returns a `Properties` object representing the names and values of the output properties defined using **`<xsl:output>`** elements in the stylesheet. The keys of these properties will be strings defined in the `OutputKeys` class; the values will be the values defined in the stylesheet. Note that output properties that are determined dynamically will not be returned: for example, if the method attribute of **`<xsl:output>`** is defaulted, the system doesn't know at compile-time whether the output will be XML or HTML.
`Transformer newTransformer() [TCE]`	Creates a `Transformer` object, which can be used to effect the transformation defined in this stylesheet.

javax.xml.transform.sax.TemplatesHandler

A **`TemplatesHandler`** is a SAX `ContentHandler` that treats the stream of SAX events supplied to it as the contents of a stylesheet. When the full document has been supplied, the stylesheet is compiled, and the compiled stylesheet can be retrieved using the `getTemplates()` method.

This provides an alternative to calling `TransformerFactory.newTemplates()` and supplying a `SAXSource` as the source of the stylesheet. The case for using a `TemplatesHandler` arises when the source of the SAX events is something other than a SAX `XMLReader`; for example, when the stylesheet is the output of another transformation, in which case the source of the SAX events is a TrAX `Transformer`. In this situation the `TemplatesHandler` can be wrapped into a `SAXResult` and used as the `Result` of the earlier transformation.

A `TemplatesHandler` is always created using the `newTemplatesHandler()` method of a `SAXTransformerFactory`. As well as the methods defined in the SAX `ContentHandler` interface, it provides the following additional methods:

Method	Description
`String getSystemId()`	Gets the system identifier of the stylesheet.
`Templates getTemplates()`	Returns the `Templates` object created by compiling the supplied document as a stylesheet.
`void setSystemId()`	Sets the system identifier of the stylesheet. A system identifier is needed if relative URIs (for example in **`<xsl:include>`** or **`<xsl:import>`** elements) need to be resolved.

javax.xml.transform. TransformerFactoryConfigurationError

A **`TransformerFactoryConfigurationError`** (the specification writers must be good typists) represents an error in configuring the XSLT processor, as distinct from an error in the stylesheet itself.

Note that this is an `Error` rather than an `Exception`, which means that an application is not expected to take any recovery action.

The only methods available are:

Method	Description
`String getMessage()`	Gets the error message
`Exception getException()`	Gets any nested exception

javax.xml.transform.Transformer

A **`Transformer`** represents the collection of resources needed to perform a transformation of a `Source` to a `Result`. This includes the compiled stylesheet, the parameter values, and the output properties, as well as details such as an `ErrorListener` and a `URIResolver`.

This interface is analogous to the `IXSLProcessor` class in Microsoft's MSXML3 API.

A `Transformer` is always created by calling the `newTransformer()` method of either the `Templates` object, or the `TransformerFactory` object.

A transformer can be used to perform more than one transformation, but it is not thread-safe: you should not start one transformation until another has finished. If you want to perform several transformations in parallel, obtain several `Transformers` from the same `Templates` object.

The principal method is **`transform()`**, which takes two arguments, representing the `Source` and the `Result`. There are several different kinds of `Source` defined, and several kinds of `Result`. These are described elsewhere in this appendix.

The full set of methods is as follows. The exception codes `[IAE]` and `[TE]` refer to `IllegalArgumentException` and `TransformerException` respectively.

Method	Description
`void clearParameters()`	Clear all parameters set using `setParameter()`
`ErrorListener getErrorListener()`	Gets the `ErrorListener` for this transformation.
`java.util.Properties getOutputProperties()` `[IAE]`	Gets the output properties defined for this transformation. This will be a combination of those defined in the stylesheet and those defined using `setOutputProperty()` and `setOutputProperties()`.
`String getOutputProperty( String)` `[IAE]`	Gets a specific output property defined for this transformation. The argument should be one of the constants defined in `OutputKeys`, or a vendor-specific property name.
`Object getParameter(String)`	Gets the value of a parameter defined for this transformation.
`URIResolver getURIResolver()`	Gets the `URIResolver` used for this transformation, or null if none has been supplied.
`void setErrorListener( ErrorListener)` `[IAE]`	Sets the `ErrorListener` to be used to handle errors reported during this transformation.
`void setOutputProperties( java.util.Properties)` `[IAE]`	Sets output properties for the result of this transformation. These properties override any values set using **`<xsl:output>`** in the stylesheet. The property names will normally be constants defined in **`OutputKeys`**, or vendor-defined properties, but they can also be user-defined properties provided they are namespace-qualified. Names are namespace-qualified using the «`{uri}localname`» notation, in the same way as parameters.
`void setOutputProperty( String, String)` `[IAE]`	Sets a specific output property for the result of this transformation.
`void setParameter( String, Object)`	Supplies a parameter for the transformation. The first argument corresponds to the parameter name, as defined in a global **`<xsl:param>`** element in the stylesheet; if this is namespace-qualified, it should be written in the form «`{uri}local-name`». The second argument is the parameter value. It is likely (though not mandatory) that processors will use the same rules for converting Java objects to XPath values as they use for the return values of Java external functions. These rules are described in Chapter 8.
`void setURIResolver( URIResolver)`	Sets the `URIResolver` to be used to resolve all URIs encountered during this transformation, especially when evaluating the **`document()`** function.

Method	Description
void transform(Source, Result) [TE]	Performs the transformation. Source and Result are interfaces, allowing a wide range of different types of Source and Result to be supplied.

javax.xml.transform.TransformerConfigurationException

This class defines a compile-time error, generally an error in the stylesheet. It is a subclass of TransformerException. It has the same methods as its parent class, TransformerException.

There are several constructors defined, but since this object will usually be created by the XSLT processor itself, I won't list them here.

javax.xml.transform.TransformerException

A TransformerException represents an error which might be detected either at compile-time or at run-time. The exception may contain any or all of the following:

- A message explaining the error.
- A nested exception, generally containing additional information about this error. (Actually, despite the name getException(), this need not be an Exception object: it can be any Throwable, allowing an Error as well as an Exception.)
- A SourceLocator, indicating where in the stylesheet the error occurred.
- A cause. To be honest, I don't know why the designers of this interface felt it necessary to allow a nested exception and a cause to be recorded separately; but they did, and the information is there if you want to look at it.

There are several constructors defined, but since this object will usually be created by the XSLT processor itself, I won't list them here.

The methods available are:

Method	Description
Throwable getCause()	Gets the cause of the exception, if any
Throwable getException()	Gets the nested exception, if any
String getLocationAsString()	Constructs a String representing the location of the error
SourceLocator getLocator()	Gets the SourceLocator, if any, that identifies where the error occurred
String getMessageAndLocation()	Constructs a String that combines information about the error and information about where it occurred
void initCause(Throwable)	Sets the cause of this exception
void setLocator(SourceLocator)	Sets a SourceLocator identifying where the error occurred

The printStackTrace() methods inherited from the standard Exception class are overridden so that they show not only the execution stack at the point where the TransformerException occurred, but also the stack trace of any nested Exception.

javax.xml.transform.TransformerFactory

Like the SAXParserFactory and DocumentBuilderFactory in the javax.xml.parsers package, described in the first part of this appendix, this factory class enables you to select a specific vendor's XSLT implementation.

The first thing an application must do is to obtain a TransformerFactory, which it can do by calling the static method TransformerFactory.newInstance(). Different vendors of XSLT processors will each implement their own subclass of TransformerFactory, and this method call determines which vendor's processor your application will end up using. If there are several available, the one that is used is based on the following decision process:

- Use the value of the system property javax.xml.transform.TransformerFactory if it is available. You can set system properties using the -D option on the java command line, or by calling System.setProperty() from your application.
- Look for a properties file $JAVA_HOME/lib/jaxp.properties, and within this file, for the property named javax.xml.parsers.TransformerFactory.
- Use the services API, which is part of the JAR specification.

It is likely that when you install a particular XSLT processor, it will contain a file in its .jar archive that makes that particular processor the default, so if you don't do anything to select a specific processor, the one chosen will depend on the order of files and directories on your class path.

Once you have got a TransformerFactory, you can use a number of methods to configure it. Finally, you can call the newTemplates() method to compile a stylesheet, or the newTransformer() method to obtain a Transformer directly (if you only want to use the compiled stylesheet once).

The methods available are shown below. As with other methods, the exceptions thrown are indicated by a list of codes, which are explained in the table on page 848 at the start of this appendix.

Method	Description
Source getAssociatedStyleSheet(Source, String media, String title, String charset) [TCE]	Within the XML source document identified by the Source argument, finds the **<?xml-stylesheet?>** processing instruction corresponding to the media, title, and charset parameters (any of which may be null), and returns a Source representing this stylesheet.

Method	Description
`Object getAttribute(String)` [IAE]	Gets a vendor-specific configuration property.
`ErrorListener getErrorListener()`	Gets the default error listener that will be used for transformations. If none has been set, this will be a vendor-supplied `ErrorListener`.
`boolean getFeature(String)`	Gets information about the features supported by this implementation. Features are defined by constants within other classes, for example `getFeature(SAXResult.FEATURE)` returns `true` if the processor supports output to a SAX `ContentHandler`.
`URIResolver getURIResolver()`	Gets the default `URIResolver` that will be used for transformations.
`static TransformerFactory newInstance()` [TFCE]	Returns an instance of the vendor-specific `TransformerFactory`, selected according to the rules given above.
`Templates newTemplates(Source)` [TCE]	Compiles the stylesheet provided in the given `Source`, returning a `Templates` object as a representation of the compiled stylesheet.
`Transformer newTransformer()` [TCE]	Creates a `Transformer` that will perform an identity transformation.
`Transformer newTransformer(Source)` [TCE]	A shortcut method equivalent to calling `newTemplates(Source).newTransformer()`
`void setAttribute(String, Object)` [IAE]	Sets a vendor-specific configuration property.
`void setErrorListener(ErrorListener)` [IAE]	Defines the `ErrorListener` to be used for error handling.
`void setURIResolver(URIResolver)`	Defines the `URIResolver` to be used for resolving URIs contained in the stylesheet or source document.

javax.xml.transform.sax.TransformerHandler

A **`TransformerHandler`** receives SAX events representing a source document. It performs a transformation on this source document, and writes the results of the transformation to a given `Result` object.

The `TransformerHandler` interface extends three SAX event handling interfaces; the `ContentHandler`, the `LexicalHandler`, and the `DTDHandler` It needs to act as a `LexicalHandler` so that it can handle comments in the source document, and it needs to act as a `DTDHandler` so that it can ignore comments in the DTD, and so that it can find out about unparsed entity declarations in the DTD.

Using a `TransformerHandler` is an alternative to creating a `Transformer` and using a `SAXSource` to define the input document. This alternative approach is particularly useful when the source of SAX events is something other than a SAX `XMLReader`. For example, the source of SAX events might be another TrAX transformation, or it might be any other piece of software that allows a `ContentHandler` to be nominated to receive results.

A `TransformerHandler` is always created using the `newTransformerHandler()` method of a `SAXTransformerFactory`.

In addition to the methods defined in the SAX `ContentHandler`, `LexicalHandler`, and `DTDHandler` interfaces, a `TransformerHandler` offers the following methods:

Method	Description
`String getSystemId()`	Gets the system identifier defined for the source document.
`Transformer getTransformer()`	Gets the underlying Transformer. This can be used to set parameters and output properties for the transformation.
`void setResult(Result) [IAE]`	Sets the output destination for the transformation.
`void setSystemId(String)`	Sets the system identifier for the source document. This will be used as a base URI to resolve any relative URIs contained in the document.

javax.xml.transform.URIResolver

`URIResolver` is an interface; you can write a class that implements this interface and supply it to the `setURIResolver()` method of the `TransformerFactory` or `Transformer` classes. When the XSLT processor has to find an XML document using a URI specified in **`<xsl:include>`**, **`<xsl:import>`**, or in the **`document()`** function, it will call any user-supplied `URIResolver` to do the work. The `URIResolver` can treat the URI any way it likes, and it returns the required document as a `Source` object: typically a `SAXSource`, a `DOMSource`, or a `StreamSource`.

For example, if the stylesheet called «`document('db:employee=517541')`», your `URIResolver` could interpret this URI as a database query and return an XML document containing the result as a rowset.

The interface defines only one method:

Method	Description
`Source resolve(String, String) [TE]`	The first argument is a relative URI, the second is the base URI against which it is resolved. The method returns a `Source` containing the requested document, or throws a `TransformerException` if it cannot retrieve it. It may also return null, indicating that the default `URIResolver` should be used.

Note: there is a practical problem that the TrAX interface does not address, namely the XSLT rule that if you call the **document()** function twice to fetch the same absolute URI, the same document should be returned each time. Since the `URIResolver` accepts the relative URI and base URI as separate arguments, but does not actually return an absolute URI, it's not entirely clear whether it is the responsibility of the processor or the `URIResolver` to enforce this rule, especially when the URI is in a format that the XSLT processor itself does not recognize, as in the example above.

Note also that the arguments are supplied in the opposite order from those of the Java `java.net.URL` class.

Examples

This section provides some simple examples of applications that use the TrAX API in different ways to control a transformation.

Example 1: Transformation Using Files

This example (`FileTransform.java`) performs a single transformation, reading the source document and stylesheet from files, and sending the XML output to another file.

```
import javax.xml.transform.*;
import javax.xml.transform.stream.*;
import java.io.File;

public class FileTransform {

    public static void main(String[] args) throws Exception {
        File source = new File(args[0]);
        File style = new File(args[1]);
        File out = new File(args[2]);

        TransformerFactory factory = TransformerFactory.newInstance();
        Transformer t = factory.newTransformer(new StreamSource(style));
        t.transform(new StreamSource(source), new StreamResult(out));
    }
}
```

This is a minimal TrAX application.

The Java examples in this section are provided on the Wrox web site download for this book in source form only. That's deliberate: you'll learn more if you have to compile them before running them. In particular, you need to have a TrAX-conformant XSLT processor such as Saxon or Xalan properly installed and on your classpath, and if you haven't got this right, you'll get much clearer error messages when you try to compile the code than you get when you try to run it.

Assuming you have installed the Sun Java JDK, you can compile this application by the command:

```
javac  FileTransform.java
```

This assumes that the directory containing the Java source file is the current directory. Once you have compiled the code, you can run it from the command line, for example:

```
java  FileTransform  source.xml  style.xsl  out.html
```

Of course, this is not a very professionally-written application. It will fall over with a stack trace if incorrect arguments are supplied, if either of the input files doesn't exist, or if errors occur during the transformation: but it's a start. My aim in these examples is to show how the main TrAX classes work, not to teach you professional Java programming.

Because some people like to type examples exactly as they are written in the book, the folder containing the Java applications also contains specimen XML and XSL files called `source.xml` and `style.xsl`. So if you make this folder your current directory, you should be able to type the command line above exactly as shown. But of course, the Java application will handle any source file and any stylesheet.

> *In my examples, I've supplied relative URIs such as* `source.xml` *as arguments. Many of the examples in the JAXP 1.1 specification do the same, and both Saxon and Xalan accept them. But this will probably only work if the SAX parser accepts a relative URI as the system identifier supplied to an* `InputSource` *object, despite the fact that the SAX specification states explicitly that it ought to be an absolute URI.*

Example 2: Supplying Parameters and Output Properties

This example, `Parameters.java`, enhances the previous example:

- It allows a stylesheet parameter to be supplied from the command line
- It modifies the output properties defined in the stylesheet
- It directs the output to `System.out` instead of to a file

The `main()` method of the enhanced application looks like this:

```
public static void main(String[] args) throws Exception {
    File source = new File(args[0]);
    File style = new File(args[1]);
    String title = args[2];

    TransformerFactory factory = TransformerFactory.newInstance();
    Transformer t = factory.newTransformer(new StreamSource(style));
    t.setParameter("title", title);
    t.setOutputProperty(OutputKeys.INDENT, "no");
    t.transform(new StreamSource(source), new StreamResult(System.out));
}
```

This version of the program can be run using a command such as the following. The third argument on the command line (written in quotes because it contains spaces) is now a parameter value for the stylesheet, instead of the output file name.

```
java Parameters source.xml style.xsl "New organization structure"
```

Comparing the output with that of the previous example, note that the HTML is no longer indented, and that the contents of the **<title>** and **<h1>** elements have changed. And, of course, the output is written to the console this time.

Example 3: Holding Documents in Memory

In this example we will hold both the stylesheet and the source document in memory so they can be used repeatedly. In principle this would allow us to run different source documents past the same stylesheet, or to use different stylesheets to transform the same source document, but in practice, to keep the example simple, we'll use the same source document and stylesheet repeatedly, changing only the parameters to the transformation. We'll do one transformation using each of the parameters supplied on the command line.

To keep the source document in memory, we'll create a DOM. The natural way of doing this would be to use the `DocumentBuilder` class defined in the first section of this appendix; but I'd prefer to stick to using the TrAX interfaces in these examples, so I'll do it a different way. TrAX makes it very easy to do an identity transform, and to build the DOM, all we need is an identity transform that takes the serial file as input and produces the DOM as output.

We could also keep the stylesheet it memory as a DOM, but that would mean validating and compiling it each time it is used. It's better to keep the compiled stylesheet, that is, the `Templates` object.

The main program of this example (`Repeat.java`) looks like this:

```
public static void main(String[] args) throws Exception {
     File source = new File(args[0]);
     File style = new File(args[1]);

     TransformerFactory factory = TransformerFactory.newInstance();

     // Build a DOM using an identity transform
     Transformer builder = factory.newTransformer();
     DOMResult result = new DOMResult();
     builder.transform(new StreamSource(source), result);
     Document doc = (Document)result.getNode();

     // Compile the stylesheet
     Templates templates = factory.newTemplates(new StreamSource(style));

     // do one transformation for each parameter supplied
     for (int i=2; i<args.length; i++) {
          Transformer t = templates.newTransformer();
          System.out.println("======= TITLE = " + args[i] + "=======");
          t.setParameter("title", args[i]);
          t.transform(new StreamSource(source), new StreamResult(System.out));
     }
}
```

You can run this application from the command line with a command such as:

```
java Repeat source.xml style.xsl one two three four
```

This will run the transformation four times, producing output HTML with the title set to «one», «two», «three», and «four» in turn.

This application is quite unrealistic, but the same principle of keeping source documents and stylesheets in memory can often be used to achieve significant performance benefits in a servlet environment.

Example 4: Using the <?xml-stylesheet?> Processing Instruction

The previous examples have all specified the source document and the stylesheet separately. However, as we saw in Chapter 3, it is possible for a source XML document to identify its preferred stylesheet using an **`<?xml-stylesheet?>`** processing instruction at the start of the source XML. This example shows how to extract the relevant stylesheet using the TrAX API: specifically, the `getAssociatedStylesheet()` method provided by the `TransformerFactory` object.

The **`main()`** method of this example (`Associated.java`) is:

```
public static void main(String[] args) throws Exception {
    File input = new File(args[0]);
    StreamSource source = new StreamSource(input);

    TransformerFactory factory = TransformerFactory.newInstance();

    // Get the associated stylesheet for the source document

    Source style =
            factory.getAssociatedStylesheet(source, null, null, null);

    // Use this to do the transformation

    Transformer t = factory.newTransformer(style);
    t.transform(source, new StreamResult(System.out));
}
```

Specifying null values for the media, title, and charset arguments of **`getAssociatedStylesheet()`** selects the default stylesheet for the document. If the document has multiple **`<?xml-stylesheet?>`** processing instructions it is possible to use these parameters to choose more selectively.

You can run this example with the command:

```
java Associated source.xml
```

Example 5: A SAX Pipeline

It can often be useful to place an XSLT transformation within a SAX pipeline. A pipeline consists of a series of stages, each of which implements the SAX2 interface `XMLFilter`. The filters are connected together so that each filter looks like a SAX2 `ContentHandler` (a receiver of SAX events) to the previous stage in the pipeline, and looks like an `XMLReader` (a supplier of SAX events) to the following stage. Some of these filters might be XSLT filters, others might be written in Java or implemented using other tools.

In our example (`Pipeline.java`) we will use a three-stage pipeline. The first stage will be a Java-written filter whose job is to convert all the element names in the document to uppercase, recording the original name in an attribute. The second stage is an XSLT transformation that copies some elements through unchanged and removes others, based on the value of another attribute. The final stage is another Java-written filter that restores the element names to their original form.

I've invented this example for the purpose of illustration, but there is some rationale behind it. In XML, uppercase and lowercase are distinct, so **<b>** and **<B>** are quite distinct element names. But the legacy of HTML means you may sometimes want to do a transformation in which **<b>** and **<B>** are handled in the same way. This isn't easy to achieve in XSLT, so we do the pre- and post-processing in Java to get round this.

Let's start with the two Java-written XMLFilters. These are written as subclasses of the SAX helper class `XMLFilterImpl`. We only need to implement the `startElement()` and `endElement()` methods; the other methods simply pass the events through unchanged.

The pre-filter looks like this. It normalizes the name of the element to lowercase, and saves the supplied local name and QName as additional attributes.

```
private class PreFilter extends XMLFilterImpl {

        public void startElement (String uri, String localName, String qName,
                            Attributes atts)
            throws SAXException {
                String newLocalName = localName.toLowerCase();
                String newQName = qName.toUpperCase();
                AttributesImpl newAtts =
                    (atts.getLength()>0 ?
                        new AttributesImpl(atts) :
                        new AttributesImpl());
                newAtts.addAttribute("", "old-local-name",
                          "old-local-name", "CDATA", localName);
                newAtts.addAttribute("", "old-qname",
                          "old-qname", "CDATA", qName);
                super.startElement(uri, newLocalName, newQName, newAtts);
            }

            public void endElement (String uri, String localName, String qName)
            throws SAXException {
                String newLocalName = localName.toLowerCase();
                String newQName = qName.toUpperCase();
                super.endElement(uri, newLocalName, newQName);
            }
        }
```

The post-filter is very similar; the only difference is that because the original element name is needed by the `endElement()` code as well as `startElement()`, the `startElement()` code (which gets the names from the attribute list) saves them on a stack where `endElement` can pick them up later.

```
    private class PostFilter extends XMLFilterImpl {

        public Stack stack;

        public void startDocument() throws SAXException {
            stack = new Stack();
            super.startDocument();
        }

        public void startElement (String uri, String localName, String qName,
                        Attributes atts)
            throws SAXException {

                String originalLocalName = localName;
                String originalQName = qName;
                AttributesImpl newAtts = new AttributesImpl();
                for (int i=0; i<atts.getLength(); i++) {
                    String name = atts.getQName(i);
                    String val = atts.getValue(i);
                    if (name.equals("old-local-name")) {
                        originalLocalName = val;
                    } else if (name.equals("old-qname")) {
                        originalQName = val;
                    } else {
                        newAtts.addAttribute(
                                atts.getURI(i),
                                atts.getLocalName(i),
                                name,
                                atts.getType(i),
                                val);
                    }
                }
                super.startElement(uri, originalLocalName,
                                            originalQName, newAtts);
                stack.push(originalLocalName);
                stack.push(originalQName);
            }

            public void endElement (String uri, String localName, String qName)
            throws SAXException {
                String originalQName = (String)stack.pop();
                String originalLocalName = (String)stack.pop();
                super.endElement(uri, originalLocalName, originalQName);
            }
    }
```

Now we can build the pipeline, which actually has five stages:

- The XML parser itself, which we can get using the `ParserFactory` mechanism described at the start of this appendix.
- The pre-filter.
- The XSLT transformation, constructed using the stylesheet held in `filter.xsl`.
- The post-filter.

- The serializer. The serializer is obtained from the TransformerFactor and is actually a TransformerHandler that performs an identity transformation with a StreamResult as its output.

As with any SAX2 pipeline, the first stage is an XMLReader, the last is a ContentHandler, and each of the intermediate stages is an XMLFilter. Each stage is linked to the previous stage using setParent(), except that the ContentHandler at the end is linked in by calling setContentHandler() on the last XMLFilter. Finally, the pipeline is activated by calling the parse() method on the last XMLFilter, which in our case is the post-filter.

Here is the code that builds the pipeline and runs a supplied source file through it:

```
public void run(String input) throws Exception {
    StreamSource source = new StreamSource(new File(input));
    File style = new File("filter.xsl");

    TransformerFactory factory = TransformerFactory.newInstance();
    if (!factory.getFeature(SAXTransformerFactory.FEATURE_XMLFILTER)) {
        System.err.println("SAX Filters are not supported");
    } else {
        SAXTransformerFactory saxFactory = (SAXTransformerFactory)factory;
        XMLFilter pre = new PreFilter();

        // substitute your chosen SAX2 parser here, or use the
        // SAXParserFactory to get one
        pre.setParent(new com.icl.saxon.aelfred.SAXDriver());

        XMLFilter filter = saxFactory.newXMLFilter(new StreamSource(style));
        filter.setParent(pre);

        XMLFilter post = new PostFilter();
        post.setParent(filter);

        TransformerHandler serializer = saxFactory.newTransformerHandler();
        serializer.setResult(new StreamResult(System.out));
        Transformer trans = serializer.getTransformer();
        trans.setOutputProperty(OutputKeys.METHOD, "xml");
        trans.setOutputProperty(OutputKeys.INDENT, "yes");

        post.setContentHandler(serializer);
        post.parse(source.getSystemId());
    }
}
```

For the example I've given the class a trivial main program as follows:

```
public static void main(String[] args) throws Exception {
    new Pipeline().run(args[0]);
}
```

And you can execute it as:

```
java  Pipeline  mixed-up.xml
```

The results are sent to standard output.

Summary

In this appendix I have given an overview of the JAXP 1.1 interfaces.

I started, for the sake of completeness, with a quick tour of the JAXP facilities for controlling SAX and DOM parsers, found in package `javax.xml.parsers`.

I then gave detailed descriptions of the classes and methods in package `javax.xml.transform` and its subsidiary packages: the Transformation API for XML, or TrAX.

Finally, I showed some simple examples of TrAX in action, in extremely simple applications.

The benefit of TrAX is that it allows you to write Java applications that invoke XSLT transformations without committing your application to a particular XSLT processor. At the time of writing, TrAX interfaces are already available in Saxon and Xalan, even though the specification is still a working draft. Further implementations can be expected to follow.

Glossary

This glossary gathers together some of the more common technical terms used in this book. These terms are not all defined in the XSLT or XPath specifications, some of them are borrowed from XML or other standards in the XML family, and others have been invented for the purposes of this book. So for each definition, I also tell you where the term comes from.

The definitions, however, are my own; in some cases the original specifications have a much more formal definition, but in other cases they are surprisingly vague.

Ancestor Axis — XPath

The ancestor axis selects the parent of the context node, its parent, and so on up to and including the root node. The axis is in reverse document order.

Ancestor-or-Self Axis — XPath

The ancestor-or-self axis selects the context node followed by all the nodes on the ancestor axis. The axis is in reverse document order.

Attribute — XML

A name=value pair appearing in an element's start tag, for example «`category="grocery"`».

Attribute Axis — XPath

The attribute axis selects all the attributes of the context node. If the context node is not an element, the axis will be empty.

Attribute Node XPath

A node in a tree that represents an attribute in an XML document. There will be an attribute node attached to an element node for each attribute defined in the start tag of the corresponding element in the original XML document, other than an attribute acting as a namespace declaration. There will also be attribute nodes for attributes given a default value in the Document Type Definition. The string value of the node is the value of the attribute.

Attribute Set XSLT

A named collection of `<xsl:attribute>` instructions, which when invoked using the `use-attribute-sets` attribute of `<xsl:element>` or `<xsl:copy>`, or the `xsl:use-attribute-sets` attribute of a literal result element, generates a set of attribute nodes to be added to the current output element.

Attribute Value Template XSLT

An attribute value template is an attribute in the stylesheet that can contain both fixed and variable parts. The fixed parts are written as ordinary characters, while the variable parts are written between curly braces: for example «`file="{$dir}/{$fname}.html"`» would evaluate to «`file="out/page.html"`» if the variables `$dir` and `$fname` have the values «`out`» and «`page`» respectively. Attribute value templates can be used for any attribute of a literal result element, but on XSLT elements they can be used only for those attributes that explicitly allow them.

Axis XPath

An axis is a direction of travel through the tree. Starting from a particular context node, an axis defines a list of nodes reached from that origin. For example the ancestor axis returns the parent, grandparent, and so on up to the root of the tree, while the following-sibling axis returns all the nodes that appear after the context node and share the same parent.

Base URI XSLT

Every node has an associated Base URI. For an element, this is the absolute URI of the XML external entity containing the element's start and end tags (most often, of course, this will be the document entity). For other node types, it is defined by reference to an associated element node, typically its parent. The Base URI of an element can also be set explicitly by using the `xml:base` attribute. The Base URI of a node is used when expanding a relative URI defined in that node, for example a relative URI in an `href` attribute is considered to be relative to the Base URI of the parent element.

Boolean XPath

One of the allowed data types for the value of an XPath expression. It takes the value true or false.

Built-in Template Rule

XSLT

A template rule that is not explicitly defined in the stylesheet, but which is implicitly available to process a node if there is no explicit template rule that matches it.

CDATA Section

XML

A sequence of characters in an XML document enclosed between the delimiters «`<![CDATA[`» and «`]]>`»; within a CDATA section all characters represent text content rather than markup, except for the sequence «`]]>`».

Character Reference

XML

A representation of a character using its decimal or hexadecimal Unicode value, for example «`
`» or «`↤`». Normally used for characters that are difficult or impossible to enter directly at the keyboard.

Child Axis

XPath

The child axis selects all the immediate children of the context node. These can include elements, text nodes, comments, and processing instructions, but not attributes or namespace nodes.

Comment

XML

An item in an XML document that is conventionally used to carry extraneous information that is not part of the document proper. Written between the delimiters «`<!--`» and «`-->`».

Comment Node

XPath

A node in a tree representing an XML comment. The string-value of the node is the text of the comment.

Context Node

XPath

For an XPath expression contained directly in the stylesheet (for example, an expression in the `select` attribute of `<xsl:value-of>`, or between curly braces in an attribute value template), the context node is the same as the current node. For an XPath expression used as a predicate within a path expression, the context node is the node for which the predicate is being tested. The context node can be retrieved using the expression «`.`».

Context Position

XPath

For an XPath expression contained directly in the stylesheet, the context position is the position of the current node in the current node list, all positions being numbered from one. For an XPath expression used as a predicate in a step, the context position is the position of the context node among all the nodes selected by that step of the path expression, in the order of that step's axis. The context position determines the value of the `position()` function, and is also used in evaluating a numeric predicate such as «`[1]`».

Context Size — XPath

For an XPath expression contained directly in the stylesheet, the context size is the number of nodes in the current node list. For an XPath expression used as a predicate in a step, the context size is the number of nodes selected by that step of the path expression. The context size determines the value of the `last()` function.

Current Node — XSLT

A node in a source tree becomes the current node when it is processed using `<xsl:apply-templates>` or `<xsl:for-each>`. The current node is accessed directly by using the `current()` function. Except within a predicate of a path expression, the current node is the same as the context node, so it can also be accessed using the expression «`.`».

Current Node List — XSLT

The current node list is a list (an ordered set) of nodes in the source document tree. A new current node list is established by the select expression of `<xsl:apply-templates>` or `<xsl:for-each>`. By default the current node list is in document order, but it may be in a different order if an `<xsl:sort>` element is present. When an XPath expression in the stylesheet is evaluated, the position of the current node in the current node list determines the context position (the value of the `position()` function), and the size of the current node list determines the context size (the value of the `last()` function).

Current Output Destination — This book

The XSLT specification speaks of instructions such as `<xsl:value-of>` and `<xsl:element>` writing nodes to the result tree. But while an `<xsl:variable>` element is being instantiated, any output is actually redirected to the result tree fragment that will form the value of this variable. In this book we have therefore chosen to refer to whichever tree is currently being written to as the current output destination. In the XSLT 1.1 draft (and in many XSLT 1.0 products, using vendor extensions) it is possible to generate multiple result trees.

Current Template Rule — XSLT

When `<xsl:apply-templates>` selects a template rule to process a particular node, that template rule becomes the current template rule. It remains the current template rule through calls of `<xsl:call-template>`, but not though calls of `<xsl:for-each>`. The current template rule is used only in deciding which template to invoke when `<xsl:apply-imports>` is called.

Default Namespace Declaration — XML

Takes the form of an XML attribute `xmlns="uri"`. Declares that within its scope, an element name with no explicit prefix will be associated with a particular namespace URI. The default namespace is used only for element names; other objects with no prefix (for example, attributes) have a null namespace URI.

Descendant Axis XPath

The descendant axis selects all the children of the context node, their children, and so on, in document order.

Descendant-or-Self Axis XPath

The descendant-or-self axis selects the context node followed by all the nodes on the descendant axis.

Document Element XML

The outermost element of a document, the one that contains all other elements. The XML standard also refers to this as the root element, but it must not be confused with the root node in the XPath tree model: the root node is the parent of the document element, and represents the document itself.

Document Order XPath

The nodes in a node-set can always be sorted into document order. For elements from the same document, document order is the same as the order of the start tags in the original source. In terms of the tree structure, a node is ordered after its preceding siblings, and these are ordered after their parent node. The ordering of attribute and namespace nodes, and of nodes from different source documents, is not fully defined.

Document Type Definition (DTD) XML

The definition of the structure of an XML document, or a collection of XML documents. May be split into an external subset, held in a separate file, and an internal subset, embedded within the document itself.

Document XML

A parsed entity that conforms to the XML syntax for a `Document` is said to be a well-formed document; a document that also obeys the rules in its Document Type Definition is said to be valid.

Element XML

A logical unit within an XML document, delimited by start and end tags, for example `<publisher>Wrox Press</publisher>`; an empty element may also be written in abbreviated form, for example `<publisher name="Wrox"/>`.

Element Node XPath

A node in a tree that represents an element in an XML document. The parent of the element node is either the containing element or the root of the tree; its children are the element nodes, text nodes, comment nodes, and processing instruction nodes derived from the immediate content of the XML element.

Embedded Stylesheet XSLT

A physical stylesheet that does not constitute an entire XML document in its own right, but which is embedded as an `<xsl:stylesheet>` element within some larger XML (or perhaps non-XML) document.

Entity Reference XML

A reference to an internal or external entity, generally in the form «`&name;`».

Entity XML

A physical unit of information that may be referenced within an XML document. Internal entities are embedded within the document in its Document Type Definition; external entities are generally held as a separate file. A parsed entity contains text with XML markup; an unparsed entity contains binary data. A general entity contains material for inclusion in the document; a parameter entity contains material for inclusion in the Document Type Definition.

Expanded Name XML Namespaces

An identifier obtained from a `QName` by replacing the namespace prefix with the full namespace URI of the namespace to which it refers. An expanded name has two components, the namespace URI and the local name. There is no standard convention for displaying an expanded name, though in some interfaces such as TrAX, expanded names are written in the form «`{namespace-uri}local-name`»."

Expression XPath

An XPath construct that can be evaluated to yield a string, a number, a Boolean, a node-set, or a result tree fragment. Used in many contexts such as the `select` attribute of `<xsl:for-each>`, `<xsl:value-of>`, and `<xsl:variable>`, and the `test` attribute of `<xsl:if>` and `<xsl:when>`. Expressions are also used between curly braces in attribute value templates.

Extension Element XSLT

An element within a template body that is defined by a product vendor, a user, or a third party, but which otherwise behaves like an XSLT instruction. The XSLT Recommendation defines how extension elements are instantiated but not how they are implemented.

Extension Function XSLT

A function defined by a product vendor, a user, or a third party, which can be called from within an XPath expression. The XSLT Recommendation defines how extension functions are called but not how they are implemented.

Following Axis XPath

The following axis selects all the nodes that follow the context node with the exception of attribute and namespace nodes, and the node's own descendants. The axis is in document order.

Following-Sibling Axis XPath

The following-sibling axis selects all the nodes that follow the context node and that share the same parent node, in document order.

Function XPath

A procedure that can be called from within an XPath expression; it takes arguments and returns a result. Functions cannot be defined using XPath, only invoked from XPath. A function is either a core function defined in the XPath or XSLT recommendations, or an extension function provided by the vendor or the user.

Global Variable XSLT

A variable defined in a top-level `<xsl:variable>` element. Global variables are available anywhere in the logical stylesheet, unless masked by a local variable of the same name, or a global variable of the same name and higher import precedence.

ID XML

An attribute of type ID has a value which is unique within the document (that is, different from any other ID attribute). It is an ID by virtue of being declared as such in the DTD. It is only guaranteed unique if the document is valid (XSLT is not constrained to operate only on valid documents). Elements can be accessed using their ID by means of the `id()` function. Attributes of type IDREF have no special significance in XSLT.

Import Precedence XSLT

A stylesheet that is loaded using `<xsl:import>` has lower import precedence than the stylesheet doing the importing. The import precedence affects all the top-level elements in that stylesheet, and is used when deciding which top-level elements to use. For example, if two global variables have the same name, the one with higher import precedence is used.

Instantiate XSLT

Instructions and template bodies in XSLT are not executed, obeyed, or activated: they are said to be instantiated. This term is chosen to avoid any connotation that execution must be sequential.

Instruction — XSLT

One of a number of XSLT elements that is permitted to appear directly within a template body, for example `<xsl:variable>`, `<xsl:choose>`, and `<xsl:message>`. Not all XSLT elements are instructions, for example `<xsl:param>` and `<xsl:when>` are not: this is because these can only appear in a defined context.

Literal Result Element — XSLT

A literal result element is an element appearing within a template body in a stylesheet that is not an XSLT instruction or an extension element. When the template body is instantiated, a literal result element is copied to the current output destination and its content (which is also a template body) is instantiated in turn.

Local Variable — XSLT

A variable defined within a template body. A local variable is accessible only from the following siblings of the `<xsl:variable>` element that defines the variable, and from their descendants. This is analogous to the normal rule in block-structured programming languages.

Mode — XSLT

Modes partition the set of template rules in a stylesheet, so that the same nodes can be processed more than once using different rules each time. The mode named on the call of `<xsl:apply-templates>` must match the mode named on the `<xsl:template>` element that is invoked.

Named Template — XSLT

An `<xsl:template>` element in the stylesheet with a `name` attribute. A named template may be invoked using an `<xsl:call-template>` instruction.

Namespace — XML Namespaces

A named collection of names. The namespace is named using a URI, which is intended to be formed in such a way as to ensure global uniqueness, but which, in practice, may be any string. Within a particular region of a document, a namespace is also identified by a local name called a prefix; different prefixes can be used to refer to the same namespace in different documents or even within the same document. A name (of an element or attribute in XML, and of a variable, template, mode etc in XSLT) belongs to a specific namespace, and two names can be considered equivalent only if they belong to the same namespace.

Namespace Axis — XPath

The namespace axis selects all the namespace nodes belonging to the context node. If the context node is not an element, the axis will be empty. For elements, there is one namespace node for every namespace that is in scope for the element, whether it relates to a namespace declaration that was defined on this element or on a containing element.

Namespace Declaration — XML Namespaces

A construct in an XML document which declares that within a particular region of the document, a given namespace prefix will be used to refer to the namespace with a particular URI. There are two forms of namespace declaration: `xmlns="uri"` to declare the default namespace (the one with a null prefix), and `xmlns:prefix="uri"` to declare a namespace with a non-null prefix. Both are written in the form of XML attributes and apply to the element they are on and all descendant elements, unless overridden.

Namespace Node — XPath

A node in a tree that represents the binding of a namespace prefix to a namespace URI. A namespace node belongs to an element called its parent: it applies only to that element and not to any descendant elements.

XML Namespace

A short name used to identify a namespace within a particular region of a stylesheet, so called because it is most often used as the prefix of a `QName` (the part before the colon). Different prefixes can be used to identify the same namespace, and in different contexts the same prefix can be used to identify different namespaces.

Namespace URI — XML Namespaces

A URI used to identify a namespace. Namespace URIs are unusual in that there is no actual resource that can be obtained using the URI; the URI is simply a unique identifier. In practice, any string can be used as a namespace URI, though «`http://`» URLs are often used to give some prospect of uniqueness.

NaN — XPath

Not-a-Number. This is one of the possible values of a variable whose data type is Number. It results from an operation whose result is not numeric, for example «`number('apple')`».

Node — XPath

An object on a tree. There are seven types of node: attribute nodes, comment nodes, element nodes, namespace nodes, processing instruction nodes, root nodes, and text nodes.

Node-set XPath

A node-set is an unordered collection of distinct nodes from one or more trees. It may be empty, and it may be heterogeneous in the sense that it contains a mixture of nodes of different types.

Number XPath

One of the allowed data types for the value of an XPath expression. It is a floating point number as defined by IEEE 754.

Output Method XSLT

XSLT defines three output methods, xml, html, and text. The output method controls the way in which the result tree is output (or serialized) as a stream of characters or bytes.

Parameter XSLT

A variable whose value is supplied by the caller. A global parameter is a global variable whose value can be set (in a vendor-defined way) when the stylesheet is executed. A local parameter is defined within an `<xsl:template>` element, and its value can be set when the template is invoked using `<xsl:apply-templates>` or `<xsl:call-template>`.

Path Expression XPath

A path expression is an expression that selects a set of nodes in the source tree. It defines an initial node-set, from which selection starts, and a sequence of steps which define navigation paths from the initial nodes to further nodes. The final result is the set of nodes reached by following each of the steps in turn For example, the path expression «`./parent::*`» has an initial node-set containing the context node «`.`», and a single step which navigates to the parent element of that node.

Pattern XSLT

A construct that defines a condition which every node either satisfies or does not satisfy. The syntax for a Pattern is a subset of the syntax for an XPath expression. Patterns are used in only three XSLT elements: `<xsl:template>`, `<xsl:key>`, and `<xsl:number>`.

Precedence XSLT

see Import Precedence

Preceding Axis XPath

The preceding axis selects all the nodes that precede the context node, in reverse document order, with the exception of attribute and namespace nodes, and the node's own ancestors.

Preceding-Sibling Axis XPath

The preceding-sibling axis selects all the nodes that precede the context node and that share the same parent node, in reverse document order.

Predicate XPath

An expression used to filter which nodes are selected by a particular step in a path expression, or to select a subset of the nodes in a node-set. A Boolean expression selects the nodes for which the predicate is true; a numeric expression selects the node at the position given by the value of the expression, for example «`[1]`» selects the first node.

Prefix XML Namespaces

see Namespace Prefix

Principal Node Type XPath

Every axis has a principal node type. For most axes, the principal nodes are Elements. For the attribute axis, the principal node type is Attribute, and for the namespace axis, it is Namespace. The principal node type determines the type of nodes selected by the node test «*»: for example, «`following-siblings::*`» selects elements, while «`namespace::*`» selects namespace nodes.

Priority XSLT

Every template rule has a priority. The priority is expressed as a floating-point number. The priority may be specified explicitly, using the `priority` attribute of the `<xsl:template>` element; if it is omitted a default priority is allocated based on the pattern. The priority is used to decide which template to instantiate when several template rules match the same node: a rule with numerically higher priority is used in preference to one with lower priority.

Processing Instruction XML

An item in an XML document that is conventionally used to carry instructions to the software that receives the document and processes it. Written between the delimiters «`<?`» and «`?>`». Note that the XML declaration at the start of a document, and the text declaration at the start of an external parsed entity, are not processing instructions even though they use the same delimiters.

Processing Instruction Node XPath

A node in a tree representing an XML processing instruction.

QName XML Namespaces

A qualified name. It is either a simple name (an `NCName`) or a name preceded by a namespace prefix and a colon.

Result Tree XSLT

The output of a stylesheet. A stylesheet defines a transformation from a source tree to a result tree. Several products have extensions that allow multiple result trees to be created. The final stage of processing is normally to serialize the result tree as a stream of characters or bytes: this is controlled by the selected output method.

Result Tree Fragment XSLT

In XSLT 1.0, **Result Tree Fragment** is the data type of the temporary tree created by instantiating the content of a non-empty `<xsl:variable>` element. In the XSLT 1.1 working draft, the data type of a temporary tree becomes simply a node-set, which contains a single node, the root of the tree.

Root Node XPath

The top-most node in a tree. If the tree represents a well-formed XML document the root node will have exactly one element node as a child, representing the document element, and no text nodes as children. In other cases (for example result tree fragments) it may have zero or more element node children, and zero or more text node children: I refer to such a document as being **well-balanced**. In both cases the root node may also have comment nodes and processing instruction nodes as children.

Simplified Stylesheet This book

Referred to in XSLT as the *Literal Result Element as Stylesheet Facility*, a simplified stylesheet is a stylesheet consisting solely of a literal result element which is instantiated using the root of the source document as the current node.

Source Document XPath

The principal source document is the XML document to which the stylesheet is being applied. Secondary source documents can be loaded using the `document()` function.

Step XPath

A step is used within a path expression to navigate from one node to a particular set of nodes. The step is defined by an axis, giving the direction of navigation, a node test, which defines constraints on the type of and names of the target nodes, and zero or more predicates, which define arbitrary constraints that the target nodes must satisfy.

String XPath

One of the allowed data types for the value of an XPath expression. It is a sequence of zero or more Unicode characters (the same character set as is used in XML).

String-value XPath

Every node has a string-value. For a text node the string-value is the textual content; for an element it is the concatenation of the string-values of its descendant text nodes (that is, the textual content of the element after stripping all markup). The string-value of a node is output by the instruction `<xsl:value-of select=".">`.

Stylesheet — XSLT

This term is used to refer either to a single `<xsl:stylesheet>` element and its contents (called in this book a stylesheet module), or to a stylesheet with all the stylesheets that it loads using `<xsl:include>` and `<xsl:import>` elements (called a stylesheet program).

Template Body — This book

A sequence of XSLT instructions, extension elements, literal result elements, and text nodes, forming the content of an `<xsl:template>` element or of various other elements in the stylesheet. When the template body is instantiated, any instructions and extension elements are instantiated according to the rules for each one, while any literal result elements and text nodes are copied to the current output destination. In the XSLT Recommendation the term used is simply *Template*; I have used *Template Body* to avoid confusion with `<xsl:template>` elements.

Template Rule — XSLT

An `<xsl:template>` element in the stylesheet with a `match` attribute. A template rule may be invoked using the `<xsl:apply-templates>` instruction; for each selected node, the appropriate template rule is determined based on a number of criteria including the match pattern and the template rule's import precedence and priority.

Temporary Tree — This book

A tree constructed in the course of processing a stylesheet, by instantiating a non-empty `<xsl:variable>` element. In the XSLT 1.0 specification this object (and its data type) is known as a result tree fragment. In the XSLT 1.1 working draft, the data type becomes simply a node-set, and the object itself is given no special name, so we invented one.

Text Node — XPath

A node in a tree representing character data (called PCDATA in XML) within an XML document. Adjacent text nodes will always be merged into a single node. Character references and entity references occurring within the original text will have been replaced by their expansions.

Top-level Element — XSLT

An element in a stylesheet that is an immediate child of the `<xsl:stylesheet>` element.

Tree — XPath

An abstract data structure representing the information content of an XML document. The tree always has a single root node (which contrary to the botanical analogy, is always depicted at the top). The structure of nodes in the tree need not follow the rules for a well-formed document in XML, for example, there may be several element nodes as children of the root.

Unparsed Entity — XML

An unparsed entity is an entity declared in the Document Type Definition with an associated notation. Such entities are unparsed because they generally contain binary data such as images, rather than XML. A function, `unparsed-entity-uri()`, is available in XSLT to access the unparsed entities associated with a source document.

URI — Internet standards

Uniform Resource Identifier: a generalization of the URLs (Uniform Resource Locators) used to uniquely address resources such as web pages on the Internet.

Variable Binding — XPath

The declaration of a variable, in an `<xsl:variable>` or `<xsl:param>` element, in conjunction with the current value of that variable.

Variable Reference — XPath

A reference to a variable within an expression, in the form `$name`.

Well-balanced — XML Fragment Interchange

An XML fragment is well-balanced if there is an end tag that matches every start tag. This is a less strict constraint than being well-formed: a well-balanced fragment does not have to have a single element that encloses all the others. XSLT and XPath are defined so they will work on any trees representing a well-balanced XML fragment. The XML and XSLT standards don't use this terminology; instead they refer to the rules for an *external general parsed entity*.

Well-formed — XML

A document is well-formed if it follows the syntax rules in the XML specification. These include the rule that there must be a single outermost element that encloses all others. The XML output of an XSLT stylesheet is not required to be well-formed, only to be well-balanced.

Whitespace — XML

Whitespace is any contiguous sequence of tab, carriage return, newline, and space characters. A whitespace node is a text node whose string-value consists solely of whitespace.

Index A – Elements

A note on the index.

There are three indexes in this book: Index A – Elements, Index B – Functions and Index C – General. Indexes A and B are flat indexes intended as quick references. The General index has detailed entries arranged hierarchically, covering the entire scope of the book, including elements and functions even though these are listed in their own indexes as well.

Elements

Index B - Functions

Functions

Index C - General

Symbols

A

B

C

D

E

F

J

K

L

M

N

O

P

Q

T

U

Z